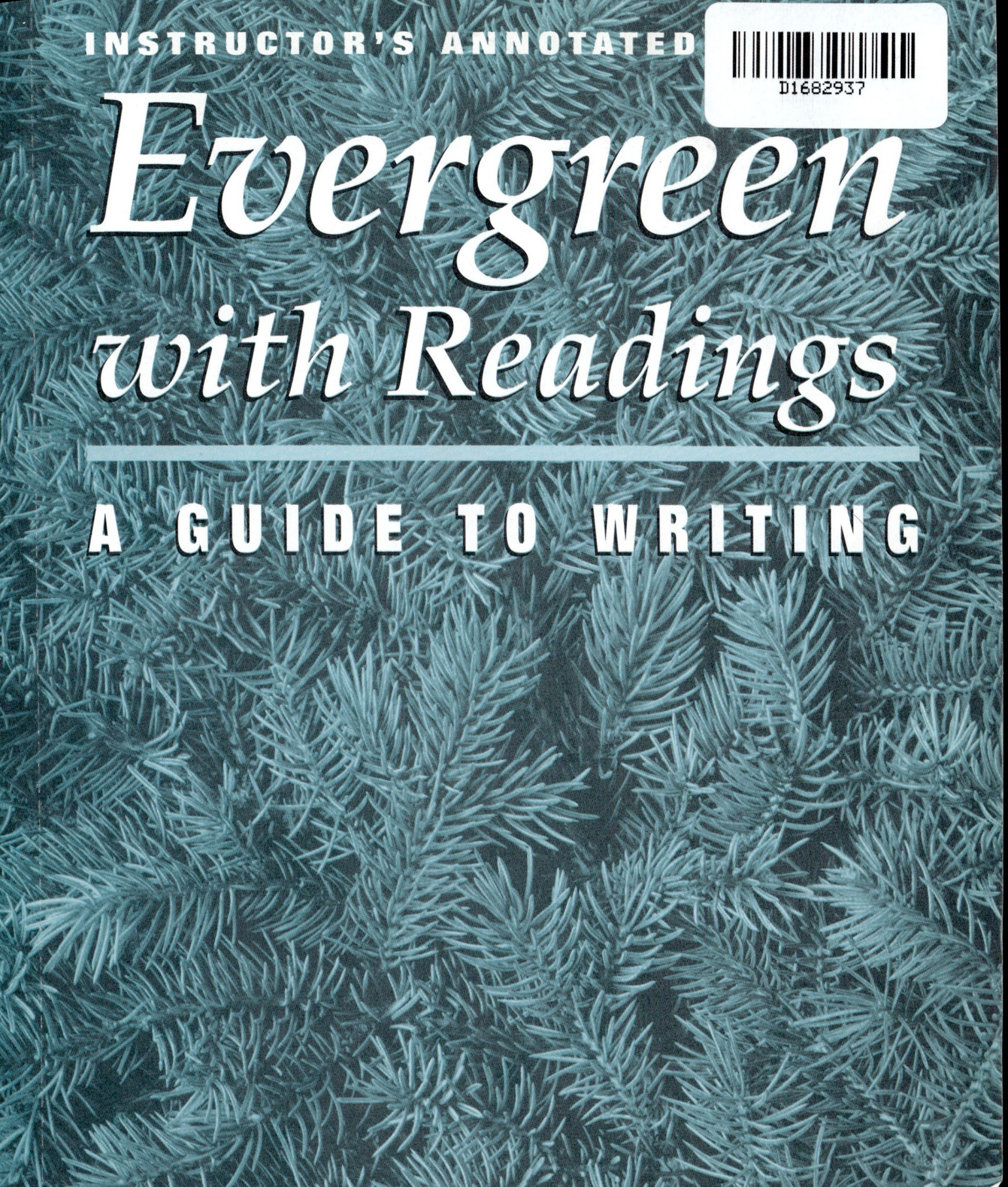

INSTRUCTOR'S ANNOTATED

Evergreen
with Readings

A GUIDE TO WRITING

As part of Houghton Mifflin's ongoing commitment to the environment, this text has been printed on recycled paper.

INSTRUCTOR'S ANNOTATED EDITION

Evergreen
with Readings

A GUIDE TO WRITING

SIXTH EDITION

Susan Fawcett

Alvin Sandberg

HOUGHTON MIFFLIN COMPANY   BOSTON   NEW YORK

Senior Sponsoring Editor: Mary Jo Southern
Senior Associate Editor: Ellen Darion
Senior Project Editor: Chere Bemelmans
Senior Production/Design Coordinator: Sarah Ambrose
Senior Manufacturing Coordinator: Priscilla Bailey
Senior Marketing Manager: Nancy Lyman
Senior Designer: Henry Rachlin
Editorial Assistants: Danielle Richardson and Joy Park

Cover design: Harold Burch, Harold Burch Design, New York City
Cover image: Francisco Villaflor/Photonica

Photo credits: We are grateful to the following individuals for permission to reproduce their photographs in this text: page 41: *The Umbrella Maker* by Patricia Hansen, watercolor, 42″ × 29″; page 50: © Corbis-Bettmann; page 83: © James Carroll; page 94: © John Nordell/Index Stock—The Picture Cube; page 99: © Grant Heilman; page 108: © Anne-Marie Webert/The Stock Market; page 109: Corbis-Bettmann; page 127: © Jeff Greenburg/Stock Boston; page 132: © Deborah Kahn Kalas/Stock Boston; page 133: © Michael Zide; page 163: © Shrank/The Independent, London, England; Cartoonists and Writers Syndicate, New York; page 218: The Florida Anti-Tobacco Campaign; page 294: © James Carroll; page 310; *Crocodile Village* by Milan Kunc, 1985, oil on canvas, 120 × 120 cm; page 429: *Half-Dome, Winter,* photograph by Ansel Adams. © 1999 by the Trustees of the Ansel Adams Publishing Rights Trust. All rights reserved.

Text credits: pages 492–493: "How Sunglasses Spanned the World" from *Panati's Extraordinary Origins of Everyday Things* by Charles Panati. Copyright © 1987 by Charles Panati. Reprinted by permission of HarperCollins Publishers, Inc. and Ellen Levine Literary Agency. Text credits continue on page 544.

Copyright © 2000 by Houghton Mifflin Company. All rights reserved.

No part of this work may be reproduced or transmitted in any form or by any means, electronic or mechanical, including photocopying and recording, or by any information storage or retrieval system without the prior written permission of the copyright owner unless such copying is expressly permitted by federal copyright law. With the exception of nonprofit transcription in Braille, Houghton Mifflin is not authorized to grant permission for further uses of copyrighted selections reprinted in this text without the permission of their owners. Permission must be obtained from the individual copyright owners as identified herein. Address requests for permission to make copies of Houghton Mifflin material to College Permissions, Houghton Mifflin Company, 222 Berkeley Street, Boston, MA 02116-3764.

Printed in the U.S.A.

Library of Congress Catalog Card Number: 99-72004

Student Edition ISBN: 0-395-95847-4
Instructor's Annotated Edition ISBN: 0-395-95848-2

1 2 3 4 5 6 7 8 9-WBC-03 02 01 00 99

Contents

Preface xi

Unit 1 Getting Started 2

1 Exploring the Writing Process 3
- **Part A** The Writing Process 3
- **Part B** Subject, Audience, and Purpose 4

2 Prewriting to Generate Ideas 6
- **Part A** Freewriting 6
- **Part B** Brainstorming 9
- **Part C** Clustering 10
- **Part D** Asking Questions 11
- **Part E** Keeping a Journal 13

Unit 1 Writers' Workshop: *Using Just One of Your Five Senses, Describe a Place* 16

Unit 2 Discovering the Paragraph 18

3 The Process of Writing Paragraphs 19
- **Part A** Defining and Looking at the Paragraph 19
- **Part B** Narrowing the Topic and Writing the Topic Sentence 24
- **Part C** Generating Ideas for the Body 29
- **Part D** Selecting and Dropping Ideas 30
- **Part E** Arranging Ideas in a Plan or an Outline 31
- **Part F** Writing and Revising the Paragraph 33

4 Achieving Coherence 43
- **Part A** Coherence Through Order 43
- **Part B** Coherence Through Related Sentences 55

Unit 2 Writers' Workshop: *Pay Tribute to an Exceptional Person* 66

Unit 3 Developing the Paragraph 68

5 Illustration 69
Checklist: The Process of Writing an Illustration Paragraph 76
Suggested Topic Sentences for Illustration Paragraphs 76

6 Narration 77
Checklist: The Process of Writing a Narrative Paragraph 83
Suggested Topics for Narrative Paragraphs 84

7 *Description* 85
Checklist: The Process of Writing a Descriptive Paragraph 94
Suggested Topics for Descriptive Paragraphs 95

8 *Process* 96
Checklist: The Process of Writing a Process Paragraph 104
Suggested Topics for Process Paragraphs 105

9 *Definition* 106
Part A Single-Sentence Definitions 106
Part B The Definition Paragraph 112
Checklist: The Process of Writing a Definition Paragraph 116
Suggested Topics for Definition Paragraphs 117

10 *Comparison and Contrast* 118
Part A The Contrast and the Comparison Paragraphs 118
Checklist: The Process of Writing a Contrast or Comparison Paragraph 128
Suggested Topics for Contrast or Comparison Paragraphs 128
Part B The Comparison-Contrast Paragraph 129
Working Through the Comparison-Contrast Paragraph 132
Suggested Topics for Comparison-Contrast Paragraphs 133

11 *Classification* 134
Checklist: The Process of Writing a Classification Paragraph 141
Suggested Topics for Classification Paragraphs 142

12 *Cause and Effect* 143
Checklist: The Process of Writing a Cause and Effect Paragraph 150
Suggested Topics for Cause and Effect Paragraphs 151

13 *Persuasion* 152
Checklist: The Process of Writing a Persuasive Paragraph 164
Suggested Topics for Persuasive Paragraphs 165

Unit 3 Writers' Workshop: *Give Advice to College Writers* 166

Unit 4   *Writing the Essay* 168

14 *The Process of Writing an Essay* 169
Part A Looking at the Essay 169
Part B Writing the Thesis Statement 173
Part C Generating Ideas for the Body 177

Part D Ordering and Linking Paragraphs in the Essay 183
Part E Writing and Revising Essays 189
Checklist: The Process of Writing an Essay 195
Suggested Topics for Essays 196

15 *Types of Essays* 197

Part A The Illustration Essay 197
Part B The Narrative Essay 200
Part C The Descriptive Essay 202
Part D The Process Essay 204
Part E The Definition Essay 206
Part F The Comparison or Contrast Essay 208
Part G The Classification Essay 211
Part H The Cause and Effect Essay 213
Part I The Persuasive Essay 216

16 *The Introduction, the Conclusion, and the Title* 220

Part A The Introduction 220
Part B The Conclusion 223
Part C The Title 225

17 *Writing Under Pressure: The Essay Examination* 227

Part A Budgeting Your Time 228
Part B Reading and Understanding the Essay Question 230
Part C Choosing the Correct Paragraph or Essay Pattern 233
Part D Writing the Topic Sentence or the Thesis Statement 235
Checklist: The Process of Writing the Essay Question 237

18 *Special College Skills: Summary and Quotation* 238

Part A Avoiding Plagiarism 238
Part B Writing a Summary 239
Checklist: The Process of Writing a Summary 242
Part C Using Direct and Indirect Quotation 243

Unit 4 Writers' Workshop: Analyze a Social Problem 248

Unit 5 *Improving Your Writing* 250

19 *Revising for Consistency and Parallelism* 251

Part A Consistent Tense 251
Part B Consistent Number and Person 256
Part C Parallelism 261

20 *Revising for Sentence Variety* 267

Part A Mix Long and Short Sentences 267
Part B Use a Question, a Command, or an Exclamation 269
Part C Vary the Beginnings of Sentences 270

viii Contents

    Part D Vary Methods of Joining Ideas 275
    Part E Review and Practice 290

21 *Revising for Language Awareness* 295
    Part A Exact Language: Avoiding Vagueness 295
    Part B Concise Language: Avoiding Wordiness 301
    Part C Fresh Language: Avoiding Triteness 304
    Part D Figurative Language: Similes and Metaphors 306

22 *Putting Your Revision Skills to Work* 311

Unit 5 Writers' Workshop: Examine the Bright (or Dark) Side of Family Life 318

Unit 6 *Reviewing the Basics* 320

23 *The Simple Sentence* 321
    Part A Defining and Spotting Subjects 321
    Part B Spotting Prepositional Phrases 322
    Part C Defining and Spotting Verbs 324

24 *Coordination and Subordination* 327
    Part A Coordination 327
    Part B Subordination 330
    Part C Semicolons 333
    Part D Conjunctive Adverbs 335
    Part E Review 337

25 *Avoiding Sentence Errors* 342
    Part A Avoiding Run-Ons and Comma Splices 342
    Part B Avoiding Fragments 346

26 *Present Tense (Agreement)* 356
    Part A Defining Subject-Verb Agreement 356
    Part B Three Troublesome Verbs in the Present Tense: *To Be, To Have, To Do* 359
    Part C Special Singular Constructions 361
    Part D Separation of Subject and Verb 362
    Part E Sentences Beginning with *There* and *Here* 363
    Part F Agreement in Questions 364
    Part G Agreement in Relative Clauses 365

27 *Past Tense* 367
    Part A Regular Verbs in the Past Tense 367
    Part B Irregular Verbs in the Past Tense 368
    Part C A Troublesome Verb in the Past Tense: *To Be* 371
    Part D Troublesome Pairs in the Past Tense: *Can/Could, Will/Would* 372

28 The Past Participle 376

- **Part A** Past Participles of Regular Verbs 376
- **Part B** Past Participles of Irregular Verbs 378
- **Part C** Using the Present Perfect Tense 382
- **Part D** Using the Past Perfect Tense 384
- **Part E** Using the Passive Voice (*To Be* and the Past Participle) 385
- **Part F** Using the Past Participle as an Adjective 387

29 Nouns 390

- **Part A** Defining Singular and Plural 390
- **Part B** Signal Words: Singular and Plural 392
- **Part C** Signal Words with *Of* 394

30 Pronouns 396

- **Part A** Defining Pronouns and Antecedents 396
- **Part B** Making Pronouns and Antecedents Agree 397
- **Part C** Referring to Antecedents Clearly 401
- **Part D** Special Problems of Case 404
- **Part E** Using Pronouns with *-Self* and *-Selves* 407

31 Prepositions 411

- **Part A** Working with Prepositional Phrases 411
- **Part B** Prepositions in Common Expressions 413

32 Adjectives and Adverbs 418

- **Part A** Defining and Using Adjectives and Adverbs 418
- **Part B** The Comparative and the Superlative 420
- **Part C** A Troublesome Pair: *Good/Well* 423

33 The Apostrophe 427

- **Part A** The Apostrophe for Contractions 427
- **Part B** The Apostrophe for Ownership 429
- **Part C** Special Uses of the Apostrophe 431

34 The Comma 433

- **Part A** Commas for Items in a Series 433
- **Part B** Commas with Introductory Phrases, Transitional Expressions, and Parentheticals 434
- **Part C** Commas for Appositives 436
- **Part D** Commas with Nonrestrictive and Restrictive Clauses 437
- **Part E** Commas for Dates and Addresses 438
- **Part F** Minor Uses of the Comma 440

35 Mechanics 443

- **Part A** Capitalization 443
- **Part B** Titles 445

Contents

Part C Direct Quotations 447
Part D Minor Marks of Punctuation 449

36 *Putting Your Proofreading Skills to Work* 452

Unit 6 Writers' Workshop: *Adopt a New Point of View* 458

Unit 7 *Strengthening Your Spelling* 460

37 *Spelling* 461

Part A Suggestions for Improving Your Spelling 461
Part B Computer Spell Checkers 462
Part C Spotting Vowels and Consonants 463
Part D Doubling the Final Consonant (in Words of One Syllable) 463
Part E Doubling the Final Consonant (in Words of More Than One Syllable) 465
Part F Dropping or Keeping the Final *E* 466
Part G Changing or Keeping the Final *Y* 467
Part H Adding *-S* or *-ES* 468
Part I Choosing *IE* or *EI* 469
Part J Spelling Lists 470

38 *Look-Alikes/Sound-Alikes* 473

Unit 7 Writers' Workshop: *Discuss a Time When Diverse People Were United* 488

Unit 8 *Reading Selections* 490

Reading Strategies for Writers 491
How Sunglasses Spanned the World 492
Only Daughter Sandra Cisneros 494
My Outing Arthur Ashe 497
The Lady of the Ring Rene Denfeld 500
Neat People Versus Sloppy People Suzanne Britt 502
How to Get the Most Out of Yourself Alan Loy McGinnis 504
Beauty: When the Other Dancer Is the Self Alice Walker 508
Hunger of Memory Richard Rodriguez 513
Some Thoughts About Abortion Anna Quindlen 517
Food for Thought Dave Barry 520
One More Lesson Judith Ortiz Cofer 522
A Brother's Murder Brent Staples 526
In Search of Bruce Lee's Grave Shanlon Wu 528
The Plot Against People Russell Baker 531
Road Rage Andrew Ferguson 533

Quotation Bank 538
Acknowledgments 544
ESL Reference Guide 545
Index 547
Rhetorical Index 552

Preface

"*Evergreen* works." Again and again, we hear this comment from instructors and students alike, and we consider it the greatest possible compliment. *Evergreen with Readings* combines in one volume the new Sixth Edition of our popular college writing text *Evergreen* and fourteen high-interest reading selections. Based on our classroom experience at Bronx Community College of the City University of New York, *Evergreen* was designed for students who need to improve the writing skills so necessary to success in college and in most careers. The text's clear, paced lessons, numerous high-interest practices, and engaging writing assignments have guided more than one and a half million students through the process of writing effectively, from prewriting to final draft.

By choosing *Evergreen with Readings,* those instructors who wish to include reading in their writing classes may select from richly varied and provocative readings by such authors as Sandra Cisneros, Arthur Ashe, Russell Baker, Anna Quindlen, Alice Walker, and Dave Barry. Each selection is accompanied by a headnote, glosses, critical thinking questions, and writing assignments, some of them collaborative.

In this exciting Sixth Edition—marking both the year 2000 and *Evergreen*'s twentieth birthday—we have kept the carefully honed lessons, flow of practices, and overall organization that have served students so well over the years. However, we have extensively reviewed and updated the text, replacing numerous activities and models and occasionally adjusting instructional priorities.

In doing so, we listened closely to the suggestions of college faculty across the country and weighed the kinds of academic and job-related challenges that our students will face once they complete this course. Our goal has been to take an excellent book and make it even more motivating, useful, and engaging than before.

Specifically, we have enhanced *Evergreen*'s academic focus with a new chapter on cause and effect, a much-expanded and reorganized chapter on summarizing and quoting, and more wide-ranging content (research on twins, underwater archeology, job search techniques, date rape, comets and asteroids, and more). In addition, we have included more samples of inspiring student writing; added more collaborative and critical thinking activities; selectively enriched writing, revising, and proofreading coverage; and replaced more models, practices, and writing assignments than ever before. Other changes include weaving references to writing on computers throughout the text, reversing Units 4 and 5 so that paragraph instruction flows directly into essay instruction, adding more practice on sentence errors plus a sentence fragment chart, and upgrading many photographs, cartoons, and other visual prompts for thinking and writing.

Special Features of *Evergreen*, Sixth Edition

Expanded Academic Focus

- **New Coverage of Cause and Effect Writing.** Unit 3 now includes a chapter on cause and effect paragraphs. A corresponding section in Chapter 15, "Types of Essays," teaches students to write essays analyzing causes and effects.

- **New Chapter on Summary and Quotation.** Chapter 18, "Special College Skills: Summary and Quotation," defines plagiarism and includes much-expanded material on how to summarize and quote from outside sources.

More Student Writing

- **New Writers' Workshops.** This versatile feature at the end of every unit showcases a student-authored paragraph or essay, carefully processed with peer-editing questions and followed by group work and writing ideas. Keyed to the subject matter of each unit and ideal for group discussion, these workshops reinforce writing and revising skills and inspire student writers by example.
- **More Student Models.** Because students are often motivated by the fine work of their peers, more student models, in addition to professional models, are used throughout the text. These represent a range of levels, from finished writing to work needing revision.

Enriched Coverage of the Writing Process

- **New Material on Controlling Idea and Revising for Support.** New coverage of the controlling idea has been added to our paragraph- and essay-writing instruction, with emphasis on the controlling idea in the topic sentence or thesis statement. At the urging of instructors, we also have added more practices in which students revise poorly developed paragraphs and essays.
- **New Chapter, "Putting Your Proofreading Skills to Work."** A new chapter of mixed-error proofreading practice now concludes Unit 6, "Reviewing the Basics." Here students correct six high-interest selections, each containing a random, real-world mix of errors.

More New High-Interest Content Than Ever Before

- **High-Interest Models and Practices.** Guided by our Faculty Advisory Board and users of the text, we have carefully reviewed and replaced many of the models and content-based practice sets so important to *Evergreen*'s effectiveness. Fresh subjects include young entrepreneurs, James Escalante's student math stars, how technology helps Stephen Hawking, insect sexual attraction, high schools of the twenty-first century, Oprah's book club, *Latina* magazine's founder, the moon as a tourist destination, soul and hip-hop, how famous authors beat writer's block, Mexico's Day of the Dead, and the Guggenheim Museum's recent motorcycle show.
- **Four New Reading Selections.** We have replaced four readings with strong new selections, according to instructor and student feedback: Sandra Cisneros on becoming a writer, Andrew Ferguson on the epidemic of road rage, Dave Barry on school science projects, and Rene Denfeld on the lessons she learned from boxing.

New Collaborative and Critical-Thinking Activities

- **Peer Revising.** Chapter 3 now includes instruction on peer editing, with a Peer Feedback Sheet to help students respond specifically to each other's work. In addition, the Writers' Workshops offer multiple opportunities for collaborative work.
- **Improved Visual Prompts for Thinking and Writing.** This edition includes more stimulating visual images for critical analysis and writing, such as a billboard campaign to stop teen smoking, a British cartoon about America's armed children, and several paintings by contemporary artists.

Extensive Ancillary Package

Available on adoption of the text, the following ancillaries provide the instructor with excellent support material and expand teaching options. New to this edition is the Evergreen Web Site, which includes the Evergreen Community (a bulletin board where users can exchange ideas about teaching with *Evergreen*), additional tests and exercises, links, and tips on teaching developmental English.

- *Instructor's Annotated Edition*
- *Test Bank*
- *Computerized Diagnostic/Mastery Tests*
- *Computerized Test Bank*
- *Evergreen Web Site including the Evergreen Community*
- *Answer Key*

Organization of the Text

Evergreen's self-contained chapters and units can be taught in any order. Unit 1 provides an overview of the writing process, audience, and purpose and then introduces five prewriting techniques. Unit 2 guides students through the paragraph-writing process: planning, writing topic sentences, generating ideas, organizing, making smooth transitions, and revising. Unit 3 moves on to the rhetorical modes most often required in college writing (illustration, narration, description, process, definition, comparison/contrast, classification, cause/effect, and persuasion). In Unit 4, the techniques of paragraph writing are applied step by step to the process of writing essays, answering essay examination questions, and summarizing and quoting from sources. Unit 5 covers the more subtle skills of revising for consistency, sentence variety, and language awareness. Unit 6 thoroughly reviews basic grammar, highlighting such major problem areas as verbs, sentence boundaries, punctuation, and mechanics; Unit 7 covers spelling and homonyms. A reader containing fourteen professional selections and a Quotation Bank—a mini-reader of great short quotations for student use—conclude the text. *Evergreen*'s full range of materials and flexible organization adapt easily to almost any course design and to a wide range of student needs. Because each chapter is self-contained, the text also works well for tutorials, laboratory work, and self-teaching.

Acknowledgments

We wish to thank those people whose thoughtful comments and suggestions helped us develop this Sixth Edition.

Carlo Annese, Bergen Community College

Kathleen Beauchene, Community College of Rhode Island

Kathleen S. Britton, Florence-Darlington Technical College

Kathryn L. Cid, Lincoln Technical Institute

Nancy B. Culberson, Georgia College & State University

Donald Edge, Camden County College

Donna M. Farrow, Miami-Dade Community College–Kendall Campus

Eddye Gallagher, Tarrant County Junior College

Cliff Gardiner, Augusta State University

Elizabeth Boote Griffey, Florida Community College at Jacksonville

Sandra K. Hall, Corning Community College

Bonita Hilton, Broward Community College

Michael Hricik, Westmoreland County Community College

Brenda Kelly, Pensacola Junior College

Qian Lu, Pima Community College

Patricia A. Malinowski, Finger Lakes Community College

Dorothy Reade, North Harris College

David Rollison, College of Marin

Sharon Shapiro, Naugatuck Valley Community Technical College

Linda Whisnant, Guilford Technical Community College

We are grateful to our exceptional editors at Houghton Mifflin, who always go the distance to create the best possible book. Special thanks to Mary Jo Southern, Senior Sponsoring Editor, who has long believed in *Evergreen* and its mission; to Ellen Darion, Senior Associate Editor, whose many gifts include expert problem solving, a wicked sense of humor, and the ability to steer us all smoothly through the inevitable snags; and to Chere Bemelmans, our superb Senior Project Editor, who sees all—or almost all—as she manages the transformation of messy manuscript into beautiful printed pages. We are the happy beneficiaries of Chere's high standards and keen eye and share her devotion to the Chocolate Force. Harriett Prentiss, our Development Editor, enthusiastically stepped into this complicated revision and helped it evolve, contributing organizational skills, wisdom, and sometimes her formidable writing talents.

In addition, Marilyn Weissman and Nancy Brandwein helped with high-quality research and writing for some of the content-based exercises.

To the English Department faculty and students of Bronx Community College, we owe a special debt of gratitude. Many of the excellent student paragraphs and essays in this book were written in BCC classrooms and later won the college newspaper's "Writer of the Month" contest; each year, winners and finalists are published in booklet form with the help of Dr. Larraine Fergenson. Dr.

Bernard Witlieb read *Evergreen* pages for accuracy, lending his sharp eye and rich store of knowledge, and Carol Zavin kindly helped us track student authors.

We thank Bruce Carson for expert assistance in securing art permissions; watercolorist Patricia Hansen for the use of her painting and for her extraordinary efforts to take an excellent photograph of it; the Crispin Porter & Bogusky advertising agency for the use of its witty truth-or-lies billboard photograph; and Harriet Fawcett, whose art books inspired several of our selections.

Susan Fawcett thanks her husband, Richard Donovan, for sharing his love, humor, and invigorating thoughts over many good years. She dedicates her work on this revision to her beloved father, Millard F. Fawcett, who died on February 21, 1999. He was vivid and courageous—an inventor, photographer, small business owner, sportsman, and stylish wearer of hats.

Alvin Sandberg thanks Beth for her encouragement and support and Miriam for her many suggestions for improvements to the manuscript. He also thanks Marilyn Weissman for her editorial assistance.

S. F.
A. S.

Suggestions for the Teacher of Writing

Student Attitude and Motivation

The students in a basic writing course usually represent a mix of levels, ages, and often, ethnic groups—a pool of varied experience that can be used to good purpose in class. Many of these students, however, may enter the classroom with negative attitudes about writing and about themselves as writers. Past experience may have convinced them that writing is a magical ability one either does or does not possess and that writing courses are, ipso facto, painful, frustrating ordeals in which only the teacher knows the rules. They may fear that any attempt at writing will provoke a volley of red marks.

Fortunately, these attitudes can be dealt with and even converted to positive motivation if the writing instructor is aware of them and designs strategies that take them into account. Writing students can be motivated (or not) by a number of factors that the instructor can to some extent control. Very important are the instructor's own attitudes and expectations. Conveying by actions as well as words the belief that students can and will improve their writing will affect student performance positively. Students are also motivated by a learning environment that encourages mutual support. The instructor can set the tone for constructive peer criticism and help create an atmosphere in which everyone works together to solve writing problems and build writing skills.

The effectiveness of books and materials can also spark or squelch motivation; a textbook that addresses students on their terms and really teaches what they need to know cannot help but motivate them. And at the heart of any writing course are the writing assignments themselves, their subject matter, wording, and purpose.

Perhaps the strongest motivator is the student's own belief in good writing skills as an attainable source of personal power. Again, the student's fear, plus inaccurate perceptions of his or her capabilities, may block this belief (Janine Bempechat, "Learning from Poor and Minority Students Who Succeed in School," *Harvard Education Newsletter,* May/June 1999). Usually, however, as the term progresses and students are helped to see improvement, their inner motivation will grow. You can use class discussions, writing assignments, and written material from your students' jobs and lives to point out the importance of writing skills to their daily survival as students, employees, consumers, and concerned citizens.

In the material that follows, these factors will be discussed in more depth and illustrated with suggestions and exercises from our classroom experience.

The First Weeks of Class

One of the most important tasks facing the writing instructor during the first weeks of class is the creation of an effective learning environment. We try to create a writers' community based on sharing, discussion, ungraded writing, and group activities.

Consider spending the entire first class getting to know one another. One exercise that students enjoy is Sixty-Second Autobiographies. Break the class into groups of four or five students, making sure that someone in each group has a watch with a second hand. Have each group member in turn tell as much about himself or herself as possible in one minute; you can demonstrate (while a student times you) speaking as fast as you can and setting the tone for participation. Such activities, if you feel comfortable with them, are great icebreakers and can legitimize risk taking and even acting a little foolish—both potential assets in a writing course.

Another get-acquainted exercise involves short writings. Go once around the room, having each person say the name by which he or she would like to be called. Then ask students to write for five minutes about their own names—whether they like them or not, where their names came from, and so forth. Let volunteers read some or all of what they have written. Often such sharing is contagious, but at this point it should be optional. Assure the students before they write that papers will not be graded.

In general, the more students write, the better. Frequent in-class writings are especially useful early in the term because they dispel fears about writing and provide you with an accurate picture of student performance in a controlled setting. Because paragraphs and short assignments are less intimidating to write and to read aloud than longer essays, they can be assigned almost daily. We have had good luck with topics like "My Finest Hour," "A Valued Possession," and "Why I Like (or Dislike) My Job."

Early on, as an introduction to the writing process, we have the class try freewriting and focused freewriting. We explain that writing requires two different skills—*creative* and *critical*. Each is best used at different phases of the writing process. Freewriting is a creative, or idea-generating, method. Later, the writer can go over a freewriting with a critical eye, selecting good ideas, rearranging, rewriting. (For more on using and processing freewriting, see the notes for Chapter 2, "Prewriting to Generate Ideas.")

After a paper is read aloud in class, encourage students to say what they liked about it, being as specific as possible. In this way, the class can begin to build its own definition of "powerful writing." From the very start, guided discussions of student work (and later, written models) can give students an idea of what to aim for as writers and how to think and respond critically as readers.

Consider returning the first few papers with comments but no grades. Some instructors grade no papers at all for the first week or two, preferring to comment fully and specifically, especially pointing out an individual's strengths. In any case, these early papers will help you ascertain the level of the class so you can select the appropriate textbook chapters and sequence of lessons.

Reproducing and Discussing Student Work

We find it worthwhile to reproduce student work, either by retyping and photocopying it or by using an overhead projector. Basic writing students need practice in *seeing* and paying close attention. Furthermore, students usually love to see their work in print, and successful peer writings are a great inspiration to the whole class.

Always choose papers that are good in some way and whose strengths and weaknesses relate to the current lesson. Ask students to underline sections that seem especially strong or confusing and to give specific reasons for their opinions. *Which words* make this line so vivid? Just *why* is this paragraph so moving? *Why* is this conclusion unclear? Stress *effect* rather than correctness.

In-class revising sessions are very helpful to students, who, like all of us, spot errors and awkwardness more easily in other people's work. Urging students to think critically about one another's writing and to suggest improvements can sharpen their own sense of correctness and style. Approach in-class revision in the spirit of shared problem solving. Let the class argue the merits of any suggested change. The important point for students to grasp is that the writer needs to make reasoned choices.

In these discussions, you should model and reinforce good editing skills. Through questions and discussion, help students avoid the "hasty closure" that often characterizes basic-skills learners—that is, their tendency to rush through uncomfortable new tasks.

Critical Thinking in the Writing Classroom

"I think best with a pencil in my hand," wrote Anne Morrow Lindbergh, one of many writers who have commented on the relationship between writing and thinking. This textbook embodies our assumption that both creative and critical thinking are integral to the writing process. Writing makes order out of chaos; if the process succeeds, we have thought and written our way to greater clarity.

The rhetorical modes themselves reflect ways of thinking—ways of sorting, organizing, and categorizing ideas. The same is true of the notion of general and specific, thesis statement or topic sentence and support, the techniques of order—time, space, importance—and of transitions among ideas. All are ways of presenting ideas in relationship (parallel, subordinate, and so forth). Teaching students consciously, step by step, how to read a rough draft and to cull, rearrange, and present ideas is teaching them to think critically. Ideally, writing assignments and class discussions will underscore this connection by posing problems to be solved, guiding student criticism of one another's writing, and analyzing ads, readings, and news events to separate emotionalism from thinking. Nobody said this was easy. One of our students, pressed to reason something out on her own, exclaimed, "I hate thinking. Thinking is hard!"

A caution: Peter Elbow has warned against an overemphasis on objectivity and audience, noting that too much early concern about what others will think can inhibit the writing process and that some of the best writing largely ignores audience (*Pretext: A Journal of Rhetorical Theory*, Spring 1990). We try to impress upon students the importance of keeping separate the creative and the critical phases of the writing process.

Writing Exercises and Assignments

Seek a variety of writing topics and assignments. Clearly, not every student will be inspired by every topic, and different approaches will give all students a chance to perform well. At the same time, students should be reminded that good writing can be done on just about any subject; we use focused freewriting, collaborative brainstorming, series of questions, and so forth, to show students how to direct a topic toward areas that interest them. *Evergreen with Readings* and the notes to the instructor suggest a number of paragraph and essay assignments. You will no doubt have others.

You will probably assign more personal topics early in the course, as students often write most easily about their own lives. As the term progresses and more formal topics are assigned, you may need to spend extra class time making sure that students grasp particular modes of organization or relationships between ideas. Unused to thinking and writing in an orderly way, many students at first have trouble here. Class analysis of written models and discussion of relevant practices in the text can be invaluable. Further, ask the author of a successful paper to share with classmates how he or she "got it."

Occasionally link writing assignments to techniques you are teaching—consistency, parallelism, and so forth—urging students to pay attention to one or two techniques and marking papers with an eye to these techniques. In addition, combine grammar review and paragraph writing. For example, if you have just reviewed verb agreement, assign a five- or ten-minute writing exercise. Place a student in front of the class and ask the other students to create a verbal portrait in the present tense. ("Wanda shifts from side to side and pops gum. Every time she catches my eye, she grins and turns away . . .") Have volunteers read their paragraphs while the class listens for the verbs and checks verb agreement.

As you move into more abstract assignments, students' enjoyment need not fade. Have them classify the people they are dating, or urge them to define a term that matters to them. To relate thinking and writing skills to the real world, bring in sets of facts about American eating habits, statistics on school violence, a collection of advertisements. Have students analyze these, looking for and articulating patterns. Government publications can be wonderful resources for the writing instructor: the *Statistical Abstract of the United States*, the survey on women and work by the National Commission on Working Women, and so on. Introduce your students to almanacs, reference books, and sources of entertaining or bizarre information, like Charles Panati's *Panati's Extraordinary Origins of Everyday Things* (HarperCollins, 1989). A useful book that will help students find information on nearly any topic is Robert I. Berkman's *Find It Fast: How to Uncover Expert Information on Any Subject,* Fourth Edition (Harper, 1997). Of course, your college librarian can help you open a world of print and electronic information to your students.

Group Work

The writing process lends itself to collaboration. We use an approach that takes advantage of the full class as a group to provide an audience beyond the teacher, to inspire by example, to model and practice the writing process, to hone reading and speaking skills, to build team skills, and so forth. The new Writers' Workshops concluding each unit embody this approach. In addition, small groups of five or six students, established early in the term, serve as a home base for developing writers, a place to get air time, test early written drafts, and collaboratively brainstorm or edit. One way to balance democracy with quality control in peer-group feedback is to use a peer feedback sheet, a page of questions that each group member fills out and hands to the author of the draft under discussion.

Some instructors use small groups occasionally, after full-group discussions have trained students' critical eyes and ears. Other instructors base the entire course on small peer groups. For more information, see Kenneth Bruffee's *Collaborative Learning: Higher Education, Interdependence, and the Authority of Knowledge*, Second Edition, (Johns Hopkins University Press, 1998).

Evaluating Student Performance

Balancing writing-process instruction and grammar work, the basic-writing teacher encourages students and yet realistically assesses their written performance. However, many students enter our classes unwilling to write much, assuming that the more they write, the more errors they will make. We have found it effective to note strengths as well as weaknesses throughout the term, pointing out what the student does particularly well or what has improved, not just what is still wrong. Responding to content as well as to errors helps keep a balance. A number of instructors and English departments these days favor evaluating student progress on the basis of entire portfolios of writing.

Even with this approach, a developing writer will be overwhelmed by receiving a paper covered with red marks. Ellery Sedgwick writes in the *Journal of Developmental Education*, "A considerable body of research indicates that intensive marking of most or all errors is at least inefficient and quite possibly counterproductive" ("Alternatives to Teaching Formal, Analytical Grammar," January 1989). Consider marking errors and problem areas cumulatively, adding one or two at a time as the term progresses and new material is taught. Stress writing itself as the context for grammar instruction. Whatever your system, explain it clearly to your students so they will not be surprised when you mark errors that you did not mark before. Help students see their individual writing patterns; have them chart the errors made in each paper and review the chart before revising. The Student Answer Key that accompanies this text provides you with the flexibility to let students check some of their own work. In any case, use instructor-student conferences to teach writing skills, evaluate students' work, and apprise students of their progress.

Suggestions for Using *Evergreen with Readings*

Organization of the Text

Evergreen with Readings moves from an overview of the writing process and a presentation of prewriting techniques in Unit 1 to the basics of writing and organizing paragraphs in Unit 2. Unit 3 presents more sophisticated modes of development, and Unit 4 applies the principles of good writing and the developmental modes to the essay, the essay-examination question, and the summary. Unit 5 teaches the skills of revising for consistency, parallelism, sentence variety, and language awareness. Units 6 and 7 provide grammar and spelling review with abundant practices. Each unit concludes with a Writers' Workshop, showcasing a real student paragraph or essay processed with peer-editing questions and a group task. Fourteen professional Reading Selections, each accompanied by discussion questions and writing assignments, and a Quotation Bank conclude the text.

The organization of the text suggests one possible way to structure a course in basic composition. However, because chapters and units are self-contained, they can be taught in any order that suits the individual instructor and the needs of a particular class. Within the text, on-page cross-references direct student and instructor to relevant material in other chapters. A very complete table of contents and index further expand options.

We focus on the paragraph as a model and move to a discussion of the full-length essay, but if you wish to do so, you can teach the essay earlier in the course. The modes of development presented in Unit 3 are specifically applied to essays in Unit 4; in fact, Chapter 15 contains a sample essay, instruction, and practice for each mode taught in Unit 3. Unit 1, "Getting Started," and Unit 5, "Improving Your Writing," work equally well for paragraphs and essays.

Whatever order is followed in the course, we suggest that the chapters in Unit 3, "Developing the Paragraph," not be taught straight through but instead be integrated with the material in Units 4, 5, and 6. Likewise, the chapters in Unit 6, "Reviewing the Basics," and Unit 7, "Strengthening Your Spelling," should be assigned as needed. We find it most effective to weave the Reading Selections throughout the course, perhaps as follow-up for related chapters. Work on contrast, for example, might be followed by a contrast essay by Suzanne Britt or Judith Ortiz Cofer. Because varying the activities of any class works best, you could balance the introduction of one type of paragraph or essay by assigning a short in-class writing exercise on one day, group work on grammar or a problem of style on the next, and a reading selection and writing activity on the third.

Organization of Each Chapter

In general, each chapter of *Evergreen with Readings* moves from simple to more difficult material. Each lesson consists of explanations, examples, and practices that reinforce each skill taught and always move toward the writing of paragraphs or longer compositions. Depending on the level of the class, you may wish to assign all the practices in a particular chapter or assign them selectively. Many of the practices make effective and enjoyable full-class exercises. A checklist for writers concludes most of the chapters in Units 2, 3, and 4; you may find it useful to have students turn in checked checklists with their written assignments. Because of their carefully paced progression, most chapters work well for tutorial sessions and even self-teaching.

Organization of the Reading Selections

An introduction gives students ten strategies for reading each selection effectively and preparing for class discussion and writing. Included here in full is a short essay, "How Sunglasses Spanned the World," with sample student annotations. Fourteen other reading selections follow, each accompanied by a headnote, vocabulary work, comprehension and critical thinking questions, and writing assignments, some of them collaborative. For an in-depth discussion of each selection and for teaching suggestions, see Unit 8, "Reading Selections."

Notes on the Units and Chapters

UNIT 1   Getting Started

Unit 1 gives an overview of the writing process, including the importance of subject, audience, and purpose, and presents five techniques that writers use to get started. Here and elsewhere, as your students begin to write, stress the recursive nature of the writing process—that the steps or stages of writing need not follow a particular order and may have to be done again. The concluding Writers' Workshop reinforces the material in the unit through discussion and small-group work.

Chapter 1: Exploring the Writing Process

Chapter 1 introduces students to the writing process and its three main phases: prewriting, writing, and revising. The importance of subject, audience, and purpose is also discussed. The practices on audience and purpose make an interesting group exercise early in the term.

Chapter 2: Prewriting to Generate Ideas

This chapter introduces the student to five prewriting and exploratory techniques: freewriting, brainstorming, clustering, asking questions, and keeping a journal. Explain to students that these methods represent just one stage of the writing process: the creative, inventive stage. Stress that this stage and later critical stages should be kept separate. (One cause of writer's block is that the overeager critic rejects ideas even before they arrive on paper.) Make sure students understand that they can use one or more of these techniques on any one assignment. For example, they might use clustering followed by freewriting.

Freewriting is a fine motivational tool and a way to unlock hesitant writers, helping them experience, perhaps for the first time, the uncensored outpouring of words. Introduce Part A by doing the first freewriting in class; assign more at home. Most students get the hang of it after one or two trials, and most thoroughly enjoy it. Such freewriting should never be graded, and sharing should be optional at first. Reading freewritings dramatically demonstrates the uniqueness of each writer's voice. It is also fun.

We find it worthwhile to reproduce two or three interesting examples of freewriting from an early batch (anonymous, if the student wishes) so that students can follow on the page. Encourage them to underline words or lines that strike them as strong or funny and to look for connections of which the writer may be unaware. (See "Reproducing and Discussing Student Work" in this manual.)

Follow up with focused freewritings. Read aloud a list of five trigger words and have students write for two or three minutes about each one, trying to stick to the subject. Afterward, ask them if certain words—for whatever reason—triggered a powerful response. Inevitably the answer is yes. Have students put a check by these trigger words and note that they probably have more to say on many subjects than they thought.

The same exercise can be done with a list of five or more possible writing topics. Students should freewrite on each, underlining powerful words or ideas, but now have them choose just one of the underlined ideas and freewrite again, this time for five to ten minutes. This exercise helps students see how they can direct a topic toward ideas that have meaning to them, even when topics are assigned. Successive focused freewritings can later be used to develop weak sections in a paper. For more on freewriting, see Ken Macrorie's *Telling Writing* (Boynton/Cook Publishers, 1985).

Part B, "Brainstorming," presents another effective technique for getting ideas on paper, one used throughout *Evergreen with Readings* as an alternative or addition to freewriting. Some students prefer brainstorming to freewriting; urge them to try both and decide. Like freewriting, brainstorming can be done successively to focus and direct a topic.

"Clustering," Part C, may be especially useful to the visually oriented writer who has trouble with more linear techniques like brainstorming. Try clustering on the board to make sure your students get the hang of it.

"Asking Questions," Part D, helps many writers move beyond the obvious as they explore their ideas about a topic. With the whole class, go over the two model sequences in the text; students usually enjoy these and are helped by this process to see the possibilities. Ask whether they have additional questions they want answered about either model topic.

Part E, "Keeping a Journal," introduces students to journal writing, an activity that some instructors swear by and others largely ignore. At its best, journal writing affords privacy and freedom to the writer. To suggest the wide range of possibilities, we include two actual student journal entries, one written rather formally and the other more loosely, a kind of interior problem solving. We list a number of possible writing exercises and objectives for students to try.

For instructors who wish to emphasize critical thinking skills and move beyond personal topics, the journal can be a place for students to comment on the news or copy down facts, statistics, and quotations to write about later. One instructor has his students subscribe to *Newsweek*, which serves as the springboard for responses and commentary in their journals.

UNIT 2   Discovering the Paragraph

Unit 2 explains the basics of paragraph writing and organizing. Chapter 3 guides students through the process of writing paragraphs, stressing the topic sentence, development, and revision. Chapter 4 deals with order and coherence within the paragraph. Both chapters contain numerous written models for illustration and class discussion. The concluding Writers' Workshop reinforces the material in the unit through discussion and small-group work.

Chapter 3: The Process of Writing Paragraphs

Chapter 3 begins with a definition of the paragraph and with practices that help students understand the relationship of the topic sentence to the body. With this grounding, the student moves on to writing paragraphs of his or her own, first practicing topic sentences and then generating ideas to develop the body of a paragraph.

We have included paced material on topic sentences, stressing the importance of a controlling idea. The concepts of general and specific ideas, central to writing paragraphs and essays, cannot be assumed in the case of many students, who are simply unused to perceiving relationships between ideas.

If you start the course with Unit 1 on the writing process and prewriting techniques, you can spend the first few classes on these assignments and then begin Chapter 3, or you can integrate them with Chapter 3, in which brainstorming, freewriting, and asking questions are recommended as ways to generate ideas for the body. Whatever your approach, emphasize that the inventive and critical steps of the writing process should be kept distinct.

Part F in this chapter, "Writing and Revising the Paragraph," introduces revising for support and unity, and analyzes typical problems for the beginning writer: providing inadequate facts or details and drifting away from the subject. Although revision is not covered in greater depth until Unit 5, early on you may want to ask students to begin to revise and rewrite by checking for support and unity. Later, as they learn more writing techniques, they can revise on a more sophisticated level.

Throughout *Evergreen with Readings*, the practices support this cumulative process. Many practice sections include paragraphs to be revised with an eye to the particular skills being taught. Chapter 22 pulls together a number of these skills.

We recommend periodic in-class discussion and revision of student work. This shows students by example just how a writer uses and builds on strong parts and changes weak parts. Having students in groups revise material from the book or a fellow student's paper works well. We tell our students that revision is a gradually acquired art: the more they practice, the more they see; the more they learn, the more options they have. In addition, some instructors formalize revision by requiring students to turn in first and second drafts of each paper.

Chapter 4: Achieving Coherence

Here three basic kinds of paragraph order and four techniques for coherence are taught, each with short explanations and paced practices. Most developing writers do not think or write in an organized way, let alone use conscious signals to help a reader follow; yet most grasp and apply this material without much trouble once they are exposed to it.

As you teach this material, stress the effects of order and coherence (or disorder and incoherence) on reader understanding. If you use a student model of *dis*organization this early in the term, make sure that the paper is good in other ways; show how a potentially fine paper can be hindered by jumbled order.

One way to teach the material on order is to read aloud and discuss in class the model paragraphs for time, space, and importance, perhaps doing some of the practice exercises. Students have most trouble at first with the exercise on order of importance, but a brief discussion should clear up any confusion. For homework, assign one paragraph using whichever type of order each student wishes to try. In the next class, read some of these aloud.

You may wish to assign all or some of Part B, "Coherence Through Related Sentences," or skip it temporarily, moving on to the modes of development in Unit 3. The section on pronoun substitution can be supplemented with the material on consistent number and person in Chapter 19. The section on synonyms and substitutions makes an enjoyable and creative in-class exercise.

Perhaps the most crucial material here is that on transitional expressions. Many beginning writers simply do not use them. The transitional expressions of time, space, and order of importance are introduced in Part A of this chapter. Here the full range of transitional expressions is taught. Transitional expressions are also reinforced in every chapter of Unit 3, where those appropriate to each type of paragraph are highlighted.

Although students are usually quick to see the usefulness of transitional expressions, they lack a group of them to draw upon as they write. In this section, we include a reference list of such expressions. Urge students to keep it handy as they write and to add one or two new transitional expressions to each paper, striving for variety. Please note as well the chart of coordinating and subordinating conjunctions on page 337 of the text; most students find this very useful.

For additional instruction and practice in choosing the correct conjunction, see Chapter 20, "Revising for Sentence Variety," Chapter 24, "Coordination and Subordination," and Chapter 25, "Avoiding Sentence Errors."

UNIT 3 Developing the Paragraph

Unit 3 covers the rhetorical modes most frequently called for in college writing. Although this unit stresses paragraph writing, it dovetails perfectly with Chapter 15, "Types of Essays." Chapter 15 contains a model essay, instruction, and practice for every mode discussed in Unit 3, so the instructor who wishes to move directly from paragraph to essay may do so easily. Since the chapters in Unit 3 are self-contained, you can concentrate on those kinds of development that best meet the needs of your class, integrating these chapters, if you wish, into relevant parts of Chapter 15.

However, Chapter 5, "Illustration," should probably be covered first because the ability to use effective examples is assumed in many of the chapters that follow. In addition, "Narration," "Description," and "Process" (Chapters 6, 7, and 8) are easy for many students to grasp and therefore work well early in the course. In any case, we do not recommend that you teach all the modes rapidly one after the other; students need time to absorb this material.

Each chapter in Unit 3 consists of two sections, examination of a model and writing practice. The first section explains how the topic sentence must indicate clearly that a certain kind of paragraph will follow, how such a paragraph can be adequately developed, how a plan helps the writer organize his or her thoughts, and how transitional expressions link the ideas within the paragraph. The practice sections provide exercises designed to guide students through the writing process and to eliminate the kinds of errors students are likely to make as they first write each kind of paragraph.

The concluding Writers' Workshop, through discussion and small-group work, gives students practice in applying paragraph modes to real-life assignments.

Chapter 5: Illustration

This chapter presents three models for illustration: a topic sentence supported by several examples, by one detailed example, and by a narrative. Although the use of multiple examples may be the easiest of the three, some danger exists of losing sight of what one is attempting to illustrate. A simple way to overcome this problem is to have students reread their topic sentence as they write each example to ensure that each illustration clearly supports the general statement.

The greatest difficulty students encounter in using illustration is that often they do not completely understand the relationship between the general statement and its supporting examples. It is likely that their first attempts will read something like, "I would rather go to the movies than do almost anything else; for instance, westerns, comedies, and musicals." The thinking behind such a sentence is that "westerns, etc." are examples of the kind of movies that the writer enjoys. However, the examples called for by the topic sentence as written should demonstrate the writer's choice of movies over other activities.

While you are working on the relationship between the topic sentence and its examples, stress the point that a good topic sentence for an illustration paragraph should be a general statement that can be supported logically by examples. For example, "It is snowing outside" is a dead end; such a statement cannot be supported by relevant examples. However, "This has been the worst winter we have had in years" can be supported easily with illustrations of the bad weather. It is a useful exercise to write five or six topic sentences for paragraphs on the board and have the students identify those that lend themselves to illustration. Then have the class choose one topic sentence and brainstorm possible illustrations, selecting the best three.

Some students assume that the words *for example* can transform any group of words into a complete sentence: "For example, riding horseback through the park." You may find a review of Chapter 25, "Avoiding Sentence Errors," necessary. In addition, students tend to overuse this expression because they feel that every illustration must be tagged as such. Point out that the first example should certainly be clearly identified but that subsequent examples do not necessarily require transitional expressions.

Chapter 6: Narration

Most students easily take to writing narratives and, with a little coaching, they begin to see the rich subject matter that is available for storytelling. If your class is multicultural, draw on this resource by suggesting, for instance, that students write memorable family stories. Two areas may cause difficulty, however: each narrative should make a point and should follow a clear, usually chronological, order.

Working with students on creating a clear topic sentence for their narrative paragraph can help clarify the point of the story they are telling. Tell students that the point of their story may not be clear to them until they have written a draft or two and that the topic sentence may be written last, after the story is finished. Ask students to read Practice 1, on the photographer Horace Bristol, and discern the point. An effective way to stress purpose is to use narration to illustrate a point.

Students usually understand the importance of chronological order after they are alerted to its use. Extra work on time order can be found in Chapter 4, "Achieving Coherence."

Narration works nicely with lessons on present and past tense verbs (Chapters 26 and 27) and on tense consistency (Chapter 19, Part A).

Chapter 7: Description

Most students enjoy writing descriptions and putting their sensory impressions on paper; however, two areas in which they may need help are using exact language and logically ordering their observations. You may wish to review "Revising for Support," in Part F of Chapter 3 before your students begin to write. Chapter 21, "Revising for Language Awareness," also combines well with description. See the section in this manual on Chapter 21 for ideas on classroom exercises, writing assignments, and using poetry to teach descriptive language.

The sample paragraphs in Chapter 7 are carefully arranged according to space order so that students will see that description—like all good writing—requires a logical sequence. In class, you might have students describe the classroom itself, perhaps beginning by drawing a diagram of the room on the board and instructing students to describe one segment of the room at a time. Students also write lively descriptions of one another after any initial embarrassment passes. Consider tying descriptive topics to the demands of the college curriculum; have students accurately describe leaves or rocks, an interesting terrain, a piece of office equipment, and so forth.

Fragments occur rather often in some students' descriptive paragraphs. A topic sentence like "He was a strikingly handsome man" will often be followed by a fragment like "Very tall, curly black hair and a bronze complexion." Students who write such fragments have not yet taken the second step of putting jotted impressions into sentence form; they are actually hampered by their attempts to write exactly what they perceive as they perceive it. An exercise or two in making descriptive fragments into sentences can be very helpful; jot a number of adjectives on the board and have students transform them into complete sentences. You also may find it necessary to review Chapter 25, "Avoiding Sentence Errors."

Chapter 8: Process

This chapter discusses two kinds of process paragraphs: the how-to and the explanation paragraph. Point out that the first is often useful in the sciences—in describing an experiment, for example—and that the second may be useful in the liberal arts—in explaining a historical process, for instance.

Because the two kinds of process paragraphs require similar organizational and developmental skills, only the how-to paragraph is thoroughly analyzed with complete questions and a plan. After students have mastered the techniques of writing an effective how-to paragraph, they should be able to transfer them easily to the explanation paragraph.

Students' greatest difficulty in writing effective process paragraphs is maintaining chronological order. Therefore, in addition to using the sample paragraphs in the text, you might work a few paragraphs on the board with students. Let them call out the steps for some process they know well—tying a shoelace, doing a cartwheel, or cooking spaghetti—and they will soon notice that the first order they hit upon is probably not the correct chronological order of steps. Let the class put the steps into an ordered plan. Point out that strict chronological order leaves absolutely no margin for chance. See also "Time Order," in Part A of Chapter 4, for additional practice.

Students generally find transitional expressions denoting time fairly easy to use, but they tend to overuse them, beginning almost every sentence with *when, after, before, next,* etc. Make it clear that the order of the sentences in the paragraph indicates the sequence in which the steps are to be performed and that only a very few transitional expressions are necessary.

Finally, watch for the problem of dangling modifiers. Because giving directions usually involves a quasi command, students forget that modifiers must clearly relate to the words they modify. You may get a sentence like "Once cooked, remove the eggs from the pot." A short lesson on dangling modifiers might be helpful *before* students begin to write. For extra work, see Part D in Chapter 20, "Revising for Sentence Variety."

Chapter 9: Definition

The first part of this chapter is devoted to writing single-sentence definitions, used later as topic sentences of definition paragraphs. Because many students find accurate single-sentence definitions difficult to write, these definitions require more work than other topic sentences.

Part A presents three basic kinds of definitions: synonym, class, and negation. As definition by class is most often called for in college writing and is the most difficult to master, it requires the most explanation and practice. It helps to begin teaching definition by class on the board, drawing three-line columns to designate word, class, and distinguishing characteristics. Examples from everyday life are excellent to begin with; although students are familiar with such things as bikinis, benches, and coffee cups, they find accurately defining them challenging.

A discussion of definition by synonym can be taught as a mini-lesson on the dictionary. Definition by negation can introduce the student to the notion of second-guessing their readers by first presenting what they thought the definition was and then giving the true definition. Definition by negation can also be tied into Chapter 13, "Persuasion," in which the student learns about answering the opposition.

Part B deals with paragraphs of definition. Point out to students that the first model paragraph in this part is developed by examples—a good way to develop extended definitions. When students have some proficiency in defining terms, they often enjoy assignments like Practice 8 in Part B—defining everyday items for a group of visiting Martians. Good supplementary sources for work on definitions are technical or slang dictionaries. See also the notes in this manual on Chapter 19.

You might want to introduce your students to more poetic definitions, like these from the Quotation Bank at the end of *Evergreen with Readings*:

"Love is a fire, but whether it's going to warm your hearth or burn down your house, you can never tell."—Dorothy Parker

"Life is a succession of moments. To live each one is to succeed."—Corita Kent

"What is a friend? A single soul dwelling in two bodies."—Aristotle

Chapter 10: Comparison and Contrast

Comparison and contrast paragraphs require much practice to master, yet they are two of the most important rhetorical modes in college writing.

The plan for these paragraphs is somewhat more complex than the plans studied so far. In fact, the use of the two-column plan may be somewhat forbidding to students at first, but a few sample plans on the board should dispel their initial confusion. However, you should stress two important aspects of the plan. It must show parallel information for items A and B, and it should list this information in exactly the same order for each item. By so doing, the writer ensures that nothing is left out and nothing extraneous is added. Additional explanation may also be needed to reinforce the difference between the two methods of presenting the information in the plan: (1) all of A, followed by B or (2) skipping back and forth between A and B. One effective way of showing the importance of the choice between these two methods is to read aloud one short paragraph and one long one, both using the first method of ordering. Then ask if students can recall the various points of contrast. They will undoubtedly recall more of the short paragraph. This experiment can provide proof that the first method is better for short compositions when the reader can easily recall what has gone before.

Students should have no particular difficulty with the comparison paragraph after they have learned how to write a contrast paragraph. However, it is wise to continue using the same two-column plan to minimize the chances of excluding necessary points of comparison or adding extra unnecessary ones. The student model given here usually provokes interesting discussion.

The last paragraph taught in this chapter, the comparison-contrast paragraph, is somewhat more advanced, and you may wish to assign it only selectively. You might find it best to explain the sample paragraph in two parts, first the comparison and then the contrast. Writing each plan on a separate blackboard might demonstrate the division of the plan.

Chapter 11: Classification

One professor we know introduces classification by bringing in numerous magazine advertisements. He spreads these on a table or on the floor and asks his students to classify them into piles. Having done this, they discuss their bases of classification, and the professor suggests other possibilities they may not have thought of, such as "ads that intimidate."

Beginning writers may confuse classification with illustration. To help them make the distinction, consider using a sample illustration, like "Many people in this class have jobs." Then ask class members to volunteer as examples of students who have jobs. Next, ask the class on what basis *all* class members could be gathered into groups so that everyone in the room would fit into a particular category. Some of the obvious answers will be classification by gender, race, major, etc. Once they see that illustration means using a few examples to support a general statement and that classification means placing all items into discrete groups according to a single criterion, they should be able to handle the work of the chapter.

To clarify the nature of classification further, begin the discussion of the sample topic sentence by asking, "Can there be a gym-goer that does not fit one of the four categories mentioned in the topic sentence?" If students can answer this question correctly, they are off to a good start.

Somewhere in the middle of their classification paragraphs, many students hit upon a new method of dividing the group, and the original classification goes awry. Urge students to watch out for that problem as they create their plans, and point out that clustering often works well as a preclassification technique.

Chapter 12: Cause and Effect

The ability to discern causes and effects is extremely important in college and beyond, yet cause-and-effect analysis can be tricky. Students tend to oversimplify, overgeneralize, or even mistake causes for effects. Therefore, careful class discussion of the sample paragraphs in the text and of your own examples worked through on the blackboard is key. Consider having the full class work through Practice 1 together, analyzing and discussing a student's paragraph on date rape. Practice 2 provides useful practice in differentiating causes and effects; you might point out to students that items in the practice represent the kinds of thinking tasks they will be called upon to undertake in college and on the job. Practice 3 provides good preparation for students' own writing, moving from understanding to actual writing. We have found that students enjoy Practice 5, a collaborative task, and some are inspired to learn that their backgrounds may predispose them to entrepreneurial risk.

Because discussions of most subjects—from students addicted to computer games to fashion trends to the difference between high and low achievers—invite an examination of causes and effects, this chapter can generate great excitement and be tied to units of study, outside readings, and even mini-research projects.

Chapter 13: Persuasion

This chapter may be the most difficult one in Unit 3. Here the student has to contend not only with the usual problems of development and organization but also with the judicious use of clear and adequate evidence to convince the reader.

The sample paragraph in Chapter 13 is somewhat artificial, as it contains five basic methods of argumentation—illustration, using facts, referring to an authority, predicting consequences, and answering the opposition. This paragraph and plan should be analyzed slowly, so that students can learn to differentiate between various kinds of evidence. Examples should not be too difficult, as illustration is covered fully in Chapter 5; however, you may find a brief review helpful.

Using facts may be more of a problem because often it is not easy for beginning writers to marshal facts effectively in defense of a thesis. In addition, even the hardest facts are sometimes circumstantial and depend on a biased reading of data. Still, a valuable classroom exercise might be to write a list of "facts" on the board and ask students to distinguish between real facts and mere assumptions. After they have settled on a number of clear facts, ask how they could prove their selections valid. Many will answer that they can verify them by looking them up. Where one looks up a fact can provide a mini-lesson on the use of library, Internet, and other source material. Remind students that they must clearly state the source of any facts in their compositions. You may wish to refer students to Chapter 18, which addresses plagiarism, summary, and quotation of outside sources.

The important point to stress about referring to an authority is simply that an authority has to be an expert on the subject being discussed. Ask students to discuss television commercials in which the "authority"—a basketball player—recommends soft drinks or cereal. A useful classroom exercise is to ask a question like "Where would you go for an authority on _____?" The class should be able to say whom they would consult for authoritative and unbiased information. This exercise puts them in touch with resources available to them, in person, in print, and on-line.

Predicting the consequences and answering the opposition require critical thinking skills in part addressed in Chapter 12, "Cause and Effect." Working through an example with the full class is always an effective way to hone students' skills and rein in their tendency to exaggerate or leap to conclusions. Brief writing exercises in which students must actually argue *for* the opposition's position are excellent because many students first approach argumentation passionately convinced that their point of view is the only right one. You might ask small groups to analyze the meaning and persuasive effectiveness of the cartoon on gun-toting children.

Instructors who wish to introduce college research skills to their students often feel that lessons on persuasion are the logical place to do so. Chapter 18, "Special College Skills: Summary and Quotation," ties in nicely with this aim, teaching these two basic competencies. Further, your college librarian can help you demonstrate to students that research can be downright exciting, rather than the tedious task some expect it to be. Library resources and the Internet can open new worlds in the mustering of evidence and facts.

UNIT 4 Writing the Essay

Unit 4 shows students how they can apply effective paragraph-writing techniques to the multiparagraph essay and the essay examination. Further, this unit stresses those aspects of writing unique to the longer composition. Chapter 14 takes students through the essay-writing process; Chapter 15 applies each of the nine developmental modes discussed in Unit 3 to essay writing. Chapter 16 discusses the introduction, conclusion, and title in depth, and Chapter 17 guides students through the essay examination. Chapter 18 introduces summary writing and incorporating quotations into essays.

Instructors who introduce the essay early in the term may do so with ease; Unit 4 dovetails with the material on paragraph writing in Units 2 and 3. The Writers' Workshop at the end of this unit reinforces work on organizing an essay through discussion of a student essay and collaborative revision tasks.

Chapter 14: The Process of Writing an Essay

Part A introduces the essay and indicates that the essay and the paragraph are similar in structure—each having an introduction, a body, and a conclusion. Part B points out the importance of a controlling idea in the thesis statement and essay. The more specific the thesis statement, the easier it will be for the writer to organize his or her thoughts and for the reader to have a clear sense of what the rest of the essay will discuss. Since the concepts of structure and specificity have already been discussed in relation to the paragraph, it would be wise to assure your students that much of what they have already learned about writing effective paragraphs can be applied to writing effective essays.

Part C shows students two ways to plan the body of an essay: (1) brainstorming or freewriting ideas and then finding paragraph groups and/or (2) writing topic sentences and then planning the subsequent paragraphs. Although these methods are equally effective, one may be better suited than the other for a specific writing problem. When a student has trouble beginning an essay, he or she may find the first method helpful because the mind can run free without worrying about order or relevance. (Note that this method is used in Chapters 2 and 3.) The merit of the second method—writing topic sentences and then planning paragraphs—is that it forces the writer to eliminate irrelevant ideas early on.

Whichever option your students choose, you must make it clear to them that a good writer does not pad a paragraph in order to develop an essay. New ideas, new facts, or new examples can flesh out the essay, but pointless repetition makes for an empty and dull composition.

You may find it helpful to begin a discussion of Part D, "Ordering and Linking Paragraphs in the Essay," by briefly reviewing time, space, and order of importance, discussed in Chapter 4, "Achieving Coherence." Often, of course, one of these three orders will not work for a particular essay, and you might stress that it is then the responsibility of the writer to find a logical sequence of ideas.

Once students have begun to write short compositions, they need to know how to provide the reader with a smooth transition from paragraph to paragraph. Although Part D presents four basic methods of linking paragraphs, too often students will use one method exclusively—especially transitional expressions—with the result that every paragraph begins with *in addition, therefore,* or *in conclusion.* The practices in this part are designed to show students just how varied linking devices can be.

Part E demonstrates the process of revising an essay. The complete first and revised drafts of a student essay are shown, together with an explanation for every revision made. As with the revision material in Chapters 3 and 22, you may wish to discuss with the whole class the weaknesses of the first draft and the effectiveness of the changes before students revise their own papers.

The assignments in Part E have worked well for our students; refer students to the checklist at the end of the chapter. Once they have written a few of the assigned essays, most students will have little trouble planning and developing short essays of their own.

Chapter 15: Types of Essays

Chapter 15 dovetails with the chapters on developmental modes in Unit 3: illustration, narration, description, process, definition, comparison/contrast, classification, cause and effect, and persuasion. Each part of Chapter 15 contains a description of the uses of a particular developmental mode in college and business, a well-developed model essay processed with questions, specific tips on writing the thesis statement or body of such an essay, and a list of writing topics.

With this chapter, instructors who move from a particular paragraph pattern—comparison/contrast, for instance—to an essay using the same pattern of development can do so with ease. The value of such a procedure is that students begin to write short essays early in the term and hence lose their hesitancy about writing longer compositions. When a class is sufficiently advanced, some instructors bypass Chapter 14 and move right from selected Unit 3 chapters to Chapter 15.

Chapter 16: The Introduction, the Conclusion, and the Title

Part A covers six methods of writing introductions, but you may want to concentrate on the three or four most appropriate to the kind of writing you expect the class to do. If your class discusses readings, ask students to analyze the professionals' introductions. Part B provides only three methods of concluding, as more often than not the last idea of the theme is the conclusion, and nothing else is necessary. Part C covers the title. Make sure students understand that the title and the thesis statement are two different elements in the essay.

Be sure to stress also that although the introduction and the conclusion are important, the body is the largest and most vital part of the essay. Otherwise, students may devote too much time to polishing the introduction and conclusion and skimp on the body of the essay.

Chapter 17: Writing Under Pressure: The Essay Examination

Writing-across-the-curriculum programs underscore the need for good writing skills for all students, yet students often feel that what they write for an English instructor has no use in history, psychology, or philosophy. This chapter aims to show students that what they have learned in English can help them throughout their college and professional careers and that effective planning and writing are pragmatic skills.

Part A explains six basic steps that students can take to help them use the time allotted on an essay examination effectively. Since students often panic when they first see an examination, a review of this part will make clear to them that their grades depend both on how much they know and on how well they present their ideas.

Part B teaches careful reading and correct interpretation of examination questions. By breaking the question into its component parts, the student will know better what he or she has to do; by conceptualizing the question as a set of instructions—"the student must"—he or she stands a good chance of answering the entire question. You may wish to acquire old final examinations from other faculty members and use them in class as practice exercises; a test-taking workshop with "real exams" never fails to spark student interest.

In Part C students can directly apply to the essay examination what they have learned in Units 3 and 4. It might be a good idea to review the developmental modes that you covered in Unit 3 before going on to Part C. If there are some modes that you have not discussed, give the students a brief summary of them, if possible, so they will be able to complete the practice exercises. Stress the fact that students can apply these skills from English class to many other courses.

As Part D demonstrates, using key words from the question in the first sentence of the answer is a time-honored technique, yet many students are unaware of it. They tend to get lost in lengthy introductions and never quite answer the question. Before you begin the practice, a useful classroom exercise is to have one student devise a question—"How is the weather today?"—and have him or her call upon another student to answer the question using its key words, "The weather today is fine." Accustomed to hearing the repetition of the key words of the question in the answer, most students have no difficulty learning to write precise topic and thesis statements. In bolstering your students' exam-taking skills, stress the pertinence of the composing process to nearly all courses. In fact, under the time pressure of an exam, planning and outlining skills become even more important because there is usually little time to rewrite or recopy the answer later on. A checklist for taking essay examinations is provided.

Chapter 18: Special College Skills: Summary and Quotation

The goal of this chapter is to ease the transition from developmental writing to higher-level English and other college courses that require students to read, respond to, condense, and cite outside sources. Part A discusses plagiarism, a recurring problem that has increased with the availability of student essays on the Internet. However, students sometimes do not realize when they are plagiarizing or do not know how to incorporate references into their own writing. By discussing and practicing *how* to quote from sources, students should become more sensitive to the issue of plagiarism in general, as well as become more confident in their ability to quote appropriately from sources.

Part B guides students through the writing of a summary, helps them evaluate the effectiveness of two summaries of the same piece of writing, and provides a checklist. The single most common problem students encounter is injecting their feelings and opinions as they summarize. Stress that summarizing is purely objective reportage. Have small groups summarize one source and then read to each other and choose the best and most objective summary. The skills involved in summary writing are widely applicable in college and in the business world. An excellent assignment is asking students to summarize a reading selection that the whole class has read.

Part C shows students how to quote from outside sources to enrich their own writing. Suggesting ways in which students can use the words of others to stress important ideas, reinforce their own ideas with validation by authorities, provide interesting introductions or conclusions, or simply add sparkle to their writing "legitimizes" using the words of others and helps students avoid plagiarism. The chapter ends with several paragraphs from interesting outside sources; students practice writing direct and indirect quotations from these sources, introducing quotations in different ways, and writing summaries. The instructor who wants to familiarize students with basic research may wish to use this chapter as a means to that end.

UNIT 5   Improving Your Writing

Unit 5 contains chapters on revising for consistency, parallelism, sentence variety, and language awareness. Select those chapters that your class or individuals need. You may wish to alternate this material with the Unit 3 modes or to assign only some chapters (for example, Chapter 21) earlier in the term, as you introduce revising for exact language or description.

One way to approach the elements in this unit is to urge students to revise with them in mind. Chapters 19 through 21 include practices in which the student must revise selectively for the skill being taught. Chapter 22 demonstrates the process of revising specifically for the material in the three preceding chapters.

The Writers' Workshop at the end of this unit reinforces the revising skills covered in the unit through discussion and small-group work.

Chapter 19: Revising for Consistency and Parallelism

The need for consistency may come as a complete surprise to developing writers, who usually grasp the idea quickly, however, when they see how inconsistency confuses readers. This chapter begins with consistent tense, perhaps the most common problem for beginning writers, who may also be struggling to overcome verb errors. In teaching this material, watch for the student who cannot spot the verb at all, let alone make it consistent with other verbs. Such a student should review Chapter 23, "The Simple Sentence," and the verb chapters in Unit 6.

Consistent number and person are almost universally confusing to new writers. As you teach these principles, it is wise to go over a few practice exercises in class, encouraging students to ask questions freely. As the term progresses, reinforce these lessons by pointing out examples in student work or by spot-checking with questions. Other pronoun practice appears in Chapter 4, "Achieving Coherence," and Chapter 30, "Pronouns."

We find that "Parallelism," Part C, is an extremely useful concept for beginning writers, who quite readily understand and apply it. You may wish to assign this section by itself. Students enjoy the practices, which work especially well in class.

Chapter 20: Revising for Sentence Variety

Learning to use a variety of sentences is a matter of time and trial, as any instructor knows. This chapter is not meant to be read through and mastered in one sitting. Rather, here is a compendium of techniques. With practice, trying out one or two at a time, a writer can learn to achieve the effects he or she wants.

Stressing the writer's choice, not just correctness, we assume here that the student already possesses some knowledge of sentence basics. In fact, this chapter is designed to dovetail with and be followed up by a review of the basics in Chapters 23 and 24.

The importance of *revising* for sentence variety should be emphasized—going back over the first draft to see, for example, if there are too many short, choppy sentences or too many sentences coordinated with *and*. You might wish to have students analyze and chart the sentences in a recent paper. To gather the facts, they might number every sentence in the paper and make a grid like this:

	Length	Begins with	Type
Sentence 1	_____	_____	_____
Sentence 2	_____	_____	_____
Sentence 3	_____	_____	_____

Then each student should ask: Are most of my sentences the same number of words long? Do most begin in the same way? Do I overuse one type of sentence? The student should decide what he or she would like to change and set short-term goals for the next paper. Many word-processing programs will analyze the word-count and even the structure of the writer's sentences. This kind of feedback can be valuable and enjoyable, especially when used as a tool for improvement.

Encourage the class to refer to the review of techniques as they write their paragraphs and essays, choosing two or three techniques to try out.

Chapter 21: Revising for Language Awareness

This material may be taught as it occurs in the text or integrated with earlier chapters if you wish—for example, with the section on developing the body of a paragraph in Chapter 3, "The Process of Writing Paragraphs," or with Chapter 7, "Description."

The study of language can be illuminating to developing writers, who may believe that without a large vocabulary they cannot write powerfully. Assure them that although vocabulary building is a worthwhile pursuit, it is not the only way to improve writing. Any writer can begin by closely observing, using the senses, and searching for the right word.

Consider launching a study of exact language by showing up in class with paper cups and several large bottles of cola. Ask the students to have writing paper handy, and pour each one a cup of cola. Have them take a sip, savor the taste, and write down one word that accurately describes their *precise* experience. Then have them taste again and search for another word, repeating this process until everyone has written down at least ten words. Finally, ask them to read over their list and underline the most exact word. Often the best word is not the one they thought of first but one that emerged later. Discuss the results.

Or bring in four or five objects—a shell, a piece of bark, a metal cube, a lemon, for example—and give each one to a group of students. Ask the students to use their different senses, examine each object, and then write, capturing their experience in words. As they read aloud what they have written, list on the board key words and phrases that describe each object. Then discuss the lists, perhaps noting patterns: a preponderance of sibilant *s*'s used to describe the shell or a preponderance of words of touch, or dislike, for another object. Exercises that heighten language awareness are limited only by your imagination.

Parts B and C of this chapter, on avoiding wordiness and triteness, are especially useful to college writers. Remember that what are tired usages to you may not seem overworked to your students, so stress the obvious clichés or fad terms that lose their meaning quickly.

Well-chosen poems are another wonderful way to show the dazzling powers of language. Reproduce two or three poems, have the class discuss their meaning, then examine how the poet's word choices create certain effects. We have had good luck with Stanley Kunitz's "The Portrait," Elizabeth Bishop's "The Fish," Marianne Moore's own "The Fish," Theodore Roethke's "Old Florist" and "The Meadow Mouse"—the list is endless. See Robert Bly's anthology, *News from the Universe,* for an inspiring selection of poems.

You may wish to bring a thesaurus to class or to introduce your students to various dictionaries, vocabulary-building books, or the thesaurus feature in most word-processing programs. Dictionaries of slang terms often interest students. We find that actual vocabulary building is done most effectively by the individual student who is ready to try. One excellent tool that we recommend to all students, however, is an individual vocabulary list of new words to try out in papers.

Chapter 22: Putting Your Revision Skills to Work

This chapter builds on the basic revision process presented in Chapter 3, Part F, and shows students how to revise for the more subtle elements of good writing taught in Unit 5. Revision requires a complex of skills acquired over time; throughout *Evergreen with Readings,* the practices support this cumulative process. Chapter 22 assumes that the process of revision has been encouraged throughout the course, perhaps collaboratively in class. (See "Reproducing and Discussing Student Work" earlier in this manual.)

Chapter 22 shows the first and revised drafts of two student paragraphs, with the reasons for every change clearly marked. You may want to go over these drafts with the class, discussing the revisions, before students revise the practice essay or their own work. Collaboratively revising one sample paragraph in class also works well.

UNIT 6   Reviewing the Basics

"Reviewing the Basics" is an overview of fundamental grammar skills. Each chapter contains paced practice exercises and concludes with a review practice—usually essay length—in which students proofread for and correct particular errors. You will no doubt wish to assign these chapters to the class or to individuals as needed.

If you ask students to keep a list of their own errors and error patterns on each composition, make the point that writers have individual strengths and weaknesses and that such a record can help each student chart his or her progress or lack of it. Consistent errors in one area may force students to realize that they need extra help with specific problems. If your class has Internet access, a session on finding and using good ESL or OWL (on-line writing lab) sites might prove very useful.

The concluding Writers' Workshop reinforces the material in this unit through discussion and small-group work, affording students a chance to proofread a peer's essay and to note typical errors.

Chapter 23: *The Simple Sentence*

This chapter introduces the basic elements of the complete sentence, the subject and the verb. Part B anticipates a common problem by teaching students to spot prepositional phrases and to differentiate them from the true subject of a sentence. It might be wise to review Part B when teaching Chapter 26, "Present Tense (Agreement)," and Chapter 30, "Pronouns," because students will need a clear understanding of prepositional phrases for portions of these chapters.

Chapter 24: *Coordination and Subordination*

This chapter covers the basics of joining ideas by means of coordination and subordination. Parts C and D, "Semicolons" and "Conjunctive Adverbs," are more advanced than Parts A and B, "Coordination" and "Subordination," and you may wish to assign them selectively. A review chart in Part E, "Review," summarizes the writer's options in clear form; many students find this chart very helpful.

We believe that a thorough knowledge of coordination and subordination will help students to avoid the most common sentence errors in their own writing. These errors—run-ons, comma splices, and fragments—are covered in Chapter 25, "Avoiding Sentence Errors."

Chapter 20, "Revising for Sentence Variety," provides another logical follow-up to this chapter. After students have mastered coordination and subordination, Chapter 20 can teach them to vary the beginnings of sentences and to link ideas in other ways.

Chapter 25: *Avoiding Sentence Errors*

This chapter provides clear definitions and many examples of the three basic sentence errors: run-ons, comma splices, and fragments. The practice exercises contain individual sentences, paragraphs, and essays. The paragraph- and essay-length practices are especially useful because after students learn to spot and correct such errors in isolated sentences, they need additional work spotting them in longer pieces of writing.

Chapter 26: Present Tense (Agreement)

Chapter 26 begins with the basics of subject-verb agreement in Parts A and B and then moves quickly to more complex cases, in which some additional skill is necessary to locate the subject and make the verb agree with it. (See Chapter 23, "The Simple Sentence," for extra drills on spotting subjects.) Students' major difficulty comes from their assumption that the subject is necessarily the first or second word in a sentence or that it always directly precedes the verb. A careful working of Parts C, D, E, and F should eliminate this problem as students learn to spot the subject wherever it might appear in the sentence.

Parts E and F can be studied in conjunction with Chapter 20, "Revising for Sentence Variety." Part G may be followed up with Part D, "Commas with Nonrestrictive and Restrictive Clauses," in Chapter 34.

Chapter 27: Past Tense

This chapter briefly reviews regular verbs and includes a chart of irregular verbs. Students should be encouraged to acquire the habit of using the chart or looking up verbs they are not sure of in the dictionary.

The only verbs singled out for special attention are *to be, can,* and *will.* We feel that a thorough review of *to be* is necessary because this is the only verb requiring subject-verb agreement in the past tense and because students often confuse *was* and *were.* There is also a note about *wasn't* and *weren't,* as the addition of negative contraction endings tends to confuse students. An entire section, Part D, is devoted to *can* and *will* because students are frequently unaware that these verbs have a past tense. We have omitted the conditional mood of these verbs because the rules are subtle and complex.

A good follow-up to this chapter is Part A, "Consistent Tense," in Chapter 19.

A possible assignment for Chapters 26 and 27 is to have students write brief narratives at home—perhaps what they do on a particular morning—in the present tense. Then, in class, ask them to change all the verbs in their narratives to the past tense.

Chapter 28: The Past Participle

Part A defines the past participle and provides practice in writing the past participles of regular verbs. Be careful to note that the helping verb *to have* must agree with its subject. If necessary, refer the class to Part B, which covers the past participles of irregular verbs. Encourage students to use the chart or to consult a dictionary when they are not sure of the correct past participle form of an irregular verb.

Parts C and D introduce basic uses of the present perfect and past perfect tenses. We have omitted some of the more complex rules concerning the relationship of tenses.

Part E covers the passive voice and Part F the use of the past participle as an adjective. An effective classroom exercise is to have students change active sentences into the passive voice. However, warn students to use the passive voice sparingly in their writing, applying it only when they wish to show the passivity of the subject.

It is often difficult for students to understand that past participles can serve as adjectives because they believe a word can be one, and only one, part of speech. You might find it best to cover Part E at some later time, not directly after Parts C and D, because the many uses of the past participle may confuse students if presented all at once.

Chapter 29: Nouns

This chapter begins with lists of some common irregular plurals and then continues with signal words that indicate singular or plural. Part C covers constructions like *one of the* and *many of the,* which occasionally give students trouble. You may wish to assign this chapter or parts of it as needed.

Chapter 30: Pronouns

Once students understand the relationship between the pronoun and its antecedent, they should have little trouble with the material covered in Part B of this chapter: indefinite pronouns, special singular antecedents, and collective nouns. You may refer students to Chapter 26, Part C, "Special Singular Constructions," for related work on verb agreement. In addition, Part B, "Consistent Number and Person," in Chapter 19 contains work on pronoun reference.

More difficult for students to grasp are the problems of vague, repetitious, and ambiguous pronoun references, dealt with in Part C of Chapter 30. These errors are so much a part of informal speech that students are likely to say, "But I know what the sentence means." You might wish to give a brief talk on the difference between formal written English and informal spoken English, emphasizing that "knowing what it means" may not be sufficient for clear college writing.

Part D is fairly simple and direct; students' main difficulty here is in choosing the correct pronoun in a comparison. Once they are able to complete the comparison mentally, they should be able to choose the correct case.

Part E covers reflexive and intensive pronouns, providing a chart to help students use these forms.

Chapter 31: Prepositions

Part A covers the difference between *in* and *on* for time and place, and Part B contains a list of frequently used expressions containing prepositions. The chapter will be especially useful to ESL students, who are often baffled by the idiomatic use of prepositions in English. Memorization and review are the best approaches to this material. Students might find it helpful to mark those expressions that give them trouble and to keep their own chart of other commonly used expressions and phrases. In fact, a class chart containing expressions contributed by individuals throughout the term can be fun as well as informative.

Chapter 32: Adjectives and Adverbs

If your students have trouble grasping the difference between adjectives and adverbs, stress this distinction: Adjectives often answer the questions *What kind? Which one? How many?* Adverbs often answer the question *When? Where? To what extent?*

A good supplement to the practice provided in Part A is to have students make up two sentences, one using the adjectival and the other the adverbial form of a word. This kind of oral/aural reinforcement helps students *hear* the difference, a skill that can be transferred fairly easily to the written word. Parts B and C are straightforward, although some extra care should be taken in teaching *good/well,* so often confused in everyday speech.

Chapter 33: The Apostrophe

Students' most common error in using the apostrophe for a contraction is to misplace the apostrophe between the two contracted words. Once they realize that the apostrophe indicates a deleted letter or letters, this problem can be easily resolved. A word like *won't*, however, requires special attention because, as a contraction of *will* and *not,* it does not readily break down into its component parts.

You may run into some difficulties in teaching the apostrophe to show ownership. Many students believe that plural nouns always take the apostrophe after the *s.* Of course, with words like *children, men,* or *women,* this rule does not hold. What you should stress is that the ending of the ownership word determines where the apostrophe is placed.

After you have finished teaching the chapter, however, be prepared to find some students placing apostrophes before or after almost every final *s*. For some reason, they are apt to see ownership everywhere: "The boys' took their skates." Because the boys own their skates, the student reasons, an apostrophe is required. You may find it necessary to devote another lesson to spotting those cases in which an apostrophe is called for and those in which it is not.

Chapter 34: The Comma

You may not wish to teach this entire chapter at once; there are a number of rules here, and students may get them confused. You may prefer to teach the various uses of the comma concomitantly with Chapter 20, "Revising for Sentence Variety," and Chapter 24, "Coordination and Subordination."

Chapter 35: Mechanics

This chapter requires no special comment. You may find it helpful to link Part C, "Direct Quotations," with Chapter 13, "Persuasion," in which the student learns about quoting an authority. If you expect students to use quotations from other written sources, you may also want to link Part B, "Titles," with your lessons on persuasive writing.

Chapter 36: Putting Your Proofreading Skills to Work

This chapter caps the grammar review unit with six high-interest paragraphs and essays for mixed-error proofreading. In the preceding chapters of Unit 6, students found and corrected individual errors—those in verb agreement, for example. Here students proofread documents like those they will encounter in the real world of college and work—those containing a realistic mix of errors. For example, Proofreading Practice 1 contains run-ons, comma splices, and fragments; subject-verb agreement errors; past tense errors; and past particple errors. The problems that students have most frequently—sentence boundary errors and verb errors—are proportionately represented in these exercises. The paragraph-length practices list the types of errors that students should watch for, with chapter references in Unit 6 given for review; the essay-length practices contain random errors.

For still more practice in mixed-error proofreading, the Writers' Workshop concluding each unit provides students with an opportunity to read the work of a peer and evaluate it for such qualities as unity, coherence, support, organization, and correctness. About half the student compositions in these workshops contain grammar errors, and students are encouraged to proofread for "error patterns"—

the same error made two or more times. Thus, peer proofreaders not only realistically scrutinize a document, but get to see that writers often make habitual mistakes that can be recognized and corrected.

UNIT 7 Strengthening Your Spelling

Chapter 37: Spelling

This chapter provides students with clear explanations of some basic spelling rules and their exceptions, each reinforced with ample practice. The entire section should be taught slowly because the rules take time to digest and spelling drills can quickly become tedious.

Parts A and B might be discussed early in the term so that students can begin to keep spelling lists, devise tricks for remembering difficult words, and get in the habit of using spell-check software. Part C is often a necessary preface to further work in spelling because—depending on the level of the class—some students may not clearly understand what vowels and consonants are. Since Parts D and E deal with the doubling of consonants, they might logically be discussed with Chapter 27, "Past Tense." The rules discussed in Parts G and H can likewise be related to lessons on present-tense verbs and past-tense verbs. Part I can be assigned individually or to a class as needed.

Chapter 38: Look-Alikes/Sound-Alikes

This chapter defines and gives examples of words that writing students often confuse, like *accept/except* or *then/than.* A practice for each group provides additional work on these words. Assign sections to individuals or to the class as needed.

UNIT 8 Reading Selections

For instructors who wish to incorporate reading into their writing classes, this unit contains fourteen professional reading selections. An introduction presents "Reading Strategies for Writers," with ten useful suggestions, and contains a short essay, "How Sunglasses Spanned the World," with sample student annotations. The readings offer a range of high-interest subjects, authorial voices, and written models. At least one example of each rhetorical mode taught in this book is included; see the rhetorical index to the readings for guidance.

As you weave the readings into the course, you may wish to follow up certain chapters in the text with readings—for example, follow work on exact language with Alice Walker's "Beauty: When the Other Dancer Is the Self" or cause and effect with Andrew Ferguson's "Road Rage." Suggestions for other such linkages are given in the sections on individual readings below.

If your class is poorly prepared for reading, consider using prereading strategies to help students gain access to an essay. Short writings or small-group discussions on a topic relevant to the selection work well. As an aid to comprehension, consider having students keep a journal, perhaps a double-entry journal in which one column is devoted to notes and queries about the material itself and another is devoted to the student's own reactions and questions. Having students summarize an essay is another excellent technique; précis writing teaches important skills and improves comprehension. See the instruction and checklist in "Writing a Summary," Part B of Chapter 18. Small-group discussions guided by one or more of the Discussion and Writing Questions will help students make sense of what they have read.

Some instructors will assign the readings individually, and others may wish to use thematically linked pairs or clusters. Having students apply the ideas or style in one essay to those in another builds thinking skills and promotes a conversation of ideas. Try having students write dialogues between themselves and an author or between one author and another. Consider such clusters as these: male roles and relationships (Staples, Wu, Ashe); female roles and relationships (Cisneros, Denfeld, Walker); dealing with loss (Quindlen, Walker, Staples, Denfeld); success and failure (McGinnis, Ortiz Cofer, Walker, Staples, Cisneros); multicultural or minority experience and self-esteem (Ortiz Cofer, Rodriguez, Staples, Cisneros, McGinnis); work and careers (Ashe, Rodriguez, Denfeld, Cisneros).

Encourage students to apply themes and ideas from a reading selection to current articles from newspapers or magazines or to a film. This exercise will help them connect their reading to the "real world."

Sandra Cisneros, "Only Daughter"

This essay vividly explores the tangled issues of identity, ethnic heritage, gender, and professional calling. Cisneros is a story teller, writing her way to understanding. At the heart of this tale is the relationship between a traditional Mexican father who values sons and the talented daughter who yearns for his approval. Have students find and read aloud some of the wonderfully written details that convey the Mexican-ness of the home that shaped Cisneros. Students usually respond strongly to a discussion of familial expectations, whether high or low; some students might wish to share personal experiences of their families' expectations and whether they reacted by rebelling against or accepting the role laid out for them. Students might discuss the wounds as well as the freedoms that came to Cisneros or themselves as a result of such expectations. In Cisneros's case, what finally earned the father's attention and admiration? Cisneros's striking opening—trying to sum up her identity in one sentence—suggests an exercise in which students do the same, revising until they have it "right."

Cisneros's emotional honesty is evident in much of her writing. Students might discuss the role of honesty in all good writing. Other topics for exploration and writing might include people's reactions to the expectations of their partners, cultures, or peer groups. How does a person find his or her true professional calling? This essay works nicely with Denfeld's "The Lady of the Ring," which examines male and female expectations about boxing, or with essays by Wu and Ortiz Cofer on coping with being different. Consider having students apply the ideas on building self-esteem in Alan McGinnis's article to Sandra Cisneros. How would students rate Cisneros's self-esteem? Has she applied any of McGinnis's principles?

Arthur Ashe, "My Outing"

This moving excerpt from Ashe's autobiography, *Days of Grace*, details, through well-chosen examples, the public's response to news that Ashe had AIDS. Reactions to this disease can be so unkind that its sufferers are almost forced into secrecy, and the story of Ashe's threatened "outing" by the press opens wide the issues of privacy and the power of other people's judgments. Ironically, Ashe's announcement prompted an outpouring of sympathetic letters from people all over the world; his descriptions of some of these form the emotional heart of the essay—and no doubt one source of the "grace" referred to in the title of his book.

If you feel comfortable in doing so, you might consider raising a question implicit in this selection: Because Ashe got AIDS through a blood transfusion, were people more sympathetic than they might have been if he had contracted it in some other way? Does this attitude make any sense?

Chapters on narration or illustration might precede a discussion of this essay. Consider comparing this essay with others on loss and triumph, for example, Denfeld's "The Lady of the Ring." An interesting lesson on the power of personal letters might flow from Ashe's essay.

Rene Denfeld, "The Lady of the Ring"

This beautifully written essay explores issues of self-esteem, mentoring, and cross-gender understanding. As a prewriting exercise, students might write about or discuss stereotypes related to boxing or some other sport or to gender. Consider guiding students to discuss the stereotyped male and female roles that Denfeld explores. Why, for example, did the men feel they had to hit Denfeld as hard as they could? What stereotyped roles did they feel they had to live out? Students can then discuss the ways in which Denfeld's perceptions of the sexes change and the profound effects her new perceptions have on her life. Have them share times from their own lives when their beliefs about something or someone shifted dramatically.

Chapters on process, narration, or cause and effect could precede work with this essay. It also may be grouped with others involving role models (for example, Wu's "In Search of Bruce Lee's Grave"), with gender stereotypes (Cisneros's "Only Daughter"), with liberation from fear or self-doubt (Walker's "Beauty: When the Other Dancer Is the Self"), or with loss (Staples's "A Brother's Murder").

Suzanne Britt, "Neat People Versus Sloppy People"

Most students enjoy Britt's spoof of a contrast essay, a lighthearted look at two common human types and at the kind of thinking that stereotypes people. Does the author really think that sloppy people are morally superior? Of course, she is turning a common societal assumption on its head: that neat people are somehow superior to sloppy ones. Ask your students whether they would identify themselves as sloppy people or neat people. Do they agree with Britt's assessment of their motivation? The fact that sloppiness and procrastination can be serious and painful problems for some people adds punch to the essay. If any students have trouble catching Britt's ironic tone, an introduction to irony may be in order. Have students provide examples from daily interactions (for example, saying the words "Thanks a *lot*" when someone makes their life difficult).

Work on comparison/contrast could precede this essay. Britt here provides an excellent and humorous model of point-by-point contrast. Students may enjoy writing humorous comparison-contrast essays of their own. Encourage them to take a stand that reverses a commonly held view; they might, for example, show that people who eat junk food are morally superior to people who eat health food. Consider pairing this with Alan McGinnis's serious look at self-esteem and achievement, "How to Get the Most Out of Yourself."

Alan Loy McGinnis, "How to Get the Most Out of Yourself"

Students usually enjoy discussing this essay and applying its suggestions to their own lives. Have students note the author's use of well-chosen examples to develop his points and of periodic quotations to support his ideas. You might wish to tell your class about *Bartlett's Familiar Quotations* and other sources of interesting quotations (classified by subject and author) they could use in their writing.

The chapters on illustration or persuasion can lead into this essay. As a pre-reading exercise, you might ask students to freewrite on the topic "The Secret of Success." Ask them to comb newspapers and magazines for contemporary success stories; do McGinnis's ideas seem to apply to such stories? Later, either in discussion groups or in writing, have students choose one of McGinnis's suggestions that they feel would most help them and set a reachable goal to apply it in their own lives. Or try guiding students through a visualization exercise, having them see themselves successfully and joyfully performing some task that has given them trouble.

This essay can be combined to good effect with such personal narratives as Judith Ortiz Cofer's "One More Lesson" and Brent Staples's "A Brother's Murder" or with Suzanne Britt's humorous "Neat People Versus Sloppy People." By applying McGinnis's ideas on success and failure to the lives they read about (and to their own), students join in a conversation of ideas. Highlight this experience by having students write dialogues—for instance, between McGinnis and Staples's brother Blake.

Alice Walker, "Beauty: When the Other Dancer Is the Self"

Students are usually eager to discuss this essay, which touches on many important themes, among them the power of a disfiguring experience, family denial, and personal healing. Walker employs a series of short narratives to tell her larger story, held together by the refrain of her family's denial that she has changed. Have your students select several of Walker's narrative vignettes that they consider especially strong, noting effective description and articulating the point of each mini-narrative. Ask them to enumerate the ways in which Walker did change or was treated differently. Why did the boys in her family keep their guns and go on to own more deadly weapons? For interesting discussion or writing, ask students: What have you realized about yourself as you have raised your children?

You may want to assign the chapters on description and narration before students read this essay. Consider pairing Walker's essay with Judith Ortiz Cofer's "One More Lesson" to examine the relationship between self-esteem and school performance. You could also pair Walker's essay with Rene Denfeld's essay on personal triumph.

Richard Rodriguez, "Hunger of Memory"

You might launch a discussion of this essay by asking whether students or their family members have ever taken a job imagining it would be a certain way and, then, like Rodriguez, have been surprised by the actual experience. Rodriguez punctuates his narrative with some vivid description, as in paragraph 5 on the author's relishing of hard physical work. Ask students how sharp descriptions add realism to the story.

The narrative and descriptive chapters might precede this essay. Consider having students in groups discuss what it was that Rodriguez learned; why was the arrival of the group of Mexicans especially significant? Students might also discuss whether observing a parent's or guardian's relationship to work influenced their own career choices. Articles in current publications may provide interesting stories about minorities in the workplace.

This essay can be taught as part of a unit on work and career choices in conjunction with Judith Ortiz Cofer's "One More Lesson," Sandra Cisneros's "Only Daughter," and Rene Denfeld's "The Lady of the Ring."

Anna Quindlen, "Some Thoughts About Abortion"

So incendiary is this topic that students, like many developing thinkers, may believe that only one right position exists—their own or their parents'. The first order of business in approaching this thoughtful essay (as well as in introducing the writing of persuasive essays) may be impressing on your students that both points of view are valid.

Here is a usually illuminating exercise. Flip a coin to choose either a pro-life or a pro-choice position. Have the whole class brainstorm reasons and points in support of this position. The next day, have the class support the opposite point of view. Stress that either side can be argued eloquently. Sometimes, in fact, arguing the opposite of what one believes is actually more effective because this process keeps the focus on reasoned thought instead of mere emotion. Have students share what they felt as they thought of good points to support the "other guy's" point of view.

Quindlen's first and third paragraphs present both points of view in strong images of a shattered young woman and a newborn baby. Unlike some persuasive essays, this one reveals the author's own ambivalence; ask students whether this ambivalence strengthens or weakens Quindlen's argument. In fact, she carefully avoids the usual extremes, stating her belief that all thoughtful people find the issue difficult.

Work on persuasion could precede or follow this essay. Consider having students compare its style, tone, and approach with the persuasive essays by McGinnis and/or Ferguson.

Dave Barry, "Food for Thought"

This hilarious essay on science fair projects is a process/narrative with a hidden persuasive message: science fair projects achieve nothing—or worse than nothing. You might begin by asking students whether they or someone they know has ever been involved with a science fair project, either as a parent or a child. Was the project successful, productive, and useful, or just the opposite? Have students discuss Barry's tone and style. Do they find him humorous? Ask them specifically why. Have them cite the lines, words, or punctuation with which Barry achieves his effects. Does the humor involve irony, an unusual image, or a comparison of two things usually not thought of together?

Note Barry's commentary on the role of parents in both the first and the last paragraphs of the essay (as well as the full circle he draws by beginning and ending with blow-drying the ant). Have students find other lines in the essay that comment on the role of parents, and perhaps point out the pronouns Barry uses when he discusses carrying out the project (*we, our*). What is their significance? Also be sure that students understand that Barry writes to make a point, not only to amuse. Does his technique make the point effectively?

This essay might be paired with Baker's "The Plot Against People," a classification essay that also makes a serious point through humor.

Judith Ortiz Cofer, "One More Lesson"

This essay loosely contrasts the author's experience of modest privilege and belonging in Puerto Rico to her defensive, outsider status in Paterson, New Jersey. Cofer's descriptions are particularly rich; have students point out some specific details she uses to capture the unique experience of Christmas in Puerto Rico. What anecdotes and details capture her essential experience of Paterson? Is language mastery really central to power and success?

The chapters on description, narration, comparison/contrast, or exact language may logically precede this essay. As a prereading exercise, consider having students freewrite about the words *noise* and *silence.* Ask students whether Cofer's essay works as a contrast since it does not give parallel information about the two places. If your students come from different ethnic groups, writing about special holidays their families celebrate can help them get to know each other. You may wish to cluster this selection with other essays on the minority experience and personal power by Shanlon Wu, Richard Rodriguez, Brent Staples, and Sandra Cisneros. Alternatively, you could pair it with McGinnis's "How to Get the Most Out of Yourself," asking students whether McGinnis's insights help them answer question 3.

Brent Staples, "A Brother's Murder"

"Killing is only machismo taken to the extreme," writes Staples in the third paragraph of this essay, which raises questions about the meaning of masculinity and its relation to education and social class and about the brutal influence of the inner city. Furthermore, any reader with troubled or addicted loved ones will identify with Staples's self-questioning. Ask your students whether they believe that Brent Staples could have done more to save his brother. The essay usually stimulates strong class discussion on these themes.

As a prereading strategy, students could study the chapter on narration or form groups and compare the concepts of "masculinity" and "machismo." After discussion, have students write their own narrative that begins, as Staples's does, with a climactic event and then tells the story, as if trying to understand what happened. Assigning this piece with the essays by Wu, Ashe, and Denfeld will enrich any discussion of male identity and relationships. You might also consider pairing Staples's essay with McGinnis's essay on self-esteem and productivity. Do McGinnis's ideas shed light on the behavior of each Staples brother?

Shanlon Wu, "In Search of Bruce Lee's Grave"

In discussing this essay, you may wish to ask students about the need for heroes. Do all people need them? If your class is multicultural, many will probably relate to Wu's struggle for identity as a minority. Why does he want "instruction on how to live"? Do women in your class feel they have enough female heroes to choose from? (Does the word *heroine* carry the same connotations as does the word *hero?*)

As a prereading strategy, consider having students write about a movie they have seen many times, a TV program they watch religiously, or a hero they had in their youth. Have their heroes changed over the years? For work on the minority experience, cluster this essay with Judith Ortiz Cofer's "One More Lesson," Richard Rodriguez's "Hunger of Memory," and Sandra Cisneros's "Only Daughter." To explore male heroes and relationships, link Wu's essay with Brent Staples's "A Brother's Murder," and Arthur Ashe's "My Outing."

Russell Baker, "The Plot Against People"

This humorous essay on the perversity of inanimate objects provides an excellent example of classification, in which Baker divides objects into three wacky categories. Have students in groups analyze the essay. Do they find it humorous? Have them cite specific lines and words as they explain why or why not. A class discussion might encourage students to share frustrating experiences with objects or machines, from can openers to cars to computer software.

Work on classification or parallelism can precede this essay. You might pair this piece with Dave Barry's "Food for Thought," another humorous essay—this one with another take on science and technology.

Andrew Ferguson, "Road Rage"

This well-written and disturbing cause-and-effect essay is sure to provoke a lively class discussion. Ask students to describe their own experiences with road rage—either fury they have felt at the wheel or fury directed at them. Ask students what kinds of people, according to Ferguson, experience road rage and whether those people consider themselves dangerous. Consider having students make one list of reasons (causes) that Ferguson suggests for road rage and another list of results (effects) of road rage. Ferguson powerfully illustrates his points with examples. Have students find and discuss these examples. Which do they find most effective? To give students practice in abstract and concrete thinking, have them pick one of Ferguson's comments on road rage, illustrate it with examples they have experienced or witnessed, and show how the problem was handled or solved.

Chapters on illustration, cause and effect, or persuasion could precede work with this essay. You might also like to have students look at Chapter 16, on introductions and conclusions. Ask what Ferguson accomplishes in his last paragraph. Does the solution proposed in his last sentence provide a satisfying literary conclusion for the essay? Does it provide a realistic solution to the problem?

Because this article is so well-researched and readable, it can provide a fine introduction to basic research skills and a springboard for student writing and research. See also Chapter 18, "Special College Skills: Summary and Quotation."

Quotation Bank

The Quotation Bank that concludes *Evergreen with Readings* consists of 80 wise and witty quotations by a broad range of authors, classified under the headings Education, Work and Success, Love, Friends and Family, Ourselves in Society, and Wisdom for Living. Use these quotations to stimulate class discussion or inspire students to write. Use your creativity to tie the Quotation Bank into class work on illustration, definition, contrast, cause and effect, summary and quotation, exact language, and so forth; for example, have groups of students read through the quotations, choosing one to illustrate with examples from their experience.

Notes on the Ancillaries

Available on adoption of the text, the following ancillaries provide the instructor with excellent support material and expand teaching options. New to this edition is the Evergreen Web Site, which includes The Evergreen Community (a bulletin board where users can exchange ideas about teaching with *Evergreen*), additional tests and exercises, links, and tips on teaching Developmental English.

Instructor's Annotated Edition

Test Bank

Computerized Diagnostic/Mastery Tests

Computerized Test Bank

Evergreen Web Site including the Evergreen Community

Answer Key

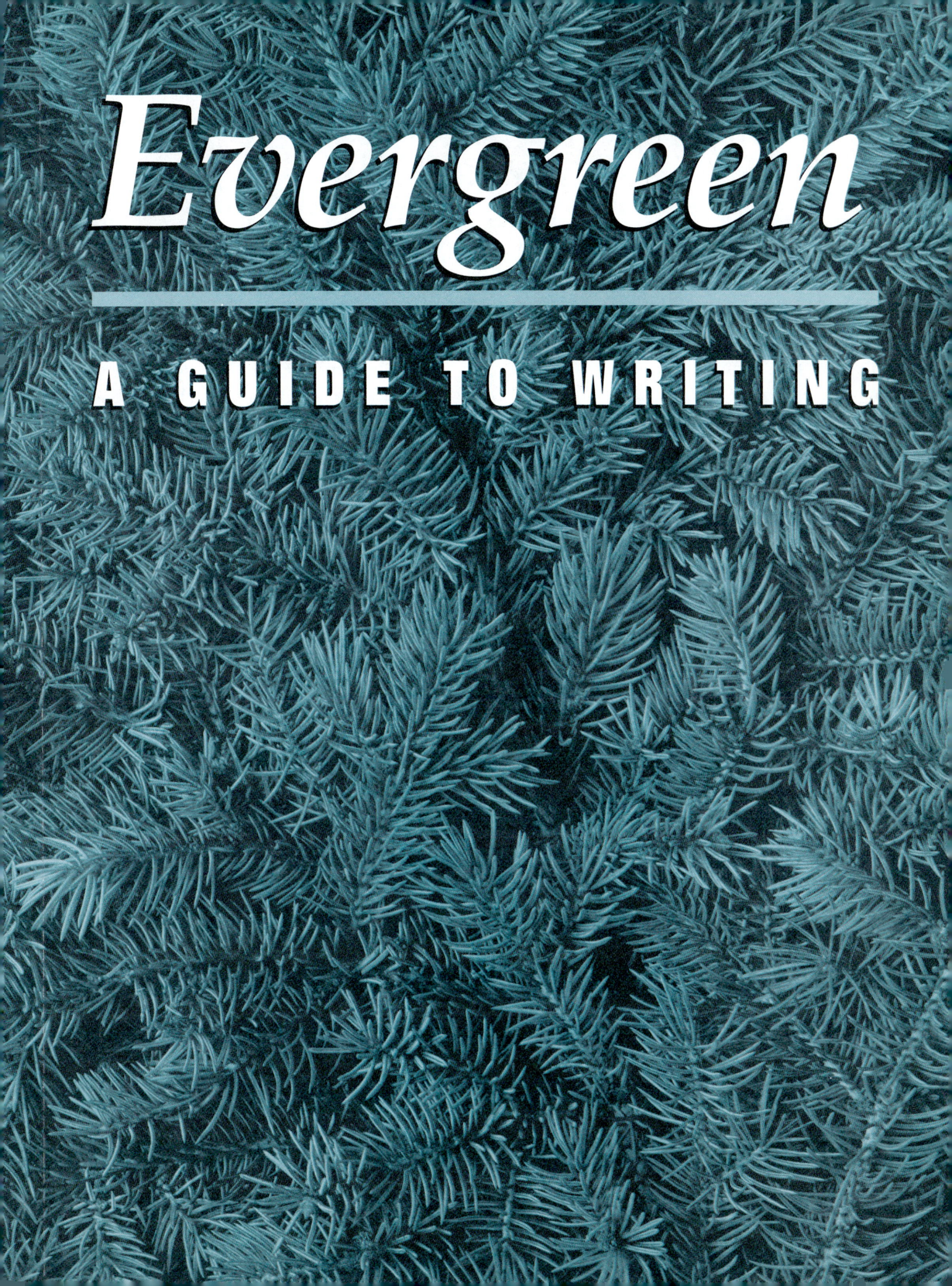

Evergreen

A GUIDE TO WRITING

UNIT 1

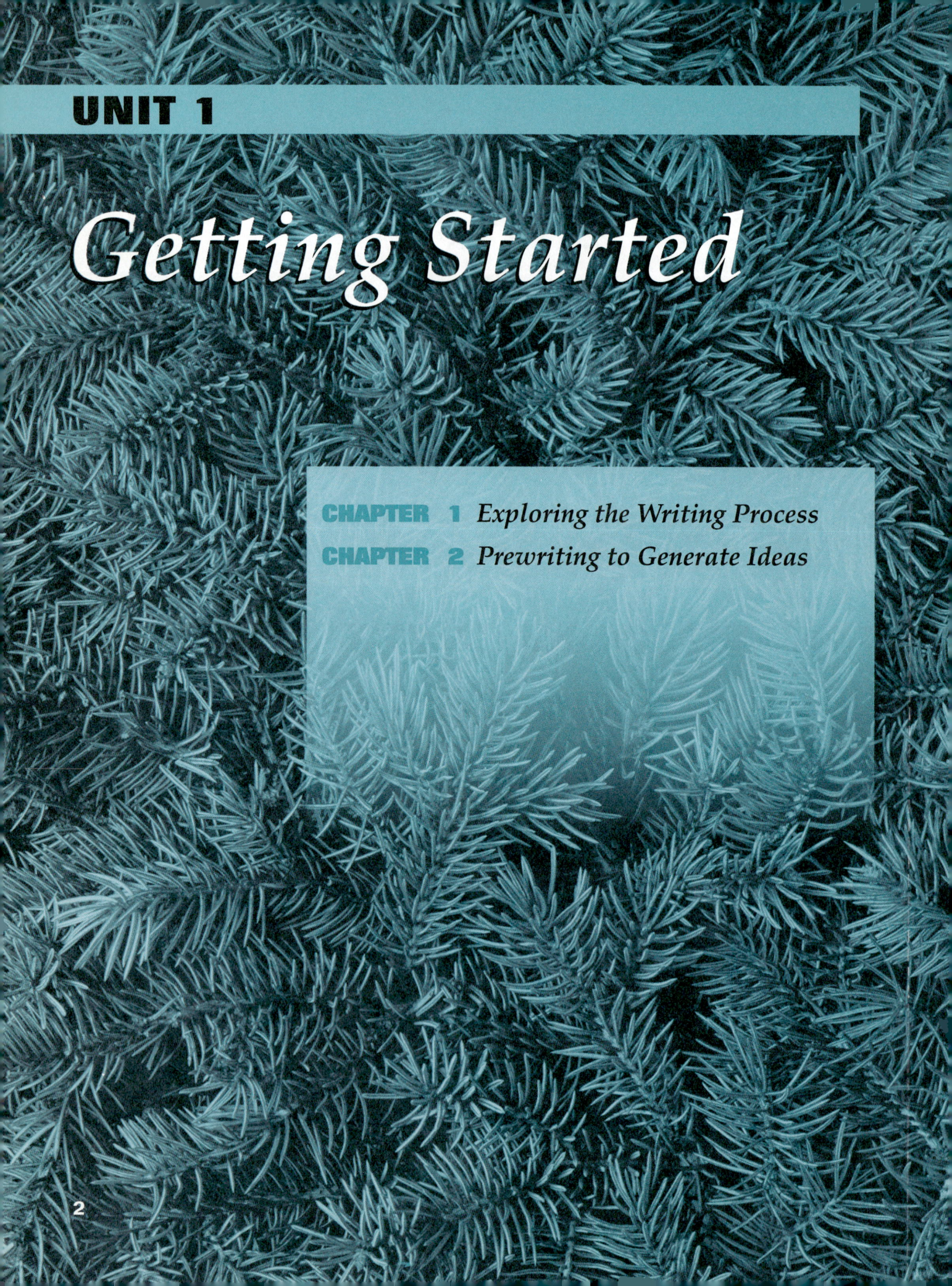

Getting Started

CHAPTER 1 *Exploring the Writing Process*
CHAPTER 2 *Prewriting to Generate Ideas*

CHAPTER 1

Exploring the Writing Process

PART A The Writing Process
PART B Subject, Audience, and Purpose

This chapter will give you a brief overview of the writing process, which is explored in greater depth throughout this book. By surveying the steps that many writers take and some of the factors they consider, you will see that writing is not a magic ability some are born with, but a skill that can be learned—the result of planning, hard work, and a positive attitude.

PART A   The Writing Process

Many students mistakenly think that good writers simply sit down and write out a perfect letter, paragraph, or essay from start to finish. In fact, writing is a **process** consisting of a number of steps:

1 Prewriting
- Thinking about possible subjects
- Freely jotting down ideas on paper or computer
- Narrowing the subject and writing it as one sentence
- Deciding which ideas to include
- Arranging ideas in a plan or an outline

2 Writing
- Writing a first draft

3 Revising
- Rethinking, rearranging, and rewriting as necessary
- Writing one or more new drafts
- Proofreading for grammar and spelling errors

Not all writers perform all the steps in this order, but most prewrite, write, revise, and proofread. Actually, writing can be a messy process of thinking, writing, reading what has been written, and rewriting. Sometimes steps overlap or must be repeated. The important thing is that writing the first draft is just one stage in the process. "I love being a writer," jokes Peter De Vries. "What I can't stand is the paperwork."

Before they write, good writers spend time **prewriting**—thinking about and planning for a paper. The first five steps on page 3 are all prewriting steps. Here writers think, let their imaginations run free, jot down ideas or list ideas on the computer, decide which ideas to use, and come up with a plan. Many beginning writers get into trouble by skipping the prewriting phase. They don't realize that doing this early work saves time and frustration later and usually creates a much better piece of writing than when students just sit down to write.

Next comes **writing** the first draft. Writers who have planned ahead are now free to concentrate on writing the best possible draft. The focus now is on presenting ideas, feelings, and experiences as convincingly as possible, rather than on correcting.

The next phase of the process—and one that many writers rush through or omit altogether—is **revising.** Experienced writers do not accept the first words that flow from their pens; they are like sculptors, shaping and reworking rough material into something meaningful. Writers do this by letting the first draft sit for five minutes, an hour, or a day. Then they read it again with a fresh, critical eye and rewrite—adding, dropping, or rearranging ideas; changing words to achieve more clarity and punch; and so on. Many writers revise two or three times until they get it right—until their writing says clearly and effectively what they want it to say. Finally, they **proofread** for grammar and spelling errors, so that their writing seems to say, "I am proud to put my name on this work."

PART B Subject, Audience, and Purpose

Early in the prewriting phase, you should give some thought to your subject, audience, and purpose.

Whenever possible, choose a **subject** that you know and care about: life in Cleveland, working with learning-disabled children, repairing motorcycles, overcoming shyness, watching a friend struggle with drug addiction, succeeding in college. You may not realize how many subjects you do know or have strong opinions about. What special experience or expertise do you have? What angers you, inspires you, saddens you? What do you love to do? The answers to these questions will suggest good subjects to write about. In college courses, instructors often assign a broad subject. Try to narrow this subject toward some specific aspect that intrigues you. If you have interest, energy, and passion about a topic, then probably your readers will, too.

Just how you approach your subject will depend on your readers—your **audience.** Ask yourself who these readers are: your classmates, your professor, other students at your college, your boss, youngsters in your community, people who probably agree with you, people who don't. Keeping your audience in mind will help you know what information to include and what to leave out. For example, if you are writing about rap music for an audience of middle-aged parents, you will explain your subject differently than you will to an audience of eighteen-year-old rap fans. What do your readers already know about your subject? What may they need or want to learn?

Next you will want to think about your **purpose** in writing. Do you want to explain something to your readers, persuade them that a certain view is correct, entertain them, tell a good story, or some combination of these? Keeping your purpose in mind will help you write more effectively. For example, if your purpose is to persuade your company to recycle its paper and glass, you may want to write about ways in which recycling will benefit the company: Recycling can earn or save money, improve the company's image, or make employees proud to work there.

PRACTICE 1

List five subjects that you might like to write about. For ideas, reread the list of possible subjects and the questions in Part B, page 4. Consider your audience and purpose: For whom are you writing? What do you want them to know about your subject? Notice how the audience and purpose will help shape your paper.

	Subject	Audience	Purpose
EXAMPLE	my recipe for chili	inexperienced cooks	to show how easy it is to make chili
1.	_____	_____	_____
2.	_____	_____	_____
3.	_____	_____	_____
4.	_____	_____	_____
5.	_____	_____	_____

PRACTICE 2

Jot down ideas for these three assignments, by yourself or with a group of classmates. Notice how your ideas and details differ, depending on the audience and purpose.

1. You have been asked to write a description of your college for local high school students. Your purpose is to encourage them to enroll in your college after graduating from high school. What kinds of information should you include? What will your audience want to know?

2. You have been asked to write a description of your college for the governor of your state. Your purpose is to persuade her or him to spend more money to improve your college. What information should you include? What will your audience want to know?

3. You have been asked to write a description of your college for your best friend, who attends a college out of state. Your purpose is to share your personal impressions and experiences. What information should you include? What will your audience want to know?

CHAPTER 2

Prewriting to Generate Ideas

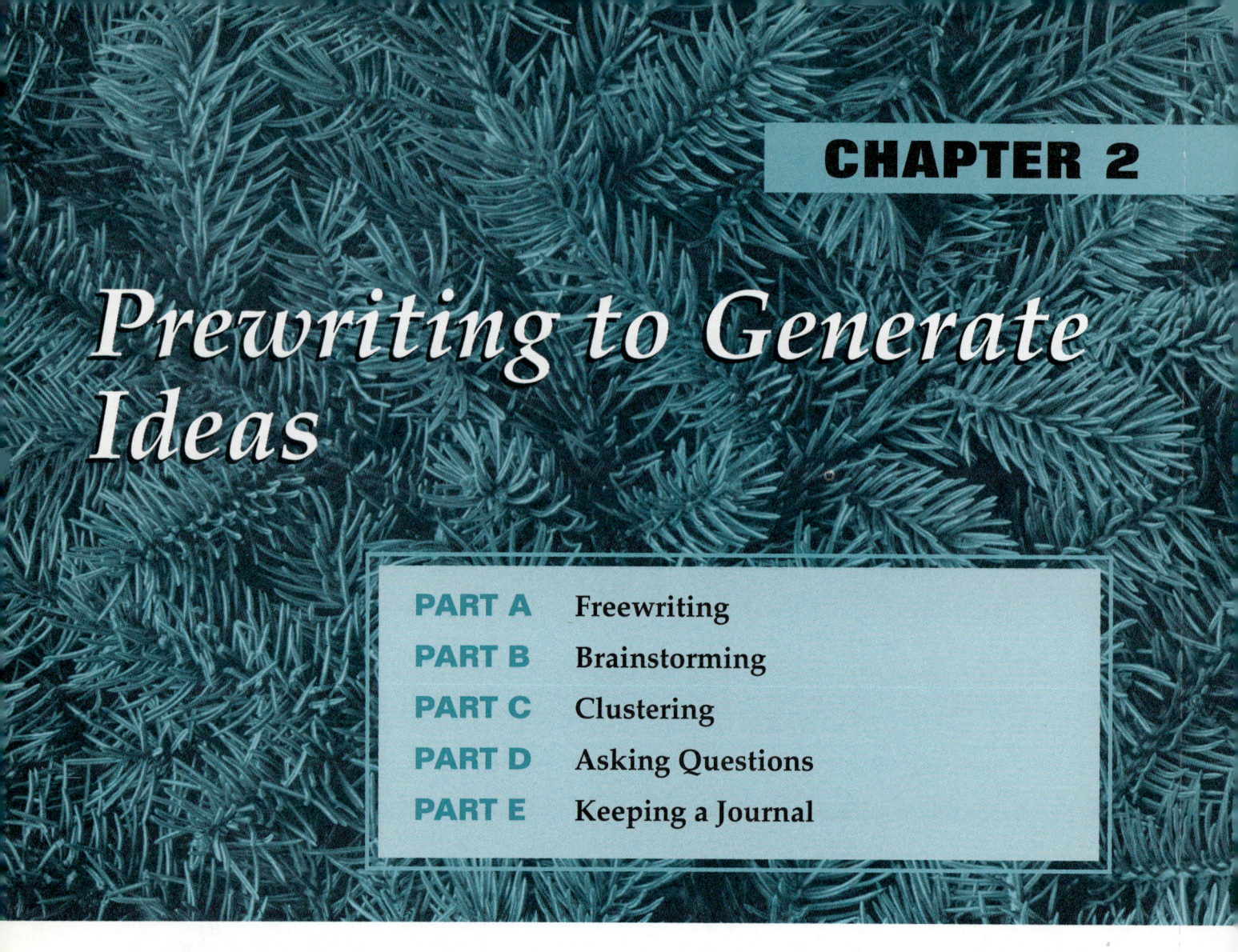

PART A	Freewriting
PART B	Brainstorming
PART C	Clustering
PART D	Asking Questions
PART E	Keeping a Journal

This chapter presents five effective prewriting techniques that will help you get your ideas onto paper (or onto the computer). These techniques can help you overcome the "blank-page jitters" that many people face when they first sit down to write. You also can use them to generate new ideas at any point in the writing process. Try all five to see which ones work best for you.

In addition, if you write on a computer, try prewriting in different ways: on paper and on computer. Some writers feel they produce better work if they prewrite by hand and only later transfer their best ideas onto the computer. Every writer has personal preferences, so don't be afraid to experiment.

PART A Freewriting

Freewriting is an excellent method that many writers use to warm up and to generate ideas. These are the guidelines: for five, ten, or fifteen minutes, write rapidly, without stopping, about anything that comes into your head. If you feel stuck, just repeat or rhyme the last word you wrote, but *don't stop writing*. And don't worry about grammar, logic, complete sentences, or grades.

The point of freewriting is to write so quickly that ideas can flow without comments from your inner critic. The *inner critic* is the voice inside that says, every time you have an idea, "That's dumb; that's no good; cross that out." Freewriting helps you tell this voice, "Thank you for your opinion. Once I have lots of ideas and words on paper, I'll invite you back for comment."

After you freewrite, read what you have written, underlining or marking any parts you like.

Here is one student's first freewriting, with his own underlinings:

> Boy I wish this class was over and I could go home and get out of this building, boy was my day miserable and this sure is a crazy thing to do <u>if a shrink could see us now</u>. My I just remember I've got to buy that CD <u>my my my</u> I am running out of stuff to write but dont worry teach because this is really the nuttiest thing but lots of fun you probably like reading this mixed up thing That girl's remark sounded dumb but impressing. You know <u>this writing sure puts muscles in your fingers</u> if I stop writing oh boy this is the most incredible assignment in the world think and write without worrying about sentence structure and other English garbage to stall you down boy that guy next to me is writing like crazy so he looks crazy you know this is outrageous I'm writing and writing I never realized the extent of mental and physical concentration it takes to do this constantly <u>dont mind the legibility of my hand my hand oh my hand is ready to drop off</u> please this is crazy crazy and too much work for a poor guy like myself. Imagine me putting on paper all I have to say and faster than a speeding bullet.

■ This example has the lively energy of many freewritings. Why do you think the student underlined what he did? Would you have underlined other words or phrases? Why?

Freewriting is a powerful tool for helping you turn thoughts and feelings into words, especially when you are unsure about what you want to say. Sometimes freewriting produces only nonsense; often, however, it can help you zoom in on possible topics, interests, and worthwhile writing you can use later.

If you are freewriting on a computer, try turning off the monitor and writing "blind." Some students find that this helps them forget about making mistakes and concentrate on getting words and ideas out fast.

PRACTICE 1

1. Set a timer for ten minutes or have someone time you. Freewrite without stopping for the full ten minutes. If you get stuck, repeat or rhyme the last word you wrote until words start flowing again but *don't stop writing!*

2. When you finish, write down one or two words that describe how you felt while freewriting.

   Sample answers: excited, liberated, creative, intense

3. Next, read your freewriting. Underline any words or lines you like—anything that strikes you as interesting, thoughtful, or funny. If nothing strikes you, that's okay.

Practice 2

Try three more freewritings at home—each one ten minutes long. Do them at different times of day or night when you have a quiet moment. If possible, use a timer. Set it for ten minutes; then write quickly and freely until it rings. Later, read over your freewritings and underline any striking lines or ideas.

Focused Freewriting

In **focused freewriting**, you simply try to focus your thoughts on one subject as you freewrite. The subject might be one assigned by your instructor, one you choose, or one you have discovered in unfocused freewriting. The goal of most writing is a polished, organized piece of writing; focused freewriting can help you generate ideas or narrow a topic to one aspect that interests you.

Here is one student's focused freewriting on the topic *someone who strongly influenced you:*

> Mr. Martin, the reason I'm interested in science. Wiry, five-foot-four-inch, hyperactive guy. A darting bird in the classroom, a circling teacher-bird, now jabbing at the knee bone of a skeleton, now banging on the jar with the brain in it. Like my brain used to feel, pickled, before I took his class. I always liked science but everything else was too hard. I almost dropped out of school, discouraged, but Martin was fun, crazy, made me think. Encouragement was his thing. Whacking his pencil against the plastic model of an eyeball in his office, he would bellow at me, "Taking too many courses! Working too many hours in that restaurant! Living everyone else's life but your own!" Gradually, I slowed down, got myself focused. Saw him last at graduation, where he thwacked my diploma with his pencil, shouting, "Keep up the good work! Live your own life! Follow your dreams!"

■ This student later used this focused freewriting—its vivid details about Mr. Martin and his influence—as the basis for an effective paper. Underline any words or lines that you find especially striking or appealing. Be prepared to explain why you like what you underline.

Practice 3

Do a three-minute focused freewriting on three of these topics:

beach   body piercing
friendship   parent (*or* child)
news   tests

Underline as usual. Did you surprise yourself by having so much to say about any one topic? Perhaps you would like to write more about that topic.

PRACTICE 4

1. Read over your earlier freewritings and notice your underlinings. Would you like to write more about any underlined words or ideas? Write two or three such words or ideas here:

   Sample answers:

   Sometimes I feel closer to my children than to my parents.

   I'm often most content on a rainy day.

2. Now choose one word or idea. Focus your thoughts on it and do a ten-minute focused freewriting. Try to stick to the topic as you write but don't worry too much about keeping on track; just keep writing.

PART B Brainstorming

Another prewriting technique that may work for you is **brainstorming** or freely jotting down ideas about a topic. As in freewriting, the purpose is to generate lots of ideas so you have something to work with and choose from. Write everything that comes to you about a topic—words and phrases, ideas, details, examples.

After you have brainstormed, read over your list, underlining interesting or exciting ideas you might develop further. As with freewriting, many writers brainstorm on a general subject, underline, and then brainstorm again as they focus on one aspect of that subject.

Here is one student's brainstorm list on the topic *e-mail:*

> everyone has it—really neat
>
> can send mail day or night
>
> not like snail mail—so slow
>
> I hate to write letters but I love to e-mail
>
> I e-mail my friends at their colleges all the time
>
> I even e-mail my little brother at home
>
> more intimate than phone calls—you can share inner thoughts
>
> Mom's always sending me e-mails
>
> she e-mails her old college friends, too
>
> people are more in touch with each other now

With brainstorming, this writer generated many ideas and started to move toward a more focused topic: *People are more in touch with each other now because of e-mail.* With a narrowed topic, brainstorming once more can help the writer generate details and reasons to support the idea.

PRACTICE 5

Choose one of the following topics that interests you and write it at the top of your paper or computer screen. Then brainstorm. Write anything that comes into your head about the topic. Just let ideas pour out fast!

1. a place I want to go back to
2. dealing with difficult people
3. an unforgettable person in politics, sports, or religious life
4. growing up
5. my best/worst job
6. a first or blind date

Once you fill a page with your list, read it over, marking the most interesting ideas. Draw arrows or highlight and move text on your screen to connect related ideas. Is there one idea that might be the subject of a paper?

PART C Clustering

Some writers use still another method—called **clustering** or **mapping**—to get their ideas onto paper. To begin clustering, simply write an idea or a topic, usually one word, in the center of a piece of paper. Then let your mind make associations, and write these associations branching out from the center.

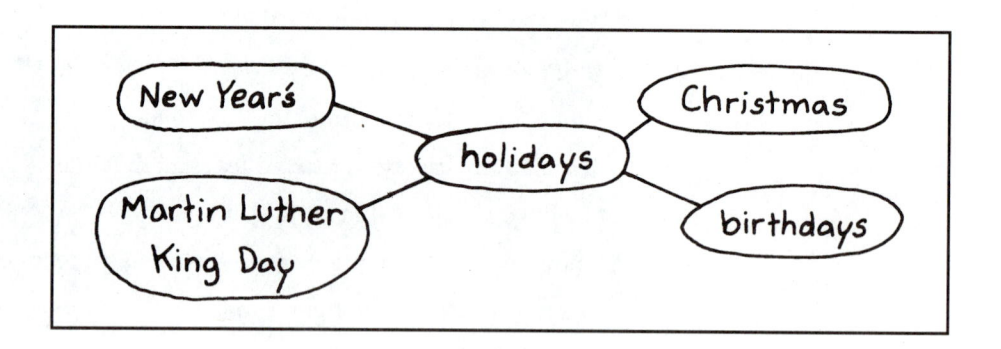

```
     New Year's              Christmas
            \               /
             \             /
              holidays
             /             \
            /               \
   Martin Luther            birthdays
    King Day
```

When one idea suggests other ideas, details, and examples, write these around it in a "cluster." After you finish, pick the cluster that most interests you. You may wish to freewrite for more ideas.

Cluster Diagram

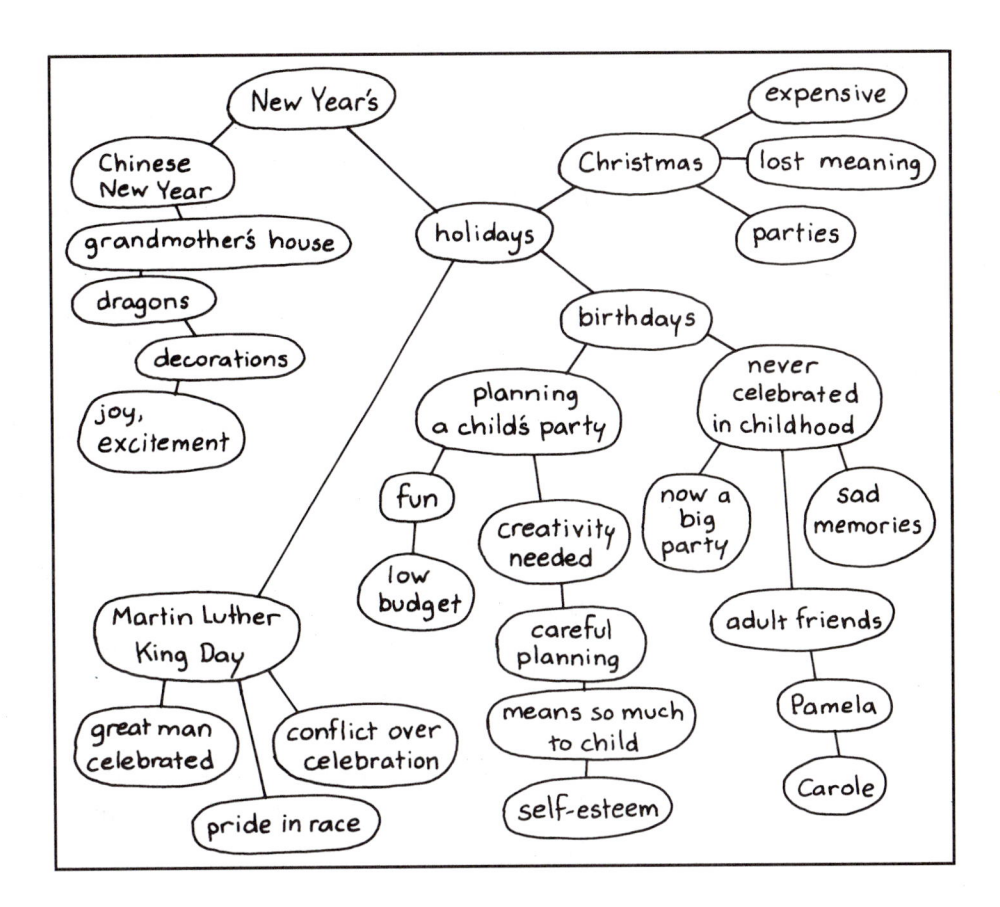

- **holidays** (center)
  - New Year's
    - Chinese New Year
      - grandmother's house
      - dragons
      - decorations
      - joy, excitement
  - Christmas
    - expensive
    - lost meaning
    - parties
  - birthdays
    - planning a child's party
      - fun
      - low budget
      - creativity needed
      - careful planning
      - means so much to child
      - self-esteem
    - never celebrated in childhood
      - now a big party
      - sad memories
      - adult friends
        - Pamela
        - Carole
  - Martin Luther King Day
    - great man celebrated
    - conflict over celebration
    - pride in race

PRACTICE 6

Choose one of these topics or another topic that interests you. Write it in the center of a piece of paper and then try clustering. Keep writing down associations until you have filled most of the page.

1. heroes
2. holidays
3. food
4. inspiration
5. a dream
6. movies

PART D   Asking Questions

Many writers get ideas about a subject by asking questions and trying to answer them. This section describes two ways of doing this.

The Reporter's Six Questions

Newspaper reporters often answer six basic questions at the beginning of an article: **Who? What? Where? When? Why? How?** Here is the way one student used these questions to explore the general subject of *sports* assigned by his instructor:

> **Who?** Players, basketball and football players, coaches, fans. Violence—I'm tired of that subject. Loyal crazy screaming fans—Giants fans.
>
> **What?** Excitement. Stadium on the day of a game. Tailgate parties. Cookouts. Incredible spreads—Italian families with peppers, stuff to spread on sandwiches. All day partying. Radios, TVs, grills, Giants caps.
>
> **Where?** Giants Stadium parking lot. People gather in certain areas—meet me in 10-B. Stadiums all over the country, same thing. People party on tailgates, in cars, on cars, plastic chairs, blankets.
>
> **When?** People arrive early morning—cook breakfast, lunch. After the game, many stay on in parking lot, talking, drinking beer. Year after year they come back.
>
> **Why?** Big social occasion, emotional outlet.
>
> **How?** They come early to get space. Some stadiums now rent parking spaces. Some families pass on season tickets in their wills!

Notice the way this writer uses the questions to focus his ideas about tailgate parties at Giants Stadium. He has already come up with many interesting details for a good paper.

Ask Your Own Questions

If the reporter's six questions seem too confining, just ask the questions *you* want answered about a subject. Let each answer suggest the next question.

Here is how one student responded to the subject of *teenage pregnancy:*

> **What do I know about teenage pregnancy?** I saw my sister's plans for her future cut short by pregnancy. She won a high-school fashion design award, was spunky, full of fun. Now, with a child to raise, she works in a diner. The father of the child disappeared two years ago.
>
> **What would I like to know?** Why do teenagers get pregnant? Teenage girls think they can't get pregnant. Teenage boys think it's macho to get a girl pregnant. Lack of knowledge of birth control methods. Teenage girls think that having a baby will keep their boyfriends from leaving them. They think that babies are fun to have around, to play with.
>
> **Where can I get more information?** Guidance counselors at my old school. Planned Parenthood. Interview my friends who had babies when they were still teenagers. Talk to my sister.
>
> **What would I like to focus on?** What interests me? I would like to know what pressures, fears, and hopes teenage girls feel that would allow them to take the chance of becoming pregnant.
>
> **What is my point of view?** I would like teenagers to be aware of how their lives will be forever changed by a pregnancy.
>
> **Who is my audience?** I would like to write for teenagers—primarily girls—to help them understand the problems of teenage pregnancy.

PRACTICE 7

Answer the reporter's six questions on one of the following topics or on a topic of your own choice.

1. drug addiction
2. sports
3. career goals
4. neighbors/neighborhood
5. music
6. family get-togethers
7. living a simple life
8. choosing a major or concentration

PRACTICE 8

Ask and answer at least five questions of your own about one of the topics in Practice 7. Use these questions if you wish: What do I know about this subject? What would I like to know? Where can I find answers to my questions? What would I like to focus on? What is my point of view about this subject? Who is my audience?

PART E Keeping a Journal

Keeping a journal is an excellent way to practice your writing skills and discover ideas for further writing. Your journal is mostly for you—a private place where you record your experiences and your inner life; it is the place where, as one writer says, "I discover what I really think by writing it down."

You can keep a journal in a notebook or on a computer. If you prefer handwriting, get yourself an attractive notebook with 8½-by-11-inch paper. If you prefer to work on a computer, just open a "Journal" folder or keep a "Journal" disk. Then every morning or night, or several times a week, write for at least fifteen minutes in this journal. Don't just record the day's events. ("I went to the store. It rained. I came home.") Instead, write in detail about what most angered, moved, or amused you that day.

Write about what you really care about—motorcycles, loneliness, working in a doughnut shop, family relationships, grades, ending or starting a relationship. You may be surprised by how much you know. Write, think, and write some more. Your journal is private, so don't worry about grammar or correctness. Instead, aim to capture your truth so exactly that someone reading your words might experience it too.

You might also carry a little 3-by-5-inch pad with you during the day for "fast sketches," jotting down things that catch your attention: a man playing drums in the street; a baby wearing a bib that reads *Spit Happens*; a compliment you receive at work; something your child just learned to do.

Every journal is unique—and usually private—but here are two sample journal entries to suggest possibilities. The first student links a quotation he has just learned to a disturbing "lesson of love":

> Apr. 11. Two weeks ago, our professor mentioned a famous quote: "It is better to have loved and lost than never to have loved at all." The words had no particular meaning for me. How wrong I was. Last Sunday I received some very distressing news that will change my life from now on.
>
> My wife has asked me why I never notified any family members except my mother of the birth of our children. My reply has been an argument or an angry stare. Our daughter Angelica is now two months shy of her second birthday, and we were also blessed with the birth of a son, who is five months old. I don't know whether it was maturity or my conscience, but last Sunday I decided it was time to let past grievances be forgotten. Nothing on this green earth would shelter me from what I was to hear that day.
>
> I went to my father's address, knocked on his door, but got no response. Nervous but excited, I knocked again. Silence. On leaving the building, I bumped into his neighbor and asked for the possible whereabouts of my father. I couldn't brace myself for the cold shock of hearing from him that my father had died. I was angry as well as saddened, for my father was a quiet and gentle man whose love of women, liquor, and good times exceeded the love of his son.
>
> Yes, it would have been better to have loved my father as he was than never to have gotten the opportunity to love such a man. A lesson of love truly woke me up to the need to hold dearly the ones you care for and overcome unnecessary grudges. "I love you, Pop, and may you rest in peace. Que Díos te guide."
>
> —Anthony Falu (Student)

In the more freely written journal entry that follows, another student writes in order to sort out her feelings. As you read, ask yourself what seems to be bothering her. Is it really a cold? Is it the cat?

> Nov. 5. The coffee and the donut can wait—not particularly in the mood for that now. Not in the mood for this journal either, but maybe I'll find out what's going on or why I feel so bad. I'm a little sleepy, have less patience lately, especially stupidity—questions asked without thinking. Why do I feel my time's wasted? Shouldn't. Just a little irritable, worried about this cold I'm getting and why Don seemed upset when I asked him about visiting his sister. I didn't sleep very well last night. Maybe the cat's at fault. She must have been cold and crawled under the covers, so I pushed her out and Don woke up. Or he shoved her off the bed when her whiskers tickled his nose and that woke me up. So we fought again. Now I'm the one who gets up at 7 a.m., and he's the one in the beautiful picture of a tired sleeping male form under the covers, calico cat curled up, sleeping off the breakfast I just gave her. Wish I didn't have to leave.

The uses of a journal are limited only by your imagination. Here are some ideas:

■ Write down your career goals and dreams; then brainstorm steps you can take to make them reality. (Notice negative thoughts—"I can't do that. That will never work." Focus on positive thoughts—"Of course I can! If X can do it, so can I.")

■ Write about a problem you are having and creative ways in which you might solve it.

CHAPTER 2 Prewriting to Generate Ideas   15

- Analyze yourself as a student. What are your strengths and weaknesses? What can you do to build on the strengths and overcome the weaknesses?
- What college course have you most enjoyed? Why?
- Who believes in you? Who seems not to believe in you? How do these attitudes make you feel?
- Imagine five other lives you might want to live. Who would you be: a figure skater? an inventor? a surgeon?
- If you could change one thing about yourself, what would it be? What might you do to change it?
- If you could spend time with one famous person, living or dead, who would it be? Why?
- List five things you would love to do if they didn't seem so crazy.
- Do you have an important secret? Kept from whom? How do you feel about keeping this secret? Why *do* people have secrets?
- Name three people you are supposed to admire; then name three you really do admire. Do the differences teach you anything about yourself?
- If money were no object, what place in the world would you visit and why? What would you do there, whom would you take, and how long would you stay?
- Use your journal as a place to think about material that you have read in a textbook, newspaper, magazine, or the Internet.
- What news story most upset you in the past month? Why?
- Write down facts that impress you—the average young American watches 18,000 TV murders before graduating from high school! Analyzing that one fact could produce a good paper.
- Record quotations that spark your interest. Suppose you jot down Abe Lincoln's statement that "most folks are as happy as they make up their minds to be." Later, thinking and writing about that thought could produce a whole paragraph or composition.
- Read through the Quotation Bank at the end of this book, and copy your five favorite quotations into your journal.

PRACTICE 9

Get a notebook or set up your computer journal. Write for at least fifteen minutes three times a week.
   At the end of each week, reread what you have written or typed. Underline sections or ideas you like and put a check mark next to subjects you might like to write more about.

PRACTICE 10

Choose one passage in your journal that you would like to rewrite and let others read. Mark the parts you like best. Now rewrite and polish the passage so you would be proud to show it to someone else.

UNIT 1   WRITERS' WORKSHOP

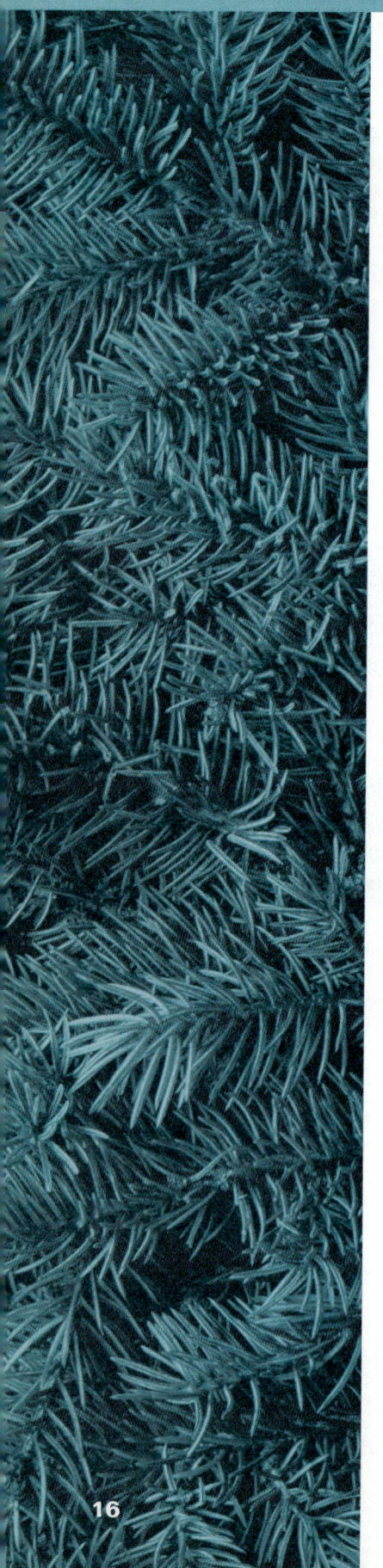

Using Just One of Your Five Senses, Describe a Place

Readers of a finished paper can easily forget that they are reading the *end result* of someone else's writing process. The writer has already thought about audience and purpose, zoomed in on a subject, and prewritten to get ideas.

Here is one student's response to the following assignment: "Using just one of the five senses—smell, hearing, taste, touch, or sight—describe a special place." In your class or group, read the paper, aloud if possible. As you read, underline words or lines that strike you as especially well written or powerful.

Noises in My Village

Orlu, my village in Nigeria, has a population of about five hundred sounds. The sounds range from the clucking of the rooster in the morning to the rumbling of people getting ready for market. You hear the shrill cry of the widow and the squeaking of the rats. At the farm, two men start a fight over land and slam each other on the ground with great thuds. Water flows with a rushing sound from the rocks into the river, and the trees whisper to themselves. People fill their earthen pots with water while children splash into the water after washing their clothes. From a distance, a lost goat bleats, "Meeee, meee." At the village square, bamboo drums sound, "Drooom, drooom." This signifies a curfew for the women. A young man tells how his friend bought a car that sounded "Vrooom, vrooom." At dusk people return from the market. One woman shouts at the top of her voice, "I forgot my palm oil keg!" and rushes to get it. After supper children gather at the village square. They clap their hands and listen to folk tales. From a distance, the town crier announces the arrival of the new moon.

—Chinwe Okorie (Student)

---

1. How effective is Ms. Okorie's paper?

   __Y__ Good topic for a college audience?   __Y__ Clear main idea?

   __Y__ Rich supporting details?   __Y__ Logical organization?

2. Does the first sentence make you want to read on? Why or why not?
   Yes. "Population of five hundred sounds" is interesting.
3. Which of the five senses does the writer emphasize? What words reveal this?
   sound
4. Discuss your underlinings with the group or class. Try to explain why a particular word or sentence is effective. For instance, the fourth sentence contains such precise words that we can almost hear the two men "*slam* each other *on the ground* with great *thuds*."

5. Would you suggest that the writer make any improvements? For instance, does the word *cluck* accurately describe the sound roosters make?

6. Last, proofread for grammar, spelling, and omitted words. Do you spot any error patterns (the same type of error made two or more times) that this student should watch out for? *Yes, 2 omitted words.*

> Of her prewriting process, Chinwe Okorie writes: "I decided to write about my village in Africa because I thought my American classmates (my audience) would find that more interesting than the local neighborhood. This paper also taught me the importance of brainstorming. I filled two whole pages with my brainstorming list, and then it was easy to pick the best details."

Group Work

Imagine that you have been given this assignment: *Using just one of the five senses, describe a special place.* Your audience will be your college writing class. Working as a group, plan a paper and prewrite. First, choose a place that your group will describe; if it is a place on campus, your instructor might even want you to go there. Second, decide whether you will emphasize sound, smell, taste, touch, or sight. Choose someone to write down the group's ideas, and then brainstorm. List as many sounds (or smells, etc.) as your group can think of. Fill at least one page. Now read back the list and put a check next to the best details; does your group agree or disagree about which ones are best?

You are well on your way to an excellent paper. Each group member can now complete the assignment, based on the list. If necessary, prewrite again for more details.

Writing and Revising Ideas

1. Using one of your five senses, describe a place. You might use a first sentence like this:

   _____ has a population of about five hundred _____.
   (place)   (smells, tastes, etc.)

2. List unusual experiences you have had that your classmates and professor might like to read about (a job, time in another country, and so on). Choose one of these and prewrite; use the prewriting method of your choice and fill at least a page with ideas.

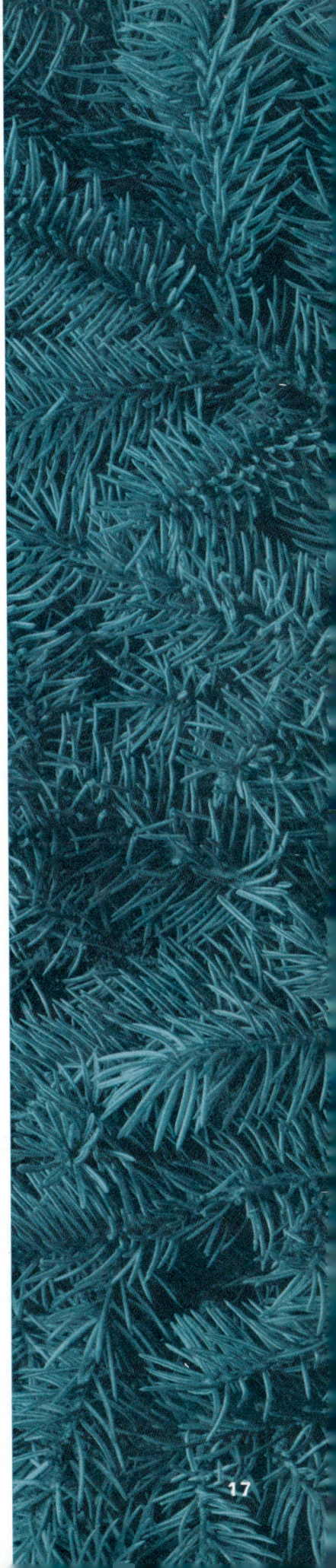

UNIT 2

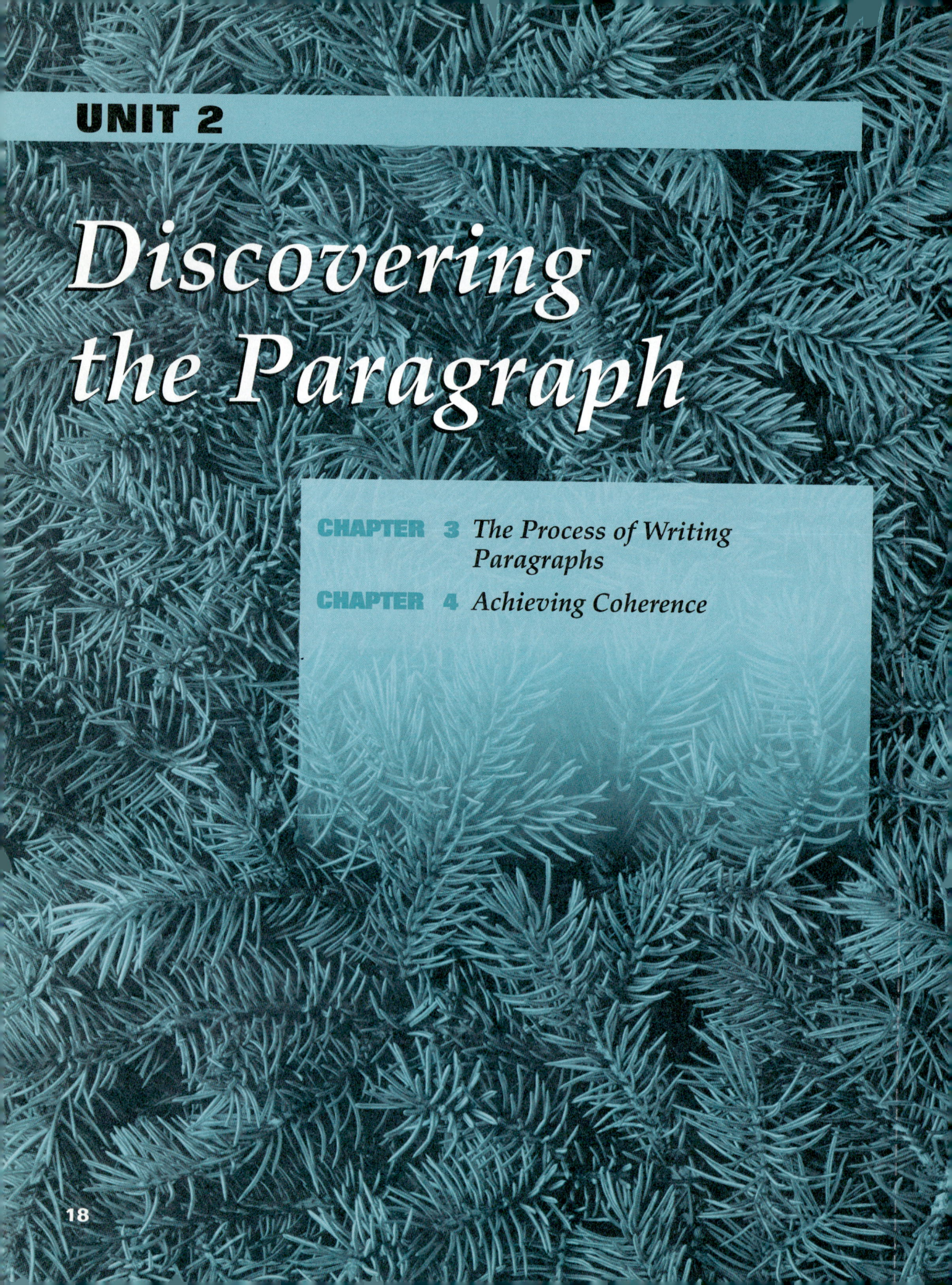

Discovering the Paragraph

CHAPTER 3 *The Process of Writing Paragraphs*

CHAPTER 4 *Achieving Coherence*

CHAPTER 3

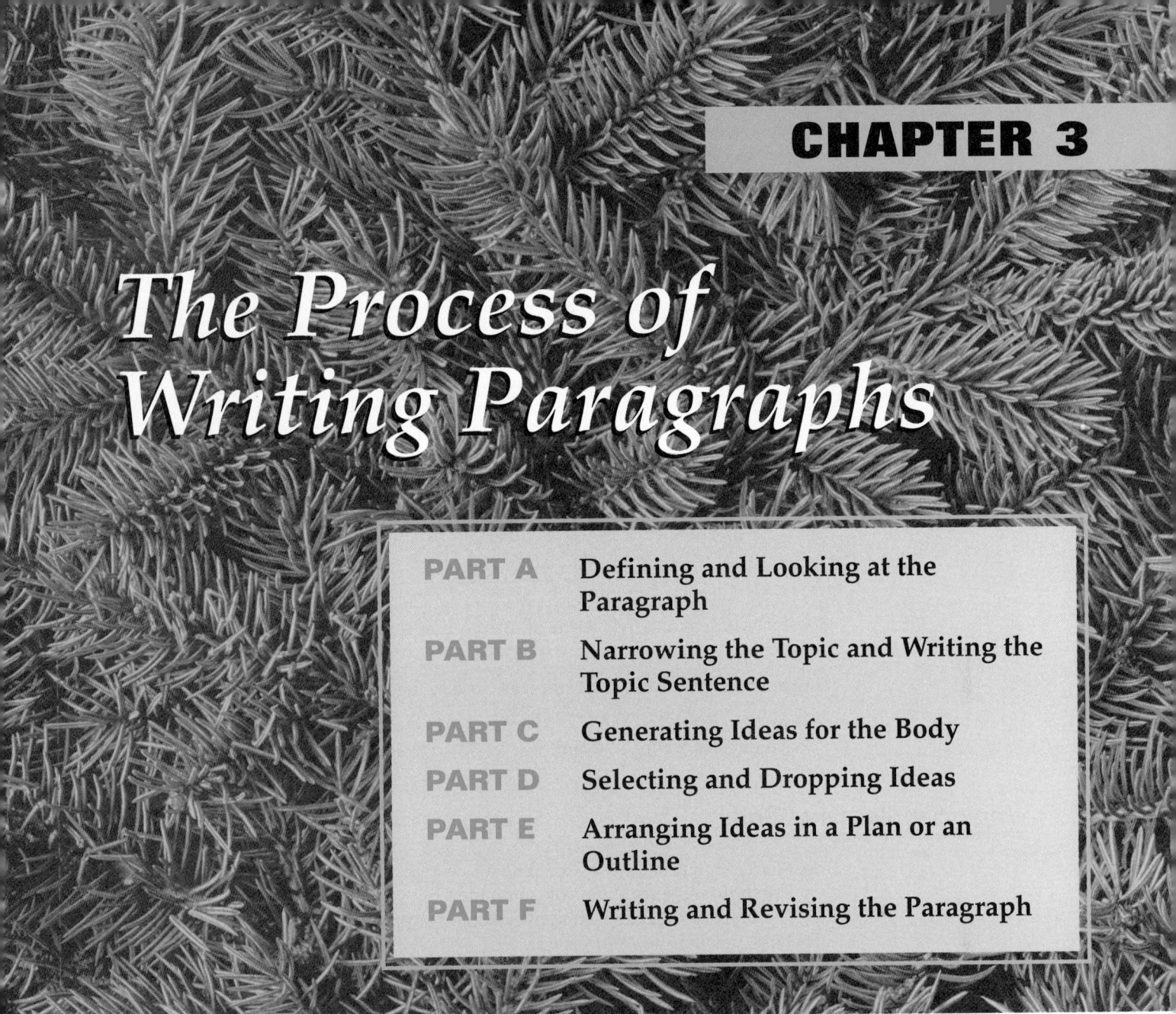

The Process of Writing Paragraphs

PART A	Defining and Looking at the Paragraph
PART B	Narrowing the Topic and Writing the Topic Sentence
PART C	Generating Ideas for the Body
PART D	Selecting and Dropping Ideas
PART E	Arranging Ideas in a Plan or an Outline
PART F	Writing and Revising the Paragraph

This chapter will guide you step by step from examining basic paragraphs to writing them. The paragraph makes a good learning model because it is short yet contains many of the elements found in longer compositions. Therefore, you easily can transfer the skills you gain by writing paragraphs to longer essays, reports, and letters.

In this chapter, you will first look at finished paragraphs and then move through the process of writing paragraphs of your own.

PART A Defining and Looking at the Paragraph

A **paragraph** is a group of related sentences that develops one main idea. Although there is no definite length for a paragraph, it is often from five to twelve sentences long. A paragraph usually occurs with other paragraphs in a longer piece of writing—an essay, an article, or a letter, for example. Before studying longer compositions, however, we will look at single paragraphs.

A paragraph looks like this on the page:

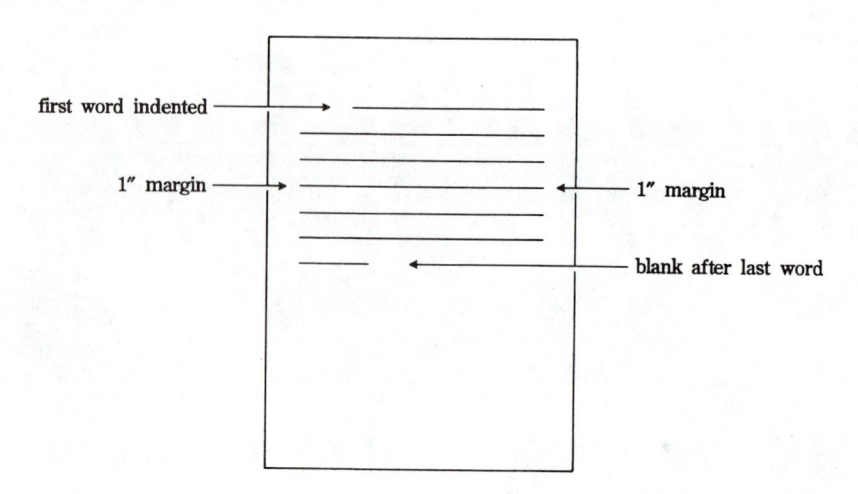

- Clearly **indent** the first word of every paragraph about 1 inch (five spaces on the computer).
- Extend every line of a paragraph as close to the right-hand margin as possible.
- However, if the last word of the paragraph comes before the end of the line, leave the rest of the line blank.

Topic Sentence and Body

Most paragraphs contain one main idea to which all the sentences relate.
The **topic sentence** states this main idea.
The **body** of the paragraph develops and supports this main idea with particular facts, details, and examples:

> I allow the spiders the run of the house. I figure that any predator that hopes to make a living on whatever smaller creatures might blunder into a four-inch-square bit of space in the corner of the bathroom where the tub meets the floor needs every bit of my support. They catch flies and even field crickets in those webs. Large spiders in barns have been known to trap, wrap, and suck hummingbirds, but there's no danger of that here. I tolerate the webs, only occasionally sweeping away the very dirtiest of them after the spider itself has scrambled to safety. I'm always leaving a bath towel draped over the tub so that the big, haired spiders, who are constantly getting trapped by the tub's smooth sides, can use its rough surface as an exit ramp. Inside the house the spiders have only given me one mild surprise. I washed some dishes and set them to dry over a plastic drainer. Then I wanted a cup of coffee, so I picked from the drainer my mug, which was still warm from the hot rinse water, and across the rim of the mug, strand after strand, was a spider web.
> —Annie Dillard, *Pilgrim at Tinker Creek*

- The first sentence of Dillard's paragraph is the **topic sentence.** It states the main idea of the paragraph: that *the spiders are allowed the run of the house.*
- The rest of the paragraph, the **body,** fully explains and supports this statement. The writer first gives a reason for her attitude toward spiders and then gives particular examples of her tolerance of spiders.

The topic sentence is more *general* than the other sentences in the paragraph. The other sentences in the paragraph provide specific information relating to the topic sentence. Because the topic sentence tells what the entire paragraph is about, *it is usually the first sentence,* as in the example. Sometimes the topic sentence occurs elsewhere in the paragraph, for example, as the sentence after an introduction or as the last sentence. Some paragraphs contain only an implied topic sentence but no stated topic sentence at all.

As you develop your writing skills, however, it is a good idea to write paragraphs that *begin* with the topic sentence. Once you have mastered this pattern, you can try variations.

PRACTICE 1

Find and underline the **topic sentence** in each of the following paragraphs. Look for the sentence that states the **main idea** of the entire paragraph. Be careful: the topic sentence is not always the first sentence.

Paragraph a

The summer picnic gave ladies a chance to show off their baking hands. On the barbecue pit, chickens and spareribs sputtered in their own fat and in a sauce whose recipe was guarded in the family like a scandalous affair. However, every true baking artist could reveal her prize to the delight and criticism of the town. Orange sponge cakes and dark brown mounds dripping Hershey's chocolate stood layer to layer with ice-white coconuts and light brown caramels. Pound cakes sagged with their buttery weight and small children could no more resist licking the icings than their mothers could avoid slapping the sticky fingers.

—Maya Angelou, *I Know Why the Caged Bird Sings*

Paragraph b

Something strange and wonderful has happened, and it challenges much of what we thought we knew about living to be very old. All over the country, the number of people who last to and beyond the age of 100—the centenarians—has been soaring. There are more than 52,000 in America today, almost three times the number in 1980. They have become the fastest-growing age group not only in this country but throughout the industrialized world. New studies show that Americans live longer after the age of 80 than other national groups. In fact, after the age of 85, the odds that you will die in the next year or two actually level off. And half of today's centenarians are in good health, both physically and mentally.

—Caryl Stern, "Who Is Old?" *Parade*

Paragraph c

Eating sugar can be worse than eating nothing. Refined sugar provides only empty calories. It contributes none of the protein, fat, vitamins or minerals needed for its own metabolism in the body, so these nutrients must be obtained elsewhere. Sugar tends to replace nourishing food in the diet. It is a thief that robs us of nutrients. A dietary emphasis on sugar can deplete the body of nutrients. If adequate nutrients are not supplied by the diet—and they tend not to be in a sugar-rich diet—they must be leached from other body tissues before sugar can be metabolized. For this reason, a U.S. Senate committee labeled sugar as an "antinutrient."

—Janice Fillip, "The Sweet Thief," *Medical Self-Care*

Paragraph d   At local noontime on the Moon, surface temperatures rise above the boiling point of water. But at night or in the shade, the temperature plummets to well below water's freezing point. Warmth does not spread on the Moon's surface, for lunar soil is made of pulverized dust that does not conduct heat well. Nor does heat move through lunar air, for the Moon has no air. Without an artificial Earth habitat such as a spacecraft or spacesuit, humans could not survive on the Moon.

—Eric Chaisson and Steve McMillan, *Astronomy Today*

PRACTICE 2

Each group of sentences below could be unscrambled and written as a paragraph. Circle the letter of the **topic sentence** in each group of sentences. Remember: The topic sentence should state the main idea of the entire paragraph and should be general enough to include all the ideas in the body.

EXAMPLE
a. Rubies were supposed to stimulate circulation and restore lost vitality.
b. Clear quartz was believed to promote sweet sleep and good dreams.
(c.) For centuries, minerals and precious stones were thought to possess healing powers.
d. Amethysts were thought to prevent drunkenness.
(Sentence c includes the ideas in all the other sentences.)

1. a. Tiger Woods first appeared on television at the age of two, winning a putting contest against comedian Bob Hope.
   b. The world took note in 1997 when he won the famous Masters Golf Championship by twelve strokes, the largest margin of victory in any major golf championship of the twentieth century.
   c. At age twenty-one, Tiger Woods was not only the youngest person but the first person of color to win the Masters.
   d. Coached by his father, Earl Woods, Tiger Woods spent his teen years honing his skills and winning one junior and amateur golf title after another.
   e. Nike featured him in a series of stylish commercials that helped give golf a younger, "cooler" image.
   (f.) Tiger Woods has become a sports legend through his exceptional talent and his role in attracting young people and minorities to the game of golf.

2. a. Though they often wield their powerful trunks aggressively, elephants are just as likely to use their trunks to offer greetings by entwining them in a "trunk shake."
   b. One of the trunk's many functions is to suck up gallons of water, which it carries to the mouth for drinking or sprays on the back like a flexible showerhead.
   (c.) An elephant's trunk is a marvel of engineering.
   d. The trunk is sensitive enough to pick up a thin dime off a concrete floor and strong enough to carry several hundred pounds of mahogany logs.

3. a. Albert Einstein, whose scientific genius awed the world, did not speak until he was four and could not read until he was nine.
   b. Inventor Thomas Edison had such severe problems reading, writing, and spelling that he was called "defective from birth," taken out of school, and taught at home.
   (c.) Many famous people have suffered from learning disabilities.
   d. Olympic diving champion Greg Louganis was teased and laughed at for his speech delay, stutter, and perceptual problems.

4. (a.) Here at Kensington College, without our student numbers, we would hardly exist.
   b. We must display our student numbers and IDs just to get onto campus.
   c. We must pencil our student numbers on computer cards in order to register for courses.
   d. When our grades are posted, the *A*'s and *F*'s go not to Felicia Watson and Bill Jenkins, Jr., but to 237–002 and 235–1147.

5. a. The left side of the human brain controls spoken and written language.
   b. The right side, on the other hand, seems to control artistic, musical, and spatial skills.
   c. Emotion is also thought to be controlled by the right hemisphere.
   (d.) The human brain has two distinct halves, or hemispheres, and in most people, each one controls different functions.
   e. Logical reasoning and mathematics are left-brain skills.
   f. Interestingly, the left brain controls the right hand and vice versa.

6. a. The better skaters glided in wide circles, playing tag or crack the whip.
   (b.) Every winter, the lake was the center of activity.
   c. People talked and shoveled snow, exposing the dark, satiny ice.
   d. Children on double runners skated in the center of the cleared area.
   e. Dogs raced and skidded among the skaters.

7. a. This college student from Los Angeles could not find pastel nail polish in the stores, so she started mixing her own.
   b. When Mohajer took samples to a trendy shop in 1995, one customer snapped up four bottles at $18 apiece.
   c. Celebrities like Alicia Silverstone started buying the polish in colors like pea green and black, with offbeat names like "Geek," "Tantrum," and "Trailer Trash."
   d. Mohajer received so many compliments that she decided to start selling her product.
   e. Soon the business was so big that Mohajer hired someone to handle the finances.
   (f.) With only a fine sense of style and a knack for mixing colors, twenty-two-year-old Dineh Mohajer created a $10-million company.

8. (a.) Male and female insects are attracted to each other by visual, auditory, and chemical means.
   b. Through its chirping call, the male cricket attracts a mate and drives other males out of its territory.
   c. Butterflies attract by sight, and their brightly colored wings play an important role in courtship.
   d. Some female insects, flies among them, release chemicals called *pheromones* that attract males of the species.

9. a. At the University of Michigan, he helped develop a flu vaccine.
   b. He served as a consultant to the World Health Organization, a branch of the United Nations that brings medical help to developing countries.
   (c.) Dr. Jonas Salk contributed much to the cure of disease.
   d. After years of research, he finally created the first effective polio vaccine.
   e. When Dr. Salk died in 1995, he was working on an AIDS vaccine.

10. a. Believe it or not, the first contact lens was drawn by Leonardo da Vinci in 1508.
    b. However, not until 1877 was the first thick glass contact actually made by a Swiss doctor.
    (c.) The journey of contact lenses from an idea to a comfortable, safe reality took nearly five hundred years.
    d. In 1948, smaller, more comfortable plastic lenses were introduced to enthusiastic American eyeglass wearers.
    e. These early glass lenses were enormous, covering the whites of the eyes.
    f. Today, contact lens wearers can choose ultra-thin, colored, or even disposable lenses.

PART B Narrowing the Topic and Writing the Topic Sentence

A writer can arrive at the goal—a finished paragraph—in several ways. However, before writing a paragraph, most writers go through a process that includes these important steps:

1. Narrowing the topic
2. Writing the topic sentence
3. Generating ideas for the body
4. Selecting and dropping ideas
5. Arranging ideas in a plan or an outline

The rest of this chapter will explain these steps and guide you through the process of writing basic paragraphs.

Narrowing the Topic

As a student, you may be assigned broad writing topics by your instructor—success, cheating in schools, a description of a person. Your instructor is giving you the chance to cut the topic down to size and choose one aspect of the topic *that interests you.*

Suppose, for example, that your instructor gives this assignment: "Write a paragraph describing a person you know." The challenge is to pick someone you would *like* to write about, someone who interests you and also would probably interest your readers.

Thinking about your *audience* and *purpose* may help you narrow the topic. In this case, your audience probably will be your instructor and classmates; your purpose is to inform or perhaps to entertain them by describing a person you want to write about.

Many writers find it useful at this point—on paper or on computer—to brainstorm, freewrite, or ask themselves questions: "What person do I love or hate or admire? Is there a family member I would enjoy writing about? Who is the funniest, most unusual, or most talented person I know?"

Let's suppose you choose Pete, an unusual person and one about whom you have something to say. But Pete is still too broad a subject for one paragraph; you could probably write pages and pages about him. To narrow the topic further, you might ask yourself, "What is unusual about him? What might interest others?" Pete's room is the messiest place you have ever seen; in fact, Pete's whole life is sloppy, and you decide that you could write a good paragraph about that. You have now narrowed the topic to just one of Pete's qualities: *his sloppiness*.

Writing the Topic Sentence

The next important step is to state your topic clearly *in sentence form*. Writing the topic sentence helps you further narrow your topic by forcing you to make a statement about it. The simplest possible topic sentence about Pete might read *Pete is sloppy*, but you might wish to strengthen it by saying, for instance, *Pete's sloppiness is a terrible habit*.

Writing a good topic sentence is an important step toward an effective paragraph because the topic sentence controls the direction and scope of the body. A topic sentence should have a clear *controlling idea* and should be a *complete sentence*.

You can think of the topic sentence as having two parts, a **topic** and a **controlling idea**. The controlling idea states the writer's point of view or attitude about the topic.

               topic   **controlling idea**

Topic sentence: Pete's sloppiness is a terrible habit.

The controlling idea helps you focus on just one aspect or point. Here are three possible topic sentences about the topic *a memorable job*.

> 1. My job in the complaint department taught me how to calm down angry people.
> 2. Two years in the complaint department persuaded me to become an assistant manager.
> 3. Working in the complaint department persuaded me to become a veterinarian.

■ These topic sentences all explore the same topic—working in a complaint department—but each controlling idea is different. The controlling idea in 1 is *taught me how to calm down angry people*.

■ What is the controlling idea in 2? *prepared me to become an assistant manager*

What is the controlling idea in 3? *persuaded me to become a veterinarian*

■ Notice the way in which the controlling idea lets the reader know what the paragraph will be about. There are many possible topic sentences for any topic, depending on the writer's interests and point of view. If you were assigned the topic *a memorable job*, what would your topic sentence be?

_____

_____

PRACTICE 3

Read each topic sentence below. Circle the topic and underline the controlling idea.

1. (A low-fat diet) provides many health benefits.
2. (MTV's *Road Rules*) is both entertaining and educational.
3. (Our football coach) works to build players' self-esteem.
4. (This campus) offers many peaceful places where students can relax.
5. (My cousin's truck) looks like something out of *Star Wars*.

As a rule, the more specific and clear your topic and controlling idea, the better the paragraph; in other words, your topic sentence should not be so broad that it cannot be developed in one paragraph. Which of these topic sentences do you think will produce the best paragraphs?

> 4. Five wet, bug-filled days at Camp Nirvana made me a fan of the great indoors.
> 5. This town has problems.
> 6. Road rage is on the rise for three reasons.

■ Topic sentences 4 and 6 are both specific enough to write a good paragraph about. In each, the topic sentence is carefully worded to suggest clearly what ideas will follow. From topic sentence 4, what do you expect the paragraph to include?

The paragraph will probably discuss how weather and insects ruined the week.

■ What do you expect paragraph 6 to include?

The paragraph will probably discuss three reasons that road rage is on the rise.

■ Topic sentence 5, on the other hand, is so broad that a paragraph could include almost anything. Just what problems does the town have? Strained relations between police and the community? Litter in public parks? Termites? The writer needs to rewrite the controlling idea, focusing on just one problem for an effective paragraph.

The topic sentence also must be a **complete sentence.** It must contain a subject and a verb, and express a complete thought.* Do not confuse a topic with a

---

* For practice in correcting fragments, see Chapter 25, "Avoiding Sentence Errors," Part B.

CHAPTER 3 The Process of Writing Paragraphs   27

topic sentence. For instance, *a celebrity I would like to meet* cannot be a topic sentence because it is not a sentence; however, it could be a title* because topics and titles need not be complete sentences. One possible topic sentence might read, *A celebrity I would like to meet is writer Julia Alvarez.*

Do not write *This paragraph will be about . . .* or *In this paper I will write about. . . .* Instead, craft your topic sentence carefully to focus the topic and let your reader know what the paragraph will contain. Make every word count.

PRACTICE 4

Put a check beside each topic sentence that is focused enough to allow you to write a good paragraph. If a topic sentence is too broad, narrow the topic according to your own interests and write a new topic sentence with a clear controlling idea.

EXAMPLES

✓ ___ Keeping a journal can improve a student's writing.

Rewrite: _____

___ This paper will be about my family.

Rewrite: *My brother Mark has a unique sense of humor.*

1. ✓ ___ Eugene's hot temper causes problems at work.

   Rewrite: _____

2. ___ This paragraph will discuss study techniques.

   Rewrite: *Organizing my study time has been difficult for me to achieve.*

3. ✓ ___ Bilingualism is a great asset in the workplace.

   Rewrite: _____

4. ✓ ___ Many beer commercials on TV imply that people need to drink in order to have a good time.

   Rewrite: _____

---

*For practice in writing titles, see Chapter 16, "The Introduction, the Conclusion, and the Title," Part C.

28 UNIT 2 Discovering the Paragraph

5. ___ Child abuse is something to think about.

   Rewrite: *Child abuse can be reduced through parenting classes.*

6. ✓ Students should not be allowed to wear short shorts or revealing clothing on campus.

   Rewrite: ___

7. ✓ Learning karate increased my self-confidence.

   Rewrite: ___

8. ✓ Companies should not read employees' e-mail.

   Rewrite: ___

PRACTICE 5

Here is a list of broad topics. Choose three that interest you from this list or from your own list on page 5. Narrow each topic, choose your controlling idea, and write a topic sentence focused enough to write a good paragraph about. Make sure that each topic sentence has a clear controlling idea and is a complete sentence.

Overcoming fears	Insider's tour of your community
Popular music	Balancing work and play
Credit cards	A person you like or dislike
An act of cowardice or courage	A time when you were (or were not) in control

1. Narrowed topic: *Overcoming fear of flying*

   Controlling idea: *Daryl boosted his career and calmed his nerves*

   Topic sentence: *Overcoming his fear of flying boosted Daryl's career and calmed his nerves.*

CHAPTER 3   The Process of Writing Paragraphs   29

2. Narrowed topic: *I dislike Tom*

   Controlling idea: *his gossiping is destructive*

   Topic sentence: *I dislike Tom because his gossiping is a destructive habit.*

3. Narrowed topic: *Lack of balance when I worked several jobs*

   Controlling idea: *during this time I become less productive*

   Topic sentence: *The more hours a week I worked in part-time jobs, the less productive I was at home and school.*

PRACTICE 6

Many writers adjust the topic sentence after they have finished drafting the paragraph. In a group of three or four classmates, study the body of each of these paragraphs to find the main, or controlling, idea. Then, working together, write the most exact and interesting topic sentence you can for each paragraph.

Paragraph a   *The Internet is growing at an amazing rate.*

In 1981, fewer than 300 computers were linked to the Internet. By 1989, the number of Internet users was fewer than 90,000. However, by 1993, more than 1 million computer users had logged on and were sending e-mail, doing research, working, and shopping in cyberspace. According to a survey conducted by *Business Week* magazine in 1997, about 60 million people in the United States alone were hooked up to the Internet. As the twenty-first century dawned, that number topped 100 million, with no end to the explosive growth in sight.

Paragraph b   *Animals occasionally rescue human beings.*

A pet parrot recently saved his owner's life. Harry Becker was watching TV in his living room when he suddenly slumped over with a heart attack. The parrot screamed loudly until Mr. Becker's wife awoke and called 911. In another reported case of animal rescue, a family cat saved six-week-old Stacey Rogers. When the cat heard the baby gasping for breath in her crib, it ran howling to alert the baby's mother, who called paramedics. Even more surprising was an event reported in newspapers around the world. In 1996 in a Chicago zoo, a female gorilla rushed to save a three-year-old boy who fell accidentally into the gorilla enclosure. Still carrying her own baby on her back, the 150-pound gorilla gently picked up the unconscious child and carried him to the cage door to be rescued. Though we might not understand why, animals sometimes help and even save us.

PART C   Generating Ideas for the Body

One good way to generate ideas for the body of a paragraph is **brainstorming**—freely jotting on paper or computer anything that relates to your topic sentence: facts, details, examples, little stories. This step might take just a few minutes, but it is one of the most important elements of the writing process. Brainstorming can provide you with specific ideas to support your topic sentence. Later you can choose from these ideas as you compose your paragraph.

Here, for example, is a possible brainstorm list for the topic sentence *Pete's sloppiness is a terrible habit*:

1. His apartment is full of dirty clothes, books, candy wrappers
2. His favorite candy—M&Ms
3. He is often a latecomer or a no-show
4. He jots time-and-place information for dates and appointments on scraps of paper that are soon forgotten
5. Stacks of old newspapers sit on chair seats
6. Socks are on the lampshades
7. Papers for classes wrinkled and carelessly scrawled
8. I met Pete for the first time in math class
9. His sister is just the opposite, very neat
10. Always late for classes, out of breath
11. He is one messy person
12. Papers stained with coffee or M&Ms

Instead of brainstorming, some writers freewrite or ask themselves questions to generate ideas for their paragraphs. Some like to perform this step on paper whereas others use a computer. Do what works best for you. If you need more practice in any of these methods, reread Chapter 2, "Prewriting to Generate Ideas."

PRACTICE 7

Now choose the topic from Part B, Practice 5, that most interests you. Write your narrowed topic, controlling idea, and topic sentence here.

Narrowed topic: _____

Controlling idea: _____

Topic sentence: _____

_____

Next, brainstorm. On paper or on computer, write anything that comes to you about your topic sentence. Just let your ideas pour out. Try to fill at least one page.

PART D Selecting and Dropping Ideas

Next, simply read over what you have written, **selecting** those ideas that relate to and support the topic sentence and **dropping** those that do not. That is, keep the facts, examples, or little stories that provide specific information about your topic sentence. Drop ideas that just **repeat** the topic sentence but that add nothing new to the paragraph.

If you are not sure which ideas to select or drop, underline the **key word** or **words** of the topic sentence, the ones that indicate the real point of your paragraph. Then make sure that the ideas that you select are related to those key words.

Here again is the brainstorm list for the topic sentence *Pete's sloppiness is a terrible habit.* The key word in the topic sentence is *sloppiness*. Which ideas would you keep? Why? Which would you drop? Why?

1. His apartment is full of dirty clothes, books, candy wrappers
2. His favorite candy—M&Ms
3. He is often a latecomer or a no-show
4. He jots time-and-place information for dates and appointments on scraps of paper that are soon forgotten
5. Stacks of old newspapers sit on chair seats
6. Socks are on the lampshades
7. Papers for classes wrinkled and carelessly scrawled
8. I met Pete for the first time in math class
9. His sister is just the opposite, very neat
10. Always late for classes, out of breath
11. He is one messy person
12. Papers stained with coffee or M&Ms

You probably dropped ideas 2, 8, and 9 because they do not relate to the topic—Pete's sloppiness. You should also have dropped idea 11 because it merely repeats the topic sentence.

PRACTICE 8

Read through your own brainstorm list from Part C, Practice 7. Select the ideas that relate to your topic sentence and drop those that do not. In addition, drop any ideas that just repeat your topic sentence. Be prepared to explain why you drop or keep each idea.

PART E Arranging Ideas in a Plan or an Outline

After you have selected the ideas you wish to include in your paragraph, you can begin to make a plan or an outline. A plan briefly lists and arranges the ideas you wish to present in your paragraph. An outline does the same thing a bit more formally, but in an outline, letters or numbers indicate the main groupings of ideas.

First, group together ideas that have something in common, that are related or alike in some way. Then order your ideas by choosing which one you want to come first, which one second, and so on.

Below is a plan for a paragraph about Pete's sloppiness:

Topic sentence: Pete's sloppiness is a terrible habit.

- His apartment is full of dirty clothes, books, candy wrappers
- Stacks of old newspapers sit on chair seats
- Socks are on the lampshades

- He jots time-and-place information for dates and appointments on scraps of paper that are soon forgotten
- He is often a latecomer or a no-show
- Always late for classes, out of breath

- Papers for classes wrinkled and carelessly scrawled
- Papers stained with coffee or M&Ms

- Do you see the logic in this arrangement? How are the ideas in each group above related? *Each group includes examples of Pete's sloppiness in one area of his life.*

- Does it make sense to discuss Pete's apartment first, his lateness second, and his written work third? Why? *Yes. The order goes from the personal to the social, which means it goes from what he does in his house to what he does when he's outside his house.*

- Once you have finished arranging ideas, you should have a clear **plan** from which to write your paragraph.*

Practice 9

On paper or on computer, arrange the ideas from your brainstorm list according to some plan or outline. First, group together related ideas; then decide which ideas will come first, which second, and so on.

Keep in mind that there is more than one way to group ideas. Think about what you want to say; then group ideas according to what your point is.

---

* For more work on order, see Chapter 4, "Achieving Coherence," Part A.

PART F   Writing and Revising the Paragraph

Writing the First Draft

The first draft should contain all the ideas you have decided to use in the order you have chosen in your plan. Be sure to start with your topic sentence. Try to write the best, most interesting, or most amusing paragraph you can, but avoid getting stuck on any one word, sentence, or idea. If you are unsure about something, put a check in the margin and come back to it later. Writing on every other line or double spacing if you write on computer will leave room for later corrections.

Once you have included all the ideas from your plan, think about adding a concluding sentence that summarizes your main point or adds a final idea. Not all paragraphs need concluding sentences. For example, if you are telling a story, the paragraph can end when the story does. Write a concluding sentence if it will help to bring your thoughts to an end for your reader.

If possible, once you have finished the first draft, set the paper aside for several hours or several days.

PRACTICE 10

Write a first draft of the paragraph you have been working on.

Revising

Revising means rethinking and rewriting your first draft and then making whatever changes, additions, or corrections are necessary to improve the paragraph. You may cross out and rewrite words or entire sentences. You may add, drop, or rearrange details.

As you revise, keep the *reader* in mind. Ask yourself these questions:

- Is my topic sentence clear?
- Can a reader understand and follow my ideas?
- Does the paragraph follow a logical order and guide the reader from point to point?
- Will the paragraph keep the reader interested?

In addition, check your paragraph for adequate support and unity, characteristics that we'll consider in the following pages.

Revising for Support

As you revise, make sure your paragraph contains excellent **support**—that is, specific facts, details, and examples that fully explain your topic sentence.

34 UNIT 2 Discovering the Paragraph

Be careful, too, that you have not simply repeated ideas—especially the topic sentence. Even if they are in different words, repeated ideas only make the reader suspect that your paragraph is padded and that you do not have enough facts and details to support your main idea properly.

Which of the following paragraphs contains the most convincing support?

Paragraph a   (1) Our run-down city block was made special by a once-vacant lot called The Community Garden. (2) The lot was planted with all sorts of plants, vegetables, and flowers. (3) There was a path curving through it. (4) We went there to think. (5) The Community Garden made our block special. (6) Though our neighborhood was known as "tough," no one ever vandalized the garden.

Paragraph b   (1) Our run-down city block was made special by a once-vacant lot called The Community Garden. (2) I'm not sure who first had the idea, but the thin soil had been fertilized, raked, and planted with a surprising assortment of vegetables and flowers. (3) Anyone interested in gardening could tend green pepper plants, string beans, fresh herbs, even corn. (4) Others planted flowers, which changed with the seasons—tall red dahlias, white and purple irises, and taxi-yellow marigolds to discourage the insects. (5) Paved with bricks no doubt left over from the building that once stood here, a narrow path curved gracefully among the plants. (6) The Community Garden was our pride, the place we went to think and to be still. (7) Though the neighborhood was known as "tough," no one ever vandalized the garden.

■ *Paragraph a* contains general statements but little specific information to support the topic sentence.

■ *Paragraph a* also contains needless repetition. What is the number of the sentence or sentences that just repeat the topic sentence?

Sentence 5

■ *Paragraph b*, however, supports the topic sentence with specific details and examples: *thin soil, fertilized, raked and planted, green pepper plants, string beans, fresh herbs, corn, red dahlias.* What other specific support does it give?

It states that others planted white and purple irises, taxi-yellow marigolds; it

describes in detail the curving path of brick and explains why people went

to the garden.

Practice 11

Check the following paragraphs for adequate support. As you read each one, decide which places need more or better support—specific facts, details, and examples. Then rewrite the paragraphs, inventing facts and details whenever necessary and dropping repetitious words and sentences.

Paragraph a   (1) My uncle can always be counted on when the family faces hardship. (2) Last year, when my mother was very ill, he was there, ready to help in every way. (3) He never has to be called twice. (4) When my father became seriously depressed, my uncle's caring made a difference. (5) Everyone respects him for his willingness to be a real "family man." (6) He is always there for us.

Paragraph b   (1) Loaning money to a friend can have negative consequences. (2) For example, Ashley, a student at Tornado Community College, agreed to lend $200 to her best friend, Jan. (3) This was a bad decision even though Ashley meant well. (4) The results of this loan were surprising and negative for Ashley, for Jan, and for the friendship. (5) Both women felt bad about it but in different ways. (6) Yes, loaning money to a friend can have very negative consequences, like anger and hurt.

Paragraph c   (1) Many television talk shows don't really present a discussion of ideas. (2) Some people who appear on these shows don't know what they are talking about; they just like to sound off about something. (3) I don't like these shows at all. (4) Guests shout their opinions out loud but never give any proof for what they say. (5) Guests sometimes expose their most intimate personal and family problems before millions of viewers—I feel embarrassed. (6) I have even heard hosts insult their guests and guests insult them back. (7) Why do people watch this junk? (8) You never learn anything from these dumb shows.

Revising for Unity

It is sometimes easy, in the process of writing, to drift away from the topic under discussion. Guard against doing so by checking your paragraph for unity; that is, make sure the topic sentence, every sentence in the body, and the concluding sentence all relate to one main idea.*

This paragraph lacks unity:

> (1) John Bryant is a prime example of someone who has used his success and expertise to help others. (2) In 1992, Bryant was a successful financial consultant in Los Angeles. (3) After the riots, Bryant, an African American, was moved to tears by the sight of South Central L.A. in ruins. (4) With $5,000 of his personal savings, he set up Operation Hope, a nonprofit banking group dedicated to rebuilding inner-city Los Angeles. (5) Since that day, Bryant has personally escorted dozens of bankers through South Central L.A. (6) Compton, California, was his birthplace. (7) His passionate appeals have persuaded forty financial institutions to fund $13 million in home loans. (8) In addition, Bryant has worked one-on-one with people who want to buy homes, teaching them to solve the personal credit problems that have stood in their way.

■ What is the number of the topic sentence in this paragraph?

Sentence 1

---

*For more work on revising, see Chapter 22, "Putting Your Revision Skills to Work."

36 UNIT 2 Discovering the Paragraph

■ Which sentence in the paragraph does not clearly relate to the topic sentence?

Sentence 6

This paragraph also lacks unity:

> (1) Quitting smoking was very difficult for me. (2) When I was thirteen, my friend Janice and I smoked in front of a mirror. (3) We practiced holding the cigarette in different ways and tried French inhaling, letting the smoke roll slowly out of our mouths and drawing it back through our noses. (4) I thought this move, when it didn't incite a fit of coughing, was particularly sexy. (5) At first I smoked only to give myself confidence on dates and at parties. (6) Soon, however, I was smoking all the time.

■ Here the topic sentence itself, sentence 1, does not relate to the rest of the paragraph. The main idea in sentence 1, that quitting smoking was difficult, is not developed by the other sentences. Since the rest of the paragraph *is* unified, a more appropriate topic sentence might read, *As a teenager, I developed the bad habit of smoking.*

PRACTICE 12

Check the following paragraphs for unity. If a paragraph has unity, write U in the blank. If not, write the number of the sentence that does not belong in the paragraph.

Paragraph a __6__ (1) The first batch of one of the world's most popular soft drinks was mixed in a backyard kettle over a hundred years ago. (2) On May 6, 1886, Dr. John Styth Pemberton heated a mixture of melted sugar, water, cocoa leaves, kola nuts, and other ingredients. (3) He planned to make one of the home-brewed medical syrups so popular at that time. (4) However, this one tasted so good that Dr. Pemberton decided to sell it as a soda fountain drink for five cents a glass. (5) The first glass of this new drink was sold at Jacob's Pharmacy in Atlanta, Georgia. (6) Atlanta was and still is a wonderful place to live. (7) Pemberton's tasty invention, Coca-Cola, caught on. (8) Today, Coca-Cola is consumed by 140,000 people every minute.

Paragraph b __4__ (1) At Paradise Produce, attractive displays of fruit and vegetables caught my eye. (2) On the left, oranges, lemons, and apples were stacked in neat pyramids. (3) In the center of the store, baskets of ripe peaches, plums, and raspberries were grouped in a kind of still life. (4) Many nutritionists believe that berries help prevent certain diseases. (5) On the right, the leafy green vegetables had been arranged according to intensity of color: dark green spinach, then romaine lettuce and parsley, next the lighter iceberg lettuce, and finally the nearly white Chinese cabbage. (6) On the wall above the greens hung braided ropes of garlic.

Paragraph c __9__ (1) Technology enables people like the famous physicist Dr. Stephen Hawking to continue working despite serious physical disabilities. (2) For thirty-five years, Dr. Hawking has lived with Lou Gehrig's disease, which attacks the muscles, but his brilliant mind works perfectly. (3) He can no longer walk, speak, or feed himself. (4) Nevertheless, a high-tech wheelchair with computer attachments allows him to continue his research and stay in touch with friends and colleagues around the world. (5) His computer is hooked up full-time to the Internet. (6) To speak, he chooses words displayed on the computer screen, and then an electronic voice machine pronounces each word. (7) A pressure-sensitive joystick even lets Dr. Hawking make his way through traffic. (8) In his home, infrared remote control operates doors, lights, and his personal entertainment center. (9) He had two children with his first wife, Jane. (10) Dr. Hawking continues to search for new ways to overcome his problems through technology.

Revising with Peer Feedback

You may wish to show or read your first draft to a respected friend. Ask this person to give an honest response, *not* to rewrite your work. Ask specific questions of your own or use this peer feedback sheet.

PEER FEEDBACK SHEET

To _____ From _____ Date _____

1. What I like about this piece of writing is _____

   _____

2. Your main point seems to be _____

   _____

3. These particular words or lines struck me as powerful:

Words or lines	I like them because
_____	_____
_____	_____
_____	_____

4. Some things aren't clear to me. These lines or parts could be improved (meaning not clear, supporting points missing, order seems mixed up, writing not lively):

Lines or parts	Need improving because
_____	_____
_____	_____
_____	_____

5. The one change you could make that would make the biggest improvement in this piece of writing is _____

   _____

Writing the Final Draft

When you are satisfied with your revisions, recopy your paper or print a fresh copy. If you are writing in class, the second draft will usually be the last one. Be sure to include all your corrections, writing neatly and legibly.

The first draft of the paragraph about Pete, showing the writer's changes, and the revised, final draft follow. Compare them.

First Draft with Revisions

Pete's sloppiness is a terrible habit. He lives by himself in a <u>small</u> apartment ^carpeted with dirty clothes, books, and candy wrappers. Stacks of papers cover the chair seats. Socks ~~are~~ ^bake! on the lampshades. When Pete makes a date or an appointment, he may jot down the time and place on a scrap of paper that is soon ^tucked into a pocket and forgotten, or—more likely—he doesn't jot down the information at all. ^As a result, Pete often arrives late, or he completely forgets to appear. His grades have suffered, too, ^because Few instructors will put up with a student who arrives out of breath ^ten minutes after class has begun and whose ^wrinkled, scrawled ~~messy~~ papers arrive (late, of course) with ^punctuated with coffee stains and melted M&Ms. ~~stains on them.~~

~~Pete's sloppiness really is a terrible habit.~~

Margin notes:
- Add details to show his sloppiness!
- how small?—better word needed
- Show consequences
- Add more details—better support
- This repeats t.s. Better conclusion needed.

Final Draft

> Pete's sloppiness is a terrible habit. He lives by himself in a one-room apartment carpeted with dirty clothes, books, and crumpled candy wrappers. Stacks of papers cover the chair seats. Socks bake on the lampshades. When Pete makes a date or an appointment, he may jot down the time and place on a scrap of paper that is soon tucked into a pocket and forgotten, or—more likely—he doesn't jot down the information at all. As a result, Pete often arrives late, or he completely forgets to appear. His grades have suffered, too, because few instructors will put up with a student who arrives out of breath ten minutes after the class has begun and whose wrinkled, carelessly scrawled papers arrive (late, of course) punctuated with coffee stains and melted M&Ms. The less Pete controls his sloppiness, the more it seems to control him.

■ Note that the paragraph contains good support—specific facts, details, and examples that explain the topic sentence.

- Note that the paragraph has unity—every idea relates to the topic sentence.
- Note that the final sentence provides a brief conclusion, so that the paragraph *feels finished*.

Proofreading

Whether you write by hand or on computer, be sure to **proofread** your final draft carefully for grammar and spelling errors. Pointing to each word as you read it will help you catch errors or words you might have left out, especially small words like *to*, *the*, or *a*. If you are unsure of the spelling of a word, consult a dictionary and run spell check if you work on a computer.* Make neat corrections in pen or print a corrected copy of your paper. Chapter 36, "Putting Your Proofreading Skills to Work," and all of Units 6 and 7 in this book are devoted to improving your proofreading skills.

PRACTICE 13

Now read the first draft of your paragraph with a critical eye. Revise and rewrite it, checking especially for a clear topic sentence, strong support, and unity.

PRACTICE 14

Exchange *revised* paragraphs with a classmate. Ask specific questions or use the Peer Feedback Sheet.

When you *give* feedback, try to be as honest and specific as possible; saying a paper is "good," "nice," or "bad" doesn't really help the writer. When you *receive* feedback, think over your classmate's responses; do they ring true?

Now **revise** a second time, with the aim of writing a fine paragraph. Proofread carefully for grammar errors, spelling errors, and omitted words.

WRITING ASSIGNMENTS

The assignments that follow will give you practice in writing basic paragraphs. In each, aim for (1) a topic sentence with a clear controlling idea and (2) a body that fully supports and develops the topic sentence.

Remember to **narrow the topic, write the topic sentence, freewrite or brainstorm, select,** and **arrange ideas** in a plan or an outline before you write. Rethink and **revise** as necessary before composing the final version of the paragraph. As you work, refer to the checklist at the end of this chapter.

Paragraph 1 *Discuss an important day in your life*

Think back to a day when you learned something important. In the topic sentence, tell what you learned. Freewrite or brainstorm to gather ideas. Then describe the lesson in detail, including only the most important steps or events in the learning process. Conclude with an insight.

---

* For tips and cautions on using a computer spell checker, see Chapter 37, Part B.

Paragraph 2 *Examine campus fashion*

What clothing and hair styles are currently in fashion on your campus? Update your readers on the look—or looks—of the moment. Focus your topic: You might write about a certain group of students who share one look, hair only, clothing styles only, and so forth. Use humor if you wish. Vivid supporting details, descriptions, and examples will help make your point. Revise your work for good support, unity, and all-around excellent writing.

Paragraph 3 *Interview a classmate about an achievement*

Write about a time when your classmate achieved something important, like winning an award for a musical performance, getting an *A* in a difficult course, or helping a friend through a hard time. To gather interesting facts and details, ask your classmate questions like these and take notes: *Is there one accomplishment of which you are very proud? Why was this achievement so important?* Keep asking questions until you feel you can give the reader a vivid sense of your classmate's triumph. In your first sentence, state the person's achievement—for instance, *Being accepted in the honors program improved Gabe's self-esteem.* Then explain specifically why the achievement was so meaningful.

Paragraph 4 *Choose an ideal job*

Decide what kind of job you are best suited for and, in your topic sentence, tell what this job is. Then give three or four reasons that will convince readers of the wisdom of your choice. Discuss any special qualifications, talents, skills, or attitudes that would make you an excellent _____. Revise your work, checking for support and unity.

Paragraph 5 *Discuss a quotation*

Look through the quotations in the Quotation Bank before the indexes in this book. Pick a quotation you especially agree or disagree with. In your topic sentence, state how you feel about the quotation. Then explain why you feel the way you do, giving examples from your own experience to support or contradict the quotation. Make sure your reader knows exactly how you feel.

Paragraph 6 *Explain a sports or music fanatic*

Do you know a sports or music fan who takes his or her loyalty and enthusiasm to an extreme? Explain this person's behavior to your readers. You might choose several details or actions that best capture his or her fanatic behavior. Or you might wish to discuss why you think a team or musical group is so important to this person. Use humor if you wish. State your controlling idea in the topic sentence and support this idea fully with details, facts, and examples.

Paragraph 7 *Discuss a childhood experience*

Choose an experience that deeply affected you. First tell exactly what happened, giving important details. Then explain the meaning this experience had for you.

Paragraph 8 *Describe a portrait*

Look closely at this painting of a young woman, "Umbrella Maker" by artist Patricia Hansen. Study the woman in the painting—her eyes, mouth, expression, and other important details. Notice the room and the umbrellas that surround her. Then write a paragraph in which you describe the painting for a reader who has never seen it. In your topic sentence, state your overall impression of the painting. Support this impression with details.

✓ CHECKLIST: The Process of Writing Basic Paragraphs

____ 1. Narrow the topic in light of your audience and purpose.

____ 2. Write a topic sentence that has a clear controlling idea and is a complete sentence. If you have trouble, freewrite or brainstorm first; then narrow the topic and write the topic sentence.

____ 3. Freewrite or brainstorm, generating facts, details, and examples to develop your topic sentence.

____ 4. Select and drop ideas for the body of the paragraph.

_____ 5. Arrange ideas in a plan or an outline, deciding which ideas will come first, which will come second, and so forth.

_____ 6. Write the best first draft you can.

_____ 7. Conclude. Don't just leave the paragraph hanging.

_____ 8. Revise as necessary, checking your paragraph for support and unity.

_____ 9. Proofread for grammar and spelling errors.

CHAPTER 4

Achieving Coherence

PART A   Coherence Through Order

PART B   Coherence Through Related Sentences

Every composition should have **coherence.** A paragraph *coheres*—holds together—when the sentences are arranged in a clear, logical *order* and when the sentences are *related* like links in a chain.

PART A   Coherence Through Order

An orderly presentation of ideas within the paragraph is easier to follow and more pleasant to read than a jumble. *After* jotting down ideas but *before* writing the paragraph, the writer should decide which ideas to discuss first, which second, which third, and so on, according to a logical order.

There are many possible orders, depending on the subject and the writer's purpose. This section will explain three basic ways of ordering ideas: **time order, space order,** and **order of importance.**

Time Order

One of the most common methods of ordering sentences in a paragraph is through **time,** or **chronological, order,** which moves from present to past or from past to present. Most stories, histories, and instructions follow the logical order of time.* The following paragraph employs time order:

---

* For work on narrative paragraphs, see Chapter 6, "Narration," and for work on process paragraphs, see Chapter 8, "Process."

43

> (1) Most Westerners are fascinated by Japanese sumo wrestling, but few understand the elaborate ritual that begins every bout. (2) *First*, the two *rikishi* (the Japanese term for "sumo wrestlers") step to the edge of the ring opposite each other, squat on their haunches, extend their arms, and clap once. (3) *Then* they go to the center of the ring; each lifts one leg sideways and stomps down on the mat. (4) *Next*, each opponent returns to his side of the ring and receives a dipper of "power-water" to rinse his mouth. (5) *At this point*, an attendant offers each a basket of unrefined salt. (6) The wrestlers walk toward the center of the ring, scattering salt to purify the ring. (7) They stop in the center, squat on their haunches with their fists on their knees, and lean toward each other, eyeball to eyeball. (8) As the fans scream and shout, the wrestlers return to the edge of the ring *one more time*. (9) The referee raises his war fan. (10) *Finally*, the fighters approach each other and begin fighting.

- The events in this paragraph are clearly arranged in the order of time. They are presented as they happen, *chronologically*.

- Throughout the paragraph, key words like *first*, *then*, *next*, and *at this point* emphasize time order and guide the reader from event to event.

Careful use of time order helps prevent confusing writing like this: *Oops, I forgot to mention that before the wrestlers scatter salt, they rinse their mouths.*

Occasionally, when the sentences in a paragraph follow a very clear time order, the topic sentence is only implied, not stated directly, as in this example:

> (1) <u>In 1905</u>, a poor washerwoman with a homemade hair product started a business—with $1.50! (2) <u>In just five years</u>, Madame C. J. Walker established offices and manufacturing centers in Denver, Pittsburgh, and Indianapolis. (3) The Madame C. J. Walker Manufacturing Company specialized in hair supplies, but Madame Walker specialized in independence for herself and for others. (4) Although she was not formally educated, she developed an international sales force, teaching her African-American agents the most sophisticated business skills. (5) <u>Eight years after starting her business</u>, Madame Walker was the first African-American woman to become a self-made millionaire. (6) In addition, she drew thousands of former farm and domestic workers into the business world. (7) One of her most original ideas was to establish "Walker Clubs," and she awarded cash prizes to the clubs with the most educational and philanthropic projects in their African-American communities. (8) <u>When she died in 1919</u>, Madame Walker left two-thirds of her fortune to schools and charities. (9) Another of her contributions also lived on. (10) <u>After her death</u>, many of her former employees used their experience to start businesses throughout the United States and the Caribbean.

- Time order gives coherence to this paragraph. Sentence 1 tells us about the beginning of Madame Walker's career as a businessperson. However, it does not express the main idea of the entire paragraph.

CHAPTER 4 Achieving Coherence 45

- What is the implied topic sentence or main idea developed by the paragraph?

  With almost nothing but natural business ability, Madame Walker achieved success and helped others.

- The implied topic sentence or main idea of the paragraph might read, *With nothing but natural business ability and vision, Madame C. J. Walker achieved history-making success for herself and others.*

- Because the writer arranges the paragraph in chronological order, the reader can easily follow the order of events in Madame Walker's life. What words and phrases indicate time order? Underline them and list them here:

  in 1905; in just five years; eight years after starting her business; when she died in 1919; after her death

PRACTICE 1

Arrange each set of sentences in logical time order, numbering the sentences 1, 2, 3, and so on, as if you were preparing to write a paragraph. Underline any words and phrases, like *first*, *next*, and *in 1692*, that give time clues.

1. __2__ <u>First</u>, turn off the appliance that caused the fuse to blow.

   __5__ <u>Finally</u>, replace with a new fuse of the same amperage.

   __4__ Remove the blown fuse by turning it from right to left.

   __1__ Changing a fuse is not difficult.

   __3__ <u>Then</u> identify the blown fuse by its clouded glass cap.

2. __5__ The judge <u>later</u> deeply regretted his part, but this sorry chapter in American history has never been forgotten.

   __2__ Two books "proving" that witches existed, by the famous Puritan ministers Increase Mather and his son Cotton Mather, further fanned the hysteria <u>in 1693</u>.

   __3__ The stage was set for the terrible Salem witchcraft trials.

   __4__ Nineteen so-called "witches and wizards" were hanged; one was pressed to death.

   __1__ <u>In 1692</u>, when two girls in Salem Village, Massachusetts, had fits, they blamed the townspeople for bewitching them.

46   UNIT 2   Discovering the Paragraph

3. __4__ Therefore, they decided to produce the reissues themselves, including three LPs by early rock legend Ritchie Valens.

__1__ In 1978 Richard Foos and Harold Bronson decided to turn their hobby of recording novelty tunes into a business, Rhino Records, Inc.

__3__ After this initial success, however, Foos and Bronson realized that many old favorites were out of print and that the original labels did not want to reissue them.

__6__ The king of reissues, Rhino Records is known today as Rhino Entertainment and includes Rhino Home Video, Rhino Movie Music, Rhino Films, and the family division Kid Rhino.

__5__ Rhino continued to produce even more reissues, including a classic seven-CD John Coltrane box set and the hugely successful twenty-five-volume *Have a Nice Day: Super Hits of the '70s*.

__2__ At first, Rhino Records was known for its unusual records and compilations, like "Pencil Neck Geek" and *The World's Worst Recordings*.

WRITING ASSIGNMENT 1

Use **time order** to give coherence to a paragraph. Choose one of the following three paragraphs. Compose a topic sentence, freewrite or brainstorm to generate ideas, and then arrange your ideas *chronologically*. You may wish to use transitional words and phrases like these to guide the reader from point to point.*

first, second	before	soon	suddenly
then	during	when	moments later
next	after	while	finally

Paragraph 1   *Narrate the first hour of your average day*

Start with getting up in the morning and continue to describe what you do for that first hour. Record your activities, your conversations, if any, and possibly your moods as you go through this hour of the morning. As you revise, make sure that events clearly follow time order.

Paragraph 2   *Record an unforgettable event*

Choose a moment in sports or in some other activity that you vividly remember, either as a participant or as a spectator. In the topic sentence, tell in a general way

---

* For a more complete list of transitional expressions, see p. 62.

what happened. (*It was the most exciting touchdown I have ever seen,* or *Ninety embarrassing seconds marked the end of my brief surfing career.*) Then record the experience, arranging details in time order.

Paragraph 3 *Relate an accident or a close call*

Focus on just a few critical moments of an accident or a close call that you experienced or witnessed, depicting the most important events in detail. Try to capture your thoughts and perceptions at the time as honestly and exactly as possible. Arrange them in time order.

Space Order

Another useful way to arrange ideas in writing is through **space order**—describing a person, a thing, or a place from top to bottom, from left to right, from foreground to background, and so on. Space order is often used in descriptive writing because it moves from detail to detail like a movie camera's eye:*

> (1) We lived on the top floor of a five-story tenement in Williamsburg, facing the BMT elevated train, or as everyone called it, the El. (2) Our floors and windows would vibrate from the El, which shook the house like a giant, roaring as if his eyes were being poked out. (3) When we went down into the street, we played on a checkerboard of sunspots and shadows, which rhymed the railroad ties above our heads. (4) Even the brightest summer day could not lift the darkness and burnt-rubber smell of our street. (5) I would hold my breath when I passed under the El's long shadow. (6) It was the spinal column of my childhood, both oppressor and liberator, the monster who had taken away all our daylight, but on whose back alone one could ride out of the neighborhood into the big broad world.
>
> —Philip Lopate, *Bachelorhood: Tales of the Metropolis*

- This paragraph uses space order.
- Sentence 1 clearly places the scene: on the *top floor* of a tenement, *facing* the elevated train.
- In sentences 3 and 4, the paragraph moves downstairs, from the apartment to the street. These sentences describe the pattern made by the sun through the tracks overhead.
- Sentence 5 moves directly *under* the railroad.

Note how words and phrases like *on the top floor, facing, down into the street, above our heads,* and *passed under* help locate the action as the paragraph *moves* from place to place.

Some paragraphs that are clearly arranged according to space order have only an implied topic sentence:

---

* For more work on space order, see Chapter 7, "Description."

> (1) On my right a woods thickly overgrown with creeper descended the hill's slope to Tinker Creek. (2) On my left was a planting of large shade trees on the ridge of the hill. (3) Before me the grassy hill pitched abruptly and gave way to a large, level field fringed in trees where it bordered the creek. (4) Beyond the creek I could see with effort the vertical sliced rock where men had long ago quarried the mountain under the forest. (5) Beyond that I saw Hollins Pond and all its woods and pastures; then I saw in a blue haze the world poured flat and pale between the mountains.
>
> —Annie Dillard, *Pilgrim at Tinker Creek*

- The main idea of this paragraph is *implied*, not stated by a topic sentence. What is the main idea? _Standing on the hill, I had a broad view of the surrounding countryside._

- The implied topic sentence or main idea of this paragraph might read, *This was the scene all around me.* Because the paragraph is so clearly arranged according to space order, the reader can easily follow it.

- Transitional phrases like *on my right* and *on my left* guide the reader from sentence to sentence. What phrases in sentences 3, 4, and 5 help guide the reader? _before me; beyond the creek; beyond that_

Practice 2

Arrange each group of details here according to **space order,** numbering them 1, 2, 3, and so on, as if in preparation for a descriptive paragraph. Be prepared to explain your choices.

1. Describe an ostrich.

    _4_ on each foot, two clawed toes of unequal length

    _2_ long neck lightly covered with down

    _3_ muscular legs that can deliver tremendously strong kicks

    _1_ sharp eyes, which spot enemies a long way off

    _5_ toenails so sharp they can disembowel prey

2. Describe an old bike.

    _3_ wide seat, adjustable in height

    _1_ nearly bald front tire, with inner tube of soft rubber

__2__ scratched handlebars, with bell and brake levers

__5__ back tire nearly flat

__4__ pedals fixed to the chain wheel

3. Describe a gift.

__3__ white rectangular box

__1__ big blue bow

__5__ flannel nightgown with Minnie Mouse designs

__4__ white tissue paper, the innermost wrapping

__2__ flowered wrapping paper

WRITING ASSIGNMENT 2

Use **space order** to give coherence to one of the following paragraphs. Compose a topic sentence, freewrite or brainstorm for more details, and then arrange them in space order. Use transitional words and phrases like these if you wish:*

on the left	above	next to
on the right	below	behind
in the middle	beside	farther out

Paragraph 1 *Describe an ostrich, a bike, or a gift*

Choose one group of details from Practice 2, formulate a topic sentence that sets the scene for them all, and use them as the basis of a paragraph. Convert the details into complete sentences, adding words if you wish.

Paragraph 2 *Describe a room in your home*

Describe a room in your home that has special meaning to you—the bedroom, the kitchen, a workroom or den. Write a topic sentence that gives the reader a sense of what the room is like. Then choose details that capture the special feeling or purpose of the room. Before you write the paragraph, arrange your details in space order.

---

* For a more complete list of transitional expressions, see p. 62.

Paragraph 3 *Describe a photograph*

Describe this unusual beach scene as clearly and exactly as you can. First, jot down the four or five most important details in the scene. Then, before you write your paragraph, arrange these details according to space order—moving from background to foreground, perhaps, or from top to bottom.

Paragraph 4   *Describe a public figure*
Choose someone you admire or like—for example, a person in the news or a television personality. Working from memory or from a photograph, choose five or six striking details to use as the basis of a paragraph that employs space order. Move from head to toe, or from face to hands, but follow a logical plan.

Order of Importance

Ideas in a paragraph can also be arranged in the **order of importance.** You may start with the most important ideas and end with the least, or you may begin with the least important idea and build to a climax with the most important one. If you wish to persuade your reader with arguments or examples, beginning with the most important points impresses the reader with the force of your ideas and persuades him or her to continue reading.*

On essay examinations and in business correspondence, be especially careful to begin with the most important idea. In those situations the reader definitely wants your important points first.

Read the following paragraph and note the order of ideas.

> (1) Louis Pasteur is revered as a great scientist for his three major discoveries. (2) Most important, this Frenchman created vaccines that have saved millions of human and animal lives. (3) The vaccines grew out of his discovery that weakened forms of a disease could help the person or animal build up antibodies that would prevent the disease. (4) The vaccines used today to protect children from serious illnesses owe their existence to Pasteur's work. (5) Almost as important was Pasteur's brilliant idea that tiny living beings, not chemical reactions, spoiled beverages. (6) He developed a process, pasteurization, that keeps milk, wine, vinegar, and beer from spoiling. (7) Finally, Pasteur found ways to stop a silkworm disease that threatened to ruin France's profitable silk industry. (8) Many medical researchers regard him as "the father of modern medicine."

■ The ideas in this paragraph are explained in the **order of importance,** from the *most important to the least important:*

What was Pasteur's most important discovery? *vaccines*

What was his next most important discovery? *pasteurization*

What was his least important one? *cure for silkworm disease*

■ Note how the words *most important, almost as important,* and *finally* guide the reader from one idea to another.

---

*See Chapter 5, "Illustration," and Chapter 13, "Persuasion."

Sometimes, if you wish to add drama and surprise to your paragraphs, you may want to begin with the least important idea and build toward a climax by saving the most important idea for last. This kind of order can help counter the tendency of some writers to state the most important idea first and then let the rest of the paragraph dwindle away.

Read the following paragraph and note the order of ideas.

> (1) El Niño, an unusual flow of warm ocean water in the Pacific, has many destructive effects. (2) Peruvian fishermen usually are the first to know that El Niño is back. (3) The warm currents prevent plankton—tiny plants and animals on which fish feed—from forming on the surface of the ocean. (4) When the plankton supply goes down, so does the fish supply. (5) Even more devastating, however, are the rainstorms that are caused by the change in water temperature. (6) Rains that normally move west "follow" the warm water east, bringing severe storms—and flooding—to North and South America. (7) But the most destructive effects of El Niño are unrelenting heat and drought. (8) Some areas in the United States, for example, have suffered temperatures of more than a hundred degrees for several months at a time. (9) Crops have been ruined, herds have been destroyed, and hundreds of people have died of heat-related causes.

- The destructive effects of El Niño that develop the topic sentence in this paragraph are discussed in the **order of importance:** *from the least to the most harmful.*

- The effects of the rainstorms are more destructive than the effects of the lessened fish supply. However, the destructive effects of heat and drought—which result in lost crops and the deaths of animals and people—are the most destructive effects of all.

- Transitional words like *more* and *most* help the reader follow clearly from one set of destructive effects to the next.

PRACTICE 3

Arrange the ideas that develop each topic sentence in their **order of importance,** numbering them 1, 2, 3, and so on. *Begin with the most important* (or largest, most severe, most surprising) and continue to the *least* important. Or reverse the order if you think that the paragraph would be more dramatic by beginning with the *least* important ideas and building toward a climax, with the most important last.

1. Cynthia Lopez's first year of college brought many unexpected expenses.

    __3 (2)__ Her English professor wanted her to own a college dictionary.

    __1 (4)__ All those term papers to write required a computer.

    __2 (3)__ She had to spend $90 for textbooks.

    __4 (1)__ Her solid geometry class required various colored pencils and felt-tipped pens.

2. Alcoholic beverages should not be sold at sporting events.

   _1 (3)_ Injuries and even deaths caused by alcohol-induced crowd violence would be eliminated.

   _3 (1)_ Fans could save money by buying soft drinks instead of beer.

   _2 (2)_ Games and matches would be much more pleasant without the yelling, swearing, and rudeness often caused by alcohol.

3. The apartment needed work before the new tenants could move in.

   _3 (2)_ The handles on the kitchen cabinets were loose.

   _1 (4)_ Every room needed plastering and painting.

   _4 (1)_ Grime marred the appearance of the bathroom sink.

   _2 (3)_ Two closet doors hung off the hinges.

WRITING ASSIGNMENT 3

Use **order of importance** to give coherence to one of the paragraphs that follow. Use transitional words and phrases like these to guide the reader along:*

first	even more	another
next	last	least of all
above all	especially	most of all

Paragraph 1 *Describe a day in which everything went right (or wrong)*

Freewrite or brainstorm to generate ideas. Choose three or four of the day's best (or worst) events and write a paragraph in which you present them in order of importance—either from the most to the least important, or from the least to the most important.

Paragraph 2 *Describe an unusual person*

Choose a person you know whose looks or actions are unusual. Write your topic sentence and generate ideas; choose three to five details about the person's looks or behavior. Arrange the details according to the order of importance—either from the most to the least important or from the least to the most important.

Paragraph 3 *Explain a goal*

Write a paragraph that begins *I want a college education* (or name some other goal) *for three reasons*. Choose the three reasons that matter most to you and arrange them in the order of importance—either from the most to the least important or from the least to the most important.

---

*For a more complete list of transitional expressions, see page 62.

UNIT 2 Discovering the Paragraph

PRACTICE 4 — Review

Decide how you would develop each of the following topic sentences into a paragraph and choose an appropriate **order** of ideas. In the blanks, state what order you would use and briefly describe your approach.

There are no "right" answers. Some topics can be developed in several ways, depending on the writer.

EXAMPLE The fields behind the barn are vibrant with color.

Order: *Space*   Approach: *Describe the colors of the fields from foreground to background.*

Order: *Time*   Approach: *Describe the different colors at three different times of day.*

Order: *Importance*   Approach: *Describe the details of color from most to least striking—or the reverse.*

1. The Peruvian band Inca Son stunned the crowd with its show-stopping performance.

    Order: *Importance*   Approach: *Name the songs that the group performed, from the most exciting to the least—or the reverse.*

2. The attic was filled with unusual objects.

    Order: *Space*   Approach: *Describe the objects from foreground to background.*

3. Three influences formed my decision to major in _____.

    Order: *Importance*   Approach: *Describe the influences from the most important to the least important—or the reverse.*

4. During my first year at college, I had to make three important changes in my life.

    Order: *Time/Importance*   Approach: *Describe the changes in the order in which they were made. Describe the changes in the order of their importance, from the most important to the least—or the reverse.*

5. One look at my dog reveals his mixed background.

    Order: *Space*   Approach: *Describe the dog from nose to tail.*

6. Gregor Mendel, an Austrian monk, performed many experiments before he discovered the laws of heredity.

Order: _Time_   Approach: _Describe Mendel's early experiments and lead up from the least important to the most important ones._

PART B Coherence Through Related Sentences

In addition to arranging ideas in a logical order, the writer can ensure paragraph coherence by linking one sentence to the next. This section will present four basic ways to link sentences: **repetition of important words, substitution of pronouns, substitution of synonyms,** and **transitional expressions.**

Repetition of Important Words and Pronouns

Link sentences within a paragraph by *repeating important words and ideas.*

> (1) A grand jury is an investigative body composed of members elected from the community. (2) It serves as a buffer between the state and the citizen. (3) The prosecutor, in many cases, brings before the grand jury the evidence gathered on a particular case. (4) The grand jury must then decide if sufficient evidence exists to hand down an indictment—the indictment being a formal charge against an accused person written by the prosecutor and submitted to a court by the grand jury. (5) With the indictment issued, the prosecutor can proceed to the arraignment.
>
> —Ronald J. Waldron et al., *The Criminal Justice System: An Introduction*

■ What important words are repeated in this paragraph?
■ The words *grand jury* appear four times, in sentences 1, 3, and 4. The word *indictment*, introduced near the end of the paragraph, appears three times, in sentences 4 and 5. The word *prosecutor* appears three times, in sentences 3, 4, and 5.
■ Repetition of these key words helps the reader follow from sentence to sentence as these terms are defined and the relationships between them are explained.

Although repetition of important words can be effective, it can also become boring if overused.* To avoid *unnecessary* repetition, substitute *pronouns* for words already mentioned in the paragraph, as this author does:

---

*For practice in eliminating wordiness (repetition of unimportant words), see Chapter 21, "Revising for Language Awareness," Part B.

> (1) For several months, Julia "Butterfly" Hill has been living in Northern California—at the top of a two-hundred-foot, one-thousand-year-old redwood. (2) A logging company wants to cut down the ancient tree, but *it* has not done so because of *her*. (3) Hill says *she* will stay atop the tree until the loggers agree to allow *it* to live out a natural life.

- The use of pronouns in this paragraph avoids unnecessary repetition. In sentence 2, the pronoun *it* refers to the antecedent* *a logging company*, and the pronoun *her* refers to *Julia "Butterfly" Hill*.
- The pronoun *she* in sentence 3 gives further coherence to the paragraph by referring to what antecedent? __Hill__
- The pronoun *it* in sentence 3 refers to what antecedent? __tree__

Use pronoun substitution together with the repetition of important words for a smooth presentation of ideas.

PRACTICE 5

What important words are repeated in the following paragraph? Underline them. Circle any pronouns that replace them. Notice the varied pattern of repetitions and pronoun replacements.

I have always considered my father a very intelligent person. His intelligence is not the type usually tested in schools; perhaps he would have done well on such tests, but the fact is that he never finished high school. Rather, my father's intelligence is his ability to solve problems creatively as they arise. Once when I was very young, we were driving through the desert at night when the oil line broke. My father improvised a light, squeezed under the car, found the break, and managed to whittle a connection to join the two severed pieces of tubing; then he added more oil and drove us over a hundred miles to the nearest town. Such intelligent solutions to unforeseen problems were typical of him. In fact, my father's brand of brains—accurate insight, followed by creative action—is the kind of intelligence that I admire and most aspire to.

---
*For more work on pronouns and antecedents, see Chapter 30, "Pronouns," Parts A, B, and C.

WRITING ASSIGNMENT 4

Paragraph 1 *Discuss success*

How do you measure *success*? By the money you make, the number or quality of friends you have? Freewrite or brainstorm for ideas. Then answer this question in a thoughtful paragraph. Give the paragraph coherence by repeating important words and using pronouns.

Paragraph 2 *Discuss a public figure*

Choose a public figure whom you admire—from the arts, politics, media, or sports—and write a paragraph discussing *one quality* that makes that person special. Name the person in your topic sentence. Vary repetition of the person's name with pronouns to give the paragraph coherence.

Synonyms and Substitutions

When you do not wish to repeat a word or use a pronoun, give coherence to your paragraph with a **synonym** or **substitution**. **Synonyms** are two or more words that mean nearly the same thing. For instance, if you do not wish to repeat the word *car*, you might use the synonym *automobile* or *vehicle*. If you are describing a sky and have already used the word *bright*, try the synonym *radiant*.

Or instead of a synonym, **substitute** other words that describe the subject. If you are writing about José Canseco, for example, refer to him as *this powerful slugger* or *this versatile outfielder*. Such substitutions provide a change from constant repetition of a person's name or a single pronoun.*

Use synonyms and substitutions together with repetition and pronouns to give coherence to your writing:

> (1) On September 10, 1990, *the main building of Ellis Island* in New York Harbor reopened as a museum. (2) Restoration of *the huge red brick and limestone structure* took eight years and cost $156 million. (3) From 1900 to 1924, *this famous immigrant station* was the first stop of millions of newcomers to American shores. (4) *The building* was finally abandoned in 1954; by 1980, *it* was in such bad condition that snow and rain fell on its floor. (5) Today, visitors can follow the path of immigrants: from a ferryboat, through the great arched doorway, into the room where the weary travelers left their baggage, up the stairway where doctors kept watch, and into the registry room. (6) Here questions were asked that determined if each immigrant could stay in the United States. (7) *This magnificent monument to the American people* contains exhibits that tell the whole immigration history of the United States.

- This paragraph effectively mixes repetition, pronouns, and substitutions. The important word *building* is stated in sentence 1 and repeated in sentence 4.

- Sentence 4 also substitutes the pronoun *it*.

- In sentence 2, *the huge red brick and limestone structure* is substituted for *building*, and a second substitution, *this famous immigrant station*, occurs in sentence 3. Sentence 7 refers to the building as *this magnificent monument to the American people* and concludes the paragraph.

---

*For more work on exact language, see Chapter 21, "Revising for Language Awareness," Part A.

58 UNIT 2 Discovering the Paragraph

Sometimes the dictionary lists synonyms. For instance, the entry for *smart* might list *clever, witty, intelligent*. An even better source of synonyms is the **thesaurus,** a book of synonyms. For example, if you are describing a city street and cannot think of other words meaning "noisy," look in the thesaurus. The number of choices will amaze you.

PRACTICE 6

Read each paragraph carefully. Then write on the lines any synonyms and substitutions that the writer has used to replace the word(s) in italics.

Paragraph 1

Rocky Mountain bighorn sheep use their massive horns as percussion instruments. During the fall rutting season, when hormone changes bring on the breeding urge, 250-pound rams square off in violent, head-butting matches to determine which gains leadership of the herd and pick of the ewes. Duelists rear on hind legs, then drop to all fours and, heads down, charge at full speed.

—*National Geographic*

Rocky Mountain bighorn sheep are also referred to as __250-pound rams__ and __duelists__.

Paragraph 2

According to sports writer Ian Stafford, the British hold the record for winning the world's *oddest competitions*. In one of these bizarre events, contestants contort their faces and are judged on their ugliness. One competitor removed half his dentures and reversed the other half, rolled his eyes, and tucked his nose into his mustache and upper lip to achieve prize-winning ugliness. Another of these eccentric contests is snail racing. Opponents in this case are, of course, snails, which are placed in the center of a thirteen-inch cloth circle. The first to reach the edge of the circle wins. The race often takes four to five minutes, although the all-time champion (owned and trained by an English seven-year-old) finished the course in two minutes. Toe wrestling, bog snorkeling, worm charming—the British have emerged as unconquered rivals in all of these so-called sports. Perhaps you think that sports writer Ian Stafford should win first prize in the Biggest Liar in the World Competition. No, every one of these outlandish games exists. You can check them all out on the Internet.

Oddest competitions are also referred to as __bizarre events__, __eccentric contests__, __so-called sports__, and __outlandish games__.

Paragraph 3

When Lewis and Clark made their way through what is now North Dakota, the Shoshone Indian woman named *Sacajawea* and her French-Canadian husband joined the team of explorers. Because the expedition was traveling with a Native American, other tribes did not attack the group. In fact, one tribe even supplied horses to help the explorers and their interpreter cross the Rocky Mountains. This invaluable team member taught the men how to find medicine and food in the wilderness and once even saved the records of the journey when a canoe overturned during a storm. Sacajawea reached the Pacific Ocean with Lewis and Clark in 1805. Her fame eventually spread; one of the best-known monuments to her is a statue in Portland, Oregon.

Sacajawea is also referred to as __a Native American__, __their interpreter__, and __this invaluable team member__.

CHAPTER 4 Achieving Coherence 59

PRACTICE 7

Give coherence to the following paragraphs by thinking of appropriate synonyms or substitutions for the words in italics. Then write them in the blanks.

Paragraph 1 Christopher Reeve's story includes an extraordinary twist of fate. This *star* played Superman, the fictional hero who inspired fans with his ability to overcome obstacles and save others from harm. How ironic that this _Hollywood heartthrob_ was paralyzed from the neck down in a horse-jumping accident in 1995 and now personifies that superhuman perseverance himself. Before his accident, Reeve was not only a(n) _famous actor_ but a pianist, an athlete who performed his own film stunts, a pilot, and an all-round outdoorsman. Now he depends on a ventilator to breathe and operates his wheelchair by sipping or puffing on a straw. Since his accident, however, this _brave man_ has directed and narrated award-winning films, written the best-selling autobiography *Still Me*, and inspired thousands of people through speeches and interviews. He also has raised millions of dollars for research on spinal cord injuries. Christopher Reeve has become a(n) _hero_ of a different kind; his heroism depends not on physical strength but on courage, optimism, and a sense of purpose.

Paragraph 2 Much evidence shows that the urge to take a midafternoon *nap* is natural to humans. Sleep researchers have found that volunteer subjects, kept in underground rooms where they cannot tell the time, need a _sleep break_ about twelve hours after the halfway point of their main sleep. For example, if people sleep from midnight till 6:00 A.M., they'll be ready for a _relaxing doze_ at 3:00 the next afternoon. Other studies show that people have less trouble taking a _snooze_ in midafternoon than at any other daylight time. In many countries with warm climates, citizens take their daily _siesta_ in the afternoon. Even stressed Americans take an average of two afternoon naps a week.

Paragraph 3   According to the experts, those who learn about *money* early in life usually make sound financial decisions as adults. How then can parents give children the knowledge and experience they need? Well, even preschoolers can feed <u>coins</u> into parking meters and pay phones. Young children will become interested in clipping coupons if parents give them the <u>cash</u> saved off the regular prices. Children of seven and eight can learn about <u>finances</u> by managing an allowance. By the age of ten or so, kids become fascinated by the idea of having a bank account of their own and earning interest on their <u>savings</u>. In other words, parents can provide children with learning experiences about money at almost every age and stage of their lives. However, if your children won't accept any gift but stocks for their birthday presents, you may have carried the concept too far!

WRITING ASSIGNMENT 5

As you do the following assignments, try to achieve paragraph coherence by using repetition, pronouns, synonyms, and substitutions.

Paragraph 1   *Discuss your favorite form of relaxation*
Tell what you like to do when you have free time. Do you like to get together with friends? Do you like to go to a movie or to some sporting event? Or do you prefer to spend your time alone, perhaps listening to music or reading? Maybe you like to get outdoors and do something active, like play a game of pickup basketball or go rollerblading.
   Whatever your favorite free-time activity, name it in your topic sentence. Be sure to tell what makes your choice of activity *relaxing*. Then give your paragraph coherence by using pronouns and synonyms such as *take it easy, rest,* and *unwind.*

Paragraph 2   *Describe your ideal mate*
Decide on three or four crucial qualities that your ideal husband, wife, or friend would possess, and write a paragraph describing this extraordinary person. Use repetition, pronouns, and word substitutions to give coherence to the paragraph. For example, *My ideal husband . . . he . . . my companion.*

Paragraph 3   *React to a quotation*
Choose a quotation from the Quotation Bank before the indexes in this book, one you strongly agree or disagree with. Write a paragraph explaining why you feel that way. As you write, refer to the quotation as a *wise insight* or a *silly idea*— depending on what you think of it. Use other substitutions to refer to the quotation without repeating it or calling it *the quotation.*

Transitional Expressions

Skill in using transitional expressions is vital to coherent writing. **Transitional expressions** are words and phrases that point out the exact relation between one idea and another, one sentence and another. Words like *therefore, however, for example*, and *finally* are signals that guide the reader from sentence to sentence. Without them, even orderly and well-written paragraphs can be confusing and hard to follow.

The transitional expressions in this paragraph are italicized:

> (1) Zoos in the past often contributed to the disappearance of animal populations. (2) Animals were cheap, and getting new ones was easier than providing the special diet and shelter necessary to keep captive animals alive. (3) *Recently, however*, zoo directors have begun to realize that if zoos themselves are to continue, they must help save many species from extinction. (4) *As a result*, some zoos have begun to redefine themselves as places where endangered species can be protected and even revived. (5) The Basel Zoo in Switzerland, *for example*, selects endangered species and encourages captive breeding. (6) If zoos continue such work, perhaps they can, like Noah's ark, save some of earth's wonderful creatures from extinction.

- Each transitional expression in the previous paragraph links, in a precise way, the sentence in which it appears to the sentence before. The paragraph begins by explaining the destructive policies of zoos in the past.

- In sentence 3, two transitional expressions of contrast—*recently* (as opposed to the past) and *however*—introduce the idea that zoo policies have *changed*.

- The phrase *as a result* makes clear that sentence 4 is a *consequence* of events described in the previous sentence(s).

- In sentence 5, *for example* tells us that the Basel Zoo is *one particular illustration* of the previous general statement.

As you write, use various transitional expressions, together with the other linking devices, to connect one sentence to the next. Well-chosen transitional words also help stress the purpose and order of the paragraph.

Particular groups of transitional expressions are further explained and demonstrated in each chapter of Unit 3. However, here is a combined partial list for handy reference as you write.

Purpose	Transitional Expressions
to add	also, and, and then, as well, besides, beyond that, first (second, third, last, and so on), for one thing, furthermore, in addition, moreover, next, what is more
to compare	also, as well, both (neither), in the same way, likewise, similarly
to contrast	although, be that as it may, but, even though, however, in contrast, nevertheless, on the contrary, on the other hand, whereas, yet
to concede (a point)	certainly, granted that, of course, no doubt, to be sure
to emphasize	above all, especially, indeed, in fact, in particular, most important, surely
to illustrate	as a case in point, as an illustration, for example, for instance, in particular, one such, yet another
to place	above, below, beside, beyond, farther, here, inside, nearby, next to, on the far side, opposite, outside, to the east (south, and so on)
to qualify	perhaps, maybe
to give a reason or cause	as, because, for, since
to show a result or effect	and so, as a consequence, as a result, because of this, consequently, for this reason, hence, so, therefore, thus
to summarize	all in all, finally, in brief, in other words, lastly, on the whole, to sum up
to place in time	after a while, afterward, at last, at present, briefly, currently, during, eventually, finally, first (second, and so on), gradually, immediately, in the future, later, meanwhile, next, now, recently, soon, suddenly, then

PRACTICE 8

Carefully determine the *exact relationship* between the sentences in each pair below. Then choose from the list a **transitional expression** that clearly expresses this relationship and write it in the blank. Pay attention to punctuation and capitalize the first word of every sentence.*

1. No one inquired about the money found in the lobby. __Consequently__, it was given to charity.

---

* For practice using conjunctions to join ideas, see Chapter 24, "Coordination and Subordination."

CHAPTER 4   Achieving Coherence   63

2. First, cut off the outer, fibrous husk of the coconut. __Then__ poke a hole through one of the dark "eyes" and sip the milk through a straw.

3. The English Department office is on the fifth floor. __Next__ to it is a small reading room.

4. Some mountains under the sea soar almost as high as those on land. One underwater mountain in the Pacific, __for example__, is only 500 feet shorter than Mount Everest.

5. All citizens should vote. Many do not, __however__.

6. Mrs. Dalworth enjoys shopping in out-of-the-way thrift shops. __Furthermore__, she loves bargaining with the vendors at outdoor flea markets.

7. In 1887, Native Americans owned nearly 138 million acres of land. By 1932, __in contrast__, 90 million of those acres were owned by whites.

8. Kansas corn towered over the fence. __Beside__ the fence, a red tractor stood baking in the sun.

9. Most street crime occurs between 2:00 and 5:00 A.M. __For this reason__, do not go out alone during those hours.

10. Dr. Leff took great pride in his work at the clinic. __Nevertheless__, his long hours often left him exhausted.

11. Few scientists have worked so creatively with a single agricultural product. __Besides__ peanut oil and peanut butter, George Washington Carver developed literally hundreds of uses for the peanut.

12. We waited in our seats for over an hour. __Finally__ the lights dimmed, and the Fabulous String Band bounded on stage.

PRACTICE 9

Add **transitional expressions** to this essay to guide the reader smoothly from sentence to sentence. To do so, consider the relationship between sentences (shown in parentheses). Then write the transitional word or phrase that best expresses this relationship.

Math Stars

James Escalante was teaching physics in his native Bolivia when political unrest made him flee to the United States. In East Los Angeles, where he settled, he learned English and ____eventually____ (time) found a job teaching mathematics at Garfield High School. Garfield was known for its gangs, drugs, and low academic ratings. Teaching in this environment was difficult, ____but____ (contrast) Escalante persisted, taking a tough, humorous approach to motivate his classes. ____For example____ (illustration), many students remember the day he chopped up an apple with a meat cleaver to teach percentages.

Only five students showed up for his first calculus class, but four of them went on to pass the advanced placement test for college credit. Escalante's students continued to succeed. Suddenly, ____however____ (contrast), fourteen of them were accused of cheating. Twelve agreed to take an even more difficult test; ____furthermore____ (addition), all twelve passed. The incident received considerable media attention and ____as a result____ (result), became the subject of the film *Stand and Deliver*. ____Most important____ (emphasis), at a time when only 2 percent of U.S. seniors were taking the advanced placement test, all of Escalante's students were taking it—and 80 percent of them were passing.

PRACTICE 10   Review

Most paragraphs achieve coherence through a variety of linking devices: repetition, pronouns, substitutions, and transitional expressions. Read the following paragraphs with care, noting the kinds of linking devices used by each writer. Answer the questions after each paragraph.

Paragraph 1   (1) The blues is the one truly American music. (2) Born in the Mississippi Delta, this twelve-bar cry of anguish found its durable, classic form in the searing soliloquies of poor black men and women who used it to ventilate all the aches and pains of their condition—the great Bessie Smith, Robert Johnson, Ma Rainey, Lightnin' Hopkins and Son House, Mississippi John Hurt, John Lee Hooker and

CHAPTER 4   Achieving Coherence   **65**

Blind Lemon Jefferson. (3) And, ever since, the blues has served as the wellspring of every major movement in this country's popular music.

—Paul D. Zimmerman with Peter Barnes et al.,
"Rebirth of the Blues," *Newsweek*

1. What important words appear in both the first and the last sentence?
   the blues

2. In sentence 2, *the blues* is referred to as *this twelve-bar cry of anguish.*

3. What transitional expressions are used in sentence 3? *and; ever since*

Paragraph 2   (1) Mrs. Zajac seemed to have a frightening amount of energy. (2) She strode across the room, her arms swinging high and her hands in small fists. (3) Taking her stand in front of the green chalkboard, discussing the rules with her new class, she repeated sentences, and her lips held the shapes of certain words, such as "homework," after she had said them. (4) Her hands kept very busy. (5) They sliced the air and made karate chops to mark off boundaries. (6) They extended straight out like a traffic cop's, halting illegal maneuvers yet to be perpetrated. (7) When they rested momentarily on her hips, her hands looked as if they were in holsters. (8) She told the children, "One thing Mrs. Zajac expects from each of you is that you do *your* best." (9) She said, "Mrs. Zajac gives homework. (10) I'm sure you've all heard. (11) The old meanie gives homework." (12) *Mrs. Zajac.* (13) It was in part a role. (14) She worked her way into it every September.

—Tracy Kidder, *Among Schoolchildren*

1. What important words are repeated in this paragraph? *Mrs. Zajac,*
   hands, homework

2. What word does *they* in sentences 5 and 6 refer to? *hands*

Paragraph 3   (1) More important perhaps than the recipes and ideas that flowed into the home through cookbooks and magazines were the conveniences that began more and more to appear in the kitchen. (2) <u>First</u> it was the icebox. (3) <u>Next</u> it was running hot water, along with the cold. (4) <u>Then</u> it was the gas stove, a frightening apparatus for the uninitiated—<u>and then, just as soon as</u> mastery of its dials and heat had been achieved, along came the electric stove to sow confusion again. (5) The icebox gave way to the refrigerator and the freezer. (6) <u>And</u> out of Clarence Birdseye's observation that Eskimos in Labrador froze their meat and fish evolved the quick-freezing of various foodstuffs, a revolution of the first order in American cooking.

—*Foods of the World/American Cooking,*
Time-Life Books Inc.

1. Underline the transitional expressions in this paragraph.

2. What *order* of ideas does the paragraph employ? *time order*

UNIT 2   WRITERS' WORKSHOP

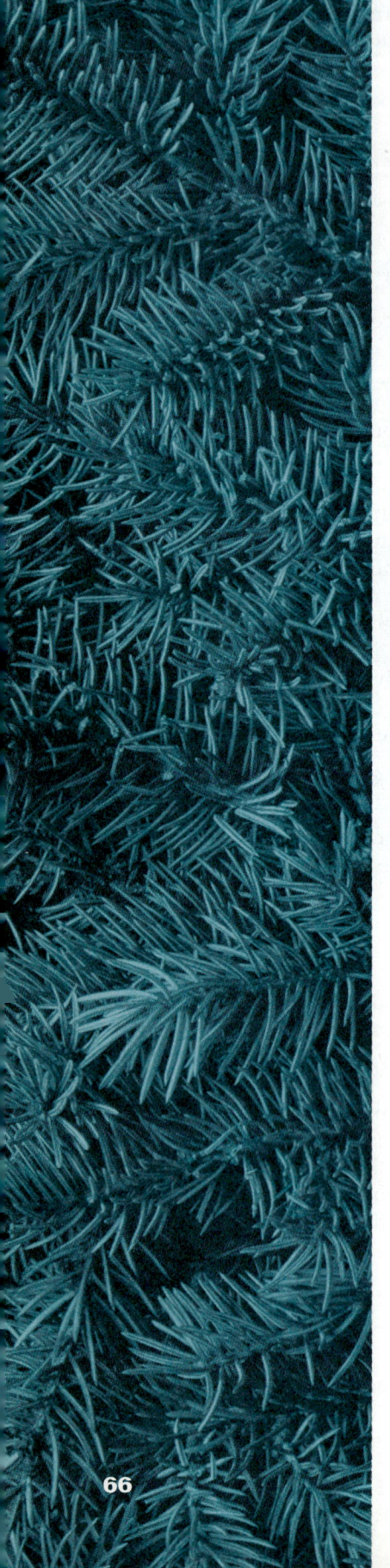

Pay Tribute to an Exceptional Person

In this unit, you learned that most good paragraphs have a clear topic sentence, convincing support, and an order that makes sense. In your group or class, read this student's paragraph, aloud if possible. Underline any parts you find especially well written. Put a check next to anything that might be improved.

Making Mittens Out of Sweaters

~~This paper will be about my grandmother.~~ My grandmother, Mary Bell Auld, was exceptional in her ability to "make do." She made tasty meals out of the cheapest ingredients and grew fresh vegetables in coffee cans on the fire escape. She could fix just about anything. Once I watched her take our kitchen clock apart and repair it. When she couldn't afford a new mop head, she made one out of rags. She sewed our clothes by hand and was always darning someone's shirt or socks. One winter, we didn't have any gloves, and it was bitterly cold outside. I remember her taking an old wool sweater from the hamper, placing my hands over one of the sleeves, and drawing a pattern for mittens. She cut them out, sewed them with tiny stitches, turned them on the other side, and presto, I had mittens. She cut off the other sleeve, tied the top, rolled and stitched the edge, and there was my matching hat. Today my grandmother lives on in me. From her, I learned to be independent and creative, and if ever I am overcome by one of the curves that life throws me, I am not down for long.

—Crystal Standish (Student)

1. How effective is this paragraph?

    _Y/N_ Clear topic sentence?   _Y_ Good supporting details?

    _Y_ Logical organization?   _Y_ Effective conclusion?

2. Which sentence, if any, is the topic sentence? Is sentence 1 as good as the rest of the paragraph? If not, what revision advice would you give the writer?
   #2 is t.s. Drop #1.
3. Does this student provide adequate support for her main idea? Why or why not? *Y*

4. Discuss your underlinings with the group or class. Which parts of this paragraph did you find most powerful? Explain as specifically as possible why. For example, the detail about growing vegetables on a fire escape vividly supports the topic sentence.

5. Although the subject of the paragraph is the writer's grandmother, the two concluding sentences focus on the writer herself. Has Ms. Standish drifted away from her main idea or written an interesting conclusion? Justify your position.

6. Do you see any error patterns (one error made two or more times) that this student needs to watch out for)? *No*

Group Work

In your group or class, make a plan of Ms. Standish's paragraph. How many points does she use to support her topic sentence? Which point is developed more fully than the others? Why do you think the writer does this? Is this effective or not? How can a writer know whether a paragraph has good support or needs better support? List three ways.

Writing and Revising Ideas

1. Pay tribute to an exceptional person.
2. Discuss the ways in which someone from the past lives on in you.

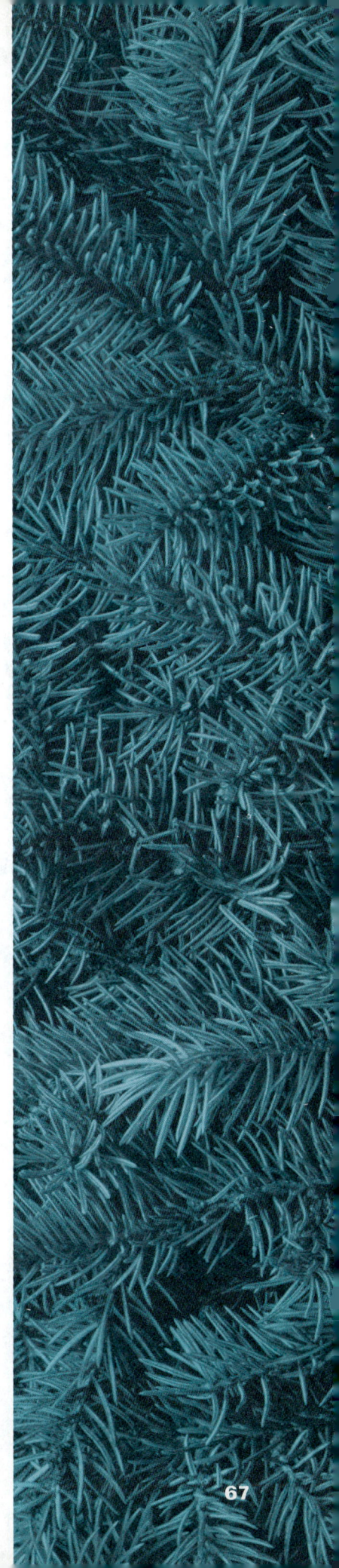

UNIT 3

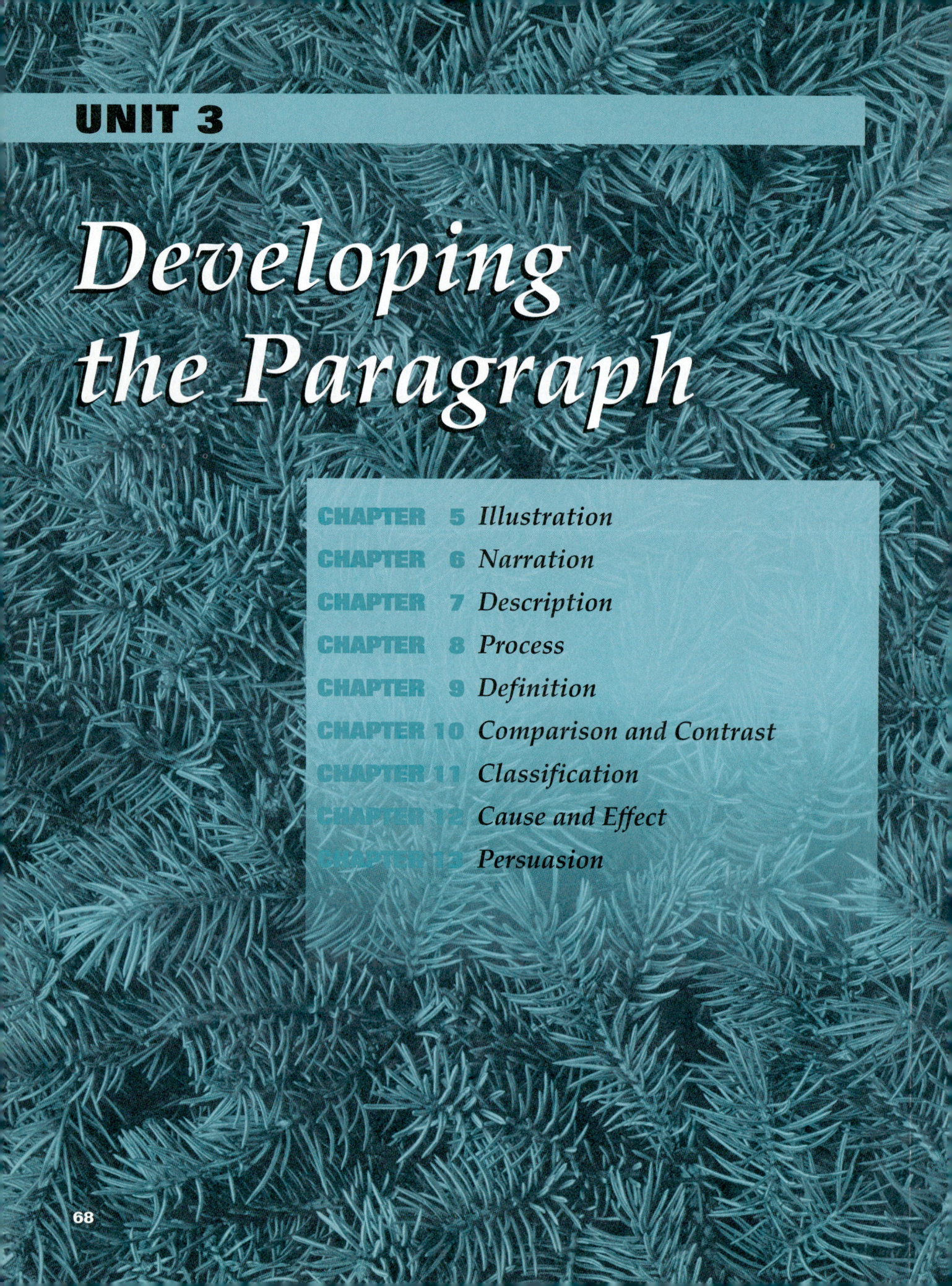

Developing the Paragraph

CHAPTER 5	Illustration
CHAPTER 6	Narration
CHAPTER 7	Description
CHAPTER 8	Process
CHAPTER 9	Definition
CHAPTER 10	Comparison and Contrast
CHAPTER 11	Classification
CHAPTER 12	Cause and Effect
CHAPTER 13	Persuasion

CHAPTER 5

Illustration

To **illustrate** is to explain a general statement by means of one or more specific *examples*.

Illustration makes what we say more vivid and more exact. Someone might say, "My math professor is always finding crazy ways to get our attention. Just yesterday, for example, he wore a high silk hat to class." The first sentence is a general statement about this professor's unusual ways of getting attention. The second sentence, however, gives a specific example of something he did that *clearly shows* what the writer means.

Writers often use illustration to develop a paragraph. They explain a general topic sentence with one, two, three, or more specific examples. Detailed and well-chosen examples add interest, liveliness, and power to your writing.

Topic Sentence

Here is the topic sentence of a paragraph that is later developed by examples:

> Great athletes do not reach the top by talent alone but by pushing themselves to the limit and beyond.

- The writer begins an illustration paragraph with a topic sentence that makes a general statement.
- This generalization may be obvious to the writer, but if he or she wishes to convince the reader, some specific examples would be helpful.

69

Paragraph and Plan

Here is the entire paragraph:

> Great athletes do not reach the top by talent alone but by pushing themselves to the limit and beyond. For instance, champion figure skater Michelle Kwan is her own worst critic, studying every practice on video in order to perfect her performance. During one practice, when she flubbed a double axel, she repeated the jump over and over until the ice cleaners urged her off the ice. "Winning isn't about miracles on ice," she says. "It's all about training." Another example is tennis great Pete Sampras, whose relaxed attitude hides a punishing work ethic. For 90 to 150 minutes a day, he rallies with a tennis pro and then works out with a strength and conditioning coach for another 60 to 90 minutes. Even Chicago Bulls superstar Michael Jordan, who has been called the most gifted athlete of all time, was a relentlessly hard worker and perfectionist. He and two teammates practiced *before* every team practice. Each day from pre-season camp to the last Finals game, Jordan was in his gym with a trainer by 8 A.M., sweating through a tough routine created by exercise scientists; then he hit the court. Like many top athletes, he turned his talent into greatness through sheer hard work.

■ How many examples does the writer use to develop the topic sentence?

three

■ Who are they?

Michelle Kwan, Pete Sampras, and Michael Jordan

Before completing this illustration paragraph, the writer probably made an outline or plan like this:

Topic Sentence: Great athletes do not reach the top by talent alone but by pushing themselves to the limit and beyond.

Example 1:   Michelle Kwan

—studies practices on video

—repeated one jump until thrown off the ice

—quote ("not about miracles but training")

Example 2:   Pete Sampras

—relaxed attitude hides work ethic

—90–150 minutes rallying with a pro

—then 60–90 minutes working out

Example 3:   Michael Jordan

—most gifted but also relentlessly hard worker

—practiced before practice!

—8 A.M. scientific workout, then practice on the court

■ Note that each example clearly relates to and supports the topic sentence.

Instead of using three or four examples to support the topic sentence, the writer may prefer instead to discuss one single example:

> Many schools in the twenty-first century will look more like elegant shopping malls than like old-fashioned school buildings. The new Carl Sandburg High School in Chicago is just one example. Now being redesigned, the school will feature a main library with the comfortable, open layout of a super-bookstore like Barnes & Noble or Borders. The physical education facilities will include rock-climbing walls and other features now seen in health clubs. Carl Sandburg's cafeteria will be laid out like a food court, not only giving students more choices, but eliminating the long lunch lines that caused delays in the old high school. Retailers have learned how to create attractive, practical public spaces, and many modern school planners think it's time that school officials learned the same lessons.

■ What is the general statement? *Many schools in the twenty-first century will look more like elegant shopping malls than like old-fashioned school buildings.*

■ What specific example does the writer give to support the general statement?

Carl Sandburg High School

The single example may also be a **narrative**,* a *story* that illustrates the topic sentence.

> Aggressive drivers not only are stressed out and dangerous, but often they save no time getting where they want to go. Recently I was driving south from Oakland to San Jose. Traffic was heavy but moving. I noticed an extremely aggressive driver jumping lanes, speeding up and slowing down. Clearly, he was in a hurry. For the most part, I remained in one lane for the entire forty-mile journey. I was listening to a new audiotape and daydreaming. I enjoyed the trip because driving gives me a chance to be alone. As I was exiting off the freeway, the aggressive driver crowded up behind me and raced on by. Without realizing it, I had arrived in San Jose ahead of him. All his weaving, rapid acceleration, and putting families at risk had earned him nothing except perhaps some high blood pressure and a great deal of wear and tear on his vehicle.
>
> —Adapted from Richard Carlson, *Don't Sweat the Small Stuff*

■ What general statement does the aggressive driver story illustrate?

Aggressive drivers not only are stressed out and dangerous, but often they save no time getting where they want to go.

■ Note that this narrative follows time order.[†]

---

[*] For more on narrative, see Chapter 6, "Narration," and Chapter 15, "Types of Essays," Part B.
[†] For more work on time order, see Chapter 4, "Achieving Coherence," Part A.

Transitional Expressions

The simplest way to tell your reader that an example is going to follow is to say so: "*For instance*, Michelle Kwan . . ." or "The new Carl Sandburg High School is *just one example*." This partial list should help you vary your use of **transitional expressions** that introduce an illustration:

Transitional Expressions for Illustration	
for instance	another instance of
for example	another example of
an illustration of this	another illustration of
a case in point is	here are a few examples
to illustrate	(illustrations, instances)

■ Be careful not to use more than two or three of these transitional expressions in a single paragraph.*

PRACTICE 1

Read each of the following paragraphs of illustration. Underline each topic sentence. Note in the margin how many examples are provided to illustrate each general statement.

Paragraph 1

(3 examples)

Random acts of kindness are those little sweet or grand lovely things we do for no reason except that, momentarily, the best of our humanity has sprung . . . into full bloom. When you spontaneously give an old woman the bouquet of red carnations you had meant to take home to your own dinner table, when you give your lunch to the guitar-playing beggar who makes music at the corner between your two subway stops, when you anonymously put coins in someone else's parking meter because you see the red "Expired" medallion signalling to a meter maid—you are doing not what life requires of you, but what the best of your human soul invites you to do.

—Daphne Rose Kingma, *Random Acts of Kindness*

Paragraph 2

(4 examples)

There are many quirky variations to lightning. A "bolt from the blue" occurs when a long horizontal flash suddenly turns toward the earth, many miles from the storm. "St. Elmo's Fire," often seen by sailors and mountain climbers, is a pale blue or green light caused by weak electrical discharges that cling to trees, airplanes, and ships' masts. "Pearl lightning" occurs when flashes are broken into segments. "Ball lightning" can be from an inch to several feet in diameter. Pearls and balls are often mistaken for flying saucers or UFOs, and many scientists believe they are only optical illusions.

—Reed McManus, *Sierra Magazine*

---

*For a complete essay developed by illustration, see "Libraries of the Future—Now," Chapter 15, Part A.

PRACTICE 2

Each example in a paragraph of illustration must clearly relate to and support the general statement. Each general statement in this practice is followed by several examples. Circle the letter of any example that does *not* clearly illustrate the generalization. Be prepared to explain your choices.

EXAMPLE The museum contains many fascinating examples of African art.
   a. It houses a fine collection of Ashanti fertility dolls.
   b. Drums and shamans' costumes are displayed on the second floor.
   ⓒ The museum building was once the home of Frederick Douglass. (The fact that the building was once the home of Frederick Douglass is *not an example* of African art.)

1. Amelia Earhart dared to act beyond the limits of what society thought a woman could or should do.
   ⓐ She saw her first plane at the Iowa State Fair.
   b. She became a pilot and mechanic, entering the all-male world of aviation.
   c. She presented her new husband with a marriage contract that gave both partners considerable freedom.

2. Today's global companies sometimes find that their product names and slogans can translate into embarrassing bloopers.
   a. Pepsi's slogan "Come alive with the Pepsi Generation" didn't work in Taiwan, where it meant "Pepsi will bring your ancestors back from the dead."
   b. When General Motors introduced its Chevy Nova in South America, company officials didn't realize that *no va* in Spanish means "it won't go."
   c. In Chinese, the Kentucky Fried Chicken slogan "finger-lickin' good" means "eat your fingers off."
   ⓓ Nike runs the same ad campaign in several countries, changing the ad slightly to fit each culture.

3. Stone Age cave dwellers left amazing paintings on the walls of over two hundred European caves.
   a. The walls of the now-famous cave at Lascaux, France, glow with multi-colored animals and human figures painted some 25,000 years ago.
   ⓑ Cave dwellers in China left evidence of the human use of fire 400,000 years ago.
   c. Using mineral pigments mixed with fat, Stone Age artists also adorned the cave walls at Altamira, Spain, with graceful animal paintings.

4. Some writers use strange tricks to overcome writer's block and keep their ideas flowing.
   a. To help himself choose the right word, the German playwright and poet Schiller sniffed rotten apples that he kept inside his desk.
   b. Benjamin Franklin believed that he had to write in the nude to do his best work, and he often wrote in the bathtub.
   ⓒ Argentinian writer Jorge Luis Borges went blind, but he kept creating brilliant stories packed with learning, philosophy, and magic.
   d. To inspire herself before she started writing, Dame Edith Sitwell would lie for a while each morning in an open coffin.

5. In the Arizona desert, one sees many colorful plants and flowers.
    a. Here and there are patches of pink clover.
    b. Gray-green saguaro cacti rise up like giant candelabra.
    (c.) Colorful birds dart through the landscape.
    d. Bright yellow poppies bloom by the road.

6. Many important inventions were rejected when they were first introduced.
    a. Chester Carlson was laughed at for his dry copy process, xerography, but it later made him rich and gave a company its name, Xerox.
    (b.) The invention of NutraSweet happened accidentally in 1965 when a chemist noticed that a chemical he had spilled tasted sweet.
    c. When John Holland first invented the submarine in the late 1800s, the Navy saw no use for it and treated him like a kook.

7. The United States offers many unusual tourist attractions for those who venture off the beaten path.
    a. Visitors to Mitchell, South Dakota, can stop at the Mitchell Corn Palace, a castle covered with murals made of corn, grass, and grain.
    (b.) One of the most popular tourist stops in the country is the Washington Monument in Washington, D.C.
    c. Hard-core Elvis fans can visit the Elvis Museum in Pigeon Forge, Tennessee, to see Elvis's razor, hair dryer, and nasal spray applicator.
    d. On Route 115 in Colorado, drivers can gawk at the World's Largest Hercules Beetle, a giant bug made of plaster.

8. Many months in our calendar take their names from Roman gods or heroes.
    a. Mars, the Roman war god, gave his name to March.
    b. January was named for Janus, the god of doorways, whose two faces looked both forward and back.
    c. August honors Augustus, the first Roman emperor and the second Caesar.
    (d.) December took its name from *decem*, the Latin word meaning "ten," and was the tenth month in the Roman calendar.

PRACTICE 3

The secret of good illustration lies in well-chosen, well-written examples. Think of one example that illustrates each of the following general statements. Write out the example in sentence form (one to three sentences) as clearly and exactly as possible.

1. A few contemporary singers work hard to send a positive message.

    Example: *Will Smith, for example, describes the joys of fatherhood and praises the city of Miami in just two of his top-selling tracks.*

2. In a number of ways, this college makes it easy for working students to attend.

CHAPTER 5   Illustration   75

Example: *The college offers many courses on Saturdays and Sundays.*

3. Believing in yourself is 90 percent of success.

   Example: *My friend Paco owns a successful restaurant today because his enthusiasm and confidence attracted investors.*

4. Many teenagers believe they must have expensive designer clothing.

   Example: *My nephew has a closet full of Tommy and Nautica clothes that his mother cannot really afford.*

5. Growing up in a large family can teach the value of compromise.

   Example: *The five Hanson children take turns choosing what game they will all play.*

6. A number of shiny classic cars cruised up and down Ocean Drive.

   Example: *The robin's egg blue 1955 Thunderbird convertible had gleaming chrome bumpers and a white top.*

7. Children say surprising things.

   Example: *My daughter said that she couldn't sit in her car seat because the Wizard of Oz was already sitting there.*

8. Sadly, gun violence has affected many Americans.

   Example: *My neighbor Paul has used a wheelchair since being shot by a mugger last year.*

✓ CHECKLIST: The Process of Writing an Illustration Paragraph

Refer to this checklist of steps as you write an illustration paragraph of your own.

_____ 1. Narrow the topic in light of your audience and purpose.

_____ 2. Compose a topic sentence that can honestly and easily be supported by examples.

_____ 3. Freewrite or brainstorm to find six to eight examples that support the topic sentence. If you wish to use only one example or a narrative, sketch out your idea. (You may want to freewrite or brainstorm before you narrow the topic.)

_____ 4. Select only the best two to four examples and drop any examples that do not relate to or support the topic sentence.

_____ 5. Make a plan or an outline for your paragraph, numbering the examples in the order in which you will present them.

_____ 6. Write a draft of your illustration paragraph, using transitional expressions to show that an example or examples will follow.

_____ 7. Revise as necessary, checking for support, unity, logic, and coherence.

_____ 8. Proofread for errors in grammar, punctuation, sentence structure, spelling, and mechanics.

Suggested Topic Sentences for Illustration Paragraphs

1. Some lucky people love their jobs.
2. In my family, certain traditions (or values or beliefs) are very important.
3. Painful experiences can sometimes teach valuable lessons.
4. Using animated animals and humor, some beer commercials seem to target minors.
5. Some unusual characters live in my neighborhood.
6. Soap operas "hook" viewers in several ways.
7. Many enjoyable activities in this area are inexpensive or even free.
8. Celebrities who have overcome illness or tragedy can inspire others.
9. A sense of humor can make difficult times easier to bear.
10. Sexual harassment is a fact of life for some employees.
11. Some professors are masters at helping their students learn.
12. Many sites on the Internet offer free grammar help (greeting cards, medical information, and so on).
13. Sometimes a chance meeting can change a person's life.
14. Choose a quotation from the Quotation Bank at the end of this book. First, state whether you think this saying is true; then use an example from your own or others' experience to support your view.
15. Writer's choice: _____

CHAPTER 6

Narration

To **narrate** is to tell a story that explains what happened, when it happened, and who was involved.

A news report may be a narrative about how Congress voted, what the president did, or how a man was rescued from a burning building. When you read a bedtime story to your children, you are reading them a narrative.

In a letter to a friend, you might want to write a narrative detailing how you were hired for your new job; your narrative could emphasize the fact that your relaxed and confident manner throughout the interview impressed your future employer. Or you might wish to retell what happened on your first skiing trip, when a minor accident proved to you that you prefer tamer recreation.

However, no matter what your narrative is about, it must make a *point:* It must clearly tell what you want your reader to learn or take away from the story.

Topic Sentence

Here is the topic sentence of a **narrative** paragraph:

> A birthday gift I received years ago has become a lasting symbol of love.

- The writer begins a narrative paragraph with a topic sentence that tells the point of the narrative.

- What is the point of this narrative? *to show how the gift has become a lasting symbol of love*

77

Paragraph and Plan

Here is the entire paragraph:

> A birthday gift I received years ago has become a lasting symbol of love. It was a cold day during my first year in college. My birthday had just passed, and I hadn't heard from my best friend, Linda, who had moved away two years before. A card and a present would have been nice, but what I really wanted from her was a hug. Suddenly the doorbell rang. I ran downstairs and signed the receipt that the letter carrier held out—in return for a package from Linda! I pulled off all the wrappings—and stared. Then, because I didn't know whether to laugh or cry, I ended up doing some of each. Linda's gift was a sweater, but this sweater had something extra. Attached to each cuff was a cutout of one of Linda's hands, and the hands in the box were arranged in a hug around the sweater. I loved the sweater, but I didn't wear it for months because I couldn't bear to unpin the hands, which would have looked pretty silly just dangling from my cuffs. Then I got an idea. I'm not an artist, but I decided to make a collage. I got hours of pleasure painting a background and then cutting, arranging, and pasting photographs and magazine pictures, along with the hands, into what is surely a unique piece of artwork. I eventually wore out the sweater, but the collage has hung in every place I've ever lived. Every time I look at it, I feel hugged, loved, and comforted.

- The body of a narrative paragraph is developed according to time, or chronological, order.* That is, the writer explains the narrative—the entire incident—as a series of small events or actions in the order in which they occurred. By keeping to strict chronological order, the writer helps the reader follow the story more easily and avoids interrupting the narrative with *But I forgot to mention that before this happened....*

- What smaller events make up this narrative? *My birthday passed; I didn't hear from my best friend; a package arrived with a sweater from Linda; I didn't wear the sweater; I made a collage; I wore out the sweater; the collage has been with me ever since.*

Before writing this narrative paragraph, the writer may have brainstormed or freewritten to gather ideas, and then she may have made an outline or a plan like this:

Topic sentence: A birthday gift I received years ago has become a lasting symbol of love.

    Event 1:   My birthday passed.

    Event 2:   I didn't hear from best friend, Linda.

                    —would have liked card or present

                      —really wanted hug

---

*For more work on time, see Chapter 4, "Achieving Coherence," Part A.

Event 3: The letter carrier came with a package.

Event 4: The present was from Linda.

—laughed and cried

—sweater had hands

—hands were arranged in a hug

Event 5: I didn't wear the sweater.

Event 6: I made a collage.

Event 7: I wore out the sweater.

Event 8: I've hung the collage everywhere I've lived.

- Note that all of the events occur in chronological order.
- Also note that the first two events present background information: They tell what led up to receiving the gift.
- Finally, note that the specific details of certain events (like events 2 and 4) make the narrative more vivid.

Transitional Expressions

Because narrative paragraphs tell a story in **chronological** or **time order,** transitional expressions that indicate time can be useful.*

Transitional Expressions for Narratives		
after	finally	soon
as (soon as)	later	then
before	meanwhile	upon
during	next	when
first	now	while

PRACTICE 1

Read the following narrative paragraph carefully and answer the questions.

Horace Bristol might be the only photographer to owe his fame to his child's book report. Before he became an architect, Bristol had been a documentary journalist. One day his teenage son was writing a book report on *The Grapes of Wrath,* John Steinbeck's novel about an Oklahoma farm family forced off their drought-stricken land during the 1930s. He asked his father if he'd ever read the book. Not

---

* For a complete essay developed by narration, see "Maya Lin's Vietnam War Memorial," Chapter 15, "Types of Essays," Part B.

80 UNIT 3 Developing the Paragraph

only had he read it, Bristol replied, he had dreamed up the idea for it, recruited Steinbeck to write it, and photographed thousands of real farm families forced to leave their homes. After revealing his past to his son, Bristol the photographer came out of hiding. Hoping to sell a few of his photographs, he was soon astounded by the prices they commanded. Encouraged, he took up his camera once again. Since then the photographs of Horace Bristol have become famous. His images of despair during the Depression, heroism in the Pacific during World War II, and postwar poverty and hope in rural Korea are among the greatest photographs of the twentieth century.

1. What is the point of the narrative? *Bristol's unusual debt to his son's book report*

2. What events make up this narrative paragraph? *Bristol had once been a documentary journalist; son asked whether Bristol had read The Grapes of Wrath; Bristol revealed his role in creating the novel; came out of hiding as a photographer; photos sold for high prices; started taking pictures again; photos have become famous.*

PRACTICE 2

Here are three plans for narrative paragraphs. The events in the plans are not in correct chronological order. The plans also contain events that do not belong in each story. Number the events in the proper time sequence and cross out any irrelevant ones.

1. Aesop's fable about a dog and his reflection teaches a lesson about greed.

    _3_ He thought he saw another dog with another piece of meat in his mouth, so he decided to get that one too.

    _5_ Now the dog had nothing at all to eat.

    _1_ A dog was happily carrying a piece of meat in his mouth.

    ___ ~~The dog was brown with white spots.~~

CHAPTER 6 Narration **81**

__2__ While crossing a bridge, he saw his reflection in the water of a running brook.

__4__ When he snapped at the reflection, the meat dropped from his mouth into the water and sank.

2. In 1897, Lena Jordan performed the first triple somersault on the flying trapeze, but for years she did not get credit.

   __2__ For the next sixty-six years, all the record books listed Clarke as the record holder, not Jordan.

   __1__ When a second person, a man named Ernest Clarke, managed a triple somersault in 1909, he received national attention.

   __4__ Only recently did the *Guinness Book of World Records* give Jordan sole credit for the first triple somersault in circus history.

   ____ ~~The first free-fall parachute jump from an airplane was also made by a woman.~~

   __3__ In 1975, the *Guinness Book of World Records* finally listed Lena Jordan's achievement, but only in addition to Clarke's.

3. The Civil War battle between two iron-covered ships, on March 9, 1862, changed sea warfare forever.

   __2__ Two hours into the battle, the *Monitor* ran out of ammunition and moved into shallow water to reload.

   __4__ After four hours, the *Merrimack*, her hull leaking and her smokestack broken, escaped from the scene of battle.

   __3__ When the *Monitor* returned with guns loaded, the *Merrimack* lured her into deep water and then suddenly swung around and rammed her, leaving barely a dent.

   ____ ~~The Civil War lasted from 1861 to 1865.~~

   __5__ At the end of the conflict, neither ironclad ship had really won, but the wooden fighting ship was a thing of the past.

   __1__ At first, the two ships—the North's *Monitor* and the South's *Merrimack*—just circled each other like prehistoric monsters, firing at close range but causing no damage.

PRACTICE 3

Here are topic sentences for three narrative paragraphs. Make a plan for each paragraph, placing the events of the narrative in the proper time sequence.

1. When I was _____, help came from an unexpected source.

2. Sometimes, seemingly unimportant events can prove to be of great importance.

3. Last year, _____ learned something surprising about himself/herself.

CHAPTER 6   Narration   83

PRACTICE 4

You have been given the photo below and asked to tell the story behind it. That is, you must invent a brief narrative that explains this mysterious picture. What are these people looking at so intently and why? Your narrative can be serious, funny, or otherworldly. First, list the main events and include them in chronological order. State the point of your narrative in the topic sentence, which you may wish to place last rather than first in your paragraph.

✓ CHECKLIST: The Process of Writing a Narrative Paragraph

Refer to this checklist of steps as you write a narrative paragraph of your own.

____ 1. Narrow the topic in light of your audience and purpose.

____ 2. Compose a topic sentence that tells the point of the story.

____ 3. Freewrite or brainstorm for all of the events and details that might be part of the story. (You may want to freewrite or brainstorm before you narrow the topic.)

____ 4. Select the important events and details; drop any that do not clearly relate to the point in your topic sentence.

____ 5. Make a plan or an outline for the paragraph, numbering the events in the correct time (chronological) sequence.

____ 6. Write a draft of your narrative paragraph, using transitional expressions to indicate time sequence.

____ 7. Revise as necessary, checking for support, unity, logic, and coherence.

____ 8. Proofread for errors in grammar, punctuation, sentence structure, spelling, and mechanics.

Suggested Topics for Narrative Paragraphs

1. A favorite family story
2. A lesson in tolerance
3. A fulfilled ambition
4. A few moments that changed someone's life
5. A laugh at yourself
6. A breakthrough (emotional, physical, or spiritual)
7. An experience in another country
8. A first day at college (or at a new job)
9. A triumphant (or embarrassing) moment
10. The first time you met an important friend
11. A serious decision
12. A strange dream
13. Something you or another person dared to do
14. An incident that made you happy (or proud)
15. Writer's choice: _____

CHAPTER 7

Description

To **describe** something—a person, a place, or an object—is to capture it in words so others can imagine it or see it in their mind's eye.

The best way for a writer to help the reader get a clear impression is to use language that appeals to the senses: sight, sound, smell, taste, and touch. For it is through the senses that human beings experience the physical world around them, and it is through the senses that the world is most vividly described.

Imagine, for instance, that you have just gone boating on a lake at sunset. You may not have taken a photograph, yet your friends and family can receive an accurate picture of what you have experienced if you *describe* the pink sky reflected in smooth water, the creak of the wooden boat, the soothing drip of water from the oars, the occasional splash of a large bass jumping, the faint fish smells, the cool and darkening air. Writing down what your senses experience will teach you to see, hear, smell, taste, and touch more acutely than ever before.

Description is useful in English class, the sciences, psychology—anywhere that keen observation is important.

Topic Sentence

Here is the topic sentence of a descriptive paragraph:

> On November 27, 1922, when archaeologist Howard Carter unsealed the door to the ancient Egyptian tomb of King Tut, he stared in amazement at the fantastic objects heaped all around him.

■ The writer begins a descriptive paragraph by pointing out what will be described. What will be described in this paragraph?

the fantastic objects in King Tut's tomb

■ The writer can also give a general impression of this scene, object, or person. What overall impression of the tomb does the writer provide?

The writer gives the impression that the heaps of fantastic objects in King Tut's tomb were an amazing sight.

Paragraph and Plan

Here is the entire paragraph:

> On November 27, 1922, when archaeologist Howard Carter unsealed the door to the ancient Egyptian tomb of King Tut, he stared in amazement at the fantastic objects heaped all around him. On his left lay the wrecks of at least four golden chariots. Against the wall on his right sat a gorgeous chest brightly painted with hunting and battle scenes. Across from him was a gilded throne with cat-shaped legs, arms like winged serpents, and a back showing King Tut and his queen. Behind the throne rose a tall couch decorated with animal faces that were half hippopotamus and half crocodile. The couch was loaded with more treasures. To the right of the couch, two life-sized statues faced each other like guards. They were black, wore gold skirts and sandals, and had cobras carved on their foreheads. Between them was a second sealed doorway. Carter's heart beat loudly. Would the mummy of King Tut lie beyond it?

■ The overall impression given by the topic sentence is that the tomb's many objects were amazing. List three specific details that support this impression.

wrecks of four golden chariots

chest painted with hunting and battle scenes

gilded throne with cat-shaped legs

■ Note the importance of words that indicate richness and unusual decoration in helping the reader visualize the scene.* List as many of these words as you can:

golden, gorgeous, brightly painted, gilded, cat-shaped legs, winged serpents,

animal faces that were half hippopotamus and half crocodile, treasures, life-sized

statues, gold skirts and sandals, cobras carved on their foreheads

---

* For more work on vivid language, see Chapter 21, "Revising for Language Awareness."

■ This paragraph, like many descriptive paragraphs, is organized according to space order.* The author uses transitional expressions that show where things are. Underline the transitional expressions that indicate place or position.

Before composing this descriptive paragraph, the writer probably brainstormed and freewrote to gather ideas and then made an outline or a plan like this:

Topic sentence: On November 27, 1922, when archaeologist Howard Carter unsealed the door to the ancient Egyptian tomb of King Tut, he stared in amazement at the fantastic objects heaped all around him.

1.	To the left:	chariots —wrecked —golden
2.	To the right:	a gorgeous chest —brightly painted with hunting and battle scenes
3.	Across the room:	a throne —gilded —cat-shaped legs —arms like winged serpents
4.	Behind the throne:	a couch —decorated with faces that were half hippopotamus and half crocodile
5.	To the right of the couch:	two life-sized statues —black —gold skirts and sandals —cobras carved on foreheads
6.	Between the two statues:	a second sealed doorway
7.	Conclusion:	expectation that King Tut's mummy was beyond the second door

■ Note how each detail supports the topic sentence.

Transitional Expressions

Since space order is often used in description, **transitional expressions** indicating place or position can be useful:

Transitional Expressions Indicating Place	
next to, near	on top, beneath
close, far	toward, away
up, down, between	left, right, center
above, below	front, back, middle

---

*For more work on space order and other kinds of order, see Chapter 4, "Achieving Coherence," Part A.

88 UNIT 3 Developing the Paragraph

Of course, other kinds of order are possible. For example, a description of a person might have two parts: details of physical appearance and details of behavior.*

PRACTICE 1

Read the following paragraph carefully and answer the questions.

The woman who met us had an imposing beauty. She was tall and large-boned. Her face was strongly molded, with high cheekbones and skin the color of mahogany. She greeted us politely but did not smile and seemed to hold her head very high, an effect exaggerated by the abundant black hair slicked up and rolled on the top of her head. Her clothing was simple, a black sweater and skirt, and I remember thinking that dressed in showier garments, this woman would have seemed overwhelming.

1. What overall impression does the writer give of the woman?

    The impression is that the woman had a regal and imposing beauty.

2. What specific details support this general impression? *tall; high cheekbones; mahogany skin; head held high; hair piled high on head; unsmiling expression*

3. What kind of order does the writer use? *space order*

PRACTICE 2

It is important that the details in a descriptive paragraph support the overall impression given in the topic sentence. In each of the following plans, one detail has nothing to do with the topic sentence; it is merely a bit of irrelevant information. Find the irrelevant detail and circle the letter.

---

* For a complete essay developed by description, see "The Day of the Dead," Chapter 15, Part C.

CHAPTER 7 Description 89

1. Miami's Calle Ocho Festival, named after S.W. 8th Street in Little Havana, is a giant Latino street party.
    a. as far as the eye can see on S.W. 8th Street, thousands of people stroll, eat, and dance
    b. on the left, vendors sell hot pork sandwiches, *pasteles* (spiced meat pies), and fried sweets dusted with powdered sugar
    c. up close, the press of bare-limbed people, blaring music, and rich smells
    (d.) during the 1980s, Dominican merengue music hit the dance clubs of New York
    e. on the right, two of many bands play mambo or merengue music

2. In my mind's eye is a plan for the perfect workout room.
    a. complete Nautilus set in center
    b. StairMaster near the door
    c. on shelf above the StairMaster, a color TV
    (d.) exercise helps me think more clearly
    e. hot tub with view of woods through one-way glass
    f. spotless blue carpet

3. In the photograph from 1877, Chief Joseph looks sad and dignified.
    a. long hair pulled back, touched with gray
    b. dark eyes gaze off to one side, as if seeing a bleak future
    c. strong mouth frowns at the corners
    d. ceremonial shell necklaces cover his chest
    (e.) Nez Percé tribe once occupied much of the Pacific Northwest

4. On the plate lay an unappetizing hamburger.
    a. burned bun, black on the edges
    (b.) burger cost two dollars
    c. fat dripping from the hamburger onto the plate
    d. parts of burger uncooked and partially frozen
    e. sour smell of the meat

5. An illegal dump site has spoiled the field near the edge of town.
    a. fifty or more rusting metal drums, some leaking
    b. pools of green-black liquid on the ground
    (c.) in the distance, view of the mountains
    d. wildflowers and cottonwood trees dead or dying
    e. large sign reading "Keep Out—Toxic Chemicals"

PRACTICE 3

Here is a list of topic sentences for descriptive paragraphs. Give five specific details that would support the overall impression given in each topic sentence. Appeal to as many of the senses as possible. Be careful not to list irrelevant bits of information.

UNIT 3 Developing the Paragraph

EXAMPLE Stopped in time by the photographer, my mother appears confident.

Details:
a. her hair swept up in a sophisticated pompadour
b. a determined look in her young eyes
c. wide, self-assured smile
d. her chin held high
e. well-padded shoulders

(These five details support *confident* in the topic sentence.)

1. This was clearly a music lover's room.
   a. a grand piano at one end
   b. music stand with flute laid across it
   c. shelves of books about music
   d. CD player on one shelf with collection of discs
   e. stacks of music on a desk

2. The prizefighter looked tough and fearless.
   a. bulging muscles in his arms
   b. jaws set
   c. teeth clenched
   d. hair bristling
   e. feet firmly on the ground

3. Spaghetti and meatballs were splattered all over the white kitchen.

   a. *blotches of sauce on wall behind stove*

   b. *pool of sauce on stove top*

   c. *crusted saucepan in sink*

   d. *stray spaghetti hanging off edge of stove*

   e. *plates on counter with leftover spaghetti spilling over them*

4. The auto repair shop was alive with activity.

   a. *a car rising on a hydraulic lift*

   b. *one tired-looking worker hammering out dents on a car*

   c. *two men repainting a green truck*

   d. *one woman checking the exhaust system of a car*

   e. *telephone constantly ringing as customers called for appointments*

5. The buildings on that street look sadly rundown.

   a. *paint peeling from weathered old buildings*

   b. *some windows broken or covered with cardboard*

c. *other windows covered with dirt and grease*

d. *sagging roofs with loose tiles*

e. *screen doors open or attached by only one hinge*

6. The beach on a hot summer day presented a constant show.

   a. *children running and splashing in the water*

   b. *sunbathers rubbing lotion on themselves*

   c. *dogs chasing sticks and balls*

   d. *vendors selling soda and ice-cream bars*

   e. *sea gulls circling and diving for food*

7. During the first week of classes, the college bookstore is wall-to-wall confusion.

   a. *crowds of students pushing to get into the store*

   b. *cartons of books clogging the aisles*

   c. *spilled piles of books on the shelves*

   d. *students shouting out their orders to harried salespeople*

CHAPTER 7 Description   93

e. _separate, but unmarked, registers for cash, check, or credit card sales_

8. The automobile seemed like something from the next century.

   a. _streamlined body_

   b. _hidden headlights and wipers_

   c. _complicated instrument control panel_

   d. _a computerized voice telling passengers to fasten their seat belts_

   e. _dark-tinted windows_

PRACTICE 4

Pick the description you like best from Practice 3. Prewrite for more details if you wish. Choose a logical order in which to present the best details, make a plan or an outline, and then write an excellent descriptive paragraph.

PRACTICE 5

Describe the photograph on page 94. In your topic sentence state your overall impression of the scene and those in it. What do you think they are watching—what is the mood? Then support this impression with a detailed description—facial expressions, clothing, and so on.

Make your description as vivid as you can, so that readers who have not seen the photograph can visualize it in their minds' eye.

You may wish to use space order to organize these details, moving from left to right, top to bottom, or front to back.

✓ CHECKLIST: The Process of Writing a Descriptive Paragraph

Refer to this checklist of steps as you write a descriptive paragraph of your own.

____ 1. Narrow the topic in light of your audience and purpose.

____ 2. Compose a topic sentence that clearly points to what you will describe or gives an overall impression of the person, object, or scene.

____ 3. Freewrite or brainstorm to find as many specific details as you can to capture your subject in words. Remember to appeal to your readers' senses. (You may want to freewrite or brainstorm before you narrow the topic.)

____ 4. Select the best details and drop any irrelevant ones.

____ 5. Make a plan or an outline for the paragraph, numbering the details in the order in which you will present them.

____ 6. Write a draft of your descriptive paragraph, using transitional expressions wherever they might be helpful.

____ 7. Revise as necessary, checking for support, unity, logic, and coherence.

____ 8. Proofread for errors in grammar, punctuation, sentence structure, spelling, and mechanics.

Suggested Topics for Descriptive Paragraphs

1. An unusual man or woman: for example, an athlete, an entertainer, someone with amazing hair or clothing, or a teacher you won't forget
2. A public place: emergency room, library, fast-food restaurant, town square, or theater lobby
3. The face of someone in the news
4. A shop that sells only one type of item: cheese, computer software, Western boots, car parts, flowers
5. An animal, a bird, or an insect you have observed closely
6. Someone or something you found yourself staring at
7. A photograph of yourself as a child
8. A scene of peace (or of conflict)
9. A room that reveals something about its owner
10. An intriguing outdoor scene
11. A possession you value
12. An interesting person you have seen on campus
13. Your favorite dinner
14. A neighborhood personality
15. Writer's choice: _____

CHAPTER 8

Process

Two kinds of **process paragraphs** will be explained in this chapter: the how-to paragraph and the explanation paragraph.

The **how-to paragraph** gives the reader directions on how he or she can do something: how to install a software program, how to get to the airport, or how to make tasty barbecued ribs. The goals of such directions are the installed software, the arrival at the airport, or the great barbecued ribs. In other words, the reader should be able to do something after reading the paragraph.

The **explanation paragraph**, on the other hand, tells the reader how a particular event occurred or how something works. For example, an explanation paragraph might explain how an internal combustion engine works or how palm trees reproduce. After reading an explanation paragraph, the reader is not expected to be able to do anything, just to understand how it happened or how it works.

Process writing is useful in history, business, the sciences, psychology, and many other areas.

Topic Sentence

Here is the topic sentence of a *how-to paragraph*:

> Careful preparation before an interview is the key to getting the job you want.

- The writer begins a how-to paragraph with a topic sentence that clearly states the goal of the process—what the reader should be able to do.
- What should the reader be able to do after he or she has read the paragraph following this topic sentence?

The reader should be able to prepare for a job interview.

Paragraph and Plan

Here is the entire paragraph:

> "Luck is preparation meeting opportunity," it has been said, and this is true for a job interview. Careful preparation before an interview is the key to getting the job you want. The first step is to learn all you can about the employer. Read about the company in its brochures or in newspaper and magazine articles. A reference librarian can point you to the best sources of company information. You can also find company web sites and other useful material on the Internet. Second, as you read, think about the ways your talents match the company's goals. Third, put yourself in the interviewer's place, and make a list of questions that he or she will probably ask. Employers want to know about your experience, training, and special skills, like foreign languages. Remember, every employer looks for a capable and enthusiastic team player who will help the firm succeed. Fourth, rehearse your answers to the questions out loud. Practice with a friend or a tape recorder until your responses sound well prepared and confident. Finally, select and prepare a professional-looking interview outfit well in advance to avoid the last-minute panic of a torn hem or stained shirt. When a job candidate has made the effort to prepare, the interviewer is much more likely to be impressed.

■ The topic sentence is the second sentence. In the first sentence, the writer has used a quotation to open the paragraph and spark the reader's interest.

■ The body of the how-to paragraph is developed according to time, or chronological, order.* That is, the writer gives directions in the order in which the reader is to complete them. Keeping to a strict chronological order avoids the necessity of saying, *By the way, I forgot to tell you . . .* , or *Whoops, a previous step should have been to. . . .*

■ How many steps are there in this how-to paragraph and what are they?

There are five steps: (1) Learn about the company, (2) match your talents to the company's goals, (3) list interviewer questions, (4) practice answering them, (5) prepare your outfit.

Before writing this how-to paragraph, the writer probably brainstormed or freewrote to gather ideas and then made an outline or a plan like this:

---

* For more work on order, see Chapter 4, "Achieving Coherence," Part A.

Topic sentence: Careful preparation before an interview is the key to getting the job you want.

Step 1:	Learn about the employer —read company brochures, papers, magazines —reference librarian can help —check company web site
Step 2:	Think how your talents match company goals
Step 3:	List interviewer questions —think about experience, training, special skills —employers want capable team players
Step 4:	Rehearse your answers out loud —practice with friend or tape recorder
Step 5:	Select your interview outfit —avoid last-minute panic —avoid torn hem, stained shirt
Conclusion:	interviewer more likely to be impressed

■ Note that each step clearly relates to the goal stated in the topic sentence.

The second kind of process paragraph, the *explanation paragraph*, tells how something works, how it happens, or how it came to be:

> Many experts believe that recovery from addiction, whether to alcohol or other drugs, has four main stages. The first stage begins when the user finally admits that he or she has a substance abuse problem and wants to quit. At this point, most people seek help from groups like Alcoholics Anonymous or treatment programs because few addicts can "get clean" by themselves. The next stage is withdrawal, when the addict stops using the substance. Withdrawal can be a painful physical and emotional experience, but luckily, it does not last long. After withdrawal comes the most challenging stage—making positive changes in one's life. Recovering addicts have to learn new ways of spending their time, finding pleasure and relaxation, caring for their bodies, and relating to spouses, lovers, family, and friends. The fourth and final stage is staying off drugs. This open-ended part of the process often calls for ongoing support or therapy. For people once defeated by addiction, the rewards of self-esteem and a new life are well worth the effort.

■ What process does the writer explain in this paragraph? _The writer explains how people recover from addiction._

■ How many stages or steps are explained in this paragraph? _four_

CHAPTER 8   Process   **99**

■ What are they? *(1) deciding to quit, (2) withdrawing from substance,*

   (3) changing one's life, (4) staying off drugs

■ Make a plan of the paragraph in your notebook.

    Just as the photographs on this page show each stage in the process of a chick hatching, so your process paragraph should clearly describe each step or stage for the reader. Before you write, try to visualize the process as if it were a series of photographs.*

---

*For complete essays developed by process, see "How to Prepare for a Final Exam," Chapter 15, Part D, and "Bottle Watching," page 172.

Transitional Expressions

Since process paragraphs rely on **chronological order**, or **time sequence**, words and expressions that locate the steps of the process in time are extremely helpful.

Transitional Expressions for Process

Beginning a Process	Continuing a Process		Ending a Process
(at) first	second, third step	when	finally
initially	until	while	at last
begin by	after(ward)	as soon as	
	then	as	
	next	upon	
	later	during	
	before	meanwhile	

PRACTICE 1

Read the following how-to paragraph carefully and answer the questions.

If your dog barks too much, the Humane Society recommends an easy way to solve the problem. All you need is a plant mister—a small spray bottle—filled with water and kept handy. First and most important, respond immediately every time your dog barks unnecessarily. Instantly say, "Quiet, Pluto," or whatever the dog's name is, giving one or two squirts of water in the dog's face. Be sure to do this while the dog is barking. Waiting until the dog stops barking may confuse it. If the dog moves away, say, "Quiet" again as you move toward the dog and give it one more squirt of water. Second, repeat this procedure every time the dog barks without a good reason. The dog will soon learn that your saying "Quiet" comes with a squirt of water. Usually two days—about five to ten water treatments—are enough. Third, as time goes by, use the spray bottle only if the dog forgets—that is, rarely. Throughout the training process, remember to be consistent, using the spray technique every single time, and don't forget to reassure your dog that you two are still friends by petting it when it is quiet.

—Eleanor Steiger (Student)

1. What should you be able to do after reading this paragraph?

    You should be able to teach your dog to stop unnecessary barking.

2. Are any "materials" necessary for this process? *The only item is a spray bottle.*

3. How many steps are there in this paragraph? List them.

   three (1) squirt the dog in the face the minute it barks, (2) repeat this every time for a day or two, (3) thereafter, squirt only when the dog forgets. Also, the writer says, "throughout the process"—be consistent and pet the dog when quiet.

4. What order does the writer employ? *time order*

PRACTICE 2

Here are five plans for process paragraphs. The steps for the plans are not in the correct chronological order. The plans also contain irrelevant details that are not part of the process. Number the steps in the proper time sequence and cross out any irrelevant details.

1. Starting your own rock band is a difficult process.

   _3_ After the group has mastered five songs, it should make a demo tape.

   _1_ The first step is finding friends and local musicians with the same musical taste and vision.

   _4_ Send the demo tapes to local clubs, bars, and DJs, and follow up in person to try to line up some gigs.

   _2_ Each band member should choose a main instrument, and only one or two should sing, to avoid chaos on stage.

   ___ ~~When Ginger Spice left the Spice Girls, it definitely shook up the whole group.~~

   _5_ With persistence, multiple performances, and a small dose of talent, your band might develop a following.

2. Stress, which is your body's response to physical or mental pressures, occurs in three stages.

   _2_ In the resistance stage, your body works hard to resist or handle the threat, but you may become more vulnerable to other stressors, like flu or colds.

   _3_ If the stress continues for too long, your body uses up its defenses and enters the exhaustion stage.

   ___ ~~Trying to balance college courses, parenthood, and work is sure to cause stress.~~

   _1_ During the alarm stage (also called *fight or flight*), your body first reacts to a threat by releasing hormones that increase your heart rate and blood pressure, create muscle tension, and supply quick energy.

3. Chewing gum is made entirely by machine.

   __3__ Then the warm mass is pressed into thin ribbons by pairs of rollers.

   __1__ First, the gum base is melted and pumped through a high-speed spinner that throws out all impurities.

   ____ ~~The gum base makes the gum chewy.~~

   __2__ Huge machines mix the purified gum with sugar, corn syrup, and flavoring, such as spearmint, peppermint, or cinnamon.

   __5__ Finally, machines wrap the sticks individually and then package them.

   __4__ Knives attached to the last rollers cut the ribbons into sticks.

4. Many psychologists claim that marriage is a dynamic process consisting of several phases.

   __2__ Sooner or later, romance gives way to disappointment as both partners really see each other's faults.

   __1__ Idealization is the first phase, when two people fall romantically in love, each thinking the other is perfect.

   __5__ The last phase occurs as the couple face their late years as a twosome once again.

   __3__ The third phase is sometimes called the productivity period, when two people work at parenting and career development.

   ____ ~~Men and women may have different expectations in a marriage.~~

   __4__ As the children leave home and careers mature, couples may enter a stage when they rethink their lives and goals.

5. Because turtles are cold-blooded animals, they hibernate during the winter.

   __2__ After finding the right place, they dig their winter home, bury themselves in the mud, and fall into a deep sleep.

   __1__ As the weather turns cold, turtles begin to seek a spot in the mud near a pond to spend the winter.

   ____ ~~Contrary to popular opinion, turtles make charming pets.~~

   __4__ With the onset of spring, the ice on the pond melts and the thawing mud awakens these buried creatures to new life.

   __3__ Throughout the winter, their metabolism remains low.

CHAPTER 8   Process   **103**

PRACTICE 3

Here are topic sentences for five process paragraphs. Make a plan for each paragraph, listing in proper time sequence all the steps that would be necessary to complete the process. Now choose one plan and write an excellent process paragraph. *Answers will vary.*

1. Although I'm still not the life of the party, I took these steps to overcome my shyness at parties.

   Two weeks before the next party, I told myself that others were as shy as I was.

   One week before the party, I selected clothes I feel comfortable in to wear

   to the party.

   On my way to the party, I rehearsed some conversation topics.

   At the party, I introduced myself to three new people.

   _____

2. _Registration_ is/was a very complicated (or simple) process.

   I picked the four courses I wanted to take.

   My adviser was in her office when I went to get her signature.

   The line at the registrar's office was short when I arrived.

   None of the courses I wanted was full, so I didn't have to choose alternatives.

   _____

   _____

3. Ted learned _business skills_ in stages over a period of time.

   As a child after school, he watched his parents run their candy shop.

   In high school, he spent afternoons selling shoes at his uncle's store.

   He took several sales and marketing courses in college.

   In his senior year, Ted made excellent money selling health products out

   of his home.

   Finally, he opened his own T-shirt store in the mall after graduation.

4. Good kids turning bad: it is a process occurring all over the country.

   It usually begins with a good kid in a bad situation, in a dangerous neighborhood or school.

   The child may do the right thing but be mocked or beaten up by peers for studying or even attending class.

   After a while, the pressure or effort may be too much, and the child stops caring about schoolwork or joins a gang.

   Now, without skills, he or she has no future, and easy money from drug sales or other crimes may start to look good.

5. My morning routine gets me out of the house in twenty minutes.

   Brushing my teeth, shaving, and showering follow one another so quickly that they are like one step.

   While toweling off, I decide what I will wear and think of everything I need to take for the day.

   Next I race to the kitchen to make breakfast and feed the cats.

   I eat breakfast in bits while dressing and packing up my knapsack.

✔ CHECKLIST: The Process of Writing a Process Paragraph

Refer to this checklist of steps as you write a process paragraph of your own.

____ 1. Narrow the topic in light of your audience and purpose.

____ 2. Compose a topic sentence that clearly states the goal or end result of the process you wish to describe.

____ 3. Freewrite or brainstorm to generate steps that might be part of the process. (You may want to freewrite or brainstorm before you narrow the topic.)

____ 4. Drop any irrelevant information or steps that are not really necessary for your explanation of the process.

____ 5. Make an outline or a plan for your paragraph, numbering the steps in the correct time (chronological) sequence.

____ 6. Write a draft of your process paragraph, using transitional expressions to indicate time (chronological) sequence.

____ 7. Revise as necessary, checking for support, unity, logic, and coherence.

____ 8. Proofread for errors in grammar, punctuation, sentence structure, spelling, and mechanics.

Suggested Topics for Process Paragraphs

1. How to relax or meditate
2. How to establish credit
3. How to break up with (or attract) someone
4. How an important discovery was made
5. How to find information in the library's electronic card catalogue (or reference book section)
6. How to be a good friend
7. How someone landed a wonderful job
8. How to prepare your favorite dish
9. How to shop on a budget for a computer (or clothes, school supplies, and so on)
10. How to appear smarter than you really are
11. How to break an unhealthy habit
12. How a team won an important game
13. How to get the most out of a visit to the doctor
14. How to choose a major
15. Writer's choice: _____

CHAPTER 9

Definition

PART A Single-Sentence Definitions
PART B The Definition Paragraph

To **define** is to explain clearly what a word or term means.

As you write, you will sometimes find it necessary to explain words or terms that you suspect your reader may not know. For example, *net profit* is the profit remaining after all deductions have been taken; a *bonsai* is a dwarfed, ornamentally shaped tree. Such terms can often be defined in just a few carefully chosen words. However, other terms—like *courage, racism,* or *a good marriage*—are more difficult to define. They will test your ability to explain them clearly so that your reader knows exactly what you mean when you use them in your writing. They may require an entire paragraph for a complete and thorough definition.

In this chapter, you will learn to write one-sentence definitions and then whole paragraphs of definition. The skill of defining clearly will be useful in such courses as psychology, business, the sciences, history, and English.

PART A Single-Sentence Definitions

There are many ways to define a word or term. Three basic ways are **definition by synonym, definition by class,** and **definition by negation.**

Definition by Synonym

The simplest way to define a term is to supply a **synonym,** a word that means the same thing. A good synonym definition always uses an easier and more familiar word than the one being defined.

1. *Gregarious* means *sociable.*
2. *To procrastinate* means *to postpone needlessly.*
3. A *wraith* is a *ghost* or *phantom.*
4. *Adroitly* means *skillfully.*

Although you may not have known the words *gregarious, procrastination, wraith,* and *adroitly* before, the synonym definitions make it very clear what they mean.

A synonym should usually be the same part of speech as the word being defined, so it could be used as a substitute. *Gregarious* and *sociable* are both adjectives; *to procrastinate* and *to postpone* are verb forms; *wraith, ghost,* and *phantom* are nouns; *adroitly* and *skillfully* are adverbs.

5. Quarterback Payton Manning *adroitly* moved his team up the field.
6. Quarterback Payton Manning *skillfully* moved his team up the field.

■ In this sentence *skillfully* can be substituted for *adroitly.*

Unfortunately, it is not always possible to come up with a good synonym definition.

Definition by Class

The **class** definition is the one most often required in college and formal writing—in examinations, papers, and reports.

The class definition has two parts. First, the writer places the word to be defined into the larger **category,** or **class,** to which it belongs.

7. *Lemonade* is a *drink . . .*
8. An *orphan* is a *child . . .*
9. A *dictatorship* is a *form of government . . .*

Second, the writer provides the **distinguishing characteristics** or **details** that make this person, object, or idea *different* from all others in that category. What the reader wants to know is what *kind* of drink is lemonade? What *specific* type of child is an orphan? What *particular* form of government is a dictatorship?

10. *Lemonade* is a drink *made of lemons, sugar, and water.*
11. An *orphan* is a child *without living parents.*
12. A *dictatorship* is a form of government *in which one person has absolute control over his or her subjects.*

108 UNIT 3 Developing the Paragraph

Here is a class definition for the action pictured: A slam-dunk is a basket that is scored when the shooter leaps high, forcefully throwing the basketball through the rim from above.

Think of class definitions as if they were in chart form:

Word	Category or Class	Distinguishing Facts or Details
lemonade	drink	made of lemons, sugar, and water
orphan	child	without living parents
dictatorship	form of government	one person has absolute control over his or her subjects

When you write a class definition, be careful not to place the word or term in too broad or vague a category. For instance, saying that lemonade is a *food* or that an orphan is a *person* will make your job of zeroing in on a distinguishing detail more difficult.

Besides making the category or class as limited as possible, be sure to make your distinguishing facts as specific and exact as you can. Saying that lemonade is a drink *made with water* or that an orphan is a child *who has lost family members* is not specific enough to give your reader an accurate definition.

Definition by Negation

A definition by **negation** means that the writer first says what something is not, and then says what it is.

> 13. A *good parent* does not just feed and clothe a child but loves, accepts, and supports that child for who he or she is.
>
> 14. *College* is not just a place to have a good time but a place to grow intellectually and emotionally.
>
> 15. *Liberty* does not mean having the right to do whatever you please but carries the obligation to respect the rights of others.

Definitions by negation are extremely helpful when you think that the reader has a preconceived idea about the word you wish to define. You say that *it is not* what the reader thought, but that *it is* something else entirely.

Here is a definition by negation: The fax machine is not the revolutionary new office machine that people think but an invention patented in 1863 and used to send words and pictures between the United States and France.

Practice 1

Write a one-sentence definition by **synonym** for each of the following terms. Remember, the synonym should be more familiar than the term being defined.

1. *irate:* To be irate is to be angry.

2. *to elude:* To elude someone is to keep away from him or her.

3. *pragmatic:* To be pragmatic is to be practical.

4. *fiasco:* A fiasco is a disaster.

5. *elated:* To be elated is to be overjoyed.

Practice 2

Here are five **class definitions**. Circle the category and underline the distinguishing characteristics in each. You may find it helpful to make a chart.

1. A *haiku* is a (Japanese poem) that has seventeen syllables.
2. A *homer* is a (referee) who unconsciously favors the home team.
3. An *ophthalmologist* is a (doctor) who specializes in diseases of the eye.
4. The *tango* is a (ballroom dance) that originated in Latin America and is in 2/4 or 4/4 time.
5. *Plagiarism* is (stealing) writing or ideas that are not one's own.

Practice 3

Define the following words by **class definition**. You may find it helpful to use this form: "A _____ (noun) is a _____ (class or category) that _____ (distinguishing characteristic)."

1. *hamburger:* A hamburger is a sandwich that consists of a split bun and a ground beef patty.

2. *bikini:* A bikini is a two-piece swimsuit that is very scanty.

3. *snob:* A snob is a person who thinks he or she is, and acts as if he or she were, socially superior to others.

4. *mentor:* A mentor is a counselor who guides, teaches, and assists another person.

5. *adolescence:* Adolescence is the period of life between puberty and maturity.

PRACTICE 4

Write a one-sentence definition by **negation** for each of the following terms. First say what each term is not; then say what it is.

1. *hero:* A hero is not someone with great athletic ability or wealth but a person admired for his or her acts of morality and fine character.

2. *final exam:* A final exam is not just a way to make students suffer but an enforced review of everything learned in the course.

3. *self-esteem:* Self-esteem does not mean conceit but rather a healthy respect for oneself.

4. *intelligence:* Intelligence is not knowledge in a specific area; it is the capacity to acquire and apply knowledge.

5. *freedom of speech:* Freedom of speech is not just a phrase we learn in history class; it is a right guaranteed to each American to express his or her beliefs in public.

PART B The Definition Paragraph

Sometimes a single-sentence definition may not be enough to define a word or term adequately. In such cases, the writer may need an entire paragraph in which he or she develops the definition by means of examples, descriptions, comparisons, contrasts, and so forth.

Topic Sentence

The topic sentence of a definition paragraph is often one of the single-sentence definitions discussed in Part A: definition by synonym, definition by class, definition by negation.

Here is the topic sentence of a definition paragraph:

> *Ambivalence* can be defined as a feeling or attitude that is both positive and negative at the same time.

- What kind of definition does the topic sentence use?

  class

- To what larger category or class does *ambivalence* belong?

  feeling or attitude

- What are the distinguishing details about *ambivalence* that make it different from all other feelings or attitudes?

  It is both positive and negative at the same time.

Paragraph and Plan

Here is the entire paragraph:

> *Ambivalence* can be defined as a feeling or attitude that is both positive and negative at the same time. For instance, a young woman might feel *ambivalent* about motherhood. She may want to have a child yet fear that motherhood will use up energy she would like to spend on her career. Or a Michigan man who is offered a slightly higher salary in Arizona might be ambivalent about moving. He and his family don't want to leave their friends, their schools, and a city they love. On the other hand, they are tempted by a larger income and by Arizona's warm climate and clean air. Finally, two people may have ambivalent feelings about each other, loving and disliking each other at the same time. It hurts to be together, and it hurts to be apart; neither situation makes them happy. As these examples show, the double tug of ambivalence can complicate decision making.

■ One effective way for a writer to develop the body of a definition paragraph is to provide examples.*

■ What three examples does this writer give to develop the definition in the topic sentence?

young woman ambivalent about motherhood; man ambivalent about moving;

two people ambivalent about each other

■ By repeating the word being defined—or a form of it—in the context of each example, the writer helps the reader understand the definition better: A young woman might feel *ambivalent*, a Michigan man might be *ambivalent*, and two people may have *ambivalent* feelings.

Before writing the paragraph, the writer probably brainstormed or freewrote to gather ideas and then made an outline or a plan like this:

Topic sentence: *Ambivalence* can be defined as a feeling or attitude that is both positive and negative at the same time.

Example 1: A young woman
—wants to have a child
—yet fears motherhood will use up career energy

Example 2: Michigan man and his family
—don't want to leave friends, schools, city
—are tempted by income, climate, clean air

Example 3: Two people
—love each other
—also dislike each other

Conclusion: Ambivalence can complicate decisions.

■ Note that each example in the body of the paragraph clearly relates to the definition in the topic sentence.

Although examples are an excellent way to develop a definition paragraph, other methods of development are also possible. For instance, you might compare and contrast[†] *love* and *lust*, *assertiveness* and *aggressiveness*, or *the leader* and *the follower*. You could also combine definition and persuasion.[‡] Such a paragraph might begin *College is a dating service* or *Alcoholism is not a moral weakness but a disease*. The rest of the paragraph would have to persuade readers that this definition is valid.

There are no transitional expressions used specifically for definition paragraphs. Sometimes phrases like *can be defined as* or *can be considered* or *means that* can help alert the reader that a definition paragraph will follow.[§]

---

* For more work on examples, see Chapter 5, "Illustration."
† For more work on contrast, see Chapter 10, "Comparison and Contrast."
‡ For more work on persuasion, see Chapter 13, "Persuasion."
§ For an entire essay developed by definition, see "Winning," Chapter 15, Part E.

114 UNIT 3 Developing the Paragraph

PRACTICE 5

Read the following paragraph carefully and then answer the questions.

A feminist is *not* a man-hater, a masculine woman, a demanding shrew, or someone who dislikes housewives. A feminist is simply a woman or man who believes that women should enjoy the same rights, privileges, opportunities, and pay as men. Because society has deprived women of many equal rights, feminists have fought for equality. For instance, Susan B. Anthony, a famous nineteenth-century feminist, worked to get women the right to vote. Today, feminists want women to receive equal pay for equal work. They support a woman's right to pursue her goals and dreams, whether she wants to be an astronaut, athlete, banker, or full-time homemaker. On the home front, feminists believe that two partners who work should equally share the housework and child care. Because the term is often misunderstood, some people don't call themselves feminists even though they share feminist values. But courageous feminists of both sexes continue to speak out for equality.

1. The definition here spans two sentences. What kind of definition does the writer use in sentence 1? _definition by negation_

2. What kind of definition appears in sentence 2? _definition by class_

3. The paragraph is developed by describing some key beliefs of feminists. What are these? _equal rights, equal pay for equal work, freedom to pursue goals and dreams, working couples' sharing housework and child care_

4. Which point is supported by an example? _Feminists have fought for equality. Example: Susan B. Anthony_

5. Make a plan or an outline of the paragraph.

   Topic sentence(s): *A feminist is* not *a man-hater, a masculine woman, a demanding shrew, or someone who dislikes housewives. A feminist is simply a woman or man who believes that women should enjoy the same rights, privileges, opportunities, and pay as men.*

   —fights for equal rights

   —wants equal pay for equal work

   —wants freedom for women to pursue goals and dreams

—believes working partners should share housework, child care

—some people afraid to call themselves feminists

PRACTICE 6

Read the following paragraphs and answer the questions.

Induction is reasoning from particular cases to general principles; that is, the scientific method: you look at a number of examples, then come to a general conclusion based on the evidence. For instance, having known twenty-five people named Glenn, all of whom were men, you might naturally conclude, through induction, that all people named Glenn are men. The problem with inductive reasoning here, however, is Glenn Close, the movie actress.

Deduction is reasoning from the general to the particular. One starts from a statement known or merely assumed to be true and uses it to come to a conclusion about the matter at hand. Once you know that all people have to die sometime and that you are a person, you can logically deduce that you, too, will have to die sometime.

—Judy Jones and William Wilson, "100 Things Every College Graduate Should Know," *Esquire*

1. What two terms are defined? *induction and deduction*

2. What kind of definition is used in both topic sentences? *class definition*

3. In what larger category do the writers place both induction and deduction? *reasoning*

4. What example of induction do the writers give? *Glenn as a man's name*

5. What example shows the *problem* with induction? *a woman—the actress Glenn Close*

6. What example of deduction do the writers give? *that every person must die*

PRACTICE 7

Here are some topic sentences for definition paragraphs. Choose one that interests you and make a plan for a paragraph, using whatever method of development seems appropriate.

1. An optimist is someone who usually expects the best from life and from people.
2. Prejudice means prejudging people on the basis of race, creed, age, or sex—not on their merits as individuals.
3. A wealthy person does not necessarily have money and possessions, but he or she might possess inner wealth—a loving heart and a creative mind.
4. Registration is a ritual torture that students must go through before they can attend their classes.
5. Bravery and bravado are very different character traits.

PRACTICE 8

The Martians have landed. You have been chosen to answer their questions about several things they have noticed on Earth. Since they can read English but cannot speak it, you must write a clear paragraph defining one of the following: *money, clothes, computers, cars, the president of the United States*. Begin with a one-sentence definition; then discuss, giving examples and details that fully define the word or term for your Martian readers.

✓ CHECKLIST: The Process of Writing a Definition Paragraph

Refer to this checklist of steps as you write a definition paragraph of your own.

____ 1. Narrow the topic in light of your audience and purpose.

____ 2. Compose a topic sentence that uses one of the three basic methods of definition discussed in this chapter: synonym, class, or negation.

____ 3. Decide on the method of paragraph development that is best suited to what you want to say.

____ 4. Freewrite or brainstorm to generate ideas that may be useful in your definition paragraph. (You may want to freewrite or brainstorm before you narrow the topic.)

____ 5. Select the best ideas and drop any ideas that do not clearly relate to the definition in your topic sentence.

____ 6. Make a plan or an outline for your paragraph, numbering the ideas in the order in which you will present them.

____ 7. Write a draft of your definition paragraph, using transitional expressions wherever they might be helpful.

____ 8. Revise as necessary, checking for support, unity, logic, and coherence.

____ 9. Proofread for errors in grammar, punctuation, sentence structure, spelling, and mechanics.

Suggested Topics for Definition Paragraphs

1. A self-starter
2. The loner (or life of the party, perfectionist, big mouth, Internet addict)
3. Country and western music (or rock, gospel, Celtic, or some other type of music)
4. Confidence
5. A dead-end job
6. A good marriage (or a good partner, parent, or friend)
7. The racing-car (or fashion, football, credit-card, computer-game, or other) fanatic
8. An interesting term you know from reading (*placebo, UFO, apartheid, hubris,* and so forth)
9. Spring break
10. A racist (sexist, terrorist, artist, philanthropist, or other *-ist*)
11. The night person (or morning person)
12. Integrity
13. A technical term you know from work or a hobby
14. A slang term you or your friends use
15. Writer's choice: _____

CHAPTER 10

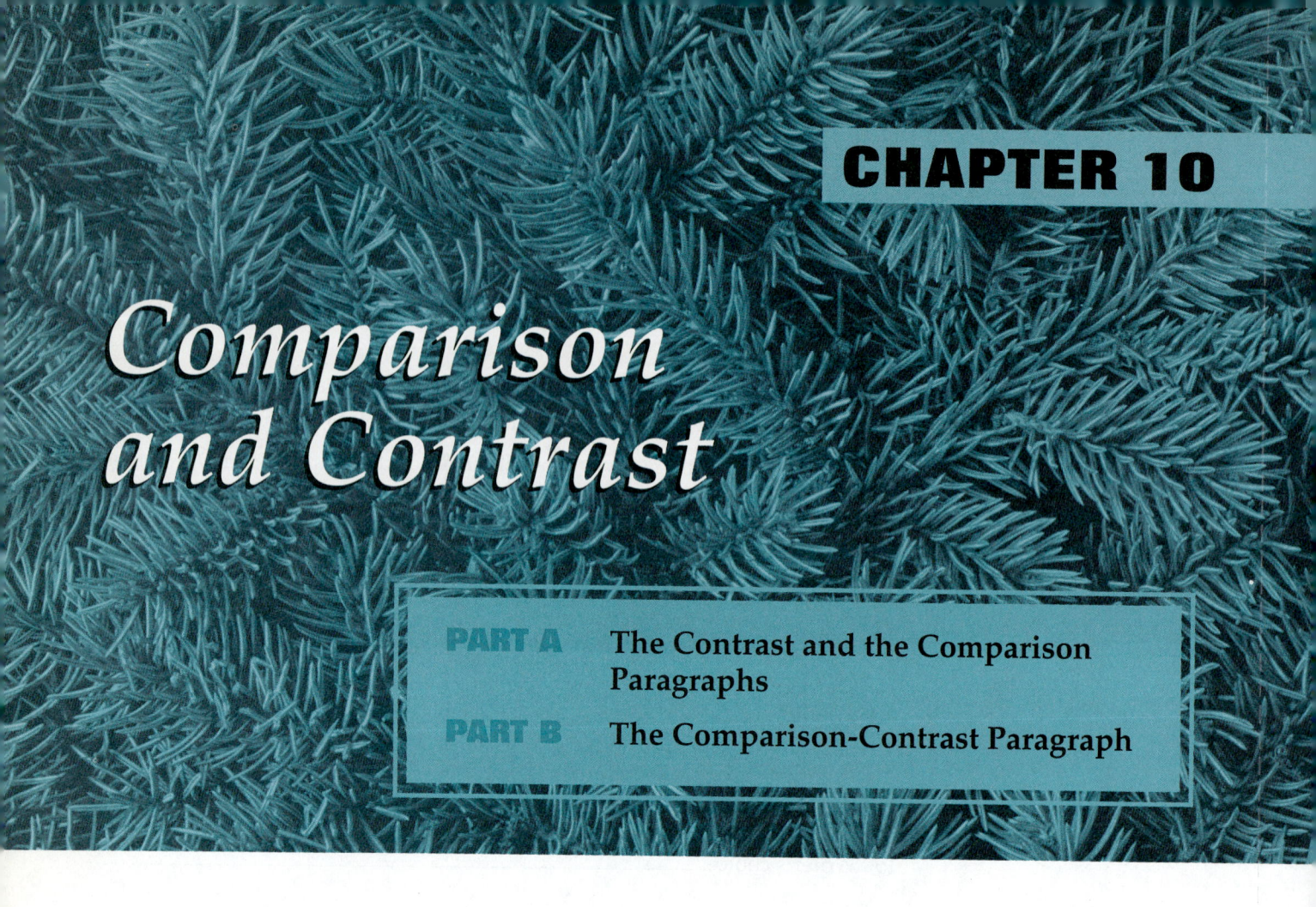

Comparison and Contrast

PART A   The Contrast and the Comparison Paragraphs

PART B   The Comparison-Contrast Paragraph

To **contrast** two persons, places, or things is to examine the ways in which they are different. To **compare** them is to examine the ways in which they are similar.

Contrast and comparison are useful skills in daily life, work, and college. When you shop, you often compare and contrast. For instance, you might compare and contrast two dishwashers to get the better value. In fact, the magazine *Consumer Reports* was created to help consumers compare and contrast different product brands.

Your employer might ask you to compare and contrast two computers, two telephone services, or two shipping crates. Your job is to gather information about the similarities and differences to help your employer choose one over the other. In nearly every college course, you will be expected to compare and contrast—two generals, two types of storm systems, two minerals, or two painters of the same school.

PART A   The Contrast and the Comparison Paragraphs

Topic Sentence

Here is the topic sentence of a contrast paragraph:

> Although soul and hip-hop both spring from African-American roots, they are very different musical expressions.

- The writer begins a contrast paragraph with a topic sentence that clearly states what two persons, things, or ideas will be contrasted.

- What two things will be contrasted?

    soul and hip-hop

- What word or words in the topic sentence make it clear that the writer will contrast soul and hip-hop?

    very different

Paragraph and Plan

Here is the entire paragraph:

> Although soul and hip-hop both spring from African-American roots, they are very different musical expressions. Soul music borrows from gospel and rhythm and blues. The singer's voice, backed up by live instruments, soars with emotion, with soul. This music captures the optimism of its time—the civil rights movement of the 1960s and hope for social change. There are two types of soul—the smooth Detroit style of the Supremes, Stevie Wonder, and the Temptations and the more gritty, gospel-driven Memphis style of Otis Redding and Booker T and the MGs. Soul music is upbeat and often joyful; its subjects are love and affirmation of the human condition. On the other hand, hip-hop (or rap) draws on hard rock, funk, and techno. The rapper chants rhymes against a driving instrumental background that may be prerecorded. Rap grew out of the New York ghettos in the late 1970s and the 1980s, when crack and guns flooded "the hood" and many dreams seemed broken. Of the rival East and West Coast rappers, New Yorkers include Grandmaster Flash, LL Cool J, and the murdered Biggie Smalls, while Los Angeles rappers include Ice Cube and the murdered Tupac Shakur. The subjects of hip-hop are racism, crime, and poverty. Both soul and hip-hop claim to "tell it like it is." Hip-hop's answer to the soulful Four Tops is the Furious Four. What's in a name? Perhaps the way the listener experiences reality.
>
> —Maurice Bosco (Student)

- The writer first provides information about (A) soul music and then gives contrasting parallel information about (B) hip-hop.

- What information about (A) soul does the writer provide in the first half of the paragraph? *The writer discusses musical influences, sound, time period, types, and subjects.*

- What contrasting parallel information does the writer provide about hip-hop in the second half of the paragraph? *The writer discusses the same five points: influences, sound, time period, types, and subjects.*

- Why do you think the writer chose to present the points of contrast in this order? _It makes sense to describe the sound and historical background of each kind of music first._

- Note that the last four sentences provide a thoughtful conclusion. What final point does the writer make? _that the two kinds of music express two views of reality_

Before composing the paragraph, the writer probably brainstormed or freewrote to gather ideas and then made an outline or a plan like this:

Topic sentence: Although soul and hip-hop both spring from African-American roots, they are very different musical expressions.

Points of Contrast	A. Soul	B. Hip-Hop
1. influences	gospel, R&B	rock, funk, techno
2. sound	soaring voice, live instruments	chanted rhymes; instrumentals may be prerecorded
3. time period	1960s, civil rights, hope for change	1970s–80s, crack, guns
4. types	Detroit, Memphis	New York, Los Angeles
5. subjects	love, affirmation	racism, crime, poverty

Organized in this manner, the plan for this contrast paragraph helps the writer make sure that the paragraph will be complete. That is, if the historical period of soul is discussed, that of hip-hop must also be discussed, and so on, for every point of contrast.

Here is another way to write the same paragraph:

> Although soul and hip-hop both spring from African-American roots, they are very different musical expressions. Soul music borrows from gospel and rhythm and blues, whereas hip-hop (or rap) draws on hard rock, funk, and techno. The soul singer's voice, backed up by live instruments, soars with emotion, with soul; however, the rapper chants rhymes against a driving instrumental background that may be prerecorded. Soul music captures the optimism of its time—the civil rights movement of the 1960s and hope for social change. On the other hand, hip-hop grew out of the New York ghettos in the late 1970s and the 1980s, when crack and guns flooded "the hood" and many dreams seemed broken. There are two types of soul—the smooth Detroit style of the Supremes, Stevie Wonder, and the Temptations and the more gritty, gospel-driven Memphis style of Otis Redding and Booker T and the MGs. Of the rival East and West Coast rappers, New Yorkers include Grandmaster Flash, LL Cool J, and the murdered Biggie Smalls, while Los Angeles rappers include Ice Cube and the murdered Tupac Shakur. Whereas soul music's subjects are love and affirmation of the human condition, the subjects of hip-hop are racism, crime, and poverty. Both soul and hip-hop claim to "tell it like it is." Hip-hop's answer to the soulful Four Tops is the Furious Four. What's in a name? Perhaps the way the listener experiences reality.

- Instead of giving all the information about soul music and then going on to hip-hop, this paragraph moves back and forth between soul and hip-hop, dealing with *each point of contrast separately.*

Use either one of these two patterns when writing a contrast or a comparison paragraph:

> 1. Present all the information about **A** and then provide parallel information about **B**:
>
> **First all A:**   point 1
>   point 2
>   point 3
>
> **Then all B:**   point 1
>   point 2
>   point 3

- This pattern is good for paragraphs and for short compositions. The reader can easily remember what was said about *A* by the time he or she gets to *B*.

> 2. Move back and forth between **A** and **B**. Present one point about **A** and then go to the parallel point about **B**. Then move to the next point and do the same:
>
> **First A,** point 1;   **then B,** point 1
>
> **First A,** point 2;   **then B,** point 2
>
> **First A,** point 3;   **then B,** point 3

- The second pattern is better for longer papers, where it might be hard for the reader to remember what the writer said about *A* by the time he or she gets to *B* a few paragraphs later. By going back and forth, the writer makes it easier for the reader to keep the contrasts or comparisons in mind.

What you have learned so far about planning a contrast paragraph holds true for a comparison paragraph as well. Just remember that a **contrast** *stresses differences* whereas a **comparison** *stresses similarities.*

Here is a comparison paragraph:

> "Two birds of a feather," so the family describes my mother and me, and it's true that we have much in common. We share the same honey-colored skin, hazel eyes, and pouting mouth. I like to think I've inherited her creative flair. Though we were poor, she taught me that beauty requires style, not money, and I see her influence in my small apartment, which I have decorated with colorful fabrics and my own paintings. One similarity alarms me, however: both my mother and I were battered wives. She believed a woman's place is with her husband, so she stayed with my father despite the abuse. Eventually, he left us. Soon after I married, my husband hit me for the first time. Shocked to think that the secret pain of my mother's life would now be mine, I took the initiative, got counseling, and left him. Two birds of a feather, my mother and I, but not in this.
>
> —Janice Wilson (Student)

- What words in the topic sentence does the writer use to indicate that a comparison will follow? _"Two birds of a feather," much in common_

- In what ways are the writer and her mother similar? _They look alike; both are creative; both were battered wives._

- What transitional words stress the similarities? _the same, one similarity, both_

- What pattern of presentation does the writer use? _The writer uses the A-B, A-B, A-B pattern._

- What one point of *contrast* serves as a strong punch line for the paragraph? _The writer left an abusive husband whereas her mother had stayed with one._

- Make a plan or an outline of this comparison paragraph.

Transitional Expressions

Transitional expressions in contrast paragraphs stress opposition and difference:

Transitional Expressions for Contrast	
although	on the other hand
whereas	in contrast
but	while
however	yet
conversely	unlike

Transitional expressions in comparison paragraphs stress similarities:

Transitional Expressions for Comparison	
in the same way	just as . . . so
and, also, in addition	similarly
as well as	like
both, neither	too
each of	the same

As you write, avoid using just one or two of these transitional expressions. Learn new ones from the list and practice them in your paragraphs.*

PRACTICE 1

Read the following paragraph carefully and answer the questions.

Certain personality traits, like whether a person is more reactive or proactive, can predict success or its opposite. In his book *The Seven Habits of Highly Effective People*, Steven Covey writes that reactive people tend to sit back and wait for life or circumstances to bring them opportunities. They react instead of act. When good things happen, they are happy, but when bad things happen, they feel like victims. Reactive people often say things like, "There's nothing I can do," "I can't because . . . ," and "If only." In the short term, reactive people might feel comfortable playing it safe, holding back, and avoiding challenges; in the long term, though, they are often left dreaming. On the other hand, proactive people know that they have the power to choose their responses to whatever life brings. They act instead of react: If things aren't going their way, they take action to help create the outcome they desire. Proactive people can be recognized by their tendency to say things like "Let's consider the alternatives," "I prefer," "We can," and "I will." In the short term, proactive people might face the discomfort of failing because they take on challenges, set goals, and work toward them. But in the long term, Covey says, proactive people are the ones who achieve their dreams.

1. Can you tell from the topic sentence whether a contrast or comparison will follow? *The words* more reactive or proactive *and* success or its opposite *suggest contrast.*

2. What two personality types are being contrasted? *reactive and proactive*

3. What information does the writer provide about reactive people? *They sit and wait; react not act; say things like "There's nothing I can do"; avoid discomfort in the short term but are left dreaming.*

4. What parallel information does the writer provide about proactive people? *They know they have power; take positive action; say things like "We can" and "I will"; face discomfort but often achieve their dreams.*

5. What pattern does the writer of this paragraph use to present the contrasts? *all A, then all B*

6. What transitional expression does the writer use to stress the shift from *A* to *B*? *On the other hand*

---

*For an entire essay developed by comparison-contrast, see "Two Childhoods," Chapter 15, Part F.

PRACTICE 2

This paragraph is hard to follow because it lacks transitional expressions that emphasize contrast. Revise the paragraph, adding transitional expressions of contrast. Strive for variety. *Answers may vary.*

The city of Bangalore, India, is a jarring mixture of new and old. Bangalore has become a world center of the computer software industry, and companies like IBM, Dell, and Hewlett Packard have built dozens of gleaming new buildings. ~~The~~ *In contrast, the* rutted dirt roads are choked with oxcarts, and three-wheeled taxis belch black fumes. Over breakfast each morning at the Taj Residency Hotel, Indian programmers chat with American engineers about the latest piece of computer code. ~~Sandal-clad~~ *Yet, sandal-clad* women carry baskets of tools on their heads at a nearby construction site, and workers drag a huge pipe into place, using only ropes. Each night, teams of programmers send their work by satellite uplink to teams on the other side of the earth. ~~They~~ *However, they* must rely on diesel generators because power outages lasting two to three hours occur almost every day.

PRACTICE 3

Below are three plans for contrast paragraphs. The points of contrast in the second column do not follow the same order as the points in the first column. In addition, one detail is missing. First, number the points in the second column to match those in the first. Then fill in the missing detail.

1. Shopping at a Supermarket

1. carries all brands
2. lower prices
3. open seven days a week
4. little personal service
5. no credit

Shopping at a Local Grocery

_4_ personal service
_3_ closed on Sundays
_2_ prices often higher
_1_ doesn't carry all brands
_5_ credit available for steady customers

2. My Son

1. fifteen years old
2. likes to be alone

My Daughter

_4_ good at making minor household repairs
_2_ likes to be with friends

3. reads a lot   _3_ doesn't like to read

4. is an excellent cook   _5_ expects to attend a technical college

5. wants to go to chef school   _1_ seventeen years old

3. Job A   **Job B**

1. good salary   _3_ three-week vacation

2. office within walking distance   _4_ work on a team with others

3. two-week vacation   _2_ one-hour bus ride to office

4. work alone   _6_ health insurance

5. lots of overtime   _5_ no overtime

6. no health insurance   _1_ good salary

PRACTICE 4

Here are five topics for either contrast or comparison paragraphs. Compose two topic sentences for each topic, one for a possible contrast paragraph and one for a possible comparison paragraph. *Answers will vary.*

Topic	Topic Sentences
EXAMPLE Two members of my family	A. My brother and sister have different attitudes toward exercise.
	B. My parents are alike in that they're easygoing.
1. Two friends or coworkers	A. Tom Bogyo and Amanda Gill have very different attitudes toward success.
	B. Although Sylvia and Miako excel at different sports, both are talented athletes.
2. Two kinds of music or dancing	A. Jazz and classical music are performed in very different ways.
	B. Appalachian folk songs and

126 UNIT 3 Developing the Paragraph

                                                                                             Protestant hymns have several common features.

3. You as a child and you as an adult   A. *I am less selfish than I was as a child.*

                                                                                            B. *As an adult, I have some of the same dislikes I had as a child.*

4. Two vacations   A. *Some people like to relax on vacation, but others like to spend most of their time sightseeing.*

                                                                                            B. *My vacations in both Barbados and Sun Valley included miles of walking.*

5. Two teachers   A. *Mr. Larkin tends to be friendly toward his students while Mr. Jordan is a bit standoffish.*

                                                                                            B. *Professors Hazard and Jodice, as a rule, involve their classes in lively discussions.*

PRACTICE 5

Here are four topic sentences for comparison or contrast paragraphs. For each topic sentence, think of one supporting point of comparison or contrast and explain that point in one or two sentences. *Answers will vary.*

1. When it comes to movies (TV shows, books, entertainment), Demetrios and Arlene have totally different tastes.

   Demetrios loves action and violence whereas Arlene will leave the theater at the first sight of blood on the screen.

2. The average bowl of chili and my family's Texas chili have little in common besides beans.

CHAPTER 10 Comparison and Contrast   127

The average chili is pleasantly spicy whereas my family's chili will make you cry and will clear your sinuses for a week.

3. Although there are obvious differences, the two neighborhoods (blocks, homes) have much in common.

   The large house has an extensive and beautiful garden. The smaller house also has a garden, less extensive but equally colorful.

4. Paying taxes is like having a tooth pulled.*

   Both are painful. It hurts to write that tax check and to have that tooth pulled. But by doing both, we avoid worse pain in the future.

PRACTICE 6

Now choose one of the topic sentences you wrote in Practice 4, or write a new topic sentence. Develop three or four points of comparison or contrast to support your topic sentence, and make a plan for the paragraph, numbering points in the order you wish to present them.

WRITING ASSIGNMENT 1

Study this photograph of a sunbather at the Indiana Dunes National Lakeshore. Then write a paragraph *contrasting* the man and his rather unusual surroundings.

---

*For more work on this kind of comparison, see Chapter 21, "Revising for Language Awareness," Part D.

Notice the man's posture, clothing, and apparent mood. How do these differ from the scene on the dunes behind him? In your topic sentence, state your overall impression. Then support this main idea with details. Remember to conclude your paragraph; don't just stop abruptly.

✓ CHECKLIST: The Process of Writing a Contrast or Comparison Paragraph

Refer to this checklist of steps as you write a contrast or comparison paragraph of your own.

    1. Narrow the topic in light of your audience and purpose.

    2. Compose a topic sentence that clearly states that a contrast or a comparison will follow.

    3. Freewrite or brainstorm to generate as many points of contrast or comparison as you can think of. (You may want to freewrite or brainstorm before you narrow the topic.)

    4. Choose the points you will use, and drop any details that are not really part of the contrast or the comparison.

    5. List parallel points of contrast or of comparison for both *A* and *B*.

    6. Make a plan or an outline, numbering all the points of contrast or comparison in the order in which you will present them in the paragraph.

    7. Write a draft of your contrast or comparison paragraph, using transitional expressions that stress either differences or similarities.

    8. Revise as necessary, checking for support, unity, logic, and coherence.

    9. Proofread for errors in grammar, punctuation, sentence structure, spelling, and mechanics.

Suggested Topics for Contrast or Comparison Paragraphs

1. Compare or contrast two attitudes toward money (the spendthrift and the miser) or marriage (the confirmed single and the committed partner).
2. Compare or contrast two young children parented in different ways.
3. Compare or contrast a job you hated and a job you loved.
4. Compare or contrast two athletes in the same sport.
5. Compare or contrast the same scene at two times of day.
6. Compare or contrast two high schools or colleges that you have attended (perhaps one in the United States and one in a different country).
7. Compare or contrast two ways to treat a cold, flu, or headache—Western medicine and some alternative.

8. Compare or contrast your *expectations* of a person, place, or situation and *reality*.

9. Compare or contrast your best friend and your spouse or partner.

10. Writer's choice: _____

PART B The Comparison-Contrast Paragraph

Sometimes an assignment will call for you to write a paragraph that both compares and contrasts, one that stresses both similarities and differences.

Here is a comparison-contrast paragraph:

> Although contemporary fans would find the game played by the Knickerbockers—the first organized baseball club—similar to modern baseball, they would also note some startling differences. In 1845, as now, the four bases of the playing field were set in a diamond shape, ninety feet from one another. Nine players took the field. The object of the game was to score points by hitting a pitched ball and running around the bases. The teams changed sides after three outs. However, the earlier game was also different. The umpire sat at a table along the third base line instead of standing behind home plate. Unlike the modern game, the players wore no gloves. Rather than firing the ball over the plate at ninety miles an hour, the pitcher gently tossed it underhand to the batter. Since there were no balls and strikes, the batter could wait for the pitch he wanted. The game ended, not when nine innings were completed, but when one team scored twenty-one runs, which were called "aces."

■ How are the Knickerbockers' game and modern baseball similar?

Both have four bases ninety feet apart in a diamond shape, nine players; both score points by runs; both have three outs.

■ How are these two versions of the game different? *In Knickerbockers' game, umpire sat at a table on third base line, players wore no gloves, pitcher gently tossed the ball, there were no balls and strikes, a team needed twenty-one "aces" to win, and there were no innings. In modern game, umpire stands at home plate, pitcher fires the ball, there are balls and strikes, team with the most runs wins, and game is composed of nine innings.*

- What transitional expressions in the paragraph emphasize similarities and differences? _although, as now, however, unlike, rather than, not when, but when_

Before composing this comparison-contrast paragraph, the writer probably brainstormed or freewrote to gather ideas and then made a plan like this:

Topic sentence: Although contemporary fans would find the game played by the Knickerbockers—the first organized baseball club—similar to modern baseball, they would also note some startling differences.

Comparisons	Knickerbockers	Modern Game
Point 1	four bases, ninety feet apart, in diamond shape	
Point 2	nine players	
Point 3	scoring points	
Point 4	three outs	

Contrasts	Knickerbockers	Modern Game
Point 1	umpire sat at third base line	umpire at home plate
Point 2	no gloves	gloves
Point 3	pitcher gently tossed ball	pitcher fires ball at plate
Point 4	no balls and strikes	balls and strikes
Point 5	twenty-one "aces" to win, no innings	most runs to win, nine innings

- A plan such as this makes it easier for the writer to organize a great deal of material.
- The writer begins by listing all the points of comparison—how the Knickerbockers' game and modern baseball are similar. Then the writer lists all the points of contrast—how they are different.

PRACTICE 7

Here is a somewhat longer comparison and contrast (two paragraphs). Read it carefully and answer the questions.

No meal eaten in the Middle East ends without coffee or tea, but coffee takes precedence most of the time. Coffee is a social beverage, offered to guests by housewives and to customers by merchants; to refuse it borders upon insult.

There are two distinct but similar ways of preparing it, Turkish and Arabic. Both are served black, in cups the size of a demitasse or smaller. And both are brewed by starting with green beans, roasting them to a chocolate brown color, pulverizing them at once, either with mortar and pestle or in a handsome cylindrical coffee mill of chased brass, and quickly steeping them in boiling water.

The Turkish version is made in a coffee pot that has a long handle to protect the fingers from the fire and a shape narrowing from the bottom to the open neck to intensify the foaming action as the coffee boils up. Water, sugar and coffee are stirred together to your taste; then, at the first bubbling surge, the pot is whisked from the fire. It is returned briefly one or two more times to build up the foamy head, which is poured into each cup in equal amounts, to be followed by the rest of the brew, grounds and all. The dregs soon settle to the bottom, and the rich, brown coffee that covers them is ready to be enjoyed, with more sugar if you like. The Arabs prepare coffee in a single boil; they almost never use sugar; they pour the liquid into a second pot, leaving the sediment in the first, and then add such heady spices as cloves or cardamon seeds.

—*Foods of the World/Middle Eastern Cooking,*
Time-Life Books

1. What two things does this writer contrast and compare? *The writer contrasts and compares the Turkish and the Arabic methods of preparing coffee.*

2. What words indicate that both contrast *and* comparison will follow?
distinct but similar

3. How are Arabic and Turkish coffee similar? *Both are served black in small cups; both start with green beans that are roasted dark brown and then immediately ground and steeped in boiling water.*

4. How are Arabic and Turkish coffee different? *Turkish coffee is boiled several times and is served with sugar and the dregs in the cup. Arabic coffee is boiled once and served with spices rather than sugar and grounds.*

5. On a separate sheet of paper, make a plan or an outline for these paragraphs.

WRITING ASSIGNMENT 2

On this page and the next are photos of two couples. Study closely the details of facial expression, gesture, clothing, and so forth. For a paragraph that both *compares and contrasts* the two couples, jot down possible similarities and differences. Ask yourself, "What is my impression of each pair? How do they seem to be getting along with each other? How are the couples alike and how are they different?" Then plan and write your paragraph.

If you prefer, write a paragraph comparing and contrasting the two women *or* the two men.

✔ WORKING THROUGH THE COMPARISON-CONTRAST PARAGRAPH

You can work through the comparison-contrast paragraph in the same way that you do a comparison or a contrast paragraph. Follow the steps in the earlier checklist, but make certain that your paragraph shows both similarities and differences.

Suggested Topics for Comparison-Contrast Paragraphs

1. Compare and contrast two ways to prepare for an examination.
2. Compare and contrast the requirements for two jobs or careers.
3. Compare and contrast your life now with your life five years ago.
4. Compare and contrast two films on similar subjects.
5. Compare and contrast learning something from experience and learning something from books.
6. Compare and contrast two singers or musicians.
7. Compare and contrast parties, weddings, or funerals in two different cultures.
8. Compare and contrast two popular television programs of the same type (newscasts, situation comedies, talk shows, and so on).
9. Compare and contrast two attitudes toward one subject (firearms, education, immigration, welfare, and so forth).
10. Writer's choice: _____

CHAPTER 11

Classification

To **classify** is to gather into types, kinds, or categories according to a single basis of division.

Mailroom personnel, for example, might separate incoming mail into four piles: orders, bills, payments, and inquiries. Once the mail has been divided in this manner—according to which department should receive each pile—it can be efficiently delivered.

The same information can be classified in more than one way. The Census Bureau collects a variety of data about the people living in the United States. One way to classify the data is by age group—the number of people under eighteen, between eighteen and fifty-five, over fifty-five, and over seventy. Such information might be useful in developing programs for college-bound youth or for the elderly. Other ways of dividing the population are by geographic location, occupation, family size, level of education, and so on.

Whether you classify rocks by their origin for a geology course or children by their stages of growth for a psychology course, you will be organizing large groups into smaller, more manageable units that can be explained to your reader.

Topic Sentence

Here is the topic sentence for a classification paragraph:

> Gym-goers can be classified according to their priorities at the gym as sweaty fanatics, fashionites, busybodies, or fit normals.

- The writer begins a classification paragraph with a topic sentence that clearly states what group of people or things will be classified.
- What group of people will be classified? *gym-goers*
- Into how many categories will they be divided? What are the categories?

  four: sweaty fanatics, fashionites, busybodies, and fit normals

134

Paragraph and Plan

Here is the entire paragraph:

> Gym-goers can be classified according to their priorities at the gym as sweaty fanatics, fashionites, busybodies, and fit normals. Sweaty fanatics take gym-going to the extreme. They hog the machines, drip sweat everywhere, and barely look up if someone falls off the treadmill beside them. Occasionally, they will stare at the mirror, admiring the muscle group they are working on. The fashionites also admire their own reflections, but they barely break a sweat. For them, the gym is just another excuse to buy clothes. They wear perfectly matched workout clothes with color-coordinated sweat bands and gym shoes. The third group, the busybodies, can't stop talking. Whether it's making idle chitchat or correcting another exerciser's form on a machine, they seem unable to shut up. Not even headphones and one-word answers can stop the busybodies from babbling. Luckily, the fit normals keep things from getting too far out of control. They come to the gym to work out, stay healthy, and go home, but they remember that basic good manners apply in every setting.
>
> —Laurie Zamot (Student)

- On what basis does the writer classify gym-goers?   *their priorities at the gym*

- What information does the writer provide about the first type, sweaty fanatics?
  They hog machines, drip sweat, and don't notice anyone but themselves.

- What information does the writer provide about the second type, fashionites?
  They admire themselves, barely sweat, come to show off their outfits.

- What information does the writer provide about the third type, busybodies?
  They can't stop talking, even when others wear headphones and grunt.

- What information does the writer provide about the fourth type, the fit normals?   *They balance things by working out but not forgetting good manners.*

- Why do you think the writer discusses fit normals last?   *The writer starts with crazier and funnier types; the normals keep them all from going out of control.*

Before composing the paragraph, the writer probably brainstormed or free-wrote to gather ideas and then made a plan like this:

Topic sentence: Gym-goers can be classified according to their priorities at the gym as sweaty fanatics, fashionites, busybodies, or fit normals.

Type 1:   Sweaty fanatics
—hog machines; drip sweat
—barely look if someone falls
—stare in mirror, admiring muscles

Type 2:   Fashionites
—admire themselves but don't sweat
—excuse to buy clothes
—matched workout clothes
—coordinating sweat bands and gym shoes

Type 3:   Busybodies
—can't stop talking, advising
—headphones, short answers don't work

Type 4:   Fit normals
—keep things from going out of control
—work out, go home
—remember good manners even in gym

■ Note that the body of the paragraph discusses all four types of gym-goers mentioned in the topic sentence and does not add any new ones.

This classification paragraph sticks to a single method of classification: *the priorities of gym-goers at the gym*. If the paragraph had also discussed a fourth category—*left-handed gym-goers*—the initial basis of classification would fall apart because *left-handedness* has nothing to do with *the priorities of different gym-goers*.

The topic sentence of a classification paragraph usually has two parts: the *topic* and the *basis of classification*. The basis of classification is the controlling idea: it *controls* how the writer will approach the topic. Stating it in writing will help keep the paragraph on track.

There is no set rule about which category to present first, second, or last in a classification paragraph. However, the paragraph should follow some kind of **logical sequence** from the most to least outrageous, least to most expensive, from the largest to the smallest category, and so on.*

Transitional Expressions

Transitional expressions in classification paragraphs stress divisions and categories:

---

* For more work on order, see Chapter 4, "Achieving Coherence," Part A. For a complete essay developed by classification, see "The Potato Scale," Chapter 15, Part G.

Transitional Expressions for Classification	
can be divided	the first type
can be classified	the second kind
can be categorized	the last category

PRACTICE 1

Read the following paragraph carefully and answer the questions.

    Judges can be divided, on the basis of their written opinions, into three categories: conservative, liberal, and centrist. Although all judges respect the law, conservative judges have an especially strong belief in the importance of the law and the history surrounding it. They believe that real justice comes only from strictly applying the law to the facts of a case, whether or not the outcome seems fair to an individual. On the other hand, liberal judges look beyond a rigid reading to the "spirit of the law" in their search for real justice in a case. They might broadly interpret the law in order to champion individual rights. The outcome of the case matters more to them than the letter of the law. Finally, centrist judges walk the middle ground between conservative and liberal. They do not apply the law as rigidly as conservative judges, yet they are not as willing as liberal judges to apply the law loosely. Having different types of judges helps balance our legal system; their differing views help protect both the law and individual rights.

1. How many categories are there, and what are they?

    three; conservative, liberal, and centrist judges

2. On what basis does the writer classify judges?

    their written opinions

3. Make a plan of the paragraph on a separate sheet of paper.

PRACTICE 2

Each group of things or persons on the following page has been divided according to a single basis of classification. However, one item in each group does not belong—it does not fit that single basis of classification.
    Read each group of items carefully; then circle the letter of the one item that does *not* belong. Next write the single basis of classification that includes the rest of the group.

EXAMPLE Shirts
- a. cotton
- b. suede
- ⓒ short-sleeved
- d. polyester

material they are made of

1. Shoes
   - a. flat heels
   - b. 2-inch heels
   - ⓒ patent leather heels
   - d. 3-inch heels

   height of heels

2. Beds
   - a. double
   - b. twin
   - ⓒ feather
   - d. king

   size

3. Students
   - ⓐ talkative in class
   - b. very hard working
   - c. goof-offs
   - d. moderately hard working

   how hard they work

4. Contact lenses
   - ⓐ soft
   - b. green
   - c. brown
   - d. lavender

   color

5. Apartments
   - a. two-bedroom
   - b. three-bedroom
   - ⓒ penthouse
   - d. studio apartment

   number of bedrooms

6. Dates
   - ⓐ very good-looking
   - b. sometimes pay
   - c. always pay
   - d. expect me to pay

   financial arrangements

7. Milk
   - a. 2 percent fat
   - b. whole
   - ⓒ chocolate
   - d. 1 percent fat

   amount of fat

8. Drivers
   - a. obey the speed limit
   - ⓑ teenage drivers
   - c. speeders
   - d. creepers

   how fast they drive

PRACTICE 3

Any group of persons, things, or ideas can be classified in more than one way, depending on the basis of classification. For instance, students in your class can be classified on the basis of height (short, average, tall) or on the basis of class participation (often participate, sometimes participate, never participate). Both of these groupings are valid classifications of the same group of people.

Think of two ways in which each of the following groups could be classified.

CHAPTER 11 Classification

Answers will vary.

EXAMPLE

Group		Basis of Classification
Bosses	(A)	how demanding they are
	(B)	how generous they are
1. Members of my family	(A)	how old they are
	(B)	how emotional they are
2. Hurricanes	(A)	how much damage they do in dollars
	(B)	how strong the winds are
3. Fans of a certain sport	(A)	how many games they attend
	(B)	how long they have been fans
4. Vacations	(A)	how much activity they involve
	(B)	how expensive they are
5. Fitness magazines	(A)	how much nutrition is covered
	(B)	how they seem to define fitness

PRACTICE 4

Listed below are three groups of people or things. Decide on a single basis of classification for each group and the categories that would develop from your basis of classification. Finally, write a topic sentence for each of your classifications. *Answers will vary.*

EXAMPLE

Group	Basis of Classification	Categories
Professors at Pell College	methods of instruction	1. lectures
		2. class discussions
		3. both

Topic Sentence: Professors at Pell College can be classified according to their methods of instruction: those who lecture, those who encourage class discussion, and those who do both.

UNIT 3 Developing the Paragraph

Group	Basis of Classification	Categories
1. Car owners	how clean they keep their cars	very neat
		moderately neat
		not neat at all

Topic sentence: Most car owners can be classified according to how clean they keep their vehicles: those whose cars are very neat, those whose cars are moderately neat, and those whose cars are not neat at all.

2. Credit-card users	how much they use their cards	use only in emergencies
		use in moderation
		charge themselves into debt and into trouble

Topic sentence: Credit-card users fall into three categories: those who use their cards only in emergencies, those who use their cards in moderation, and those who charge themselves into debt and into trouble.

3. Ways of reacting to crisis	how much emotion shown	people who cry or yell
		people who talk calmly
		people who don't talk at all

Topic sentence: People react to crises in very different ways: by crying or yelling, by talking calmly, or by remaining completely silent.

PRACTICE 5

Now choose the classification in Practice 4 that most interests you and make a plan or outline for a paragraph on a separate sheet of paper. As you work, make sure that you have listed all possible categories for your basis of classification. Remember, every car owner or credit card user should fit into one of your categories. Finally, write your paragraph, describing each category briefly and perhaps giving an example of each.

PRACTICE 6

In a group of four or five classmates, choose one of these topics:

> friends
> restaurants (or food sources) on or near campus
> places to study

Now discuss various ways in which you could classify the members of this group; list at least ten ways. For example, you could classify *friends* on the basis of their generosity, loyalty, or supportiveness. Now, from your list, choose the classification that most interests your group and make a plan for a paragraph. Write down a clear *basis of classification* and three to five possible *categories or groups* based on that classification; make sure your categories include every person or place in the larger group. Your instructor may want each group to explain its classification plan to the whole class.

Next, each group member can write a paragraph based on the plan. As you draft and revise, adjust your topic sentence and categories, and refer to the checklist.

✔ CHECKLIST: The Process of Writing a Classification Paragraph

Refer to this checklist of steps as you write a classification paragraph.

____ 1. Narrow the topic in light of your audience and purpose. Think in terms of a group of people or things that can be classified easily into types or categories.

____ 2. Decide on a single basis of classification. This basis will depend on what information you wish to give your audience.

____ 3. Compose a topic sentence that clearly shows what you are dividing into categories or types. If you wish, your topic sentence can state the basis on which you are making the classification and the types that will be discussed in the paragraph.

____ 4. List the categories into which the group is being classified. Be sure that your categories cover all the possibilities. Do not add any new categories that are not logically part of your original basis of classification.

_____ 5. Freewrite, cluster, or brainstorm to generate information, details, and examples for each of the categories. (You may want to prewrite before you narrow the topic.)

_____ 6. Select the best details and examples, and drop those that are not relevant to your classification.

_____ 7. Make a plan or an outline for your paragraph, numbering the categories in the order in which you will present them.

_____ 8. Write a draft of your classification paragraph, using transitional expressions wherever they may be helpful.

_____ 9. Revise as necessary, checking for support, unity, logic, and coherence.

_____ 10. Proofread for errors in grammar, punctuation, sentence structure, spelling, and mechanics.

Suggested Topics for Classification Paragraphs

1. People waiting in a line
2. Jobs
3. Women or men you date
4. Clothing in your closet
5. Friends
6. Students in a particular class
7. Problems facing college freshmen or someone new to a job
8. College classes or instructors
9. Ways to prevent school violence
10. Neighbors or coworkers
11. Kinds of success
12. Performers of one type of music
13. Kinds of marriages
14. Brands of jeans, backpacks, cola drinks, or some other product
15. Writer's choice: _____

CHAPTER 12

Cause and Effect

The ability to think through **causes and effects** is a key to success in many college courses, jobs, and everyday situations. Daily we puzzle over the **causes** of, or reasons for, events: What caused one brother to drop out of school and another to succeed brilliantly? What causes Jenine's asthma attacks? Why did the stock market plunge 300 points?

Effects are the *results* of a cause or causes. Does playing violent computer games affect a child's behavior? What are the effects of being a twin, keeping a secret, or winning the lottery?

Most events worth examining have complex, not simple, causes and effects. That is, they may have several causes and several effects. Certainly, in many fields, questions of cause and effect challenge even the experts: *What will be the long-term effects of the breakup of the former Soviet Union? What causes the HIV virus to disappear from the blood of some infected babies?* (This one answer could help save millions of lives.)

Topic Sentence

Here is the topic statement of a cause and effect paragraph; the writer has chosen to break the information into two sentences.

> What killed off the dinosaurs—and 70 percent of life on earth—65 million years ago? According to recent research, this massive destruction had three causes.

■ The writer begins a cause and effect paragraph by clearly stating the subject and indicating whether causes or effects will be discussed. What is the subject of this paragraph? Will causes or effects be the focus? _what killed the dinosaurs, causes_

143

- The writer states the topic in two sentences rather than one. Is this effective? Why or why not? (A single sentence might read, "According to recent research, the massive destruction of dinosaurs and other creatures 65 million years ago had three causes.") *Starting with a question sparks the reader's interest.*

- Words like *causes, reasons,* and *factors* are useful to show causes. Words like *effects, results,* and *consequences* are useful to show effects.

Paragraph and Plan

Here is the entire paragraph:

> What killed off the dinosaurs—and 70 percent of life on earth—65 million years ago? According to recent research, this massive destruction had three causes. Dr. Peter Ward of the University of Washington reports that the first cause was simple "background extinction." This is the normal disappearance of some animals and plants that goes on all the time. Second, a drop in sea level during this period slowly destroyed about 25 percent more of the world's species. Last and most dramatic, a comet as big as Manhattan smashed into the earth near Mexico's Yucatan peninsula, literally shaking the world. The huge buried crater left by this comet was found in 1991. Now Dr. Ward has proved that ash and a rare metal from that fiery crash fell around the globe. This means that the impact, fires, smoke, and ash quickly wiped out the dinosaurs and much of life on earth. This great "die-off" cleared the way for mammals to dominate the earth.

- How many causes does this writer give for the destruction of the dinosaurs and other species? What are they? *three: background extinction; drop in sea level; huge comet*

- Did the writer make up these ideas? If not, who or what is the source of the information? *no; Dr. Peter Ward, University of Washington*

- What transitional words introduce each of the three causes? *the first cause; second; last and most dramatic*

- What kind of order is used in this paragraph?* *order of importance*

Before writing the paragraph, the writer probably jotted a plan like this:

Topic sentence: According to recent research, this massive destruction had three causes.

—write a catchy introductory sentence?

—mention time, 65 million years ago

---

* For more work on order, see Chapter 4, "Achieving Coherence," Part A.

Cause 1:	"background extinction"
	—normal disappearance of animals and plants
	—give credit to Dr. Ward
Cause 2:	drop in sea level
	—25 percent more species destroyed
Cause 3:	giant comet hit earth
	—big as Manhattan
	—crater found in 1991 near Yucatan peninsula
	—now Ward proves ash and rare metal circled globe
	—this comet destroyed dinosaurs and others
Conclusion:	"die-off" cleared way for mammals
	—OR tie to current news and films about comet danger

Other paragraphs examine *effects*, not causes. Either they try to predict future effects of something happening now, or they analyze past effects of something that happened earlier, as does this paragraph:

> For Christy Haubegger, the lack of Latina role models had life-changing consequences. As a Mexican-American girl adopted by Anglo parents, Christy found no reflection of herself in teen magazines or books. One result of seeing mostly blonde, blue-eyed models was an increase in her adolescent insecurities. A more damaging effect was Christy's confusion as she wondered what career to pursue; there were no Hispanic role models in schoolbooks to suggest possible futures for this excellent student. Even at Stanford Law School, Christy and her friends missed the inspiration and encouragement of professional Latina role models. At Stanford, Christy began to see this problem as an opportunity. She decided to start a national magazine that would showcase talented and successful Latinas. The 27-year-old made a detailed business plan and, incredibly, won the financial backing of the CEO of *Essence* magazine. In 1996, the first issue of *Latina* hit the newstands—the very positive consequence of an old loneliness.

- Underline the topic sentence in this paragraph.

- For Ms. Haubegger, the lack of Latina role models caused "life-changing consequences." What effects are discussed? *increased adolescent insecurities; no professional role models; her decision to start* Latina *magazine*

- What order does the writer follow? *time order*

- Notice that the paragraph first discusses negative effects and then a positive one.

Before you write about causes or effects, do some mental detective work. First, search out the three most important causes or effects. For example, if you are trying to understand the causes of a friend's skiing accident, you might consider the snow conditions that day, whether he took unnecessary risks, and whether he had been drinking.

Causes	Effect	Further Effects
ice on the ski slope		can't drive
J. took steep course	→ J. breaks his leg →	can't play sports
had two beers		decides to read more

In exploring the effects of something, consider both short-term and long-term effects and both negative and positive effects. (Although Jay could *not* do many things, perhaps he took advantage of his recovery time to read more or to learn a new computer program.)

Avoiding Problems in Cause and Effect Writing

1. **Do not oversimplify.** Avoid the trap of naming one cause for a complex problem: *Why did they divorce? Because she is a hothead.* Or *The reason that reading scores have fallen in the school is television.* Searching for the three most important causes or effects is a good way to avoid oversimplifying.

2. **Do not confuse time order with causation.** If your eye starts watering seconds after the doorbell rings, you cannot assume that the doorbell made your eye water. Were you peeling onions? Is it allergy season? Do you need to wet your contact lenses?

3. **Do not confuse causes and effects.** This sounds obvious, but separating causes and effects can be tricky. (Is Rita's positive attitude the cause of her success in sales or the result of it?)

Transitional Expressions

These transitional expressions are helpful in cause and effect paragraphs, which often imply order of importance or time order:*

Transitional Expressions	
To Show Causes	**To Show Effects**
the first cause (second, third)	one important effect
the first reason (second, third)	another result
yet another factor	a third outcome
because	as a result
is caused by	consequently
results from	then, next, therefore, thus, so

---

*To read an essay of cause and effect, see "Why I Stayed and Stayed," Chapter 15, Part H.

PRACTICE 1

Read this paragraph and answer the questions.

Sadly, this college is part of a national trend: Date rape is on the rise. <u>To stop date rape, college administrators and students must understand and deal with its possible causes.</u> First, some fraternities and male peer groups on campus promote an attitude of disrespect toward women. This mentality sets the stage for date rape. Second, alcohol and drugs erode good judgment and self-control. The kegs, barrels, and bags consumed at many parties here put students at risk, including the risk of date rape. A third cause of date rape is miscommunication between men and women. Men and women often have different ideas of what date rape is or even if it exists. We need campus workshops in which we can discuss this issue openly and come to some understanding between the sexes. Date rape is a serious problem that can ruin lives. We can make a difference by addressing the causes of date rape: the male mentality of disrespect, heavy campus use of alcohol and drugs, and the differing views of men and women.

—Michael White Moon (Student)

1. Underline the topic sentence. Does this paragraph discuss the causes or effects of date rape? _causes_

2. Do you agree with this student's analysis of the problem? Would you name other causes, and if so, which? _Answers will vary._

3. On a separate sheet of paper, make a plan of this paragraph.

4. Does Mr. White Moon discuss the three causes in a logical order? Why or why not? _yes, causes are "layered": disrespectful attitudes set the scene; alcohol erodes judgment; lack of communication is the final factor_

PRACTICE 2

To practice separating cause from effect, write the cause and the effect contained in each item below.

EXAMPLE Fewer people are attending concerts at the Boxcar Theater because ticket prices have nearly doubled.

Cause: _ticket prices nearly doubled_

Effect: _fewer people attending concerts_

1. A thunderstorm was approaching, so we moved our picnic into the van.

   Cause: _thunderstorm approaching_

   Effect: _picnic in the van_

2. Seeing my father suffer because he could not read motivated me to excel in school.

   Cause: saw my father suffer because he could not read

   Effect: I excelled in school.

3. One study showed that laughter extended the lives of cancer patients.

   Cause: laughter

   Effect: extended lives of cancer patients

4. Americans are having fewer children and doing so later in life. Some experts believe this is why they are spending more money every year on their pets.

   Cause: Americans having fewer children later

   Effect: spending more money on pets

5. According to Celtics coach Rick Pitino, what turns talent into greatness is hard work.

   Cause: hard work

   Effect: Talent becomes greatness.

6. Many doctors urged that trampolines be banned because of an "epidemic" of injuries to children playing on them.

   Cause: children playing on trampolines

   Effect: epidemic of injuries

7. I bought this glow-in-the-dark fish lamp for one reason only: it was on sale.

   Cause: lamp was on sale

   Effect: I bought it.

8. As more people spend time surfing the Internet, television viewing is declining for the first time in fifty years.

   Cause: more people surfing the Internet

   Effect: first decline in TV viewing in fifty years

9. Wild animals in South African game parks can bring in millions of tourist dollars; consequently, the government is trying to save many species.

   Cause: wild animals bringing in millions from tourists

   Effect: government of South Africa trying to save many species

10. For years, Charboro cigarettes outsold all competitors as a result of added ammonia. This ammonia gave smokers' brains an extra "kick."

Cause: *Charboro added ammonia.*

First effect: *Smokers got an extra kick.*

Second effect: *Charboro outsold all competitors.*

PRACTICE 3

List three causes *or* three effects to support each topic sentence below. First, read the topic sentence to see whether causes or effects are called for. Then think, jot, and list your three best ideas. *Answers will vary.*

1. The huge success of Barbie (or some other toy, game, or product) has a number of causes. _____

2. There are several reasons why AIDS continues to spread among teenagers, despite widespread knowledge about the deadly nature of the disease. _____

3. Reading books by authors of many nationalities, instead of just American and English authors, has many positive (or negative) effects on American students. _____

PRACTICE 4

Now choose one topic from Practice 3 that interests you and write a paragraph of cause or effect on notebook paper. Before you write a draft, think and make a plan. Have you chosen the three most important causes or effects and decided on an effective order in which to present them? As you write, use transitional expressions to help the reader follow your ideas.

PRACTICE 5

In a group of four or five classmates, read this passage aloud. Then follow the directions below.

Creative risk takers are often high achievers who tend to start their own businesses or become leaders in some other way. Researchers have identified two different types of home environments that tend to produce creative risk takers: (1) "high expectation families" who enthusiastically support the child and expect great things from him or her and (2) very poor, alcoholic, or broken homes where the child receives almost no support and few positive expectations.

Your group should analyze possible reasons why households of the *second* type tend to produce creative risk takers. Write down your three best reasons. Your instructor might wish to have you report your theories to the class.

✔ CHECKLIST: The Process of Writing a Cause and Effect Paragraph

Refer to this checklist as you write a cause and effect paragraph.

—— 1. Narrow the topic in light of your audience and purpose. Think of a subject that can be analyzed for clear causes or effects.

—— 2. Decide whether you will emphasize causes or effects. What information would be most interesting to your audience?

—— 3. Compose a topic sentence that states the subject and indicates whether causes or effects will be discussed.

—— 4. Now freewrite, brainstorm, or cluster to find at least three possible causes or effects. Do your mental detective work. At this stage, think of all possible causes; think of short- and long-term effects, as well as positive and negative effects.

—— 5. Select the best causes or effects with which to develop your paragraph. Drop those that are not relevant.

—— 6. Make a plan or an outline for your paragraph, numbering the causes or effects in the order in which you will present them.

—— 7. Write a first draft of your cause and effect paragraph, explaining each point fully so that your reader understands just how *X* caused *Y*. Use transitional expressions to emphasize these relationships.

—— 8. Revise as necessary, checking for good support, unity, logic, and coherence. Does your paragraph have an interesting opening sentence?

_____ 9. Proofread for errors in grammar, punctuation, sentence structure, spelling, and mechanics. Especially watch for your personal error patterns.

Suggested Topics for Cause and Effect Paragraphs

1. Reasons why someone made an important decision
2. Reasons why some people cheat in college
3. Causes of an act of courage or cowardice
4. Causes of a marriage or divorce (friendship or end of a friendship)
5. Reasons for doing volunteer work
6. Causes or effects of membership in a group (choir, band, sports team, church, or gang)
7. Causes or effects of dropping out of school (or attending college)
8. Effects of e-mail or a computer on a person's life
9. Effects of having a certain boss (or teacher, parent, or leader)
10. Effects of a superstition or prejudice
11. Effects of the death of a loved one
12. Effects (positive or negative) of a habit or practice
13. Effects of living in a repressive country or home
14. Effects of living in a rural (or urban, mountainous, flat, rich, poor, or ethnically diverse) place
15. Writer's choice: _____

CHAPTER 13

Persuasion

To persuade is to convince someone that a particular opinion or point of view is the correct one.

Any time you argue with a friend, you are each trying to persuade, to convince, the other that your opinion is the right one. Commercials on television are another form of persuasion. Advertisers attempt to convince viewers that the product they sell—whether a deodorant, a soft drink, or an automobile—is the best one to purchase.

You will often have to persuade in writing. For instance, if you want a raise, you will have to write a persuasive memo to convince your employer that you deserve one. You will have to back up, or support, your request with proof, listing important projects you have completed, noting new responsibilities you have taken upon yourself, or showing how you have increased sales.

Once you learn how to persuade logically and rationally, you will be less likely to accept the false, misleading, and emotional arguments that you hear and read every day. Persuasion is vital in daily life, in nearly all college courses, and in most careers.

Topic Sentence

Here is the topic sentence of a persuasive paragraph:

> Passengers should refuse to ride in any vehicle driven by someone who has been drinking.

- The writer begins a persuasive paragraph by stating clearly what he or she is arguing for or against. What will this persuasive paragraph argue against?

    This paragraph will argue against riding with a driver who has been drinking.

- Words like *should*, *ought*, and *must* (and the negatives *should not*, *ought not*, and *must not*) are especially effective in the topic sentence of a persuasive paragraph.

152

Paragraph and Plan

Here is the entire paragraph:

> Passengers should refuse to ride in any vehicle driven by someone who has been drinking. First and most important, such a refusal could save lives. The National Council on Alcoholism reports that drunk driving causes 25,000 deaths and 50 percent of all traffic accidents each year. Not only the drivers but the passengers who agree to travel with them are responsible. Second, riders might tell themselves that some people drive well even after a few drinks, but this is just not true. Dr. Burton Belloc of the local Alcoholism Treatment Center explains that even one drink can lengthen the reflex time and weaken the judgment needed for safe driving. Other riders might feel foolish to ruin a social occasion or inconvenience themselves or others by speaking up, but risking their lives is even more foolish. Finally, by refusing to ride with a drinker, one passenger could influence other passengers or the driver. Marie Furillo, a student at Central High School, is an example. When three friends who had obviously been drinking offered her a ride home from school, she refused, despite the driver's teasing. Hearing Marie's refusal, two of her friends got out of the car. Until the laws are changed and a vast re-education takes place, the bloodshed on American highways will probably continue. But there is one thing people can do: They can refuse to risk their lives for the sake of a party.

- The first reason in the argument **predicts the consequence.** If passengers refuse to ride with drinkers, what will the consequence be?

    Lives could be saved.

- The writer also supports this reason with **facts.** What are the facts?

    Drunk driving causes 25,000 deaths and 50 percent of all traffic accidents each year.

- The second reason in the argument is really an **answer to the opposition.** That is, the writer anticipates the critics. What point is the writer answering?

    The writer is answering the point that some people believe they drive well even after having a few drinks.

- The writer supports this reason by **referring to an authority.** That is, the writer gives the opinion of someone who can provide unbiased and valuable information about the subject. Who is the authority and what does this person say?

    Dr. Burton Belloc of the Alcoholism Treatment Center notes that even one drink affects a driver's reflexes.

- The third reason in the argument is that risking your life is foolish. This reason is really another **answer to the opposition.** What point is the writer answering?

    The writer is answering the point that people hesitate to be "party poopers."

- The final reason in the argument is that one passenger could influence others. What **example** does the writer supply to back up this reason?

  Marie Furillo refused a ride home from school because the driver had been drinking. Her refusal influenced the two passengers to get out of the car.

- Persuasive paragraphs either can begin with the most important reason and then continue with less important ones, or they can begin with the least important reasons, saving the most important for last.* This paragraph begins with what the author considers *most* important. How can you tell?

  The writer states that the first point is the most important.

Before composing this persuasive paragraph, the writer probably brainstormed or freewrote to gather ideas and then made an outline or a plan like this:

Topic sentence: Passengers should refuse to ride in any vehicle driven by someone who has been drinking.

Reason 1: Refusal could save lives (**predicting a consequence**).
—statistics on deaths and accidents (**facts**)
—passengers are equally responsible

Reason 2: Riders might say some drinkers drive well—not true (**answering the opposition**).
—Dr. Belloc's explanation (**referring to authority**)

Reason 3: Others might feel foolish speaking up, but risking lives is more foolish (**answering the opposition**).

Reason 4: One rider might influence other passengers.
—Marie Furillo (**example**)

Conclusion: Bloodshed will probably continue, but people can refuse to risk their lives.

- Note how each reason clearly supports the topic sentence.

Transitional Expressions

The following transitional expressions are helpful in persuasive paragraphs:

Transitional Expressions for Persuasion

Give Reasons	Answer the Opposition	Draw Conclusions
first (second, third)	of course	therefore
another, next	some may say	thus
last, finally	nevertheless	hence
because, since, for	on the other hand	consequently
	although	

---

* For work on order of importance, see Chapter 4, "Achieving Coherence," Part A.

Methods of Persuasion

The drinking-and-driving example showed the basic kinds of support used in persuasive paragraphs: **facts, referring to an authority, examples, predicting the consequences,** and **answering the opposition.** Although you will rarely use all of them in one paragraph, you should be familiar with them all. Here are some more details:

1. **Facts: Facts** are simply statements of *what is.* They should appeal to the reader's mind, not just to the emotions. The source of your facts should be clear to the reader. If you wish to prove that children's eyesight should be checked every year by a doctor, you might look for supporting facts in appropriate books and magazines, or you might ask your eye doctor for information. Your paper might say, "Many people suffer serious visual impairment later in life because they received insufficient or inadequate eye care when they were children, according to an article in *Better Vision.*"*

    Avoid the vague "everyone knows that" or "it is common knowledge that" or "they all say." Such statements will make your reader justifiably suspicious of your "facts."

2. **Referring to an authority:** An **authority** is an expert, someone who can be relied on to give unbiased facts and information. If you wish to convince your readers that asthma is a far more serious illness than most people realize, you might speak with an emergency-room physician about the numbers of patients treated for asthma attacks, or you might quote experts from the literature of national organizations like the Asthma and Allergy Foundation of America or the American Lung Association. These are all excellent and knowledgeable authorities whose opinions on medical matters would be considered valid and unbiased.

    Avoid appealing to "authorities" who are interesting or glamorous but who are not experts. A basketball player certainly knows about sports, but probably knows little about cameras or cookware.

3. **Examples:** An **example** should clearly relate to the argument and should be typical enough to support it.† If you wish to convince your reader that high schools should provide more funds than they do for women's sports, you might say, "Jefferson High School, for instance, has received inquiries from sixty female students who would be willing to join a women's basketball or baseball team if the school could provide the uniforms, the space, and a coach."

    Avoid examples that are not typical enough to support your general statement. That your friend was once bitten by a dog does not adequately prove that all dogs are dangerous pets.

4. **Predicting the consequence: Predicting the consequence** helps the reader visualize what will occur if *something does or does not happen.* To convince your readers that a college education should be free to all qualified students, you might say, "If bright but economically deprived students cannot attend college because they cannot afford it, our society will be robbed of their talents."

    Avoid exaggerating the consequence. For instance, telling the reader, "If you don't eat fresh fruit every day, you will never be truly healthy," exaggerates the consequences of not eating fresh fruit and makes the reader understandably suspicious.

---

* For more work on summarizing and quoting outside sources, see Chapter 18.

† For more work on examples, see Chapter 5, "Illustration."

5. **Answering the opposition: Answering possible critics** shows that you are aware of the opposition's argument and are able to respond to it. If you wish to convince your readers that your candidate is the best on the ballot, you might say, "Some have criticized him for running a low-key campaign, but he feels that the issues and his stand on them should speak for themselves."

Avoid calling the opposition "fools" or "crooks." Attack their ideas, not them.

Considering the Audience

In addition to providing adequate proof for your argument, pay special attention to the **audience** as you write persuasively. In general, we assume that our audience is much like us—reasonable people who wish to learn the truth. But because argument can evoke strong feelings, directing your persuasive paper toward a particular audience can be helpful. Consider just *what kind of evidence* this audience would respond to. For instance, if you were attempting to persuade parents to volunteer their time to establish a local Scout troop, you might explain to them the various ways in which their children would benefit from the troop. In other words, show these parents how the troop is important to *them*. You might also say that you realize how much time they already spend on family matters and how little spare time they have. By doing so, you let them know that you understand their resistance to the argument and that you are sympathetic to their doubts. When you take your audience into consideration, you will make your persuasive paragraph more convincing.*†

PRACTICE 1

Read the following persuasive paragraph carefully and answer the questions.

American women should stop buying so-called women's magazines because these publications lower their self-esteem. First of all, publications like *Glamour* and *Cosmo* appeal to women's insecurities and make millions doing it. Topics like "Ten Days to Sexier Cleavage" and "How to Attract Mr. Right" lure women to buy seven million copies a month, reports Claire Ito in *The Tulsa Chronicle,* May 4, 1999. The message: women need to be improved. Second, although many people—especially magazine publishers—claim these periodicals build self-esteem, they really do the opposite. One expert in readers' reactions, Deborah Then, says that almost all women, regardless of age or education, feel worse about themselves after reading one of these magazines. Alice, one of the women I spoke with, is a good example: "I flip through pictures of world-class beauties and six-foot-tall skinny women, comparing myself to them. In more ways than one, I come up short." Finally, if women spent the money and time these magazines take on more self-loving activities—studying new subjects, developing mental or physical fitness, setting goals and daring to achieve them—they would really build self-worth. Sisters, seek wisdom, create what you envision, and above all, know that you can.

—Rochelle Revard (Student)

---

* For more work on audience, see Chapter 1, "Exploring the Writing Process," Part B.
† For a complete essay developed by persuasion, see "Stopping Youth Violence: An Inside Job," Chapter 15, Part I.

1. What is this paragraph arguing for or against? _The paragraph argues that women should stop buying women's magazines._

2. What audience is the writer addressing? _women_

3. Which reason is supported by facts? _the first reason_

   What are the facts, and where did the writer get them? _Women buy seven million copies a month, according to Claire Ito, The Tulsa Chronicle, May 4, 1999._

4. Which reason answers the opposition? _the second reason_

5. Which reason is supported by an example? _the second reason_

   What is the example? _Alice, one of the women interviewed_

6. Which reason appeals to an authority? _the second reason_

   Who is the authority? _Deborah Then, expert in readers' reaction_

PRACTICE 2

Read the following paragraph carefully and answer the questions.

  This state should offer free parenting classes, taught by experts, to anyone who wishes to become a parent. First and most important, such parenting classes could save children's lives. Every year, over two million American children are hurt, maimed, or killed by their own parents, according to the National Physicians Association. Some of these tragedies could be prevented by showing parents how to recognize and deal with their frustration and anger. Next, good parenting skills do not come naturally, but must be learned. Dr. Phillip Graham, chairman of England's National Children's Bureau, says that most parents have "no good role models" and simply parent the way they were parented. The courses would not only improve parenting skills but might also identify people at high risk of abusing their children. Third, critics might argue that the state has no business getting involved in parenting, which is a private responsibility. However, the state already makes decisions about who is a fit parent—in the courts, child-protection services, and adoption agencies—but often this is too late for the well-being of the child. Finally, if we do nothing, the hidden epidemic of child abuse and neglect will continue. We train our children's teachers, doctors, day-care workers, and bus drivers. We must also educate parents.

1. What is this paragraph arguing for or against? _It is arguing that the state should offer free parenting courses to all prospective parents._

2. Which reason appeals to an authority for support? _reason two_

   Who is the authority? _Dr. Phillip Graham, chairman of England's National Children's Bureau_

3. Which reason answers the opposition? _reason three_

4. Which reason includes facts? What is the source of these facts? _reason one; the National Physicians Association_

5. What consequence does the writer predict will occur if parenting classes are not offered? _Reason four predicts that the "hidden epidemic of child abuse and neglect" will continue._

6. Does this writer convince you that parenting classes might make a difference? If you were writing a persuasion paragraph to oppose or support this writer, what would your topic sentence be? _____

PRACTICE 3

So far you have learned five basic methods of persuasion: **facts, referring to an authority, examples, predicting the consequence,** and **answering the opposition.** Ten topic sentences for persuasive paragraphs follow. Write one reason in support of each topic sentence, using the method of persuasion indicated. *Answers will vary.*

Facts

1. A stop sign should be placed at the busy intersection of Hoover and Palm streets.

   Reason: _In the last three months, there have been fifteen accidents at this intersection._

2. People should not get married until they are at least twenty-five years old.

   Reason: _Statistics show that 75 percent of couples who marry before that age eventually divorce._

CHAPTER 13   Persuasion   159

Referring to an Authority

(If you cannot think of an authority offhand, name the kind of person who would be an authority on the subject.)

3. These new Sluggo bats will definitely raise your batting average.

   Reason: *According to coach Bill Bartlett of the Madison College baseball team, the design and weighting of these bats allow for a better swing—by any batter.*

4. Most people should get at least one hour of vigorous exercise three times a week.

   Reason: *Dr. Pamela Lu of the Fitness Research Corporation notes that regular exercise can help prevent heart attacks and other life-threatening afflictions.*

Examples

5. Pet animals should be allowed in children's hospital rooms because they speed healing.

   Reason: *Adam, a cancer patient who was deeply depressed, began to recover once his doctor allowed his silky terrier, Cola, to visit him.*

6. Mace and pepper spray should be legalized because they can prevent crime without causing permanent injury.

   Reason: *My cousin was given pepper spray by her police-officer father. When a man grabbed her at a bus stop, she was able to spray him and get away safely.*

Predicting the Consequence

7. Companies should (should not) be allowed to conduct random drug testing on employees.

   Reason: *If companies can perform such tests, innocent people will be embarrassed, inconvenienced, and disrespected.*

160 UNIT 3 Developing the Paragraph

8. The federal government should (should not) prohibit the sale of handguns through the mail.

   Reason: *Without such a prohibition, anyone, no matter how unstable, could obtain a handgun.*

Answering the Opposition

(State the opposition's point of view and then refute it.)

9. This college should (should not) drop its required-attendance policy.

   Reason: *Although some might argue that students would quickly stop going to class, most students would make responsible decisions to attend classes and to get an education.*

10. Teenagers should (should not) be required to get their parents' permission before being allowed to have an abortion.

    Reason: *Although some teenagers may make mature and informed decisions, not all teenagers are able to make such important decisions by themselves.*

PRACTICE 4

Each of the following sentences tells what you are trying to persuade someone to do. Beneath each sentence are four reasons that attempt to convince the reader that he or she should take this particular course of action. Circle the letter of the reason that seems *irrelevant, illogical,* or *untrue*.

1. If you wanted to persuade someone to do holiday shopping earlier, you might say that
   a. shopping earlier saves time.
   b. more gifts will be in stock.
   c. stores will not be overly crowded.
   d. the Back Street Boys shop early.

2. If you wanted to persuade someone to buy a particular brand of cereal, you might say that
   a. it is inexpensive.
   b. it contains vitamins and minerals.

CHAPTER 13 Persuasion 161

   c. it comes in an attractive box. *(circled)*
   d. it makes a hearty breakfast.

3. If you wanted to persuade someone to move to your town, you might say that
   a. two new companies have made jobs available.
   b. by moving to this town, he or she will become the happiest person in the world. *(circled)*
   c. there is a wide selection of housing.
   d. the area is lovely and still unpolluted.

4. If you wanted to persuade someone to vote for a particular candidate, you might say that
   a. she has always kept her promises to the voters.
   b. she has lived in the district for thirty years.
   c. she has substantial knowledge of the issues.
   d. she dresses very fashionably. *(circled)*

5. If you wanted to persuade someone to learn to read and speak a foreign language, you might say that
   a. knowledge of a foreign language can be helpful in the business world.
   b. he or she may want to travel in the country where the language is spoken.
   c. Ricky Martin sings in two languages. *(circled)*
   d. being able to read great literature in the original is a rewarding experience.

6. If you wanted to persuade someone to quit smoking, you might say that
   a. smoking is a major cause of lung cancer.
   b. smoking stains teeth and softens gums.
   c. ashtrays are often hard to find. *(circled)*
   d. this bad habit has become increasingly expensive.

PRACTICE 5

As you write persuasive paragraphs, make sure that your reasons can withstand close examination. Here are some examples of *invalid* arguments. Read them carefully. Decide which method of persuasion is being used and explain why you think the argument is invalid. Refer to the list on pages 155–156.

1. Men make terrible drivers. That one just cut right in front of me without looking.

   Method of persuasion: _example_

   Invalid because _the example of one careless male driver isn't enough to support a general statement about all male drivers_

2. Many people have become vegetarians during the past ten or fifteen years, but such people have lettuce for brains.

   Method of persuasion: _answering the opposition_

162 UNIT 3 Developing the Paragraph

   Invalid because *the writer attacks the opposition rather than*

   countering the benefits of vegetarianism

3. Candy does not really harm children's teeth. Tests made by scientists at the Gooey Candy Company have proved that candy does not cause tooth decay.

   Method of persuasion: *referring to an authority*

   Invalid because *the scientists are employed by a candy company*

   and may therefore be biased

4. Stealing pens and pads from the office is perfectly all right. Everyone does it.

   Method of persuasion: *example*

   Invalid because *saying "everyone does it" is vague and does not*

   justify stealing

5. We don't want _____ in our neighborhood. We had a _____ family once, and they made a lot of noise.

   Method of persuasion: *example*

   Invalid because *generalizations about an entire ethnic, religious, etc.,*

   group based on one family's behavior are not convincing

6. If our city doesn't build more playgrounds, a crime wave will destroy our homes and businesses.

   Method of persuasion: *predicting the consequence*

   Invalid because *this argument exaggerates the consequence*

7. Studying has nothing to do with grades. My brother never studies and still gets *A*'s all the time.

   Method of persuasion: *example*

   Invalid because *one person's experience doesn't adequately support*

   such a broad statement

8. Women bosses work their employees too hard. I had one once, and she never let me rest for a moment.

   Method of persuasion: *example*

   Invalid because *a single example cannot justify this sweeping statement*

9. The Big Deal Supermarket has the lowest prices in town. This must be true because the manager said on the radio last week, "We have the lowest prices in town."

   Method of persuasion: <u>*referring to an authority*</u>

   Invalid because <u>*the "authority" cited was advertising the store,*</u>
   <u>*not stating research findings*</u>

10. If little girls are allowed to play with cars and trucks, they will grow up wanting to be men.

    Method of persuasion: <u>*predicting the consequence*</u>

    Invalid because <u>*the writer cannot support such a sweeping*</u>
    <u>*prediction with facts*</u>

PRACTICE 6

In a group of four or five classmates, discuss the meaning of this cartoon. Like many cartoons, this one expresses a strong point of view. What issue in American life is this British cartoonist commenting on? What point is he making? Working together, write down the cartoon's "topic sentence" and argument. How effective—how persuasive—is this cartoon?

WRITING ASSIGNMENT

To help you take a stand for a persuasive paragraph of your own, try the following exercises on notebook paper:

1. List five things you would like to see changed at your college.
2. List five things you would like to see changed in your home *or* at your job.
3. List five things that annoy you or make you angry. What can be done about them?
4. Imagine yourself giving a speech on national television. What message would you like to convey?

From your lists, pick one topic you would like to write a persuasive paragraph about and write the topic sentence here:

Sample answer: The college library should be open all day on Sundays.

Now make a plan or an outline for a paragraph on a separate sheet of paper. Use at least two of the five methods of persuasion. Arrange your reasons in a logical order, and write the most persuasive paragraph you can.

✓ CHECKLIST: The Process of Writing a Persuasive Paragraph

Refer to this checklist of steps as you write a persuasive paragraph of your own.

___ 1. Narrow the topic in light of your audience and purpose. What do you wish to persuade your reader to believe or do?

___ 2. Compose a topic sentence that clearly states your position for or against. Use *should, ought, must,* or their negatives.

___ 3. Freewrite or brainstorm to generate all the reasons you can think of. (You may want to freewrite or brainstorm before you narrow the topic.)

___ 4. Select the best three or four reasons and drop those that do not relate to your topic sentence.

___ 5. If you use *facts,* be sure that they are accurate and that the source of your facts is clear. If you use an *example,* be sure that it is a valid one and adequately supports your argument. If you *refer to an authority,* be sure that he or she is really an authority and *not biased.* If one of your reasons *predicts the consequence,* be sure that the consequence flows logically from your statement. If one of your reasons *answers the opposition,* be sure to state the opposition's point of view fairly and refute it adequately.

___ 6. Make a plan or an outline for the paragraph, numbering the reasons in the order in which you will present them.

___ 7. Write a draft of your persuasive paragraph, using transitional expressions wherever they may be helpful.

___ 8. Revise as necessary, checking for support, unity, logic, and coherence.

___ 9. Proofread for errors in grammar, punctuation, sentence structure, spelling, and mechanics.

Suggested Topics for Persuasive Paragraphs

A list of possible topic sentences for persuasive paragraphs follows. Pick one statement and decide whether you agree or disagree with it. Modify the topic sentence accordingly. Then write a persuasive paragraph that supports your view, explaining and illustrating from your own experience, your observations of others, or your reading.

1. Companies should not be allowed to read their employees' e-mail.
2. Occasional arguments are good for friendship.
3. A required course at this college should be _____ (Great American Success Stories, Survey of World Art, How to Use the Internet, or another).
4. The families of AIDS patients are the hidden victims of AIDS.
5. Condom machines should be permitted on campus.
6. People should laugh more because laughter heals.
7. Expensive weddings are an obscene waste of money.
8. Single people should not be allowed to adopt children.
9. Some college football (soccer, basketball, and so on) programs send the message that academic excellence is not important.
10. TV talk shows trivialize important social issues.
11. _____ is the most _____ (hilarious, educational, mindless, racist) show on television.
12. To improve academic achievement, this town should create same-sex high schools (all boys, all girls).
13. People convicted of drunk driving should lose their licenses for one year.
14. _____ (writer, singer, or actor) has a message that more people need to hear.
15. Writer's choice: _____

UNIT 3   WRITERS' WORKSHOP

Give Advice to College Writers

When you are assigned a writing task, take a few minutes to think about the different types of paragraphs you have studied in this unit. Could a certain type of paragraph help you present your ideas more forcefully? You might ask yourself, "Would a paragraph developed by examples work well for this topic? How about a paragraph of cause and effect?"

When he received the assignment "Give advice to other college writers," this student not only made use of one paragraph pattern he had learned, but he added something of his own—humor. In your class or group, read his work, aloud if possible, underlining any lines that you find especially funny or effective.

English Students, Listen Up!

You may think that years of school have taught you how to put off writing a paper; however, true procrastination is an art form, and certain steps must be followed to achieve the status of Master Procrastinator. The first step is to come up with a good reason to put off writing the paper. Reasons prevent others from hassling you about your procrastination. A reason should not be confused with an excuse. An excuse would be, "I am too tired." A reason would be, "It is important that I rest in order to do the best possible job." The second step is to come up with a worthwhile task to do before starting the paper. If you put off writing your paper by watching Baywatch. You will feel guilty. *Baywatch, you* On the other hand, if you put off writing your paper by helping your child do his or her homework or by doing three weeks' worth of laundry or by organizing your sock drawer, there will be no guilt. After completing your worthwhile task. You will be hungry. In order to have *task, you* the energy necessary to write the paper, you will need to eat something. The true artist can make this third step last even longer by either cooking a meal or going out for food. It is important not to risk your energy level by simply eating a bowl of cereal or a ketchup sandwich. After you eat, the fourth step is to prepare the space in which you will write the paper. This includes cleaning all the surfaces, sharpening pencils. And making sure the lighting is exactly right. You may *pencils, and* think that after this fourth step is completed, you will have no choice but to start your paper, but you do if you have done the other steps correctly. It is now too late in the day to start your paper. The fifth step is, of course, to go to bed and start over with step one in the morning.

—Thomas Capra (Student)

1. How effective is this paragraph?

   ___Y___ Clear topic sentence?   ___Y___ Good supporting details?

   ___Y___ Logical organization?   ___Y___ Effective conclusion?

2. What type of paragraph development does Mr. Capra use here? How do you know? Does the topic sentence indicate what kind of paragraph will follow?
   process; topic sentence says "certain steps must be followed"
3. One step in the process of becoming a Master Procrastinator contains a *contrast*. Which step? What two things are contrasted? *step one; reason and excuse*
4. Discuss your underlinings with the group or class. Tell what parts of the paragraph you like best, explaining as specifically as possible why. For example, the mention of a ketchup sandwich in step three adds an extra dash of humor.
5. Although this writer is having fun, procrastination is a serious problem for some people. Do you think Mr. Capra is writing from experience? Why or why not?
6. This otherwise excellent writer makes the same grammar error three times. Can you spot and correct the error pattern that he needs to avoid? *three sentence fragments*

Group Work

In your group or class, make a chart like the one below, listing all the types of paragraph development that you have studied. Now suppose that you have been assigned the topic *procrastination*. Discuss how different paragraphs could be developed on the subject of procrastination, each one using a different paragraph pattern. For instance, you could *illustrate* procrastination by discussing examples of procrastinators you have known. Fill in the chart with one idea per paragraph type. Then share your group's ideas with the whole class.

Topic: Procrastination

Method of development:	A paragraph could
Illustration	give two to three examples of procrastinators.
Narration	
Description	
Process	
Definition	
Comparison and Contrast	
Classification	
Cause and Effect	
Persuasion	

Writing and Revising Ideas

1. Give advice to college writers. Use humor if you wish.
2. Discuss procrastination, using one kind of paragraph development that you studied this term.

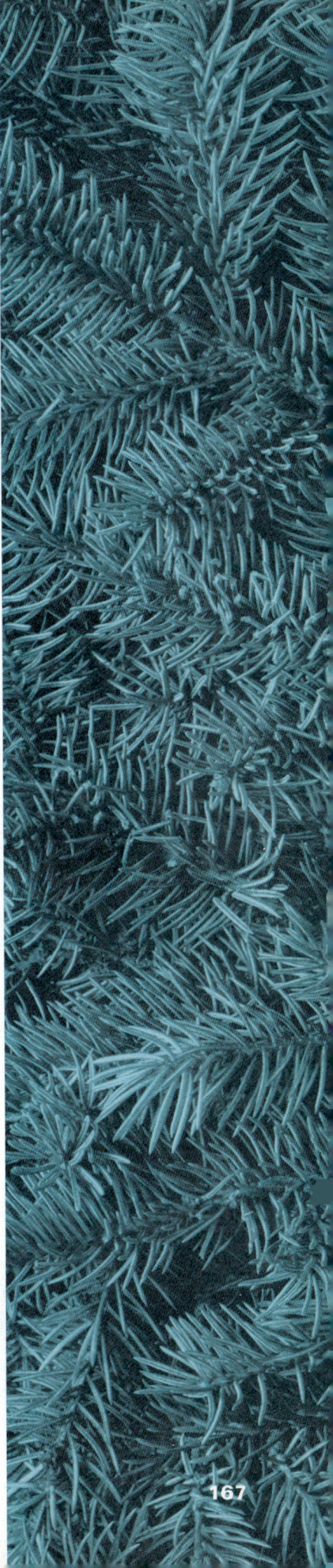

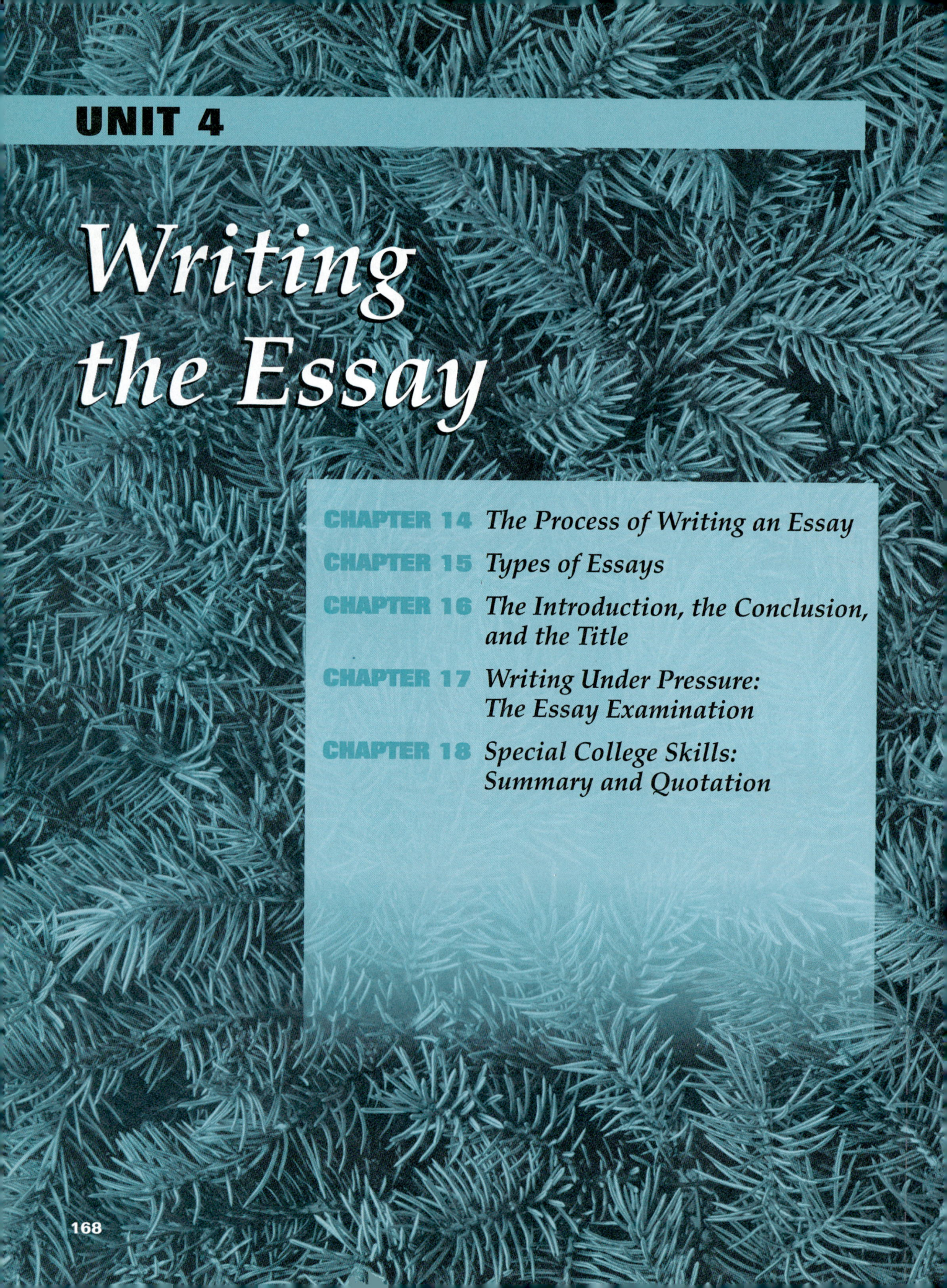

UNIT 4

Writing the Essay

CHAPTER 14 The Process of Writing an Essay
CHAPTER 15 Types of Essays
CHAPTER 16 The Introduction, the Conclusion, and the Title
CHAPTER 17 Writing Under Pressure: The Essay Examination
CHAPTER 18 Special College Skills: Summary and Quotation

CHAPTER 14

The Process of Writing an Essay

PART A   Looking at the Essay
PART B   Writing the Thesis Statement
PART C   Generating Ideas for the Body
PART D   Ordering and Linking Paragraphs in the Essay
PART E   Writing and Revising Essays

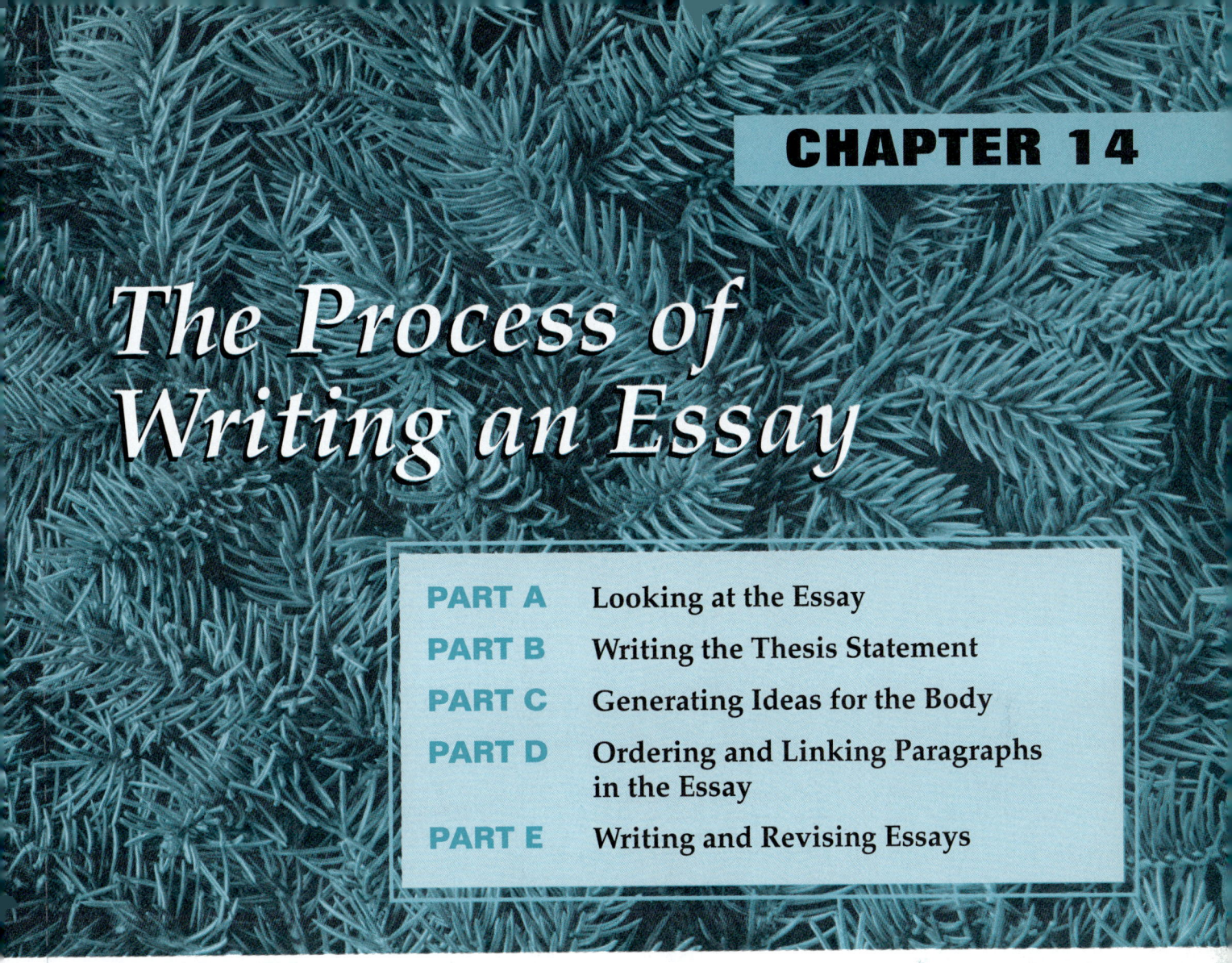

Although writing effective paragraphs will help you complete short-answer exams and do brief writing assignments, much of the time—in college and in the business world—you will be required to write essays and reports several paragraphs long. Essays are longer and contain more ideas than the single paragraphs you have practiced so far, but they require many of the same skills that paragraphs do.

This chapter will help you apply the skills of paragraph writing to the writing of short essays. It will guide you from a look at the essay and its parts through the planning and writing of essays.

PART A   Looking at the Essay

An **essay** is a group of paragraphs about one subject. In many ways, an essay is like a paragraph in longer, fuller form. Both have an introduction, a body, and a conclusion. Both explain one main, or controlling, idea with details, facts, and examples. An essay is not just a padded paragraph, however. An essay is longer because it contains more ideas.

169

The paragraphs in an essay are part of a larger whole, so each one has a special purpose.

- The **introductory paragraph*** opens the essay and tries to catch the reader's interest. It usually contains a **thesis statement,** one sentence that states the main idea of the entire essay.

- The **body** of an essay consists of one, two, three, or more paragraphs, each one making a different point about the main idea.

- The **conclusion**† brings the essay to a close. It might be a sentence or a paragraph long.

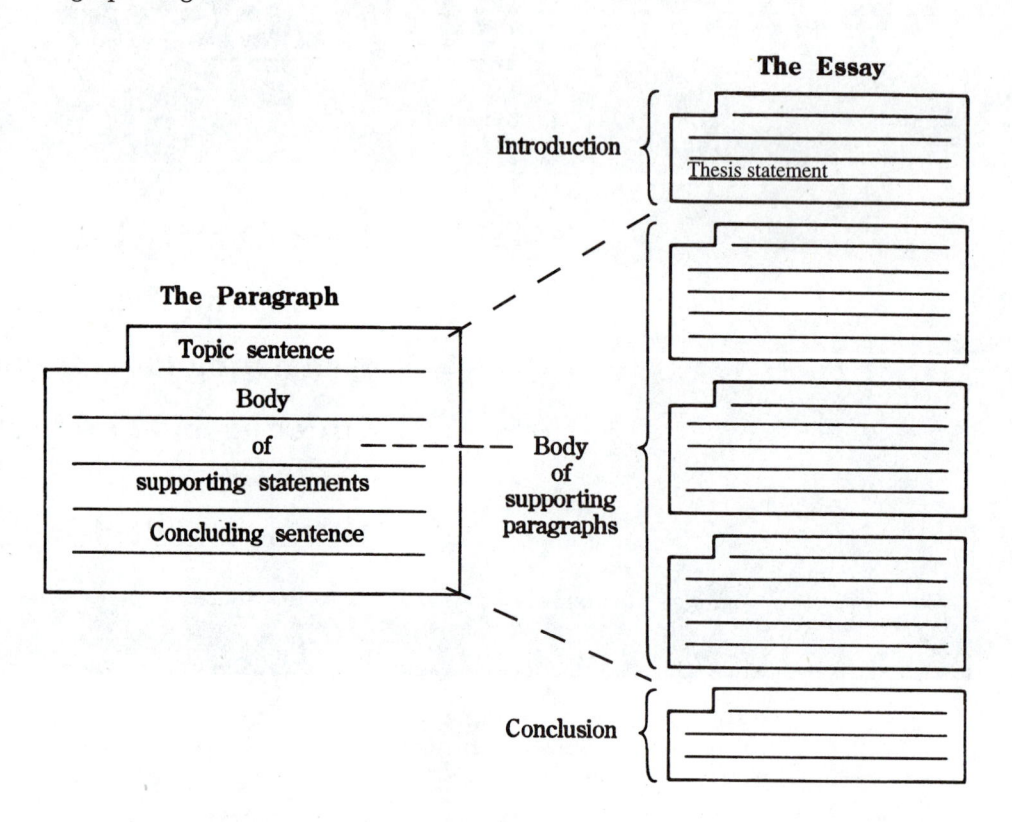

Here is a student essay:

Sunlight

(1) An old proverb says, "He who brings sunlight into the lives of others cannot keep it from himself." Students who volunteer through the Center for Community Service often experience this wisdom firsthand. By giving their time and talents to the local community, these students not only enrich the lives of others, but they receive many surprising benefits for themselves.

(2) Most important, volunteering can bring a sense of empowerment, a knowledge that we can make a difference. This is significant because many students feel passive and hopeless about "the way things are." My first volunteer assignment was working with a group of troubled teenagers. Together we transformed a dismal vacant lot into a thriving business. The three-acre lot in the

---

* For more work on introductions, see Chapter 16, "The Introduction, the Conclusion, and the Title."

† For more work on conclusions, see Chapter 16, "The Introduction, the Conclusion, and the Title."

South Bronx, surrounded by abandoned buildings, was full of junk and heaps of wood. One teenager kicked a piece of wood and said, "Why don't we chop this up and sell it?" We surprised him by taking his idea seriously. We helped these young men, some of whom already had rap sheets, to chop up the wood, bundle it, contact restaurants with wood-burning ovens, and make deliveries. The restaurants, most of them very elegant, were happy to get cheap firewood, and the teenagers were thrilled to be treated like businesspeople. Most rewarding for me was seeing the changes in Raymond, "Mr. Apathy," as he took on a leading role in our project.

(3) Second, the volunteer often gains a deeper understanding of others. Another student, Shirley Miranda, worked with SHARE, a food cooperative that distributes bulk food once a month to its members. SHARE does not give food as charity; rather, each person does a job like unloading trucks at 5 a.m. on delivery day or packing boxes in exchange for healthy, inexpensive food. For Shirley, SHARE was a lesson in human relationships. Reflecting on her service, she wrote: "I learned that people may sometimes need guidance with dignity rather than total dependency on others. I saw that true teamwork is based on people's similarities, not their differences." SHARE so impressed Shirley that she worked in the program through her graduation.

(4) Finally, volunteering can be a way to "try on" a work environment. Sam Mukarji, an engineering student, volunteers on Saturdays as a docent, or guide, at the Museum of Science and Industry, which he describes as "my favorite place on the planet." Sam admires the creative uses of science in this museum, such as the virtual-reality experience of piloting an airplane. When many visitors asked Sam how the exhibit was put together, he suggested that the museum include signs explaining the technology. His idea was accepted, and he was asked to help implement it. Struggling to explain the exhibit in a clear way taught Sam how important writing skills are, even for an engineering major. Now he is paying closer attention to his English assignments and has discovered that working in a science museum would be his "dream job."

(5) Stories like these are not unusual at the Center for Community Service. Whenever the volunteers meet there, we always seem to end up talking about the positive ways in which volunteering has changed our lives. The Center is in a cinder-block basement without a single window, but it is filled with sunlight.

- The last sentence in the introduction is the *thesis statement*. Just as a topic sentence sets forth the main idea of a paragraph, so the thesis statement sets forth the main idea of the whole essay. It must be *general enough to include the topic sentence of every paragraph in the body*.

- Underline the topic sentence of each supporting paragraph. Each topic sentence introduces one *benefit* that volunteers receive.

- Note that the thesis and topic sentences of paragraphs 2, 3, and 4 make a rough *plan* of the entire essay:

1. INTRODUCTION and Thesis statement: By giving their time and talents to the local community, these students not only enrich the lives of others, but they receive many surprising benefits for themselves.

2. Topic sentence: Most important, volunteering can bring a sense of empowerment, a knowledge that we can make a difference.

3. Topic sentence: Second, the volunteer often gains a deeper understanding of others.

4. Topic sentence: Finally, volunteering can be a way to "try on" a work environment.

5. CONCLUSION

■ Note that every topic sentence supports the thesis statement. Every paragraph in the body discusses in detail one *benefit* that students receive from volunteering. Each paragraph also provides an *example* to explain that benefit.

■ The last paragraph *concludes* the essay by mentioning sunlight, a reference to the proverb in paragraph 1.

PRACTICE 1

Read this student essay carefully and then answer the questions.

Bottle Watching

(1) Every time I see a beer bottle, I feel grateful. This reaction has nothing to do with beer. The sight reminds me of the year I spent inspecting bottles at a brewery. That was the most boring and painful job I've ever had, but it motivated me to change my life.

(2) My job consisted of sitting on a stool and watching empty bottles pass by. A glaring light behind the conveyor belt helped me to spot cracked bottles or bottles with something extra—a dead grasshopper, for example, or a mouse foot. I was supposed to grab such bottles with my hooked cane and break them before they went into the washer. For eight or nine hours a day that was all I did. I got dizzy and sore in the eyes. I longed to fall asleep. I prayed that the conveyor would break down so the bottles would stop.

(3) After a while, to put some excitement into the job, I began inventing little games. I would count the number of minutes that passed before a broken bottle would come by, and I would compete against my own past record. Or I would see how many broken bottles I could spot in one minute. Once, I organized a contest for all the bottle watchers with a prize for the best dead insect or animal found in a bottle—anything to break the monotony of the job.

(4) After six months at the brewery, I began to think hard about my goals for the future. Did I want to spend the rest of my life looking in beer bottles? I realized that I wanted a job I could believe in. I wanted to use my mind for better things than planning contests for bleary-eyed bottle watchers. I knew I had to hand in my hook and go back to school.

(5) Today I feel grateful to that terrible job because it motivated me to attend college.

—Pat Barnum (Student)

CHAPTER 14 The Process of Writing an Essay   173

1. Which sentence in the introductory paragraph is the thesis statement? _That was the most boring and painful job I've ever had, but it motivated me to change my life._

2. Did Mr. Barnum's introduction catch and hold your interest? Why or why not? _Yes; the first sentence is surprising and makes you want to read on._

3. Underline the topic sentences in paragraphs 2, 3, and 4.

4. What is the controlling idea of paragraph 2? _description of his duties on the job_

5. What is the controlling idea of paragraph 3? What examples support this idea? _games Barnum invented to add excitement; examples are competing against his record, counting broken bottles, prize for best dead critter_

6. What do you like best about this essay? What, if anything, would you change? _____

PART B Writing the Thesis Statement

The steps in the essay-writing process are the same as those in the paragraph-writing process: **narrow the topic, write the thesis statement, generate ideas for the body,** and **organize them.** However, in essay writing, planning on paper and prewriting are especially important because an essay is longer than a paragraph and more difficult to organize.

Narrowing the Topic

The essay writer usually starts with a broad subject and then narrows it to a manageable size. An essay is longer than a paragraph and gives the writer more room to develop ideas; nevertheless, the best essays, like the best paragraphs, are often quite specific. For example, if you are assigned a four-hundred-word essay titled "A Trip I Won't Forget," a description of your recent trip to Florida would be too broad a subject. You would need to *narrow* the topic to just one aspect of the trip. Many writers list possible narrowed subjects on paper or on computer:

1. huge job of packing, more tiring than the trip
2. how to pack for a trip with the children without exhausting yourself
3. Disney World, more fun for adults than for children
4. our afternoon of deep-sea fishing: highlight of the trip
5. terrible weather upsetting many of my sightseeing plans

Any one of these topics is narrow enough and specific enough to be the subject of a short essay. If you had written this list, you would now consider each narrowed topic and perhaps freewrite or brainstorm possible ways to support it.

Keeping your audience and purpose in mind may also help you narrow your topic. Your audience here might be your instructor and classmates; your purpose might be to inform (by giving tips about packing) or to entertain (by narrating a funny or a dramatic incident). Having considered your topic, audience, and purpose, you would then choose the topic that you could best develop into a good essay.

If you have difficulty with this step, reread Chapter 2, "Prewriting to Generate Ideas."

Writing the Thesis Statement

The thesis statement—like the topic sentence in a paragraph—further focuses the narrowed subject because it must clearly state, in sentence form, the writer's **controlling idea**—the main point, opinion, or angle that the rest of the essay will support and discuss.

Narrowed subject:	My job at the brewery
Controlling idea:	So bad it changed my life
Thesis statement:	That was the most boring and painful job I've ever had, but it motivated me to change my life.

■ This thesis statement has a clear controlling idea. From it, we expect the essay to discuss specific ways in which this job was boring and painful and how it motivated a change.

The thesis statement and its controlling idea should be as **specific** as possible. By writing a specific thesis statement, you focus the subject and give yourself and your readers a clear idea of what will follow. Here are three ways to make a vague thesis statement more specific.

1. As a general rule, replace vague words with more exact words* and replace vague ideas with more exact information:

Vague thesis statement:	My recent trip to Florida was really bad.
Revised thesis statement:	My recent trip to Florida was disappointing because the weather upset my sightseeing plans.

■ The first thesis statement above lacks a clear controlling idea. The inexact words *really bad* do not say specifically enough *why* the trip was bad or what the rest of the essay might discuss.

■ The second thesis statement is more specific. The words *really bad* are replaced by the more exact word *disappointing*. In addition, the writer has added more complete information about why the trip was disappointing. From this thesis statement, it is clear that the essay will discuss how the weather upset the writer's plans.

---

*For more practice in choosing exact language, see Chapter 21, "Revising for Language Awareness," Part A.

2. Sometimes you can make the thesis statement more specific by stating the natural divisions of the subject. If a subject naturally has two, three, or four divisions, stating these in the thesis can set up an outline for your entire essay:

Vague thesis statement:	The movie *Southern Smoke* seemed phony.
Revised thesis statement:	The costumes, the dialogue, and the plot of the movie *Southern Smoke* all seemed phony.

■ The first thesis statement above gives little specific direction to the writer or the reader.

■ The second thesis statement, however, actually sets up a plan for the whole essay. The writer has divided the subject into three parts—the costumes, the dialogue, and the plot—and he or she will probably devote one paragraph to discussing the phoniness of each one, following the order in the thesis statement.

3. Avoid a heavy-handed thesis statement that announces, "Now I will write about . . ." or **"This essay will discuss. . . ."** Don't state the obvious. Instead, craft a specific thesis statement that will capture the reader's interest and control what the rest of your essay will be about. Make every word count.

PRACTICE 2

Revise each vague thesis statement, making it more specific. Remember, a good thesis statement should have a clear controlling idea and indicate what the rest of the essay will be about. *Answers will vary.*

EXAMPLE Watching TV news programs has its good points.

Watching news programs on TV can make one a more informed and responsible citizen.

1. The library at this college is bad.

   Our college library has short hours, cranky librarians, and few books.

2. A visit to the emergency room can be interesting.

   A late-night visit to the emergency room can shed light on the activities and problems of teenagers.

3. There are many unusual people in my family.

   My aunt and uncle, who once traveled the world as circus acrobats, are the most unusual members of my family.

4. School uniforms are a good idea.

   To reduce competition and school crime, students at Highland Middle School should be required to wear uniforms.

5. I will write about my job, which is very cool.

   Working as an administrative assistant at JamVision has allowed me to meet many young musicians in the Chicago area.

6. Professors should teach better.

   Some professors at State College should prepare more completely and spend more time on difficult material.

7. You can learn a lot by observing children.

   You can learn a lot about children's developing social sense by observing three-year-olds at play.

8. Sketching caricatures is a great hobby.

   Sketching caricatures relaxes me, brings out my creativity, and allows me to earn extra money.

PRACTICE 3

Eight possible essay topics follow. Pick three that interest you. For each one, **narrow** the topic, choose your **controlling idea,** and then compose a specific **thesis statement.** *Answers will vary.*

an addictive habit	a problem on campus or at work
when parents work	a story or issue in the news now
a volunteer experience	handling anger (or other emotion)
the value of pets	a time when you surprised yourself

EXAMPLE Subject: *handling anger*

Narrowed subject: *my angry adolescence*

Controlling idea: *channeling adolescent anger into art*

Thesis statement: *In a photography workshop for "at-risk" teenagers, I learned that anger can be channeled positively into art.*

1. Subject: _____

   Narrowed subject: _____

Controlling idea: _____

Thesis statement: _____
_____

2. Subject: _____

   Narrowed subject: _____

   Controlling idea: _____

   Thesis statement: _____
   _____

3. Subject: _____

   Narrowed subject: _____

   Controlling idea: _____

   Thesis statement: _____
   _____

PART C Generating Ideas for the Body

The thesis statement sets forth the main idea of the entire essay, but it is the **body** of the essay that must fully support and discuss that thesis statement. In composing the thesis statement, the writer should already have given some thought to what the body will contain. Now he or she should make a **plan** or an **outline** that includes the following:

1. Two to four main ideas to support the thesis statement
2. Two to four topic sentences stating these ideas
3. A plan for each paragraph in the body (developed in any of the ways explained earlier in this book)
4. A logical order in which to present these paragraphs

Different writers create such plans in different ways. Some writers brainstorm or freewrite ideas and then find paragraph groups. Others first write topic sentences and then plan paragraphs.

1. Brainstorm ideas and then find paragraph groups. Having written the thesis statement, some writers brainstorm on paper or on the computer—they jot down any ideas that develop the thesis statement, including main ideas, specific details, and examples, all jumbled together. Only after creating a long list do they go back over it, drop any ideas that do not support the thesis statement, and then look for "paragraph groups."

Suppose, for instance, that you have written this thesis statement: *Although people often react to stress in harmful ways, there are many positive ways to handle stress.* By brainstorming and then dropping ideas that do not relate, you might eventually produce a list like this:

work out

dig weeds or rake leaves

call a friend

talking out problems relieves stress

jogging

many sports ease tension

go to the beach

take a walk

taking breaks, long or short, relieves stress

talk to a shrink if the problem is really bad

escape into a hobby—photography, bird watching

go to a movie

talk to a counselor at the college

talk to a minister, priest, rabbi, etc.

many people harm themselves trying to relieve stress

they overeat or smoke

drinking too much, other addictions

do vigorous household chores—scrub a floor, beat the rugs, pound pillows

doing something physical relieves stress

some diseases are caused by stress

take a nap

some people blow up to help tension, but this hurts their relationships

Now read over the list, looking for groups of ideas that could become paragraphs. Some ideas might become topic sentences; others might be used to support a topic sentence. How many possible paragraphs can you find in this list?

four

PRACTICE 4

From the list, make a **plan** or an **outline** for an essay that supports the thesis statement *Although people often react to stress in harmful ways, there are many positive ways to handle stress.*

Plan four paragraphs for the body of the essay. Find four paragraph groups in the list and determine the main idea of each paragraph; then write a topic sentence stating this main idea.

Now arrange the topic sentences in an order that makes sense. Under each topic sentence, list supporting examples or details. *Answers will vary.*

1. INTRODUCTION and Thesis statement: Although people often react to stress in harmful ways, there are many positive ways to handle stress.

2. Topic sentence: *Many people actually harm themselves trying to relieve stress.*

   (examples) *overeat; smoke; drink too much; get stress-induced diseases; blow up at others*

3. Topic sentence: *For some people, doing something physical is a positive way to relieve stress.*

   (examples) *walk; jog; work out; vigorous household chores; dig weeds or rake leaves*

4. Topic sentence: *Taking breaks, long or short, is another positive way to relieve stress.*

   (examples) *take a nap; escape into a hobby; go to a movie, to the beach*

5. Topic sentence: *Discussing one's problems can relieve stress and sometimes resolve the cause of it.*

   (examples) *call a friend; talk to a minister, etc.; talk to a counselor at the college; talk to a therapist if necessary*

6. CONCLUSION: *Stress is a fact of life, and we all react to it whether we know it or not. We should incorporate these positive responses into our lives so that we can live more happily and more productively.*

■ Does every topic sentence support the thesis statement?
■ Have you arranged the paragraphs in a logical order?

2. Write topic sentences and then plan paragraphs. Sometimes a writer can compose topic sentences directly from the thesis statement without extensive jotting first. This is especially true if the thesis statement itself shows how the body will be divided or organized. Such a thesis statement makes the work of planning paragraphs easy because the writer has already broken down the subject into supporting ideas or parts:

| Thesis statement: | Because the student cafeteria has many problems, the college should hire a new administrator to see that it is properly managed in the future. |

■ This thesis statement contains two main ideas: (1) that the cafeteria has many problems and (2) that a new administrator should be hired. The first idea states the problem and the second offers a solution.

From this thesis statement, a writer could logically plan a two-paragraph body, with one paragraph explaining each idea in detail. He or she might compose two topic sentences as follows:

Thesis statement:	Because the student cafeteria has many problems, the college should hire a new administrator to see that it is properly managed in the future.
Topic sentence:	Foremost among the cafeteria's problems are unappetizing food, slow service, and high prices.
Topic sentence:	A new administrator could do much to improve these terrible conditions.

These topic sentences might need to be revised later, but they will serve as guides while the writer further develops each paragraph.

The writer might develop the first paragraph in the body by giving **examples*** of the unappetizing foods, slow service, and high prices.

He or she could develop the second paragraph through **process**,† by describing the **steps** that the new administrator could take to solve the cafeteria's problems. The completed essay **plan** might look like this:

1. INTRODUCTION and Thesis statement: Because the student cafeteria has many problems, the college should hire a new administrator to see that it is properly managed in the future.

2. Topic sentence: Foremost among the cafeteria's problems are unappetizing food, slow service, and high prices.

    Problem 1: Food is unappetizing

    —sandwiches with tough meat, stale bread
    —salads with wilted lettuce, tasteless tomatoes
    —hot meals often either overcooked or undercooked

    Problem 2: Service is slow

    —students wait 30 minutes for sandwiches
    —students wait 15 minutes just for a cup of coffee
    —have to gulp meals to get to class on time

    Problem 3: Prices too high

    —sandwiches overpriced
    —coffee or tea costs $1.50

3. Topic sentence: A new administrator could do much to improve these terrible conditions.

    Step 1. Set minimum quality standards

    —personally oversee purchase of healthful food
    —set and enforce rules about how long food can be left out

---

* For more work on developing paragraphs with examples, see Chapter 5, "Illustration."
† For more work on developing paragraphs by process, see Chapter 8, "Process."

—set cooking times for hot meals

Step 2. Reorganize service lines

—study which lines are busiest at different times of the day
—shift cooks and cashiers to those lines
—create a separate beverage line

Step 3. Lower prices

—better food and faster service would attract more student customers
—cafeteria could then lower prices

4. CONCLUSION

Note that the order of paragraphs logically follows the order in the thesis statement, discussing first the problem and then the solution.

The writer now has a clear plan from which to write the first draft of the essay.

PRACTICE 5

Write from two to four topic sentences to support *three* of the thesis statements that follow. (First you may wish to brainstorm or freewrite on paper or on computer.) Make sure that every topic sentence really supports the thesis statement and that every one could be developed into a good paragraph. Then arrange your topic sentences in a **plan** in the space provided. *Answers will vary.*

EXAMPLE Before you buy a computer, do these three things.

Topic sentence: *Decide how much you can spend, and determine your price range.*

Topic sentence: *Examine the models that are within your price range.*

Topic sentence: *Shop around; do not assume that all computer dealers are created equal.*

1. I vividly recall the sights, smells, and tastes of *the baking table at the county fair.*

Topic sentence: *Everywhere was a smorgasbord of homemade cakes, pies, cookies, and bread.*

Topic sentence: *The enticing fragrances of yeast, spices, fruit, and chocolate were heavy in the air.*

Topic sentence: *Some of the bakers proudly offered samples of their freshly baked wares.*

Topic sentence: _____

2. Living alone has both advantages and disadvantages.

   Topic sentence: *When you live alone, you can make spur-of-the-moment decisions about what you want to do.*

   Topic sentence: *Living by yourself, you can keep your apartment as neat or as sloppy as you like.*

   Topic sentence: *Living alone allows you to eat whatever and whenever you want.*

   Topic sentence: *Living alone, however, makes you especially vulnerable to crime.*

3. Doing well at a job interview requires careful planning.

   Topic sentence: *First, learn as much as possible about the company at which you are interviewing.*

   Topic sentence: *Try to anticipate the kinds of questions the interviewer might ask.*

   Topic sentence: *Choose appropriate clothing to wear at the interview.*

   Topic sentence: *Get a good night's sleep and practice relaxation techniques.*

4. *Jewelry making* _____ is a fascinating and profitable hobby.

   Topic sentence: *Jewelry making provides an outlet for creative energies.*

Topic sentence: _One can always work on new designs and experiment with new materials._

Topic sentence: _There is a large and growing market for handmade jewelry._

Topic sentence: _____

5. My three children have individual techniques for avoiding housework.

Topic sentence: _Bob always remembers that he needs to go somewhere important._

Topic sentence: _Zena suddenly becomes eager to do her homework._

Topic sentence: _Bill says he will help but procrastinates until someone else does his work for him._

Topic sentence: _____

PRACTICE 6

Now choose *one* thesis statement you have written, or write one now, and develop a plan for an essay of your own. (For ideas, reread the thesis statements you wrote for Practice 3, p. 176.) Your plan should include your thesis statement, two to four topic sentences, and supporting details, facts, and examples. Brainstorm or freewrite every time you need ideas; revise the thesis statement and the topic sentences until they are sharp and clear.

PART D Ordering and Linking Paragraphs in the Essay

An essay, like a paragraph, should have **coherence.** That is, the paragraphs in an essay should be arranged in a clear, logical order and should follow one another like links in a chain.

Ordering Paragraphs

It is important that the paragraphs in your plan, and later in your essay, follow a **logical order.** The rule for writers is this: Use your common sense and plan ahead. *Do not* leave the order of your paragraphs to chance.

The types of order often used in single paragraphs—**time order, space order,** and **order of importance***—can sometimes be used to arrange paragraphs within an essay. Essays about subjects that can be broken into stages or steps, with each step discussed in one paragraph, should be arranged according to *time. Space order* is used occasionally in descriptive essays. A writer who wishes to save the most important or convincing paragraph for last would use *order of importance.* Or he or she might wish to reverse this order and put the most important paragraph first.

Very often, however, the writer simply arranges paragraphs in whatever order makes sense in the particular essay. Suppose, for example, that you have written the thesis statement *Action heroes Jackie Chan and Michelle Yeow have much in common,* and you plan three paragraphs with these topic sentences:

> Unlike other action heroes, they both do their own stunts.
>
> Both were popular in Asia long before they were discovered by Western movie audiences.
>
> By poking fun at themselves in their movies, both tweak the heroic image of the action star.

Because doing their own stunts and poking fun at themselves both deal with their style in the movies, it would seem logical to arrange these two paragraphs one after the other. Once the reader has read about who they are and how they approach action movies, it makes sense to end with their early popularity in Asia. A logical order of paragraphs, then, might be the following:

1. INTRODUCTION and Thesis statement: Action heroes Jackie Chan and Michelle Yeow have much in common.
2. Topic sentence: Unlike other action heroes, they both do their own stunts.
3. Topic sentence: By poking fun at themselves in their movies, both tweak the heroic image of the action star.
4. Topic sentence: Both were popular in Asia long before they were discovered by Western movie audiences.
5. CONCLUSION

Finally, if your thesis statement is divided into two, three, or four parts, the paragraphs in the body should follow the order in the thesis; otherwise, the reader will be confused. Assume, for instance, that you are planning three paragraphs to develop the thesis statement *Using a CD-ROM encyclopedia for the first time can be overwhelming, exciting, and educational.*

Paragraph 2 should discuss   *its overwhelming aspects*.

Paragraph 3 should discuss   *its exciting aspects*.

Paragraph 4 should discuss   *its educational aspects*.

---

*For more work on time order, space order, and order of importance, see Chapter 4, "Achieving Coherence," Part A.

PRACTICE 7

Plans for three essays follow, each containing a thesis statement and several topic sentences in scrambled order. Number the topic sentences in each group according to an *order that makes sense*. Be prepared to explain your choices.

1. Thesis statement: The practice of tai chi can improve one's concentration, health, and peace of mind.

    Topic sentences:
    - __2__ In several ways, tai chi boosts physical health.
    - __3__ Peace of mind increases gradually as one becomes less reactive.
    - __1__ Concentrating on the movements of tai chi in practice promotes better concentration in other areas of life.

2. Thesis statement: The fastest-growing job markets through the year 2005 will be in the computer and medical fields.

    Topic sentences:
    - __3__ Numerous job openings also exist for home health aides, physical therapists, and occupational therapists.
    - __1__ The sources of these career opportunities are the rapid growth of the Internet and a generation of aging baby boomers needing more medical care.
    - __2__ Skilled computer engineers, systems analysts, and technical support personnel will find many job opportunities to choose from.

3. Thesis statement: The history of European contact with the Karaja Indians of Brazil is one of violence and exploitation.

    Topic sentences:
    - __2__ The Karaja, exposed to European diseases during the nineteenth century, were reduced in numbers by 90 percent.
    - __1__ During the eighteenth century, the *bandeirantes* led attacks on Karaja villages to get slaves.
    - __3__ Since the turn of the twentieth century, Brazilian pioneers have increasingly used Indian territory as grazing land.

PRACTICE 8

Now, go over the essay plan that you developed in Practice 6 and decide which paragraphs should come first, which second, and so forth. Does time order, space order, or order of importance seem appropriate to your subject? Number your paragraphs accordingly.

Linking Paragraphs

Just as the sentences within a paragraph should flow smoothly, so the paragraphs within an essay should be clearly **linked** one to the next. As you write your essay, do not make illogical jumps from one paragraph to another. Instead, guide your reader. Link the first sentence of each new paragraph to the thesis statement or to the paragraph before. Here are four ways to link paragraphs:

1. Repeat key words or ideas from the thesis statement.
2. Refer to words or ideas from the preceding paragraph.
3. Use transitional expressions.
4. Use transitional sentences.

1. Repeat key words or ideas from the thesis statement.* The topic sentences in the following essay plan repeat key words and ideas from the thesis statement.

Thesis statement:	Spending time in nature can promote inner peace and a new point of view.
Topic sentence:	A stroll in the woods or a picnic by the sea often brings feelings of inner peace and well-being.
Topic sentence:	Natural places can even give us a new point of view by putting our problems in perspective.

- In the first topic sentence, the words *feelings of inner peace* repeat, in slightly altered form, words from the thesis statement. The words *a stroll in the woods or a picnic by the sea* refer to the idea of *spending time in nature*.

- Which words in the second topic sentence repeat key words or ideas from the thesis statement?

natural places, new point of view

2. Refer to words or ideas from the preceding paragraph. Link the first sentence of a new paragraph to the paragraph before, especially by referring to words or ideas near the end of the paragraph. Note how the two paragraphs are linked in the following passage:

> (1) Would you rather take the risk of starting your own business than work for someone else? Would you prefer an insecure job with a large income over a secure job with an average income? Do you have a high energy level? If you answered yes to these questions, you might have some of the traits of what Dr. Frank Farley calls the "Type T" personality.
>
> (2) According to Farley, Type T people ("T" stands for "Thrill") are creative risk takers. He believes that as much as 30 percent of the American public falls into this category. "They are the great experimenters of life," declares Farley. "They break the rules."
>
> —Ira Peck and Larry F. Krieger, *Sociology: The Search for Social Patterns*

---

* For more work on repetition of key words, see Chapter 4, "Achieving Coherence," Part B. See also "Synonyms and Substitutions" in the same section.

■ What words and groups of words in paragraph 2 clearly refer to paragraph 1?

Farley, Type T people, and "T" stands for "Thrill"

3. Use transitional expressions.* Transitional expressions—words like *for example, therefore,* and *later on*—are used within a paragraph to show the relationship between sentences. Transitional expressions can also be used within an essay to show the relationships between paragraphs:

> (1) The house where I grew up was worn out and run-down. The yard was mostly mud, rock hard for nine months of the year but wet and swampy for the other three. Our nearest neighbors were forty miles away, so it got pretty lonely. Inside, the house was shabby. The living room furniture was covered in stiff, nubby material that had lost its color over the years and become a dirty brown. Upstairs in my bedroom, the wooden floor sagged a little further west every year.
>
> (2) *Nevertheless,* I love the place for what it taught me. There I learned to thrive in solitude. During the hours I spent alone, when school was over and the chores were done, I learned to play the guitar and sing. Wandering in the fields around the house or poking under stones in the creek bed, I grew to love the natural world. Most of all, I learned to see and to appreciate small wonders.

■ The first paragraph describes some of the negative details about the writer's early home. The second paragraph *contrasts* the writer's attitude, which is positive. The transitional expression *nevertheless* eases the reader from one paragraph to the next by pointing out the exact relationship between the paragraphs.

■ Transitional expressions can also highlight the *order* in which paragraphs are arranged.† Three paragraphs arranged in time order might begin: *First . . . , Next . . . , Finally. . . .* Three paragraphs arranged in order of importance might begin: *First . . . , More important . . . , Most important. . . .* Use transitional expressions alone or together with other linking devices.

4. Use transitional sentences. From time to time, you may need to write an entire sentence of transition to link one paragraph to the next, as shown in this passage:

> (1) Dee Kantner and Violet Palmer are hardly radicals, but they have helped bring about a revolution in sports. In 1995, both were experienced referees in women's college basketball and in the newly created Women's National Basketball Association, the WNBA. Although they were the top women in their profession, they wanted the prize all great referees want—to work in the NBA. In 1997, they won that prize, becoming the first women to referee regular-season games in the NBA and in professional football, hockey, and baseball.
>
> (2) *Achieving this goal, however, created a new challenge.* The two women now faced the criticism and even taunts of male players and coaches. Former Chicago Bulls coach Phil Jackson stated publicly that gender got them into NBA, not qualifications. Dennis Rodman shouted negative comments

---

*For a complete list of transitional expressions, see Chapter 4, "Achieving Coherence," Part B. See also the chapters in Unit 3 for ways to use transitional expressions in each paragraph and essay pattern.

†For more work on transitional expressions of time, space, and importance, see Chapter 4, "Achieving Coherence," Part A.

> on the court. Kenny Anderson responded to a foul call by telling Kantner to keep her eyes on the game and off his pants. Yet Kantner and Palmer have kept their cool, above all, focusing on the game. When asked how they can curb the behavior of quick-tempered players like Rodman, Charles Barkley, and Anthony Mason, Palmer told a reporter, "Confrontation is part of being a referee. If they cross a line, they get a technical foul."

- In paragraph 1, Kantner and Palmer achieve their goal. In paragraph 2, they face the reaction of the all-male NBA. The topic sentence of paragraph 2 is the second sentence: *The two women now faced the criticism and even taunts of male players and coaches.*

- The first sentence of paragraph 2 is actually a **sentence of transition** that eases the reader from success to a new challenge. (Note that it includes a transitional expression of contrast, *however*.)

Use all four methods of linking paragraphs as you write your essays.

PRACTICE 9

Read the essay that follows, noting the paragraph-to-paragraph *links*. Then answer the questions.

Skin Deep

(1) What do Johnny Depp, Lady Randolph Churchill, Whoopi Goldberg, and Charles Manson all have in common? Perhaps you guessed tattoos: body decorations made by piercing the skin and inserting colored pigments. In fact, tattoos have a long and nearly worldwide history, ranging from full-body art to a single heart, from tribal custom to pop-culture fad.

(2) The earliest known tattoo was found on the mummy of an Egyptian priestess dating back to 2200 B.C. Tattoos were also used in the ancient world to decorate Japanese noblemen, mark Greek spies, and hide expressions of fear on Maori tribesmen in New Zealand. Full-body tattooing was practiced for centuries in the South Seas; in fact, the word *tattoo* comes from the Tahitian word *tattaw*. In medieval times, small tattoos were common in Europe. For instance, in 1066, after the famous Battle of Hastings, the only way that the body of the Anglo Saxon King Harold could be identified was by the word *Edith* tattooed over his heart.

(3) For the next 600 years, however, Europeans lost interest in tattoos. Then, in the 1700s, explorers and sailors rekindled public excitement. Captain Cook, returning from a trip to Tahiti in 1761, described the wonders of tattoos. Cook enthusiastically paraded a heavily tattooed Tahitian prince named Omai through England's finest drawing rooms. People were intrigued by the colorful flowers, snakes, and geographical maps covering Omai's body. Although large tattoos were too much for the British, the idea of a pretty little bee or royal crest on the shoulder was very appealing. Tattooing remained popular with Europe's royalty and upper classes through the nineteenth century. The Prince of Wales, the Duke of York, Tsar Nicholas of Russia, and Winston Churchill's mother all had tattoos.

(4) When tattooing first reached America, on the other hand, its image was definitely not refined. American soldiers and sailors, feeling lonely and patriotic during World War II, visited tattoo parlors in South Pacific ports and came home with *Mother* or *Death Before Dishonor* inked into their arms. Soon motorcyclists started getting tattoos as part of their rebellious, macho image. The process was painful, with a high risk of infection, so the more elaborate a cyclist's bloody dagger or skull and crossbones, the better.

(5) Tattooing did not remain an outlaw rite of passage for long. Safer and less painful methods developed in the 1970s and 1980s brought tattooing into the American mainstream, especially among the young. Designs ranged from one butterfly to black-and-white patterns like Native American textiles to flowing, multicolored, stained-glass designs. With the media documenting the tattoos of the rich and famous, tattooing became a full-blown fad by the 1990s. Now the onetime symbols of daring have become so common that many rebels are having their tattoos removed. About one third of all the work performed by tattoo artists in the United States is "erasing" unwanted tattoos.

1. What transitional expressions does this writer use to link paragraphs? (Find at least two.) *For the next 600 years, however; on the other hand*

2. How does the writer link paragraphs 1 and 2? *Tattoo repeats key word in paragraph 1; "earliest known" refers to "long history"*

3. How does the writer link paragraphs 4 and 5? *Transitional sentence in 5; "outlaw rite of passage" refers to motorcyclists in 4*

PART E Writing and Revising Essays

Writing the First Draft

Now you should have a clear plan or outline from which to write your first draft. This plan should include your thesis statement, two to four topic sentences that support it, details and facts to develop each paragraph, and a logical order. Write on every other line to leave room for later corrections, including all your ideas and paragraphs in the order you have chosen to present them. Explain your ideas fully, but avoid getting stuck on a particular word or sentence. When you have finished the draft, set it aside, if possible, for several hours or several days.

PRACTICE 10

Write a first draft of the essay you have been working on in Practices 6 and 8.

Revising and Proofreading

Revising is perhaps the most important step in the essay-writing process. Revising an essay involves the same principles as revising a paragraph.* Read your first draft slowly and carefully to yourself—aloud if possible. Imagine you are a reader who has never seen the paper before. As you read, underline trouble spots, draw arrows, and write in the margins, if necessary, to straighten out problems.

Here are some questions to keep in mind as you revise:

1. Is my thesis statement clear?
2. Does the body of the essay fully support my thesis statement?
3. Does the essay have unity; does every paragraph relate to the thesis statement?
4. Does the essay have coherence; do the paragraphs follow a logical order?
5. Are my topic sentences clear?
6. Does each paragraph provide good details, well-chosen examples, and so on?
7. Is the language exact, concise, and fresh?
8. Are my sentences varied in length and type?
9. Does the essay conclude, not just leave off?

If possible, ask a **peer reviewer**—a trusted classmate or friend—to read your paper and give you feedback. Of course, this person should not rewrite or correct the essay but should simply tell you which parts are clear and which parts are confusing.

To guide your peer reviewer, you might ask him or her to use the Peer Feedback Sheet on page 37 or to answer these questions in writing:

1. What do you like about this piece of writing?
2. What seems to be the main point?
3. Which parts could be improved (meaning unclear sentences, supporting points missing, order mixed up, writing not lively, and so forth)? Please be specific.
4. What one change would most improve this essay?

Proofreading and Writing the Final Draft

Next, carefully **proofread** the draft for grammar and spelling. Check especially for those errors you often make: verb errors, comma splices, and so forth.† If you are unsure about the spelling of a word, check a dictionary or use the spellcheck on your computer.

Finally, neatly recopy your essay or print out a final copy on 8½-by-11-inch paper. Write on one side only. When you finish, proofread the final copy.

The following sample essay by a student shows his first draft, the revisions he made, and the revised draft. Each revision has been numbered and explained to give you a clear idea of the thinking process involved.

---

*For more work on revising, see Chapter 3, "The Process of Writing Paragraphs," Part F, and Chapter 22, "Putting Your Revision Skills to Work."

†For practice proofreading for individual errors, see chapters in Unit 6; for mixed-error proofreading, see Chapter 36.

First Draft

Portrait of a Bike Fanatic

(1) I first realized how serious Diane was when I joined her on a long trip one Sunday afternoon. Her bike looked new, so I asked her if it was. When she told me she had bought it three years ago, I asked her how she kept it looking so good. She showed me how she took good care of it.

(2) Diane had just about every kind of equipment I've ever seen. She put on her white crash helmet and attached a tiny rearview mirror on it—the kind the dentist uses to check out the backs of your teeth. She put a warning light on her left leg. She carried a whole bag full of tools. When I looked into it, I couldn't believe how much stuff was in there (wrenches, inner tubes, etc.)—tools to meet every emergency. I was tempted to see if it had a false bottom.

(3) I had no idea she was such a bike nut. We rode thirty miles and I was exhausted. Her equipment was something else, but useful because she had a flat and was able to fix it, saving our trip.

(4) She doesn't look like a bike fanatic, just a normal person. You'd never guess that her bike has more than 10,000 miles on it.

(5) As we rode, Diane told me about her travels throughout the Northeast (Cape Cod, Vermont, Penn., New York). Riding to work saved her money, kept her in shape. Her goal for the next summer was a cross-country tour over the Rockies!

(6) Our trip was no big deal to her but to me it was something. I might consider biking to work because it keeps you in shape. But basically I'm lazy. I drive a car or take the bus. I do like to walk though.

Revisions

Portrait of a Bike Fanatic

① Add intro and thesis

② about bicycling

③ thirty-mile

④ Describe in detail

⑤ For example,

I first realized how serious Diane was ② when I joined her on a ③ ~~long~~ trip one Sunday afternoon. Her bike looked new, so I asked her if it was. When she told me she had bought it three years ago, I asked her how she kept it looking so good. ~~She showed me how she took good care of it.~~

Diane had just about every kind of equipment I've ever seen. ⑤ For example, She put on her white crash helmet and attached a tiny rearview mirror on it—the kind the dentist uses to ~~check out~~ ⁶ examine the backs of your teeth. She ⁷ strapped to , just below the knee ~~put a warning light on~~ her leg.

⁸ Mention trip location

> She carried a whole bag full of tools. When I looked into it, I couldn't believe how much stuff was in there (wrenches, inner tubes, etc.)—tools to meet every emergency. I was tempted to see if it had a false bottom.

⁹ New ¶ on tools, flat tire

¹⁰ ~~I had no idea she was such a bike nut. We rode thirty miles and I was exhausted.~~ Her equipment was something else, but useful because she had a flat and was able to fix it, saving our trip.

¹¹ Combine into one ¶ on tools

¹² Move to intro?

She doesn't look like a bike fanatic, just a normal person. You'd never guess that her bike has more than 10,000 miles on it.

¹³ Describe in detail. Make interesting!

As we rode, Diane told me about her travels throughout the Northeast (Cape Cod, Vermont, Penn., New York). Riding to work saved her money, kept her in shape. Her goal for the next summer was a cross-country tour over the Rockies!

¹⁴ Better conclusion needed

Our trip was no big deal to her, but to me it was something. ~~I might consider biking to work because it keeps you in shape. But basically I'm lazy. I drive a car or take the bus. I do like to walk though.~~

¹⁵ Drop. Irrelevant

Reasons for Revisions

1. No thesis statement. Add catchy introduction. (introduction and thesis statement)
2. Add *bicycling*. What she is serious *about* is not clear. (exact language)
3. Tell *how* long! (exact language)
4. Expand this; more details needed. (support, exact language)
5. Add transition. (transitional expression)

6. Wrong tone for college essay. (exact language)

7. Find more active verb; be more specific. (exact language)

8. Conclude paragraph; stress time order. (order)

9. This section is weak. Add one paragraph on tools. Tell story of flat tire? (paragraphs, support)

10. Drop! Repeats thesis. Not really a paragraph. (unity, paragraphs)

11. Put this in tools paragraph. Order is mixed up. (order)

12. Put this in introduction? (order)

13. Add details; make this interesting! (support, exact language)

14. Write a better conclusion. (conclusion)

15. Drop! Essay is about Diane and biking, not my bad exercise habits. (unity)

Final Draft

Portrait of a Bike Fanatic

(1) You'd never guess that the powder-blue ten-speed Raleigh had more than 10,000 miles on it. And you'd never guess that the tiny woman with the swept-back hair and the suntanned forearms had ridden those miles over the last two years, making trips through eleven states. But Diane is a bicycle fanatic.

(2) I first realized how serious Diane was about bicycling when I joined her on a thirty-mile trip one Sunday afternoon. Her bike looked new, so I asked her if it was. When she told me she had bought it three years ago, I asked her how she kept it looking so good. From her saddlebag she took the soft cloth that she wiped the bike down with after every long ride and the plastic drop cloth that she put over it every time she parked it outdoors overnight.

(3) Diane had just about every kind of bike equipment I've ever seen. For example, she put on her white crash helmet and attached a tiny rearview mirror to it—the kind the dentist uses to examine the backs of your teeth. She strapped a warning light to her left leg, just below the knee. Then we set off on our trip, starting at Walden Pond in Concord and planning to go to the Wayside Inn in Sudbury and back again before the sun set.

(4) We were still in Concord when Diane signaled me to stop. "I think I have a flat," she said. I cursed under my breath. I was sure that would mean the end of our trip; we'd have to walk her bike back to the car and she'd have to take it to the shop the next day. But she reached into her saddlebag again, and out came a wrench and a new tube. Before I knew it, she took the rear wheel off the bike, installed the new tube, and put the wheel back on. I began to wonder what else was in that saddlebag. When I asked, she showed me two sets of wrenches, another spare inner tube, two brake pads, a can of lubricating oil, two screwdrivers, a roll of reflective tape, extra bulbs for her headlight and taillight, and an extra chain. She had so much in the bag, I was tempted to see if it had a false bottom. Diane is one of those bicyclists who have tools to meet any emergency and know how to use them.

(5) As we rode along, Diane told me about her travels throughout the Northeast. She had taken her bike on summer vacations on Cape Cod and fall foliage tours in Vermont. She had ridden all over Pennsylvania and upstate New York, covering as much as seventy miles in a single day. She also rode to and from work every day, which she said saved money, kept her in shape, and helped her start each day feeling good. Her goal for the next summer, she said, was a cross-country tour. "All the way?" I asked. "What about the Rockies?" "I know," she said. "What a challenge!"

(6) Our trip took a little less than three hours, but I'm sure Diane was slowing down to let me keep up with her. When we got back to the parked car, I was breathing hard and had worked up quite a sweat. Diane was already there waiting for me, looking as if she did this every day—which she does. For Diane, riding a bike is as easy and natural as walking is for most people. Look out, Rockies.

PRACTICE 11

Now, carefully read over the first draft of your essay from Practice 10 and **revise** it, referring to the checklist of questions on page 190. You might wish to ask a peer reviewer for feedback before you revise. Ask specific questions or use the peer feedback sheet on page 37. Take your time and write the best essay you can. Once you are satisfied, **proofread** your essay for grammar and spelling errors. Neatly write the final draft or print a final copy.

WRITING ASSIGNMENTS

The assignments that follow will give you practice in writing essays. In each, concentrate on writing a clear thesis statement and a full, well-organized body. Because introductions and conclusions are not discussed until Chapter 16, you may wish to begin your essay with the thesis statement and conclude as simply as possible.

Before you write, make a plan or an outline that includes

- a clear thesis statement
- two to four topic sentences that support the thesis statement
- details, facts, and examples to develop each paragraph
- a logical order of paragraphs

1. Some college students cheat on their papers and exams; some people cheat on the job. Why do people cheat? What are the advantages and disadvantages of cheating? Does cheating pay off? Does it achieve the end that the cheater desires? Focus on cheating at college or at work, and choose one main idea to write about. You might wish to use examples to support your thesis. Plan your essay carefully on paper—before you write it.

2. Interview a classmate (or, if you do this assignment at home, someone with an unusual skill). As you talk to the person, look for a thesis: ask questions, take notes. What stands out about the person? Is there an overall impression or idea that can structure your essay? Use your descriptive powers. Notice the person's looks, clothes, typical expressions, and gestures. Later, formulate a thesis statement about the person, organize your ideas, and write.

3. Do you feel that certain television programs show stereotypical women, African Americans, Hispanics, or members of any other group instead of believable people? Examine and discuss just one such program and one group of people. What situations, words, and actions by the TV characters are stereotypical, not real? Focus your subject, make a plan, and write a well-organized essay.

    You might wish to construct a thesis statement divided in this way: On the television program _(name show)_, _(name group)_ are often portrayed as being _(name stereotype)_.

4. Give advice to the weary job hunter. Describe the most creative job-hunting strategies you have ever tried or heard about. Support your thesis statement with examples, or consider using time order to show a successful job-hunting day in the life of the expert, you.

5. For better or worse, sex education begins at home—whether or not parents speak about the subject, whether parents' words reinforce or contradict the message of their own behavior. How do you think a parent should handle this responsibility? Be as specific as possible, including details from your own and your friends' experiences to make your point.

6. Draw upon your romantic misfortunes to give dating advice to others. Think back to the two, three, or four most disastrous dates you ever had. Relive the unhappy details, the disappointment, the shock, and take notes; look for a pattern, a thesis, that can pull these isolated bad times together. Now write an excellent paper in which you tell what happened to you and share your hard-earned wisdom with those seeking love—or at least, a first-run movie and popcorn.

7. Have you ever had a close call with death? Describe the experience and its effect, if any, on your attitudes and actions since. If it has had little or no effect on you, try to explain why. Be sure to unify your essay with a clear thesis statement.

8. Many children have working parents; in fact, mothers of young children make up 45 percent of the American work force. How do you think children are affected when both parents work or when their single parent works? Focus your discussion on one aspect of this topic that you can discuss fully in a short essay—on the positive and/or negative emotional effects on children, on the way day care affects children, and so forth.

✔ CHECKLIST: The Process of Writing an Essay

____ 1. Narrow the topic in light of your audience and purpose. Be sure you can discuss this topic fully in a short essay.

____ 2. Write a clear thesis statement. If you have trouble, freewrite or brainstorm first; then narrow the topic and write the thesis statement.

____ 3. Freewrite or brainstorm, generating facts, details, and examples to support your thesis statement.

____ 4. Plan or outline your essay, choosing from two to four main ideas to support the thesis statement.

____ 5. Write a topic sentence that expresses each main idea.

___ 6. Decide on a logical order in which to present the paragraphs.

___ 7. Plan the body of each paragraph, using all you learned about paragraph development in Unit 2 of this book.

___ 8. Write the first draft of your essay.

___ 9. Revise as necessary, checking your essay for support, unity, and coherence. Refer to the list of revision questions on page 190.

___ 10. Proofread carefully for grammar, punctuation, sentence structure, spelling, and mechanics.

Suggested Topics for Essays

1. The career for which I am best suited
2. This college's worst problem (propose a solution)
3. A special or unusual person
4. A valuable discipline or practice (lifting weights, rock climbing, meditating, or other)
5. Why many Americans don't read the newspaper (vote, value education, or read poetry)
6. The best (or worst) teacher I ever had
7. Music videos (choose one performer or group, one type of music, or one TV show)
8. A lesson in diversity, race, or difference
9. The joys of homework (or housework or some other supposedly unpleasant task)
10. How to resolve a disagreement peacefully
11. An important film (book, magazine, or program)
12. The best gift I ever gave (or received)
13. Three ways that cigarette ads hook kids
14. Should courts require a one-year "cooling-off" period before a divorce?
15. Writer's choice: _____

CHAPTER 15

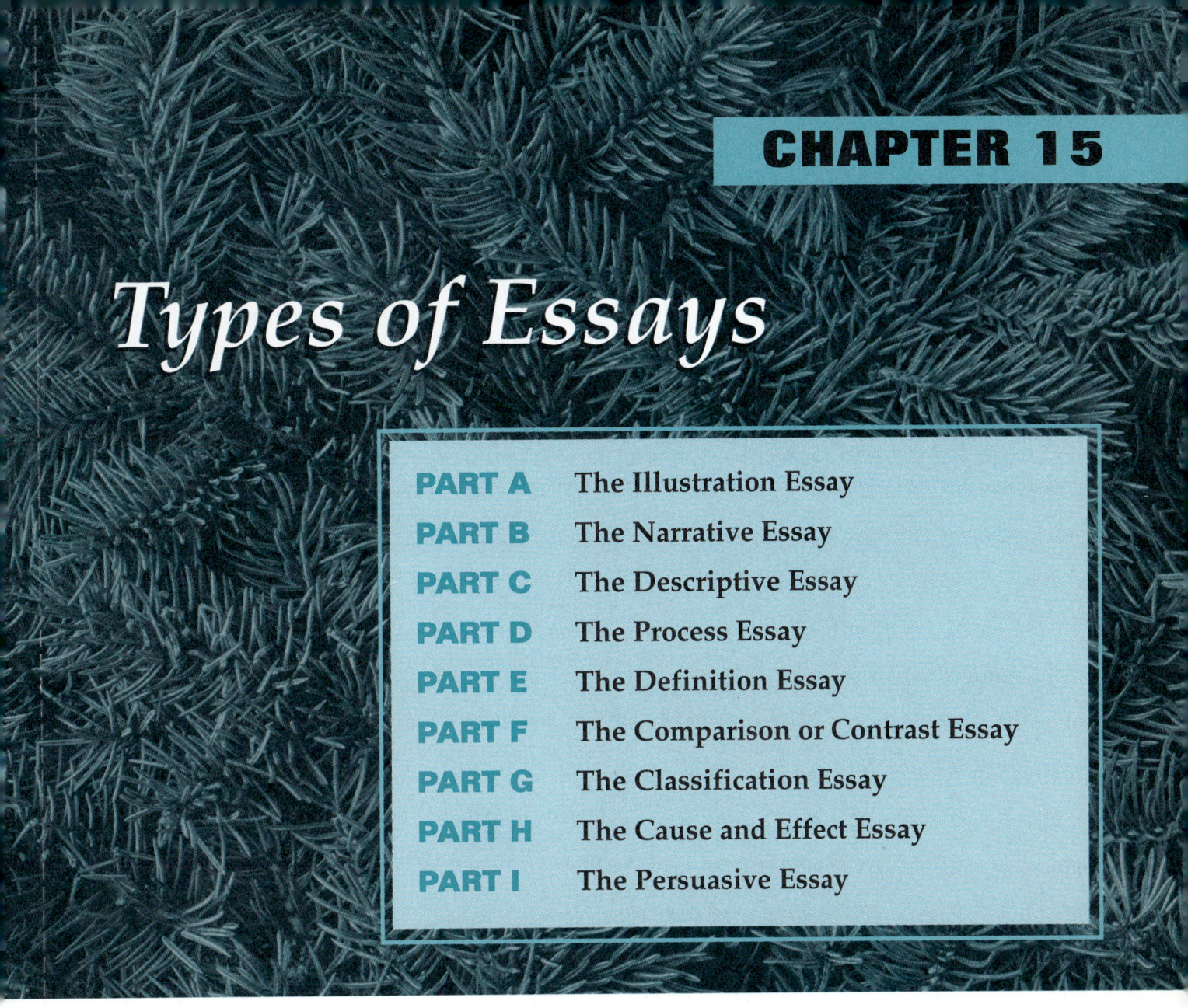

Types of Essays

PART A   The Illustration Essay
PART B   The Narrative Essay
PART C   The Descriptive Essay
PART D   The Process Essay
PART E   The Definition Essay
PART F   The Comparison or Contrast Essay
PART G   The Classification Essay
PART H   The Cause and Effect Essay
PART I   The Persuasive Essay

Because an essay is like an expanded paragraph, the methods for developing and organizing a paragraph that you learned in Unit 3—illustration, process, and so forth—can also be used to develop an entire essay. The rest of this chapter will show you how.

PART A   The Illustration Essay

The **illustration** essay is one of the most frequently used in college writing and in business. For papers and exams in history, psychology, health, English, and other subjects, you will often be asked to develop a main point with examples. In a letter of job application, you might wish to give examples of achievements that demonstrate your special skills.

Here is an illustration essay:

Libraries of the Future—Now

(1) When you think of the word *library*, do you picture an old-fashioned building, dusty books, and stern librarians? Think instead of an electronic theme park for readers, where people from tots to seniors can not only read books from the stacks around them, but explore cyberspace from one of many computer terminals. Imagine yourself calling up documents from libraries around the world or working with other students on multimedia projects. In fact, the future has arrived in a few pioneering libraries that are using technology to offer more resources to library users than ever before.

(2) For instance, the San Francisco Public Library is helping its diverse community enter the information age. At San Francisco's many branch libraries, visitors can now surf the Internet from public terminals, but the hub of the system is the $140 million San Francisco Main Public Library building, which opened in 1996. The seven-story building features 300 computer terminals where users can access catalogues, databases, and the World Wide Web. Another 1,100 users can plug their own laptops into the library's outlets. The huge children's book room has many more computers on child-sized tables. The San Francisco Library appears to be achieving its goal. In its first year, library visits jumped from 1.1 million to 2.1 million, and the number of library-card holders tripled.

(3) A second example of today's high-tech libraries is the private Vatican Library in Rome. The Vatican, headquarters of the Roman Catholic Church, has one of the finest collections of manuscripts and books in the world. The entire catalogue of this collection is now available on the Internet. Yet until recently, only about 2,000 scholars a year could come to Rome and examine such costly treasures as an ancient text handwritten on antelope skin or a perfect Gutenberg Bible. Now, with help from IBM, the Vatican is making digital images of these documents. In an underground, atom bomb–proof vault where the originals are kept, two technicians are scanning one page at a time with a special camera. Soon anyone will be able to see 20,000 rare, perfectly colored images and to enlarge the tiniest details on his or her computer screen.

(4) An even more futuristic library is the University of Michigan's new Media Union. Besides holding the University's art and architecture libraries, the 225,000-square-foot Media Union contains 500 computer workstations, computer training areas, four interactive multimedia classrooms, video and sound production facilities, a theater, a virtual reality and animation lab, a gallery, and, last but not least, books. Students can experience virtual worlds in dance, engineering, art, architecture, and computer science. Imagine two engineering students playing with 3-D designs of a century-old bridge to come up with a dynamic new form or a dance student moving with a virtual dance performance in real time. This exciting library lets people in many fields work together on new creations.

(5) These three unique libraries are helping to adapt the printed past to a digital future. However, they are still the exception, not the rule. Transforming our libraries requires millions of private and public dollars. As citizens, we can urge our elected officials to support the efforts of libraries as they help move all our citizens into the information age. When many of us were children, libraries opened the door to a world of dreams through books. The high-tech libraries of the future will open doors we cannot yet imagine.

- The **thesis statement** of an illustration essay states the writer's central point—a general statement that the rest of the essay will develop with examples.

- Which sentence in the introductory paragraph is the thesis statement?

   In fact, the future has arrived in a few pioneering libraries that are using technology to offer more resources to library users than ever before.

- How many examples does the writer use to develop the thesis statement? What are they?

   three: San Francisco Public Library, Vatican Library, and University of Michigan Media Union

- Underline the topic sentence of each supporting paragraph.

- The thesis statement and topic sentences setting forth the three examples create a **plan** for this essay. The writer no doubt made such a plan or an outline before she wrote the first draft.

   Before writing an illustration essay, you may wish to reread Chapter 5, "Illustration." As you pick a topic and plan your illustration essay, make sure your thesis statement can be richly developed by examples. Then brainstorm or freewrite, jotting down as many possible examples as you can think of; choose the best two or three examples. If you devote one paragraph to each example, each topic sentence should introduce the example to be developed. As you revise, make sure you have fully discussed each example, including all necessary details and facts.

PRACTICE 1

Choose a topic from the following list or use a topic that you or your instructor has chosen. Write an illustration essay, referring to the essay checklist at the end of Chapter 14.

Suggested Topics: The Illustration Essay

1. Good deeds that backfired
2. Inventions that probably will shape the twenty-first century
3. Failure as the best teacher
4. TV talk show hosts who send a positive message (or who _____)
5. Small events that changed lives
6. Memorable neighbors (professors, friends, and so on)
7. Currently cool hairstyles or clothing styles
8. Unusual places to go on dates (or to study, de-stress, get married, and so on)
9. Successful (or unsuccessful) college students
10. Musicians or artists of a particular group (R&B, tropical Latin, surrealist, French impressionist, and so on)
11. Writer's choice: _____

PART B The Narrative Essay

The narrative essay is used frequently in college writing. For instance, in a history course you might be assigned a paper on the major battles of World War I or be given an essay examination on the story of women's struggle to gain the right to vote. An English teacher may ask you to write a composition in which you retell a meaningful incident or personal experience. In all of these instances, your ability to organize facts and details in clear chronological, or time, order—to tell a story well—will be a crucial factor in the success of your paper.

Here is a narrative essay:

Maya Lin's Vietnam War Memorial

(1) The Vietnam War was the longest war in United States history, lasting from 1965 until 1975. Also our most controversial war, it left a deep wound in the nation's conscience. The creation of the Vietnam War Memorial helped heal this wound and put an unknown architecture student into the history books.

(2) In 1980, when the call went out for designs for a Vietnam War Memorial, no one could have predicted that as many as 14,000 entries would be submitted. The rules were clear. The memorial had to be contemplative, harmonize with its surroundings, list the names of those dead or missing, and—most important—make no political statement about the war. When the judges, all well-known architects and sculptors, met in April 1981, they unanimously chose entry number 1026. The winner was Maya Lin, a twenty-one-year-old Asian-American architecture student who, ironically, was too young to have had any direct experience of the war.

(3) Lin envisioned shining black granite slabs embedded in a long V-shaped trench, with one end pointing toward the Lincoln Memorial and the other toward the Washington Monument. She defined the trench as a cut in the earth, "an initial violence that in time would heal." Names would be carved into the granite in the order of the dates on which the soldiers had died or disappeared. Lin felt that finding a name on the memorial with the help of a directory would be like finding a body on a battlefield.

(4) Although her design satisfied all the contest criteria and was the judges' clear favorite, it aroused much controversy. Some critics called it a "black gash of shame and sorrow," labeling it unpatriotic, unheroic, and morbid. They were upset that the memorial contained no flags, no statues of soldiers, and no inscription other than the names. Privately, some complained that Lin was too young to win the contest—and that she was female besides. She fought back. She claimed that a flag would make the green area around the memorial look like a golf course and that a traditional statue on her modern structure would be like a mustache drawn on someone else's portrait. At last, a compromise was reached: A flag and a statue were added to the memorial, and the critics withdrew their complaints. On Veterans Day, November 11, 1982, the Vietnam War Memorial was finally dedicated.

(5) Since then, the memorial has become the most popular site in Washington, D.C. Some visit to see the monument and pay tribute to those who died in the war. Others come to locate and touch the names of loved ones. As they stand before the wall, they also learn the names of those who served and died with their relatives and friends. When the rain falls, all the names seem to disappear.

Visitors often leave memorials of their own—flowers, notes to the departed, bits of old uniforms. A place of national mourning and of love, Maya Lin's monument has helped heal the wounds of the Vietnam War.

- The **thesis statement** of a narrative essay gives the point of the essay.
- What is the thesis statement of the essay?

  The creation of the Vietnam War Memorial helped heal this wound and put an

  unknown architecture student into the history books.

- Paragraphs 2, 4, and 5 of this essay tell in chronological order the incidents of the narrative.
- What are the incidents?

  the call for designs, the judges' decision, the controversy, the dedication, the

  healing result

- What is the main idea of paragraph 3?

  a description of Maya Lin's design

- Paragraph 1 provides background information that helps the reader understand the narrative.
- What background material is given in this paragraph?

  The Vietnam War was the longest and most controversial war in U.S. history.

Before writing a narrative essay, you may wish to reread Chapter 6, "Narration." Make sure that your thesis statement clearly states the point of your narrative. Organize all the incidents and details in chronological, or time, order, in general beginning with the earliest event and ending with the latest. Be sure to supply any necessary background information. As you plan your essay, pay careful attention to paragraphing; if your narrative consists of just a few major incidents, you may wish to devote one paragraph to each one. Use transitional expressions that indicate time order to help your reader follow the narrative easily.

PRACTICE 2

Choose a topic from the following list or use a topic that you or your instructor has chosen. Write a narrative essay, referring to the essay checklist at the end of Chapter 14.

Suggested Topics: The Narrative Essay

1. A risk that paid off
2. How someone chose his or her career
3. The story behind a key scientific discovery or invention
4. An event that changed your view of yourself

5. An unforgettable incident you witnessed
6. An important historical event
7. A time someone acted with courage or cowardice
8. The plot line of a movie or TV show you would like to produce
9. Learning a new language (or other subject or skill)
10. Someone's battle with a serious illness
11. Writer's choice: _____

PART C The Descriptive Essay

Although paragraphs of **description** are more common than whole essays, you will sometimes need to write a descriptive essay. In science labs, you may need to describe accurately cells under a microscope or a certain kind of rock. In business, you might have to describe a product or piece of equipment. Travel writers frequently use description, and personal letters often call on your descriptive powers.

Here is a descriptive essay:

The Day of the Dead

(1) The most important holiday in Mexico is the Day of the Dead, *El Día de Los Muertos*. Surprisingly, this holiday is anything but depressing. In the weeks before, Mexicans excitedly prepare to welcome the souls of the dead, who come back each year to visit the living. From October 31 through November 2 this year, I attended this fiesta with my roommate Manuel. By sharing Day of the Dead activities in his family's home, in the marketplace, and in a cemetery, I have observed that Mexicans, unlike other North Americans, accept and celebrate death as a part of life.

(2) For this holiday, the home altar, or *ofrenda*, lovingly celebrates the dead. In the Lopez home, a trail of marigold petals and the rich smell of incense led us from the front door to the altar. The bright orange marigold blooms, the flowers of the dead, also trimmed a card table overflowing with everything the dead would need to take up their lives again. For Manuel's Uncle Angel there was a fragrant bowl of mole,* a glass of tequila, cigars, playing cards, and two Miles Davis jazz CDs. For Manuel's cousin Lucia, who died at eighteen months, there was a worn stuffed puppy, a coral blanket, and a bowl of the rice pudding she loved. Heavy black and yellow beeswax candles threw a soft glow on photos of Angel and Lucia. It was as if the dead had never left and would always have a place of honor.

(3) While death is given an honored place in the home, it is celebrated with humor and mockery in the marketplace. Here the skeleton, or *calavera*, rules. Shops sell sugar skulls, humorous bone figures, and even skeletons made of flowers. At the candy store, Manuel's niece picked out a white chocolate skull decorated with blue icing and magenta sequins in the eye sockets. In many bakeries, skull-and-crossbones designs decorated the delicious "bread of the dead." Most impressive were the stalls filled with *calacas*, handmade wooden skeletons,

---

*mole: a spicy sauce made with unsweetened chocolate

some no bigger than my thumb. The shelves showed a lively afterlife where skeleton musicians played in a band; skeleton writers tapped bony fingers on tiny typewriters, and teenage skeletons hoisted boom boxes on their matchstick-sized shoulder bones.

(4) On the evening of November first, reverence and fun combined in an all-night vigil at the cemetery. On a path outside the cemetery gate, rows of vendors sold soft drinks and cotton candy as if it were a sporting event. Men drank a strong fermented cactus beverage called *pulque* and played cards at picnic tables. The loud music of a mariachi band serenaded the dead, who would come back to eat the food laid out for them on the graves. Old grandmothers wearing hand-woven shawls mourned and wept while children chased each other around the pink- and blue-painted graves. Nobody scolded the children. Life and death did not seem so separate.

(5) While I have always felt fearful in cemeteries at home, there I felt excited and hopeful. When a soft breeze made the rows of candles flicker, I wondered if the souls of the children, the *angelitos*, had come back, laughing and giggling. Or was it the real children I heard laughing? I really didn't know. But I felt more alive than ever, waiting for the dead to arrive in a dusty cemetery in Mexico.

—Jason Eady (Student)

■ The **thesis statement** of a descriptive essay says what will be described and sometimes gives an overall impression of it or tells how the writer will approach the subject. Which sentence in the introductory paragraph is the thesis statement?

By sharing Day of the Dead activities in his family's home, in the marketplace, and in a cemetery, I have observed that Mexicans, unlike other North Americans, accept and celebrate death as a part of life.

■ Each paragraph in the body of this essay describes one scene or aspect of the topic. How many scenes or aspects are described, and what are they?

three scenes: the home altar, the marketplace and shops, and the village cemetery

■ What kind of **order** does the writer follow in organizing paragraph 2?

space order: petals leading door to altar, marigolds trim the altar, offerings for Angel and Lucia, photos

■ Paragraph 5 completes and **concludes** the essay. How effective is this student's conclusion?

Very effective. He movingly describes the laughter of children—or angelitos. He has so well described the fiesta that we can see why he felt "more alive" in that cemetery.

■ Note that the thesis statement and topic sentences make a **plan** for the whole essay.

Before writing an essay of description, you may wish to reread Chapter 7, "Description." Make sure that your thesis statement clearly sets forth the precise subject your essay will describe. Use your senses—sight, smell, hearing, taste, and touch—as you jot down ideas for the body. As you plan, pay special attention to organizing details and observations; space order is often the best way to organize a description. As you revise, pay special attention to the richness and exactness of your language and details; these are what make good descriptions come alive.

PRACTICE 3

Choose a topic from the following list or use a topic that you or your instructor has chosen. Write an essay of description, referring to the essay checklist at the end of Chapter 14.

Suggested Topics: The Descriptive Essay

1. The decorations and rituals of a holiday you know
2. A person or animal you have closely observed
3. The scene of a historic event or battle as you imagine it
4. A school, church, prison, store, gym, or other public place
5. A tourist attraction or a place of natural beauty
6. College classrooms in the twenty-first century
7. A computer, motorcycle, or piece of equipment from your job
8. A place you know from travel or reading
9. Your family portrait
10. A scene you will never forget
11. Writer's choice: _____

PART D The Process Essay

The **process** essay is frequently used in college and business. In psychology, for example, you might describe the stages of personality development. In history, you might explain the process of electing a president or how a battle was won or lost, while in business, you might set forth the steps of an advertising campaign. In science labs, you will often have to record the stages of an experiment.

Here is a process essay:

How to Prepare for a Final Exam

(1) At the end of my first semester at college, I postponed thinking about final examinations, desperately crammed the night before, drank enough coffee to keep the city of Cincinnati awake, and then got C's and D's. I have since realized that the students who got A's on their finals weren't just lucky; they knew how to *prepare.* There are many different ways to prepare for a final examination, and each individual must perfect his or her own style, but over the years, I have developed a method that works for me.

(2) First, when your professor announces the date, time, and place of the final—usually at least two weeks before—ask questions and take careful notes on the answers. What chapters will be covered? What kinds of questions will the test contain? What materials and topics are most important? The information you gather will help you study more effectively.

(3) Next, survey all the textbook chapters the test will cover, using a highlighter or colored pen to mark important ideas and sections to be studied later. Many textbooks emphasize key ideas with boldface titles or headlines; others are written so that key ideas appear in the topic sentences at the beginning of each paragraph. Pay attention to these guides as you read.

(4) Third, survey your class notes in the same fashion, marking important ideas. If your notes are messy or disorganized, you might want to rewrite them for easy reference later.

(5) Fourth, decide approximately how many hours you will need to study. Get a calendar and clearly mark off the hours each week that you will devote to in-depth studying. If possible, set aside specific times: Thursday from 1 to 2 p.m., Friday from 6 to 8 p.m., and so on. If you have trouble committing yourself, schedule study time with a friend; but pick someone as serious as you are about getting good grades.

(6) Fifth, begin studying systematically, choosing a quiet place free from distractions in which to work—the library, a dorm room, whatever helps you concentrate. One of my friends can study only in his attic; another, in her car. As you review the textbook and your notes, ask yourself questions based on your reading. From class discussions, try to spot the professor's priorities and to guess what questions might appear on the exam. Be creative; one friend of mine puts important study material on cassette tapes, which he plays walking to and from school.

(7) Finally, at least three days before the exam, start reviewing. At the least opportunity, refer to your notes, even if you are not prepared to digest all the material. Use the moments when you are drinking your orange juice or riding the bus; just looking at the material can promote learning. By the night before the exam, you should know everything you want to know—and allow for a good night's sleep!

(8) By following these simple procedures, you may find, as I do, that you are the most prepared person in the exam room, confident that you studied thoroughly enough to do well on the exam.

—Mark Reyes (Student)

- The **thesis statement** in a process essay tells the reader what process the rest of the essay will describe.
- What is the thesis statement in this essay?

  There are many different ways to prepare for a final examination, and each individual must perfect his or her own style, but over the years, I have developed a method that works for me.

- What process will be described?

  preparing for a test

- How many steps make up this process, and what are they?

  six: ask questions about the test, survey the chapters to be tested, survey

  class notes, plan studying times, begin studying systematically, review

  material

- What kind of order does the writer use to organize his essay?

  chronological order

Before writing a process essay, you may wish to reread Chapter 8, "Process." The thesis statement should clearly set forth the process you intend to describe. As you plan your essay, jot down all the necessary steps or stages and put them in logical order. As you revise, make sure you have fully and clearly explained each step so that a reader who may not be familiar with the subject matter can follow easily. Clear language and logical organization are the keys to good process writing. Pay special attention to paragraphing; if the process consists of just three or four steps, you may wish to devote one paragraph to each step. If the steps are short or numerous, you will probably wish to combine two or three steps in each paragraph.

PRACTICE 4

Choose a topic from the list below or use a topic that you or your instructor has chosen. Write a process essay, referring to the essay checklist at the end of Chapter 14.

Suggested Topics: The Process Essay

1. How someone achieved success
2. How to prepare for a trip (backpacking, a weekend in Las Vegas, and so on)
3. How to get in shape
4. How a cell phone can ruin a date (or other social occasion)
5. How to get action on a community problem
6. How to teach a child a skill or value
7. The yearly cycle of a crop (corn, wheat, oranges, cocoa, and so on)
8. How to impress the boss
9. A process you learned in another course (stages of human moral development, how a lake becomes a meadow, and so on)
10. How to get an A in _____
11. Writer's choice: _____

PART E The Definition Essay

Although paragraphs of **definition** are more common in college writing than essays are, you may at some time have to write a definition essay. In a computer course, for example, you might be called on to define *Internet* and *intranet*. In psychology, you might need to define the *Oedipus complex,* or in biology, the terms *DNA* or *spontaneous remission.*

Here is a definition essay:

Winning

(1) The dictionary defines winning as "achieving victory over others in a competition, receiving a prize or reward for achievement." Yet some of the most meaningful wins of my life were victories over no other person, and I can remember winning when there was no prize for performance. To me, winning means overcoming obstacles.

(2) My first experience of winning occurred in elementary school gym. Nearly every day, after the preparatory pushups and squat-thrusts, we had to run relays. Although I had asthma as a child, I won many races. My chest would burn terribly for a few minutes, but it was worth it to feel so proud—not because I'd beaten others or won a prize, but because I'd overcome a handicap. (By the way, I "outgrew" my asthma by age eleven.)

(3) In high school, I had another experience of winning. Although I loved reading about biology, I could not bring myself to dissect a frog in lab. I hated the smell of the dead animals, and the idea of cutting them open disgusted me. Every time I tried, my hands would shake and my stomach would turn. Worst of all, my biology teacher reacted to my futile attempts with contempt. After an upsetting couple of weeks, I decided to get hold of myself. I realized that I was overreacting. "The animals are already dead," I told myself. With determination, I swept into my next lab period, walked up to the table, and with one swift stroke, slit open a frog. After that, I excelled in biology. I had won again.

(4) I consider the fact that I am now attending college winning. To get here, I had to surmount many obstacles, both outside and inside myself. College costs money, and I don't have much of it. College takes time, and I don't have much of that either with a little son to care for. But I overcame these obstacles and a bigger one still—lack of confidence in myself. I had to keep saying, "I won't give up." And here I am, winning!

(5) These examples should clarify what winning means to me. I don't trust anything that comes too easily. In fact, I expect the road to be rocky, and I appreciate a win more if I have to work, sacrifice, and overcome. This is a positive drive for me, the very spirit of winning.

—Audrey Holmes (Student)

- The **thesis statement** of a definition essay tells the reader what term will be defined and usually defines it as well.

- Which sentence in the introductory paragraph is the thesis statement?

  To me, winning means overcoming obstacles.

- What is the writer's definition of *winning*?

  Winning to this writer means overcoming obstacles.

- Underline the topic sentences of paragraphs 2, 3, and 4.

- How do paragraphs 2, 3, and 4 develop the thesis statement?

    They give examples of how the writer overcame obstacles in her life.

- What order does the writer follow in paragraphs 2, 3, and 4?

    time order

Before writing a definition essay, you may wish to reread Chapter 9, "Definition." Choose a word or term that truly interests you, one about which you have something to say. Decide what type of definition you will use and write the thesis statement, which should state and define your term. Then brainstorm ideas to explain your definition. Consider using two or three examples to develop the term—the way the writer does in the preceding essay—devoting one paragraph to each example. As you revise, make sure your writing is very clear, so the reader knows exactly what you mean.

PRACTICE 5

Choose a topic from the following list or one that you or your instructor has chosen. Write a definition essay, referring to the essay checklist at the end of Chapter 14.

Suggested Topics: The Definition Essay

1. A special term from sports, music, art, science, or technology
2. Tolerance
3. A friend
4. An environmental term (*endangered species, wind chill, global warming,* and so on)
5. A breed of dog or other animal
6. Sexual harassment
7. Maturity
8. A slang term in current use
9. A term from another language (*salsa, joi de vivre, machismo, zeitgeist,* and so on)
10. A disease or medical condition
11. Writer's choice: _____

PART F The Comparison or Contrast Essay

Essays of **comparison** or **contrast** are frequently called for in college courses. In an English or a drama class, you might be asked to contrast two of Shakespeare's villains—perhaps Iago and Claudius. In psychology, you might have to contrast the training of the clinical psychologist and that of the psychiatrist, or in history, to compare ancient Greek and Roman religions.

Does the following essay compare or contrast?

Two Childhoods

(1) When I was young, my mother told me stories about her childhood. I loved her tales and still think of them. It was intriguing to hear about life thirty years before mine began. What fascinated me most, however, were the differences between her youth and mine.

(2) My mother grew up in the country. She spent most of her young years on a farm in South Carolina, surrounded by animals, orchards, cane fields, and agricultural machinery. By the time she was six, she was a walking agricultural textbook. Hers was a simple, serene, and comfortable life within a close-knit, neighborly environment. My mother's days were filled with swimming in nearby rivers and lakes, climbing and falling off trees, scooter riding down country lanes, playing marbles with siblings and friends, bird watching and mending of wings, and building fences and tree houses.

(3) My childhood, on the other hand, was spent in New York City, without animals, scenic surroundings, or close-knit neighbors. Mine was a lifestyle of fast activity crammed into a tight schedule. Nature was replaced by shops and businesses, trees by tall buildings. My knowledge was not based on the simple things at hand, but on expensive toys, the latest clothes, and the newest sneakers. Compared with my mother's country existence, my city childhood seems humdrum—a constant series of trips to the park or movies, visits to the grocery store or shopping center, picnics at the amusement park or beach, and a few birthday parties thrown in.

(4) Just as our lifestyles differed, so too did our personalities. Relatives say that my mother was a loving, caring child who was always willing to help. She was praised for being clever and vibrant, levelheaded and respectful to others. My mother was strong willed and spoke her mind when she saw fit, but she placed few demands on her parents for toys or fancy clothes. Somehow her environment, which had instilled in her an appreciation of nature and living things, was enough.

(5) I, on the other hand, was considered a bit too extroverted, selfish, and stubborn. I reveled in being petulant, pigheaded, demanding, and unstable. Although I could be loving, I cleverly used this trait to my advantage in an attempt to manipulate my parents and get the beautiful toys and clothes I wanted. After all, these gave me all the aesthetic appreciation I needed. In fact, I was a brazenfaced brat.

(6) Looking back, I think it would have been wonderful as a child to have fallen off a few trees or driven a scooter at maniacal speeds or even milked a cow or crushed some coffee beans in a mortar. Yes, that would have been wonderful. It really would have been.

—Cheryl Parris (Student)

- The **thesis statement** of a comparison or contrast essay tells what two persons or things will be compared or contrasted.
- What is the thesis statement of this essay?

What fascinated me most, however, were the differences between her youth

and mine.

- Will this essay compare or contrast the two people? What word or words in the thesis indicate this?

  contrast; differences

- Does the writer discuss all points about A and then all points about B, or skip back and forth from A to B?

  skips back and forth from A to B

- Note that the thesis statement and topic sentences make a **plan** for this essay.

Before you plan or outline your essay, you may wish to reread Chapter 10, "Comparison and Contrast." Bear in mind, as you choose a subject, that the most interesting essays usually compare two things that are different or contrast two things that are similar. Otherwise, you run the risk of saying the obvious ("Cats and dogs are two different animals").

Here are a few tips to keep in mind as you write your thesis statement: Don't just say that A and B are similar or different; instead, say *in what way* A and B are similar or different, as the writer does on page 209. You may wish to use this form for a contrast thesis: *Although A and B have this similarity, they are different in these ways.* And for a comparison: *Although A and B are unlike in this way, they are similar in these ways.*

As you plan the body of your essay, you may wish to make a chart of all your points of comparison or contrast. In any case, if you discuss the food, service, price, and atmosphere of Restaurant A, you must discuss the food, service, price, and atmosphere of Restaurant B as well.

In your essay, you can first discuss A (one paragraph), then discuss B (one paragraph), or you can skip back and forth between A and B (one paragraph on point one, A and B, one paragraph on point two, A and B, and one paragraph on point three, A and B). Refer to the charts in Chapter 10, page 121.

Practice 6

Choose a topic from the list below or use a topic that you or your instructor has chosen. Write either a comparison or a contrast essay, referring to the essay checklist at the end of Chapter 14.

Suggested Topics: The Comparison or Contrast Essay

1. Two entertainers, athletes, philosophers, politicians, or other public figures
2. Your mother's or father's childhood and your own
3. Two cultural attitudes about one subject
4. A neighborhood store and a chain store (bookstore, restaurant, music store, and so on)
5. Two cars, computers, or other machines
6. Two views on a controversial issue
7. Two houses or apartments that you know well
8. A traditional doctor and an alternative healer
9. A book and a movie made from that book

10. Two pets

11. Writer's choice: _____

PART G The Classification Essay

The **classification** essay is useful in college and business. In music, for example, you might have to classify Mozart's compositions according to the musical periods of his life. A retail business might classify items in stock according to popularity—how frequently they must be reordered.

Although the classification essay is usually serious, the pattern can make a good humorous essay, as this essay shows:

The Potato Scale

(1) For years, television has been the great American pastime. Nearly every household has at least one TV, which means that people are spending time watching it, unless, of course, they bought it to serve as a plant stand. Television viewers can be grouped in many ways—by the type of shows they watch (but there is no accounting for taste) or by hours per week of watching (but that seems unfair since a working, twelve-hour-a-week viewer could conceivably become a fifty-hour-a-week viewer if he or she were out of a job). So I have developed the Potato Scale. The four major categories of the Potato Scale rank TV viewers on a combination of leisure time spent watching, intensity of watching, and the desire to watch versus the desire to engage in other activities.

(2) First, we have the True Couch Potatoes. They are diehard viewers who, when home, will be found in front of their televisions. They no longer eat in the dining room, and if you visit them, the television stays on. *TV Guide* is their Bible. They will plan other activities and chores around their viewing time, always hoping to accomplish these tasks in front of the tube. If a presidential address is on every channel but one, and they dislike the president, they will tune in that one channel, be it Bugs Bunny reruns or Polynesian barge cooking. These potatoes would never consider turning off the box.

(3) The second group consists of the Pseudo Couch Potatoes. These are scheduled potatoes. They have outside interests and actually eat at the table, but for a certain period of time (let's say from seven to eleven in the evening), they will take on the characteristics of True Couch Potatoes. Another difference between True and Pseudo Potatoes deserves note. The True Potato must be forced by someone else to shut off the television and do something different; however, if the Pseudo Potato has flipped through all the channels and found only garbage, he or she still has the capacity to think of other things to do.

(4) Third, we have the Selective Potatoes. These more discriminating potatoes enjoy many activities, and TV is just one of them. They might have a few shows they enjoy watching regularly, but missing one episode is not a world-class crisis. After all, the show will be on next week. They don't live by *TV Guide,* but use it to check for interesting specials. If they find themselves staring at an awful movie or show, they will gladly, and without a second thought, turn it off.

(5) The fourth group consists of Last Resort Potatoes. These people actually prefer reading, going to the theater, playing pickup basketball, walking in the woods, and many other activities to watching television. Only after they have exhausted all other possibilities or are dog tired or shivering with the flu, will they click on the tube. These potatoes are either excessively choosy or almost indifferent to what's on, hoping it will bore them to sleep.

(6) These are the principal categories of the Potato Scale, from the truly vegetable to the usually human. What type of potato are you?

—Helen Petruzzelli (Student)

- The **thesis statement** in a classification essay tells the reader what group will be classified and on what basis.

- This entire essay **classifies** people on the basis of their television viewing habits. Which sentence is the thesis statement?

  The four major categories of the Potato Scale rank TV viewers . . . to engage in other activities.

- Into how many categories are TV viewers divided?

  four

- Each paragraph in the body of the essay discusses one of four categories, which the writer names. What are they?

  1: *True Couch Potatoes*

  2: *Pseudo Couch Potatoes*

  3: *Selective Potatoes*

  4: *Last Resort Potatoes*

- The thesis statement and the topic sentences setting forth the four categories create a **plan** for the essay. The writer no doubt made the plan before she wrote the first draft.

- Can you see the logic in the writer's *order* of paragraphs? That is, why does she present True Couch Potatoes first, Pseudo Potatoes second, Selective Potatoes third, and Last Resort Potatoes last?

  She moves from people who watch TV the most to those who watch it the least.

Before writing your classification essay, you may wish to reread Chapter 11, "Classification." Choose a topic that lends itself to classification and carefully determine your basis of classification. Your thesis statement should state clearly the group you will classify and your basis of classification. As you plan, make sure that all your categories (three or four is a good number) reflect that basis of classification. Discuss one category per paragraph, including enough examples, details, and facts to let the reader completely understand your ideas.

PRACTICE 7

Choose a topic from the following list or use a topic that you or your instructor has chosen. Write a classification essay, referring to the essay checklist at the end of Chapter 14.

Suggested Topics: The Classification Essay

1. Members of your family
2. People studying in the library
3. Stories on the front page of the newspaper
4. Drivers
5. Soap operas
6. Teenagers whom you interview about their hopefulness or the lack of it (or their belief in education, thoughts about gangs, and so on)
7. Restaurants, music stores, or shoe stores in your neighborhood
8. Criminals
9. Your coworkers
10. People in a movie theater
11. Writer's choice: _____

PART H The Cause and Effect Essay

Essays of **cause and effect** are among the most important kinds of essays to master because knowing how to analyze the causes and consequences of events will help you succeed in college, at work, and in your personal life. What *caused* a historic battle, an increase in homelessness since the 1980s, or two friends' breaking apart? How will a certain child be *affected* by owning a computer, spending time at Sunshine Day Care, or being teased because he loves to dance? In business, the success of every company and product relies on a grasp of cause and effect in the marketplace. Why does this brand of sneaker outsell all others? What causes employees to want to work hard? How will the Internet affect business in 2015?

Here is an essay of cause and effect. As you will see, this writer's eventual understanding of causes and effects might have saved her life.

Why I Stayed and Stayed

(1) It has been proven that about 1.8 million women are battered each year, making battery the single largest cause of injury to women in the United States. Domestic violence can be physical, emotional, verbal, financial, or sexual abuse from a partner you live with. I suffered from most of these abuses for almost ten years. I have had black eyes, busted lips, bruises, and scars on my face. He had affairs with other women, yet he claimed that he loved me. People ask, "Why did you wait so long to leave him?" I stayed for many reasons.

(2) First, I was born in a country that is male-dominated. Many of my people accept violence against women as a part of life. I grew up seeing hundreds of women staying in violent relationships for the sake of their children. They wanted their children to grow up with a father at home. Relatives convinced these women to try to make their marriages work. This was all I knew.

(3) Another reason I stayed was that I was afraid to make changes in my life. I had been with him so long that I thought I had nowhere to go. I depended on

him to provide me and my child with food and shelter. How could I manage on my own? Of course, the longer I believed these things, the more my self-confidence withered.

(4) Finally, I stayed because I was isolated. I felt ashamed to talk about the problem, believing it was somehow my fault. Fear was isolating, too. Living in a violent home is very frightening. Like many women, I was afraid to say anything to anyone, thinking he would get upset. If I just kept quiet, maybe he wouldn't hurt me. But nothing I did made any difference.

(5) When I finally realized that the abuse was not going to stop, I decided to do something about it. I was finally ready to end my pain. I began to talk to people and learn about ways to get help.

(6) On April 24 of this year, I fought back. When he punched me in the eye, I called 911. Thank God for changes in the way domestic violence cases are now being handled. The police responded quickly. He was arrested and taken to jail, where he waited for two days to go to court. The next day, I went to the courthouse to press charges. I spoke to the district attorney in charge, asking for an order of protection. This order forbids him from having any verbal or physical contact with me.

(7) It is very hard to see someone you love being taken away in handcuffs, but I had to put my safety and my child's well-being first. Although he is now out of jail, I feel safe with my order of protection; however, I understand that court orders sometimes do not stop abusers. These are very difficult days for me, but I pray that time will heal my wounds. I cry often, which helps my pain. But an innocent life depends on me for guidance, and I cannot let her down.

(8) Every case is different, and you know your partner better than anyone, but help is out there if you reach for it. Most cities have a twenty-four-hour hotline. There is help at this college at the PASS Center and the Department of Student Development. You can go to a shelter, to a friend, to your family. These people will not fail you. You too can break the chain.

—Fadima (Student, last name withheld by request)

■ The **thesis statement** in a cause and effect essay identifies the subject and tells whether causes or effects will be emphasized. What is this writer's thesis statement? Will she emphasize causes or effects?

I stayed for many reasons; causes

■ How many causes does the writer discuss, and what are they?

three: upbringing, fear of change, isolation

■ Although some essays discuss either causes or effects, this one does both. Paragraph 5 marks a turning point, her decision to take action. What positive effects of this new decision does she discuss? Are there any negative effects?

reached out for help and information, fought back by calling 911 and getting

order of protection, acted for her daughter's welfare; negative feelings, sadness

and guilt

- Before she wrote this essay, the writer probably made a plan like this:

   Introduction and thesis statement
   Reasons for staying with abusive partner — upbringing, fear of change, isolation
   Decision to leave
   Effects of leaving abusive partner — reached out for help, fought back (911, order of protection), acted for daughter
   Advice for women in the same situation — sadness, guilt

- What order does this essay follow?

  time

- Do you think paragraph 8 makes an effective conclusion?

  good information but might seem anticlimactic after dramatic personal story

Before writing an essay of cause or effect, reread Chapter 12, "Cause and Effect," especially the section called "Avoiding Problems in Cause and Effect Writing." Choose a subject that lends itself to analysis of causes or effects; see the topic lists in Chapter 12 and this chapter for ideas. Think on paper or on computer, listing many possible causes or effects; then choose the best three or four. Don't forget to consider short- and long-term effects, as well as positive and negative effects. Decide on a logical order—probably time order or order of importance.

PRACTICE 8

Choose a topic from the following list or one that your instructor has chosen. Write a cause and effect essay, referring to the checklist at the end of Chapter 14.

Suggested Topics: The Cause and Effect Essay

1. What are the reasons for the popularity of a product, musical group, or game?
2. What caused you to do something you are not proud of?
3. Analyze the main causes of a serious problem in society.
4. Analyze the effects of shyness on someone's life (or anger, pride, curiosity or the lack of it, and so on).
5. What are the effects of a tragedy?
6. What are the effects of a new experience (a trip, military service, living in another country, dorm life)?
7. What causes a hurricane, tornado, or other natural disaster?
8. Choose an event in history that interests you and analyze its causes.
9. What effects did an early failure or success (in public speaking, sports, and so on) have on someone you know?
10. How does being unusual looking affect one's daily life?
11. Writer's choice: _____

PART 1   The Persuasive Essay

Persuasive essays are the essay type most frequently called for in college and business. That is, you will often be asked to take a stand on an issue—legalized abortion, capital punishment, whether a company should invest in on-site child care—and then try to persuade others to agree with you. Examination questions asking you to "agree or disagree" are really asking you to take a stand and make a persuasive case for that stand—for example, "World War II was basically a continuation of World War I. Agree or disagree." You are asked to muster factual evidence to support your stand.

Here is a persuasive essay:

Stopping Youth Violence: An Inside Job

(1) Every year, nearly a million twelve- to nineteen-year-olds are murdered, robbed, or assaulted—many by their peers—and teenagers are more than twice as likely as adults to become the victims of violence, according to the Children's Defense Fund. Although the problem is far too complex for any one solution, teaching young people conflict-resolution skills—that is, nonviolent techniques for resolving disputes—seems to help. To reduce youth violence, conflict-resolution skills should be taught to all children before they reach junior high school.

(2) First and most important, young people need to learn nonviolent ways of dealing with conflict. In a dangerous society where guns are readily available, many youngsters feel they have no choice but to respond to an insult or an argument with violence. If they have grown up seeing family members and neighbors react to stress with verbal or physical violence, they may not know that other choices exist. Robert Steinback, a *Miami Herald* columnist who works with at-risk youth in Miami, writes that behavior like carrying a weapon or refusing to back down gives young people "the illusion of control," but what they desperately need is to learn real control—for example, when provoked, to walk away from a fight.

(3) Next, conflict-resolution programs have been shown to reduce violent incidents and empower young people in a healthy way. Many programs and courses around the country are teaching teens and preteens to work through disagreements without violence. Tools include calmly telling one's own side of the story and listening to the other person without interrupting or blaming—skills that many adults don't have! Conflict Busters, a Los Angeles public school program, starts in the third grade; it trains students to be mediators, helping peers find their own solutions to conflicts ranging from "sandbox fights to interracial gang disputes," according to *Youthwatch: Statistics on Violence*, October 1999. Schools in Claremont, Connecticut, run a conflict-resolution course written by Dr. Luz Rivera, who said in a phone interview that fewer violent school incidents have been reported since the course began. Although conflict resolution is useful at any age, experts agree that students should first be exposed before they are hit by the double jolts of hormones and junior high school.

(4) Finally, although opponents claim that this is a "Band-Aid" solution that does not address the root causes of teen violence—poverty, troubled families, bad schools, and drugs, to name a few—in fact, conflict-resolution training saves lives now. The larger social issues must be addressed, but they will take years to solve, whereas teaching students new attitudes and "people skills" will empower them

immediately and serve them for a lifetime. For instance, fourteen-year-old Verna, who once called herself Vee Sinister, says that Ms. Rivera's course has changed her life: "I learned to stop and think before my big mouth gets me in trouble. I use the tools with my mother, and guess what? No more screaming at home."

(5) The violence devastating Verna's generation threatens everyone's future. One proven way to help youngsters protect themselves from violence is conflict-resolution training that begins early. Although it is just one solution among many, this solution taps into great power: the hearts, minds, and characters of young people.

- The **thesis statement** in a persuasive essay clearly states the issue to be discussed and the writer's position on it. What is the thesis statement?

    To reduce youth violence, conflict-resolution skills should be taught to all children before they reach junior high school.

- This introduction includes *facts*. What is the source of these facts and why does the writer include them here?

    Children's Defense Fund. These facts show how serious a problem youth crime is.

- Sometimes a writer needs to define terms he or she is using. What term does the writer define?

    conflict-resolution skills

- How many reasons does this writer give to back up the thesis statement?

    three

- Notice that the writer presents one reason per paragraph.

- Which reasons refer to an *authority*?

    reason 1 and reason 2

- Who are these authorities?

    Robert Steinback, Miami Herald columnist who works with youth, and Dr. Luz Rivera, who wrote a conflict-resolution course

- How is the second reason supported?

    by examples

- What is the source of information on Conflict Busters?

    Youthwatch: Statistics on Violence, October 1999

- Which reason is really an *answer to the opposition*?

    reason 3

218   UNIT 4   Writing the Essay

- This reason also uses an *example*. What or who is the example?

  <u>Verna, a student whose life changed</u>

- Note that the thesis statement and topic sentences make up a plan or an outline for the whole essay.

Before writing an essay of persuasion, reread Chapter 13, "Persuasion." Craft your thesis statement carefully. Devote one paragraph to each reason, developing each paragraph fully with facts and discussion. Use some of the methods of persuasion discussed in Chapter 13: *facts, referring to an authority, examples, predicting the consequence,* and *answering the opposition*. Revise for clarity and support, and remember, ample factual support is the key to successful persuasion. An excellent way to find interesting factual support is to do some basic research—for example, to find books or magazine articles by or about experts on your subject or even to conduct your own interviews, as does the author of "Stopping Youth Violence: An Inside Job."*

PRACTICE 9

In a group of four or five classmates, study this billboard. It is part of a campaign to persuade young people in Florida *not to smoke*.

Now have someone record your group's answers to these questions:

1. How effective—how persuasive—is the antismoking message of this billboard? Why?

---

* For information on summarizing and quoting outside sources, see Chapter 18, "Special College Skills: Summary and Quotation."

2. Do you think the intended audience of teens and young people will get the message? Why or why not?

3. The tobacco industry spends billions for ads that make smoking seem glamorous and grown-up. Does this picture successfully *oppose the tobacco industry's claim* that smoking is glamorous?

4. If your group were designing a billboard to persuade young people *not to smoke*, what would your message be?

PRACTICE 10

Choose a topic from the list below or one that your instructor has chosen. Make sure your thesis statement takes a clear stand. Write a persuasive essay, referring to the checklist at the end of Chapter 14.

Suggested Topics: The Persuasive Essay

1. Parents should routinely test their children's urine for evidence of drug use.
2. Computer and Internet classes should be given to every child in this state.
3. All animal testing of medicines should be banned, even if it will save human lives.
4. Every college student should be required to give three credit hours' worth of community service a year.
5. Only minority police should patrol minority neighborhoods.
6. A college education is (not) worth the time and money.
7. Gay couples should be allowed to adopt children.
8. Naturalized citizens should be allowed to run for president.
9. To better prepare students for the world of work, this college should do three things.
10. Illegal aliens in the United States should be entitled to receive basic health services.
11. Writer's choice: _____

CHAPTER 16

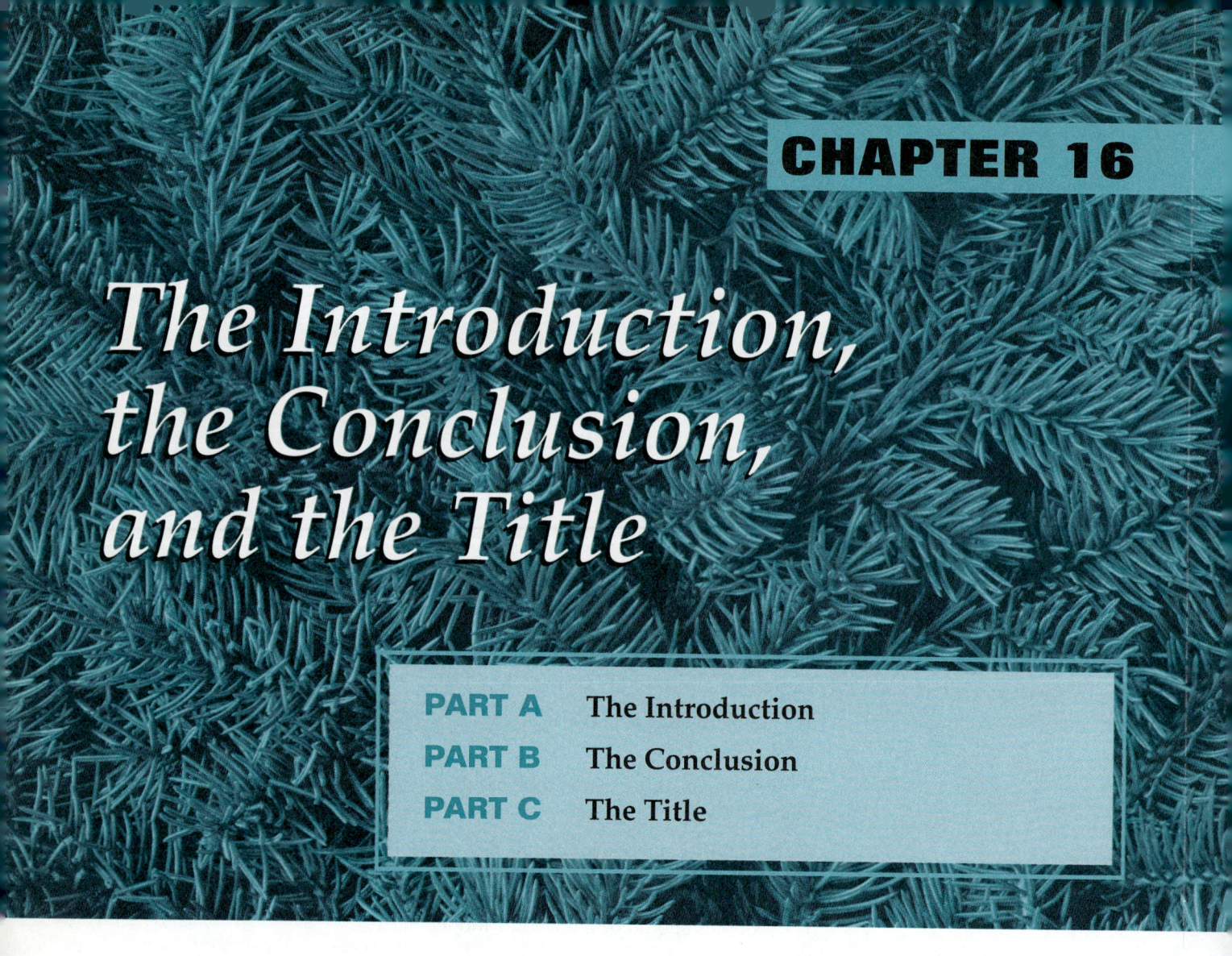

The Introduction, the Conclusion, and the Title

PART A	The Introduction
PART B	The Conclusion
PART C	The Title

PART A   The Introduction

An **introduction** has two functions in an essay. First, it contains the **thesis statement** and, therefore, tells the reader what central idea will be developed in the rest of the paper. Since the reader should be able to spot the thesis statement easily, it should be given a prominent place—for example, the first or the last sentence in the introduction. Second, the introduction has to interest the reader enough that he or she will want to continue reading the paper.

Sometimes the process of writing the essay will help clarify your ideas about how best to introduce it. So once you have completed your essay, you may wish to revise and rewrite the introduction, making sure that it clearly introduces the essay's main idea.

There is no best way to introduce an essay, but you should certainly avoid beginning your work with "I'm going to discuss" or "This paper is about." You needn't tell the reader you are about to begin; just begin!

Here are six basic methods for beginning your composition effectively. In each example, the thesis statement is italicized.

1. **Begin with a single-sentence thesis statement.** A single-sentence thesis statement can be effective because it quickly and forcefully states the main idea of the essay:

> *Time management should be a required course at this college.*

■ Note how quickly and clearly a one-sentence thesis statement can inform the reader about what will follow in the rest of the essay.

2. **Begin with a general idea and then narrow to a specific thesis statement.** The general idea gives the reader background information or sets the scene. Then the topic narrows to one specific idea—the thesis statement. The effect is like a funnel, from wide to narrow.

> Few Americans stay put for a lifetime. We move from town to city to suburb, from high school to college in a different state, from a job in one region to a better job elsewhere, from the home where we raise our children to the home where we plan to live in retirement. *With each move we are forever making new friends, who become part of our new life at that time.*
>
> —Margaret Mead and Rhoda Metraux, "On Friendship," in *A Way of Seeing*

■ What general idea precedes the thesis statement and then leads the reader to focus on the specific main point of the essay?

Americans move often.

3. **Begin with an illustration.** One or more brief illustrations in the introduction of an essay make the thesis statement more concrete and vivid:

> Lisette Flores-Nieves, a thirty-three-year-old consumer affairs representative for Colgate-Palmolive in New York City, was turned down when she first applied for a job at the company. But she was undaunted. "The original job was filled, but I believe in convincing people and letting them know where I stand." She decided to keep phoning the human resources staff, and as it turned out, a new position opened up and Flores-Nieves was hired. "This is all because I'm very assertive and persistent. After all, what can you lose?"
>
> *As job openings with America's top corporations continue to decrease in number and recruiters become more selective, entry-level job seekers need to be more creative and aggressive in their planning and hunting.*
>
> —Irene Middleman Thomas, "First Steps: Advice for Creating Your Own Opportunities," *Hispanic*

■ What example does the writer provide to make the thesis statement more concrete?

the example of Lisette Flores-Nieves

4. **Begin with a surprising fact or idea.** A surprising fact or idea arouses the reader's curiosity about how you will support this initial startling statement.

> *Millions of law-abiding Americans are physically addicted to caffeine—and most of them don't even know it.* Caffeine is a powerful central nervous system stimulant with substantial addiction potential. When deprived of their caffeine, addicts experience often severe withdrawal symptoms, which may include a throbbing headache, disorientation, constipation, nausea, sluggishness, depression, and irritability. As with other addictive drugs, heavy users develop a tolerance and require higher doses to obtain the expected effect.
>
> —Tom Ferguson and Joe Graedon, "Caffeine," *Medical Self-Care*

■ Why are the facts in this introduction likely to startle or surprise the reader?

So many people drink caffeine-containing beverages that they think caffeine is harmless.

5. **Begin with a contradiction.** In this type of introduction, your thesis statement contradicts what many or most people believe. In other words, your essay will contrast your opinion with the widely held view.

> Almost all of us have heard of the Amish, the religious sect that separates itself from the world and rejects modern conveniences and advanced technology. We imagine people wearing hand-sewn clothing and living in homes without refrigerators, dishwashers, televisions, and telephones. However, the Amish have been buying and using cell phones for years. They also use in-line skates, power-operated grass cutters, and gas grills for barbecuing. The Amish employ such conveniences when they do not interfere with family life. Cell phones, for example, are kept outside the home and are used for business purposes only. *The Amish people look at every modern-day convenience and accept it only if it works to bring together, not drive apart, members of the family and community.*
>
> —Adapted from Howard Rheingold, "Look Who's Talking," *Wired*

■ What widely held view does the author present?

the view that Amish people reject all modern-day conveniences and technology

■ How does he contradict this idea?

He lists modern-day conveniences that the Amish, in fact, use.

6. **Begin with a direct quotation.** A direct quotation is likely to catch your reader's attention and to show that you have explored what others have to say about the subject. You can then proceed to agree or to disagree with the direct quotation.

> "Speech is silver; silence is golden," according to an old Swiss saying. In a close relationship, however, silence often loses value. If we speak about certain issues, we may endanger the relationship; but if we do not speak, the relationship may become static and tense until the silence takes on a life of its own. Such silences are corrosive. They eat at the innards of intimacy until, often, *the silence itself causes the very rupture or break-up that we've tried to avoid by keeping silent.*
>
> —Adapted from Michael Ventura,
> "Don't Even Think About It," *Psychology Today*

■ Does the author agree or disagree with the Swiss saying?

The author seems to disagree when it comes to close relationships.

Of course, definitions, comparisons, or any of the other kinds of devices you have already studied can also make good introductions. Just make sure that the reader knows exactly which sentence is your thesis statement.

WRITING ASSIGNMENT 1

Here are five statements. Pick three that you would like to write about and compose an introduction for each one. Use any of the methods for beginning compositions discussed in this chapter thus far.

1. Cell phones in cars can be dangerous.
2. Noise is definitely a form of pollution.
3. Serious illness—our own or a loved one's—sometimes can bring surprising blessings.
4. Studying with someone else can pay off in better grades.
5. My college should offer a three-day course in "How to _____."

PART B   The Conclusion

A conclusion signals the end of the essay and leaves the reader with a final thought. As with the introduction, you may wish to revise and rewrite the conclusion once you have completed your essay. Be certain your conclusion flows logically from the body of the essay.

Like introductions, conclusions can take many forms, and the right one for your essay depends on how you wish to complete your paper—with what thought you wish to leave the reader. However, never conclude your paper with "As I said in the beginning," and try to avoid the overused "In conclusion" or "In summary." Don't end by saying you are going to end; just end!

Here are three ways to conclude an essay.

1. **End with a call to action.** The call to action says that in view of the facts and ideas presented in this essay, the reader should *do something*.

> Thus, birdwatchers must work together to keep track of numbers and types of all birds—not just endangered species. Through BirdSource, a program that will revolutionize the monitoring of bird populations, you can join the growing number of volunteer birders across the country who report their sightings every day, online. Go to http://birdsource.cornell.edu. By sharing your observations, you can help assemble important data on the distribution, migratory pathways, and population trends of North American birds, almost instantly and on a scale that was impossible before the Internet.
>
> —Adapted from John Flicker, "Tracking Birds on the Net," *Audubon*

■ What does the writer want the reader to do?

The writer wants the reader to report bird sightings, using BirdSource.

2. **End with a final point.** The final point can tie together all the other ideas in the essay; it provides the reader with the sense that the entire essay has been leading up to this one final point.

> Students who follow their hearts in choosing majors will most likely end up laboring at what they love. They're the ones who will put in the long hours and intense effort that achievement requires. And they're the ones who will find the sense of purpose that underlies most human happiness.
>
> —Lynne V. Cheney, "Students of Success," *Newsweek*

■ With what final point does Cheney end her article?

She concludes by stating that students who choose majors with their hearts will probably find work they love.

3. **End with a question.** By ending with a question, you leave the reader with a final problem that you wish him or her to think about.

> Illness related to chemical dumping is increasing in Larkstown, yet only a handful of citizens have joined the campaign to clean up the chemical dump on the edge of town and to stop further dumping. Many people say that they don't want to get involved, but with their lives and their children's futures at stake, can they afford not to?

■ What problem does the writer's final question point to?

the problem of passivity: people's not wanting to "get involved"

WRITING ASSIGNMENT 2

Review two or three essays that you have written recently. Do the conclusions bring the essays to clear ends? Are those conclusions interesting? How could they be improved? Using one of the three strategies taught in this section, write a new conclusion for one of the essays.

PART C The Title

If you are writing just one paragraph, chances are that you will not need to give it a title, but if you are writing a multiparagraph essay, a title is definitely in order.

The title is centered on the page above the body of the composition and separated from it by several blank lines (about 1 inch of space), as shown here.

```
                    Title               ← about 1½"
                                        ← about 1"
    If you are writing just one
paragraph, chances are that
you will not be required to
give it a title, but if you are
writing a multiparagraph
theme, a title is definitely in
order.
    The title is centered on the
page above the body of the
theme and separated from it by
several blank lines (about 1 inch
of space).
```

- *Do not* put quotation marks around the title of your own paper.
- *Do not* underline or italicize the title of your own paper.
- Remember, unlike the topic sentence, the title is not part of the first paragraph; in fact, it is usually only four to five words long and is rarely an entire sentence.

A good title has two functions: to suggest the subject of the essay and to spark the reader's interest. Although the title is the first part of your essay the reader sees, the most effective titles are usually written *after* the essay has been completed.

To create a title, reread your essay, paying special attention to the **thesis statement** and the **conclusion**. Try to come up with a few words that express the main point of your paper.

Here are some basic kinds of titles.

1. **The most common title used in college writing is the no-nonsense descriptive title.** In this title, stress key words and ideas developed in the essay:

The Search for Identity in Orwell's *1984*

Advantages and Disadvantages of Buying on Credit

The Role of Chlorophyll in Photosynthesis

2. **Two-part titles are also effective.** Write one or two words stating the general subject, and then add several words that narrow the topic:

> Legal Gambling: Pro and Con
>
> Tito Puente: King of Latin Music

3. **Write the title as a rhetorical question.** Then answer the question in your essay:

> What Can Be Done About the High Price of Higher Education?
>
> Are Athletes Setting Bad Examples?

4. **Relate the title to the method of development used in the essay** (see Unit 3 and Chapter 15):

Illustration:	Democracy in Action
	Three Roles I Play
Narration:	The Development of Jazz
	Sandra Cisneros: The Making of a Storyteller
Description:	Portrait of a Scientist
	A Waterfront Scene
Process:	How to Get Organized
	How to Get in Shape Fast
Definition:	What It Means to Be Unemployed
	A Definition of Love
Comparison:	Two Country Stars Who Crossed Over
	Strange Realities: *Star Wars* and *X Files*
Contrast:	Pleasures and Problems of Owning a Home
	Montreal: City of Contrasts
Classification:	Three Types of Soap Operas
	What Kind of Risk Taker Are You?
Cause and Effect:	What Causes Whales to Beach Themselves?
	The Effects of Divorce on Children
Persuasion:	Pornography Should Be Banned
	The Need for Metal Detectors in Our Schools

Use this list the next time you title a paper.

WRITING ASSIGNMENT 3

Review two or three essays that you have written recently. Are the titles clear and interesting? Applying what you've learned in this chapter, write a better title for at least one paper.

CHAPTER 17

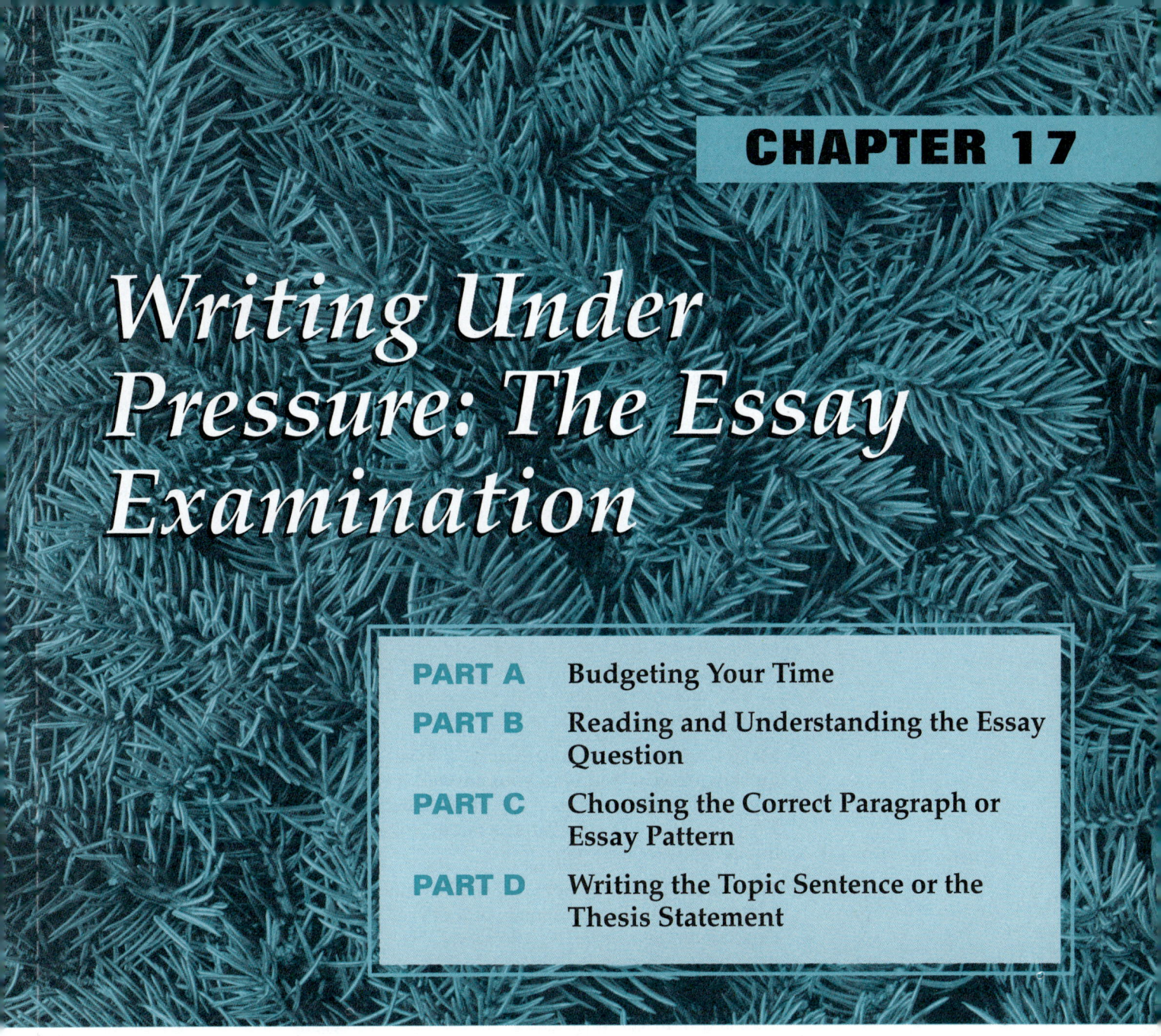

Writing Under Pressure: The Essay Examination

PART A	Budgeting Your Time
PART B	Reading and Understanding the Essay Question
PART C	Choosing the Correct Paragraph or Essay Pattern
PART D	Writing the Topic Sentence or the Thesis Statement

Being able to write under pressure is a key skill both in college and in the workplace. Throughout your college career, you will be asked to write **timed papers** in class and to take **essay examinations.** In fact, many English programs base placement and passing on timed essay exams. Clearly, the ability to write under pressure is crucial.

An **essay question** requires the same writing skills that a student uses in composing a paragraph or an essay. Even in history and biology, how well you do on an essay test depends partly on how well you write; yet many students, under the pressure of a test, forget or fail to apply what they know about good writing. This chapter will improve your ability to write under pressure. Many of the sample exam questions on the following pages were taken from real college examinations.

PART A Budgeting Your Time

To do well on a timed essay or an essay test, it is not enough to know the material. You must also be able to call forth what you know, organize it, and present it in writing—all under pressure in a limited time.

Since most essay examinations are timed, it is important that you learn how to **budget** your time effectively so that you can devote adequate time to each question *and* finish the test. The following six tips will help you use your time well.

1. **Make sure you know exactly how long the examination lasts.** A one-hour examination may really be only fifty minutes; a two-hour examination may last only one hour and forty-five minutes.

2. **Note the point value of all questions and allot time accordingly to each question.** That is, allot the most time to questions that are worth the most points and less time to ones that are worth fewer.

3. **Decide on an order in which to answer the questions.** You do not have to begin with the first question on the examination and work, in order, to the last. Instead, you may start with the questions worth the most points. Some students prefer to begin with the questions they feel they can answer most easily, thereby guaranteeing points toward the final grade on the examination. Others combine the two methods. No matter which system you use, be sure to allot enough time to the questions that are worth the most points—whether you do them first or last.

4. **Make sure you understand exactly what each question asks you to do; then quickly prewrite and plan your answer.** It is all-important to take a breath, study the question, and make a quick scratch outline or plan of your answer *before you start to write.* Parts B through D of this chapter will guide you through these critical steps.

5. **Time yourself.** As you begin a particular question, calculate when you must be finished with that question in order to complete the examination, and note that time in the margin. As you write, check the clock every five minutes so that you remain on schedule.

6. **Finally, do not count on having enough time to recopy your work.** Skip lines and write carefully so that the instructor can easily read your writing as well as any neat corrections you might make.

PRACTICE 1

Imagine that you are about to take the two-hour history test shown below. Read the test carefully, noting the point value of each question, and then answer the questions that follow the examination. *Answers may vary.*

> Part I   Answer both questions. 15 points each.
>
> 1. Do you think that the Versailles Peace Treaty was a "harsh" one? Be specific.
>
> 2. List the basic principles of Karl Marx. Analyze them in terms of Marx's claim that they are scientific.

> Part II Answer two of the following questions. 25 points each.
>
> 3. Describe the origins of, the philosophies behind, and the chief policies of either Communist Russia or Fascist Italy. Be specific.
>
> 4. What were the causes of Nelson Mandela's presidential victory in South Africa in 1994?
>
> 5. European history of the nineteenth and twentieth centuries has been increasingly related to that of the rest of the world. Why? How? With what consequences for Europe?
>
> Part III Briefly identify ten of the following. 2 points each.
>
> a. John Locke
> b. Franco-Prussian War
> c. Stalingrad
> d. Cavour
> e. Manchuria, 1931
> f. Entente Cordiale
> g. Existentialism
> h. Jacobins
> i. The Opium Wars
> j. Social Darwinism
> k. The Reform Bill of 1832
> l. The most interesting reading you have done this term (from the course list)

1. Which part would you do first and why? *I would do Part II first because it is worth the most points (50).*

   How much time would you allot to the questions in this part and why? *I would allot approximately half of my time because it is half of the exam.*

2. Which part would you do second and why? *I would do Part I second because it is worth 30 points.*

   How much time would you allot to the questions in this part and why? *I would allot about half my remaining time because this part is about one-fourth of the exam.*

3. Which part would you do last and why? *I would do Part III last because it is worth the least number of points (20). Also, I would get some credit for each item that I answer correctly; if I run out of time, my score would be hurt less on this kind of question than on an essay question.*

How much time would you allot to the questions in this part and why?

I would allot most of my remaining time, answering all of the questions I could. I'd save some time to review my other answers.

PART B Reading and Understanding the Essay Question

Before you begin writing, carefully examine each question to decide exactly what your purpose is: that is, what the instructor expects you to do.

> Question: Using <u>either</u> Communist China or Nazi Germany as a model,
> (a) <u>describe</u> the characteristics of a totalitarian <u>state</u>, and
> (b) <u>explain</u> how such a state was <u>created</u>.

- This question contains three sets of instructions.
- First, you must use "either Communist China or Nazi Germany as a model." That is, you must **choose** *one or the other* as a model.
- Second, you must **describe**, and third, you must **explain**.
- Your answer should consist of two written parts, a **description** and an **explanation**.

It is often helpful to underline the important words, as shown in the box above, to make sure you understand the entire question and have noted all its parts.

> The student must   (1) <u>choose</u> to write about <u>either</u> Communist China or Nazi Germany, not both; (2) <u>describe</u> the totalitarian state; (3) <u>explain</u> how such a state was created.

PRACTICE 2

Read each essay question and underline key words. Then, on the lines beneath the question, describe in your own words exactly what the question requires: (1) What directions does the student have to follow? (2) How many parts will the answer contain?

EXAMPLE What were the <u>causes</u> of the Cold War? What were its chief <u>episodes</u>? <u>Why</u> has there not been a "<u>hot</u>" war?

Student must   *(1) tell what caused the Cold War (two or more causes), (2) mention main events of Cold War, (3) give reasons why we haven't had a full-scale war. The essay will have three parts: causes, main events, and reasons.*

CHAPTER 17 Writing Under Pressure: The Essay Examination **231**

1. State Newton's First Law and give examples from your own experience.

    Student must *(1) write out Newton's First Law and (2) give examples of the law from his or her own experience. The essay will have two parts: the law and examples.*

2. Choose one of the following terms. Define it, give an example of it, and then show how it affects *your* life: (a) freedom of speech, (b) justice for all, (c) equal opportunity.

    Student must *(1 and 2) define and give an example of one term: freedom of speech, justice for all, or equal opportunity and (3) show how it affects his or her life. The essay will have three parts: a definition, an example, and effects.*

3. Shiism and Sunni are the two great branches of Islam. Discuss the religious beliefs and the politics of each branch.

    Student must *(1) discuss the religious beliefs and the politics of Shiism and (2) discuss the religious beliefs and the politics of Sunni. The essay will have two parts: Shiism and Sunni.*

4. Name and explain four types of savings institutions. What are three factors that influence one's choice of a savings institution?

    Student must *(1) identify and describe four types of savings institutions and (2) name three factors influencing one's choice of a savings institution. The essay will have two parts: types and factors.*

5. Steroids: the athlete's "unfair advantage." Discuss.

    Student must *(1) explain what advantage steroids offer to athletes and (2) explain why the advantage is considered unfair. The essay will have two parts: explanation of advantage and explanation of why advantage is unfair.*

6. Discuss the causes and consequences of the Broad Street cholera epidemic in mid–nineteenth-century London. What was the role of Dr. John Snow?

232   UNIT 4   Writing the Essay

Student must *(1) discuss the causes of the Broad Street cholera epidemic, (2) discuss its consequences, and (3) explain Dr. Snow's role. The essay will have three parts: causes, effects, and role of Snow.*

7. Define the Monroe Doctrine of the early nineteenth century and weigh the arguments for and against it.

    Student must *(1) define the Monroe Doctrine, (2) evaluate the arguments for it, and (3) evaluate the arguments against it. The essay will have three parts: definition, arguments for, and arguments against.*

8. The sixteenth century is known for the Renaissance, the Reformation, and the Commercial Revolution. Discuss each event, showing why it was important to the history of Western civilization.

    Student must *discuss the historical importance of (1) the Renaissance, (2) the Reformation, and (3) the Commercial Revolution. The essay will have three parts: the Renaissance, the Reformation, and the Commercial Revolution.*

9. Erik Erikson has theorized that adult actions toward children may produce either (a) trust or mistrust, (b) autonomy or self-doubt, (c) initiative or guilt. Choose one of the pairs above and give examples of the kinds of adult behavior that might create these responses in a child.

    Student must *(1) choose one pair of terms, (2) give examples of adult behavior that might create trust (autonomy, initiative) in a child, and (3) give examples of adult behavior that might create mistrust (self-doubt, guilt) in a child. The essay will have two parts: behavior creating positive traits and behavior creating negative traits.*

10. Simón Bolívar may not have been as great a hero as he was believed to be. Agree or disagree.

    Student must *(1) state the "heroic" traits that Bolívar was believed to have had and (2) give reasons supporting or contradicting that portrayal. The essay will have two parts: an explanation of Bolívar's "heroic" traits and the supporting or opposing evidence.*

_____

_____

_____

PART C Choosing the Correct Paragraph or Essay Pattern

Throughout this book, you have learned how to write various types of paragraphs and compositions. Many examinations will require you simply to **illustrate, define, compare,** and so forth. How well you answer questions may depend partly on how well you understand these terms.

> 1. *Illustrate* "behavior modification."
> 2. *Define* "greenhouse effect."
> 3. *Compare* Agee and Nin as diarists.

■ The key words in these questions are *illustrate, define,* and *compare*—**instruction words** that tell you what you are supposed to do and what form your answer should take.

Here is a review list of some common instruction words used in college examinations.

1. Classify:	Gather into categories, types, or kinds according to a single basis of division (see Chapter 11).
2. Compare:	Point out similarities (see Chapter 10). Instructors often use *compare* to mean point out both *similarities* and *differences.*
3. Contrast:	Point out differences (see Chapter 10).
4. Define:	State clearly and exactly the meaning of a word or term (see Chapter 9). You may be required to write a single-sentence definition or a full paragraph. Instructors may use *identify* as a synonym for *define* when they want a short definition.
5. Discuss: (analyze, describe, or explain)	Often an instructor uses these terms to mean "thoughtfully examine a subject, approaching it from different angles." These terms allow the writer more freedom of approach than many of the others.
6. Discuss causes:	Analyze the reasons or causes for something; answer the question *Why?* (see Chapter 12).
7. Discuss effects:	Analyze the effects, consequences, or results of something (see Chapter 12).
8. Evaluate:	Weigh the pros and cons, advantages and disadvantages (see Chapters 10 and 13).

234 UNIT 4 Writing the Essay

9. **Identify:** Give a capsule who-what-when-where-why answer. Sometimes *identify* is a synonym for *define*.

10. **Illustrate:** Give one or more examples (see Chapter 5).

11. **Narrate:** Follow the development of something through time, event by event (see Chapters 6 and 8).
    (trace)

12. **Summarize:** Write the substance of a longer work in condensed form (see Chapter 18, Part B).

13. **Take a stand:** Persuade; argue for a particular position (see Chapter 13).

PRACTICE 3

You should have no trouble deciding what kind of paragraph or composition to use if the question uses one of the terms just defined—*contrast, trace, classify,* and so on. However, questions are often worded in such a way that you have to discover what kind of paragraph or essay is required. What kind of paragraph or essay is required by each of the following questions?

EXAMPLE What is *schizophrenia*? (Write a paragraph to. . . .)   *define*

1. In one concise paragraph, give the main ideas of Simone de Beauvoir's famous book *The Second Sex*.   *summarize*

2. What is the difference between veins and arteries?   *contrast*

3. Follow the development of Wynton Marsalis's musical style.   *narrate*

4. How do jet- and propeller-driven planes differ?   *contrast*

5. Who or what is each of the following: the Gang of Four, Ho Chi Minh, Tiananmen Square?   *identify* or *define*

6. Explain the causes of the American Civil War.   *discuss causes*

7. Explain what is meant by "magical realism."   *define*

8. Take a stand for or against legalizing marijuana in this country. Give reasons to support your stand.   *persuade, give reasons*

9. Give two recent instances of military hazing that you consider "out of control."   *illustrate*

10. Divide into groups the different kinds of web sites giving out medical information.   *classify*

PART D Writing the Topic Sentence or the Thesis Statement

A good way to ensure that your answer truly addresses itself to the question is to compose a topic sentence or a thesis statement that contains the key words of the question.

Question: How do fixed-rate and adjustable-rate mortgages differ?

- The key words in this question are *fixed-rate* and *adjustable-rate mortgages,* and *differ.*
- What kind of paragraph or essay would be appropriate for this question?

    a paragraph or essay of contrast

Topic sentence or *thesis statement of answer:* Fixed-rate and adjustable-rate mortgages differ in three basic ways.

- The answer repeats the key words of the question: *fixed-rate, adjustable-rate, mortgages,* and *differ.*

PRACTICE 4

Here are eight examination questions. Write a topic sentence or thesis statement for each question by using the question as part of the answer. Pretend that you know all the material. Even though you may not know anything about the subjects, you should be able to formulate a topic sentence or thesis statement based on the question. *Answers may vary.*

1. Do you think the Dawes Allotment Act was fair to Native Americans?

    Topic sentence or thesis statement: *The Dawes Allotment Act was unfair (fair) to Native Americans, for several reasons.*

2. Contrast high school requirements in Jamaica with those in the United States.

    Topic sentence or thesis statement: *High school requirements in Jamaica are more demanding than those in the United States.*

3. What steps can a busy person take to reduce the destructive impact of stress in his or her life?

Topic sentence or thesis statement: *A busy person can take several steps to help reduce the destructive impact of stress in his or her life.*

4. Gay couples should be allowed to adopt children. Agree or disagree with this statement.

   Topic sentence or thesis statement: *Gay couples definitely should be allowed to adopt children.*

5. Assume that you manage a small shop that sells men's apparel. What activities would you undertake to promote the sale of sportswear?

   Topic sentence or thesis statement: *As manager of a small shop that sells men's apparel, I would do three things to promote the sale of sportswear.*

6. The U.S. government should cover the medical costs of AIDS. Agree or disagree with this statement.

   Topic sentence or thesis statement: *The U.S. government should cover the medical costs of AIDS.*

7. The state should subsidize students in medical school because the country needs more doctors. Agree or disagree with this statement.

   Topic sentence or thesis statement: *The state should not subsidize students in medical school.*

8. Does religion play a more vital role in people's lives today than it did in your parents' generation?

   Topic sentence or thesis statement: *Religion plays a more vital role in people's lives today than it did in my parents' generation.*

✔ **CHECKLIST: The Process of Writing the Essay Question**

___ 1. Survey the test and note the point value for each question.

___ 2. Calculate how much time you need for each question. Then check the clock as you write so that you complete all the questions.

___ 3. Read each question carefully, underlining important words.

___ 4. Determine how many parts the answer should contain.

___ 5. Considering your audience (usually the teacher) and purpose, choose the paragraph or essay pattern that would best answer the question.

___ 6. Write a topic sentence or a thesis statement that repeats the key words of the question.

___ 7. Quickly freewrite or brainstorm ideas on scrap paper and arrange them in a logical order, making a scratch outline or plan.

___ 8. Write your paragraph or essay neatly, skipping lines so you will have enough room to make corrections.

CHAPTER 18

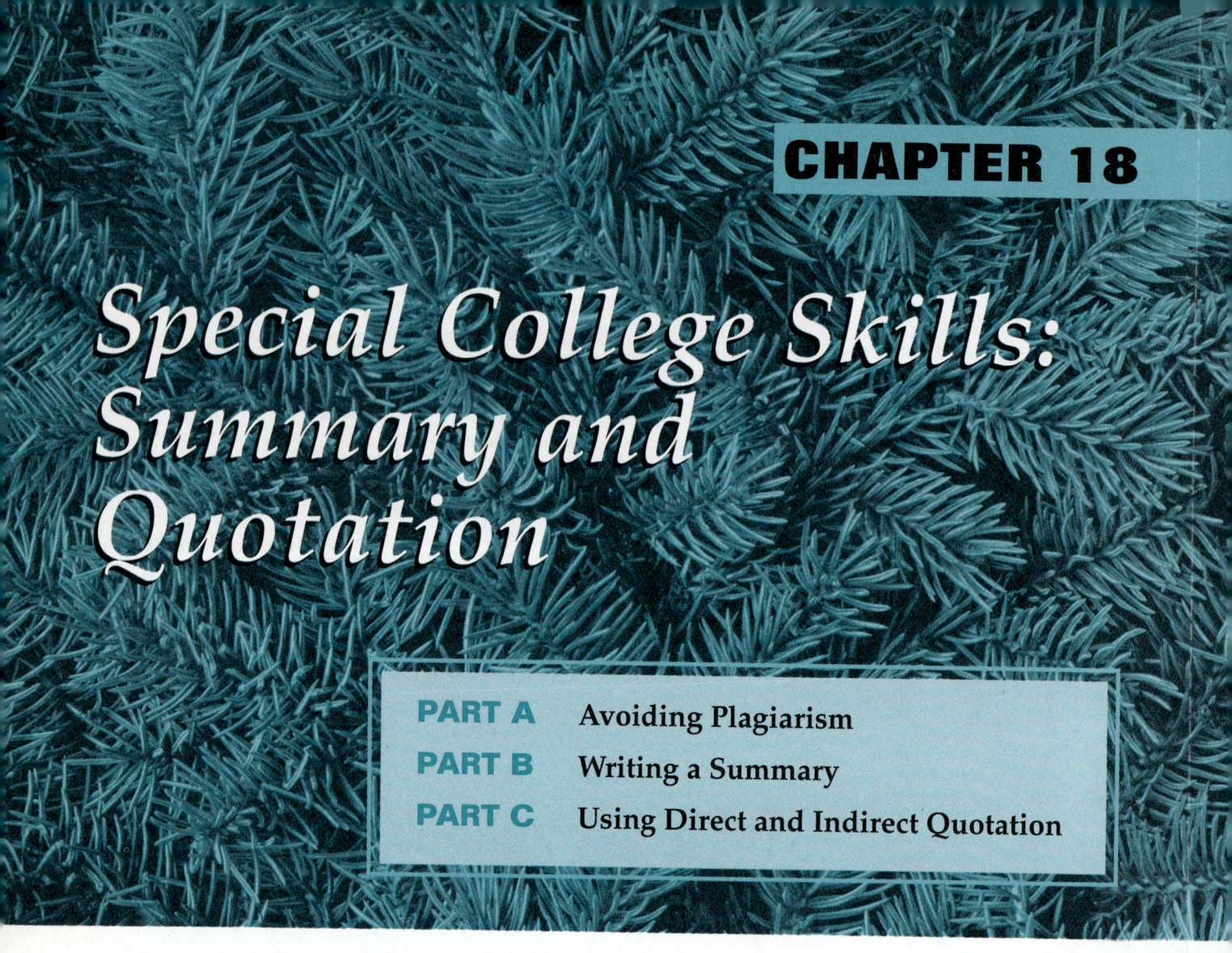

Special College Skills: Summary and Quotation

PART A   Avoiding Plagiarism
PART B   Writing a Summary
PART C   Using Direct and Indirect Quotation

In some college courses, you will write papers without using **outside sources**—that is, sources other than yourself that provide information on a subject (for example, books, articles, Internet sites, or people). However, many college courses and jobs require that you refer to outside sources as you write reports, essays, and research papers. In addition, information from outside sources can vastly enrich your writing with facts, statistics, experts' ideas, and more.

Two important skills that will help you use outside sources effectively are **writing summaries** and **quoting others. Summarizing** requires you to condense information and present it clearly in your own words. **Quotation** allows you to enliven your writing with other people's words and thoughts (giving credit, of course, to the original author).

PART A   Avoiding Plagiarism

Before we discuss summarizing and quoting, it is all-important that you understand—so you can avoid—**plagiarism.** Plagiarism means passing off someone else's words or ideas as your own. Whether intentional or careless, plagiarism is stealing. A college student who plagiarizes a paper may be expelled from

CHAPTER 18 Special College Skills: Summary and Quotation 239

the course or from college. Whatever your career may be, publishing material that you copied from someone else is a crime.

To avoid plagiarism, you must give proper credit to the original author, as this chapter shows. Meanwhile, keep this simple rule in mind: **Always tell your reader the source of any words and ideas not your own.**

PART B Writing a Summary

A **summary** presents the main idea and supporting points of a longer work *in much shorter form*. It might be one sentence, one paragraph, or several paragraphs long, depending on the length of the original and the nature of your assignment.

Summarizing is important both in college and at work. In a persuasive essay, you might summarize the ideas of an expert whose views support one of your points. A professor might ask you to summarize a book, a market survey, or even the plot of a film—that is, to condense it in your own words, presenting only the highlights. Of course, many essay exams also call for written summaries.

Compare this short newspaper article—the *source*—with the *summary* that follows:

Source

Paul Recer, "Dogs Tamed 100,000 Years Ago," *The Miami Herald*, June 13, 1997, p. 9A.

Fido may be cute, cuddly, and harmless. But in his genes, he's a wolf.

Researchers tracing the genetic family tree of man's best friend have confirmed that domestic dogs, from petite poodles to huge elkhounds, descended from wolves that were tamed 100,000 years ago.

"Our data show that the origin of dogs seems to be much more ancient than indicated in the archaeological record," said Robert K. Wayne of UCLA, the leader of a team that tested the genes from 67 dog breeds and 62 wolves on four continents.

Wayne said the study showed so many DNA changes that dogs had to have diverged genetically from wolves 60,000 to more than 100,000 years ago.

The study suggests that primitive humans living in a hunting and gathering culture tamed wolves and then bred the animals to create the many different types of dogs that now exist.

Summary

Dogs began evolving from wolves between 60,000 and 100,000 years ago, reports Paul Recer in *The Miami Herald* ("Dogs Tamed 100,000 Years Ago," June 13, 1997, p. 9A). Apparently, humans tamed wolves far earlier than was previously thought. Researchers at UCLA, led by Robert K. Wayne, came to these conclusions after studying the genes of sixty-seven breeds of dogs and sixty-two wolves on four continents.

■ Notice that sentence 1 states the author, title, source, and date of the original article. Sentence 1 also states the main idea of the article. What is its main idea?

Dogs began evolving from wolves 60,000 to 100,000 years ago.

- What evidence supports this idea?

  a recent UCLA study

- The original is short, so the summary is very short—just three sentences long.

- Note that the summary writer does not add her own opinions about dogs or evolution but simply states the main ideas of the source. Unlike many kinds of writing, a summary should not contain your personal opinions and feelings.

Preparing to Write a Summary

The secret of writing a good summary is clearly understanding the original. If you doubt this, try to summarize out loud Chapter 3 of your biology book. To summarize well, you have to know the subject matter.

Before you summarize a piece of writing, notice the title and subtitle, if there is one; these often state the main idea. Read quickly for meaning; then carefully read the work again, underlining or jotting down notes for yourself. What is the author's thesis or main point? What points does he or she offer in support? Be careful to distinguish between the most and least important points; your summary should include only the most important ones.

To help you understand *what the author thinks is important,* notice which ideas get the most coverage. Read with special care the topic sentence of each paragraph and the first and last paragraphs of the work. If you are summarizing a magazine article or a textbook chapter, the subheads (often in boldface type) point out important ideas.

Your written summary should include the following:

1. The author, title, and source of the original

2. The main idea or thesis of the original, in your own words

3. The most important supporting ideas or points of the original, in your own words

Try to present the ideas in your summary in proportion to those in the original. For instance, if the author devotes one paragraph to each of four ideas, you might give one sentence to each idea. When you finish, compare your summary with the original, to avoid plagiarism; that is, make sure you have not just copied the phrasing and sentences of the original.

A summary differs from much other writing in that it *should not* contain your feelings or opinions—just the facts. Your job is to capture the essence of the original, with nothing added.

Following are two summaries of the student essay in Chapter 15, Part F, of this book. Which do you think is the better summary, A or B? Be prepared to say specifically why.

Summary A

(1) In "Two Childhoods" (printed in *Evergreen*, 6th Edition, by Susan Fawcett and Alvin Sandberg, Houghton Mifflin Company, 2000), student Cheryl Parris contrasts her mother's childhood on a farm in South Carolina and her own childhood in New York City. (2) As a child, the author's mother enjoyed simple, slow-paced country activities like swimming in rivers and mending birds' wings whereas Ms. Parris's fast-paced youth was

CHAPTER 18 Special College Skills: Summary and Quotation **241**

crammed with such urban activities as movie-going, parties, and shopping. (3) Their personalities differed as much as—and perhaps because of—their lifestyles. (4) As a girl, the mother was known as caring, respectful, and content with nature and invented games. (5) Ms. Parris, however, describes herself as "petulant, pigheaded, demanding, and unstable"—very focused on material possessions. (6) Now she seems to have examined her values, however, and wishes her childhood had been more like her mother's.

Summary B (1) This excellent essay is by Ms. Cheryl Parris, student. (2) I enjoyed reading about Cheryl's mother, who grew up on a farm in South Carolina. (3) When Cheryl was young, her mother told stories about her own childhood. (4) Cheryl loved those tales and still thinks of them. (5) It was intriguing to hear about life thirty years before her life began. (6) What fascinated her most, however, were the differences between the mother's youth and hers. (7) The mother's days were filled with swimming in nearby lakes and rivers, climbing and falling off trees. (8) Life in the country is definitely easier than life in the city. (9) Although the rural pace of life is slower, nature can teach you many things. (10) Cheryl lived in the city, so she missed out. (11) I liked the writer's honesty; she admits that she was not a nice child.

■ The test of a good summary is how well it captures the original. Does A or B better summarize Ms. Parris's essay? Why?

A is better because it summarizes the original and does not insert the opinions of

the summarizer.

■ If you picked A, you are right. Sentence 1 states the author and title of the essay, as well as the title, authors, publisher, and date of the book in which it appears. Sentence 1 also states the main idea of the original, which *contrasts* the mother's childhood with the writer's. Does any sentence in B state the main idea of the original essay?

no

■ Compare the original with the two summaries. How many points of contrast does A include? B? *A includes two points of contrast; B includes none.*

■ Does each writer summarize the essay *in his or her own words*? If not, which sentences might seem plagiarized? *A does; B plagiarizes sentences 4, 5, 6, and 7.*

■ Writer A once quotes Ms. Parris directly. How is this shown? Why do you think the summary writer chose this sentence to quote?

Quotation marks set off Ms. Parris's words in sentence 5; these words are richly

descriptive and somewhat humorous.

- Do both summaries succeed in keeping personal opinion out? If not, which sentences contain the summary writer's opinion? _A succeeds, but writer B inserts personal opinion in sentences 1, 2, 8, 9, and 11._

PRACTICE 1

Form a group with three or four other classmates, and choose just one of the following essays to summarize: "Libraries of the Future—Now" (Chapter 15, Part A); "The Day of the Dead" (Chapter 15, Part C); "Stopping Youth Violence: An Inside Job" (Chapter 15, Part I); or "Skin Deep" (Chapter 14, Part D). Read your chosen essay in the group, aloud if possible. Then each person should write a one-paragraph summary of it, referring to the following checklist (15–20 minutes).

Now read your finished summaries aloud to your group. How well does each writer briefly capture the meaning of the original? Has he or she kept out personal opinion? What suggestions for improvement can you offer? Your instructor may wish to have the best summary in each group read aloud to the whole class.

PRACTICE 2

Flip through a copy of a current magazine: *Newsweek, People, Essence, Wired,* or another. Pick one article that interests you, read it carefully, and write a one- to three-paragraph summary of the article, depending on how long the article is. The points you include in your summary should reflect the emphasis of the original writer. Try to capture the essence of the article. Remember to give your source at the beginning, to keep out personal opinion, and to check your summary for plagiarism. Refer to the checklist.

✓ CHECKLIST: The Process of Writing a Summary

___ 1. Notice the title and subtitle of the original; do these state its main idea?

___ 2. Read the original quickly for meaning; then carefully read it again, underlining important ideas and jotting down notes for yourself.

___ 3. Determine the author's thesis or main idea.

___ 4. Now find the main supporting points. Subheads (if any), topic sentences, and the first and last paragraphs of the original may help you find key points.

___ 5. Write your topic sentence or thesis statement, stating the author's thesis, title, source, and date of the original.

___ 6. In your own words, give the author's most important supporting points, in the same order in which the author gives them. Keep the same proportion of coverage as the original.

CHAPTER 18   Special College Skills: Summary and Quotation   **243**

—— 7. Write your summary, skipping lines so you will have room to make corrections.

—— 8. Now revise, asking yourself, "Will my summary convey to someone who has never read the original the author's main idea and key supporting points?"

—— 9. Proofread, making neat corrections above the lines.

—— 10. Compare your final draft with the original to avoid plagiarism.

PART C   Using Direct and Indirect Quotation

Sometimes you will want to quote an outside source directly. A quotation might be part of a summary or part of a longer paper or report. Quoting the words of others can add richness and authority to your writing; in fact, that is why we include a Quotation Bank at the end of this book—a kind of minireader of great thoughts. Use short quotations in these ways:

- Use a quotation to stress a key idea.
- Use a quotation to lend expert opinion to your argument.
- Use a quotation to provide a catchy introduction or conclusion.
- Use a quotation about your topic that is wonderfully written and "quotable" to add interest.

However, avoid using very long quotations or too many quotations. Both send the message that you are filling up space because you don't have enough to say. Of course, to avoid plagiarism, you always must credit the original author or speaker.

Here are some methods for introducing quotations:

Ways to Introduce Quotations

Ms. Taibi says, . . .   Ms. Taibi writes, . . .

One expert notes that . . .   . . . , one authority reports.

In a recent *Times* article,
Russell Baker observes . . .

Following are a passage from a well-known book and two ways that students quoted the author:

Source   Dr. Deborah Prothrow-Stith, *Deadly Consequences* (HarperPerennial 1991), p. 34.

On film or videotape, violence begins and ends in a moment. "Bang bang, you're dead." Then the death is over. This sense of action-without-consequences replicates and reinforces the dangerous "magical" way many children think. Do the twelve- and fourteen-year-olds who are shooting each other to death in Los Angeles, Chicago, or Washington, D.C., really understand that death is permanent, unalterable, final, tragic? Television certainly is not telling them so.

Two students who wrote about the effects of TV violence correctly quoted Dr. Prothrow-Stith as follows:

Direct Quotation

> "This sense of action-without-consequences replicates and reinforces the dangerous 'magical' way many children think," writes Dr. Deborah Prothrow-Stith in *Deadly Consequences* (p. 34).

Indirect Quotation

> In *Deadly Consequences*, Dr. Deborah Prothrow-Stith points out that TV and movie violence, which has no realistic consequences, harms children by reinforcing the magical way in which they think (p. 34).

- The first sentence gives Dr. Prothrow-Stith's exact words inside quotation marks. This is direct quotation. Note the punctuation.

- The second sentence uses the word *that* and gives the *meaning* of Prothrow-Stith's words without quotation marks. This is indirect quotation. Note the punctuation.

- Both correctly quote the writer and credit the source. (See Chapter 35, Parts B and C, for more on correctly writing titles and punctuating quotations.)

PRACTICE 3

Following are passages from three sources. Read each one, and then, as if you were writing a paper, quote two sentences from each, one directly quoting the author's words and one indirectly quoting the author's ideas. Review the boxed ways to introduce quotations and try several methods. Finally, write a brief summary of each passage. Check your work to avoid plagiarism.

Source 1 Institute of Noetic Sciences with William Poole, *The Heart of Healing* (Turner Publishing, Inc. 1993), p. 134.

In most cultures throughout history, music, dance, rhythmic drumming, and chanting have been essential parts of healing rituals. Modern research bears out the connection between music and healing. In one study, the heart rate and blood pressure of patients went down when quiet music was piped into their hospital coronary care units. At the same time, the patients showed greater tolerance for pain and less anxiety and depression. Similarly, listening to music before, during, or after surgery has been shown to promote various beneficial effects—from alleviating anxiety to reducing the need for sedation by half. When researchers played Brahms' "Lullaby" to premature infants, these babies gained weight faster and went home from the hospital sooner than babies who did not hear the music. Music may also affect immunity by altering the level of stress chemicals in the blood. An experiment at Rainbow Babies and Children's Hospital found that a single thirty-minute music therapy session could increase the level of salivary IgA, an immunoglobulin that protects against respiratory infections.

CHAPTER 18 Special College Skills: Summary and Quotation 245

Direct quotation: _____

Indirect quotation: _____

Summary:

_____

Source 2   Ira Peck and Larry F. Krieger, *Sociology: The Search for Social Patterns* (Scholastic 1989), p. 181.

Identical twins account for about one in every 250 births. In a recent project at the Minnesota Center for Twin and Adoption Research, scientists conducted an exhaustive study of 350 pairs of identical twins reared apart. Identical twins who are reared apart can provide important clues for understanding the factors that influence personality and behavior. Since they have the same genetic background yet live in different environments, these identical twins help clarify the influence of heredity and environment on a variety of character traits. Each pair of twins answered 15,000 items on a comprehensive multidimensional personality questionnaire. Investigators then compared these results with answers given by the general population.

The results suggest an important genetic influence on some personality traits. For example, on the basis of their tests, researchers estimate that 61 percent of extroversion is inherited. The data also indicated that the traits of conformity, optimism, and cautiousness were 50 to 60 percent inherited. Heredity played a less significant role in other traits. Aggressiveness, ambitiousness, orderliness, and social closeness were only 33 to 48 percent inherited.

Direct quotation: _____

Indirect quotation: _____

Summary:

_____

_____

_____

_____

_____

Source 3   Samantha Baldwin, "Sky Primer," *Boulder Views,* December 12, 1999, pp. 8–9.

Besides the nine known planets, our universe contains billions of other bodies. Among them are asteroids and comets. Both are of interest to scientists because they are thought to be unspoiled primal bodies that hold clues to the origin of the solar system. They are also responsible for nearly all of the many direct hits that Earth and its moon have sustained over millions of years. In 1997, news that a huge asteroid might hit Earth in 2028 (soon corrected) intensified people's curiosity about asteroids and comets.

Although their name means "starlike," asteroids are not stars. They are chunks of rock that orbit the sun. Upwards of 4,000 have been catalogued, most of them fairly small. The largest known asteroid, Ceres, is about 940 kilometers across. Most asteroids orbit in the asteroid belt between Mars and Jupiter, and astronomers think of them as moving in "families." Some do cross the Earth's orbit.

Comets are sometimes called "dirty snowballs" because they are chunks of ice that grow long, glowing tails as they approach the sun. Comets can be classified by their tails. Type I tails are made of ionized molecules, while Type II tails are made of dust particles that reflect sunlight. Although the core of a comet may be quite small—perhaps a few kilometers in diameter—their tails can be millions of miles long.

About once every 100,000 years, a huge asteroid or comet might hit the Earth, with devastating results. The chances of this happening are slim. Astronomers are currently watching about 200 large asteroids and about 12 comets. What worries some sky-watchers, however, are the 2,000 giant asteroids and countless comets that humans don't yet know about.

Direct quotation: _____

_____

Indirect quotation: _____

_____

Summary:

_____
_____
_____
_____
_____
_____

UNIT 4 WRITERS' WORKSHOP

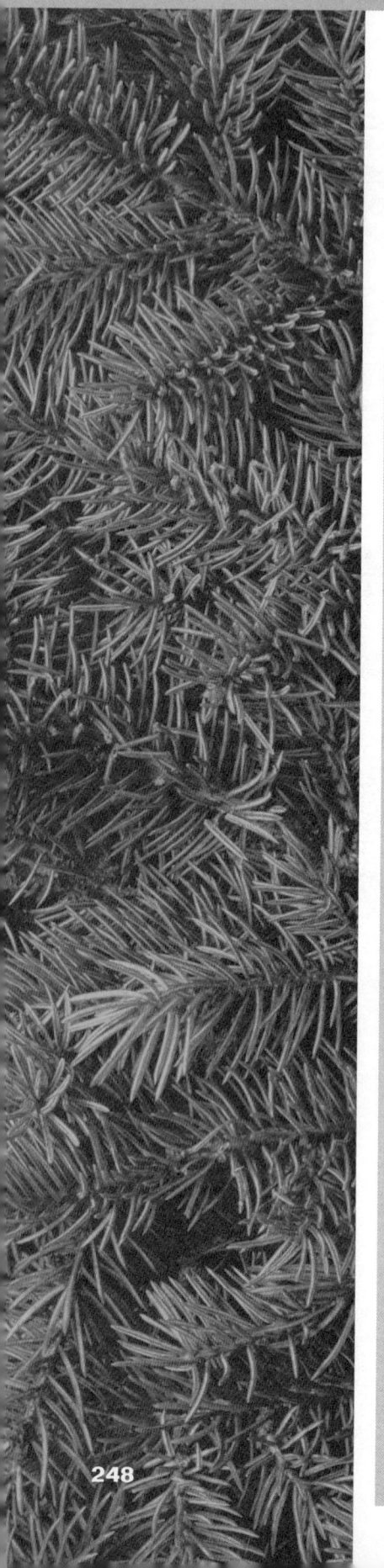

Analyze a Social Problem

Because essays are longer and more complex than paragraphs, organizing an essay can be a challenge, even for experienced writers. Techniques like having a clear *controlling idea*, a good *thesis statement*, and a *plan or an outline* all help an essay writer manage the task. Another useful approach is dividing the subject into three parts, as one student does here. In your group or class, read the essay, aloud if possible, underlining the parts you find most powerful and paying special attention to organization.

It's Great to Get Old

(1) I knock at the door and patiently await an answer. I listen and hear the thump of a cane on the hard wood floor, edging slowly toward the door. "It's great to get old," my grandmother says facetiously[1] as she opens the door, apologizing for making me wait. Through her I learn firsthand the problems of the aged. Loneliness, lack of money, and ailing health are just some of the problems old people must deal with.

(2) For one thing, loneliness seems endemic[2] among old people in America. With difficulty getting around, many spend most of their time confined to their apartments, awaiting visits from family or friends. Through my grandmother, I realize that as much as old people's families may care about them, the family members obviously have lives of their own and cannot visit as much as old persons would like. And when people are very old, most of their friends have already died, so they spend most of their time alone.

(3) Poor health is also a major problem. Any number of physical ailments create a problem. Cataracts, for example, are a common eye problem among old people. Health problems can make life very difficult for an old person.

(4) Last but not least is the financial burden old people must cope with. The rising costs of basic necessities such as food, housing, and health care are especially difficult for old people to meet. Sadly, most are forced to compromise what they need for what they can afford. Take, for example, an old person who buys pounds of inexpensive pasta for dinner every night. While the person may need other nutrients, the person forfeits this need for what the person can afford. Financial problems also make life very difficult for an old person.

(5) There is no easy way to ease the problems of the aged. Simply being aware of them is an important step in the right direction. If we turn our attention and compassion toward the elderly, we can begin to help them find solutions.

—Denise Nelley (Student)

---

[1]facetiously: humorously

[2]endemic: typical in a certain place or population

1. How effective is Ms. Nelley's essay?

   __Y__ Strong thesis statement?   __Y/N__ Good supporting details? *(see 5 below)*
   __Y/N__ Logical organization?   __Y__ Effective conclusion?
   (see 4 below)

2. Did the introductory paragraph catch your interest? Explain why or why not.

3. What is the controlling idea of the essay? What is the thesis statement?
   last sentence in first paragraph

4. This writer has skillfully organized her ideas. Her thesis names three problems facing the elderly. What are they? Does the body of the essay discuss these three problems in the same order that the thesis names them? If not, what changes would you suggest?

5. Are the three problems fully explained in paragraphs 2, 3, and 4? That is, does Ms. Nelley provide enough support for each problem? If not, what revision suggestions would you give the writer, especially for paragraph 3?*

6. This student movingly presents some problems of the elderly. Do you think she should have included solutions? Why or why not?

7. Can you spot any error patterns (the same error two or more times) that this student should watch out for? *no*

GROUP WORK

In your group or class, evaluate (or grade) Ms. Nelley's essay. Then, based on your evaluation, decide what changes or revisions would most improve the essay, and revise it accordingly, as if it were your own. If your group wishes to add any new ideas or support, brainstorm together and choose the strongest ideas. Rewrite as needed.

When you are done, evaluate the essay again, with your changes.

WRITING AND REVISING IDEAS

1. Discuss the ways in which a loved one's experience has taught you about a problem (addiction, AIDS, disability, and so on).
2. Analyze a social problem (crowded classrooms or shoplifting, for example).

---

*Prewrite again for more support on health problems. Develop paragraph 3 as fully as 2 and 4. Revise to avoid using the word "problem" four times.

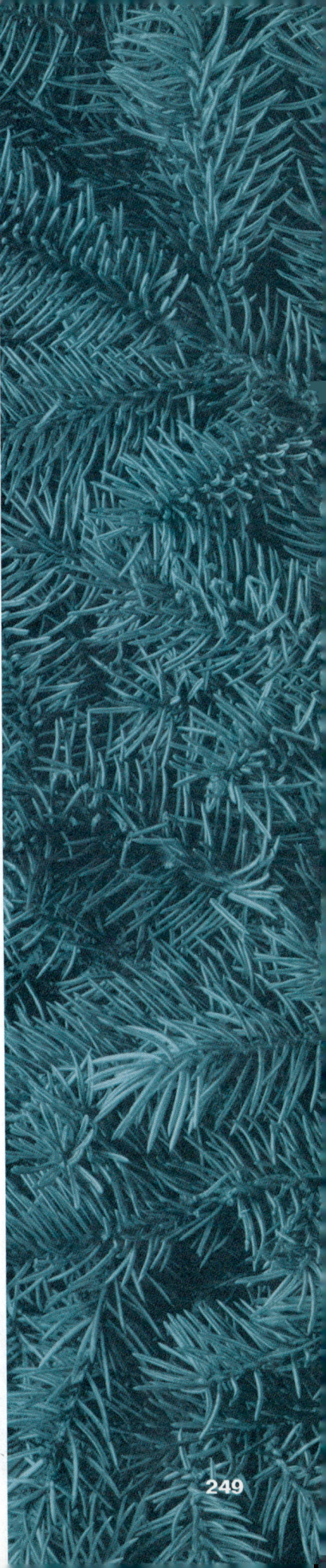

UNIT 5

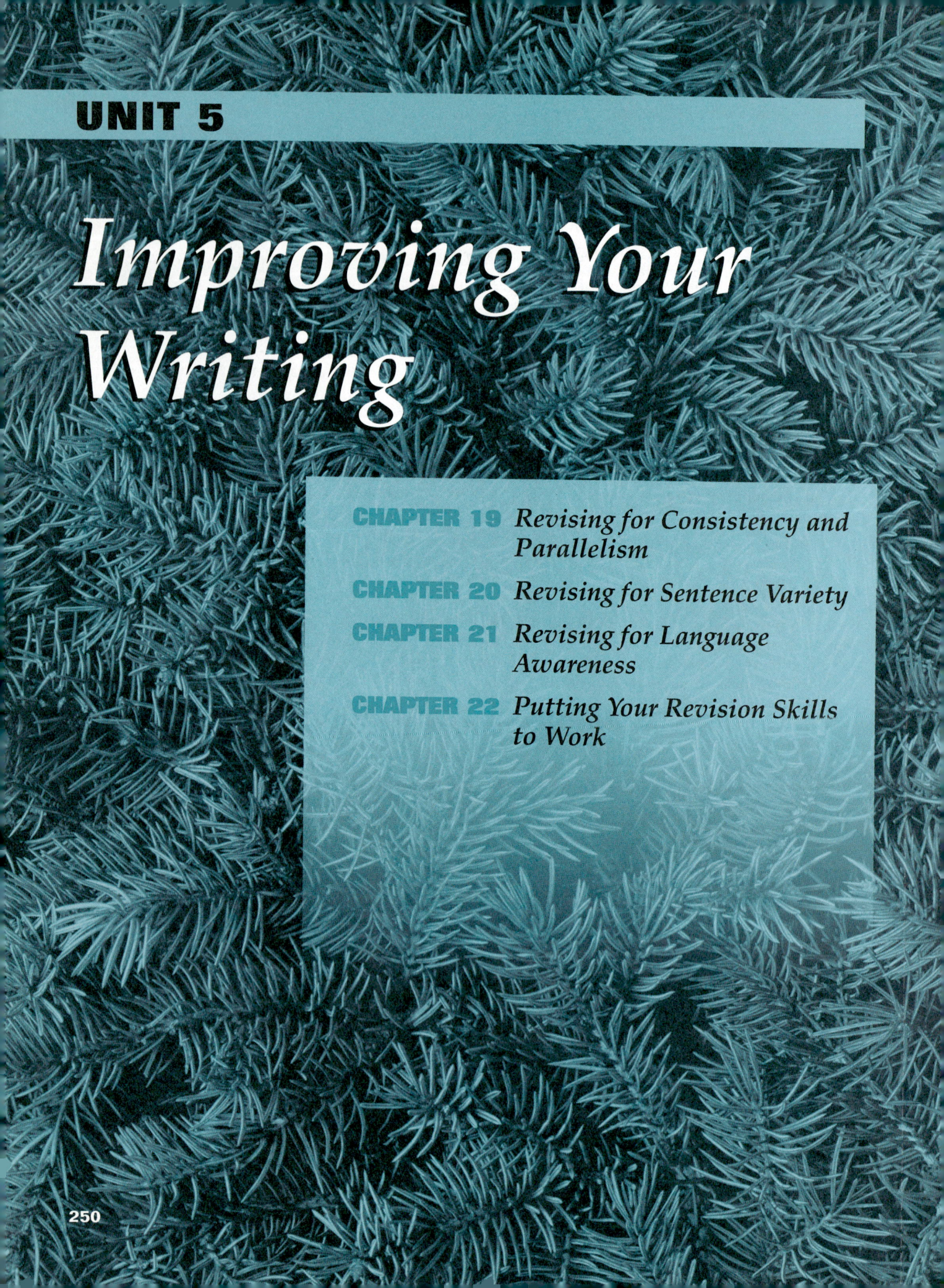

Improving Your Writing

CHAPTER 19 *Revising for Consistency and Parallelism*

CHAPTER 20 *Revising for Sentence Variety*

CHAPTER 21 *Revising for Language Awareness*

CHAPTER 22 *Putting Your Revision Skills to Work*

CHAPTER 19

Revising for Consistency and Parallelism

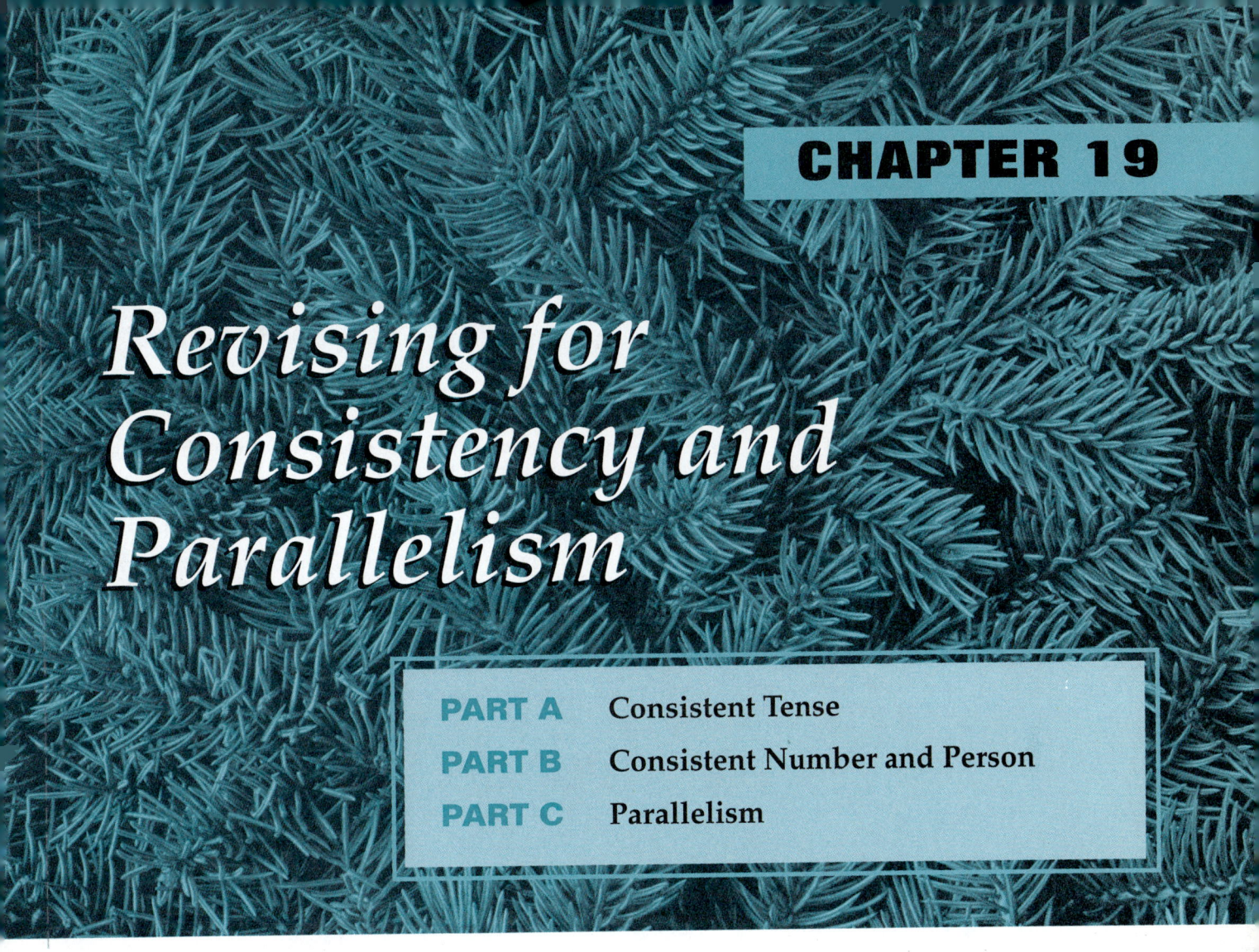

> **PART A** Consistent Tense
> **PART B** Consistent Number and Person
> **PART C** Parallelism

All good writing is **consistent.** That is, each sentence and paragraph in the final draft should move along smoothly without confusing shifts in **tense, number,** or **person.** In addition, good writing uses **parallel structure** to balance two or more similar words, phrases, or clauses.

Although you should be aware of consistency and parallelism as you write the first draft of your paragraph or essay, you might find it easier to **revise** for them—that is, to write your first draft and then, as you read it again later, check and rewrite for consistency and parallelism.

PART A Consistent Tense

Consistency of tense means using the same verb tense whenever possible throughout a sentence or an entire paragraph. Do not shift from one verb tense to another—for example, from present to past or from past to present—unless you really mean to indicate different times.

> 1. Inconsistent tense: We *stroll* down Bourbon Street as the jazz bands *began* to play.
> 2. Consistent tense: We *strolled* down Bourbon Street as the jazz bands *began* to play.
> 3. Consistent tense: We *stroll* down Bourbon Street as the jazz bands *begin* to play.

- Sentence 1 begins in the present tense with the verb *stroll* but then slips into the past tense with the verb *began*. The tenses are inconsistent since both actions (strolling and beginning) occur at the same time.

- Sentence 2 is consistent. Both verbs, *strolled* and *began*, are now in the past tense.

- Sentence 3 is also consistent, using the present tense forms of both verbs, *stroll* and *begin*. The present tense here gives a feeling of immediacy, as if the action is happening now.*

Of course, you should use different verb tenses in a sentence or paragraph if they convey the meaning that you wish to convey:

> 4. Last fall I *took* English 02; now I *am taking* English 13.

- The verbs in this sentence accurately show the time relationship between the two classroom experiences.†

Practice 1

Read the following sentences carefully for meaning. Then correct any inconsistencies of tense by changing the verbs that do not accurately show the time of events.

EXAMPLE I took a deep breath and opened the door; there stands a well-dressed man with a large box.

Consistent: I took a deep breath and opened the door; there ~~stands~~ *stood* a well-dressed man with a large box.

or

Consistent: I ~~took~~ *take* a deep breath and ~~opened~~ *open* the door; there stands a well-dressed man with a large box.

1. Two seconds before the buzzer sounded, Allan Houston sank a basket from midcourt, and the crowd ~~goes~~ *went* wild.

---

* For more work on spotting verbs, see Chapter 23, "The Simple Sentence," Part C.
† For more work on particular verb tenses and forms, see Chapters 26, 27, and 28.

CHAPTER 19 Revising for Consistency and Parallelism   253

2. Nestlé introduced instant coffee in 1938; it ~~takes~~ *took* eight years to develop this product.

3. We ~~expand~~ *expanded* our sales budget, doubled our research, and soon saw positive results.

4. For twenty years, Dr. Dulfano observed animal behavior and ~~seeks~~ *sought* clues to explain the increasing violence among human beings.

5. I knew how the system ~~works~~ *worked*.

6. I was driving south on Interstate 90 when a truck ~~approaches~~ *approached* with its high beams on.

7. Two brown horses ~~graze~~ *grazed* quietly in the field as the sun rose and the mist disappeared.

8. Lollie had a big grin on her face as she ~~walks~~ *walked* over and kicked the Coke machine.

9. Maynard ~~stormed~~ *storms* down the hallway, goes right into the boss's office, and shouts, "I want curtains in my office!"

10. The nurses quietly paced the halls, making sure their patients ~~rest~~ *rested* comfortably.

PRACTICE 2

Inconsistencies of tense are most likely to occur within paragraphs and longer pieces of writing. Therefore, it is important to revise your writing for tense consistency. Read this paragraph for meaning. Then revise, correcting inconsistencies of tense by changing incorrect verbs.

It was 1850. A poor German-born peddler named Levi Strauss came to San Francisco, trying to sell canvas cloth to tentmakers. By chance he met a miner who complained that sturdy work pants ~~are~~ *were* hard to find. Strauss had an idea, ~~measures~~ *measured* the man, and ~~makes~~ *made* him a pair of canvas pants. The miner loved his new breeches, and Levi Strauss ~~goes~~ *went* into business. Although he ordered more canvas, what he ~~gets is~~ *got was* a brown French cloth called *serge de Nimes*, which Americans soon called "denim." Strauss liked the cloth but had the next batch dyed blue. He became successful selling work pants to such rugged men as cowboys and lumberjacks. In the 1870s, hearing about a tailor in Nevada adding copper rivets to a pair of the pants to make them stronger, Strauss ~~patents~~ *patented* the idea. When he died in 1902, Levi Strauss was famous in California, but the company ~~keeps~~ *kept* growing. In the 1930s, when Levi's jeans became popular in the East, both men and women ~~wear~~ *wore* them. By the 1990s, people all over the world were buying 85 million pairs of jeans a year.

PRACTICE 3

The following paragraph is written in the past tense. Rewrite it in consistent present tense; make sure all verbs agree with their subjects.*

The tension built as I got into my car. I sat down, breathed deeply, and went through the motions of changing gears, practicing for the race. The seconds crawled by. I heard my heart pound and felt my stomach churning. I stared ahead at the long stretch of road equivalent to a quarter mile. My opponent entered his car, looked at me with a smirk on his face, and gave me the thumbs-down signal. I paid no attention to his teasing but wiped my hands on my shirt. I flexed my fingers and gripped the wheel. The race was about to begin.

The tension builds as I get into my car. I sit down, breathe deeply, and go through the motions of changing gears, practicing for the race. The seconds crawl by. I hear my heart pound and feel my stomach churning. I stare ahead at the long stretch of road equivalent to a quarter mile. My opponent enters his car, looks at me with a smirk on his face, and gives me the thumbs-down signal. I pay no attention to his teasing but wipe my hands on my shirt. I flex my fingers and grip the wheel. The race is about to begin.

PRACTICE 4

The following paragraph is written in the present tense. Rewrite it in consistent past tense.†

On the night of December 2, 1777, in Philadelphia, a woman stands breathlessly at a closed door in her house. While she listens at the keyhole, the British soldiers inside plan a surprise attack on George Washington's army. On the

---

* For more work on agreement, see Chapter 26, "Present Tense (Agreement)."
† For more work on the past tense, see Chapter 27, "Past Tense."

morning of December 4, carrying an empty flour sack, Lydia Darragh sets out. As she passes the British soldiers who occupy the town, she tells them she is on her way to buy flour. She walks five miles to the miller's, leaves her sack to be filled, and then heads toward the American camp. On the road, she meets American Colonel Thomas Craig and gives him her message. Craig gallops off to warn Washington of the danger—and Darragh goes back to pick up her flour. When British General Howe marches his army out of Philadelphia that night, the American troops are ready for the attack. Although Lydia Darragh's actions help the Americans win the Revolutionary War, she is never suspected.

> On the night of December 2, 1777, in Philadelphia, a woman stood breathlessly at a closed door in her house. While she listened at the keyhole, the British soldiers inside planned a surprise attack on George Washington's army. On the morning of December 4, carrying an empty flour sack, Lydia Darragh set out. As she passed the British soldiers who occupied the town, she told them she was on her way to buy flour. She walked five miles to the miller's, left her sack to be filled, and then headed toward the American camp. On the road, she met American Colonel Thomas Craig and gave him her message. Craig galloped off to warn Washington of the danger—and Darragh went back to pick up her flour. When British General Howe marched his army out of Philadelphia that night, the American troops were ready for the attack. Although Lydia Darragh's actions helped the Americans win the Revolutionary War, she was never suspected.

PRACTICE 5

Longer pieces of writing often use both the past tense and the present tense. However, switching correctly from one tense to the other requires care. Read the following essay carefully and note when a switch from one tense to another is logically necessary. Then revise verbs as needed.

A Quick History of Chocolate

Most of us now take solid chocolate—especially candy bars—so much for granted that we find it hard to imagine a time when chocolate didn't exist. However, this delicious food ~~becomes~~ *became* an eating favorite only about one hundred and fifty years ago.

The ancient peoples of Central America began cultivating cacao beans almost three thousand years ago. A cold drink made from the beans ~~is~~ *was* served to

Hernando Cortés, the Spanish conqueror, when he ~~arrives~~ *arrived* at the Aztec court of Montezuma in 1519. The Spaniards took the beverage home to their king. He ~~likes~~ *liked* it so much that he kept the formula a secret. For the next one hundred years, hot chocolate was the private drink of the Spanish nobility. Slowly, it ~~makes~~ *made* its way into the fashionable courts of France, England, and Austria. In 1657, a Frenchman living in London opened a shop where devices for making the beverage ~~are~~ *were* sold at a high price. Soon chocolate houses appeared in cities throughout Europe. Wealthy clients met in them, sipped chocolate, conducted business, and ~~gossip~~ *gossiped*.

During the 1800s, chocolate became a chewable food. The breakthrough ~~comes~~ *came* in 1828 when cocoa butter was extracted from the bean. Twenty years later, an English firm mixed the butter with chocolate liquor, which ~~results~~ *resulted* in the first solid chocolate. Milton Hershey's first candy bar ~~come~~ *came* on the scene in 1894, and Tootsie Rolls hit the market two years later. The popularity of chocolate bars ~~soar~~ *soared* during World War I when they ~~are~~ *were* given to soldiers for fast energy. M&Ms gave the industry another boost during World War II; soldiers needed candy that wouldn't melt in their hands.

On the average, Americans today eat ten pounds of hard chocolate a year. Their number-one choice is Snickers, which ~~sold~~ *sells* more than a billion bars every year. However, Americans consume far less chocolate than many Western Europeans. The average Dutch person ~~gobbled~~ *gobbles* up more than fifteen pounds a year while a Swiss ~~packed~~ *packs* away almost twenty pounds. Chocolate is obviously an international favorite.

PART B Consistent Number and Person

Just as important as verb tense consistency is consistency of **number** and **person**.

CHAPTER 19   Revising for Consistency and Parallelism   257

Consistency of Number

Consistency of number means avoiding confusing shifts from singular to plural or from plural to singular within a sentence or paragraph. Choose *either* singular *or* plural; then be *consistent*.

1. Inconsistent number:	*The wise jogger* chooses *their* running shoes with care.
2. Consistent number:	*The wise jogger* chooses *his* or *her* running shoes with care.
3. Consistent number:	*Wise joggers* choose *their* running shoes with care.

- Since the subject of sentence 1, *the wise jogger,* is singular, use of the plural pronoun *their* is *inconsistent*.

- Sentence 2 is *consistent*. The singular pronoun *his* (or *her*) now clearly refers to the singular *jogger*.

- In sentence 3, the plural number is used *consistently*. *Their* clearly refers to the plural *joggers*.

If you begin a paragraph by referring to a small-business owner as *she,* continue to refer to *her* in the **third person singular** throughout the paragraph:

> The small-business owner . . . . ; she . . . .
> . . . . The law may not protect *her* . . . .
> . . . . Therefore, *she* . . . .

Do not confuse the reader by shifting unnecessarily to *they* or *you*.

PRACTICE 6

Correct any inconsistencies of **number** in the following sentences.* Also make necessary changes in verb agreement.

EXAMPLE A singer must protect ~~their~~ *his or her* voice.

1. An individual's self-esteem can affect ~~their~~ *his or her* performance.

2. Jorge started drinking diet sodas only last November, but already he hates the taste of ~~it~~ *them*.

3. The headlines encouraged us, but we feared that ~~it wasn't~~ *they weren't* accurate.

4. The defendant who wishes to do so may ask a higher court to overturn ~~their~~ *his or her* conviction.

---

*For more practice in agreement of pronouns and antecedents, see Chapter 30, "Pronouns," Part B.

5. Dreams fascinate me; ~~it is~~ *they are* like another world.

6. If ~~a person doesn't~~ *people don't* know how to write well, they will face limited job opportunities.

7. Oxford University boasts of the great number of ancient manuscripts ~~they own~~ *it owns*.

8. Always buy corn and tomatoes when ~~it is~~ *they are* in season.

9. The average American takes ~~their~~ *his or her* freedom for granted.

10. ~~Women have~~ *A woman has* more opportunities than ever before. She is freer to go to school, get a job, and choose the kind of life she wants.

Consistency of Person

Consistency of person—closely related to consistency of number—means using the same *person*, or indefinite pronoun form, throughout a sentence or paragraph whenever possible.

> *First person* is the most personal and informal in written work: (singular) *I*, (plural) *we*
>
> *Second person* speaks directly to the reader: (singular and plural) *you*
>
> *Third person* is the most formal and most frequently used in college writing: (singular) *he, she, it, one, a person, an individual, a student*, and so on; (plural) *they, people, individuals, students*, and so on

Avoid confusing shifts from one person to another. Choose one, and then be *consistent*. When using a noun in a general way—*a person, the individual, the parent*—be careful not to slip into the second person, *you*, but continue to use the third person, *he or she*.

> 4. Inconsistent person: A *player* collects $200 when *you* pass "Go."
>
> 5. Consistent person: A *player* collects $200 when *he or she* passes "Go."
>
> 6. Consistent person: *You* collect $200 when *you* pass "Go."

- In sentence 4, the person shifts unnecessarily from the third person, *a player*, to the second person, *you*. The result is confusing.

- Sentence 5 maintains consistent third person. *He or she* now clearly refers to the third person subject, *a player*.

- Sentence 6 is also consistent, using the second person, *you*, throughout.

Of course, inconsistencies of person and number often occur together, as shown in the next box.

CHAPTER 19 Revising for Consistency and Parallelism   259

7.	Inconsistent person and number:	Whether *one* enjoys or resents commercials, *we* are bombarded with them every hour of the day.
8.	Consistent person and number:	Whether *we* enjoy or resent commercials, *we* are bombarded with them every hour of the day.
9.	Consistent person and number:	Whether *one* enjoys or resents commercials, *he or she* (or *one*) is bombarded with them every hour of the day.

- Sentence 7 shifts from the third person singular, *one*, to the first person plural, *we*.
- Sentence 8 uses the first person plural consistently.
- Sentence 9 uses the third person singular consistently.

PRACTICE 7

Correct the shifts in **person** in these sentences. If necessary, change the verbs to make them agree with any new subjects.

EXAMPLE One should eliminate saturated fats from ~~your~~ *one's* diet.

1. Sooner or later, most addicts realize that ~~you~~ *they* can't just quit when ~~you~~ *they* want to.

2. One problem facing students on this campus is that ~~a person doesn't~~ *they don't* know when the library will be open and when it will be closed.

3. One should rely on reason, not emotion, when ~~they are~~ *he or she is* forming opinions about such charged issues as abortion.

4. I have reached a time in my life when what others expect is less important than what ~~one~~ *I* really ~~wants~~ *want* to do.

5. Members of the orchestra should meet after the concert and bring ~~your~~ *their* instruments and music.

6. The wise mother knows that she is asking for trouble if ~~you let~~ *she lets* a small child watch violent television shows.

7. The student who participates in this program will spend six weeks in Spain and Morocco. ~~You~~ *He or she* will study the art and architecture firsthand, working closely with an instructor.

8. You shouldn't judge a person by the way ~~they dress~~. *he or she dresses*

9. If you have been working that hard, ~~one needs~~ *you need* a vacation.

10. People who visit the Caribbean for the first time are struck by the lushness of the landscape. The sheer size of the flowers and fruit amazes ~~you~~ *them*.

PRACTICE 8

The following paragraph consistently uses the third person singular—*the salesperson, he or she,* and so on. For practice in revising for consistency, rewrite the paragraph in **consistent third person plural**. Begin by changing *the salesperson* to *salespeople* or *salesclerks*. Then change verbs, nouns, or pronouns as necessary.

The salesperson is crucial to a customer's satisfaction or dissatisfaction with a particular store. In reality, the salesperson acts as the store's representative or ambassador; often he or she is the only contact a customer has with the store. Thousands of dollars may be spent in advertising to woo customers and build a favorable image, only to have this lost by the uncaring salesclerk.

—Robert F. Hartley, *Retailing: Challenge and Opportunity*

Salespeople are crucial to a customer's satisfaction or dissatisfaction with a particular store. In reality, salespeople act as the store's representatives or ambassadors; often they are the only contacts a customer has with the store. Thousands of dollars may be spent in advertising to woo customers and build a favorable image, only to have this lost by uncaring salesclerks.

PRACTICE 9

Revise the following essay for inconsistencies of person and number. Correct any confusing shifts (changing words if necessary) to make the writing clear and *consistent* throughout.

Immortality in Wax

"Madame Tussaud's. Come and find out who's in. And who's out." That's what English radios advertise to lure visitors to a most unusual show—a display of the rich, the famous, and the infamous in the form of lifelike wax statues. Nearly three million line up each year to rub shoulders with the images of historic and contemporary celebrities. ~~You~~ [They] make Madame Tussaud's the most popular paid tourist attraction in England.

Visitors are treated to some of Madame Tussaud's original handiwork, as well as to other figures that have been added over the past two hundred years. All told, tourists can see and be photographed with more than four hundred eerily lifelike statues. In the Grand Hall, ~~one~~ [they] can view British royalty standing with past and present leaders of other countries. The very popular Chamber of Horrors introduces ~~you~~ [them] to the most notorious criminals of all time. The Conservatory houses entertainers, from Marilyn Monroe and Joan Collins to Madonna and Brad Pitt.

Each month, a committee decides who should be added to or taken out of the collection. A celebrity is chosen for ~~your~~ [his or her] fame, recognizability, and publicity potential. ~~You are~~ [He or she is] invited to sit for moldings. Each image takes about six months to complete, at a cost of more than $32,000. The celebrity usually poses with ~~their~~ [his or her] finished statue for the press. Then the figure is put on display. Entertainers who have sat for moldings recently include John Travolta and Cybill Shepherd, the first American television comic actress in Madame Tussaud's. Newly represented political figures include Nelson Mandela and the Dalai Lama.

PART C   Parallelism

Parallelism, or **parallel structure**, is an effective way to add smoothness and power to your writing. **Parallelism** is a balance of two or more similar words, phrases, or clauses.

Compare the two versions of each of these sentences:

> 1. She likes dancing, swimming, and to jog.
> 2. She likes *dancing, swimming,* and *jogging*.
> 3. The cable runs across the roof; the north wall is where it runs down.
> 4. The cable runs *across the roof* and *down the north wall*.
> 5. He admires people with strong convictions and who think for themselves.
> 6. He admires people *who have strong convictions* and *who think for themselves*.

- Sentences 2, 4, and 6 use **parallelism** to express parallel ideas.
- In sentence 2, *dancing, swimming,* and *jogging* are parallel; all three are the *-ing* forms of verbs, used here as nouns.
- In sentence 4, *across the roof* and *down the north wall* are parallel prepositional phrases, each consisting of a preposition and its object.
- In sentence 6, *who have strong convictions* and *who think for themselves* are parallel clauses beginning with the word *who*.

Sometimes two entire sentences can be parallel:

> In a democracy we are all equal before the law. In a dictatorship we are all equal before the police.
>
> —Millor Fernandes

- In what way are these two sentences parallel? <u>Both use the same format:</u>

  "In a _____ we are all equal before the _____."

Certain special constructions require parallel structure:

> 7. The fruit is *both* tasty *and* fresh.
> 8. He *either* loves you *or* hates you.
> 9. Yvette *not only* plays golf *but also* swims like a pro.
> 10. I would *rather* sing in the chorus *than* perform a solo.

Each of these constructions has two parts:

   both . . . and

   (n)either . . . (n)or

   not only . . . but also

   rather . . . than

The words, phrases, or clauses following each part must be parallel:

   tasty . . . fresh

   loves you . . . hates you

   plays golf . . . swims like a pro

   sing in the chorus . . . perform a solo

PRACTICE 10

Rewrite each of the following sentences, using parallel structure to accent parallel ideas.

EXAMPLE The summer in Louisiana is very hot and has high humidity.

<u>The summer in Louisiana is very hot and humid.</u>

CHAPTER 19   Revising for Consistency and Parallelism   **263**

1. Teresa is a gifted woman—a chemist, does the carpentry, and she can cook.

   Teresa is a gifted woman—a chemist, a carpenter, and a cook.

2. The shape of the rock, how big it was, and its color reminded me of a small elephant.

   The rock's shape, size, and color reminded me of a small elephant.

3. He is an affectionate husband, a thoughtful son, and kind to his kids.

   He is an affectionate husband, a thoughtful son, and a kind father.

4. Marvin was happy to win the chess tournament and he also felt surprised.

   Marvin was happy and surprised to win the chess tournament.

5. Dr. Tien is the kindest physician I know; she has the most concern of any physician I know.

   Dr. Tien is the kindest and most concerned physician I know.

6. Joe would rather work on a farm than spending time in an office.

   Joe would rather work on a farm than spend time in an office.

7. Every afternoon in the mountains, it either rains or there is hail.

   Every afternoon in the mountains, it either rains or hails.

8. *Sesame Street* teaches children nursery rhymes, songs, how to be courteous, and being kind.

   Sesame Street teaches children nursery rhymes, songs, courtesy, and kindness.

9. Alexis would rather give orders than taking them.

   Alexis would rather give orders than take them.

UNIT 5 Improving Your Writing

10. His writing reveals not only intelligence but also it is humorous.

    His writing reveals not only intelligence but also humor.

PRACTICE 11

Write one sentence that is parallel to each sentence that follows, creating pairs of parallel sentences. *Answers will vary.*

EXAMPLE On Friday night, she dressed in silk and sipped champagne.

On Monday morning, she put on her jeans and crammed for a history test.

1. When he was twenty, he worked seven days a week in a fruit store.

   When he was forty, he worked four days a week as the owner of a chain of fruit stores.

2. The child in me wants to run away from problems.

   The adult in me knows I must face them.

3. The home team charged enthusiastically onto the field.

   The visiting team sat dejectedly in the dugout.

4. "Work hard and keep your mouth shut" is my mother's formula for success.

   "Nothing ventured, nothing gained" is mine.

5. The men thought the movie was amusing.

   The women thought it was insulting.

PRACTICE 12

The following paragraph contains both correct and faulty parallel structures. Revise the faulty parallelism.

During World War II, United States Marines who fought in the Pacific possessed a powerful ∧ weapon ~~that was also unbeatable~~: Navaho Code Talkers.
                                              and unbeatable

Creating a secret code, Code Talkers sent and ~~were translating~~ *translated* vital military information. Four hundred twenty Navahos memorized the code, *and used* ~~and it was used by them~~. It consisted of both common Navaho words and ~~there were also~~ about four hundred invented words. For example, Code Talkers used the Navaho words for *owl, chicken hawk,* and *swallow* to describe different kinds of aircraft. Because Navaho is a complex *and uncommon* language ~~that is also uncommon~~, the Japanese military could not break the code. Although Code Talkers helped the Allied Forces win the war, their efforts were not publicly recognized until the code was declassified in 1968. On August 14, 1982, the first Navaho Code Talkers Day honored these heroes, who not only had risked their lives but also ~~been developing~~ *had developed* one of the few unbroken codes in history.

PRACTICE 13

The following essay contains both correct and faulty parallel structures. Revise the faulty parallelism.

Nellie Bly

As a writer for the *New York World* in the 1880s, Nellie Bly was one of the leading journalists of her time. With determination and ~~courageously~~ *courage*, she pioneered what we now call the "media event." Nellie's most renowned exploit was her famous *and daring* trip ~~that was daring~~ around the world.

Nellie bet her publisher that she could beat the fictional record set by Phineas Fogg in Jules Verne's novel *Around the World in Eighty Days*. Moreover, her telegraphed reports of the trip would boost newspaper sales. Nellie left Jersey City on November 14, 1889, and ~~to travel~~ *traveled* first to England, France, and ~~the land of~~ Italy. From there, she journeyed over the Mediterranean Sea and the Indian Ocean to Ceylon. After stops in Singapore, Hong Kong, and ~~also in~~ Tokyo, she set sail for San Francisco. During this leg of the journey, she almost lost her bet. First, low winds delayed the sailing; then powerful storms ~~were striking~~ *struck* at sea. Adopting the motto "We'll win or die for Nellie Bly," the crew managed to get the ship to America. An easy cross-country train trip ~~that was fast~~, fast returned Nellie Bly to New York on January 25, 1890. Her trip had lasted seventy-two days, six hours, and ~~there were~~ eleven minutes.

Nellie arrived home a great hero and ~~to be~~ a national figure. Cheering crowds greeted her, songs were dedicated to her, toys were named after her, and ~~there were~~ parades ~~that~~ were organized in her honor. She embarked on a national tour, making speeches about her travels and ~~to fascinate~~ fascinating crowds with her tales. Nellie had shown the world that a gutsy American woman could travel the world alone, quickly, and ~~with safety~~ safely.

CHAPTER 20

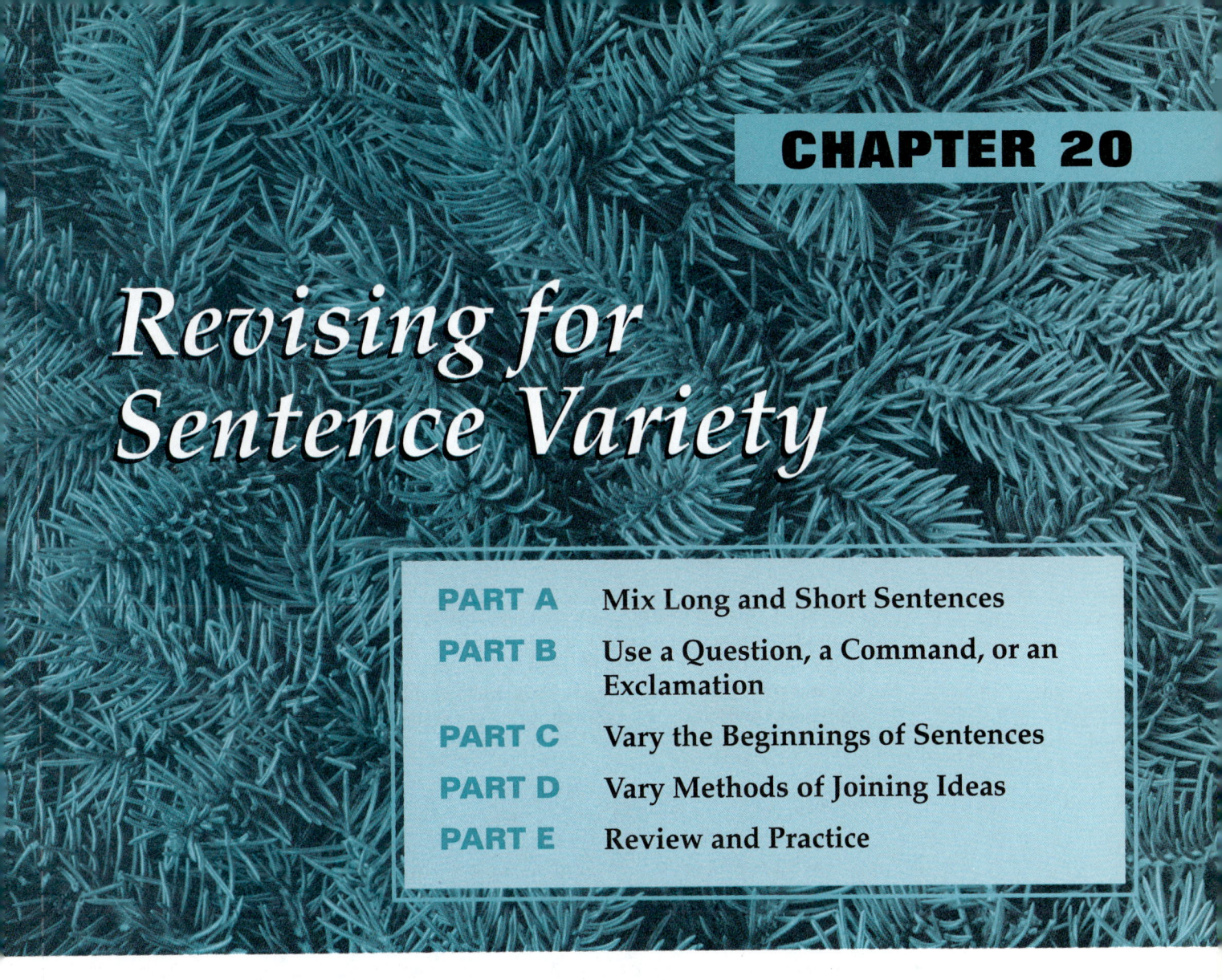

Revising for Sentence Variety

PART A   Mix Long and Short Sentences
PART B   Use a Question, a Command, or an Exclamation
PART C   Vary the Beginnings of Sentences
PART D   Vary Methods of Joining Ideas
PART E   Review and Practice

Good writers pay attention to **sentence variety.** They notice how sentences work together within a paragraph, and they seek a mix of different sentence lengths and types. Experienced writers have a variety of sentence patterns from which to choose. They try not to overuse one pattern.

This chapter will present several techniques for varying your sentences and paragraphs. Some of them you may already know and use, perhaps unconsciously. The purpose of this chapter is to make you more conscious of the **choices** available to you as a writer.

Remember, you achieve sentence variety by practicing, by systematically **revising** your papers and by trying out new types of sentences or combinations of sentences.

PART A   Mix Long and Short Sentences

One of the basic ways to achieve sentence variety is to use both long and short sentences. Beginning writers tend to overuse short, simple sentences, which quickly become monotonous. Notice the length of the sentences in the following paragraph:

268 UNIT 5 Improving Your Writing

> (1) There is one positive result of the rising crime rate. (2) This has been the growth of neighborhood crime prevention programs. (3) These programs really work. (4) They teach citizens to patrol their neighborhoods. (5) They teach citizens to work with the police. (6) They have dramatically reduced crime in cities and towns across the country. (7) The idea is catching on.

The sentences in the paragraph above are all nearly the same length, and the effect is choppy and almost childish. Now read this revised version, which contains a variety of sentence lengths.

> (1) One cause of the falling crime rate in some cities is the growth of neighborhood crime prevention programs. (2) These programs really work. (3) By patrolling their neighborhoods and working with the police, citizens have shown that they can dramatically reduce crime. (4) The idea is catching on.

This paragraph is more effective because it mixes two short sentences, 2 and 4, and two longer sentences, 1 and 3. Although short sentences can be used effectively anywhere in a paragraph or an essay, they can be especially useful as introductions or conclusions, like sentence 4 above. Note the powerful effect of short sentences used between longer ones in the paragraph that follows. Underline the short sentences.

> (1) I recall being told, when I first moved to Los Angeles and was living on an isolated beach, that the Indians would throw themselves into the sea when the bad wind blew. (2) <u>I could see why.</u> (3) The Pacific turned ominously glossy during a Santa Ana period, and one woke in the night troubled not only by the peacocks screaming in the olive trees but by the eerie absence of surf. (4) <u>The heat was surreal.</u> (5) The sky had a yellow cast, the kind of light sometimes called "earthquake weather." (6) My only neighbor would not come out of her house for days, and there were no lights at night, and her husband roamed the place with a machete. (7) One day he would tell me that he had heard a trespasser, the next a rattlesnake.
>
> —Joan Didion, *Slouching Towards Bethlehem*

PRACTICE 1

Revise and rewrite the following paragraph in a variety of sentence lengths. Recombine sentences in any way you wish. You may add connecting words or drop words, but do not alter the meaning of the paragraph. Compare your work with a fellow student's. *Answers will vary.*

The park is alive with motion today. Joggers pound up and down the boardwalk. Old folks watch them from the benches. Couples row boats across the lake. The boats are green and wooden. Two teenagers hurl a Frisbee back and forth. They yell and leap. A shaggy white dog dashes in from nowhere. He snatches the red disk in his mouth. He bounds away. The teenagers run after him.

The park is alive with motion today. Joggers pound up and down on the

boardwalk, and old folks watch them from the benches. Couples row green wooden boats across the lake. On the nearby grass, two teenagers hurl a Frisbee back and forth, yelling and leaping. Suddenly, a shaggy white dog dashes in from nowhere, snatches the red disk in his mouth, and bounds away. The teenagers run after him.

PART B Use a Question, a Command, or an Exclamation

The most commonly used sentence is the **declarative sentence,** which is a statement. However, an occasional carefully placed **question, command,** or **exclamation** is an effective way to achieve sentence variety.

The Question

> *Why did I become a cab driver?* First, I truly enjoy driving a car and exploring different parts of the city, the classy avenues and the hidden back streets. In addition, I like meeting all kinds of people, from bookmakers to governors, each with a unique story and many willing to talk to the back of my head. Of course, the pay isn't bad and the hours are flexible, but it's the places and the people that I love.

This paragraph begins with a question. The writer does not really expect the reader to answer it. Rather, it is a **rhetorical question,** one that will be answered by the writer in the course of the paragraph. A rhetorical question used as a topic sentence can provide a colorful change from the usual declarative sentences: *Is America really the best-fed nation in the world? What is courage? Why do more young people take drugs today than ever before?*

The Command and the Exclamation

> (1) Try to imagine using failure as a description of an animal's behavior. (2) Consider a dog barking for fifteen minutes, and someone saying, "He really isn't very good at barking, I'd give him a C." (3) How absurd! (4) It is impossible for an animal to fail because there is no provision for evaluating natural behavior. (5) Spiders construct webs, not successful or unsuccessful webs. (6) Cats hunt mice; if they aren't successful in one attempt, they simply go after another. (7) They don't lie there and whine, complaining about the one that got away, or have a nervous breakdown because they failed. (8) Natural behavior simply is! (9) So apply the same logic to your own behavior and rid yourself of the fear of failure.
>
> —Dr. Wayne W. Dyer, *Your Erroneous Zones*

The previous paragraph begins and ends with **commands,** or **imperative sentences.** Sentences 1, 2, and 9 address the reader directly and have as their implied subject *you.* They tell the reader to do something: *(You) try to imagine . . . , (you) consider . . . , (you) apply. . . .* Commands are most frequently used in giving directions,* but they can be used occasionally, as in the previous paragraph, for sentence variety.

Sentences 3 and 8 in the Dyer paragraph are **exclamations,** sentences that express strong emotion and end with an exclamation point. These should be used very sparingly. In fact, some writers avoid them altogether, striving for words that convey strong emotion instead.

Be careful with the question, the command, and the exclamation as options in your writing. Try them out, but use them—especially the exclamation—sparingly.

WRITING ASSIGNMENT 1

On a separate piece of paper, write a paragraph that begins with a rhetorical question. Choose one of the questions below or compose your own. Be sure that the body of the paragraph really does answer the question.

1. How has college (or anything else) changed me?
2. Is marriage worth the risks?
3. Do some MTV videos encourage the mistreatment of women?
4. Why do we do things that we know are bad for us?
5. Should people pamper their pets?

PART C Vary the Beginnings of Sentences

Begin with an Adverb

Since the first word of many sentences is the subject, one way to achieve sentence variety is by occasionally starting a sentence with a word or words other than the subject.

For instance, you can begin with an **adverb:**†

1. He *laboriously* dragged the large crate up the stairs.
2. *Laboriously,* he dragged the large crate up the stairs.
3. The contents of the beaker *suddenly* began to foam.
4. *Suddenly,* the contents of the beaker began to foam.

■ In sentences 2 and 4, the adverbs *laboriously* and *suddenly* are shifted to the first position. Notice the difference in rhythm that this creates, as well as the slight change in meaning: Sentence 2 emphasizes *how* he dragged the crate—*laboriously;* sentence 4 emphasizes the *suddenness* of what happened.

---

* For more work on giving directions, see Chapter 8, "Process."
† For more work on adverbs, see Chapter 32, "Adjectives and Adverbs."

CHAPTER 20 Revising for Sentence Variety 271

- A comma usually follows an adverb that introduces a sentence; however, adverbs of time—*often, now, always*—do not always require a comma. As a general rule, use a comma if you want the reader to pause briefly.

PRACTICE 2

Rewrite the following sentences by shifting the adverbs to the beginning. Punctuate correctly.

EXAMPLE He skillfully prepared the engine for the race.

Skillfully, he prepared the engine for the race.

1. Two deer moved silently across the clearing.

   Silently, two deer moved across the clearing.

2. The chief of the research division occasionally visits the lab.

   Occasionally, the chief of the research division visits the lab.

3. Proofread your writing always.

   Always proofread your writing.

4. Children of alcoholics often marry alcoholics.

   Often children of alcoholics marry alcoholics.

5. Jake foolishly lied to his supervisor.

   Foolishly, Jake lied to his supervisor.

PRACTICE 3

Begin each of the following sentences with an appropriate adverb. Punctuate correctly. *Answers may vary.*

1. *Cautiously,* the detective approached the ticking suitcase.

2. *Enthusiastically,* Martina Hingis powered a forehand past her opponent.

3. *Yesterday* she received her check for $25,000 from the state lottery.

4. *Reluctantly,* he left the beach.

5. *Slowly,* the submarine sank out of sight.

PRACTICE 4

Write five sentences of your own that begin with adverbs. Use different adverbs from those in Practices 2 and 3; if you wish, use *graciously, absent-mindedly, cheerfully, furiously, sometimes*. Punctuate correctly. *Sample answers:*

1. *Graciously, Rosa offered us use of her vacation home.*
2. *Absent-mindedly, he left the tickets at home.*
3. *Cheerfully, Jim whistled as he waxed the car.*
4. *Furiously, she slammed the door.*
5. *Sometimes I go for long walks on the beach.*

Begin with a Prepositional Phrase

A **prepositional phrase** is a group of words containing a **preposition** and its **object** (a noun or pronoun). *To you, in the evening,* and *under the old bridge* are prepositional phrases.*

Preposition	Object
to	you
in	the evening
under	the old bridge

Here is a partial list of prepositions:

Common Prepositions

about	beneath	into	throughout
above	beside	near	to
across	between	of	toward
against	by	on	under
among	except	onto	up
at	for	out	upon
behind	from	over	with
below	in	through	without

For variety in your writing, begin an occasional sentence with a prepositional phrase:

---

* For work on spotting prepositional phrases, see Chapter 31, "Prepositions."

> 5. Charles left the room *without a word*.
> 6. *Without a word*, Charles left the room.
> 7. A fat yellow cat lay sleeping *on the narrow sill*.
> 8. *On the narrow sill*, a fat yellow cat lay sleeping.

- In sentences 6 and 8, the prepositional phrases have been shifted to the beginning. Note the slight shift in emphasis that results. Sentence 6 stresses that Charles left the room *without a word*, and 8 stresses the location of the cat, *on the narrow sill*.
- Prepositional phrases that begin sentences are usually followed by commas. However, short prepositional phrases need not be.

Prepositional phrases are not always movable; rely on the meaning of the sentence to determine whether they are movable:

> 9. The dress *in the picture* is the one I want.
> 10. Joelle bought a bottle *of white wine for dinner*.

- *In the picture* in sentence 9 is a part of the subject and cannot be moved. *In the picture the dress is the one I want* makes no sense.
- Sentence 10 has two prepositional phrases. Which one *cannot* be moved to the beginning of the sentence? Why?

    Of white wine cannot be moved because it describes the word bottle and should therefore follow it.

PRACTICE 5

Underline the prepositional phrases in each sentence. Some sentences contain more than one prepositional phrase. Rewrite each sentence by shifting a prepositional phrase to the beginning. Punctuate correctly.

EXAMPLE A large owl <u>with gray feathers</u> watched us <u>from the oak tree</u>.

From the oak tree, a large owl with gray feathers watched us.

1. The coffee maker turned itself on <u>at seven o'clock sharp</u>.

    At seven o'clock sharp, the coffee maker turned itself on.

274 UNIT 5 Improving Your Writing

2. A growling Doberman paced behind the chainlink fence.

   Behind the chainlink fence, a growling Doberman paced.

3. A man and a woman held hands under the street lamp.

   Under the street lamp, a man and a woman held hands.

4. They have sold nothing except athletic shoes for years.

   For years, they have sold nothing except athletic shoes.

5. A group of men played checkers and drank iced tea beside the small shop.

   Beside the small shop, a group of men played checkers and drank iced tea.

PRACTICE 6

Begin each of the following sentences with a different prepositional phrase. Refer to the list and be creative. Punctuate correctly. *Answers will vary.*

1. *From the à la carte menu,* we ordered potato skins, salad, and beer.

2. *At the far table,* a woman in horn-rimmed glasses balanced her checkbook.

3. *After work,* everyone congratulated Jim on his promotion.

4. *In the museum,* one can see huge sculptures in wood, metal, and stone.

5. *Over our heads,* three large helium-filled balloons drifted.

PRACTICE 7

Write five sentences of your own that begin with prepositional phrases. Use these phrases if you wish: *in the dentist's office, between them, at my wedding, under that stack of books, behind his friendly smile.* Punctuate correctly. *Answers will vary.*

1. *In the dentist's office, the patients waited nervously.*

2. *Between them, they own ten homes.*

3. *At my wedding, we had a live orchestra.*

4. *Under that stack of books, you'll find the grocery list.*

5. *Behind his friendly smile, he is a dishonest salesman.*

PART D Vary Methods of Joining Ideas*

Join Ideas with a Compound Predicate

A sentence with a **compound predicate** contains more than one verb, but the subject is *not* repeated before the second verb. Such a sentence is really composed of two simple sentences with the same subject:

> 1. The nurse entered.
> 2. The nurse quickly closed the door.
> 3. The nurse *entered* and quickly *closed* the door.

- *The nurse* is the subject of sentence 1, and *entered* is the verb; *the nurse* is also the subject of sentence 2, and *closed* is the verb.

- When these sentences are combined with a compound predicate in sentence 3, *the nurse* is the subject of both *entered* and *closed* but is not repeated before the second verb.

- No comma is necessary when the conjunctions *and, but, or,* and *yet* join the verbs in a compound predicate.

A compound predicate is useful in combining short, choppy sentences:

> 4. He serves elaborate meals.
> 5. He never uses a recipe.
> 6. He serves elaborate meals yet never uses a recipe.
> 7. Aviators rarely get nosebleeds.
> 8. They often suffer from backaches.
> 9. Aviators rarely get nosebleeds but often suffer from backaches.

- Sentences 4 and 5 are joined by *yet*; no comma precedes *yet*.
- Sentences 7 and 8 are joined by *but*; no comma precedes *but*.

---

*For work on joining ideas with coordination and subordination, see Chapter 24, "Coordination and Subordination."

UNIT 5 Improving Your Writing

PRACTICE 8

Combine each pair of short sentences into one sentence with a compound predicate. Use *and*, *but*, *or*, and *yet*. Punctuate correctly. *Answers will vary.*

EXAMPLE Toby smeared peanut butter on a thick slice of white bread.
He devoured the treat in thirty seconds.

Toby smeared peanut butter on a thick slice of white bread and devoured the treat in thirty seconds.

1. Americans eat more than 800 million pounds of peanut butter.
   They spend more than $1 billion on the product each year.

   Americans eat more than 800 million pounds of peanut butter and spend more than $1 billion on the product each year.

2. Peanut butter was first concocted in the 1890s.
   It did not become the food we know for thirty years.

   Peanut butter was first concocted in the 1890s but did not become the food we know for thirty years.

3. George Washington Carver did not discover peanut butter.
   He published many recipes for pastes much like it.

   George Washington Carver did not discover peanut butter yet published many recipes for pastes much like it.

4. The average American becomes a peanut butter lover in childhood.
   He or she loses enthusiasm for it later on.

   The average American becomes a peanut butter lover in childhood but loses enthusiasm for it later on.

5. Older adults regain their passion for peanut butter.
   They consume great quantities of the delicious stuff.

   Older adults regain their passion for peanut butter and consume great quantities of the delicious stuff.

Practice 9

Complete the following compound predicates. *Do not repeat* the subjects. *Answers will vary.*

1. Three Korean writers visited the campus and _met with aspiring novelists_.

2. The singer breathed heavily into the microphone but _didn't sing a note_.

3. Take these cans to the recycling center or _move to a hotel_.

4. The newspaper printed the story yet _didn't check the facts first_.

5. Three men burst into the back room and _threw confetti on the surprised card players_.

Practice 10

Write five sentences with compound predicates. Be careful to punctuate correctly. *Sample answers:*

1. _Tonight I plan to study for my exam and start writing my paper._
2. _Many people like to cook but do not like to clean up._
3. _We could see a movie or go out to dinner._
4. _Mike loves to sail yet cannot swim._
5. _Renée can drive a car but has never parallel parked._

Join Ideas with an *-ing* Modifier

An excellent way to achieve sentence variety is by occasionally combining two sentences with an *-ing* modifier.

> 10. He peered through the microscope.
> 11. He discovered a squiggly creature.
> 12. *Peering through the microscope,* he discovered a squiggly creature.

- Sentence 10 has been converted to an *-ing* modifier by changing the verb *peered* to *peering* and dropping the subject *he*. *Peering through the microscope* now introduces the main clause, *he discovered a squiggly creature*.

- A comma sets off the *-ing* modifier from the word it refers to, *he*. To avoid confusion, the word referred to must appear in the immediately following clause.

An *-ing* modifier indicates that two actions are occurring at the same time. The main idea of the sentence should be contained in the main clause, not in the *-ing* modifier. In the preceding example, the discovery of the creature is the main idea, not the fact that someone peered through a microscope.

Be careful; misplaced *-ing* modifiers can result in confusing sentences: *He discovered a squiggly creature peering through the microscope.* (Was the creature looking through the microscope?)

Convert sentence 13 into an *-ing* modifier and write it in the blank:

> 13. We drove down Tompkins Road.
> 14. We were surprised by the number of "for sale" signs.
> 15. *Driving down Tompkins Road*_____, we were surprised by the number of "for sale" signs.

- The new *-ing* modifier is followed directly by the word to which it refers, *we*.

PRACTICE 11

Combine the following pairs of sentences by converting the first sentence into an *-ing* modifier. Make sure the subject of the main clause directly follows the *-ing* modifier. Punctuate correctly.

EXAMPLE Jake searched for his needle-nose pliers.
He completely emptied the tool chest.

Searching for his needle-nose pliers, Jake completely emptied the tool chest.

1. She installed the air conditioner.
   She saved herself $50 in labor.

   Installing the air conditioner, she saved herself $50 in labor.

2. The surgeons raced against time.
   The surgeons performed a liver transplant on the child.

   Racing against time, the surgeons performed a liver transplant on the child.

CHAPTER 20 Revising for Sentence Variety 279

3. They conducted a survey of Jackson Heights residents.
   They found that most opposed construction of the airport.

   Conducting a survey of Jackson Heights residents, they found that most opposed construction of the airport.

4. Three flares spiraled upward from the little boat.
   They exploded against the night sky.

   Spiraling up from the little boat, three flares exploded against the night sky.

5. Virgil danced in the Pennsylvania Ballet.
   Virgil learned discipline and self-control.

   Dancing in the Pennsylvania Ballet, Virgil learned discipline and self-control.

6. The hen squawked loudly.
   The hen fluttered out of our path.

   Squawking loudly, the hen fluttered out of our path.

7. The engineer made a routine check of the blueprints.
   He discovered a flaw in the design.

   Making a routine check of the blueprints, the engineer discovered a flaw in the design.

8. Dr. Jackson opened commencement exercises with a humorous story.
   He put everyone at ease.

   Opening commencement exercises with a humorous story, Dr. Jackson put everyone at ease.

PRACTICE 12

Add either an introductory *-ing* modifier *or* a main clause to each sentence. Make sure that each *-ing* modifier refers clearly to the subject of the main clause.
Sample answers:

EXAMPLE *Reading a book a week*, Jeff increased his vocabulary.

Exercising every day, *I lost five pounds*.

1. *Finally finishing her report*, she felt a sense of accomplishment.

280 UNIT 5 Improving Your Writing

2. Growing up in Hollywood, _he was not dazzled by movie stars_____.

3. _Talking over their differences at last_____, the father and son were reconciled.

4. Interviewing his relatives, _Jason collected many family stories_____.

5. _Moving slowly on its long chain_____, the wrecking ball swung through the air and smashed into the brick wall.

Practice 13

Write five sentences of your own that begin with -*ing* modifiers. Make sure that the subject of the sentence follows the modifier and be careful of the punctuation. *Answers will vary.*

1. _Giving myself a pep talk, I sat down to study Japanese._

2. _Crossing the street for the first time, the child carefully looked both ways._

3. _Practicing with her roommate's manual, Ellen finally learned to use WordPerfect._

4. _Rummaging through his drawers, Joe found a stack of unpaid bills._

5. _Jogging the last mile, Ben got so tired that he had to stop._

Join Ideas with a Past Participial Modifier

Some sentences can be joined with a **past participial modifier**. A sentence that contains a *to be* verb and a **past participle*** can be changed into a past participial modifier:

---

* For more work on past participles, see Chapter 28, "The Past Participle."

> 16. Judith *is trapped* in a dead-end job.
>
> 17. Judith decided to enroll at the local community college.
>
> 18. *Trapped in a dead-end job,* Judith decided to enroll at the local community college.

- Sentence 16 has been made into a past participial modifier by dropping the helping verb *is* and the subject *Judith*. The past participle *trapped* now introduces the new sentence.

- A comma sets off the past participial modifier from the word it modifies, *Judith*. To avoid confusion, the word referred to must directly follow the modifier.

Be careful; misplaced past participial modifiers can result in confusing sentences: *Packed in dry ice, Steve brought us some ice cream.* (Was Steve packed in dry ice?)

Sometimes two or more past participles can be used to introduce a sentence:

> 19. The term paper *was revised* and *rewritten*.
>
> 20. It received an A.
>
> 21. *Revised and rewritten,* the term paper received an A.

- The past participles *revised* and *rewritten* become a modifier that introduces sentence 21. What word(s) do they refer to?

    the term paper

PRACTICE 14

Combine each pair of sentences into one sentence that begins with a past participial modifier. Convert the sentence containing a form of *to be* plus a past participle into a past participial modifier that introduces the new sentence.

EXAMPLE Duffy was surprised by the interruption.
He lost his train of thought.

Surprised by the interruption, Duffy lost his train of thought.

1. My mother was married at the age of sixteen.
   My mother never finished high school.

   Married at the age of sixteen, my mother never finished high school.

2. The 2:30 flight was delayed by an electrical storm.
   It arrived in Lexington three hours late.

   Delayed by an electrical storm, the 2:30 flight arrived in Lexington three hours late.

282 UNIT 5 Improving Your Writing

3. The old car was waxed and polished.
   It shone in the sun.

   Waxed and polished, the old car shone in the sun.

4. The house was built by Frank Lloyd Wright.
   It has become famous.

   Built by Frank Lloyd Wright, the house has become famous.

5. The Nineteenth Amendment was ratified in 1920.
   It gave women the right to vote.

   Ratified in 1920, the Nineteenth Amendment gave women the right to vote.

6. The manuscript seems impossible to decipher.
   It is written in code.

   Written in code, the manuscript seems impossible to decipher.

7. Dr. Bentley will address the premed students.
   He has been recognized for his contributions in the field of immunology.

   Recognized for his contributions in the field of immunology, Dr. Bentley will address the premed students.

8. Mrs. Witherspoon was exhausted by night classes.
   She declined the chance to work overtime.

   Exhausted by night classes, Mrs. Witherspoon declined the chance to work overtime.

PRACTICE 15

Complete each sentence by filling in *either* the past participial modifier *or* the main clause. Remember, the past participial modifier must clearly refer to the subject of the main clause.

EXAMPLE Wrapped in blue paper and tied with string, *the gift arrived*.

Chosen to represent the team, Phil proudly accepted the trophy.

1. Made of gold and set with precious stones, *the snuffbox was a wonder to behold*.

CHAPTER 20 Revising for Sentence Variety 283

2. Overwhelmed by the response to her ad in *The Star*, _Marietta limited the number of people she would interview to ten_.

3. _Tired of junk mail_, Tom left no forwarding address.

4. _Laden with parcels from a shopping trip_, we found a huge basket of fresh fruit on the steps.

5. Astonished by the scene before her, _Consuela reached for the telephone and dialed 911_.

PRACTICE 16

Write five sentences of your own that begin with past participial modifiers. If you wish, use participles from this list:

thrilled	moved	seen	honored
shocked	dressed	hidden	bent
awakened	lost	stuffed	examined
annoyed	found	pinched	rewired

Make sure that the subject of the sentence clearly follows the modifier.
Sample answers:

1. _Awakened by the fire alarm, the hotel guests rushed outside._

2. _Annoyed by Louise's failure to keep appointments, I decided to stop calling her._

3. _Dressed in her ballet costume, the little girl performed for her parents._

4. _Lost for several hours, the hikers were cold and tired when they were rescued._

5. _Hidden in the back of the closet, my favorite shoes were lost for weeks._

Join Ideas with an Appositive

A fine way to add variety to your writing is to combine two choppy sentences with an appositive. An **appositive** is a word or group of words that renames or describes a noun or pronoun:

> 22. Carlos is the new wrestling champion.
> 23. He is a native of Argentina.
> 24. Carlos, *a native of Argentina,* is the new wrestling champion.

- *A native of Argentina* in sentence 24 is an appositive. It renames the noun *Carlos*.
- An appositive must be placed either directly *after* the word it refers to, as in sentence 24, or directly *before* it, as follows:

> 25. *A native of Argentina,* Carlos is the new wrestling champion.

- Note that an appositive is set off by commas.

Appositives can add versatility to your writing because they can be placed at the beginning, in the middle, or at the end of a sentence. When you join two ideas with an appositive, place the idea you wish to stress in the main clause and make the less important idea the appositive:

> 26. Naomi wants to become a fashion model.
> 27. She is the daughter of an actress.
> 28. *The daughter of an actress,* Naomi wants to become a fashion model.
> 29. FACT made headlines for the first time only a few years ago.
> 30. FACT is now a powerful consumer group.
> 31. FACT, *now a powerful consumer group,* made headlines for the first time only a few years ago.
> 32. Watch out for Smithers.
> 33. He is a dangerous man.
> 34. Watch out for Smithers, *a dangerous man.*

Using an appositive to combine sentences eliminates unimportant words and creates longer, more fact-filled sentences.

Practice 17

Combine the following pairs of sentences by making the *second sentence* an appositive. Punctuate correctly.

These appositives should occur at the *beginning* of the sentences.

EXAMPLE My uncle taught me to use watercolors.
He is a well-known artist.

A well-known artist, my uncle taught me to use watercolors.

1. Dan has saved many lives.
   He is a dedicated fire fighter.

   A dedicated fire fighter, Dan has saved many lives.

2. Acupuncture is becoming popular in the United States.
   It is an ancient Chinese healing system.

   An ancient Chinese healing system, acupuncture is becoming popular in the United States.

3. The Cromwell Hotel was built in 1806.
   It is an elegant example of Mexican architecture.

   An elegant example of Mexican architecture, the Cromwell Hotel was built in 1806.

These appositives should occur in the *middle* of the sentences. Punctuate correctly.

EXAMPLE His American history course is always popular with students.
It is an introductory survey.

His American history course, an introductory survey, is always popular with students.

4. The Korean Ping-Pong champion won ten games in a row.
   She is a small and wiry athlete.

   The Korean Ping-Pong champion, a small and wiry athlete, won ten games in a row.

5. The pituitary is located below the brain.
   It is the body's master gland.

   The pituitary, the body's master gland, is located below the brain.

6. The elevator shudders violently and begins to rise.
   It is an ancient box of wood and hope.

   The elevator, an ancient box of wood and hope, shudders violently and begins to rise.

These appositives should occur at the *end* of the sentences. Punctuate correctly.

EXAMPLE   I hate fried asparagus.
It is a vile dish.

I hate fried asparagus, a vile dish.

7. Jennifer flaunted her new camera.
   It was a Nikon with a telephoto lens.

   Jennifer flaunted her new camera, a Nikon with a telephoto lens.

8. At the intersection stood a hitchhiker.
   He was a young man dressed in a tuxedo.

   At the intersection stood a hitchhiker, a young man dressed in a tuxedo.

9. We met for pancakes at the Cosmic Cafe.
   It was a greasy diner on the corner of 10th and Vine.

   We met for pancakes at the Cosmic Cafe, a greasy diner at the corner of 10th and Vine.

Practice 18

Write six sentences using appositives. In two sentences, place the appositive at the *beginning*; in two sentences, place the appositive in the *middle*; and in two sentences, place it at the *end*. Sample answers:

1. An avid sailor, my brother-in-law dreams of owning a thirty-foot sailboat.

2. A state champion, that runner is supposed to win the marathon.

3. We serve vichyssoise, a cold potato soup, on hot summer days.

4. We stayed in Grantham, a small town in New Hampshire, for our vacation.

5. You can buy camping gear in Cherry Hill, the next town over.

6. The tall woman standing on the dock is Isabel, my mother's neighbor.

Join Ideas with a Relative Clause

Relative clauses can add sophistication to your writing. A **relative clause** begins with *who*, *which*, or *that* and describes a noun or pronoun. It can join two simple sentences in a longer, more complex sentence:

> 35. Jack just won a scholarship from the Arts Council.
> 36. He makes wire sculpture.
> 37. Jack, *who makes wire sculpture,* just won a scholarship from the Arts Council.

- In sentence 37, *who makes wire sculpture* is a relative clause, created by replacing the subject *he* of sentence 36 with the relative pronoun *who*.
- *Who* now introduces the subordinate relative clause and connects it to the rest of the sentence. Note that *who* directly follows the word it refers to, *Jack*.

The idea that the writer wishes to stress is placed in the main clause, and the subordinate idea is placed in the relative clause. Study the combinations in sentences 38 through 40 and 41 through 43.

> 38. Carrots grow in cool climates.
> 39. They are high in vitamin A.
> 40. Carrots, *which* are high in vitamin A, grow in cool climates.
> 41. He finally submitted the term paper.
> 42. It was due six months ago.
> 43. He finally submitted the term paper *that* was due six months ago.

- In sentence 40, *which are high in vitamin A* is a relative clause, created by replacing *they* with *which*. Which word in sentence 40 does *which* refer to?

    carrots

- What is the relative clause in sentence 43?

    that was due six months ago

- Which word does *that* refer to?

    term paper

Punctuating relative clauses can be tricky; therefore, you will have to be careful:*

> 44. Claude, *who grew up in Haiti,* speaks fluent French.

---

*For more practice in punctuating relative clauses, see Chapter 34, "The Comma," Part D.

- *Who grew up in Haiti* is set off by commas because it adds information about Claude that is not essential to the meaning of the sentence. In other words, the sentence would make sense without it: *Claude speaks fluent French.*
- *Who grew up in Haiti* is called a **nonrestrictive clause.** It does not restrict or provide vital information about the word it modifies.

> 45. People *who crackle paper in theaters* annoy me.

- *Who crackle paper in theaters* is not set off by commas because it is vital to the meaning of the sentence. Without it, the sentence would read, *People annoy me;* yet the point of the sentence is that people *who crackle paper in theaters* annoy me, not all people.
- *Who crackle paper in theaters* is called a **restrictive clause** because it restricts the meaning of the word it refers to, *people.*

Note that *which* usually begins a nonrestrictive clause and *that* usually begins a restrictive clause.

Practice 19

Combine each pair of sentences by changing the second sentence into a relative clause introduced by *who, which,* or *that.* Remember, *who* refers to persons, *that* refers to persons or things, and *which* refers to things.

These sentences require **nonrestrictive relative clauses.** Punctuate correctly.

EXAMPLE My cousin will spend the summer hiking in the Rockies.
She lives in Indiana.

My cousin, who lives in Indiana, will spend the summer hiking in the Rockies.

1. Scrabble has greatly increased my vocabulary.
   It is my favorite game.

   Scrabble, which is my favorite game, has greatly increased my vocabulary.

2. Contestants on game shows often make fools of themselves.
   They may travel thousands of miles to play.

   Contestants on game shows, who may travel thousands of miles to play, often make fools of themselves.

3. Arabic is a difficult language to learn.
   It has a complicated verb system.

   Arabic, which has a complicated verb system, is a difficult language to learn.

CHAPTER 20 Revising for Sentence Variety **289**

The next sentences require **restrictive relative clauses.** Punctuate correctly.

EXAMPLE He described a state of mind.
I have experienced it.

He described a state of mind that I have experienced.

4. The house is for sale.
   I was born in it.

   The house that I was born in is for sale.

5. My boss likes reports.
   They are clear and to the point.

   My boss likes reports that are clear and to the point.

6. People know how intelligent birds are.
   They have owned a bird.

   People who have owned a bird know how intelligent birds are.

PRACTICE 20

Combine each pair of sentences by changing one into a relative clause introduced by *who*, *which*, or *that*. Remember, *who* refers to persons, *that* refers to persons or things, and *which* refers to things.

Be careful of the punctuation. (Hint: *Which* clauses are usually set off by commas and *that* clauses are usually not.)

1. Her grandfather enjoys scuba diving.
   He is seventy-seven years old.

   Her grandfather, who is seventy-seven years old, enjoys scuba diving.

2. You just dropped an antique pitcher.
   It was worth two thousand dollars.

   You just dropped an antique pitcher that was worth two thousand dollars.

3. Parenthood has taught me acceptance, forgiveness, and love.
   It used to terrify me.

   Parenthood, which used to terrify me, has taught me acceptance, forgiveness, and love.

4. James Fenimore Cooper was expelled from college.
   He later became a famous American novelist.

   James Fenimore Cooper, who was expelled from college, later became a famous American novelist.

5. The verb *to hector* means "to bully someone."
   It derives from a character in Greek literature.

   The verb to hector, *which derives from a character in Greek literature, means "to bully someone."*

PART E Review and Practice

Before practicing some of the techniques of sentence variety discussed in this chapter, review them briefly:

1. Mix long and short sentences.
2. Add an occasional question, command, or exclamation.
3. Begin with an adverb: *Unfortunately,* the outfielder dropped the fly ball.
4. Begin with a prepositional phrase: *With great style,* the pitcher delivered a curve.
5. Join ideas with a compound predicate: The fans *roared and banged* their seats.
6. Join ideas with an *-ing* modifier: *Diving chin first onto the grass,* Johnson caught the ball.
7. Join ideas with a past participial modifier: *Frustrated by the call,* the batter kicked dirt onto home plate.
8. Join ideas with an appositive: Beer, *the cause of much rowdiness,* should not be sold at games.
9. Join ideas with a relative clause: Box seats, *which are hard to get for important games,* are frequently bought up by corporations.

Of course, the secret of achieving sentence variety is practice. Choose one, two, or three of these techniques to focus on and try them out in your writing. Revise your paragraphs and essays with an eye to sentence variety.

PRACTICE 21

Revise and then rewrite this essay, aiming for sentence variety. Vary the length and pattern of the sentences. Vary the beginnings of some sentences. Join two sentences in any way you wish, adding appropriate connecting words or dropping unnecessary words. Punctuate correctly. *Answers will vary.*

Little Richard, the King of Rock 'n' Roll

With "A-Wop-Bop-A-Loo-Bop-A-Lop-Bam-Boom," Little Richard hit the U.S. music scene on September 14, 1955. It has never been the same since. He had almost insane energy. He wore flamboyant clothes. He defined the rebellious behavior at the heart of rock 'n' roll. He has influenced countless performers. These performers include the Beatles, Mick Jagger and the Rolling Stones, David Bowie, and the artist formerly known as Prince.

Richard Wayne Penniman was born on December 5, 1932, in Macon, Georgia. He was the third of thirteen children. He sang gospel music with his siblings. They were called the Penniman Singers. Richard was a wild and independent child. He left home at fourteen. During his teens, he traveled throughout Georgia with musical shows of all kinds. These included "Dr. Hudson's Medicine Show" and the "Tidy Jolly Steppers." He appeared in "Sugarfoot Sam from Alabam." Here he played "Princess Lavonne" and wore a dress. He sang with B. Brown and his orchestra. He was called "Little Richard" for the first time.

By 1955, Richard had developed his own musical style. It combined gospel with rhythm and blues. At its center was a wild scream of pure joy. He had developed a stage style as well. It combined outrageous costumes, a mile-high pompadour, thick mascara, manic piano-playing, and uninhibited hip-swinging. "Tutti Frutti" made him an overnight sensation. Over the next two years, he produced one hit after another. Fans will never forget such classics as "Long Tall Sally," "Slippin' and Slidin'," "Rip It Up," "Lucille," and "Good Golly Miss Molly."

Richard had a five-year lull. He resurfaced in 1962. He became a cult figure for the next thirteen years. He was called "The Prince of Clowns" and "The King of Rock 'n' Roll." His behavior on and off the stage became more and more outrageous. In one show, he would dress as Queen Elizabeth. In the next show, he would dress as the pope. He once wore a suit covered with small mirrors. It prevented him from sitting in a car. His followers treated him royally. He was seated on a throne and crowned with jewels. He was carried into restaurants like a king.

Between 1957 and 1962, and then again in 1975, Little Richard had a spiritual awakening. The demon of rock 'n' roll dropped alcohol, drugs, and sexual promiscuity. He took on a devout lifestyle. He became an evangelist. He went to work for a Bible company. During these times, he returned to singing the gospel music of his youth.

Little Richard is still going strong. In 1992, he released an album for children, *Shake It All About.* It featured extremely lively remakes of children's classics. It has sold more than 250,000 copies. It introduced Little Richard's musical style to a new generation. In 1993, he performed at the presidential inaugural celebration. In 1997, he received the Award of Merit at the American Music Awards. At that time, he proclaimed, "I never burned out. Rock still lifts my spirit and gives me joy and an energy force."

Little Richard, the King of Rock 'n' Roll

With "A-Wop-Bop-A-Loo-Bop-A-Lop-Bam-Boom," Little Richard hit the U.S. music scene on September 14, 1955. It has never been the same since. With his almost insane energy and flamboyant clothes, he defined the rebellious behavior at the heart of rock 'n' roll. He has influenced countless performers, including the Beatles, Mick Jagger and the Rolling Stones, David Bowie, and Prince.

Richard Wayne Penniman was born on December 5, 1932, in Macon, Georgia. The third of thirteen children, he sang gospel music with his siblings. They were called the Penniman Singers. Richard was a wild and independent child who left home at fourteen. During his teens, he traveled throughout Georgia with musical shows of all kinds. These included "Dr. Hudson's Medicine Show" and the "Tidy Jolly Steppers." Playing "Princess Lavonne" and wearing a dress, he appeared in "Sugarfoot Sam from Alabam." When he sang with B. Brown and his orchestra, he was called "Little Richard" for the first time.

By 1955, Richard had developed his own musical style that combined gospel with rhythm and blues. At its center was a wild scream of pure joy. He had developed a stage style as well; it combined outrageous costumes, a mile-high pompadour, thick mascara, manic piano-playing, and uninhibited hip-swinging. "Tutti Frutti" made him an overnight sensation; then, over the next two years, he produced one hit after another. Fans will never forget such classics as "Long Tall Sally," "Slippin' and Slidin'," "Rip It Up," "Lucille," and "Good Golly Miss Molly."

After a five-year lull, Richard resurfaced in 1962. As a cult figure for the next thirteen years, he was called "The Prince of Clowns" and "The King of Rock 'n' Roll." His behavior on and off the stage became more and more outrageous. In one show, he would dress as Queen Elizabeth; in the next show, he would dress as the pope. He once wore a suit covered with small mirrors that prevented him from sitting in a car. His followers treated him royally. Seated on a throne and crowned with jewels, he was carried into restaurants like a king.

Between 1957 and 1962, and then again in 1975, Little Richard had a spiritual awakening. The demon of rock 'n' roll dropped alcohol, drugs, and sexual promiscuity. He took on a devout lifestyle and became an evangelist, working for a Bible company. During these times, he returned to singing the gospel music of his youth.

Little Richard is still going strong. In 1992, he released Shake It All About, which featured extremely lively remakes of children's classics. Selling more than 250,000 copies, it introduced Little Richard's musical style to a new generation. In 1993, he performed at the presidential inaugural celebration. In 1997, when he received the Award of Merit at the American Music Awards, he proclaimed, "I never burned out. Rock still lifts my spirit and gives me joy and an energy force."

Writing Assignment

Study this photograph of a wedding; then write a paragraph explaining how this scene came about. Invent a story of how the couple met, their courtship, and their decision to marry.

In your topic sentence, state the general feeling or mood of the photograph. Then tell the story behind the picture. Revise your paragraph, paying special attention to sentence variety. Try to vary sentence types and lengths.

CHAPTER 21

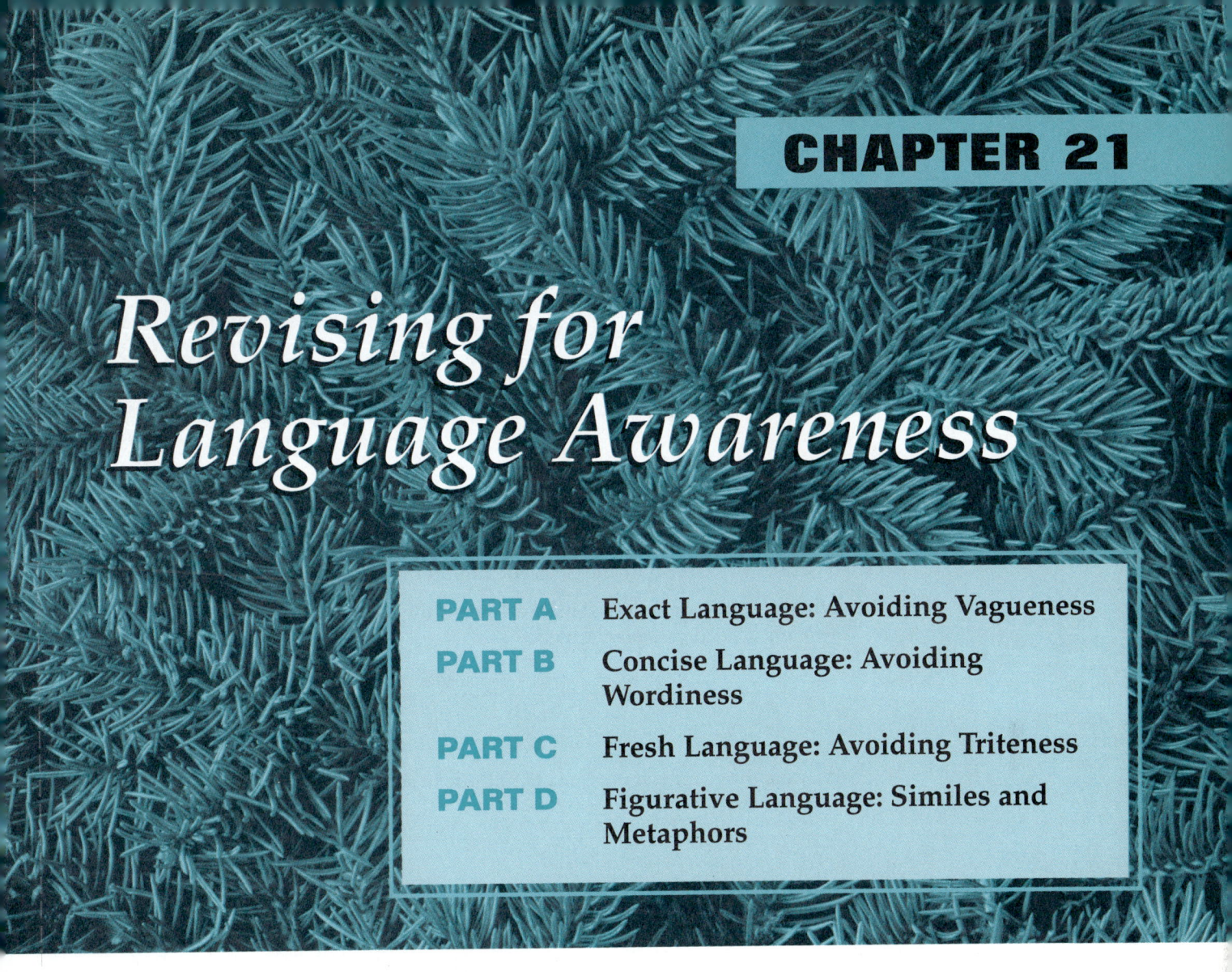

Revising for Language Awareness

PART A	Exact Language: Avoiding Vagueness
PART B	Concise Language: Avoiding Wordiness
PART C	Fresh Language: Avoiding Triteness
PART D	Figurative Language: Similes and Metaphors

Although it is important to write grammatically correct English, good writing is more than just correct writing. Good writing has life, excitement, and power. It captures the attention of the reader and compels him or her to read further.

The purpose of this chapter is to increase your awareness of the power of words and your skill at making them work for you. The secret of effective writing is **revision.** *Do not settle* for the first words that come to you, but go back over what you have written, replacing dull or confusing language with exact, concise, fresh, and sometimes figurative language.

PART A   Exact Language: Avoiding Vagueness

Good writers express their ideas as *exactly* as possible, choosing *specific, concrete,* and *vivid* words and phrases. They do not settle for vague terms and confusing generalities.

Which sentence in each of the following pairs gives the more *exact* information? That is, which uses specific and precise language? Which words in these sentences make them sharper and more vivid?

> 1. A car went around the corner.
> 2. A battered blue Mustang careened around the corner.
> 3. Janet quickly ate the main course.
> 4. Janet devoured the plate of ribs in two and a half minutes.
> 5. The president did things that caused problems.
> 6. The president's military spending increased the budget deficit.

- Sentences 2, 4, and 6 contain language that is *exact*.

- Sentence 2 is more exact than sentence 1 because *battered blue Mustang* gives more specific information than the general term *car*. The verb *careened* describes precisely how the car went around the corner, fast and recklessly.

- What specific words does sentence 4 substitute for the more general words *ate*, *main course*, and *quickly* in sentence 3?

  devoured, *plate of ribs*, and *two and a half minutes*

  Why are these terms more exact than those in sentence 3?

  They tell exactly how Janet ate, what she ate, and how quickly she ate it.

- What words in sentence 6 make it clearer and more exact than sentence 5?

  military spending; increased the budget deficit

Concrete and detailed writing is usually exciting as well and makes us want to read on, as does this passage by Toni Morrison, who won the Nobel Prize for literature:

> It is called the suburbs now, but when black people lived there it was called the Bottom. One road, shaded by beeches, oaks, maples, and chestnuts, connected it to the valley. The beeches are gone now, and so are the pear trees where children sat and yelled down through the blossoms at passersby. Generous funds have been allotted to level the stripped and faded buildings that clutter the road from Medallion up to the golf course. They are going to raze the Time and a Half Pool Hall, where feet in long tan shoes once pointed down from chair rungs. A steel ball will knock to dust Irene's Palace of Cosmetology, where women used to lean their heads back on sink trays and doze while Irene lathered Nu Nile into their hair. Men in khaki work clothes will pry loose the slats of Reba's Grill, where the owner cooked in her hat because she couldn't remember the ingredients without it.
>
> —Toni Morrison, *Sula*

CHAPTER 21 Revising for Language Awareness **297**

Now compare a similar account written in general and inexact language:

> It is called the suburbs now, but when black people lived there it was called the Bottom. One road, shaded by big trees, connected it to the valley. Many of the trees are gone now. Generous funds have been allotted to level the buildings on the road from Medallion up to the golf course. They are going to knock down the pool hall, the beauty parlor, and the restaurant.

You do not need a large vocabulary to write exactly and well, but you do need to work at finding the right words to fit each sentence. As you revise, cross out vague or dull words and phrases and replace them with more exact terms. When you are tempted to write *I feel good*, ask yourself exactly what *good* means in that sentence: *relaxed? proud? thin? in love?* When people walk by, do they *flounce, stride, lurch, wiggle,* or *sneak?* When they speak to you, do people *stammer, announce, babble, murmur,* or *coo?* Question yourself as you revise; then choose the right words to fit that particular sentence.

PRACTICE 1

Lively verbs are a great asset to any writer. The following sentences contain four overused general verbs—*to walk, to see, to eat,* and *to be.* In each case, replace the general verb in parentheses with a more exact verb *chosen to fit the context of the sentence.* Use a different verb in every sentence. Consult a dictionary or thesaurus* if you wish. *Answers will vary.*

EXAMPLES

In no particular hurry, we __strolled__ (walked) through the botanical gardens.

Jane __fidgets__ (is) at her desk and watches the clock.

1. With guns drawn, three police officers __crept__ (walked) toward the door of the warehouse.

2. As we stared in fascination, an orange lizard __crawled__ (walked) up the wall.

3. The four-year-old __teetered__ (walked) onto the patio in her mother's high-heeled shoes.

4. A furious customer __strode__ (walked) into the manager's office.

5. Two people who __witnessed__ (saw) the accident must testify in court.

6. We crouched for hours in the underbrush just to __spy__ (see) a rare white fox.

7. Three makeshift wooden rafts were __spotted__ (seen) off the coast this morning.

8. For two years, the zoologist __studied__ (saw) the behavior of bears in the wild.

---

*A thesaurus is a book of *synonyms*—words that have the same or similar meanings.

298   UNIT 5   Improving Your Writing

9. There was the cat, delicately __munching__ (eating) my fern!

10. Senator Gorman astounded the guests by loudly __slurping__ (eating) his soup.

11. All through the movie, she __crunched__ (ate) hard candies in the back row.

12. Within seconds, Dan had bought two tacos from a street vendor and __gulped__ (eaten) them both.

13. During rush hour, the temperature hit 98 degrees, and dozens of cars __stalled__ (were) on the highway.

14. A young man __lies__ (is) on a stretcher in the emergency room.

15. Workers who __sit__ (are) at desks all day should make special efforts to exercise.

16. Professor Nuzzo __paced__ (was) in front of the blackboard, excited about this new solution to the math problem.

PRACTICE 2

The following sentences contain dull, vague language. Revise them using vivid verbs, specific nouns, and colorful adjectives. As the examples show, you may add and delete words. *Answers will vary.*

EXAMPLES   A dog lies down in the shade.

A mangy collie flops down in the shade of a parked car.

My head hurts.

My head throbs.

I have shooting pains in the left side of my head.

1. Everything about the man looked mean.

   Even the angle of the shifty-eyed stranger's hat looked mean.

2. I feel good today for several reasons.

   I feel giddy today because it's Saturday, it's springtime, and I'm in love.

CHAPTER 21 Revising for Language Awareness   299

3. A woman in unusual clothes went down the street.

   A six-foot-tall woman in flowing African robes strode regally down the street.

4. The sunlight made the yard look pretty.

   The streaming sunlight painted every corner of the yard in technicolor.

5. What the company did bothered the townspeople.

   The company's dumping practices enraged the townspeople.

6. The pediatrician's waiting room was crowded.

   The pediatrician's waiting room overflowed with whining children and impatient parents.

7. As soon as he gets home from work, he hears the voice of his pet asking for dinner.

   The minute he walks in the door from work, his ears are assailed by Rover's piteous yelps begging for dinner.

8. The noises of construction filled the street.

   A cacophony of jackhammers, diesel engines, and rumbling dump trucks rose from the construction site.

9. When I was sick, you were helpful.

   When I had the flu for a week, you brought me chicken soup every day.

10. This college does things that make the students feel bad.

    The inadequate security in the college's dormitories worries and angers many students.

PRACTICE 3

A word that works effectively in one sentence might not work in another sentence. In searching for the right word, always consider the **context** of the sentence into which the word must fit. Read each of the following sentences for meaning. Then circle the word in parentheses that *most exactly fits* the context of the sentence.

EXAMPLE The alchemist cautiously (threw, (dripped), held) the liquid mercury onto copper in order to make it look like gold.

1. Alchemy, an early form of chemistry, was a (course, way, (science)) that flourished from ancient times until around 1700.

2. It was based on the (knowledge, (belief), fact) that a metal could be converted into another element.

3. Alchemists considered gold the ((perfect), nicest, shiniest) metal.

4. Therefore, their goal was to ((transform), redo, make) base metals, like lead, into gold.

5. They searched ((eagerly), high and low, lots) for the "philosopher's stone," the formula that would make this change possible.

6. All "philosopher's stones" consisted of sulphur and mercury; the trick was to discover the proper way to ((combine), destroy, mix up) the two.

7. Over time, alchemy incorporated various ((aspects), things, stuff) of astrology and magic.

8. For example, certain metals were (the same as, (equated with), sort of like) specific heavenly bodies—gold with the sun or silver with the moon.

9. One famous alchemist proudly (said, muttered, (boasted)) that he could magically transform winter into summer.

10. Many alchemists went to work for greedy princes and kings, who always (liked, (lusted for), thought about) more gold.

11. It was dangerous work though; more than one alchemist was (done away with, (executed), knocked off) because he could not produce gold.

12. In their search for gold, however, some alchemists (foolishly, hopefully, (accidentally)) made valid scientific discoveries that led to the development of modern chemistry.

PRACTICE 4

The following paragraph begins a mystery story. Using specific and vivid language, revise the paragraph to make it as exciting as possible. Then finish the story; be careful to avoid vague language. *Answers will vary.*

The weather was bad. I was in the house alone, with a funny feeling that something was going to happen. Someone knocked at the door. I got up to answer it and found someone outside. She looked familiar, but I didn't know from where or when. Then I recognized her as a person from my past. I let her in although I was not sure I had done the right thing.

PART B Concise Language: Avoiding Wordiness

Concise writing comes quickly to the point. It avoids **wordiness**—unnecessary and repetitious words that add nothing to the meaning.

Which sentence in each of the following pairs is more *concise*? That is, which does *not* contain unnecessary words?

1. Because of the fact that the watch was inexpensive in price, he bought it.
2. Because the watch was inexpensive, he bought it.
3. In my opinion I think that the financial aid system at Ellensville Junior College is in need of reform.
4. The financial aid system at Ellensville Junior College needs reform.
5. On October 10, in the fall of 1999, we learned the true facts about the robbery.
6. On October 10, 1999, we learned the facts about the robbery.

■ Sentences 2, 4, and 6 are *concise* whereas sentences 1, 3, and 5 are *wordy*.

■ In sentence 1, *because of the fact that* is really a *wordy* way of saying *because*. *In price* simply repeats information already given by the word *inexpensive*.

■ The writer of sentence 3 undercuts the point with the wordy apology of *in my opinion I think*. As a general rule, leave out such qualifiers and simply state the opinion; but if you do use them, use either *in my opinion* or *I think*, not both! Sentence 4 replaces *is in need of* with one direct verb, *needs*.

■ *In the fall of* in sentence 5 is *redundant*; it repeats information already given by which word?

October

■ Why is the word *true* also eliminated in sentence 6?

Facts are always true.

Concise writing avoids wordiness, unnecessary repetition, and padding. Of course, conciseness *does not mean* writing short, bare sentences, but simply cutting out all deadwood and never using fifteen words when ten will do.

PRACTICE 5

The following sentences are *wordy*. Make them more *concise* by crossing out or replacing unnecessary words or by combining two sentences into one concise sentence. Rewrite each new sentence on the lines beneath, capitalizing and punctuating correctly.

EXAMPLES   The U.S. Census uncovers many interesting facts that have a lot of truth to them.

The U.S. Census uncovers many interesting facts.

In the year 1810, Philadelphia was called the cigar capital of the United States. The reason why was because the census reported that the city produced sixteen million cigars each year.

In 1810, Philadelphia was called the cigar capital of the United States because the census reported that the city produced sixteen million cigars each year.

1. The Constitution requires and says that the federal government of the United States must take a national census every ten years.

   The Constitution requires the federal government to take a national census every ten years.

2. At first, the original function of the census was to ensure fair taxation and representation.

   The original function of the census was to ensure fair taxation and representation.

3. Since the first count in 1790, however, the census has been controversial. There have been several reasons why it has been controversial.

   Since the first count in 1790, however, the census has been controversial for several reasons.

4. One reason why is because there are always some people who aren't included.

   One reason is that some people aren't included.

5. The 1990 census, for example, missed almost five million people, many of whom were homeless with no place to live.

   The 1990 census, for example, missed almost five million people, many of whom were homeless.

6. For the 2000 census, the Census Bureau considered using statistical methods. The statistical methods would have been used instead of the traditional direct head count.

   For the 2000 census, the Census Bureau considered using statistical methods instead of the traditional direct head count.

7. The Bureau would have directly counted about 90 percent of U.S. residents who live in the United States and then estimated the number and characteristics of the remainder of the rest of the people.

   The Bureau would have directly counted about 90 percent of U.S. residents and then estimated the number and characteristics of the remainder.

8. Those who opposed the idea believed that in their opinion statistical methods would have introduced new errors that were mistaken into the count.

   Those who opposed the idea believed that statistical methods would have introduced new errors into the count.

9. The distribution of $100 billion in money, as well as the balance of power in the House of Representatives, depended on how and in which manner the census was conducted.

   The distribution of $100 billion, as well as the balance of power in the House of Representatives, depended on how the census was conducted.

10. Despite controversy, the U.S. census still continues to serve a beneficial purpose that is for the good of the United States.

    Despite controversy, the census serves a beneficial purpose for the United States.

PRACTICE 6

Rewrite this essay *concisely*, cutting out all unnecessary words. Reword or combine sentences if you wish, but do not alter the meaning. *Answers may vary.*

Dr. Alice Hamilton, Medical Pioneer

At the age of forty ~~years old~~, Dr. Alice Hamilton became a pioneer in ~~the field of~~ industrial medicine. In 1910, the governor of Illinois appointed her to investigate rumors that ~~people who were doing the work~~ *workers* in Chicago's paint factories were dying from lead poisoning. The result of her investigation was the first state law ~~that was passed~~ to protect workers.

The following year, the U.S. Department of Labor hired ~~this woman,~~ Dr. Hamilton to study industrial illness throughout the country ~~of the United States~~. In the next decade, she researched ~~and studied~~ many occupational diseases, including tuberculosis among quarry workers and silicosis—clogged lungs—among sandblasters. To gather information, Dr. Hamilton went to the workplace—deep in mines, quarries, and underwater tunnels. She also spoke to the workers in their homes ~~where they lived~~.

With great zeal, Dr. Hamilton spread her message about poor health conditions on the job. ~~What happened with her reports is that they~~ *Her reports* led to new safety regulations, workmen's compensation insurance, and improved working conditions in many industries. She wrote many popular articles and spoke to groups of interested citizens. In the ~~year of~~ 1919, she became the first woman to ~~hold courses and~~ teach at Harvard University. Her textbook ~~which she wrote~~, *Industrial Poisons in the U.S.*, became the standard book on the subject. By the time she died in 1970—she was 101—she had done much to improve the plight of many working people. ~~The reason why she~~ *She* is remembered today ~~is~~ because she cared at a time when many others seemed not to care at all.

PART C — Fresh Language: Avoiding Triteness

Fresh writing uses original and lively words. It avoids **clichés,** those tired and trite expressions that have lost their power from overuse.

Which sentence in each pair that follows contains fewer expressions that you have heard or read many times before?

> 1. Some people can relate to the hustle and bustle of city life.
> 2. Some people thrive on the energy and motion of city life.
> 3. This book is worth its weight in gold to the car owner.
> 4. This book can save the car owner hundreds of dollars a year in repairs.

- You probably found that sentences 2 and 4 contained fresher language. Which words and phrases in sentences 1 and 3 have you heard or seen before, in conversation, on TV, or in magazines and newspapers? List them:

    can relate to; the hustle and bustle; worth its weight in gold

Clichés and trite expressions like the following have become so familiar that they have almost no impact on the reader. Avoid them. Say what you mean in your own words:

Cliché: She is pretty as a picture.

Fresh: Her amber eyes and wild red hair mesmerize me.

Or occasionally, play with a cliché and turn it into fresh language:

Cliché: . . . as American as apple pie.

Fresh: . . . as American as a Big Mac.

Cliché: The grass is always greener on the other side of the fence.

Fresh: "The grass is always greener over the septic tank."—Erma Bombeck

The following is a partial list of trite expressions to avoid. Add to it any others that you overuse in your writing.

Trite Expressions

at a loss for words	in this day and age
at this point in time	last but not least
better late than never	living hand to mouth
break the ice	one in a million
cold cruel world	out of this world
cool, hot, awesome	sad but true
cry your eyes out	tried and true
easier said than done	under the weather
free as a bird	work like a dog
hustle and bustle	green with envy

PRACTICE 7

Cross out clichés and trite expressions in the following sentences and replace them with fresh and exact language of your own. *Answers may vary.*

1. In 1929, toy dealer Edwin S. Lowe came across people ~~having more fun than a barrel of monkeys~~ *enjoying themselves* while playing a game at a carnival in rural Georgia.

2. A leader called out each ~~and every~~ number, and the players used beans to cover the matching numbers on their cards.

3. The winners yelled "Beano!" ~~at the top of their lungs~~ when they had filled in a row of numbers.

4. According to the carnival owner, a stranger had brought the game from Europe, so ~~it went without saying that~~ no one owned the game.

5. ~~Quick as a wink,~~ *Immediately* Lowe saw the ~~game was a winner~~ *potential of the game*.

6. As soon as he returned home, the *shrewd* businessman~~, who was as sharp as a tack,~~ began testing beano out on friends.

7. One night, instead of "Beano!" ~~a~~ *an excited* guest ~~who was beside himself with excitement~~ shouted out, "Bingo!"

8. Lowe went on to market the game as Bingo, and it sold *phenomenally* ~~like crazy~~.

9. Soon many nonprofit organizations were holding bingo tournaments as ~~a tried and true~~ *an effective* method of raising funds.

10. Because Lowe had produced only twenty-four different cards, too many people were ~~cleaning up~~ *winning*.

11. Therefore, Lowe paid a mathematics professor ~~an awesome amount~~ *a huge sum* to develop six thousand cards, each with a different combination of numbers.

12. By 1934, hundreds of thousands of Americans were playing bingo ~~like there was no tomorrow~~ *enthusiastically*.

PART D Figurative Language: Similes and Metaphors

One way to add sparkle and exactness to your writing is to use an occasional simile or metaphor. A **simile** is a comparison of two things using the word *like* or *as*:

> "He was *as ugly as* a wart." —Anne Sexton
>
> "The frozen twigs of the huge tulip poplar next to the hill clack in the cold *like* tinsnips." —Annie Dillard

A **metaphor** is a similar comparison without the word *like* or *as*:

CHAPTER 21 Revising for Language Awareness 307

> "My soul is a dark forest." —D. H. Lawrence
>
> Love is a virus.

- The power of similes and metaphors comes partly from the surprise of comparing two apparently unlike things. A well-chosen simile or metaphor can convey a lot of information in very few words.

- To compare a person to a wart, as Sexton does, lets us know quickly just how ugly that person is. And to say that *twigs clack like tinsnips* describes the sound so precisely that we can almost hear it.

- What do you think D. H. Lawrence means by his metaphor? In what ways is a person's soul like a *dark forest*?

    It is a tangle of emotions containing scary, unexplored areas.

- The statement *love is a virus* tells us something about the writer's attitude toward love. What is it? In what ways is love like a virus?

    The writer thinks that love is contagious; love is a kind of sickness with

    predictable symptoms.

Similes and metaphors should not be overused; however, once in a while, they can be a delightful addition to a paper that is also exact, concise, and fresh.

PRACTICE 8

The author of the following paragraph contrasts a fat priest and his thin parishioners. He uses at least one simile and two metaphors in his description. Underline the simile and circle the metaphors.

He was a large, juicy man, <u>soft and sappy as a melon</u>, and this sweet roundness made him appear spoiled and self-indulgent, especially when contrasted with the small, spare, <u>sticklike</u> peons* who comprised his parish. . . . Everything about them, the peons, was withered and bone-dry. Everything about him was full and fleshy and wet. (They were mummies.) (He was a whale,) beached upon the desert sands, draped in black to mourn his predicament.

—Bill Porterfield, *Texas Rhapsody*

---

* peons: farm workers or laborers of the southwest United States or Latin America

Practice 9

Think of several similes to complete each sentence that follows. Be creative! Then underline your favorite simile, the one that best completes each sentence. *Answers may vary.*

EXAMPLE My English class is like an orchestra.
the Everglades.
an action movie.
a vegetable garden.

1. Job hunting is like _____

   a game of chess.

   rock climbing.

   a plunge into cold water.

2. My room looks like _____

   yesterday's scrambled eggs.

   a shipwreck.

   a supernova.

3. Writing well is like _____

   riding down the freeway.

   sailing in a stiff wind.

   reaching the top of a mountain.

4. Marriage is like _____

   a broken record.

   a trip around the world.

   completing a puzzle.

Practice 10

Think of several metaphors to complete each sentence that follows. Jot down three or four ideas, and then underline the metaphor that best completes each sentence. *Answers may vary.*

EXAMPLE Love is a blood transfusion.
a sunrise.
a magic mirror.
a roller coaster ride.

1. Television is _____

   a bottle of sedatives.

   a false friend.

   a seducer.

2. Registration is _____

   a battlefield.

   a snakepit.

   a lesson in patience.

3. My car is _____

   a two-eyed monster.

   a goldfish bowl.

   another child.

4. Courage is _____

   a taut rope.

   a doorway.

   a searchlight.

WRITING ASSIGNMENTS

1. Good writing can be done on almost any subject if the writer approaches the subject with openness and with "new eyes." Take a piece of fruit or a vegetable—a lemon, a green pepper, a cherry tomato. Examine it as if for the first time. Feel its texture and parts, smell it, weigh it in your palm.

   Now capture your experience of the fruit or vegetable in words. First jot down words and ideas, or freewrite, aiming for the most *exact* description possible. Don't settle for the first words you think of. Keep writing. Then go back over what you have written, underlining the most exact and powerful writing. Compose a topic sentence and draft a paragraph that conveys your unique experience of the fruit or vegetable.

2. In the paragraph that follows, Don DeLillo describes a "small" experience in such rich, exact detail that it becomes alive and intriguing to the reader. Read his paragraph, underlining language that strikes you as especially *exact* and *fresh.* Can you spot the two similes? Can you find any especially vivid adjectives or unusual verbs?

   You have to know the feel of a baseball in your hand, going back awhile, connecting many things, before you can understand why a man would sit in a chair at four in the morning holding such an object, clutching it—how it fits the palm so reassuringly, the corked center making it buoyant in the hand, and the rough spots on an old ball, the marked skin, how an idle thumb likes to worry the scuffed horsehide. You squeeze a baseball. You kind of juice it or milk it. The resistance of the packed material makes you want to press harder. There's an equilibrium, an agreeable animal tension between the hard leather object and the sort of clawed hand, veins stretching with the effort. And the feel of raised seams across the fingertips, cloth contours like road bumps under the knuckle joints—how the whorled cotton can be seen as a magnified thumbprint. . . . The ball was smudged green near the Spalding trademark; it was still wearing a small green bruise where it had struck a pillar, according to the history that came with it—flaked paint from a bolted column in the left-field stands embedded in the surface of the ball.

   —Don DeLillo, *Underworld*

   Write a paragraph or essay in which you also describe a brief but interesting experience (or event), perhaps a time you observed, admired, or truly studied an object or person. As you freewrite or brainstorm, try to capture the most precise and minute details of what you experienced or what happened. Now revise your piece of writing, making the language as *exact*, *concise*, and *fresh* as you can.

3. The photo above shows a painting by Milan Kunc called "Crocodile Village." Look closely at this painting, noting the small huts on the crocodile's back, the man in the boat, and the unusual position of the moon. What overall impression or mood does the painting communicate to you? Is it peaceful, threatening, magical?

   Now write a two-paragraph composition discussing the painting. In the first paragraph, describe the painting, very specifically pointing out important details. In the second paragraph, explain what you think the painter is trying to convey by creating this picture. As you revise, make your writing as *exact*, *concise*, and *fresh* as possible so that a reader who has not seen the painting has a clear sense of it.

CHAPTER 22

Putting Your Revision Skills to Work

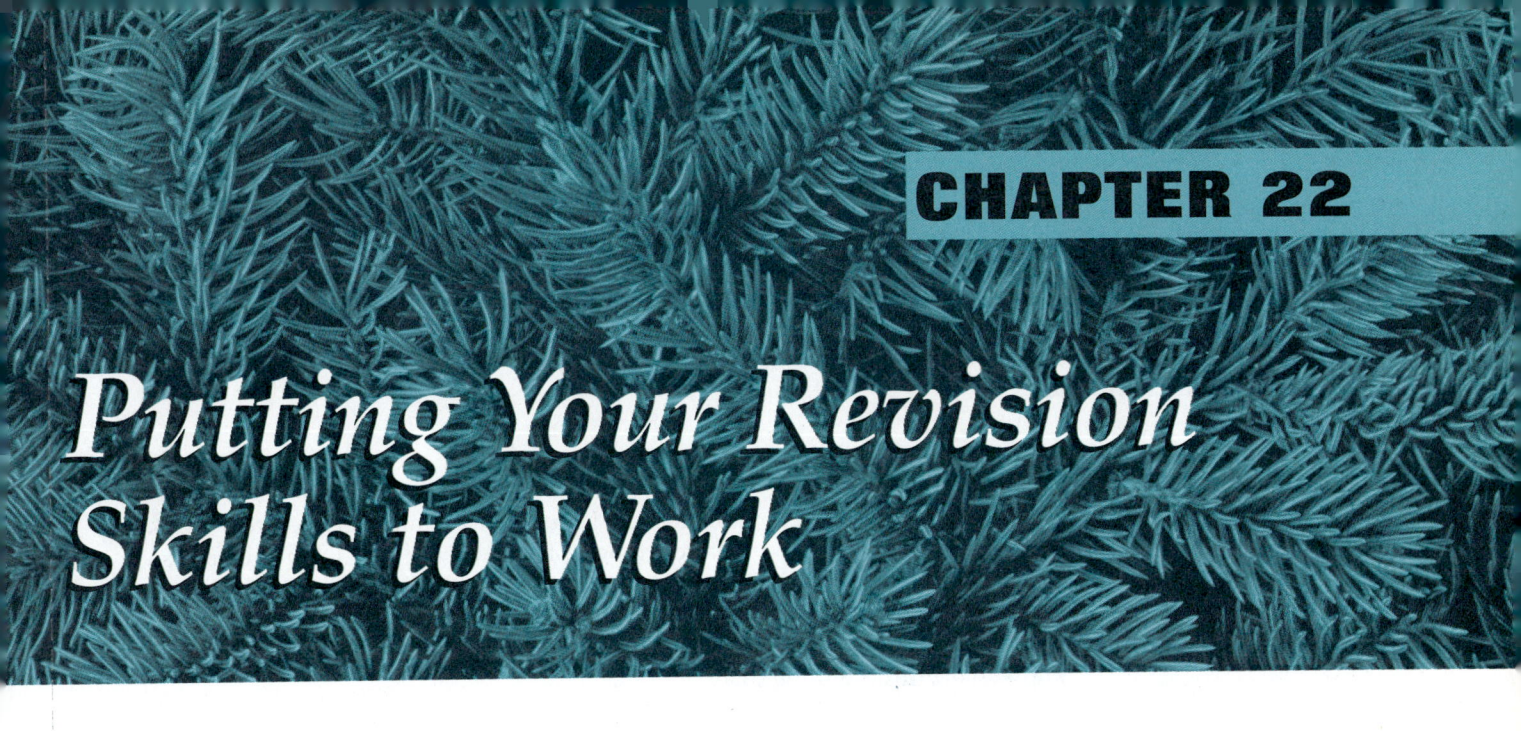

In Units 2 and 3, you learned to **revise** basic paragraphs, and in Unit 4, you learned to revise essays. All revising requires that you rethink and rewrite with such questions as these in mind:

Can a reader understand and follow my ideas?

Is my topic sentence or thesis statement clear?

Does the body of my paragraph or essay fully support the topic or thesis statement?

Does my paragraph or essay have unity? That is, does every sentence relate to the main idea?

Does my paragraph or essay have coherence? That is, does it follow a logical order and guide the reader from point to point?

Does my writing conclude, not just leave off?

Of course, the more writing techniques you learn, the more options you have as you revise. Unit 5 has moved beyond the basics to matters of style: consistency and parallelism, sentence variety, and clear, exact language. This chapter will guide you again through the revision process, adding questions like the following to your list:

Are my verb tenses and pronouns consistent?

Have I used parallel structure to highlight parallel ideas?

Have I varied the length and type of my sentences?

Is my language exact, concise, and fresh?

Many writers first revise and rewrite with questions like these in mind. They do *not* worry about grammar and minor errors at this stage. Then in a separate, final process, they **proofread*** for spelling and grammatical errors.

---

* For practice in proofreading for particular errors, see individual chapters in Units 6 and 7. For practice in proofreading for mixed errors, see Chapter 36, "Putting Your Proofreading Skills to Work."

312   UNIT 5   Improving Your Writing

Here are two sample paragraphs by students, showing the first draft, the revisions made by the student, and the revised draft of each. Each revision has been numbered and explained to give you a clear idea of the thinking process involved.

Writing Sample 1

First Draft

I like to give my best performance. I must relax completely before a show. I often know ahead of time what choreography I will use and what I'll sing, so I can concentrate on relaxing completely. I usually do this by reading, etc. I always know my parts perfectly. Occasionally I look through the curtain to watch the people come in. This can make you feel faint, but I reassure myself and say I know everything will be okay.

Revisions

(1) In order ~~I like~~ to give my best performance, I must relax completely before a show. I often know ahead of time what choreography (2) and vocals I will use, and ~~what~~ (3) during that long, last hour before curtain, ~~I'll sing;~~ so I can concentrate on relaxing (4) ~~completely.~~ I usually do this by (5) an action-packed mystery, but sometimes I joke with the other performers or just walk around backstage. reading, etc. (6) (I always know my parts perfectly.) Occasionally I (7) peek ~~look~~ (6) audience file (8) me through the curtain to watch the ~~people come~~ in. This can make ~~you~~ feel (9) "Vickie," I say, "the minute you're out there singing to the people, everything will be okay." faint, but I reassure myself, ~~and say I know everything will be okay.~~

Reasons for Revisions

1. Combine two short sentences. (sentence variety)

2. Make *choreography* and *vocals* parallel and omit unnecessary words. (parallelism)

3. Make time order clear: First discuss what I've done during the days before the performance, and then discuss the hour before performance. (time order)

4. Drop *completely*, which repeats the word used in the first sentence. (avoid wordiness)

5. This is important! Drop *etc.*, add more details, and give examples. (add examples)

6. This idea belongs earlier in the paragraph—with what I've done during the days before the performance. (order)

7. Use more specific and interesting language in this sentence. (exact language)

8. Use the first person singular pronouns *I* and *me* consistently throughout the paragraph. (consistent person)

9. Dull—use a direct quotation, the actual words I say to myself. (exact language, sentence variety)

CHAPTER 22 Putting Your Revision Skills to Work   313

Revised Draft

In order to give my best performance, I must relax completely before a show. I often know ahead of time what choreography and vocals I will use, and I always know my parts perfectly, so during that long, last hour before curtain, I can concentrate on relaxing. I usually do this by reading an action-packed mystery, but sometimes I joke with the other performers or just walk around backstage. Occasionally I peek through the curtain to watch the audience file in. This can make me feel faint, but I reassure myself. "Vickie," I say, "the minute you're out there singing to the people, everything will be okay."

—Victoria DeWindt (Student)

Writing Sample 2

First Draft

My grandparents' house contained whole rooms that my parents' house did not (pantry, a parlor, a den where Grandpa kept his loot). The furniture and things always fascinated me. Best of all was the lake behind the house. Grandpa said that Evergreen Lake had grown old just like Grandma and him, that the game fish are gone and only a few bluegills remained. But one day he let me fish. No one thought I'd catch anything, but I caught a foot-long goldfish! Grandpa said it was a goddam carp, but it was a goldfish to me and I nearly fainted with ecstasy.

Revisions

① Visiting my grandparents at Evergreen Lake was always an exotic adventure.
② Their cavernous ③
~~My grandparents'~~ house contained whole rooms that my parents' house

④ —a pantry,   with a big black grand piano, and   ⑤ The rooms
did not ~~(pantry,~~ a parlor, a den where Grandpa kept his loot). ~~The furniture~~

were furnished with musty deer heads, hand-painted candlesticks, and velvet drapes.
~~and things always fascinated me~~. Best of all was the lake behind the house.

Grandpa said that Evergreen Lake had grown old just like Grandma and

⑥ were
him, that the game fish ~~are~~ gone and only a few bluegills remained. ~~But one~~

⑦ Add new section below*
~~day he let me fish. No one thought I'd catch anything, but I caught a foot-~~

                                                B
~~long goldfish. Grandpa said it was a goddam carp,~~ but it was a goldfish to me,

⑧
and I nearly fainted with ecstasy.

*Add: But one day he rigged up a pole for me and tossed my line into the water. I sat motionless for several hours, waiting for a miracle. Suddenly I felt a tug on my line. I screeched and yanked upward. By the time Grandpa arrived on the dock, there on the surface lazily moving its fins was the biggest goldfish I had ever seen, nearly a foot long! Grandpa reached down with the net and scooped the huge orange fish out of the water. "Bring down the pail," he shouted. "It's a goddam carp."

Reasons for Revisions

1. No topic sentence; add one. (topic sentence)
2. Now *grandparents'* repeats the first sentence; use *their*. (pronoun substitution)
3. Add a good descriptive word to give the feeling of the house. (exact language)
4. Expand this; add more details. (details, exact language)
5. More details and examples needed for support! Try to capture the "exotic" feeling of the house. (details, exact language)
6. Verb shifts to present tense; use past tense consistently. (consistent tense)
7. This section is weak. Tell the story of the goldfish; try to create the sense of adventure this had for me as a kid. Quote Grandpa? (details, exact language, direct quotation)
8. Revised paragraph is getting long. Consider breaking into two paragraphs, one on the house and one on the lake.

Revised Draft

Visiting my grandparents at Evergreen Lake was always an exotic adventure. Their cavernous house contained whole rooms that my parents' house did not—a pantry, a parlor with a big black grand piano, and a den where Grandpa kept his loot. The rooms were furnished with musty deer heads, hand-painted candlesticks, and velvet drapes.

Best of all was the lake behind the house. Grandpa said that Evergreen Lake had grown old just like Grandma and him, that the game fish were gone and only a few bluegills remained. But one day he rigged up a pole for me and tossed my line into the water. I sat motionless for several hours, waiting for a miracle. Suddenly I felt a tug on my line. I screeched and yanked upward. By the time Grandpa arrived on the dock, there on the surface lazily moving its fins was the biggest goldfish I had ever seen, nearly a foot long! Grandpa reached down with the net and scooped the huge orange fish out of the water. "Bring down the pail," he shouted. "It's a goddam carp." But it was a goldfish to me, and I nearly fainted with ecstasy.

PRACTICE

Because revising, like writing, is a personal process, the best practice is to revise your own paragraphs and essays. Nevertheless, here are two first drafts that need revising.

Revise each one *as if you had written it*. Mark your revisions on the first draft, using and building on the good parts, crossing out unnecessary words, rewriting unclear or awkward sentences, adding details, and perhaps reordering parts. Then, recopy your final draft on the lines. Especially, ask yourself these questions:

Are my verb tenses and pronouns consistent?

Have I used parallel structure?

Have I varied the length and type of my sentences?

Is my language exact, concise, and fresh?

First Draft A

Home

In the South, the redbird is considered a good omen. It is not surprising to see a pair of redbirds nesting in the highest corner of the porch at 1314 Rally Road Lane. They are just two of the many visitors who found comfort under that roof. Some are drawn by the freshly baked bread that is offered to every guest. Its smell seemed to fill the house with fruity bakery scents. Others were drawn by the warmth of the owner. Her name is Louise. She stood five feet six inches. She weighs 150 pounds. She had skin of bronze and her heart was made gold. She has prominent frown lines around her nose and on her forehead. These might suggest to a stranger that she is not to be messed with. But looks can be deceiving. Louise is a friendly woman. Humor is another quality she has, and she is accepting of everyone. She teaches her children to be the same. She is careful to guide them with a gentle but steady hand. Louise's love is contagious. The little green house with pretty colored shutters welcomes a constant stream of friends, neighbors, and even nesting birds. Family members come too.

—Based on work by Linda Lupe, Student

Revised Draft A

Home

In the South, the redbird is considered a good omen, so it is not surprising to see a pair of redbirds nesting in the highest corner of the porch at 1314 Rally Road Lane. They are just two of the many visitors who find comfort under that roof. Some are drawn by the freshly baked bread that is offered to every guest. Its fragrance seems to fill the house with fruity bakery scents. Others are drawn by the warmth of the owner, whose name is Louise. Standing five feet six inches and weighing 150 pounds, she has skin of bronze and a heart of gold. The prominent frown lines around her nose and on her forehead might suggest to a stranger that she is threatening, but looks can be deceiving. In fact, Louise is friendly, funny, and accepting of everyone. She teaches her children to be the same and is careful to guide them with a gentle but steady hand. Louise's love is contagious. So the little green house with yellow shutters welcomes a constant stream of friends, neighbors, family members, and even nesting birds.

First Draft B

Breaking the Yo-Yo Syndrome

For years, I was a yo-yo dieter. I bounced from fad diets to eating binges when I ate a lot. This leaves you tired and with depression. Along the way, though, I learned a few things. As a result, I personally will never go on a diet again for the rest of my life.

First of all, diets are unhealthy. Some of the low carbohydrate diets are high in fat. Accumulating fat through meat, eggs, and the eating of cheese can raise blood levels of cholesterol and led to artery and heart disease. Other diets are too high in protein and can cause kidney ailments, and other things can go wrong with your body, too. Most diets also leave you deficient in essential vitamins and minerals that are necessary to health, such as calcium and iron.

In addition, diets are short-term. I lose about ten pounds. I wind up gaining more weight than I originally lost. I also get sick and tired of the restricted diet. On one diet, I ate cabbage soup for breakfast, lunch, and dinner. You are allowed to eat some fruit on day one, some vegetables on day two, and so on, but mostly you are supposed to eat cabbage soup. After a week, I never want to see a bowl of cabbage soup again. Because the diet was nutritionally unbalanced, I ended up craving bread, meat, and all the other foods I am not supposed to eat. Moreover, in the short-term, all one loses is water. You cannot lose body fat unless you reduce regularly and at a steady rate over a long period of time.

The last diet I try was a fat-free diet. On this diet I actually gained weight while dieting. I am surprised to discover that you can gain weight on a fat-free diet snacking on fat-free cookies, ice cream, and cheese and crackers. I also learn that the body needs fat—in particular, the unsaturated fat in foods like olive oil, nuts, avocados, and salad dressings. If a dieter takes in too little fat, you are constantly hungry. Furthermore, the body thinks it is starving, so it makes every effort to try to conserve fat, which makes it much harder for one to lose weight.

In place of fad diets, I now follow a long-range plan. It is sensible and improved my health. I eat three well-balanced meals, exercise daily, and am meeting regularly with my support group for weight control. I am much happier and don't weigh as much than I used to be.

Revised Draft B

Breaking the Yo-Yo Syndrome

For years, I was a yo-yo dieter, bouncing from fad diets to eating binges that left me tired and depressed. Along the way, though, I learned a few things. As a result, I will never go on a diet again.

First, diets are unhealthy. Some of the low carbohydrate diets are high in fat, and fat from meat, eggs, and cheese can raise blood levels of cholesterol and lead to artery and heart disease. Other diets are too high in protein and can cause kidney ailments and other disorders. Most diets also leave a person deficient in essential vitamins and minerals, such as calcium and iron.

In addition, diets are short-term. I lose about ten pounds; then I wind up gaining more weight than I originally lost. I also get bored on the restricted diet. On one diet, I ate cabbage soup for breakfast, lunch, and dinner. I was allowed to eat some fruit on day one, some vegetables on day two, and so on, but mostly I was supposed to eat cabbage soup. After a week, I never wanted to see a bowl of cabbage soup again. Because the diet was nutritionally unbalanced, I ended up craving bread, meat, and all the other foods I was not supposed to eat. Moreover, in the short term, all you lose is water. You cannot lose body fat unless you reduce steadily over a long period of time.

The last diet I tried was a fat-free diet. I was surprised to discover that you can actually gain weight snacking on fat-free cookies, ice cream, and cheese and crackers. I also learned that the body needs fat—in particular, the unsaturated fat in foods like olive oil, nuts, avocados, and salad dressings. If you take in too little fat, you are constantly hungry. Furthermore, the body thinks it is starving, so it tries to conserve fat, which makes losing weight much harder.

In place of fad diets, I now follow a long-range plan that is sensible and healthful. I eat three well-balanced meals, exercise daily, and meet regularly with my support group for weight control. I am much happier and thinner than I used to be.

UNIT 5 WRITERS' WORKSHOP

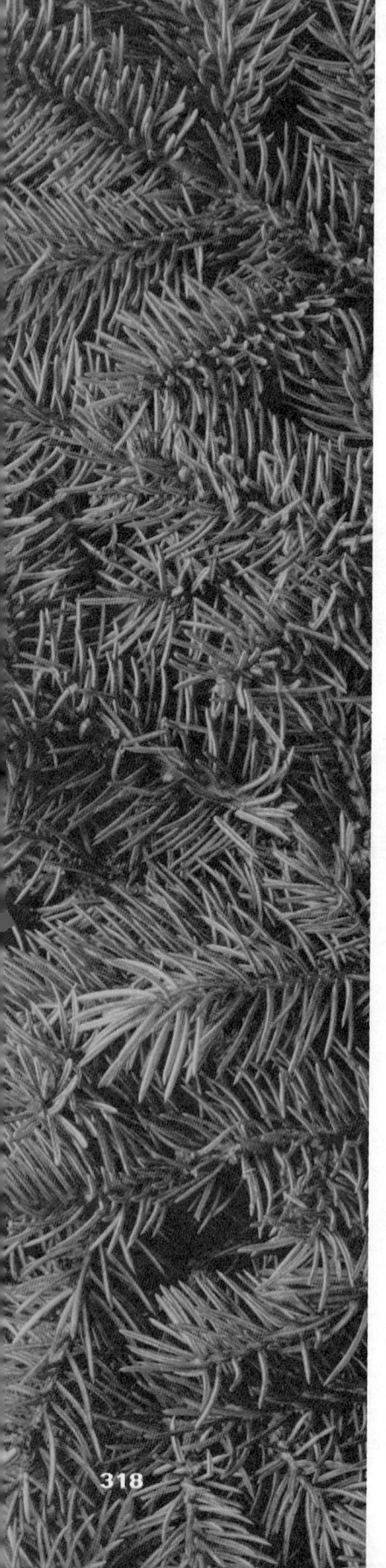

Examine the Bright (or Dark) Side of Family Life

Revising is the key to all good writing—taking the time to sit down, reread, and rethink what you have written. In this unit, you have practiced revising for consistent verb tense, consistent person, parallelism, sentence variety, and language awareness.

In your group or class, read this student's essay, aloud if possible. Underline the parts that strike you as especially effective, and put a check by anything that might need revising.

Family Secrets: Don't You Go Talking

(1) Most families have secrets, but in some families, the secrets become too important. They shape the way people think about themselves and his or her relatives. What people are not supposed to talk about can seem more real than official family history. This was true in my family. Yet when I think about some of our secrets now, they don't seem much like secrets anymore.

(2) Psychologists say that "most secrets arise out of shame." The fact that my father drank excessively brought about a certain family shame. Quiet comments were made protesting his behavior, but no one dared discuss his drinking freely. In fact, I can remember "that look" my mother would give me, meaning "Don't you go talking about nothing that goes on in this house." I couldn't understand that. It was not as if he drank at home where no one but the family could see the staggering or hear the loud profanities. Yet because he was a member of the family, we were expected to turn a blind side.

(3) Secrets help create family history, and since history is said to repeat itself, I feel it safe to say that behavior kept hidden in family secrets may be hereditary. For instance, I have heard talk among family members of an aunt who loved to gamble. As the story goes, Aunt Sally loved to gamble so much that in her ninth month of pregnancy she left her home in California and traveled to Las Vegas by bus. She wanted to play the slot machines. Aunt Sally went into labor. She refused to stop gambling. The contractions were six minutes apart. She was heavily involved in a poker game. Still she refused to leave. The labor pains were four minutes apart. Aunt Sally continued to play. She was enjoying a winning streak. She intended to see it out.

(4) Four hours and $63,000 later, Aunt Sally gives birth to a baby boy. He weighs eight pounds, eight ounces. As luck would have it, her winning hand holds a pair of eights. Aunt Sally's left palm supposedly grips one particular chip so tightly during each contraction that the imprint drew blood. Today that baby born in Vegas is said to be a gambler among gamblers. In the palm of his left hand is a birthmark, red in color and perfectly round in shape just like a poker chip. His name,

318

by the way, is Chip. I don't see how that story can be a family secret, yet after years of not being able to talk freely about certain things, a discomfort remains when these things are in fact discussed.

(5) Shame over a particular event is defined by the values of the era in which the event takes place. Although it was an earlier generation that insisted years ago that certain things need not be openly discussed in my family, the shame lives on, outliving the people. The shame is inherited, if you will. Almost 115 years ago, my great grandfather supposedly stole a handful of rice. Because of shame, I was never supposed to know about it. The story is a family secret. I guess I understand why. After all, we don't want great grand-dad's picture showing up on "America's Most Wanted" anytime now.

—Jo-Ann Jenkins (Student)

1. How effective is Ms. Jenkins's essay?

    __Y__ Strong thesis statement?   __Y__ Good supporting details?

    __Y__ Logical organization?   __Y__ Effective conclusion?

2. What do you like best about this essay? What details or sections most command your attention or make you think?

3. Although this student writes about her personal family history, she is also *thinking about the meaning* of that experience and making sense of it for herself and the reader. What ideas about family secrets does this essay include? Do you agree or disagree?

4. Does your family have secrets? What effect does this have on you or other family members?

5. Do you spot any instance of inconsistent person (paragraph 1) or wordiness (paragraph 4)?*

6. Are all the verb tenses correct, or do you notice any inconsistent tense?
   inconsistent tense in paragraph 4

7. Are there any places, especially in paragraph 3, where choppy sentences detracted from the excellent content? *yes; end of paragraph*

8. Can you spot any error patterns (the same error two or more times) that this student should watch out for? *See #6, 7 above.*

GROUP WORK

In your group, revise Ms. Jenkins's essay as if it were your own. First, decide what problems need attention. Then rewrite those parts, sentence by sentence, aiming for a truly fine paper. Share your revision with the class, explaining why you made the changes you did.

WRITING AND REVISING IDEAS

1. Examine the bright (or dark) side of family life.

2. Discuss the effects of living with a secret or a lie.

**yes;* his or her *should be* their; red in color *and* round in shape *should be* red *and* round

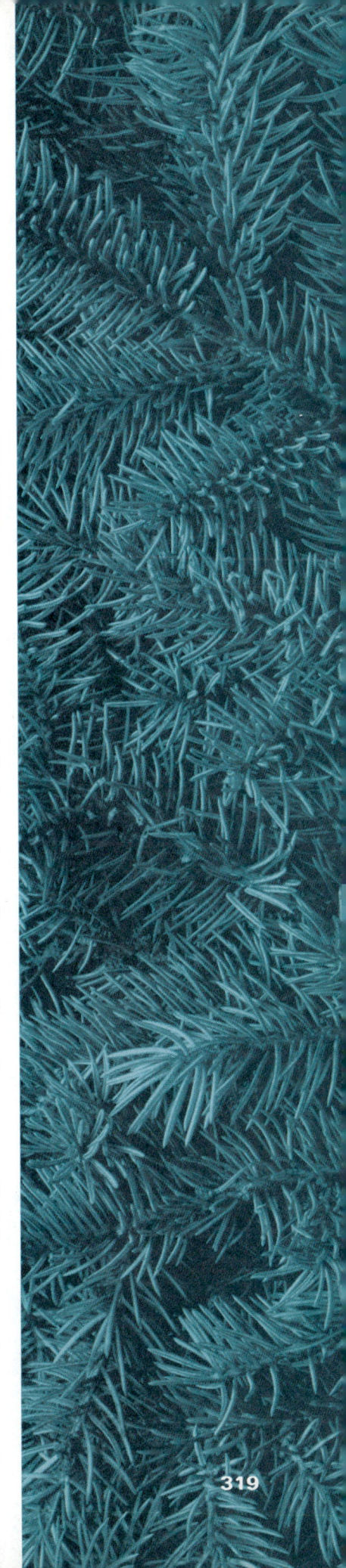

UNIT 6

Reviewing the Basics

CHAPTER 23   The Simple Sentence
CHAPTER 24   Coordination and Subordination
CHAPTER 25   Avoiding Sentence Errors
CHAPTER 26   Present Tense (Agreement)
CHAPTER 27   Past Tense
CHAPTER 28   The Past Participle
CHAPTER 29   Nouns
CHAPTER 30   Pronouns
CHAPTER 31   Prepositions
CHAPTER 32   Adjectives and Adverbs
CHAPTER 33   The Apostrophe
CHAPTER 34   The Comma
CHAPTER 35   Mechanics
CHAPTER 36   Putting Your Proofreading Skills to Work

CHAPTER 23

The Simple Sentence

> **PART A** Defining and Spotting Subjects
> **PART B** Spotting Prepositional Phrases
> **PART C** Defining and Spotting Verbs

PART A — Defining and Spotting Subjects

Every sentence must contain two basic elements: a **subject** and a **verb.**

A subject is the *who* or *what* word that performs the action or the *who* or *what* word about which a statement is made:

> 1. Three *hunters* tramped through the woods.
> 2. The blue *truck* belongs to Ralph.

- In sentence 1, *hunters,* the *who* word, performs the action—"tramped through the woods."
- In sentence 2, *truck* is the *what* word about which a statement is made—"belongs to Ralph."
- Some sentences have more than one subject, joined by *and*:

> 3. Her *aunt and uncle* love country music.

- In sentence 3, *aunt and uncle,* the *who* words, perform the action—they "love country music."
- *Aunt and uncle* is called a **compound subject.**

Sometimes an *-ing* word can be the subject of a sentence:

321

> 4. *Reading* strains my eyes.

■ *Reading* is the *what* word that performs the action—"strains my eyes."

PRACTICE 1

Circle the subjects in these sentences.

1. Do (you) know the origin and customs of Kwanzaa?
2. This African-American (holiday) celebrates black heritage and lasts for seven days—from December 26 through January 1.
3. (Maulana Karenga) introduced Kwanzaa to America in 1966.
4. In Swahili, (Kwanzaa) means "first fruits of the harvest."
5. During the holiday, (families) share simple meals of foods from the Caribbean, Africa, South America, and the American South.
6. Specific (foods) have special meanings.
7. For instance, certain (fruits and vegetables) represent the products of group effort.
8. Another important (symbol) is corn, which stands for children.
9. At each dinner, (celebrants) light a black, red, or green candle and discuss one of the seven principles of Kwanzaa.
10. These seven (principles) are unity, self-determination, collective work and responsibility, cooperative economics, purpose, creativity, and faith.

PART B Spotting Prepositional Phrases

One group of words that may confuse you as you look for subjects is the prepositional phrase. A **prepositional phrase** contains a **preposition** (a word like *at, in, of, from,* and so forth) and its **object**.

Preposition	Object
at	the beach
on	time
of	the students

CHAPTER 23 The Simple Sentence 323

The object of a preposition *cannot be* the subject of a sentence. Therefore, spotting and crossing out the prepositional phrases will help you find the subject.

> 1. The sweaters in the window look handmade.
> 2. The sweaters ~~in the window~~ look handmade.
> 3. ~~On Tuesday,~~ a carton ~~of oranges~~ was left ~~on the porch~~.

- In sentence 1, you might have trouble finding the subject. But once the prepositional phrase is crossed out in sentence 2, the subject, *sweaters,* is easy to spot.
- In sentence 3, once the prepositional phrases are crossed out, the subject, *carton,* is easy to spot.

Here are some common prepositions that you should know:

Common Prepositions			
about	before	in	through
above	behind	into	to
across	between	like	toward
after	by	near	under
along	during	of	until
among	for	on	up
at	from	over	with

PRACTICE 2

Cross out the prepositional phrases in each sentence. Then circle the subject of the sentence.

1. ~~From 6 A.M. until 10 A.M.,~~ (Angel) works out.
2. Local (buses) ~~for Newark~~ leave every hour.
3. (Three) ~~of my friends~~ take singing lessons.
4. That (man) ~~between Ralph and Cynthia~~ is the famous actor Hank the Hunk.
5. ~~Near the door,~~ a (pile) ~~of laundry~~ sits ~~in a basket~~.
6. ~~Toward evening,~~ the (houses) ~~across the river~~ disappear ~~in the thick fog~~.
7. ~~Before class,~~ (Helena and I) meet ~~for coffee~~.
8. ~~In one corner of the lab,~~ (beakers) ~~of colored liquid~~ bubbled and boiled.

PART C Defining and Spotting Verbs

Action Verbs

In order to be complete, every sentence must contain a **verb**. One kind of verb, called an **action verb,** expresses the action that the subject is performing:

> 1. The star quarterback *fumbled*.
> 2. The carpenters *worked* all day, but the bricklayers *went* home early.

- In sentence 1, the action verb is *fumbled*.
- In sentence 2, the action verbs are *worked* and *went*.*

Linking Verbs

Another kind of verb, called a **linking verb,** links the subject to words that describe or identify it:

> 3. Don *is* a fine mathematician.
> 4. This fabric *feels* rough and scratchy.

- In sentence 3, the verb *is* links the subject *Don* with the noun *mathematician*.
- In sentence 4, the verb *feels* links the subject *fabric* with the adjectives *rough* and *scratchy*.

Here are some common linking verbs:

Common Linking Verbs	
appear	feel
be (am, is, are, was, were, has been, have been, had been . . .)	look
become	seem

Verbs of More Than One Word—Helping Verbs

So far you have dealt with verbs of only one word—*fumbled, worked, is, feels,* and so on. But many verbs consist of more than one word:

---

* For work on compound predicates, see Chapter 20, "Revising for Sentence Variety," Part D.

CHAPTER 23 The Simple Sentence **325**

> 5. He *should have taken* the train home.
> 6. *Are* Tanya and Joe *practicing* the piano?
> 7. The lounge *was painted* last week.

- In sentence 5, *taken* is the main verb; *should* and *have* are the **helping verbs.**
- In sentence 6, *practicing* is the main verb; *are* is the helping verb.
- In sentence 7, *painted* is the main verb; *was* is the helping verb.*

PRACTICE 3

Underline the verbs in these sentences.

1. The ten-year-old <u>stared</u> at the cockpit of the Boeing 747.
2. Her thoughts <u>raced</u>.
3. She <u>would have loved</u> a runway takeoff or a landing.
4. However, she <u>was</u> only at the Museum of Science and Industry in Tampa, Florida, not in a real plane.
5. Science centers like this one <u>will be attracting</u> record crowds of parents and children.
6. Many of these centers <u>emphasize</u> local industry.
7. For example, the Tech Museum in California <u>introduces</u> visitors to computer technology.
8. The Louisville Science Center, on the other hand, <u>features</u> automotive games.
9. The beauty of these centers <u>lies</u> in their interactive exhibits.
10. Visitors <u>can experience</u> the latest technology firsthand and <u>can learn</u> about careers of the present and future.

PRACTICE 4

Circle the subjects and underline the verbs in the following sentences. First, cross out any prepositional phrases.

1. <u>Do</u> (you) <u>think</u> ~~of baseball~~ as America's oldest team sport?

---

* For more work on verbs in the passive voice, see Chapter 28, "The Past Participle," Part E.

2. ~~In fact,~~ (lacrosse) takes that honor.

3. (Native Americans) were playing the sport long ~~before the arrival of Europeans.~~

4. A (team) scores ~~by throwing~~ a ball ~~into the opposing team's goal.~~

5. The (goal) is ferociously guarded ~~by a goalie.~~

6. Each (player) uses a curved racket ~~with a mesh basket at its end.~~

7. Algonquin (tribes) ~~in the valley of the St. Lawrence River~~ invented the game.

8. The (Hurons and Iroquois) soon learned this demanding sport.

9. ~~By 1500,~~ the rough-and-tumble (game) was played ~~by dozens of tribes in Canada and the United States.~~

10. Sometimes (matches) would require hundreds ~~of players~~ and might last ~~for days.~~

11. (Playing) lacrosse trained young warriors ~~for battle.~~

12. ~~With this in mind,~~ the (Cherokees) named lacrosse "little brother ~~of war.~~"

13. However, (tribes) often settled their differences peaceably ~~with a lacrosse match.~~

14. French (missionaries) saw a resemblance ~~between the racket and a bishop's cross.~~

15. (They) changed the name ~~of the game from~~ *boggotaway*, the native word, ~~to~~ *lacrosse*, French ~~for the cross~~.

CHAPTER 24

Coordination and Subordination

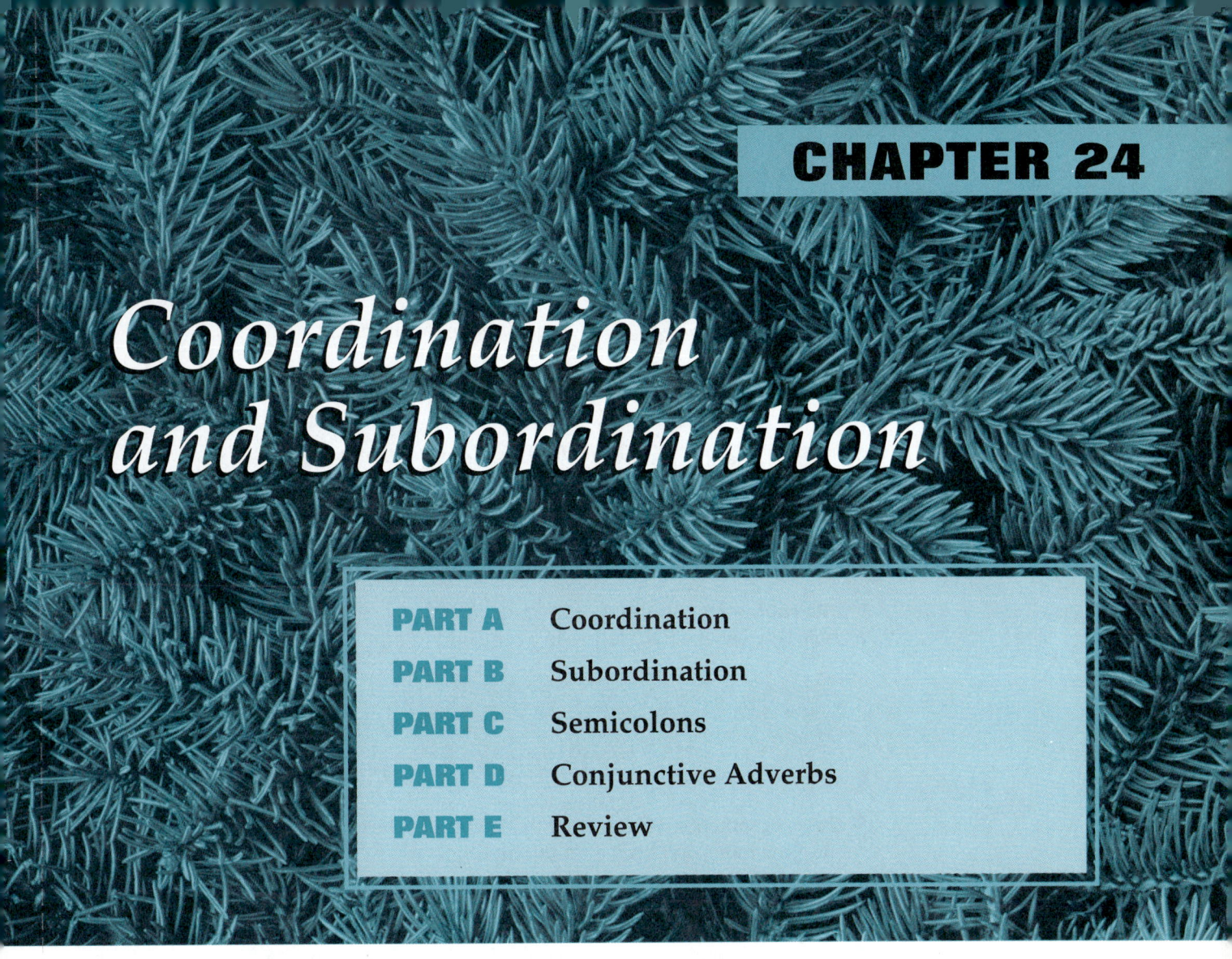

PART A   Coordination
PART B   Subordination
PART C   Semicolons
PART D   Conjunctive Adverbs
PART E   Review

PART A   Coordination

A **clause** is a group of words that includes a subject and a verb. If a clause can stand alone as a complete idea, it is an **independent clause** and can be written as a **simple sentence**.*

Here are two independent clauses written as simple sentences:

1. The dog barked all night.
2. The neighbors didn't complain.

You can join two clauses together by placing a comma and a **coordinating conjunction** between them:

---

* For more work on simple sentences, see Chapter 23, "The Simple Sentence."

3. The dog barked all night, *but* the neighbors didn't complain.

4. Let's go to the beach today, *for* it is too hot to do anything else.

- The coordinating conjunctions *but* and *for* join together two clauses.
- Note that *a comma precedes each coordinating conjunction.*

Here is a list of the most common coordinating conjunctions:

Coordinating Conjunctions

| and | for | or | yet |
| but | nor | so | |

Be sure to choose the coordinating conjunction that best expresses the *relationship* between the two clauses in a sentence:

5. It was late, *so* I decided to take a bus home.

6. It was late, *yet* I decided to take a bus home.

- The *so* in sentence 5 means that the lateness of the hour caused me to take the bus. (The trains don't run after midnight.)
- The *yet* in sentence 6 means that despite the late hour I still decided to take a bus home. (I knew I might have to wait two hours at the bus stop.)
- Note that a comma precedes the coordinating conjunction.

PRACTICE 1

Read the following sentences for meaning. Then fill in the coordinating conjunction that *best* expresses the relationship between the two clauses. Don't forget to add the comma.

1. Diners still dot the highways of the United States __, but/yet__ they are not as popular as they once were.

2. In 1872, Walter Scott of Providence, Rhode Island, decided to make prepared and cooked food easier to buy __, so__ he started selling sandwiches and pies from a large horse-drawn wagon.

3. Customers flocked to this first "diner" __, for__ the food was delicious, plentiful, and inexpensive.

4. Many did not like standing outside to eat __, so__ another businessman, Sam Jones, redecorated the wagon and invited customers inside to dine.

5. In order to widen the appeal of their diners, some owners installed stained-glass windows __, and__ other proprietors added elegant decorations.

CHAPTER 24   Coordination and Subordination   329

6. In the 1920s, narrow booths began to replace stools __, and__ diners were fixed permanently on the ground.

7. Stainless steel, efficient-looking diners were everywhere by the 1940s __, but/yet__ even this style gave way to the fancy colonial and Mediterranean designs of the 1960s.

8. Diners are not as common as they were twenty years ago __, nor__ can they compete with fast-food take-out chains like McDonald's and Wendy's.

9. Nonetheless, customers do have a choice; they can stand in line and wait for a quick hamburger __, or__ they can sit and be waited on in a diner.

10. Most choose fast food __, but/yet__ some find that the more leisurely diner still has its charm.

PRACTICE 2

Combine these simple sentences with a coordinating conjunction. Punctuate correctly.

1. My daughter wants to be a mechanic. She spends every spare minute at the garage.

    My daughter wants to be a mechanic, so she spends every spare minute at the garage.

2. Ron dared not look over the edge. Heights made him dizzy.

    Ron dared not look over the edge, for heights made him dizzy.

3. Tasha's living room is cozy. Her guests always gather in the kitchen.

    Tasha's living room is cozy, but/yet her guests always gather in the kitchen.

4. Meet me by the bicycle rack. Meet me at Lulu's Nut Shop.

    Meet me by the bicycle rack, or meet me at Lulu's Nut Shop.

5. In 1969, the first astronauts landed on the moon. Most Americans felt proud.

    In 1969, the first astronauts landed on the moon, and most Americans felt proud.

PART B Subordination

Two clauses can also be joined with a **subordinating conjunction.** The clause following a subordinating conjunction is called a **subordinate** or **dependent clause** because it depends on an independent clause to complete its meaning:

> 1. We will light the candles *when Flora arrives.*

- *When Flora arrives* is a subordinate or dependent clause introduced by the subordinating conjunction *when.*
- By itself, *when Flora arrives* is incomplete; it depends on the independent clause to complete its meaning.*

Note that sentence 1 can also be written this way:

> 2. *When Flora arrives,* we will light the candles.

- The meaning of sentences 1 and 2 is the same, but the punctuation is different.
- In sentence 1, because the subordinate clause *follows* the independent clause, *no comma* is needed.
- In sentence 2, however, because the subordinate clause *begins* the sentence, it is followed by a *comma.*

Here is a partial list of subordinating conjunctions:

Subordinating Conjunctions			
after	because	since	when(ever)
although	before	unless	whereas
as (if)	if	until	while

Be sure to choose the subordinating conjunction that *best expresses the relationship* between the two clauses in a sentence:

> 3. This course was excellent *because* Professor Green taught it.
> 4. This course was excellent *although* Professor Green taught it.

- Sentence 3 says that the course was excellent *because* Professor Green, a great teacher, taught it.
- Sentence 4 says that the course was excellent *despite the fact that* Professor Green, apparently a bad teacher, taught it.

---

* For more work on incomplete sentences, or fragments, see Chapter 25, "Avoiding Sentence Errors," Part B.

PRACTICE 3

Read the following sentences for meaning. Then fill in the subordinating conjunction that *best* expresses the relationship between the two clauses.

1. We could see very clearly last night __because__ the moon was so bright.

2. Violet read *Sports Illustrated* __while__ Daisy walked in the woods.

3. __Whenever__ it is cold outside, our new wood-burning Franklin stove keeps us warm.

4. The students buzzed with excitement __when__ Professor Hargrave announced that classes would be held at the zoo.

5. __Until__ his shoulder loosens up a bit, Ron will stay on the bench.

PRACTICE 4

Punctuate the following sentences by adding a comma where necessary. Put a C after any correct sentences.

1. More than 2,000 unfortunate infants have had a good home because Clara Hale and her daughter, Lorraine, took care of them. C

2. After she left her mother's apartment one day in 1969, Lorraine saw a woman sleeping on the street beside a baby in a crate.

3. Hale sent the woman to her mother's home because Clara had been caring for foster children for years. C

4. When Clara welcomed the baby, the seed of a new idea was planted.

5. Although many children were in need of special care, no centers existed at the time for babies born addicted to drugs and alcohol.

6. Because Clara and Lorraine established Hale House, the first such nonprofit nursery in the United States came into being.

7. Hale House became nationally known for its loving care of addicted and HIV-positive children after President Reagan praised it in 1985. C

8. Since Clara "Mother" Hale died in 1992, Dr. Lorraine Hale and her staff have continued to provide that same loving care at Hale House.

Practice 5

Combine each pair of ideas below by using a subordinating conjunction. Write each combination twice, once with the subordinating conjunction at the beginning of the sentence and once with the subordinating conjunction in the middle of the sentence. Punctuate correctly.

EXAMPLE We stayed on the beach.

The sun went down.

> We stayed on the beach until the sun went down.
>
> Until the sun went down, we stayed on the beach.

1. This cactus has flourished.
2. I talk to it every day.

> Because I talk to it every day, this cactus has flourished.
>
> This cactus has flourished because I talk to it every day.

3. Ralph takes the train to Philadelphia.
4. He likes to sit by the window.

> Whenever Ralph takes the train to Philadelphia, he likes to sit by the window.
>
> Ralph likes to sit by the window whenever he takes the train to Philadelphia.

5. I had known you were coming.
6. I would have vacuumed the guest room.

> If I had known you were coming, I would have vacuumed the guest room.
>
> I would have vacuumed the guest room if I had known you were coming.

7. He was the first person to eat a slice of meat between two pieces of bread.
8. The sandwich was named after the Earl of Sandwich.

> The sandwich was named after the Earl of Sandwich because he was the first person to eat a slice of meat between two pieces of bread.
>
> Because he was the first person to eat a slice of meat between two pieces of bread, the sandwich was named after the Earl of Sandwich.

CHAPTER 24 Coordination and Subordination 333

9. Akila was about to answer the final question.
10. The buzzer sounded.

   Akila was about to answer the final question when the buzzer sounded.

   When the buzzer sounded, Akila was about to answer the final question.

11. Few soap operas remain on the radio.
12. Daytime television is filled with them.

   Daytime television is filled with soap operas although few of them remain on the radio.

   Although few soap operas remain on the radio, daytime television is filled with them.

13. She connected the speakers.
14. The room filled with glorious sound.

   When she connected the speakers, the room filled with glorious sound.

   The room filled with glorious sound when she connected the speakers.

15. The chimney spewed black smoke and soot.
16. Nobody complained to the local environmental agency.

   Nobody complained to the local environmental agency although the chimney spewed black smoke and soot.

   Although the chimney spewed black smoke and soot, nobody complained to the local environmental agency.

PART C   Semicolons

You can join two independent clauses by placing a **semicolon** between them. The semicolon takes the place of a conjunction:

> 1. She hopes to receive good grades this semester; her scholarship depends on her maintaining a 3.5 average.
> 2. Tony is a careless driver; he has had three minor accidents this year alone.

- Each of the sentences above could also be made into two *separate sentences* by replacing the semicolon with a period.
- Note that the first word after a semicolon is *not* capitalized (unless, of course, it is a word that is normally capitalized, like someone's name).

Practice 6

Combine each pair of independent clauses by placing a semicolon between them.

1. Rush-hour traffic was worse than usual; no one seemed to mind.
2. The senator appeared ill at ease at the news conference; he seemed afraid of saying the wrong thing.
3. The new seed catalogue, a fifteen-hundred-page volume, was misplaced; the volume weighed ten pounds.
4. On Thursday evening, Stuart decided to go camping; on Friday morning, he packed his bags and left.
5. In the early 1960s, the Beatles burst on the rock scene; rock music has never been the same.
6. Ron Jackson has been promoted; he will be an effective manager.
7. This stream is full of trout; every spring men and women with waders and fly rods arrive on its banks.
8. Not a single store was open at that hour; not a soul walked the streets.

Practice 7

Each independent clause that follows is the first half of a sentence. Add a semicolon and a second independent clause. Make sure your second thought is also independent and can stand alone. *Answers will vary.*

1. At 2 A.M. I stumbled toward the ringing telephone ; it was a wrong number.

2. *People* magazine published my letter to the editor _; I am finally an author!_

3. The officer pulled over the speeding pickup truck _; the driver had three outstanding moving violations._

4. Faulkner's stories often depict life in the South _; he himself came from an old Mississippi family._

5. None of my friends can polka _; I will have to look for a new partner._

6. During the Great Depression, millions of workers were unemployed _; men selling apples on street corners were a common sight._

7. Cameras are not permitted in the museum _; I will check mine in the coatroom._

8. Bill's waiter recommended the vegetable soup _; Bill was not happy with the choice._

PART D Conjunctive Adverbs

A **conjunctive adverb** placed after the semicolon can help clarify the relationship between two clauses:

1. I like the sound of that stereo; *however,* the price is too high.
2. They have not seen that film; *moreover,* they have not been to a theater for three years.

■ Note that a comma follows the conjunctive adverb.

Here is a partial list of conjunctive adverbs.

Conjunctive Adverbs		
consequently	in fact	nevertheless
furthermore	indeed	then
however	moreover	therefore

336 UNIT 6 Reviewing the Basics

PRACTICE 8

Punctuate each sentence correctly by adding a semicolon, a comma, or both, where necessary. Put a C after any correct sentences.

1. I hate to wash my car windows; nevertheless, it's a job that must be done.
2. Sonia doesn't know how to play chess; however, she would like to learn.
3. Dean Fader is very funny; in fact, he could be a professional comedian.
4. Deep water makes Maurice nervous; therefore, he does not want to row to the middle of the lake.
5. I like this painting; the soft colors remind me of tropical sunsets. *C*
6. The faculty approved of the new trimester system; furthermore, the students liked it too. *C*
7. Bill has a cassette player plugged into his ear all day; consequently, he misses a lot of good conversations.
8. We toured the darkroom; then, we watched an actual photo shoot.

PRACTICE 9

Combine each pair of independent clauses by placing a semicolon and a conjunctive adverb between them. Punctuate correctly. *Answers may vary.*

1. The lake is quite long; however, we rowed from one end of it to the other.
2. I can still see the streaks under the fresh white paint; consequently, we will have to give the room another coat.
3. Mr. Farrington loves bluegrass music; furthermore, he plays in a local bluegrass band.
4. Jay, a tall boy, has poor eyesight; therefore, he was turned down for the basketball team.
5. Yesterday, hikers from the Nature-Walkers' Club made real progress in blazing a trail; indeed, they managed to get as far as the foot of Mt. Lookout.
6. By midnight Tien had finished tuning his engine; therefore, he still had enough time for a short nap before the race.
7. An arthroscope helps doctors examine the inside of an injured knee; consequently, the use of this instrument can prevent unnecessary surgery.
8. Rhinoceroses live in protected animal preserves; however, poachers still manage to kill a few of these magnificent beasts each year.

PART E Review

In this chapter, you have combined simple sentences by means of a **coordinating conjunction**, a **subordinating conjunction**, a **semicolon**, and a **semicolon** and **conjunctive adverb**. Here is a review chart of the sentence patterns discussed in this chapter.*

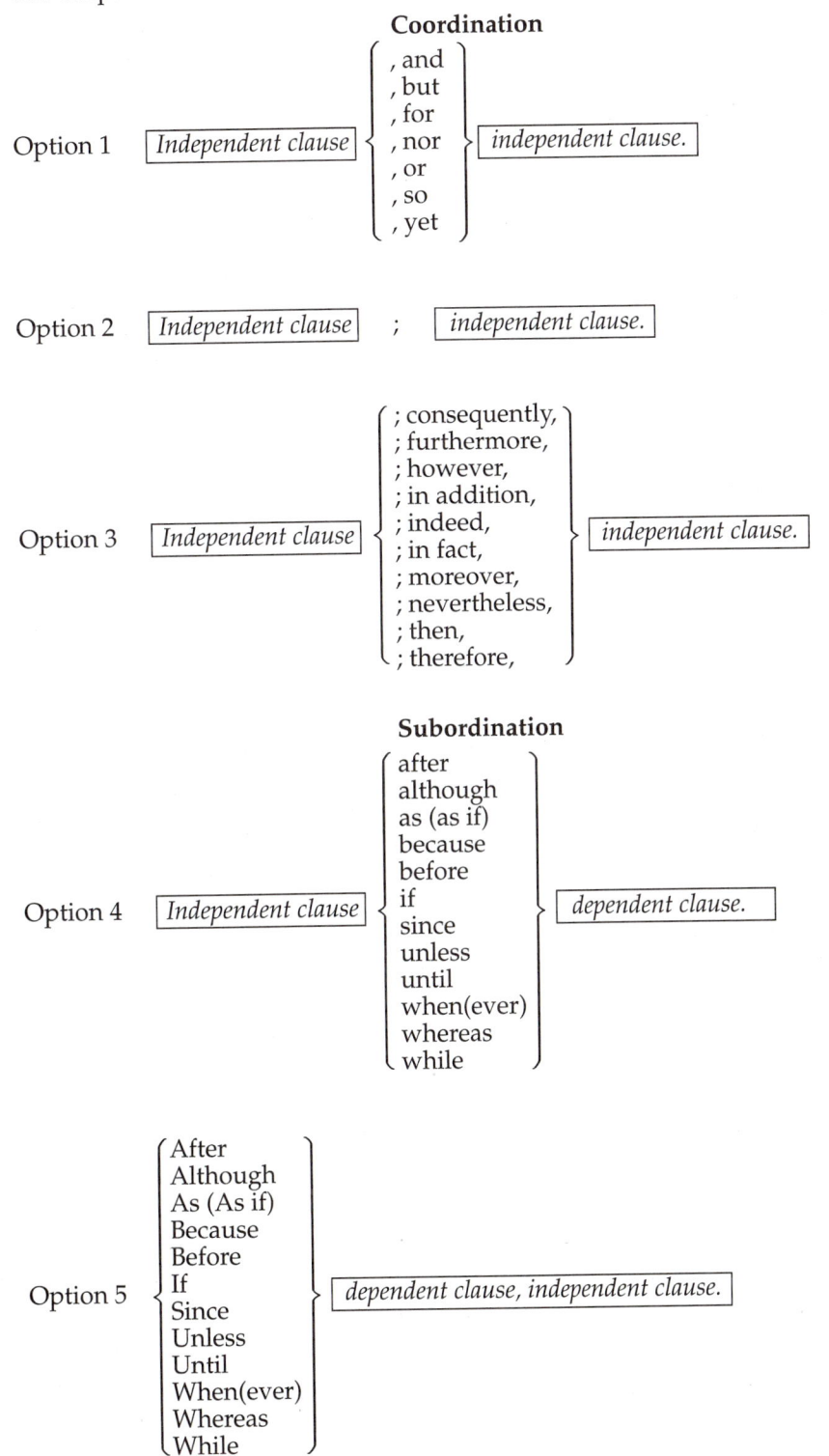

Coordination

Option 1 [Independent clause] { , and / , but / , for / , nor / , or / , so / , yet } [independent clause.]

Option 2 [Independent clause] ; [independent clause.]

Option 3 [Independent clause] { ; consequently, / ; furthermore, / ; however, / ; in addition, / ; indeed, / ; in fact, / ; moreover, / ; nevertheless, / ; then, / ; therefore, } [independent clause.]

Subordination

Option 4 [Independent clause] { after / although / as (as if) / because / before / if / since / unless / until / when(ever) / whereas / while } [dependent clause.]

Option 5 { After / Although / As (As if) / Because / Before / If / Since / Unless / Until / When(ever) / Whereas / While } [dependent clause, independent clause.]

---

* For more ways to combine sentences, see Chapter 20, "Revising for Sentence Variety," Part D.

Practice 10

Read each pair of simple sentences to determine the relationship between them. Then join each pair in three different ways, using the conjunctions or conjunctive adverbs in parentheses at the left. Punctuate correctly. *Answers will vary.*

EXAMPLE The company picnic was canceled.

Rain started to fall in torrents.

(for) *The company picnic was canceled, for the rain started to fall in torrents.*

(because) *Because the rain started to fall in torrents, the company picnic was canceled.*

(therefore) *The rain started to fall in torrents; therefore, the company picnic was canceled.*

1. My grandmother is in great shape.

    She eats right and exercises regularly.

    (for) *My grandmother is in great shape, for she eats right and exercises regularly.*

    (because) *Because my grandmother eats right and exercises regularly, she is in great shape.*

    (therefore) *My grandmother eats right and exercises regularly; therefore, she is in great shape.*

2. We just put in four hours paving the driveway.

    We need a long break and a cold drink.

    (since) *Since we just put in four hours paving the driveway, we need a long break and a cold drink.*

    (because) *We need a long break and a cold drink because we just put in four hours paving the driveway.*

    (consequently) *We just put in four hours paving the driveway; consequently, we need a long break and a cold drink.*

3. The bus schedule was difficult to read.

   Penny found the right bus.

   (but) *The bus schedule was difficult to read, but Penny found the right bus.*

   (although) *Although the bus schedule was difficult to read, Penny found the right bus.*

   (however) *The bus schedule was difficult to read; however, Penny found the right bus.*

4. Don is an expert mechanic.

   He intends to open a service center.

   (and) *Don is an expert mechanic, and he intends to open a service center.*

   (since) *Since Don is an expert mechanic, he intends to open a service center.*

   (furthermore) *Don is an expert mechanic; furthermore, he intends to open a service center.*

5. We haven't heard from her.

   We haven't given up hope.

   (but) *We haven't heard from her, but we haven't given up hope.*

   (although) *Although we haven't heard from her, we haven't given up hope.*

   (nevertheless) *We haven't heard from her; nevertheless, we haven't given up hope.*

PRACTICE 11

In your writing, aim for variety by mixing coordination, subordination, and simple sentences.* Rewrite the following paragraphs to eliminate monotonous simple sentences. First, read the paragraph to determine the relationships between

---

*For more work on sentence variety, see Chapter 20, "Revising for Sentence Variety."

ideas; then choose the conjunctions that best express these relationships. Punctuate correctly. *Answers will vary.*

Paragraph a

In 1996, Franck Goddio made the greatest discovery of his life. He found the sunken royal city of Cleopatra under the Mediterranean Sea. Almost 2000 years earlier, the fabled queen had ruled Egypt from her island palace near Alexandria. During the fourth and fifth centuries, the island gradually sank into the sea. Goddio and his high-tech team searched the sea bottom near Alexandria for two years. They found roads, temples, and palaces in a murky corner of the harbor. The silt of centuries covered the sunken treasures. They are being cleaned and left in place underwater. Goddio hopes that the Egyptian government will create an underwater museum. Cleopatra's glorious city will be preserved for generations to come.

In 1996, Franck Goddio made the greatest discovery of his life when he found the sunken royal city of Cleopatra under the Mediterranean Sea. Almost 2000 years earlier, the fabled queen had ruled Egypt from her island palace near Alexandria. During the fourth and fifth centuries, the island gradually sank into the sea. After Goddio and his high-tech team searched the sea bottom near Alexandria for two years, they found roads, temples, and palaces in a murky corner of the harbor. Although the silt of centuries covered the sunken treasures, they are being cleaned and left in place underwater. Goddio hopes that the Egyptian government will create an underwater museum, so Cleopatra's glorious city will be preserved for generations to come.

Paragraph b

Languages are disappearing all over the world. North America has two hundred Native American languages. Only about fifty have more than a thousand speakers. Europe's Celtic languages have been declining for generations. Language decline is most noticeable in tiny communities in Asia and Australia. Each isolated community speaks a different language. The population shrinks. The language begins to die out. In addition, a small community may make contact with a large one. The native language may start to fade. People use the "more important" language. It gives them better access to education, jobs, and new technology. A "powerful language" will almost always prevail over a native mother tongue.

Languages are disappearing all over the world. North America has two hundred Native American languages, but only about fifty have more than a thousand speakers. Although Europe's Celtic languages have been declining for generations, language decline is most noticeable in tiny communities in Asia and Australia. Each isolated community speaks a different language. As the population shrinks, the language begins to die out. In addition, a small community may make contact with a large one, and the native language may start to fade. People use the "more important" language because it gives them better access to education, jobs, and new technology. A "powerful language" will almost always prevail over a native mother tongue.

Paragraph c   A great star blazed in the sky. Paiea was born in Hawaii in 1758. Seers had foretold that this son of a chieftain would defeat his enemies and govern a united Hawaii. A jealous former ruler ordered the baby killed. Sympathetic courtiers hid the noble infant in a cave. There he was renamed Kamehameha. This name means "The Lonely One" or "The One Set Apart." In time, it was safe for young Kamehameha to leave the cave. He was very strong and agile. He excelled in war games. James Cook, an English sea captain, landed in Hawaii in 1778. Kamehameha had already become the most important chieftain. He gained even more power by conquering one independent island after another. With the help of English sailors, he successfully invaded Maui. Eventually, the rest of the Hawaiian islands came under his control. By 1810, this shrewd and powerful king ruled a united country. A lover of his native culture, he continued many ancient traditions of his homeland. He also borrowed many ideas from the Europeans. The prophecies at his birth had come true. He had defeated his enemies and become the sole ruler of a united Hawaii.

A great star blazed in the sky when Paiea was born in Hawaii in 1758. Seers had foretold that this son of a chieftain would defeat his enemies and govern a united Hawaii. A jealous former ruler ordered the baby killed, but sympathetic courtiers hid the noble infant in a cave. There he was renamed Kamehameha, meaning "The Lonely One" or "The One Set Apart." In time, it was safe for young Kamehameha to leave the cave. Because he was very strong and agile, he excelled in war games. When James Cook, an English sea captain, landed in Hawaii in 1778, Kamehameha had already become the most important chieftain. He gained even more power by conquering one independent island after another. With the help of English sailors, he successfully invaded Maui, and eventually the rest of the Hawaiian islands came under his control. By 1810, this shrewd and powerful king ruled a united country. A lover of his native culture, he continued many ancient traditions of his homeland; however, he also borrowed many ideas from the Europeans. The prophecies at his birth had come true, for he had defeated his enemies and become the sole ruler of a united Hawaii.

CHAPTER 25

Avoiding Sentence Errors

> **PART A** Avoiding Run-Ons and Comma Splices
>
> **PART B** Avoiding Fragments

PART A — Avoiding Run-Ons and Comma Splices

Be careful to avoid **run-ons** and **comma splices**.

A **run-on sentence** incorrectly runs together two independent clauses without a conjunction or punctuation. This error confuses the reader, who cannot tell where one thought stops and the next begins:

> 1. Run-on: My neighbor Mr. Hoffman is seventy-five years old he plays tennis every Saturday afternoon.

A **comma splice** incorrectly joins two independent clauses with a comma but no conjunction:

> 2. Comma splice: My neighbor Mr. Hoffman is seventy-five years old, he plays tennis every Saturday afternoon.

CHAPTER 25 Avoiding Sentence Errors   **343**

The run-on and the comma splice can be corrected in five ways:

Use two separate sentences.	My neighbor Mr. Hoffman is seventy-five years old. He plays tennis every Saturday afternoon.
Use a coordinating conjunction. (See Chapter 24, Part A.)	My neighbor Mr. Hoffman is seventy-five years old, but he plays tennis every Saturday afternoon.
Use a subordinating conjunction. (See Chapter 24, Part B.)	Although my neighbor Mr. Hoffman is seventy-five years old, he plays tennis every Saturday afternoon.
Use a semicolon. (See Chapter 24, Part C.)	My neighbor Mr. Hoffman is seventy-five years old; he plays tennis every Saturday afternoon.
Use a semicolon and a conjunctive adverb. (See Chapter 24, Part D.)	My neighbor Mr. Hoffman is seventy-five years old; however, he plays tennis every Saturday afternoon.

Practice 1

Some of these sentences contain run-ons or comma splices; others are correct. Put a C next to the correct sentences. Revise the run-ons and comma splices in any way you choose. Be careful of the punctuation. *Answers may vary.*

1. It was an astonishing exhibit, the Guggenheim Museum's recent show was called "The Art of the Motorcycle."

    Revised: *It was an astonishing exhibit. The Guggenheim Museum's recent show was called "The Art of the Motorcycle."*

2. Museumgoers sported leather vests and ponytails, their motorcycles jammed New York City streets.

    Revised: *Museumgoers sported leather vests and ponytails, and their motorcycles jammed New York City streets.*

3. Displayed were motorcycles through the years, including the earliest-known cycle.

    Revised: *C*

4. That was the 1868 French velocipede, it looked more like a bicycle with a steam engine under the seat than a motorcycle.

    Revised: *That was the 1868 French velocipede, but it looked more like a bicycle with a steam engine under the seat than a motorcycle.*

5. The Italian MV Agusta F4 was the latest model on display this one looked like a fantastic space machine.

    Revised: *The Italian MV Agusta F4 was the latest model on display; however, this one looked like a fantastic space machine.*

6. A 1993 Harley-Davidson stole the show it was a replica of Dennis Hopper's *Easy Rider* cycle.

    Revised: *A 1993 Harley-Davidson stole the show because it was a replica of Dennis Hopper's* Easy Rider *cycle.*

7. The show attracted more visitors than any other Guggenheim exhibit museum attendance was 45 percent higher than usual.

    Revised: *The show attracted more visitors than any other Guggenheim exhibit; in fact, museum attendance was 45 percent higher than usual.*

8. Tickets and gift-shop sales brought in more than $1 million the exhibit catalog alone sold for $85.

    Revised: *Tickets and gift-shop sales brought in more than $1 million; the exhibit catalog alone sold for $85.*

9. Although Ducati leather jumpsuits cost $1,595, museumgoers could buy their kids red plastic BMW motorcycles for $120 each.

    Revised: *C*

10. Whether motorcycles are art or not, "The Art of the Motorcycle" certainly brought many new visitors to the Guggenheim, the show was considered a huge success.

CHAPTER 25 Avoiding Sentence Errors   345

Revised: *Whether motorcycles are art or not, "The Art of the Motorcycle" certainly brought many new visitors to the Guggenheim. The show was considered a huge success.*

PRACTICE 2

Proofread the following paragraph for run-ons and comma splices. Correct them in any way you choose.

(1) Many couples today live together before they marry. (2) *Because m*/Marriage is a serious step, they want to get to know each other as well as possible. (3) However, research shows that living together is not good preparation for marriage. (4) In fact, living together usually does not lead to marriage*. It*/it leads to breakups. (5) Even happy couples are less likely to get married as time goes on. (6) If they do marry, they tend to divorce eventually*. R*/researchers cannot explain these outcomes. (7) Perhaps couples who live together are not really committed to the relationship*. P*/perhaps they find it easier to break up a household than a marriage. (8) Regardless of the reasons, statistics don't lie*. L*/living together rarely leads to a happy marriage.

PRACTICE 3

Proofread the following essay for run-ons and comma splices. Correct them in any way you choose, writing your revised essay on a separate sheet of paper. Be careful of the punctuation.

Will K. Kellogg, Least Likely to Succeed

(1) *Although*/Will Kellogg was an unlikely candidate for fame and fortune, he became one of America's great successes.

(2) The two Kellogg boys could not have been more different. (3) Will was a slow learner with few friends and interests. (4) His father pulled him from school at the age of thirteen*;* he made Will a traveling broom salesman for the family company. (5) Eight years older than Will, John Harvey Kellogg was the family genius. (6) He became a noted surgeon and head of an exclusive health resort.

(7) He treated his patients with exercise and a strict vegetarian diet; furthermore, he wrote best-selling books about healthful living.

(8) In 1880, when Will was twenty years old, Dr. John hired him to work at the resort. (9) For the next twenty-five years, Will served as his brother's flunky. (10) According to rumor, he shaved Dr. John every day and shined his shoes. (11) While John bicycled to work, Will jogged alongside getting his daily work orders. (12) Dr. John was a wealthy man, but he never paid Will more than eighty-seven dollars a month.

(13) One of the special foods at the resort was pressed wheat. (14) The brothers boiled wheat dough, and then they pressed it through rollers into thin sheets. (15) One night, they left the boiled dough out. (16) When they pressed it, it turned into flakes instead of forming sheets. (17) Will suggested that they toast the flakes. (18) Resort guests loved the new cereal, and former guests ordered it from their homes. (19) To meet the demand, the brothers opened a mail-order business; however, the snobbish Dr. John refused to sell the flakes to grocery stores.

(20) In 1906, Will finally bought out John's share of the cereal patents. He struck out on his own. (21) Will turned out to be a business genius. (22) He invented advertising techniques that made his new product, Kellogg's Corn Flakes, a household word. (23) Will K. Kellogg quickly became one of the richest persons in America.

(24) Sadly, the two brothers never reconciled. (25) In 1943, ninety-one-year-old Dr. John wrote Will an apology, but John died before the letter reached his younger brother.

PART B   Avoiding Fragments

Another error to avoid is the **sentence fragment.** A **sentence** must contain a subject and a verb and must be able to stand alone as a complete idea. A **sentence**

fragment, therefore, can be defined in terms of what it lacks: either a subject or a verb, or both—it cannot stand alone as a complete idea.

Here are common kinds of sentence fragments and ways to correct them.

Fragments with Dependent Clauses

Complete sentence:	1. Kirk decided to major in psychology.
Fragment:	2. Because human behavior had always fascinated him.

- Example 1 is a complete simple sentence.
- Example 2 is a fragment because it is a dependent clause beginning with the subordinating conjunction *because*. Furthermore, it is not a complete idea.

This fragment can be corrected in two ways:

Corrected:	3. Kirk decided to major in psychology because human behavior had always fascinated him.
	4. Kirk decided to major in psychology. Human behavior had always fascinated him.

- In sentence 3, the fragment is combined with the sentence before it.
- In sentence 4, the fragment is changed into a complete sentence.

Fragments with Relative Clauses

Complete sentence:	5. Mrs. Costa is a chemistry teacher who never runs out of creative ideas.
Fragment:	6. Who has the ability to keep her classes involved throughout the lesson.

- Example 5 is a complete sentence.
- Example 6 is a fragment because it is a relative clause beginning with *who*.*

The fragment in example 6 can be corrected in two ways, as shown below:

Corrected:	7. Mrs. Costa is a chemistry teacher who never runs out of creative ideas and who has the ability to keep her classes involved throughout the lesson.
	8. Mrs. Costa is a chemistry teacher who never runs out of creative ideas. She has the ability to keep her classes involved throughout the lesson.

---

*For more work on relative clauses, see Chapter 20, "Revising for Sentence Variety," Part D, and Chapter 26, "Present Tense (Agreement)," Part G.

- In sentence 7, the fragment is combined with the sentence before it.
- In sentence 8, the fragment is changed into a complete sentence.

Fragments with *-ing* Modifiers

Complete sentence:	9.	Daniel can always be seen on the track in the morning.
Fragment:	10.	Running a mile or two before breakfast.

- Example 9 is a complete sentence.
- Example 10 is a fragment because it lacks a subject and because an *-ing* verb form cannot stand alone without a helping verb.*

This fragment can be corrected in two ways:

Corrected:	11.	Daniel can always be seen on the track in the morning, running a mile or two before breakfast.
	12.	Daniel can always be seen on the track in the morning. He runs a mile or two before breakfast.

- In sentence 11, the fragment is combined with the sentence before it.
- In sentence 12, the fragment is changed into a complete sentence.

Fragments with Phrases

Fragment:	13.	A fine pianist.
Complete sentence:	14.	Marsha won a scholarship to Juilliard.

- Example 13 is a fragment because it lacks a verb and is not a complete idea.
- Example 14 is a complete sentence.

This fragment can be corrected in two ways:

Corrected:	15.	A fine pianist, Marsha won a scholarship to Juilliard.
	16.	Marsha is a fine pianist. She won a scholarship to Juilliard. *or* Marsha won a scholarship to Juilliard. She is a fine pianist.

- In sentence 15, the fragment is combined with the sentence after it.
- In sentence 16, the fragment is changed into a complete sentence by the addition of a verb, *is*, and a subject, *Marsha* in the first option and *she* in the second option.

---

*For more work on joining ideas with an *-ing* modifier, see Chapter 20, "Revising for Sentence Variety," Part D

Fragments with Infinitives

Complete sentence:	17. Laura has always wanted to become a travel agent.
Fragment:	18. To tell people about exotic countries that they might visit.

- Example 17 is a complete sentence.
- Example 18 is a fragment because it lacks a subject and contains only the infinitive form of the verb—*to* plus the simple form of the verb *tell*.

This fragment can be corrected in two ways:

Corrected:	19. Laura has always wanted to become a travel agent and to tell people about exotic countries that they might visit.
	20. Laura has always wanted to become a travel agent. She would find it exciting to tell people about exotic countries that they might visit.

- In sentence 19, the fragment is combined with the sentence before it.
- In sentence 20, the fragment is changed into a complete sentence.

Quick Review Chart: Types of Fragments

Type of Fragment	Example	How to Correct Them
dependent clause	Because it gets dark early.	All fragments can be fixed in one of two ways:
relative clause	Who loves computer games.	1. Add the missing subject and/or verb.
-ing modifier	Skating across the pond.	
phrase	In the attic.	2. Connect the fragment to a neighboring sentence.
infinitive	To go to the movies tonight.	

PRACTICE 4

Some of these examples are fragments; others are complete sentences. Put a C next to the complete sentences. Revise the fragments in any way you choose.
Answers will vary.

350 UNIT 6 Reviewing the Basics

EXAMPLE Leaping into the air.

Revised: _Leaping into the air, she shouted, "I won, I won!"_

1. Interviewing divorced people for her research project.

    Revised: _Interviewing divorced people for her research project, Anna made some surprising discoveries._

2. Since we live near the Colorado River.

    Revised: _We're used to tourists since we live near the Colorado River._

3. Couldn't find the group's new album.

    Revised: _Abdul looked in every record shop in town, but he couldn't find the group's new album._

4. A tall, thin man with bushy eyebrows.

    Revised: _Dad is a tall, thin man with bushy eyebrows._

5. To earn money for college.

    Revised: _To earn money for college, Sergio worked all summer as a lifeguard._

6. Ten minutes after they won the Super Bowl.

    Revised: _Ten minutes after they won the Super Bowl, the players were wildly spraying each other with champagne._

7. She has patented three of her inventions.

    Revised: _C_

8. Frantically flipping through the pages of the dictionary.

    Revised: _Jed is in the library, frantically flipping through the pages of the dictionary._

9. Someone who loves to take risks.

    Revised: _Harriet is someone who loves to take risks._

10. Although I usually ask my friends for advice.

Revised: *Although I usually ask my friends for advice, I think I had better see a professional counselor this time.*

PRACTICE 5

Proofread this paragraph for fragments. Correct them in any way you choose, either adding the fragments to other sentences or making them into complete sentences. *Answers will vary.*

(1) The sinking of the *Titanic* in 1912 has inspired fifteen motion pictures over the years, (2) ~~All~~ all of them requiring special effects. (3) What set James Cameron's *Titanic* apart, however, was his attention to detail. (4) Following the blueprints and plans for the original ship, (5) Cameron's team created scaled sets and models accurate down to the rivets. (6) Scenes of the ship in the water were made possible through the brilliant use of computer technology and a small model. (7) A larger model of the liner's huge cargo hold was needed, (8) ~~To~~ to show the ocean rushing into the ship. (9) Although the model was only a quarter as large as the original, (10) ~~It~~ it still had enough room for period luggage and a brand-new Renault. (11) The largest model was a 775-foot replica of the luxury ship, (12) ~~Which~~ which reproduced every detail, from the ship's name lettered on the façade to the chairs on the deck. (13) That set took almost a year to build, (14) ~~And~~ and a good chunk of the $287 million that Cameron spent on the most expensive movie ever made.

PRACTICE 6

Proofread this essay for fragments. Correct them in any way you choose, either adding the fragments to other sentences or making them into complete sentences. Be careful of the punctuation. *Answers will vary.*

The Regent Diamond

(1) Throughout its exciting history, (2) ~~The~~ the Regent diamond has been one of the world's most desired jewels.

(3) In 1701, the 410-carat gem was discovered in an Indian mine by a slave. (4) ~~Who~~ who risked his life to smuggle it out. (5) Slashing his leg, (6) ~~He~~ he stuffed the huge diamond into the wound and headed for the seacoast. (7) A shifty sea captain offered to sail him to freedom for half the value of the jewel. (8) When at sea, the captain stole the stone, (9) ~~And~~ and threw the slave overboard. (10) He then sold the precious rock to a powerful diamond merchant.

(11) The merchant had difficulty unloading the diamond, (12) ~~Because~~ because it was so large and because it was stolen. (13) He finally sold it to Robert Pitt, a young Englishman, (14) ~~Who~~ who had come to India seeking his fortune. (15) By the time this shrewd adventurer returned home, (16) ~~The~~ the English had nicknamed him "Diamond" Pitt and christened the stone "the Pitt."

(17) Few people believed Pitt had come by the diamond honestly, (18) ~~So~~ so he also had trouble selling it. (19) Pitt was terrified of being robbed and murdered. (20) Whenever he carried the stone, (21) ~~He~~ he disguised himself and would not sleep in the same place for more than two nights. (22) If someone recognized him, (23) ~~He~~ he would deny that he carried the stone with him. (24) It took years, (25) ~~But~~ but he finally sold his diamond in 1717 for an enormous sum to the Duke of Orleans, (26) ~~The~~ the Regent of France.

(27) Now called the Regent diamond, (28) ~~The~~ the fabulous stone was the most valuable French crown jewel. (29) In 1792, during the French Revolution, (30) ~~It~~ it disappeared, only to be found in a ditch in the middle of Paris. (31) Upon becoming emperor, (32) Napoleon had the diamond set into the hilt of his ceremonial sword. (33) In 1887 when the last French monarchy fell and the jewel collection was auctioned, (34) ~~The~~ the Regent diamond was placed in the Louvre, the famous museum in Paris, (35) ~~Where~~ where it still glitters today.

CHAPTER 25 Avoiding Sentence Errors   353

PRACTICE 7 **Review**

Proofread these paragraphs for run-ons, comma splices, and fragments. Correct the errors in any way you choose. *Answers will vary.*

Paragraph a (1) Many experts believe that before the year 2020, *the* (2) ~~The~~ moon will be a popular tourist destination. (3) Adventure travelers now might climb Mount Everest or take a canoe trip down the Amazon. *Soon* ~~soon~~ they will be paying large sums for the adventure of a lifetime, in space. (4) After careful training and space suit drills, they will rocket out of Earth's orbit and spend a day at a fuel depot, (5) *circling* ~~Circling~~ Earth and playing in zero gravity. (6) Then they will board the space ship for the two-day flight to the moon. (7) Once they land near the hotel's main airlock and check in, guests will stare at Mother Earth in the black vastness of the sky, take tours in special buses through the dusty lunar landscape, and experience the thrill of moving at one-sixth the gravity of Earth. (8) This means they will jump six times higher and feel six times lighter. (9) The week will fly by. (10) As they pack for the return trip, (11) *many* ~~Many~~ travelers will trade ten pounds of their baggage allowance for the moon rocks they've been collecting. (12) After an unforgettable final flight and decontamination, the space visitors will re-enter their lives on Earth, changed.

—Adapted from Gregory Bennett, "Your Vacation on the Moon"

Paragraph b (1) Some teenagers seem to start the day tired. *They* ~~they~~ are worn out even before they leave for school. (2) Once in class, they might doze off, even in the middle of an exciting lesson. (3) Are these students lazy? *Have* ~~have~~ they stayed out too late partying? (4) Medical research provides a different explanation for the exhaustion of these teens. (5) As children become adolescents, they develop an increased need for sleep, especially in the morning. (6) Unfortunately, most American high schools start around 7:30 A.M., *and* many students have to get up as early as 5:00 A.M. (7) Scientists suggest that if students could start school later in the day, (8) *they* ~~They~~ might get the extra sleep they need. (9) To test this theory, many schools have begun to experiment with later hours. (10) Congress is even paying the extra operating costs for schools that start after 9:00 A.M. (11) The hope is that teens will be less tired; furthermore, because schools that start later will end later, students will be off the streets and out of trouble during the late afternoon, which (12) ~~Which~~ is prime mischief time.

PRACTICE 8   Review

Proofread these two essays for run-ons, comma splices, and fragments. Correct the errors in any way you choose, writing the revised draft on a separate piece of paper. *Answers will vary.*

Words for the Wise

(1) Everyone knows that Scrabble is America's favorite word game. (2) It was invented by Alfred Butts, (3) ~~An~~ an architect who wanted to create a word game that required both luck and skill. (4) In 1938, Butts produced a board with 225 squares and 100 tiles with letters on them. (5) Each letter was worth a certain number of points, depending on how easy it was to use that letter in a word.

(6) Butts made fifty Scrabble sets by hand; he gave them to his friends, who (7) ~~Who~~ loved playing Scrabble. (8) Strangely enough, Butts could not interest a manufacturer in the game. (9) A friend of his, James Brunot, asked Butts for permission to manufacture and sell the game. (10) However, Brunot also had little success, (11) ~~Selling~~ selling only a few sets a year. (12) Then suddenly, in 1953, Scrabble caught on, and a million sets were sold that year.

(13) Butts and Brunot couldn't keep up with the demand, so they sold the rights to a game manufacturer. (14) The rest is history. Today ~~today~~ Scrabble is produced in half a dozen foreign languages; it is also used as a learning tool, (15) ~~To~~ to teach children spelling and vocabulary.

Dance Craze

(1) Do you remember the Macarena, (2) ~~Which~~ which became the hottest dance craze since the Twist? (3) After Los del Rio recorded a song in 1993 about a heartbroken seductress named Macarena, (4) ~~The~~ the tune sold more than four million

copies worldwide. (5) A duo of male musicians from Seville, Spain, (6) Los del Rio created the dance on the spot one night. (7) The audience imitated the singers; what happened next is dance-fad history. (8) Dancers bought Macarena albums, and they danced at Macarena marathons.

(9) Like the Macarena, country line dancing also spread very quickly across the United States. (10) The music is country western, but the line goes back to the conga line and the Harlem Hustle. (11) Country line dancing invites any dancer to join long lines of folks who (12) ~~Who~~ are all doing the same steps at the same time. (13) The trend was already under way when Billy Ray Cyrus's 1992 hit "Achy Breaky Heart" led to a line dance called the Achy Breaky. (14) From then on, dances like the Electric Slide, Tush Push, and Boot Scootin' Boogie sprang up on the heels of one another.

(15) Recent years have seen a revival of the big bands and the swing dancing of the 1920s and '30s. (16) Dances like the jitterbug, the Lindy Hop, and the Carolina Shag make demands on couples to (17) ~~To~~ learn complicated steps. (18) A high-energy dance form, (19) swing ~~Swing~~ requires partners to flip, slide, and dip. (20) The clothing of the period also has been revived. Dancers ~~dancers~~ often wear wide-brim fedora hats, double-breasted zoot suits, suspenders, and wing-tip shoes. (21) Because swing ~~Swing~~ clubs have sprung up practically overnight, dance studios can't keep up with the demand for lessons.

(22) Swing dancing seems to have come into the mainstream; ironically, some of its original fans are now looking for the next step. (23) Will the newest dance craze be an invention like the Macarena, or will it be a revival of an older dance, perhaps the waltz or the two-step? (24) Nobody is predicting yet what will next ignite our soles—and our souls!

CHAPTER 26

Present Tense (Agreement)

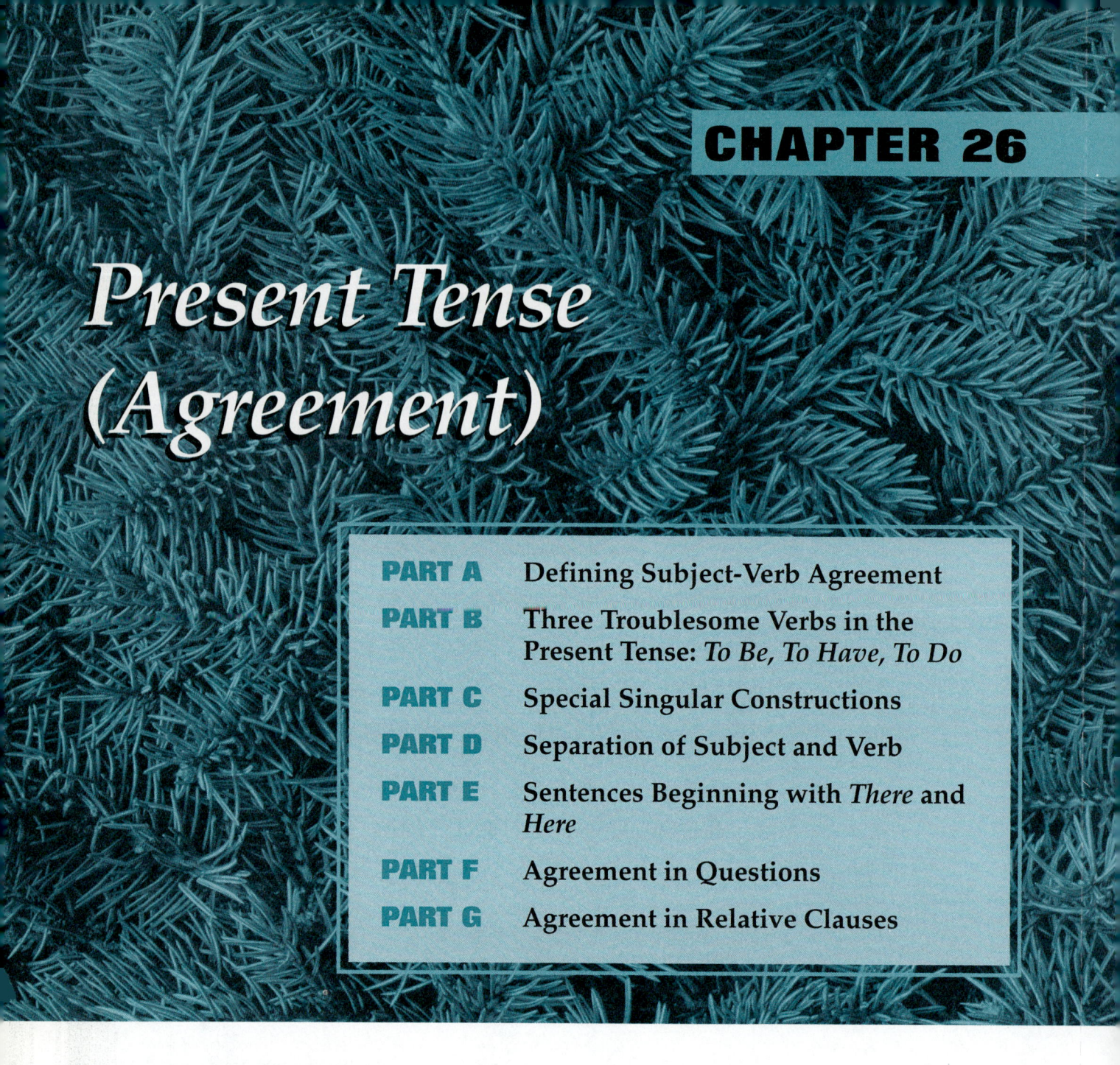

PART A	Defining Subject-Verb Agreement
PART B	Three Troublesome Verbs in the Present Tense: *To Be, To Have, To Do*
PART C	Special Singular Constructions
PART D	Separation of Subject and Verb
PART E	Sentences Beginning with *There* and *Here*
PART F	Agreement in Questions
PART G	Agreement in Relative Clauses

PART A Defining Subject-Verb Agreement

Subjects and verbs in the present tense must **agree** in number; that is, singular subjects take verbs with singular endings, and plural subjects take verbs with plural endings.

CHAPTER 26 Present Tense (Agreement)

Verbs in the Present Tense
Sample Verb: *To Leap*

	Singular		Plural	
	If the subject is	the verb is	If the subject is	the verb is
1st person:	I	leap	we	leap
2nd person:	you	leap	you	leap
3rd person:	he, she, it	leaps	they	leap

- Use an *-s* or *-es* ending on the verb only when the subject is *he, she,* or *it* or the equivalent of *he, she,* or *it*.

The subjects and verbs in the following sentences agree:

1. He *bicycles* to the steel mills every morning.
2. They *bicycle* to the steel mills every morning.
3. This student *hopes* to go to social work school.
4. The planets *revolve* around the sun.

- In sentence 1, the singular subject, *he*, takes the singular form of the verb, *bicycles*. *Bicycles* agrees with *he*.
- In sentence 2, the plural subject, *they*, takes the plural form of the verb, *bicycle*. *Bicycle* agrees with *they*.
- In sentence 3, the subject, *student*, is equivalent to *he* or *she* and takes the singular form of the verb, *hopes*.
- In sentence 4, the subject, *planets*, is equivalent to *they* and takes the plural form of the verb, *revolve*.

Subjects joined by the conjunction *and* usually take a plural verb:

5. Kirk and Quincy *attend* a pottery class at the Y.

- The subject, *Kirk and Quincy*, is plural, the equivalent of *they*.
- *Attend* agrees with the plural subject.*

---

*For work on consistent verb tense, see Chapter 19, "Revising for Consistency and Parallelism," Part A.

Practice 1

Underline the subject and circle the correct present tense verb.

1. A signed Green Bay Packers' <u>helmet</u> (**brings**, bring) in $2,000.
2. <u>Bill Gates</u> (**pays**, pay) $30.8 million for a notebook handwritten by Leonardo da Vinci.
3. Obviously, <u>autographs</u> (sells, **sell**)!
4. <u>They</u> (falls, **fall**) into three major categories—history, sports, and entertainment.
5. To a historian, an <u>autograph</u> (**means**, mean) a signed document, like a letter signed by President Lincoln.
6. For a sports fan, <u>it</u> (**includes**, include) anything signed, like a baseball or a cap.
7. In the entertainment field, <u>collectors</u> (associates, **associate**) an autograph with a signed photograph, like an eight-by-ten glossy of Jimmy Smits.
8. Some <u>people</u> (collects, **collect**) only specific items—for example, autographs of the signers of the Declaration of Independence or signed photographs of Bruce Willis.
9. Autograph <u>shops</u> (flourishes, **flourish**) in malls and airports.
10. However, <u>technology and business</u> (complicates, **complicate**) collecting.
11. For example, more and more <u>public figures</u> (uses, **use**) computers instead of pen and paper.
12. To make the situation even more complicated, an <u>autopen</u> sometimes (**confuses**, confuse) the unsuspecting buyer.
13. That <u>pen</u>, a perfect counterfeiter, automatically (**writes**, write) signatures for some celebrities.
14. Also, unlike their predecessors, <u>athletes and movie stars</u> sometimes (asks, **ask**) to be paid for their signatures.
15. Even with such problems, however, autograph <u>hounds</u> (continues, **continue**) to raise collecting to new heights.

PART B Three Troublesome Verbs in the Present Tense: *To Be, To Have, To Do*

Choosing the correct verb form of *to be*, *to have*, and *to do* can be tricky. Study these charts:

**Reference Chart—*To Be*
Present Tense**

	Singular		Plural	
	If the subject is	the verb is	If the subject is	the verb is
1st person:	I	am	we	are
2nd person:	you	are	you	are
3rd person:	he, she, it	is	they	are

**Reference Chart—*To Have*
Present Tense**

	Singular		Plural	
	If the subject is	the verb is	If the subject is	the verb is
1st person:	I	have	we	have
2nd person:	you	have	you	have
3rd person:	he, she, it	has	they	have

**Reference Chart—*To Do*
Present Tense**

	Singular		Plural	
	If the subject is	the verb is	If the subject is	the verb is
1st person:	I	do	we	do
2nd person:	you	do	you	do
3rd person:	he, she, it	does	they	do

PRACTICE 2

Write the correct present tense form of the verb in the space at the right of the pronoun.

To be	To have	To do
I _am_	we _have_	it _does_
we _are_	she _has_	they _do_
he _is_	he _has_	she _does_
you _are_	they _have_	you _do_
it _is_	I _have_	he _does_
they _are_	it _has_	we _do_
she _is_	you _have_	I _do_

PRACTICE 3

Fill in the correct present tense form of the verb in parentheses.

1. Rock climbing __is__ (to be) an extreme sport that __has__ (to have) become very popular.

2. Some beginners __have__ (to have) a terrific fear of heights, and they __are__ (to be) better off "bouldering," or climbing big rocks on or near the ground.

3. These inexperienced climbers also __do__ (to do) what is called "top roping."

4. In top roping, the beginner and an experienced climber __have__ (to have) one rope between them.

5. The experienced climber __has__ (to have) the job of taking up the slack on the ground while the beginner, or top roper, __does__ (to do) the climbing.

6. If the climber __does__ (to do) slip and fall, top roping __does__ (to do) not allow serious injury.

7. Strangely enough, even the non-outdoorsperson now __has__ (to have) a way to rock climb—indoor rock climbing.

8. Indoor climbing clubs __have__ (to have) more than tripled since 1994, and climbing walls __are__ (to be) now standard equipment in gyms around the country.

9. Some enthusiasts even __have__ (to have) climbing walls in their homes.

10. If their walls __are__ (to be) not high enough, a rolling rock wall __does__ (to do) the trick.

11. By going down as the climber __is__ (to be) going up, the rolling wall __is__ (to be) a combination of treadmill and climbing wall.

12. Indoor climbing __has__ (to have) all the benefits of outdoor rock climbing—overall body toning, stress relief, improved balance and coordination, and fun—without the danger.

PART C Special Singular Constructions

Each of these constructions takes a **singular** verb:

Special Singular Constructions		
either (of) . . .	each (of) . . .	every one (of) . . .
neither (of) . . .	one (of) . . .	which one (of) . . .

1. *Neither* of the birds *has* feathers yet.
2. *Each* of the solutions *presents* difficulties.

- In sentence 1, *neither* means *neither one*. *Neither* is a singular subject and requires the singular verb *has*.

- In sentence 2, *each* means *each one*. *Each* is a singular subject and requires the singular verb *presents*.

However, an exception to this general rule is the case in which two subjects are joined by *(n)either . . . (n)or. . . .* Here, the verb agrees with the subject closer to it:

3. Neither the teacher nor the *pupils want* the semester shortened.
4. Either the graphs or the *map has* to be changed.

- In sentence 3, *pupils* is the subject closer to the verb. The plural subject *pupils* takes the verb *want*.

- In sentence 4, *map* is the subject closer to the verb. The singular subject *map* takes the verb *has*.

362 UNIT 6 Reviewing the Basics

PRACTICE 4

Underline the subject and circle the correct verb in each sentence.

1. Each of these ferns ((needs), need) special care.
2. One of the customers always (forget, (forgets)) his or her umbrella.
3. Which one of the flights ((goes), go) nonstop to Dallas?
4. Every one of those cameras ((costs), cost) more than I can afford.
5. Either you or Doris ((is), are) correct.
6. Either of these computer diskettes (contain, (contains)) the information you need.
7. Do you really believe that one of these oysters ((holds), hold) a pearl?
8. Neither of the twins ((resembles), resemble) his parents.
9. One of the scientists ((believes), believe) he can cure baldness.
10. Each of these inventions ((has), have) an effect on how we spend our leisure time.

PART D Separation of Subject and Verb

Sometimes a phrase or a clause separates the subject from the verb. First, look for the subject; then make sure that the verb agrees with the subject.

> 1. The economist's *ideas* on this matter *seem* well thought out.
> 2. *Radios* that were made in the 1930s *are* now collectors' items.

- In sentence 1, the *ideas* are well thought out. The prepositional phrase *on this matter* separates the subject *ideas* from the verb *seem*.*
- In sentence 2, *radios* are now collectors' items. The relative clause *that were made in the 1930s* separates the subject *radios* from the verb *are*.

PRACTICE 5

Read each sentence carefully for meaning. Cross out any phrase or clause that separates the subject from the verb. Underline the subject and circle the correct verb.

---

* For more work on prepositional phrases, see Chapter 23, "The Simple Sentence," Part B.

1. The <u>plums</u> ~~in that bowl~~ (tastes, (taste)) sweet.
2. The <u>instructions</u> ~~on the package~~ (is, (are)) in French and Japanese.
3. Our new community <u>center</u>, ~~which has a swimming pool and tennis courts~~, ((keeps), keep) everyone happy.
4. The <u>lampshades</u> ~~that are made of stained glass~~ (looks, (look)) beautiful at night.
5. All the CD <u>players</u> ~~on that shelf~~ (comes, (come)) with a remote control.
6. A <u>movie</u> ~~that lasts more than three hours~~ usually ((puts), put) me to sleep.
7. The <u>man</u> ~~with the dark sunglasses~~ ((looks), look) like a typical movie villain.
8. The two <u>nurses</u> ~~who check blood pressure~~ (enjoys, (enjoy)) chatting with the patients.
9. The <u>function</u> ~~of these metal racks~~ ((remains), remain) a mystery to me.
10. The <u>lizard</u> ~~on the wall~~ ((has), have) only three legs.

PART E — Sentences Beginning with *There* and *Here*

In sentences that begin with **there** or **here,** the subject usually follows the verb:

> 1. There *seem* to be two *flies* in my soup.
> 2. Here *is* my *prediction* for the coming year.

- In sentence 1, the plural subject *flies* takes the plural verb *seem.*
- In sentence 2, the singular subject *prediction* takes the singular verb *is.*

You can often determine what the verb should be by reversing the word order: *two flies seem . . .* or *my prediction is. . . .*

PRACTICE 6

Underline the subject and circle the correct verb in each sentence.

1. There ((goes), go) <u>Tom Hanks</u>.
2. There (is, (are)) only a few <u>seconds</u> left in the game.

3. Here (**is**, are) a terrific way to save money—make a budget and stick to it!

4. There (has, **have**) been robberies in the neighborhood lately.

5. Here (is, **are**) the plantains you ordered.

6. Here (**comes**, come) Johnny, the television talk-show host.

7. There (**is**, are) no direct route to Black Creek from here.

8. There (**seems**, seem) to be something wrong with the doorbell.

9. Here (is, **are**) the teapot and sugar bowl I've been looking for.

10. There (is, **are**) six reporters in the hall waiting for an interview.

PART F   Agreement in Questions

In questions, the subject usually follows the verb:

> 1. What *is* the *secret* of your success?
> 2. Where *are* the *copies* of the review?

- In sentence 1, the subject *secret* takes the singular verb *is*.
- In sentence 2, the subject *copies* takes the plural verb *are*.

You can often determine what the verb should be by reversing the word order: *the secret of your success is . . .* or *the copies are. . . .*

PRACTICE 7

Underline the subject and circle the correct verb in each sentence.

1. How (**does**, do) the combustion engine actually work?

2. Why (is, **are**) Robert and Charity so suspicious?

3. Where (is, **are**) the new suitcases?

4. Which tour guide (have, **has**) a pair of binoculars?

5. (**Are**, Is) Dianne and Bill starting a mail-order business?

6. What (**seems**, seem) to be the problem here?

7. Why (is, **are**) those boxes stacked in the corner?

8. (**Is**, Are) the mattress factory really going to close in June?

9. How (does, **do**) you explain that strange footprint?

10. Who (is, **are**) those people on the fire escape?

PART G Agreement in Relative Clauses

A **relative clause** is a subordinate clause that begins with *who, which,* or *that*. The verb in the relative clause must agree with the antecedent of the *who, which,* or *that*.*

> 1. People *who have a good sense of humor* make good neighbors.
> 2. Be careful of a scheme *that promises you a lot of money fast*.

- In sentence 1, the antecedent of *who* is *people*. *People* should take the plural verb *have*.
- In sentence 2, the antecedent of *that* is *scheme*. *Scheme* takes the singular verb *promises*.

PRACTICE 8

Underline the antecedent of the *who, which,* or *that*. Then circle the correct verb.

1. Most patients prefer doctors who (spends, **spend**) time talking with them.

2. The gnarled oak that (**shades**, shade) the garden is my favorite tree.

3. Laptop computers, which (has, **have**) become very popular recently, are still fairly expensive.

4. My neighbor, who (**swims**, swim) at least one hour a day, is seventy years old.

5. Planning ahead, which (**saves**, save) hours of wasted time, is a good way to manage time effectively.

6. Employers often appreciate employees who (asks, **ask**) intelligent questions.

7. This air conditioner, which now (**costs**, cost) eight hundred dollars, rarely breaks down.

8. Everyone admires her because she is someone who always (**sees**, see) the bright side of a bad situation.

9. He is the man who (**creates**, create) furniture from scraps of walnut, cherry, and birch.

10. Foods that (contains, **contain**) artificial sweeteners may be hazardous to your health.

---

*For more work on relative clauses, see Chapter 20, "Revising for Sentence Variety," Part D.

PRACTICE 9 — Review

Proofread the following essay for verb agreement errors. Correct any errors by writing above the lines.

Chimp Smarts

(1) Chimpanzees sometimes seem uncannily human, especially in their use of tools and language. (2) Neither the gorilla nor the orangutan, both close relatives of the chimp, ~~exhibit~~ *exhibits* such behavior. (3) Chimps ~~employs~~ *employ* a number of tools in their everyday lives. (4) They dine by inserting sticks into insect nests and then licking their utensils clean. (5) Each of these intelligent animals also ~~crack~~ *cracks* fruit and nuts with stones. (6) What's more, chimpanzees ~~creates~~ *create* their own tools. (7) They make their eating sticks by cleaning leaves from branches. (8) They even ~~attaches~~ *attach* small sticks together to make longer rods for getting at hard-to-reach insects. (9) Some of the other tools chimps make ~~is~~ *are* fly-whisks, sponges of chewed bark, and leaf-rags to clean themselves with. (10) Scientists on safari ~~has~~ *have* observed infant chimps imitating their parents' use of these tools.

(11) Recent experiments indicate that chimpanzees probably also ~~understands~~ *understand* language though they lack the physical ability to speak. (12) There ~~are~~ *is* little doubt that they can comprehend individual words. (13) Using sign language and keyboards, some chimps in captivity use nearly two hundred words. (14) This vocabulary ~~include~~ *includes* nouns, verbs, and prepositions. (15) Hunger and affection ~~is~~ *are* needs that they have expressed by punching keyboard symbols. (16) Do chimps ~~has~~ *have* the ability to string words into sentences? (17) Intriguingly, one chimp named Lucy has shown that she ~~understand~~ *understands* the difference between such statements as "Roger tickles Lucy" and "Lucy tickles Roger."

(18) Scientists still argue about just how much language a chimpanzee truly ~~comprehend~~ *comprehends*. (19) However, no one who ~~have~~ *has* watched them closely ~~doubt~~ *doubts* the intelligence of these remarkable beings.

CHAPTER 27

Past Tense

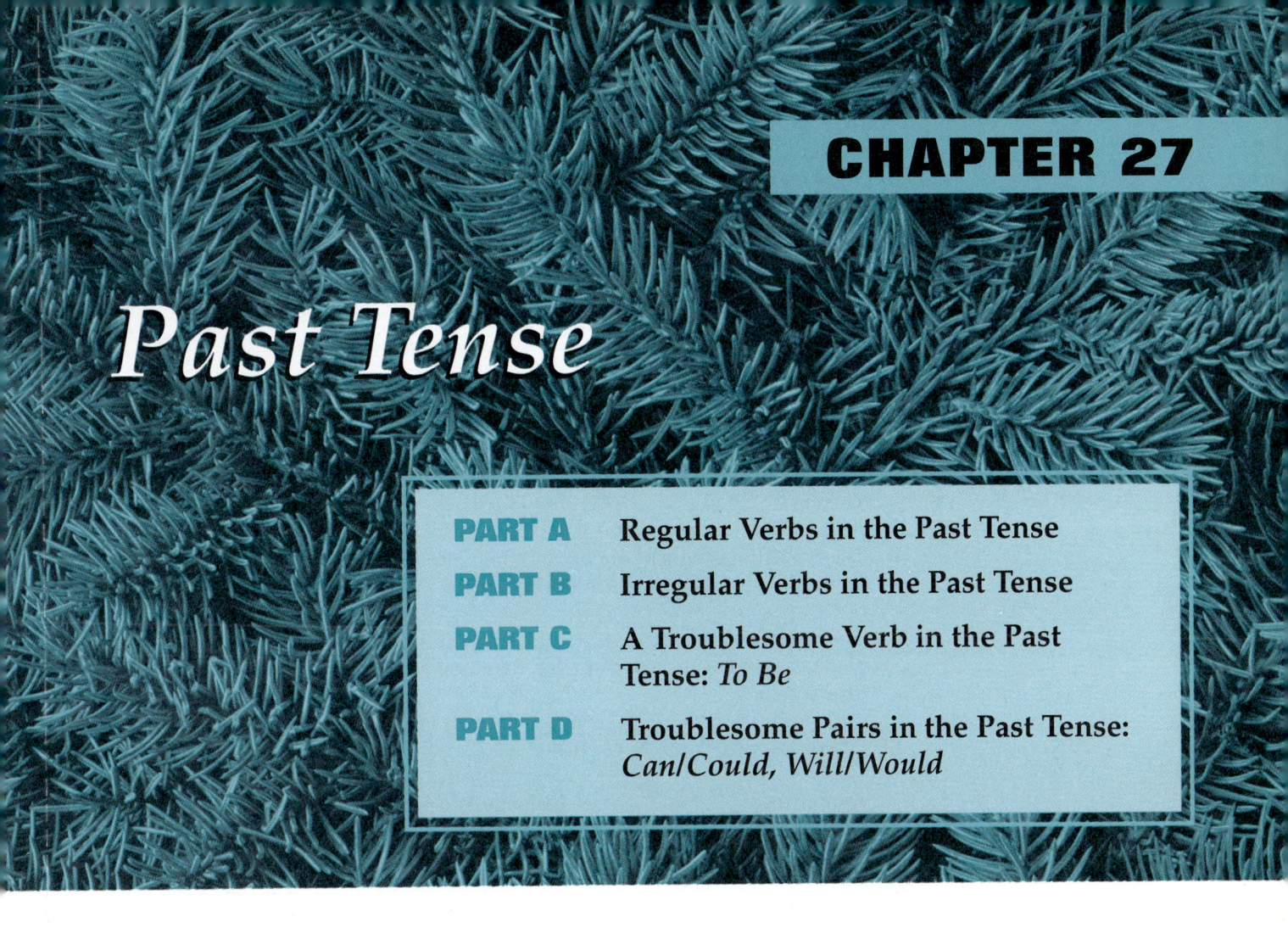

PART A   Regular Verbs in the Past Tense
PART B   Irregular Verbs in the Past Tense
PART C   A Troublesome Verb in the Past Tense: *To Be*
PART D   Troublesome Pairs in the Past Tense: *Can/Could, Will/Would*

PART A   Regular Verbs in the Past Tense

Regular verbs in the past tense take an *-ed* or *-d* ending:

1. The captain *hoisted* the flag.
2. They *purchased* lawn furniture yesterday.
3. We *deposited* a quarter in the meter.

- *Hoisted, purchased,* and *deposited* are regular verbs in the past tense.
- Each verb ends in *-ed* or *-d*.

PRACTICE 1

Fill in the past tense of the regular verbs in parentheses.*

1. I _*raised*_ (raise) my arms in a move called "embrace the tiger."

---

* If you have questions about spelling, see Chapter 37, "Spelling," Parts D, E, and F.

2. Then I __shifted__ (shift) my weight and __walked__ (walk) forward on my right foot to start the next move, "stroke the peacock's tail."

3. After stepping forward with my left foot, I __reached__ (reach) out my left hand and __pulled__ (pull) back my right arm.

4. Unfortunately, my muscles __clenched__ (clench), which __resulted__ (result) in an awkward movement.

5. Talking calmly to myself, I __relaxed__ (relax) and __started__ (start) again.

6. Then I __moved__ (move) fluidly to a new position.

7. These positions, which connect and flow into each other, __evolved__ (evolve) over the centuries into what we now call tai chi.

8. Though tai chi __developed__ (develop) from the martial arts, today it emphasizes relaxation and stress reduction in addition to flexibility and fitness.

9. I chose to practice tai chi because it __required__ (require) no special equipment, __challenged__ (challenge) me physically, and __promised__ (promise) many benefits.

10. Tai chi is excellent exercise for all ages; a recent study __showed__ (show) that when older people __performed__ (perform) it regularly, they __reduced__ (reduce) the likelihood of falling—and thus breaking bones—by almost 25 percent.

PART B Irregular Verbs in the Past Tense

Irregular verbs do not take an *-ed* or *-d* ending in the past but change internally:

1. I *wrote* that letter in ten minutes.
2. Although the orange cat *fell* from a high branch, she escaped unharmed.
3. The play *began* on time but ended fairly late.

- *Wrote* is the past tense of *write*.
- *Fell* is the past tense of *fall*.
- *Began* is the past tense of *begin*.

Here is a partial list of irregular verbs:

Reference Chart
Irregular Verbs in the Past Tense

Simple Form	Past Tense	Simple Form	Past Tense
be	was, were	leave	left
become	became	let	let
begin	began	lie	lay
blow	blew	lose	lost
break	broke	make	made
bring	brought	mean	meant
build	built	meet	met
buy	bought	pay	paid
catch	caught	put	put
choose	chose	quit	quit
come	came	read	read
cut	cut	ride	rode
deal	dealt	rise	rose
dig	dug	run	ran
dive	dove (dived)	say	said
do	did	see	saw
draw	drew	seek	sought
drink	drank	sell	sold
drive	drove	send	sent
eat	ate	shake	shook
fall	fell	shine	shone (shined)
feed	fed	sing	sang
feel	felt	sit	sat
fight	fought	sleep	slept
find	found	speak	spoke
fly	flew	spend	spent
forbid	forbade	split	split
forget	forgot	spring	sprang
forgive	forgave	stand	stood
freeze	froze	steal	stole
get	got	stink	stank
give	gave	swim	swam
go	went	take	took
grow	grew	teach	taught
have	had	tear	tore
hear	heard	tell	told
hide	hid	think	thought
hold	held	throw	threw
hurt	hurt	understand	understood
keep	kept	wake	woke (waked)
know	knew	wear	wore
lay	laid	win	won
lead	led	write	wrote

PRACTICE 2

Fill in the past tense of the regular and irregular verbs in parentheses. If you are not sure of the past tense, use the chart. Do not guess.

Entrepreneurs Did It Their Way

(1) Beth Cross and Pam Parker __worked__ (work) in the same company. (2) After they __became__ (become) friends, they __discovered__ (discover) that they both __loved__ (love) to ride horses. (3) Both women also __thought__ (think) that their riding boots were extremely uncomfortable. (4) Eventually, they __left__ (leave) their jobs, __designed__ (design) a new boot, and __began__ (begin) their own company. (5) The boots __caught__ (catch) on, sales __doubled__ (double) every year for the first four years, and they now sell boots in more than two thousand outlets in the United States, Canada, Great Britain, and Australia.

(6) Cross and Parker __went__ (go) from being employees to being entrepreneurs, individuals who start their own business. (7) These risk takers __chose__ (choose) to leave their job security so that they could try their hand at producing a new product.

(8) Duyen Le is a different type of entrepreneur, one who __followed__ (follow) his dream without ever joining a big company. (9) Le __immigrated__ (immigrate) to the United States from Vietnam. (10) Although he __expected__ (expect) to go into computer science, instead he __opened__ (open) a tiny Vietnamese restaurant in his neighborhood. (11) For years, he __got__ (get) up at five each morning to search for the spices and vegetables he couldn't afford to have delivered.

(12) When customers almost __poured__ (pour) in, a rival __challenged__ (challenge) him by opening a new Vietnamese restaurant around the corner. (13) Le simply __bought__ (buy) out his competitor. (14) Encouraged by his large number of non-Vietnamese customers, he very successfully __started__

(start) many restaurants, first in local Boston neighborhoods and then in upscale areas of the city.

(15) Not every entrepreneur _wanted_ (want) to become one. (16) However, when companies _downsized_ (downsize) in recent years, thousands of employees _lost_ (lose) their jobs. (17) They _had_ (have) to find new positions—or become entrepreneurs. (18) As it _happened_ (happen), thousands upon thousands of ordinary workers _found_ (find) greater satisfaction—and sometimes _made_ (make) far more money—when they _did_ (do) it their way!

PART C — A Troublesome Verb in the Past Tense: *To Be*

To be is the only verb that in the past tense has different forms for different persons. Be careful of subject-verb agreement:

Reference Chart—*To Be*
Past Tense

Singular		Plural	
If the subject is	the verb is	If the subject is	the verb is
1st person: I	was	we	were
2nd person: you	were	you	were
3rd person: he, she, it	was	they	were

■ Note that the first person singular form and the third person singular form are the same—*was*.

Be especially careful of agreement when adding *not* to *was* or *were* to make a contraction:

was + not = wasn't
were + not = weren't

PRACTICE 3

Circle the correct form of the verb *to be* in the past tense. Do not guess. If you are not sure of the correct form, use the chart on page 371.

1. Oprah Winfrey (**was**, were) always an avid reader.

2. In fact, books (was, **were**) sometimes her only comfort during her difficult childhood and painful adolescence.

3. When her producers (was, **were**) considering a television book club, Winfrey (**was**, were) understandably enthusiastic.

4. With a daily audience of more than twenty million, the world's most popular talk show host (**was**, were) sure she could get the whole country reading.

5. Her first book club selection (**was**, were) *The Deep End of the Ocean* by Jacquelyn Mitchard, the story of a kidnapped child.

6. The public's rush to buy books (**wasn't**, weren't) anticipated.

7. Mitchard's publishers (was, **were**) astonished to have to reprint the book nearly twenty times; all in all, 900,000 hardcovers and over 2 million paperbacks eventually (was, **were**) sold.

8. Winfrey's next book club choice (**was**, were) *Song of Solomon* by Nobel Prize winner Toni Morrison, a classic novel that (**was**, were) almost twenty years old.

9. About 300,000 copies (was, **were**) in print, but after Winfrey chose it, that figure (**was**, were) over 1,400,000.

10. Every book club pick (**was**, were) an enormous success, and even people who didn't read much found they (was, **were**) eagerly waiting for Winfrey's next selection.

PART D Troublesome Pairs in the Past Tense: Can/Could, Will/Would

Use **could** as the past tense of **can**.

> 1. Maria is extraordinary because she *can* remember what happened to her when she was three years old.
> 2. When I was in high school, I *could* do two sit-ups in an hour.

- In sentence 1, *can* shows the action is in the present.
- In sentence 2, *could* shows the action occurred in the past.

PRACTICE 4

Fill in either the present tense *can* or the past tense *could*.

1. Tom is so talented that he __can__ play most music on the piano by ear.
2. He __can__ leave the hospital as soon as he feels stronger.
3. Last week we __could__ not find fresh strawberries.
4. When we were in Spain last summer, we __could__ see all of Madrid from our hotel balcony.
5. As a child, I __could__ perform easily in public, but I __can__ no longer do it.
6. Anything you __can__ do, he __can__ do better.
7. Nobody __could__ find the guard after the robbery yesterday.
8. These days, Fred __can__ usually predict the weather from the condition of his bunions.

Use **would** as the past tense of **will**.

> 3. Roberta says that she *will* arrive with her camera in ten minutes.
> 4. Roberta said that she *would* arrive with her camera in ten minutes.

- In sentence 3, *will* points to the future from the present.
- In sentence 4, *would* points to the future from the past.

PRACTICE 5

Fill in either the present tense *will* or the past tense *would*.

1. Sean expected that he __would__ arrive at midnight.
2. Sean expects that he __will__ arrive at midnight.
3. I hope the sale at the used car lot __will__ continue for another week.
4. I hoped the sale at the used car lot __would__ continue for another week.
5. When Benny had time, he __would__ color-code his computer disks.

374 UNIT 6 Reviewing the Basics

6. When Benny has time, he __will__ color-code his computer disks.

7. The chefs assure us that the wedding cake __will__ be spectacular.

8. The chefs assured us that the wedding cake __would__ be spectacular.

PRACTICE 6 Review

Proofread the following essay for past tense errors. Then write the correct past tense form above the line.

The Warrior Queen of Jhansi

(1) The British cursed her as a devil; the people of India revered her almost as a god. (2) All agreed, however, that the Indian queen, Lakshmi Bai, ~~were~~ *was* a powerful and daring woman.

(3) Before the ruler of Jhansi died in 1853, he willed his land and title to his five-year-old son. (4) He ~~telled~~ *told* his young wife, Lakshmi Bai, to rule until their child ~~come~~ *came* of age. (5) Despite the young queen's ability and popularity, the British declared the will illegal and ~~seize~~ *seized* the kingdom. (6) Lakshmi Bai swallowed the insult and remained loyal to the British.

(7) However, throughout India, discontent against the British grew until rebellion ~~broken~~ *broke* out in 1857. (8) In Jhansi, rebels ~~taked~~ *took* the British fort and then massacred the British women and children living in the city. (9) Though the queen ~~do~~ *did* not support this bloodshed, the British held her responsible. (10) For a while in late 1857, in the absence of the British, the queen ~~gotten~~ *got* her chance to rule. (11) Rising at 3:00 A.M., she ~~spended~~ *spent* her days first attending to matters of state, then riding and training with arms, and later meditating and praying.

(12) Finally, in early 1858, the British ~~maked~~ *made* the queen an outlaw and ~~lay~~ *laid* siege to Jhansi for more than two weeks. (13) The queen heroically ~~fighted~~ *fought* for her city from a high tower where her people and the enemy ~~can~~ *could* clearly see her. (14) As the city prepared for defeat, the queen, an expert horsewoman, ~~fleed~~ *fled*. (15) After riding for four days, she at last formally ~~join~~ *joined* the rebelling forces.

(16) The queen ~~lead~~ *led* the defense at Gwalior, the last rebel stronghold. (17) Leading her men in hand-to-hand combat, she wore trousers, a silk blouse, and a red silk cap with a loose turban around it. (18) A pearl necklace that ~~were~~ *was* one of the treasures of India ~~hang~~ *hung* around her neck. (19) Mortally wounded in this battle, she immediately ~~become~~ *became* a beloved hero of the Indian nationalist movement.

CHAPTER 28

The Past Participle

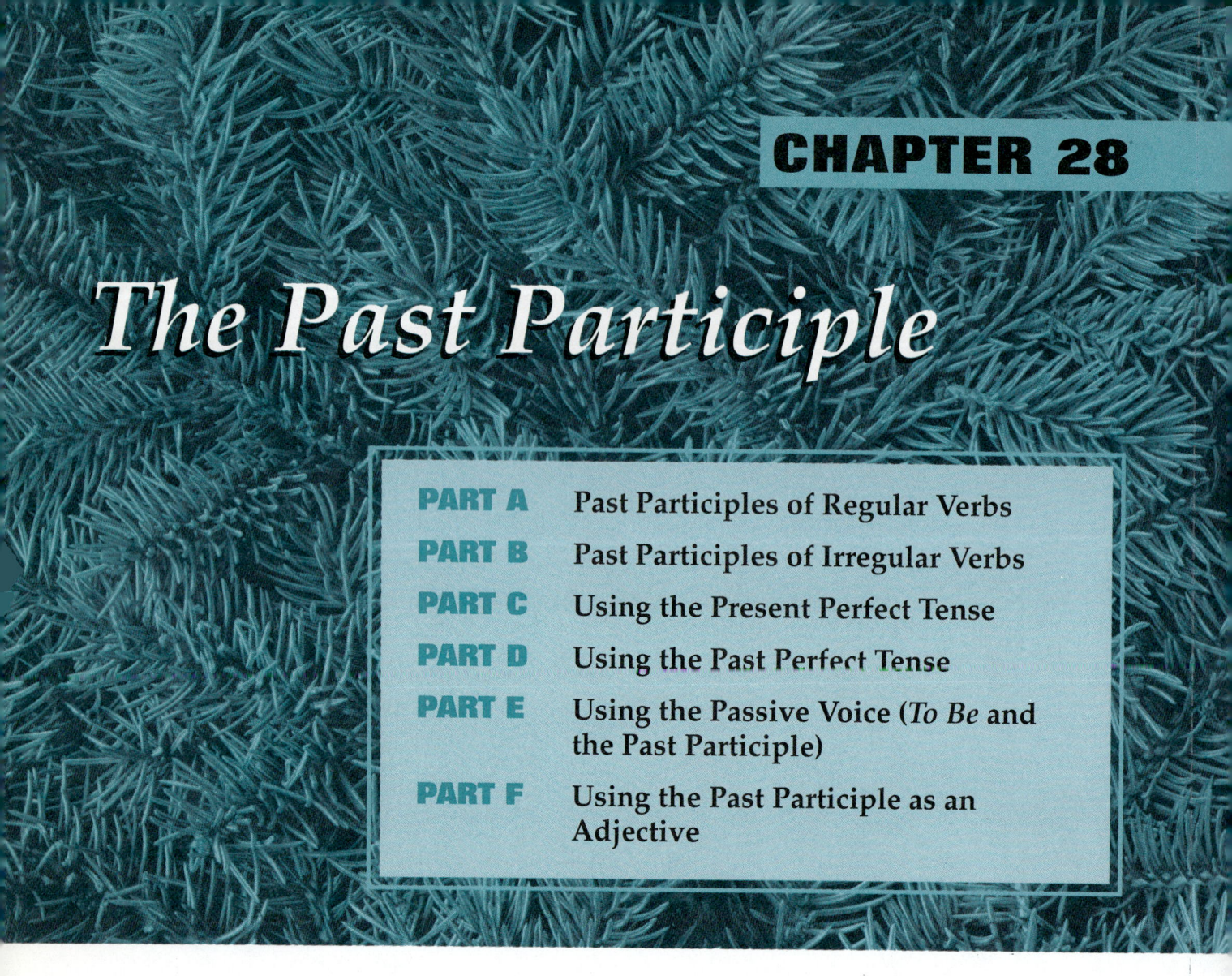

PART A   Past Participles of Regular Verbs
PART B   Past Participles of Irregular Verbs
PART C   Using the Present Perfect Tense
PART D   Using the Past Perfect Tense
PART E   Using the Passive Voice (*To Be* and the Past Participle)
PART F   Using the Past Participle as an Adjective

PART A   Past Participles of Regular Verbs

The **past participle** is the form of the verb that can be combined with helping verbs like *have* and *has* to make verbs of more than one word:

Present Tense	Past Tense	Helping Verb plus Past Participle
1. They *skate*.	1. They *skated*.	1. They *have skated*.
2. Beth *dances*.	2. Beth *danced*.	2. Beth *has danced*.
3. Frank *worries*.	3. Frank *worried*.	3. Frank *has worried*.

- *Skated, danced,* and *worried* are all past participles of regular verbs.
- Note that both the *past tense* and the *past participle* of regular verbs end in *-ed* or *-d*.

PRACTICE 1

The first sentence of each pair that follows contains a regular verb in the past tense. Fill in *have* or *has* plus the past participle of the same verb to complete the second sentence.

1. Vance locked his keys in the car.

    Vance __has__ __locked__ his keys in the car.

2. The carpenters gathered their tools from the littered floor.

    The carpenters __have__ __gathered__ their tools from the littered floor.

3. Clearly, you planned your vacation with care.

    Clearly, you __have__ __planned__ your vacation with care.

4. Twice, Dianne and Carol visited the Dominican Republic.

    Twice, Dianne and Carol __have__ __visited__ the Dominican Republic.

5. Detectives discovered the love letters in the garage.

    Detectives __have__ __discovered__ the love letters in the garage.

6. Mr. Yosufu carved this chess set out of wood.

    Mr. Yosufu __has__ __carved__ this chess set out of wood.

7. My boss impressed everyone with her ability to read Chinese.

    My boss __has__ __impressed__ everyone with her ability to read Chinese.

8. Illness interrupted his work on the film.

    Illness __has__ __interrupted__ his work on the film.

9. The windshields reflected the glow of the streetlights.

    The windshields __have__ __reflected__ the glow of the streetlights.

10. These three women studied with Madame Tebaldi.

    These three women __have__ __studied__ with Madame Tebaldi.

PART B Past Participles of Irregular Verbs

Most verbs that are irregular in the past tense are also irregular in the past participle, as shown in the box below.

Present Tense	Past Tense	Helping Verb plus Past Participle
1. We *sing*.	1. We *sang*.	1. We *have sung*.
2. Bill *writes*.	2. Bill *wrote*.	2. Bill *has written*.
3. I *think*.	3. I *thought*.	3. I *have thought*.

- Irregular verbs change from present to past to past participle in unusual ways.
- *Sung, written,* and *thought* are all past participles of irregular verbs.
- Note that the past tense and past participle of *think* are the same—*thought*.

Reference Chart
Irregular Verbs, Past and Past Participle

Simple Form	Past Tense	Past Participle
be	was, were	been
become	became	become
begin	began	begun
blow	blew	blown
break	broke	broken
bring	brought	brought
build	built	built
buy	bought	bought
catch	caught	caught
choose	chose	chosen
come	came	come
cut	cut	cut
deal	dealt	dealt
dig	dug	dug
dive	dove (dived)	dived
do	did	done
draw	drew	drawn
drink	drank	drunk
drive	drove	driven
eat	ate	eaten
fall	fell	fallen
feed	fed	fed
feel	felt	felt
fight	fought	fought
find	found	found
fly	flew	flown
forbid	forbade	forbidden
forget	forgot	forgotten
forgive	forgave	forgiven

(continued)

Reference Chart
Irregular Verbs, Past and Past Participle
(continued)

Simple Form	Past Tense	Past Participle
freeze	froze	frozen
get	got	got (gotten)
give	gave	given
go	went	gone
grow	grew	grown
have	had	had
hear	heard	heard
hide	hid	hidden
hold	held	held
hurt	hurt	hurt
keep	kept	kept
know	knew	known
lay	laid	laid
lead	led	led
leave	left	left
let	let	let
lie	lay	lain
lose	lost	lost
make	made	made
mean	meant	meant
meet	met	met
pay	paid	paid
put	put	put
quit	quit	quit
read	read	read
ride	rode	ridden
rise	rose	risen
run	ran	run
say	said	said
see	saw	seen
seek	sought	sought
sell	sold	sold
send	sent	sent
shake	shook	shaken
shine	shone (shined)	shone (shined)
sing	sang	sung
sit	sat	sat
sleep	slept	slept
speak	spoke	spoken
spend	spent	spent
split	split	split
spring	sprang	sprung
stand	stood	stood
steal	stole	stolen
stink	stank	stunk
swim	swam	swum
take	took	taken
teach	taught	taught
tear	tore	torn

(continued)

Reference Chart
Irregular Verbs, Past and Past Participle
(continued)

Simple Form	Past Tense	Past Participle
tell	told	told
think	thought	thought
throw	threw	thrown
understand	understood	understood
wake	woke (waked)	woken (waked)
wear	wore	worn
win	won	won
write	wrote	written

PRACTICE 2

The first sentence of each pair that follows contains an irregular verb in the past tense. Fill in *have* or *has* plus the past participle of the same verb to complete the second sentence.

1. Sean took plenty of time buying the groceries.

    Sean __has__ __taken__ plenty of time buying the groceries.

2. We sent our latest budget to the mayor.

    We __have__ __sent__ our latest budget to the mayor.

3. My daughter hid her diary.

    My daughter __has__ __hidden__ her diary.

4. The jockey rode all day in the hot sun.

    The jockey __has__ __ridden__ all day in the hot sun.

5. Hershey, Pennsylvania, became a great tourist attraction.

    Hershey, Pennsylvania, __has__ __become__ a great tourist attraction.

6. The company's managers knew about these hazards for two years.

    The company's managers __have__ __known__ about these hazards for two years.

7. Carrie floated down the river on an inner tube.

    Carrie __has__ __floated__ down the river on an inner tube.

8. At last, our team won the bowling tournament.

   At last, our team __has__ __won__ the bowling tournament.

9. Larry and Marsha broke their long silence.

   Larry and Marsha __have__ __broken__ their long silence.

10. Science fiction films were very popular this past year.

    Science fiction films __have__ __been__ very popular this past year.

PRACTICE 3

Complete each sentence by filling in *have* or *has* plus the past participle of the verb in parentheses. Some verbs are regular, some irregular.

1. Recently, soccer __has__ __gained__ (gain) in popularity in the United States.

2. Traditionally, most North Americans __have__ __considered__ (consider) soccer much less exciting than basketball, football, or hockey.

3. Moreover, many North American players __have__ __found__ (find) it very difficult to compete at the highest levels of the game.

4. In the 1990 World Cup, for example, the United States lost all three of its games; that defeat __has__ __haunted__ (haunt) many soccer fans.

5. However, Canadian and U.S. interest in soccer __has__ __grown__ (grow) ever since the 1994 World Cup, which was held in the United States.

6. Sports fans __have__ __seen__ (see) the enormous enthusiasm and passionate emotion that soccer arouses in such countries as Brazil, Argentina, Italy, and Portugal.

7. The United States also __has__ __demonstrated__ (demonstrate) that it is able to win games in the biggest soccer competition in the world.

8. Unexpected victories __have__ __added__ (add) even more excitement to the game, like France's defeat of Brazil in the 1998 World Cup.

9. Attention __has__ __turned__ (turn) to the 2002 World Cup, which Japan and Korea will co-host.

10. So far, every host team __has__ __won__ (win) at least one of the World Cup games played in the host country; the world will be watching to see if Japan, Korea, or both can rise to that traditional soccer feat.

PRACTICE 4

Proofread the following paragraph for past participle errors. Correct the errors by writing above the lines.

(1) Chattanooga, Tennessee, has ~~went~~ *gone* from being one of the dirtiest cities in the United States to one of the cleanest. (2) Local businesses and neighborhoods have ~~chose~~ *chosen* to join government agencies in the rehabilitation effort. (3) For example, a nonprofit organization called Chattanooga Venture has ~~brung~~ *brought* together more than a thousand residents, who have addressed problems of air pollution, downtown deterioration, and a poor economy. (4) The group has attracted "clean industry" to Chattanooga and has ~~holded~~ *held* on to environmentally sound businesses. (5) The Chattanooga Neighborhood Enterprise has ~~builded~~ *built* or ~~renovate~~ *renovated* thousands of units of inner-city housing. (6) The Tennessee River, once nothing but a source of filthy water because of the industrial sites on its banks, has ~~maked~~ *made* a complete comeback. (7) Riverwalk has reclaimed miles of waterfront, creating parks, playgrounds, and walkways. (8) In recent years, people have even ~~ate~~ *eaten* fish from the river, something many thought would never be possible again. (9) The Tennessee Aquarium—the world's largest freshwater aquarium—has opened, surrounded by art galleries, restaurants, and modern stores and residences. (10) With its free electric shuttle bus service, Chattanooga also has ~~became~~ *become* the electric bus capital of the world. (11) The city has ~~did~~ *done* such outstanding work that it has ~~winned~~ *won* an international reputation for being a leader in "sustainable development programs."

PART C Using the Present Perfect Tense

The **present perfect tense** is composed of the present tense of *to have* plus the past participle. The present perfect tense shows that an action has begun in the past and is continuing into the present.

1. Past tense:		Beatrice *taught* English for ten years.
2. Present perfect tense:		Beatrice *has taught* English for ten years.

CHAPTER 28 The Past Participle 383

- In sentence 1, Beatrice *taught* English in the past, but she no longer teaches it. Note the use of the simple past tense, *taught*.
- In sentence 2, Beatrice *has taught* for ten years and is still teaching English *now*. *Has taught* implies that the action is continuing.

PRACTICE 5

Read these sentences carefully for meaning. Then circle the correct verb—either the **past tense** or the **present perfect tense**.

1. He (directed, (has directed)) traffic for many years now.

2. Emilio lifted the rug and (has swept, (swept)) the dust under it.

3. Kelly (worked, (has worked)) in the computer industry for ten years; she now owns her own software company.

4. She ((went), has gone) to the library last night.

5. The coffee maker gurgled so loudly that the noise ((awakened), has awakened) me at 6:00 A.M.

6. For the past four years, I (enrolled, (have enrolled)) in summer school every summer.

7. We (talked, (have talked)) about the problem of your lateness for three days; it's time for you to do something about it.

8. While I was in Japan, I ((took), have taken) many photographs of shrines.

9. She ((won), has won) that contest ten years ago.

10. The boxers (fought, (have fought)) for an hour, and they look very tired.

11. He ((applied), has applied) to three colleges and attended the one with the best engineering department.

12. Raymond looked at the revised plans for his new house and ((decided), has decided) he could afford to build.

13. These useless tools ((have been), were) here for quite a while, but no one wants to throw them out.

14. The most exciting moment of the game ((occurred), has occurred) during the sudden death overtime.

15. The coauthors (worked, (have worked)) together for eight years and are now planning a new book.

PART D Using the Past Perfect Tense

The **past perfect tense** is composed of the past tense of *to have* plus the past participle. The past perfect tense shows that an action occurred further back in the past than other past action.

1. Past tense: Rhonda *left* for the movies.
2. Past perfect tense: Rhonda *had* already *left* for the movies by the time we *arrived*.

- In sentence 1, *left* is the simple past.
- In sentence 2, the past perfect *had left* shows that this action occurred even before another action in the past, *arrived*.

Practice 6

Read these sentences carefully for meaning. Then circle the correct verb—either the **past tense** or the **past perfect tense**.

1. Tony came to the office with a cane last week because he (sprained, **had sprained**) his ankle a month ago.

2. As Janice (**piled**, had piled) the apples into a pyramid, she thought, "I should become an architect."

3. Celia (finished, **had finished**) her gardening by the time I (**drove**, had driven) up in my new convertible.

4. Bonnie (operated, **had operated**) a drill press for years before she became a welder.

5. The man nervously (**looked**, had looked) at his watch and then walked a bit faster.

6. Last year Ming bought a compact disc player; he (wanted, **had wanted**) one for years.

7. Roberto told us that he (decided, **had decided**) to enlist in the Marines.

8. I (worked, **had worked**) on that essay for a week before I handed it in.

9. The caller asked whether we (received, **had received**) our free toaster yet.

10. Dianne (completed, **had completed**) college before her younger brother was old enough for the first grade.

11. Last week he told me that he (forgot, **had forgotten**) to mail the rent check.

12. As the curtain came down, everyone (**rose**, had risen) and applauded the Brazilian dance troupe.

13. Scott (**closed**, had closed) his books and went to the movies.

14. Brad missed the rehearsal on Saturday because no one (notified, **had notified**) him earlier in the week.

15. The prosecutor proved that the defendant was lying; until then I (believed, **had believed**) he was innocent.

PART E Using the Passive Voice (*To Be* and the Past Participle)

The **passive voice** is composed of the past participle with some form of *to be* (*am, is, are, was, were, has been, have been,* or *had been*). In the passive voice, the subject does not act but is *acted upon*.

Compare the passive voice with the active voice in the following pairs of sentences.

1. Passive voice:	This newspaper *is written* by journalism students.
2. Active voice:	Journalism students *write* this newspaper.
3. Passive voice:	My garden *was devoured* by rabbits.
4. Active voice:	Rabbits *devoured* my garden.

- In sentence 1, the subject, *this newspaper,* is passive; it is acted upon. In sentence 2, the subject, *students,* is active; it performs the action.
- Note the difference between the passive verb *is written* and the active verb *write.*
- However, both verbs (*is written* and *write*) are in the *present tense.*
- The verbs in sentences 3 and 4 are both in the *past tense: was devoured* (passive) and *devoured* (active).

Use the passive voice sparingly. Write in the passive voice when you want to emphasize the receiver of the action rather than the doer.

Practice 7

Fill in the correct **past participle** form of the verb in parentheses. If you are not sure, check the chart on pages 378–380.

1. The barn was _built_ (build) by friends of the family.
2. Who was _chosen_ (choose) to represent us at the union meeting?
3. These ruby slippers were _given_ (give) to me by my grandmother.
4. These jeans are _sold_ (sell) in three sizes.
5. On their weekend camping trip, Sheila and Una were constantly _bitten_ (bite) by mosquitoes and gnats.
6. It was _decided_ (decide) that Bill would work the night shift.
7. The getaway car is always _driven_ (drive) by a man in a gray fedora.
8. Her articles have been _published_ (publish) in the *Texas Monthly*.
9. Harold was _seen_ (see) sneaking out the back door.
10. A faint inscription is _etched_ (etch) on the back of the old gold watch.

Practice 8

Rewrite each sentence, changing the verb into the **passive** voice. Make all necessary verb and subject changes. Be sure to keep the sentence in the original tense.

EXAMPLE My father wore this silk hat.

This silk hat was worn by my father.

1. The goalie blocked the shot.

   The shot was blocked by the goalie.

2. The lifeguard taught us to swim.

   We were taught to swim by the lifeguard.

3. The usher warned the noisy group.

   The noisy group was warned by the usher.

4. Her rudeness hurt her reputation.

   Her reputation was hurt by her rudeness.

5. The campers folded up the tent.

   The tent was folded up by the campers.

6. The judges declared the match a draw.

   The match was declared a draw by the judges.

7. The conductor punched my ticket full of holes.

   My ticket was punched full of holes by the conductor.

8. The interviewer asked too many personal questions.

   Too many personal questions were asked by the interviewer.

PART F Using the Past Participle as an Adjective

The **past participle** form of the verb can be used as an **adjective** after a linking verb:

> 1. The window is *broken*.

- The adjective *broken* describes the subject *window*.

The **past participle** form of the verb can sometimes be used as an adjective before a noun or a pronoun.

> 2. This *fried* chicken tastes wonderful.

- The adjective *fried* describes the noun *chicken*.

PRACTICE 9

Use the past participle form of the verb in parentheses as an adjective in each sentence.

1. My __used__ (use) car was a great bargain at only $700.

2. Bob is highly __qualified__ (qualify) to install a water heater.

3. The __air-conditioned__ (air-condition) room was making everyone shiver.

4. The newly __risen__ (rise) cinnamon bread smelled wonderful.

5. Were you __surprised__ (surprise) to hear about my raise?

6. He feels __depressed__ (depress) on rainy days.

7. She knows the power of the __written__ (write) word.

388 UNIT 6 Reviewing the Basics

8. My gym teacher seems __prejudiced__ (prejudice) against short people.

9. The __embarrassed__ (embarrass) child pulled her jacket over her head.

10. We ordered __tossed__ (toss) salad, __broiled__ (broil) salmon, __mashed__ (mash) potatoes, and __baked__ (bake) apple rings.

PRACTICE 10

Proofread the following paragraph for errors in past participles used as adjectives. Correct the errors by writing above the lines.

(1) Ice palaces, magical buildings made entirely from ice, have a long history. (2) These exquisitely ~~builded~~ *built* castles first appeared in Russia. (3) The most famous one was Empress Anna's palace, constructed in 1739 on the ~~froze~~ *frozen* Neva River during one of the coldest winters ever recorded. (4) ~~Cutted~~ *Cut* blocks of ice were set in place with cranes; water, which froze in the cold air, joined the blocks so smoothly that they appeared to be all one piece. (5) Considered the most magnificently ~~craft~~ *crafted* ice palace ever, Anna's fairy-tale castle had finely ~~furnish~~ *furnished* rooms and surroundings, including sculpted trees and birds painted in natural colors. (6) Although the Russians created other ~~celebrate~~ *celebrated* ice palaces, it took more than a hundred years for this almost ~~losed~~ *lost* art form to come to North America. (7) Now, beautifully ~~carve~~ *carved* and ~~design~~ *designed* ice palaces are a major attraction of winter festivals all over the world.

PRACTICE 11   Review

Proofread the following essay for past participle errors. Correct the errors by writing above the lines.

The Man of a Thousand Faces

(1) Lon Chaney, who was ~~knowed~~ *known* as "the man of a thousand faces," was born in Colorado in 1883. (2) Both his parents were unable to hear or speak, and as a child, Chaney communicated with them through gestures and facial

expressions. (3) Later, his astonishing ability to express himself in pantomime was often ~~credit~~ *credited* to his childhood experiences with his parents.

(4) In the most famous of his many silent-film roles, Chaney played repulsive-appearing characters who made the audience feel both disgust and pity. (5) In *The Hunchback of Notre Dame,* which was ~~maked~~ *made* in 1923, Chaney played Quasimodo, a grotesquely deformed man who nevertheless aroused compassion. (6) In *The Phantom of the Opera,* which was ~~bringed~~ *brought* out two years later, Chaney played a hideous-looking composer who haunted the sewers under the Paris Opera; again he was able to make people see the man behind the ugliness.

(7) Chaney is also ~~celebrate~~ *celebrated* for his use of makeup and extraordinary disguises. (8) In *The Hunchback of Notre Dame,* for example, he wore a forty-pound rubber hump, which was ~~attach~~ *attached* to a thirty-pound breastplate. (9) A hairy rubber skin was then ~~stretch~~ *stretched* over everything. (10) His crooked nose and ~~mismatch~~ *mismatched* eyes were molded onto his face with wax.

(11) Chaney's great talents as an actor, as well as his use of those creative, if sometimes painful, disguises, have ~~gave~~ *given* him a ~~distinguish~~ *distinguished* place in the history of film. (12) Ironically, Chaney died of throat cancer when he was only forty-seven; in his last days he was ~~force~~ *forced* once again to pantomime what he wanted to communicate.

CHAPTER 29

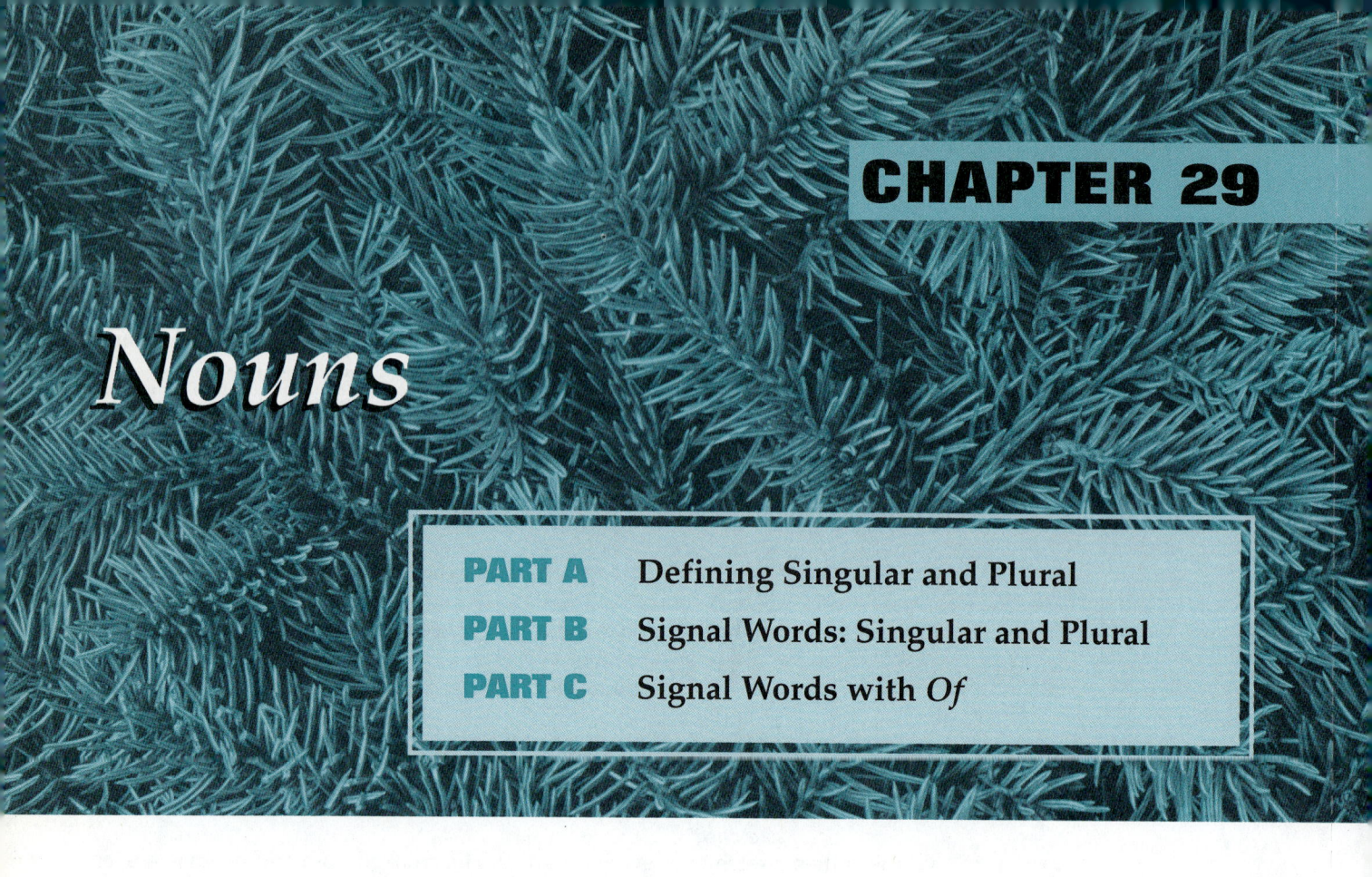

Nouns

PART A Defining Singular and Plural
PART B Signal Words: Singular and Plural
PART C Signal Words with *Of*

PART A Defining Singular and Plural

Nouns are words that refer to people, places, or things. They can be either singular or plural. **Singular** means one. **Plural** means more than one.

Singular	Plural
the glass	glasses
a lamp	lamps
a lesson	lessons

■ As you can see, nouns usually add *-s* or *-es* to form the plural.

Some nouns form their plurals in other ways. Here are a few examples:

Singular	Plural
child	children
crisis	crises
criterion	criteria
foot	feet *(continued)*

(continued) Singular	Plural
goose	geese
man	men
medium	media
memorandum	memoranda (memorandums)
phenomenon	phenomena
tooth	teeth
woman	women

These nouns ending in -f or -fe change endings to -ves in the plural:

Singular	Plural
half	halves
knife	knives
life	lives
scarf	scarves
shelf	shelves
wife	wives
wolf	wolves

Hyphenated nouns form plurals by adding -s or -es to the main word:

Singular	Plural
brother-in-law	brothers-in-law
maid-of-honor	maids-of-honor
passer-by	passers-by

Other nouns do not change at all to form the plural; here are a few examples:

Singular	Plural
deer	deer
fish	fish
moose	moose
sheep	sheep

If you are unsure about the plural of a noun, check a dictionary. For example, if you look up the noun *woman* in the dictionary, you may see an entry like this:

woman, women

The first word listed, *woman*, is the singular form of the noun; the second word, *women*, is the plural.

Some dictionaries list the plural form of a noun only if the plural is unusual. If no plural is listed, that noun probably adds *-s* or *-es*.* *Remember:* Do not add an *-s* to words that form plurals by changing an internal letter. For example, the plural of *man* is *men*, not *mens*; the plural of *woman* is *women*, not *womens*; the plural of *foot* is *feet*, not *feets*.

PRACTICE 1

Make these singular nouns plural.

1. man *men*
2. half *halves*
3. foot *feet*
4. son-in-law *sons-in-law*
5. moose *moose*
6. life *lives*
7. tooth *teeth*
8. medium *media*
9. woman *women*
10. crisis *crises*
11. passer-by *passers-by*
12. criterion *criteria*
13. shelf *shelves*
14. mouse *mice*
15. child *children*
16. father-in-law *fathers-in-law*
17. knife *knives*
18. deer *deer*
19. secretary *secretaries*
20. goose *geese*

PART B Signal Words: Singular and Plural

A **signal word** tells you whether a singular or a plural noun usually follows.

■ These signal words tell you that a singular noun usually follows:

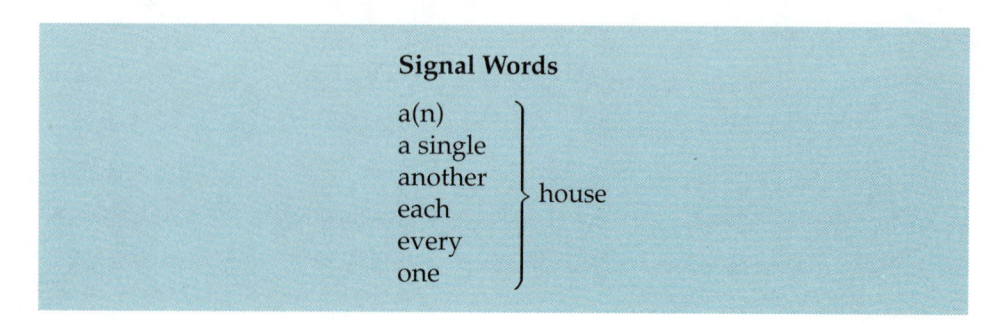

Signal Words

a(n)
a single
another } house
each
every
one

---

* For more work on spelling plurals, see Chapter 37, "Spelling," Part H.

■ These signal words tell you that a plural noun usually follows:

Signal Words

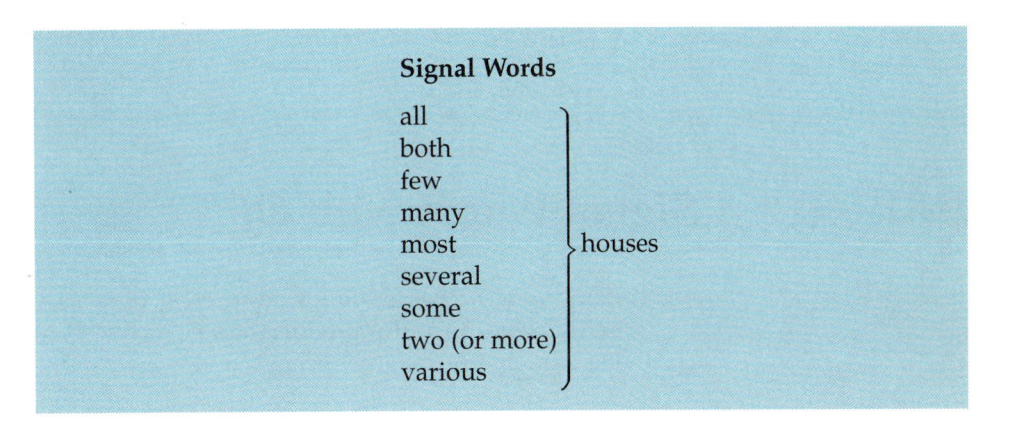

all
both
few
many
most } houses
several
some
two (or more)
various

PRACTICE 2

Some of the following sentences contain incorrect singulars and plurals. Correct the errors. Put a C after correct sentences.

1. Following the lead of celebrities like Naomi Campbell and Demi Moore, many ~~woman~~ *women* are experimenting with the body painting known as *mehndi*.

2. Although some ~~American~~ *Americans* think mehndi is a new trend, it actually dates back thousands of years in India, Africa, and the Middle East.

3. Today, every traditional Hindu ~~brides~~ *bride* still is painted to celebrate her wedding, and in Morocco, mehndi is used to ward off evil.

4. In the United States, however, mehndi customers typically have their hands, necks, ~~foots~~ *feet*, legs, or even backs painted only for the beautiful effects.

5. Most mehndi ~~painter~~ *painters* use the ancient traditional patterns in their detailed designs.

6. The paint is made by mixing crushed henna ~~leafs~~ *leaves* with tea, lemon juice, and several different oils.

7. This henna paste stays on for about twelve hours; then it cracks off and leaves a brown-orange stain that lasts about a month. *C*

8. Few mehndi ~~artist~~ *artists* can use just their fingers to create the intricate decorations.

9. Instead, they use a fine-tipped ~~funnels~~ *funnel* to paint the elaborate patterns.

10. Besides the gorgeous designs, there is another ~~bonuses~~ *bonus* for customers; they can explore mehndi's various ~~connection~~ *connections* with meditation, spirituality, good fortune, and love.

PART C   Signal Words with *Of*

Many signal words are followed by *of . . .* or *of the. . . .* Usually, these signal words are followed by a **plural** noun (or a collective noun) because they really refer to one or more from a larger group.

> one of the
> each of the   } pictures is . . .
>
> many of the
> a few of the } pictures are . . .
> lots of the

- *Be careful:* The signal words *one of the* and *each of the* are followed by a **plural** noun, but the verb is **singular** because only the signal word (*one* or *each*) is the real subject.*

> *One* of the coats *is* on sale.
>
> *Each* of the flowers *smells* sweet.

PRACTICE 3

Fill in your own nouns in the following sentences. Use a different noun in each sentence. *Answers will vary.*

1. Since Jacob wrote each of his ____exams____ with care, the A's came as no surprise.

2. You are one of the few ____people____ I know who can listen to the radio and watch television at the same time.

3. Naomi liked several of the new ____rock singers____ but remained faithful to her long-time favorites.

4. Many of the ____skateboarders____ wore Walkmans.

5. Determined to win the Salesperson of the Year award, Clyde called on all his ____clients____ two or three times a month.

---

* For more work on this type of construction, see Chapter 26, "Present Tense (Agreement)," Part C.

CHAPTER 29   Nouns   395

6. One of the _children_ was wearing a down jacket.

7. Before spring, each of these old _sheds_ will have to be demolished.

PRACTICE 4   Review

Proofread the following essay for errors in singular and plural nouns. Correct the errors above the lines.

Hot off the Press

(1) Although it was certainly not the *New York Times* or the *Washington Post*, the first newspaper was a ~~media~~ _medium_ not all that different from the papers we read today.

(2) In 59 B.C., the Roman government began to publish *Action Journal*, which carried many ~~story~~ _stories_ of social events and political activities. (3) Roman men and ~~woman~~ _women_ could read about the births of ~~childrens~~ _children_, as well as the marriages and deaths of other ~~citizen~~ _citizens_. (4) The trials of ~~thiefs~~ _thieves_ and other lawless persons—and their executions—were also described. (5) In addition, this early newspaper reviewed the many spectacular ~~show~~ _shows_ presented at the Colosseum.

(6) Several ~~century~~ _centuries_ later, on another ~~continents~~ _continent_, the Chinese government began publishing a news sheet. (7) Each government ~~officials~~ _official_ could read about social and political occurrences, as well as about court intrigues and gossip. (8) Many ~~diplomat~~ _diplomats_ also found out about natural ~~phenomenons~~ _phenomena_—like eclipses and meteors—which they believed were good or bad omens. (9) This court chronicle was the first printed newspaper. (10) It lasted for almost 1,200 ~~year~~ _years_ until the Chinese Empire fell in 1911.

(11) The main difference between both of these ~~newspaper~~ _newspapers_ and today's U.S. press is that they were state-run and state-controlled. (12) Roman and Chinese ~~authoritys~~ _authorities_ applied strict ~~criterions~~ _criteria_ of censorship to every ~~articles~~ _article_. (13) In contrast, the modern press, freely written and circulated, was begun by Dutch merchants in the two ~~city~~ _cities_ of Antwerp and Venice during the seventeenth century.

CHAPTER 30

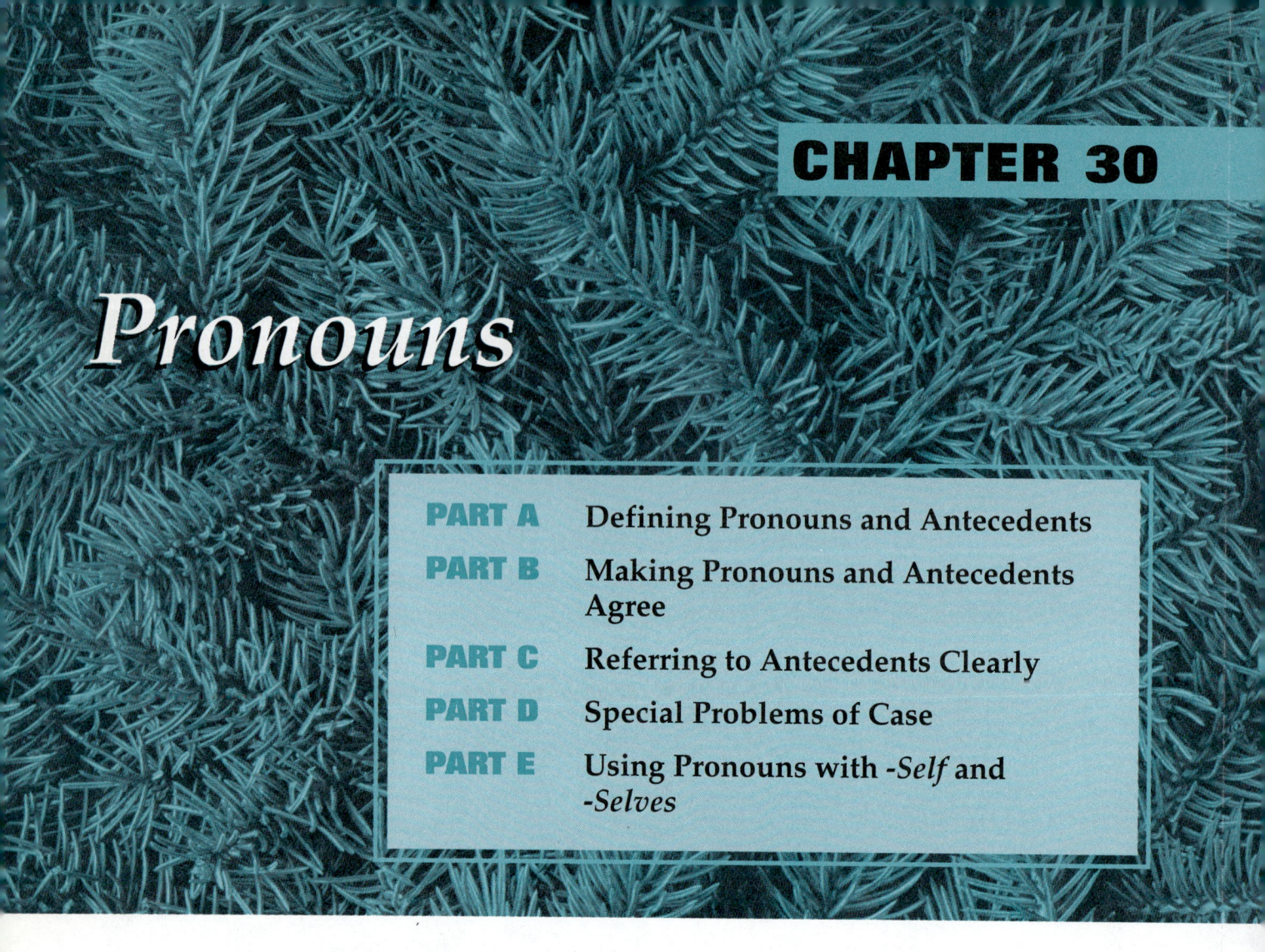

Pronouns

PART A   Defining Pronouns and Antecedents
PART B   Making Pronouns and Antecedents Agree
PART C   Referring to Antecedents Clearly
PART D   Special Problems of Case
PART E   Using Pronouns with *-Self* and *-Selves*

PART A   Defining Pronouns and Antecedents

Pronouns take the place of or refer to nouns, other pronouns, or phrases. The word that the pronoun refers to is called the **antecedent** of the pronoun.

1. *Eric* ordered *baked chicken* because *it* is *his* favorite dish.
2. *Simone and Lee* painted *their* room.
3. *I* like *camping in the woods* because *it* gives *me* a chance to be alone with *my* thoughts.

- In sentence 1, *it* refers to the antecedent *baked chicken,* and *his* refers to the antecedent *Eric.*
- In sentence 2, *their* refers to the plural antecedent *Simone and Lee.*
- In sentence 3, *it* refers to the antecedent *camping in the woods.* This antecedent is a whole phrase. *Me* and *my* refer to the pronoun antecedent *I.*

CHAPTER 30 Pronouns

PRACTICE 1

In each sentence, a pronoun is circled. Write the pronoun first and then its antecedent, as shown in the example.

EXAMPLE Have you ever wondered why we exchange rings in (our) wedding ceremonies?   _our_   _we_

1. When a man buys a wedding ring, (he) follows an age-old tradition.   _he_   _man_

2. Rich Egyptian grooms gave (their) brides gold rings five thousand years ago.   _their_   _grooms_

3. To Egyptian couples, the ring represented eternal love; (it) was a circle without beginning or end.   _it_   _ring_

4. By Roman times, gold rings had become more affordable, so ordinary people could also buy (them).   _them_   _rings_

5. Still, many a Roman youth had to scrimp to buy (his) bride a ring.   _his_   _youth_

6. The first bride to slip a diamond ring on (her) finger lived in Venice about five hundred years ago.   _her_   _bride_

7. The Venetians knew that setting a diamond in a ring was an excellent way of displaying (its) beauty.   _its_   _diamond_

8. Nowadays, a man and a woman exchange rings to symbolize the equality of (their) relationship.   _their_   _a man and a woman_

PART B Making Pronouns and Antecedents Agree

A pronoun must *agree* with its antecedent in number and person.*

> 1. When *Tom* couldn't find *his* pen, *he* asked to borrow mine.
> 2. The three *sisters* wanted to start *their* own business.

---

* For more work on pronoun agreement, see Chapter 19, "Revising for Consistency and Parallelism," Part B.

- In sentence 1, *Tom* is the antecedent of *his* and *he*. Since *Tom* is singular and masculine, the pronouns referring to *Tom* are also singular and masculine.

- In sentence 2, *sisters* is the antecedent of *their*. Since *sisters* is plural, the pronoun referring to *sisters* must also be plural.

As you can see from these examples, making pronouns agree with their antecedents is usually easy. However, three special cases can be tricky.

1. Indefinite Pronouns

anybody
anyone
everybody
everyone
nobody
no one
one
somebody
someone

Each of these words is **singular.** Any pronoun that refers to one of them must also be singular: *he, him, his, she,* or *her.*

3. *Anyone* can quit smoking if *he* or *she* wants to.
4. *Everybody* should do *his* or *her* best to keep the reception area uncluttered.

- *Anyone* and *everybody* require the singular pronouns *he, she, his,* and *her.*

In the past, writers used *he* or *him* to refer to both men and women. Now, however, many writers use *he or she, his or her,* or *him or her.* Of course, if *everyone* or *someone* is a woman, use *she* or *her*; if *everyone* or *someone* is a man, use *he* or *him.* For example:

5. *Someone* left *her* new dress in a bag on the sofa.
6. *Everyone* is wearing *his* new tie.

PRACTICE 2

Fill in the correct pronoun and circle its antecedent. Make sure each pronoun agrees in number and person with its antecedent.

1. (Anyone) can become a good cook if __he or she__ tries.
2. (Someone) dropped __her__ lipstick behind the bookcase.
3. (No one) in the mixed doubles let __his or her__ guard down for a minute.
4. (Everybody) wants __his or her__ career to be rewarding.
5. (Everyone) is entitled to __his or her__ full pension.

CHAPTER 30 Pronouns

6. (Mr. Hernow) will soon be here, so please get __his__ contract ready.

7. (One) should wear a necktie that doesn't clash with __his__ suit.

8. The movie theater was so cold that (nobody) took off __his or her__ coat.

2. Special Singular Antecedents

each (of) . . .
either (of) . . .
neither (of) . . .
every one (of) . . .
one (of) . . .

Each of these constructions is **singular.** Any pronoun that refers to one of them must also be singular.*

7. *Neither* of the two men paid for *his* ticket to the wrestling match.
8. *Each* of the houses has *its* own special charm.

- The subject of sentence 7 is the singular *neither*, not *men*; therefore, the singular masculine pronoun *his* is required.
- The subject of sentence 8 is the singular *each*, not the plural *houses*; therefore, the singular pronoun *its* is required.

PRACTICE 3

Fill in the correct pronoun and circle its antecedent. Make sure each pronoun agrees in number and person with its antecedent.

1. (Each) of the men wanted to be __his__ own boss.
2. (One) of the saleswomen left __her__ sample case on the counter.
3. (Every one) of the colts has a white star on __its__ forehead.
4. (Neither) of the actors knew __his or her__ lines by heart.
5. (Neither) of the dentists had __his or her__ office remodeled.
6. (Each) of these arguments has __its__ flaws and __its__ strengths.
7. (Every one) of the jazz bands had __its__ own distinctive style.
8. (Either) of these telephone answering machines will work very well if __it__ is properly cared for.

---

* For more work on prepositional phrases, see Chapter 23, "The Simple Sentence," Part B.

3. Collective Nouns

Collective nouns represent a group of people but are usually considered **singular.** They usually take singular pronouns.

> 9. The *jury* reached *its* decision in three hours.
> 10. The debating *team* is well known for *its* fighting spirit.

- In sentence 9, *jury* is a collective noun. Although it has several members, the jury acts as a unit—as one. Therefore, the antecedent *jury* takes the singular pronoun *its*.

- In sentence 10, why does the collective noun *team* take the singular pronoun *its*?

Here is a partial list of collective nouns:

Common Collective Nouns

class	family	panel
college	flock	school
committee	government	society
company	group	team
faculty	jury	tribe

PRACTICE 4

Read each sentence carefully for meaning. Circle the antecedent and then fill in the correct pronoun.

1. My (family) gave me all _its_ support when I went back to school.

2. The (government) should reexamine _its_ domestic policy.

3. The (college) honored _its_ oldest graduate with a reception.

4. (Eco-Wise) has just begun to market a new pollution-free detergent that _it_ is proud of.

5. The (panel) will soon announce _its_ recommendations to the hospital.

6. The two (teams) gave _their_ fans a real show.

7. The (jury) deliberated for six days before _it_ reached a verdict.

8. After touring the Great Pyramid, the (class) headed back to Cairo in _its_ air-conditioned bus.

PART C Referring to Antecedents Clearly

A pronoun must refer *clearly* to its antecedent. Avoid vague, repetitious, or ambiguous pronoun reference.

1. Vague pronoun:	At the box office, *they* said that tickets were no longer available.
2. Revised:	The cashier at the box office said....
	or
3. Revised:	At the box office, I was told....

- In sentence 1, who is *they*? *They* does not clearly refer to an antecedent.
- In sentence 2, *they* is replaced by *the cashier*.
- In sentence 3, the problem is avoided by a change of language.*

4. Repetitious pronoun:	In the article, *it* says that Tyrone was a boxer.
5. Revised:	The article says that....
	or
6. Revised:	It says that....

- In sentence 4, *it* merely repeats *article*, the antecedent preceding it.
- Use either the pronoun or its antecedent, but not both.

7. Ambiguous pronoun:	Mr. Tedesco told his son that *his* car had a flat tire.
8. Revised:	Mr. Tedesco told his son that the younger man's car had a flat tire.
9. Revised:	Mr. Tedesco told his son Paul that Paul's car had a flat tire.

- In sentence 7, *his* could refer either to Mr. Tedesco or to his son.

---

*For more work on using exact language, see Chapter 21, "Revising for Language Awareness," Part A.

Practice 5

Revise the following sentences, removing vague, repetitious, or ambiguous pronoun references. Make the pronoun references clear and specific. *Answers may vary.*

1. In this book it says that most ducks and geese travel between forty and sixty miles per hour.

    Revised: *This book says that most ducks and geese travel between forty and sixty miles per hour.*

2. On the radio they warned drivers that the Interstate Bridge was closed.

    Revised: *The radio announcer warned drivers that the Interstate Bridge was closed.*

3. Sandra told her friend that she shouldn't have turned down the promotion.

    Revised: *Sandra told her friend Janet that Janet shouldn't have turned down the promotion.*

4. In North Carolina they raise tobacco.

    Revised: *Tobacco is raised in North Carolina.*

5. The moving van struck a lamppost; luckily, no one was injured, but it was badly damaged.

    Revised: *The moving van struck a lamppost; luckily, no one was injured, but the lamppost was badly damaged.*

6. In this college, they require every entering student to take a hearing test.

    Revised: *This college requires every entering student to take a hearing test.*

7. Professor Grazel told his parrot that he had to stop chewing telephone cords.

    Revised: *Professor Grazel told his parrot to stop chewing telephone cords.*

CHAPTER 30 Pronouns 403

8. Vandalism was so out of control at the local high school that they stole sinks and lighting fixtures.

    Revised: *Vandalism was so out of control at the local high school that sinks and lighting fixtures were stolen.*

9. On the news, it said that the president hopes to present his new tax bill to Congress in the next two weeks.

    Revised: *The news broadcast reported that the president hopes to present his new tax bill to Congress in the next two weeks.*

10. Mr. Highwater informed his cousin that his wholesale rug business was a success.

    Revised: *Mr. Highwater informed his cousin Joe that Joe's wholesale rug business was a success.*

11. The saleswoman at Wigged Out, she said I look like a rock star in this wig.

    Revised: *The saleswoman at Wigged Out said that I look like a rock star in this wig.*

12. I don't watch Sunday night wrestling because they show ten commercials an hour.

    Revised: *I don't watch Sunday night wrestling because the station airs ten commercials an hour.*

13. Keiko is an excellent singer, yet she has never taken a lesson in it.

    Revised: *Keiko is an excellent singer, yet she has never taken a voice lesson.*

14. Rosalie's mother said she was glad she had decided to become a nurse.

    Revised: *Rosalie's mother said she was glad Rosalie had decided to become a nurse.*

15. At my church, they run a soup kitchen for people who need a hot meal.

    Revised: *My church runs a soup kitchen for people who need a hot meal.*

PART D Special Problems of Case

Personal pronouns take different forms depending on how they are used in a sentence. Pronouns can be **subjects**, **objects**, or **possessives**.

Pronouns used as **subjects** are in the **subjective case**:

1. *He* and *I* go backpacking together.
2. The peaches were so ripe that *they* fell from the trees.

■ *He*, *I*, and *they* are in the subjective case.

Pronouns that are **objects of verbs** or **prepositions** are in the **objective case**. Pronouns that are **subjects of infinitives** are also in the **objective case**:

3. A sudden downpour soaked *her*. (object of verb)
4. Please give this card to *him*. (object of preposition)
5. We want *them* to leave right now. (subject of infinitive)

■ *Her*, *him*, and *them* are in the objective case.

Pronouns that **show ownership** are in the **possessive case**:

6. The carpenters left *their* tools on the windowsill.
7. This flower has lost *its* brilliant color.

■ *Their* and *its* are in the possessive case.

Pronoun Case Chart

Singular	Subjective	Objective	Possessive
1st person	I	me	my (mine)
2nd person	you	you	your (yours)
3rd person	he	him	his (his)
	she	her	her (hers)
	it	it	its (its)
	who	whom	whose
	whoever	whomever	
Plural			
1st person	we	us	our (ours)
2nd person	you	you	your (yours)
3rd person	they	them	their (theirs)

Using the correct case is usually fairly simple, but three problems require special care.

1. Case in Compound Constructions

A **compound construction** consists of two nouns, two pronouns, or a noun and a pronoun joined by *and*. Make sure that the pronouns in a compound construction are in the correct case.

> 8. *Serge* and *I* went to the pool together.
> 9. Between *you* and *me*, this party is a bore.

- In sentence 8, *Serge* and *I* are subjects.
- In sentence 9, *you* and *me* are objects of the preposition *between*.

Never use *myself* as a substitute for either *I* or *me* in compound constructions.

PRACTICE 6

Determine the case required by each sentence, and circle the correct pronoun.

1. (**He**, Him) and Harriet plan to enroll in the police academy.
2. A snowdrift stood between (I, **me**) and the subway entrance.
3. Tony used the software and then returned it to Barbara and (I, **me**, myself).
4. The reporter's questions caught June and (we, **us**) off guard.
5. By noon, Julio and (**he**, him) had already cleaned the garage and mowed the lawn.
6. These charts helped (she, **her**) and (I, **me**) with our statistics homework.
7. Professor Woo gave Diane and (she, **her**) extra time to finish the geology final.
8. Between you and (I, **me**), I have always preferred country music.

2. Case in Comparisons

Pronouns that complete **comparisons** may be in the **subjective, objective,** or **possessive** case:

> 10. His son is as stubborn as *he*. (subjective)
> 11. The cutbacks will affect you more than *her*. (objective)
> 12. This essay is better organized than *mine*. (possessive)

To decide on the correct pronoun, simply complete the comparison mentally and then choose the pronoun that naturally follows:

> 13. She trusts him more than I . . . (trust him).
> 14. She trusts him more than . . . (she trusts) . . . me.

■ Note that in sentences 13 and 14, the case of the pronoun in the comparison can change the meaning of the entire sentence.

PRACTICE 7

Circle the correct pronoun.

1. Your hair is much shorter than (she, her, *hers*).
2. We tend to assume that others are more self-confident than (*we*, us).
3. She is just as funny as (*he*, him).
4. Is Hanna as trustworthy as (*he*, her)?
5. Although they were both research scientists, he received a higher salary than (*she*, her).
6. I am not as involved in this project as (*they*, them).
7. Sometimes we become impatient with people who are not as quick to learn as (*we*, us).
8. Michael's route involved more overnight stops than (us, our, *ours*).

3. Use of Who (or Whoever) and Whom (or Whomever)

Who and **whoever** are in the **subjective** case. **Whom** and **whomever** are in the **objective** case.

> 15. *Who* is at the door?
> 16. For *whom* is that gift?
> 17. *Whom* is that gift for?

■ In sentence 15, *who* is the subject.

■ The same question is written two ways in sentences 16 and 17. In both, *whom* is the object of the preposition *for*.

■ Sometimes, deciding on *who* or *whom* can be tricky:

> 18. I will give the raise to *whoever* deserves it.
>
> 19. Give it to *whomever* you like.

- In sentence 18, *whoever* is the subject in the clause *whoever deserves it*.
- In sentence 19, *whomever* is the object in the clause *whomever you like*.

If you have trouble deciding on *who* or *whom*, change the sentence to eliminate the problem.

> 20. I prefer working with people *whom* I don't know as friends.
>   or
>   I prefer working with people I don't know as friends.

PRACTICE 8

Circle the correct pronoun.

1. (**Who**, Whom) will deliver the layouts to the ad agency?

2. To (who, **whom**) are you speaking?

3. (**Who**, Whom) prefers hiking to skiing?

4. For (who, **whom**) are those boxes piled in the corner?

5. The committee will award the scholarship to (whoever, **whomever**) it chooses.

6. (Who, **Whom**) do you wish to invite to the open house?

7. At (who, **whom**) did the governor fling the cream pie?

8. I will hire (**whoever**, whomever) can use a computer and speak Korean.

PART E Using Pronouns with -*Self* and -*Selves*

Pronouns with -*self* or -*selves* can be used in two ways—as reflexives or as intensives.

A reflexive pronoun indicates that someone did something to himself or herself:

> 1. My daughter Miriam felt very grown up when she learned to dress *herself*.

- In sentence 1, Miriam did something to *herself*; she *dressed herself*.

An intensive pronoun emphasizes the noun or pronoun it refers to:

> 2. Anthony *himself* was surprised at how relaxed he felt during the interview.

■ In sentence 2, *himself* emphasizes that Anthony—much to his surprise—was not nervous at the interview.

The following chart will help you choose the correct reflexive or intensive pronoun.

	Antecedent	Reflexive or Intensive Pronoun
Singular	I	myself
	you	yourself
	he	himself
	she	herself
	it	itself
Plural	we	ourselves
	you	yourselves
	they	themselves

Note that in the plural *-self* is changed to *-selves*.

■ *Be careful:* Do not use reflexives or intensives as substitutes for the subject of a sentence.

> Incorrect: Harry and *myself* will be there on time.
>
> Correct: Harry and *I* will be there on time.

PRACTICE 9

Fill in the correct reflexive or intensive pronoun. Be careful to make pronouns and antecedents agree.

1. Though he hates to cook, André __himself__ sautéed the mushrooms.

2. Rhoda found __herself__ in a strange city with only the phone number of a cousin whom she had not seen for years.

3. Her coffee machine automatically turns __itself__ on in the morning and off in the evening.

4. The librarian and I rearranged the children's section __ourselves__.

5. When it comes to horror films, I know that you consider _yourself_ an expert.

6. They _themselves_ didn't care if they arrived on time or not.

7. After completing a term paper, I always buy _myself_ a little gift to celebrate.

8. Larry _himself_ was surprised at how quickly he grew to like ancient history.

PRACTICE 10   Review

Proofread the following essay for pronoun errors. Then write the correct pronoun above the line.

The Many Lives of Jackie Chan

(1) Few movie stars can claim a career as unusual as ~~him~~ [his]. (2) For one thing, Jackie Chan usually performs his death-defying stunts ~~hisself~~ [himself]. (3) Although he was a huge star in Asia for more than twenty years, fame eluded him in the United States until recently.

(4) Chan was born on April 7, 1954, in Hong Kong, but ~~him~~ [he] and his parents soon moved to Canberra, Australia. (5) When he was only seven, he was sent back to Hong Kong to attend the Chinese Opera Research Institute. (6) At the school, ~~they~~ [experts] trained him in singing, acting, dancing, sword fighting, acrobatics, and kung fu. (7) When the Chinese Opera Research Institute closed in 1971, ~~their~~ [its] training paid off for Chan, but not in the way his parents expected.

(8) Chan worked as a stuntman and fight choreographer and landed acting roles in several films, including Bruce Lee's *Enter the Dragon.* (9) Lee~~, he~~ died in 1973, and Chan was the natural choice to fill Lee's shoes. (10) In several films, Chan tried to imitate Lee, but the films were unsuccessful. (11) In 1978, however, Chan came up with the idea of turning Lee's tough style into comedy. (12) *Snake in the Eagle's Shadow* and *Drunken Master* were hilarious hits; ~~it~~ [they] established "kung fu comedy." (13) Jackie Chan became one of Hong Kong's most popular stars. (14) However, Hollywood directors did not appreciate Chan as a stuntman,

comedian, director, or scriptwriter when he first came to the United States in 1980. (15) Chan understood his own strengths better than ~~them~~ *they*, but he couldn't gain much filmmaking control, and every film flopped. (16) Chan returned to Hong Kong, but ~~him~~ *he* and his fans always believed he could make a U.S. comeback.

(17) When *Rumble in the Bronx,* China's most popular film ever, was dubbed in English, Chan finally began to attract attention in the United States. (18) Each of his English-dubbed films that followed worked ~~their~~ *its* way up the charts. (19) *Rush Hour,* Chan's first U.S. movie in more than thirteen years, was released in 1998. (20) Now Jackie Chan's U.S. films are being received almost as well as ~~its~~ *their* Hong Kong counterparts.

CHAPTER 31

Prepositions

PART A Working with Prepositional Phrases
PART B Prepositions in Common Expressions

PART A Working with Prepositional Phrases

Prepositions are words like *about, at, behind, into, of, on,* and *with*.* They are followed by a noun or a pronoun, which is called the **object** of the preposition. The preposition and its object are called a **prepositional phrase.**

1. Ms. Fairworth remained *in the reading room.*
2. Students *with a 3.5 grade average* will receive a special award.
3. Traffic *at this corner* is dangerously heavy.

- In sentence 1, the prepositional phrase *in the reading room* explains where Ms. Fairworth remained.
- In sentence 2, the prepositional phrase *with a 3.5 grade average* describes which students will receive a special award.
- Which is the prepositional phrase in sentence 3?

  at this corner

- What word does it describe?

  traffic

---

* For more work on prepositions, see Chapter 23, "The Simple Sentence," Part B.

411

In/On *for Time*

Two prepositions often confused are *in* and *on*. Use *in* before months not followed by a specific date, before seasons, and before years that do not include specific dates.

1. *In March,* the skating rink will finally open for business.
2. *In the summer,* I earn extra money as a lifeguard.
3. Rona expects to pay off her car *in 2005.*

Use *on* before days of the week, before holidays, and before months if a date follows.

4. *On Sunday,* the Kingston family spent the day at the beach.
5. Everyone is looking forward to the fireworks *on July Fourth.*
6. *On January 6,* Bernard left for a month of mountain climbing.

PRACTICE 1

Write either *in* or *on* in the following sentences.

1. __On__ Labor Day __in__ 1998, Mark McGwire hit his sixty-first home run of the season.

2. He thus tied the record set __in__ 1961 by Roger Maris, a record that had stood for thirty-seven years.

3. McGwire proceeded to hit his sixty-second home run the following day, breaking Maris's record set __on__ September 8, 1998.

4. __On__ the following Sunday, Sammy Sosa hit *his* sixty-first home run; McGwire and Sosa continued to bat homers in an unusually supportive competition until the season ended __on__ September 28.

5. Although McGwire set the official record at seventy home runs, the rivalry generated a level of excitement and appreciation not seen since baseball players went on strike __in__ 1994.

In/On for Place

In means *inside* a place.

> 1. Tonia put her CD player *in the bedroom.*
> 2. Many country groups got their start *in Nashville.*

On means *on top of* or *at a particular place.*

> 3. That mess *on your desk* needs to be cleared off.
> 4. Pizza Parlor will be opening a new parlor *on Highland Avenue.*

PRACTICE 2

Write either *in* or *on* in the following sentences.

1. No official records were kept of black baseball played __in__ the segregated United States of the 1930s and 1940s, but Josh Gibson is credited with season home runs of sixty-nine, seventy-five, and even eighty-four.

2. An incredibly powerful hitter, he once sent a home run so far out __on__ some railroad tracks that the mayor of the town had the homer measured—at 512 feet.

3. Gibson once hit a home run __in__ York, Pennsylvania, that landed __on__ the roof of a truck __on__ the Pennsylvania Turnpike.

4. __In__ winter league games __in__ Puerto Rico, he hit so many balls over the fences that fans hung signs __on__ the trunks of palm trees to show where the balls had landed.

5. A plaque __in__ the Baseball Hall of Fame __in__ Cooperstown, New York, estimates that Gibson hit a total of "almost 800" home runs, but other estimates say he topped 950.

PART B Prepositions in Common Expressions

Prepositions are often combined with other words to form fixed expressions. Determining the correct preposition in these expressions can sometimes be confusing. Following is a list of some troublesome expressions with prepositions. Consult a dictionary if you need help with others.

Expressions with Prepositions

Expression	Example
according to	*According to* the directions, this flap fits here.
acquainted with	Tom became *acquainted with* his classmates.
addicted to	He is *addicted to* soap operas.
afraid of	Tanya is *afraid of* flying.
agree on (a plan)	Can we *agree on* our next step?
agree to (something or another's proposal)	Roberta *agreed to* her secretary's request for a raise.
angry about or at (a thing)	Jake seemed *angry about* his meager bonus.
angry with (a person)	Sonia couldn't stay *angry with* Felipe.
apply for (a position)	By accident, the twins *applied for* the same job.
approve of	Do you *approve of* bilingual education?
argue about (an issue)	I hate *arguing about* money.
argue with (a person)	Edna *argues with* everyone about everything.
capable of	Mario is *capable of* accomplishing anything he attempts.
complain about (a situation)	Patients *complained about* the long wait to see the dentist.
complain to (a person)	Knee-deep in snow, Jed vowed to *complain to* a maintenance person.
comply with	Each contestant must *comply with* contest regulations.
consist of	This article *consists of* nothing but false accusations and half-truths.
contrast with	The light blue shirt *contrasts* sharply *with* the dark brown tie.
correspond with (write)	We *corresponded with* her for two months before we met.
deal with	Ron *deals* well *with* temporary setbacks.
depend on	Miriam can be *depended on* to say the embarrassing thing.
differ from (something)	A typewriter *differs from* a computer in many ways.
differ with (a person)	Kathleen *differs with* you on the gun control issue.
different from	Children are often *different from* their parents.
displeased with	Ms. Withers was *displeased with* her doctor's advice to eat less fat.
fond of	Ed is *fond of* his pet tarantula.
grateful for	Be *grateful for* having so many good friends.
grateful to (someone)	The team was *grateful to* the coach for his inspiration and confidence.

Expressions with Prepositions
(continued)

Expression	Example
identical with	Scott's ideas are often *identical with* mine.
inferior to	Saturday's performance was *inferior to* the one I saw last week.
in search of	I hate to go *in search of* change at the last moment before the toll.
interested in	Willa is *interested in* results, not excuses.
interfere with	That dripping faucet *interferes with* my concentration.
object to	Martin *objected to* the judge's comment.
protect against	This heavy wool scarf will *protect* your throat *against* the cold.
reason with	It's hard to *reason with* an angry person.
rely on	If Toni made that promise, you can *rely on* it.
reply to	He wrote twice, but the president did not *reply to* his letters.
responsible for	Kit is *responsible for* making two copies of each document.
sensitive to	Professor Godfried is *sensitive to* his students' concerns.
shocked at	We were *shocked at* the graphic violence in that PG-rated film.
similar to	Some poisonous mushrooms appear quite *similar to* the harmless kind.
speak with (someone)	Geraldine will *speak with* her supervisor about a raise.
specialize in	This disc jockey *specializes in* jazz of the 1920s and the 1930s.
succeed in	Oscar *succeeded in* painting the roof in less than five hours.
superior to	It's clear that the remake is *superior to* the original.
take advantage of	Celia *took advantage of* the snow day to visit the science museum.
worry about	Never *worry about* more than one problem at a time.

PRACTICE 3

Fill in the preposition that correctly completes each of the following expressions.

1. According __*to*__ his own account, Howard Schultz discovered the allure of coffee bars while on a trip to Italy.

2. When his company objected __*to*__ his idea of expanding its retail coffee business, Schultz left his employer and started his own coffee bar.

3. Customers obviously approved __of__ Schultz's decision; within six months, he was serving more than a thousand coffee lovers a day in a tiny coffee bar in Seattle.

4. __In__ search __of__ ways to expand his business, Schultz opened another store in Seattle and one in Vancouver.

5. When his former employers decided to sell their stores, Schultz immediately took advantage __of__ the opportunity to buy them out.

6. That is how Howard Schultz acquired Starbucks and became responsible __for__ turning four stores that sold coffee beans into more than 1,500 coffee bars.

7. Now, of course, Schultz's enterprise specializes __in__ all kinds of novelty coffee drinks.

8. While many people are grateful __for__ the ever-increasing variety, others complain that it interferes __with__ the magic of that strong brewed cup of "real" coffee.

PRACTICE 4   Review

Proofread this essay for preposition errors. Cross out the errors and write corrections above the lines.

Dr. Daniel Hale Williams, Pioneer Surgeon

(1) ~~On~~ *In* a lifetime of many successes, Dr. Daniel Hale Williams's greatest achievement was to pioneer open-heart surgery.

(2) Young Williams, an African American who grew up in the mid-1800s, knew poverty. (3) He relied ~~to~~ *on* his wits to get by, becoming in turn a shoemaker, musician, and barber. (4) At the age of twenty-two, he met Dr. Henry Palmer, who soon saw he was capable ~~on~~ *of* becoming a physician. (5) Williams's medical education, the usual one at the time, consisted ~~in~~ *of* a two-year apprenticeship with Dr. Palmer, followed by three years at the Chicago Medical College, where he specialized ~~on~~ *in* surgery.

(6) It was an exciting time in medicine, for surgeons had just started using antiseptics to protect patients ~~for~~ *against* infection. (7) "Dr. Dan," as he was now called, became an expert ~~on~~ *in* the new surgical techniques and a leader in Chicago's med-

ical and African-American communities. (8) In 1891, he succeeded ~~with~~ *in* opening Provident Hospital, the first interracial hospital in the United States. (9) There, African Americans were assured first-rate medical care; moreover, black interns and nurses received thorough professional training.

(10) It was to Provident Hospital that frightened friends brought James Cornish ~~in~~ *on* July 9, 1893. (11) Near death, the young man had received a deep knife gash near his heart during a fight. (12) Sensitive to the dangerous situation, Dr. Williams decided to operate immediately. (13) According ~~with~~ *to* eyewitnesses, he first made a six-inch incision and removed Cornish's fifth rib. (14) Then he repaired a torn artery and stitched up the punctured sac surrounding the heart. (15) Fifty-one days later, Cornish left the hospital, recovered and deeply grateful ~~for~~ *to* Dr. Williams ~~to~~ *for* his life. (16) The age of open-heart surgery had begun.

(17) Much lay ahead for Dr. Williams. (18) He was responsible ~~to~~ *for* reorganizing the Freedmen's Hospital at Howard University from 1894 to 1898; ~~on~~ *in* 1913, he accepted an invitation from the American College of Surgeons and succeeded ~~on~~ *in* becoming its only African-American charter member. (19) The high point of his life, however, remained that night in 1893.

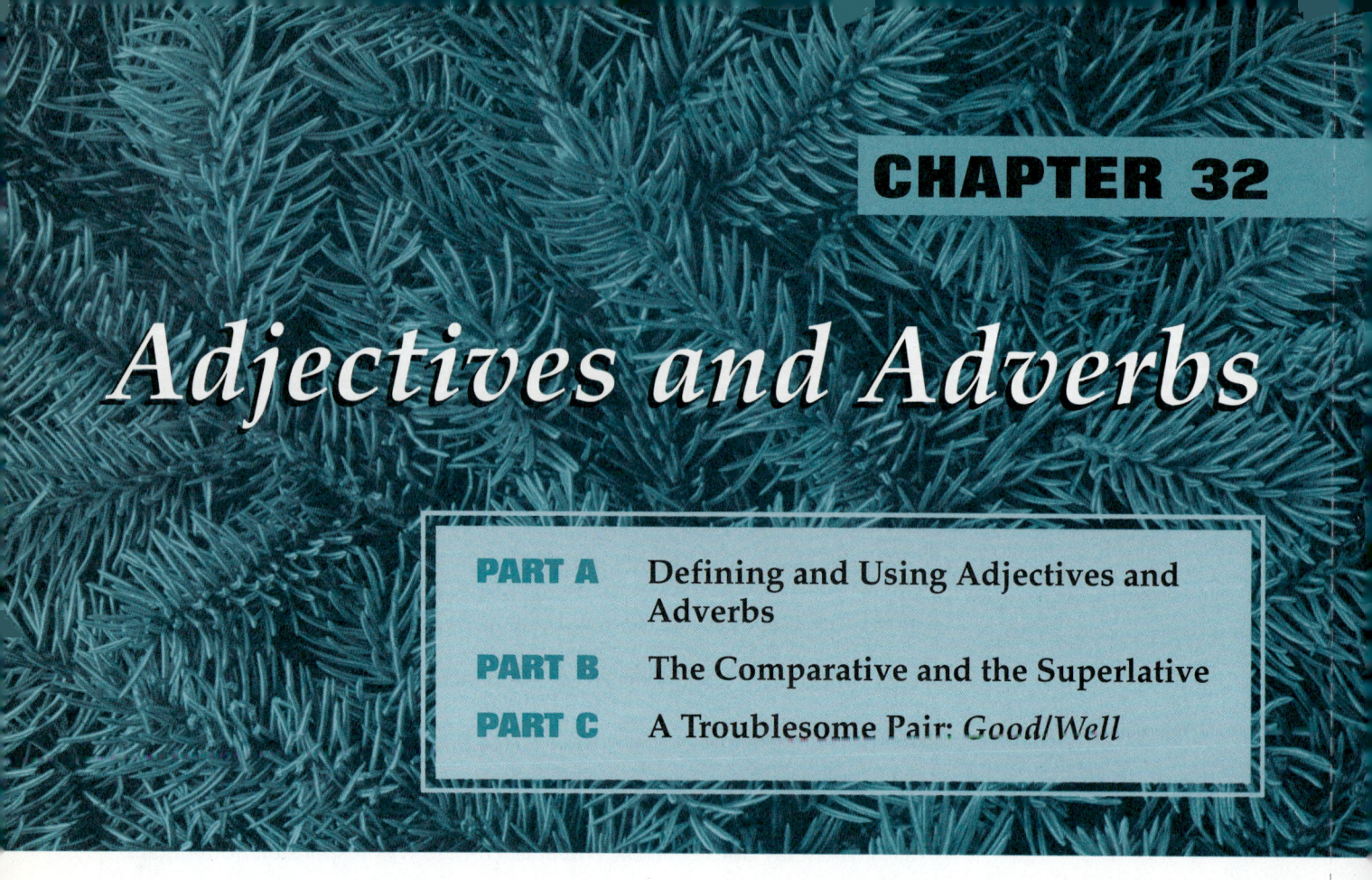

CHAPTER 32
Adjectives and Adverbs

> **PART A** Defining and Using Adjectives and Adverbs
>
> **PART B** The Comparative and the Superlative
>
> **PART C** A Troublesome Pair: *Good/Well*

PART A Defining and Using Adjectives and Adverbs

Adjectives and **adverbs** are two kinds of descriptive words. **Adjectives** describe or modify nouns or pronouns. They explain *what kind, which one,* or *how many.*

> 1. A *black* cat slept on the piano.
> 2. We felt *cheerful.*
> 3. *Three* windows in the basement need to be replaced.

- The adjective *black* describes the noun *cat.* It tells what kind of cat, a *black* one.
- The adjective *cheerful* describes the pronoun *we.* It tells what kind of mood we were in, *cheerful.*
- The adjective *three* describes the noun *windows.* It tells how many windows, *three.*

Adverbs describe or modify verbs, adjectives, and other adverbs. They tell *how, in what manner, when, where,* and *to what extent.*

4. Joe dances *gracefully*.

5. *Yesterday* Robert left for a weekend of camping.

6. Brigit is *extremely* tall.

7. He travels *very* rapidly on that skateboard.

- The adverb *gracefully* describes the verb *dances*. It tells how Joe dances, *gracefully*.
- The adverb *yesterday* describes the verb *left*. It tells when Robert left, *yesterday*.
- The adverb *extremely* describes the adjective *tall*. It tells how tall (to what extent), *extremely* tall.
- The adverb *very* describes the adverb *rapidly*, which describes the verb *travels*. It tells how rapidly he travels, *very* rapidly.

Many adjectives can be changed into adverbs by adding an *-ly* ending. For example, *glad* becomes *gladly*, *hopeful* becomes *hopefully*, *awkward* becomes *awkwardly*.

Note the pairs on this list; they are easily confused:

Adjectives	Adverbs
awful	awfully
bad	badly
poor	poorly
quick	quickly
quiet	quietly
real	really
sure	surely

8. The fish tastes *bad*.
9. It was *badly* prepared.

- In sentence 8, the adjective *bad* describes the noun *fish*.
- In sentence 9, the adverb *badly* describes the verb *was prepared*.

PRACTICE 1

Circle the correct adjective or adverb in parentheses. Remember that adjectives modify nouns or pronouns; adverbs modify verbs, adjectives, or adverbs.

1. Have you ever seen (**real**, really) emeralds?

2. Try to do your work in the library (quiet, **quietly**).

3. We will (glad, **gladly**) take you on a tour of the Crunchier Cracker factory.

4. Lee, a (high, **highly**) skilled electrician, rewired his entire house last year.

5. She made a (**quick**, quickly) stop at the photocopy machine.

6. It was (awful, **awfully**) cold today; the weather was terrible.

7. The fans from Cleveland (enthusiastic, **enthusiastically**) clapped for the Browns.

8. Are you (**sure**, surely) this bus stops in Dusty Gulch?

9. He (hasty, **hastily**) wrote the essay, leaving out several important ideas.

10. It was a funny joke, but the comedian told it (bad, **badly**).

11. Tina walked (careful, **carefully**) down the icy road.

12. Sam swims (poor, **poorly**) even though he spends as much time as he can posing on the beach.

13. Sasha the crow is an (**unusual**, unusually) pet and a (**humorous**, humorously) companion.

14. The painting is not (actual, **actually**) a Picasso; in fact, it is a (real, **really**) bad imitation.

15. It is an (extreme, **extremely**) hot day, and I (sure, **surely**) could go for some (**real**, really) orange juice.

PART B   The Comparative and the Superlative

The **comparative** of an adjective or adverb compares two persons or things:

1. Ben is *more creative* than Robert.
2. Marcia runs *faster* than the coach.

- In sentence 1, Ben is being compared with Robert.
- In sentence 2, Marcia is being compared with the coach.

The **superlative** of an adjective or adverb compares three or more persons or things:

3. Sancho is the *tallest* of the three brothers.
4. Marion is the *most intelligent* student in the class.

- In sentence 3, Sancho is being compared with the other two brothers.
- In sentence 4, Marion is being compared with all the other students in the class.

Adjectives and adverbs of one syllable usually form the **comparative** by adding *-er*. They form the **superlative** by adding *-est*.

Adjective	Comparative	Superlative
fast	fast*er*	fast*est*
smart	smart*er*	smart*est*
tall	tall*er*	tall*est*

Adjectives and adverbs of more than one syllable usually form the **comparative** by using *more*. They form the **superlative** by using *most*.

Adjective	Comparative	Superlative
beautiful	*more* beautiful	*most* beautiful
brittle	*more* brittle	*most* brittle
serious	*more* serious	*most* serious

Note, however, that adjectives that end in *-y* (like *happy, lazy,* and *sunny*) change the *-y* to *-i* and add *-er* and *-est*.

Adjective	Comparative	Superlative
happy	happ*ier*	happ*iest*
lazy	laz*ier*	laz*iest*
sunny	sunn*ier*	sunn*iest*

PRACTICE 2

Write the comparative or the superlative of the words in parentheses. Remember: Use the comparative to compare two items; use the superlative to compare more than two. Use *-er* or *-est* for one-syllable words; use *more* or *most* for words of more than one syllable.*

1. The ocean is _colder_ (cold) than we thought it would be.

2. Please read your lines again, _more slowly_ (slowly) this time.

3. Which of these two roads is the _shorter_ (short) route?

4. Which of these three highways is the _shortest_ (short) route?

5. Belkys is the _busiest_ (busy) person I know.

---

* If you have questions about spelling, see Chapter 37, "Spelling," Part G.

6. That red felt hat with feathers is the _most outlandish_ (outlandish) one I've seen.

7. Today is _warmer_ (warm) than yesterday, but Thursday was the _warmest_ (warm) day of the month.

8. The down coat you have selected is the _most expensive_ (expensive) one in the store.

9. Each one of Woody's stories is _funnier_ (funny) than the last.

10. As a rule, mornings in Los Angeles are _hazier_ (hazy) than afternoons.

11. Is Pete _taller_ (tall) than Louie? Is Pete the _tallest_ (tall) player on the team?

12. If you don't do these experiments _more carefully_ (carefully), you will blow up the chemistry lab.

13. This farmland is much _rockier_ (rocky) than the farmland in Iowa.

14. Therese says that Physics 201 is the _most challenging_ (challenging) course she has ever taken.

15. Mr. Wells is the _wisest_ (wise) and _most experienced_ (experienced) leader in the community.

PRACTICE 3

Proofread the following paragraph for comparative and superlative errors. Cross out unnecessary words and write your corrections above the lines.

(1) With the hope of making counterfeiting ~~more~~ harder than it used to be, the federal government has started to issue new currency. (2) The new $100 bill appeared in 1996, the $50 bill in 1997, and the $20 bill in 1998. (3) The currency has been designed more ~~carefuler~~ _carefully_ than it was in the past. (4) The ~~more~~ _most_ recent of the three bills, the $20, features a larger portrait of President Andrew Jackson than the one that appeared on the older twenty. (5) The picture is off center, and the numerals are bigger and ~~more~~ darker than they were. (6) All the new bills have a portrait-shaped watermark, which can be seen only when a bill is held to the light. (7) One of the ~~unusualest~~ _most unusual_ features is an embedded plastic thread that glows under ultraviolet light—red for the $100 bill, yellow for the $50, and green

for the $20. (8) Finally, the numeral in the lower right corner is printed in ink that looks green when seen straight on and black when seen from an angle. (9) Although the United States never recalls its currency, the old bills should be replaced naturally in about two years. (10) By then, everyone should be able to spot counterfeit currency more ~~easier~~ *easily* than before.

PART C A Troublesome Pair: *Good/Well*

Adjective	Comparative	Superlative
good	better	best
bad	worse	worst

Adverb	Comparative	Superlative
well	better	best
badly	worse	worst

Be especially careful not to confuse the adjective **good** with the adverb **well**:

1. Jessie is a *good* writer.
2. She writes *well*.

- *Good* is an **adjective** modifying *writer*.
- *Well* is an **adverb** modifying *writes*.

PRACTICE 4

Fill in either the adjective *good* or the adverb *well* in each blank.

1. Corned beef definitely goes __well__ with cabbage.

2. How __well__ do you understand Spanish?

3. He may not take phone messages very __well__, but he is __good__ when it comes to handling e-mail.

4. Exercise is a __good__ way to stay in shape; eating __well__ will help you maintain __good__ health.

5. Tony looks __good__ in his new beard and ponytail.

6. This is a __good__ arrangement: I wash, you dry.

7. On a rainy night, Sheila loves to curl up with a __good__ book.

8. The old Persian carpet and oak desk are a __good__ match; they go __well__ together.

9. At the finals, both teams played __well__; it was a __good__ game.

10. They are __good__ neighbors and are __well__ liked in the community.

PRACTICE 5

Fill in the correct comparative or superlative of the word in parentheses.

1. Lucinda is a __better__ (good) chemist than she is mathematician.

2. Bascomb was the __worst__ (bad) governor this state has ever had.

3. When it comes to breaking appointments, you are __worse__ (bad) than I.

4. September is the __best__ (good) month of the year for bird watching.

5. Jason used to be the __best__ (good) mechanic on the lot; now he is the __worst__ (bad).

6. Of the two sisters, Leah is the __better__ (good) markswoman.

7. You can carry cash when you travel, but using a credit card is __better__ (good).

8. Our goalie is the __best__ (good) in the league; yours is the __worst__ (bad).

9. When it comes to bad taste, movies are __worse__ (bad) than television.

10. The __worst__ part of going to a dentist is first sitting in that chair; I always feel __better__ (good) when I have said good-bye.

11. Your cold seems __worse__ (bad) than it was yesterday.

12. Gina likes rock climbing __better__ (good) than fishing; she prefers camping __best__ (good) of all.

13. A parka is the __best__ (good) protection against a cold wind; it is certainly __better__ (good) than a hat.

14. I don't think teenagers are any __worse__ (bad) now than they were in my generation.

15. Note taking is one of the __best__ (good) skills to acquire before you enter college.

PRACTICE 6   Review

Proofread the following essay for adjective and adverb errors. Correct errors by writing above the lines.

Julia Morgan, Architect

(1) Julia Morgan was one of San Francisco's ~~most~~ finest architects, as well as the first woman licensed as an architect in California. (2) In 1902, Morgan became the first woman to finish ~~successful~~ *successfully* the program in architecture at the School of Fine Arts in Paris. (3) Returning to San Francisco, she opened her own office and hired and trained a very talented staff that ~~eventual~~ *eventually* grew to thirty-five full-time architects. (4) Her first major commission was to reconstruct the Fairmont Hotel, one of the city's ~~bestest~~ *best*-known sites, which had been damaged ~~bad~~ *badly* in the 1906 earthquake. (5) Morgan earned her reputation by designing elegant homes and public buildings out of ~~inexpensively~~ *inexpensive* and available materials and by treating her clients ~~real good~~ *really well*. (6) She went on to design more than eight hundred residences, stores, churches, offices, and educational buildings, most of them in California. (7) Her ~~bestest~~ *best* customer was William Randolph Hearst, one of the country's ~~most rich~~ *richest* newspaper publishers. (8) Morgan designed newspaper buildings and more than twenty pleasure palaces for Hearst in California and Mexico. (9) She maintained a private plane and pilot to keep her moving from project to project. (10) The ~~most big~~ *biggest* and ~~famousest~~ *most famous* of her undertakings was ~~sure~~ *surely* San Simeon. (11) Morgan worked on it ~~steady~~ *steadily* for twenty years. (12) She converted a large ranch overlooking the Pacific into a hilltop Mediterranean village composed of

three of the ~~beautifullest~~ *most beautiful* guest houses in the world. (13) The ~~larger~~ *largest* of the three was designed to look like a cathedral and incorporated Hearst's fabulous art treasures from around the world. (14) The finished masterpiece had 144 rooms and was larger than a football field. (15) San Simeon is now one of the most visited tourist attractions in California and seems to grow ~~popularer~~ *more popular* each year.

CHAPTER 33

The Apostrophe

PART A   The Apostrophe for Contractions
PART B   The Apostrophe for Ownership
PART C   Special Uses of the Apostrophe

PART A   The Apostrophe for Contractions

Use the **apostrophe** in a **contraction** to show that letters have been omitted.

1. *I'll* buy that coat if it goes on sale.
2. At nine *o'clock* sharp, the store opens.

- *I'll*, a contraction, is a combination of *I* and *will*. *Wi* is omitted.
- The contraction *o'clock* is the shortened form of *of the clock*.

Be especially careful in writing contractions that contain pronouns:

Common Contractions

I + am = I'm	it + is or has = it's
I + have = I've	we + are = we're
I + will or shall = I'll	let + us = let's
you + have = you've	you + are = you're
you + will or shall = you'll	they + are = they're
he + will or shall = he'll	they + have = they've
she + is or has = she's	who + is or has = who's

427

PRACTICE 1

Proofread these sentences and above the lines, supply any apostrophes missing from the contractions.

1. Ansel Adams wasn't only a great photographer; he was also a conservationist who helped save wildlife areas and establish national parks.

2. He's best known for his dramatic scenes of the wilderness, but he also made huge technical contributions to the field of photography.

3. Because of Adams, there's now a film-exposure system that controls light and dark contrasts in every part of a photograph.

4. Adams was a talented musician who had planned to become a concert pianist; he hadn't expected a career in photography at all.

5. It's a well-known fact that the fourteen-year-old Adams took his first photo while on a family vacation trip to Yosemite National Park in 1916.

6. His decision didn't happen overnight, but he eventually realized that music wouldn't be as satisfying a field for him to work in as photography.

7. People weren't surprised when he transferred the great attention to detail that he had given his piano technique to developing sharp, clear prints.

8. What's most unusual is how Adams worked with light, space, and mood when he photographed storms, mountains, and other natural scenes.

9. Before Adams, many people couldn't believe that photography would become an art form.

10. They've been proven wrong: Adams published books about photography as well as books of his own photographs, and he established photography departments in museums and universities throughout the United States.

A photograph by Ansel Adams of Half-Dome and Merced River in Yosemite National Park appears on page 429.

PART B The Apostrophe for Ownership

Use the apostrophe to show ownership: Add an 's if a noun or an indefinite pronoun (like *someone, anybody,* and so on) does not already end in *-s:*

1. I cannot find my *friend's* book bag.
2. *Everyone's* right to privacy should be respected.
3. *John and Julio's* apartment has striped wallpaper.
4. The *children's* clothes are covered with mud.

■ The *friend* owns the book bag.
■ *Everyone* owns the right to privacy.
■ Both John and Julio own one apartment. The apostrophe follows the compound subject *John and Julio.*
■ The *children* own the clothes.

430 UNIT 6 Reviewing the Basics

Add only an apostrophe to show ownership if the word already ends in -s:*

> 5. My *aunts'* houses are filled with antiques.
> 6. The *knights'* table was round.
> 7. Mr. *Jonas'* company manufactures sporting goods and uniforms.

- My *aunts* (at least two of them) own the houses.
- The *knights* (at least two) own the table.
- *Aunts* and *knights* already end in -s, so only an apostrophe is added.
- Mr. *Jonas* owns the company. Mr. *Jonas* already ends in -s, so only an apostrophe is added.

Note that *possessive pronouns never take an apostrophe: his, hers, theirs, ours, yours, its:*

> 8. *His* car gets twenty miles to the gallon, but *hers* gets only ten.
> 9. That computer is *theirs*; *ours* is coming soon.

PRACTICE 2

Proofread the following sentences and add apostrophes where necessary to show ownership. In each case, ask yourself if the word already ends in -s. Put a C after any correct sentences.

1. Bill's bed is a four-poster.
2. Martha and David's house is a log cabin made entirely by hand.
3. Somebody's wedding ring was left on the sink.
4. During the eighteenth century, ladies' dresses were heavy and uncomfortable.
5. Have you seen the children's watercolor set?
6. Mr. James' fried chicken and rice dish was crispy and delicious.
7. The class loved reading about Ulysses' travels.
8. The Surgeon General's latest report was just released.
9. Our city's water supply must be protected.
10. He found his ticket, but she cannot find hers. *C*

---

*Some writers add an 's to one-syllable proper names that end in -s: *James's* bike.

11. Every spring, my grandmother's porch is completely covered with old furniture for sale.
12. Jack's Health Club just opened at Locust and Broad.
13. Celia's final, a brilliant study of pest control on tobacco farms, received a high grade.
14. The men's locker room is on the right; the women's is on the left.
15. It seems that your orders have been lost in transit. *C*

PART C Special Uses of the Apostrophe

Use an apostrophe in certain expressions of time:

> 1. I desperately need a *week's* vacation.

■ Although the week does not own a vacation, it is a vacation of a week—a *week's vacation*.

Use an apostrophe to pluralize letters, numbers, and words that normally do not have plurals:

> 2. Be careful to cross your *t*'s.
> 3. Your *8*'s look like *F*'s.
> 4. Don't use so many *but*'s in your writing.

Use an apostrophe to show omitted numbers:

> 5. The class of '72 held its annual reunion last week.

PRACTICE 3

Proofread these sentences and add an apostrophe wherever necessary.

1. Cross your *t*'s and dot your *i*'s.
2. I would love a month's vacation on a dude ranch.
3. Too many *and*'s make this paragraph dull.
4. Those *9*'s look crooked.
5. You certainly put in a hard day's work!

PRACTICE 4 — Review

Proofread the following essay for apostrophe errors. Correct the errors by adding apostrophes above the lines where needed and crossing out those that do not belong.

The True Story of Superman

(1) Sometimes, things just don't work out right. (2) That's how the creators of Superman felt for a long time.

(3) Superman's first home wasn't the planet Krypton, but Cleveland. (4) There, in 1933, Superman was born. (5) Jerry Siegel's story, "Reign of Superman," accompanied by Joe Shuster's illustrations, appeared in the boys' own magazine, *Science Fiction*. (6) Later, the teenagers continued to develop their idea. (7) Superman would come to Earth from a distant planet to defend freedom and justice for ordinary people. (8) He would conceal his identity by living as an ordinary person himself. (9) Siegel and Shuster hoped their character's strength and morality would boost people's spirits during the Great Depression.

(10) At first, the creators weren't able to sell their concept; then, Action Comics' Henry Donnenfield bought it. (11) In June of 1938, the first *Superman* comic hit the stands. (12) Superman's success was immediate and overwhelming. (13) Finally, Americans had a hero who wouldn't let them down! (14) Radio and TV shows, movie serials, feature films, and generations of superheros followed.

(15) While others made millions from their idea, Siegel and Shuster didn't profit from its success. (16) They produced Superman for Action Comics for a mere fifteen dollars a page until they were fired a few years later when Joe Shuster's eyes began to fail. (17) They sued, but they lost the case. (18) For a long time, both lived in poverty, but they continued to fight. (19) In 1975, Siegel and Shuster finally took their story to the press; the publicity won them lifelong pensions. (20) The two men's long struggle had ended with success.

CHAPTER 34

The Comma

PART A Commas for Items in a Series

PART B Commas with Introductory Phrases, Transitional Expressions, and Parentheticals

PART C Commas for Appositives

PART D Commas with Nonrestrictive and Restrictive Clauses

PART E Commas for Dates and Addresses

PART F Minor Uses of the Comma

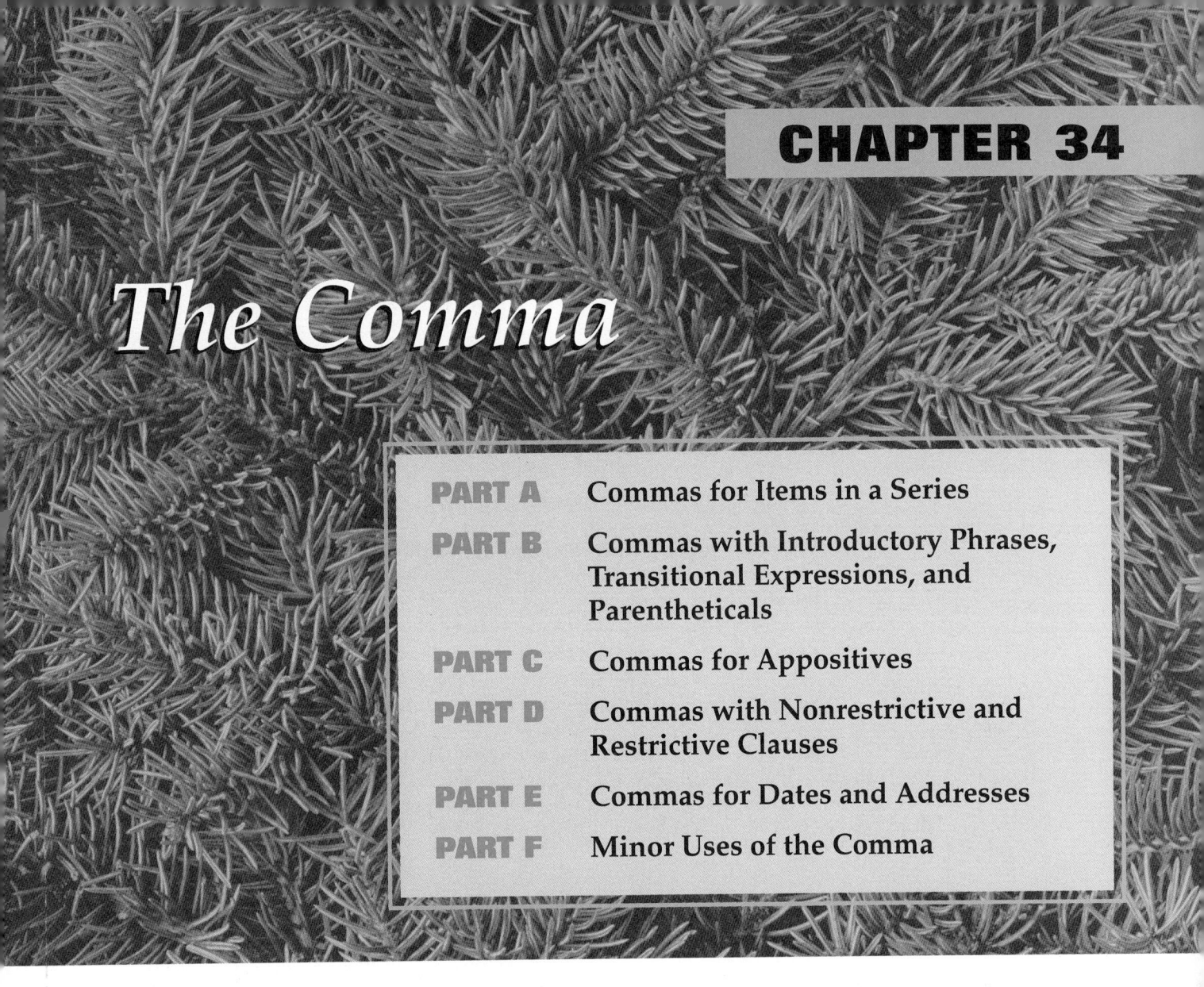

PART A Commas for Items in a Series

Use commas to separate the items in a series:*

1. You need *bolts*, *nuts*, and *screws*.
2. I will be happy to *read your poem*, *comment on it*, and *return it to you*.
3. *Mary paints pictures*, *Robert plays the trumpet*, but *Sam just sits and dreams*.

Do not use commas when all three items are joined by *and* or *or*:

4. I enjoy *biking* and *skating* and *swimming*.

---

*For work on parallelism, see Chapter 19, "Revising for Consistency and Parallelism," Part C.

PRACTICE 1

Punctuate the following sentences:

1. At the banquet, Ed served a salad of juicy red tomatoes, crunchy green lettuce, and stringless snap beans.
2. As a nursing assistant, Reva dispensed medication, disinfected wounds, and took blood samples.
3. Ali visited Santa Barbara, Concord, and Berkeley.
4. Hiking, rafting, and snowboarding are her favorite sports.
5. The police found TV sets, blenders, and blow dryers stacked to the ceiling in the abandoned house.
6. I forgot to pack some important items for the trip to the tropics: insect repellent, sunscreen, and antihistamine tablets.
7. Don't eat strange mushrooms, walk near the water, or feed the squirrels.
8. Everyone in class had to present an oral report, write a term paper, and take a final.
9. We brought a Ouija board, a Scrabble set, and a Boggle game to the party.
10. To earn a decent wage, make a comfortable home, and educate my children—those are my hopes.

PART B — Commas with Introductory Phrases, Transitional Expressions, and Parentheticals

Use a comma after most introductory phrases of more than two words:*

1. *By four in the afternoon,* everybody wanted to go home.
2. *After the game on Saturday,* we all went dancing.

---

* For more work on introductory phrases, see Chapter 20, "Revising for Sentence Variety," Part C.

Use commas to set off transitional expressions:

> 3. Ferns, *for example*, need less sunlight than flowering plants.
> 4. Instructors, *on the other hand*, receive a lower salary than assistant professors.

Use commas to set off parenthetical elements:

> 5. *By the way*, where is the judge's umbrella?
> 6. Nobody, *it seems*, wants to eat the three-bean salad.

■ *By the way* and *it seems* are called parenthetical expressions because they appear to be asides, words not really crucial to the meaning of the sentence. They could almost appear in parentheses: *(By the way) where is the judge's umbrella?*

Other common parenthetical expressions are *after all, actually, as a matter of fact,* and *to tell the truth.*

PRACTICE 2

Punctuate the following sentences:

1. Frankly, I always suspected that you were a born saleswoman.
2. General Marsh, it seems to me, trusted only one or two of his advisers.
3. At two o'clock in the morning, we were awakened by garbage cans clanging.
4. All twelve jurors, by the way, felt that the defendant was innocent.
5. On every April Fools' Day, he tries out a new, dumb practical joke.
6. In fact, Lucinda should never have written that poison-pen letter.
7. Close to the top of Mount Everest, the climbers paused for a tea break.
8. To tell the truth, that usher needs a lesson in courtesy.
9. My CD player, I'm sorry to say, gives me a shock every time I touch it.
10. These apples, to tell the truth, were organically grown in his back yard.
11. During the power blackout, people tried to help one another.

12. Near the end of the driveway, a large lilac bush bloomed and brightened the yard.

13. He prefers, as a rule, serious news programs to the lighter sitcoms.

14. To sum up, Mr. Choi will handle all the details.

15. During my three years in Minnesota, I learned how to deal with snow.

PART C Commas for Appositives

Use commas to set off appositives:*

> 1. Yoko, *our new classmate,* is our best fielder.
> 2. *A humorous and charming man,* he was a great hit with my parents.
> 3. This is her favorite food, *ketchup sandwiches.*

■ Appositive phrases like *our new classmate, a humorous and charming man,* and *ketchup sandwiches* rename or describe nouns and pronouns—*Yoko, he, food.*

> 4. The poet *Shelley* wrote "Ode to the West Wind."
> 5. Shelley's wife, *Mary,* wrote *Frankenstein.*

■ A one-word appositive is not set off by commas when it is essential to the meaning of the sentence. Without the appositive *Shelley,* we do not know which poet wrote the ode.

■ A one-word appositive is set off by commas when it is not essential to the meaning of the sentence. The name *Mary* does not affect the meaning of the sentence.

PRACTICE 3

Punctuate the following sentences.

1. Hulk Hogan, the popular wrestler and actor, advises his fans to drink milk and say their prayers.

2. Long novels, especially ones with complicated plots, force me to read slowly.

3. David, a resident nurse, hopes to become a pediatrician.

4. I don't trust that tire, the one with the yellow patch on the side.

---

* For more work on appositives, see Chapter 20, "Revising for Sentence Variety," Part D.

5. Tanzania, a small African nation, exports cashew nuts.

6. Watch out for Phil, a man whose ambition rules him.

7. Sheila, a well-known nutritionist, lectures at public schools.

8. A real flying ace, Helen will teach a course in sky diving.

9. We support the Center for Science in the Public Interest, a consumer education and protection group.

10. My husband, Bill, owns two stereos.

PART D   Commas with Nonrestrictive and Restrictive Clauses

A **relative clause** is a clause that begins with *who, which,* or *that* and modifies a noun or pronoun. There are two kinds of relative clauses: **nonrestrictive** and **restrictive.***

A **nonrestrictive relative clause** is not essential to the meaning of the sentence:

> 1. Raj, *who is a part-time aviator,* loves to tinker with machines of all kinds.

- *Who is a part-time aviator* is a relative clause describing *Raj*. It is a nonrestrictive relative clause because it is not essential to the meaning of the sentence. The point is that *Raj loves to tinker with machines of all kinds.*
- **Commas** set off the nonrestrictive relative clause.

A **restrictive relative clause** is essential to the meaning of the sentence:

> 2. People *who do their work efficiently* make good students.

- *Who do their work efficiently* is a relative clause describing *people*. It is a restrictive relative clause because it is *essential* to the meaning of the sentence. Without it, sentence 2 would read, *People make good students.* But the point is that certain people make good students—those who do their work efficiently.
- Restrictive relative clauses *do not* require commas.

PRACTICE 4

Set off the nonrestrictive relative clauses in the following sentences with commas. Note that *which* usually begins a nonrestrictive relative clause and *that* usually

---

*For more work on nonrestrictive and restrictive clauses, see Chapter 20, "Revising for Sentence Variety," Part D.

begins a restrictive clause. Remember: Restrictive relative clauses are *not* set off by commas. Write a C after each correct sentence.

1. Olive, who always wanted to go into law enforcement, is a detective in the Eighth Precinct.
2. Employees who learn to use the new computers may soon qualify for a merit raise. *C*
3. Polo, which is not played much in the United States, is very popular in England.
4. A person who always insists upon telling you the truth is sometimes a pain in the neck. *C*
5. Statistics 101, which is required for the business curriculum, demands concentration and perseverance.
6. Robin, who is usually shy at large parties, spent the evening dancing with Arsenio, who is everybody's favorite dance partner.
7. This small shop sells furniture that is locally handcrafted. *C*
8. His uncle, who rarely eats meat, consumes enormous quantities of vegetables, fruits, and grains.
9. Pens that slowly leak ink can be very messy. *C*
10. Valley Forge, which is the site of Washington's winter quarters, draws many tourists every spring and summer.

PART E Commas for Dates and Addresses

Use commas to separate the elements of an address. Note, however, that no punctuation is required between the state and ZIP code if the ZIP code is included.

1. Please send the books to *300 West Road, Stamford, CT 06860.*
2. We moved from *1015 Allen Circle, Morristown, New Jersey,* to *Farland Lane, Dubuque, Iowa.*

Use commas to separate the elements of a date:

> 3. The sociologists arrived in Tibet on *Monday, January 18, 1992,* and planned to stay for two years.
> 4. By *June 20, 2003,* I expect to have completed my B.A. in physical education.

Do not use a comma with a single-word address or date preceded by a preposition:

> 5. John DeLeon arrived *from Baltimore in January* and will be our new shortstop this season.

PRACTICE 5

Punctuate the following sentences. Write a C after each correct sentence.

1. The last few decades have seen the growth of an ancient Native American custom—the *powwow,* a gathering where tribal members dance to celebrate the circle of life. *C*

2. At hundreds of powwows across the United States and Canada, families and friends reaffirm their heritage, socialize, and compete for prize money.

3. Ten powwows were held in September 1999 alone, for example, each one with singing, chanting, drumming, and dancing. *C*

4. On Wednesday, September 1, 1999, the Permian Basin Intertribal Powwow began in Odessa, Texas.

5. On the weekend of September 4 to September 6, 1999, Native Americans and visitors could choose between the Ottawa Celebration in Miami, Oklahoma, or the Traditions in the Making Powwow in Delta, Utah.

6. The twenty-fourth Annual Fall Powwow took place on September 11 and 12, 1999, at Jefferson Barracks Park, St. Louis, Missouri.

7. The Nause Waiwash Band of Indians Native American Festival was held in Sailwinds Park, Cambridge, Maryland, on September 19 and 20, 1999.

8. Some families even spend June to September going from powwow to powwow or traveling "the Red Road." *C*

9. The Red Road is a path of commitment to living without alcohol and drugs and embracing a healthier lifestyle. *C*

10. Each year, thousands attend the powwows to dance, admire the spectacular traditional costumes, meet interesting people, or just feel part of the circle of life. *C*

11. For more information on powwows, you can contact the American Indian Heritage Foundation, 6051 Arlington Blvd., Falls Church, VA 22044.

12. Another resource is the National Native American Co-Op; the address is the Native American Trade and Information Center, P.O. Box 1000, San Carlos, AZ 85550-0301.

PART F — Minor Uses of the Comma

Use a comma after answering a question with *yes* or *no:*

1. *No,* I'm not sure about that answer.

Use a comma when addressing someone directly and specifically naming the person spoken to:

2. *Alicia,* where did you put my law books?

Use a comma after interjections like *ah, oh,* and so on:

3. *Ah,* these coconuts are delicious.

Use a comma to contrast:

4. Harold, *not Roy,* is my scuba-diving partner.

PRACTICE 6

Punctuate the following sentences.

1. Yes, I do think you will be famous one day.
2. Well, did you call a taxi?
3. The defendant, ladies and gentlemen of the jury, does not even own a red plaid jacket.
4. Cynthia, have you ever camped in the Pacific Northwest?
5. No, I most certainly will not marry you.
6. Oh, I love the way they play everything to a salsa beat.
7. The class feels, Professor Molinor, that your grades are unrealistically high.
8. He said "March," not "Swagger."
9. Perhaps, but I still don't think that the carburetor fits there.
10. We all agree, Ms. Crawford, that you are the best jazz bassist around.

PRACTICE 7 — Review

Proofread the following essay for comma errors—either missing commas or commas used incorrectly. Correct the errors above the lines.

The Pyramids of Giza

(1) The pyramids of Giza, Egypt, a wonder of the ancient world, still inspire awe. (2) Built nearly five thousand years ago, the largest of these tombs was ordered by Khu-fu, a powerful pharaoh of ancient Egypt. (3) The two smaller pyramids nearby belonged to his successors, his son Khafre and his grandson Menkaure. (4) The three pyramids—together with the Sphinx, many temples, and causeways—comprised a ceremonial complex for the dead not far from the Nile River.

(5) We marvel today at the ability of this ancient people to build such colossal structures without the benefit of work animals or machinery, not even the wheel.

(6) The Great Pyramid, for instance, is 750 square feet and 480 feet high, roughly the size of Shea Stadium filled in with solid rock to a height of forty stories. (7) More than 100,000 workers, who were probably peasants forced into service, cut two-and-a-half-ton limestone blocks from quarries on the other side of the Nile, ferried them across the river, and then dragged them up ramps to be fitted exactly in place. (8) Experts estimate that 2.3 million blocks had to be moved over a period of more than twenty years to complete the project.

(9) Perhaps the greatest wonder, however, is that these structures have lasted. (10) Countless other buildings, statues, and monuments have been constructed and admired, yet they have fallen into ruin while these magnificent structures remain. (11) The pyramids are considered all but indestructible. (12) It has been said, in fact, that they could withstand a direct hit by an atomic bomb.

CHAPTER 35

Mechanics

> **PART A**   Capitalization
> **PART B**   Titles
> **PART C**   Direct Quotations
> **PART D**   Minor Marks of Punctuation

PART A   Capitalization

Always capitalize the following: *names, nationalities, religions, races, languages, countries, cities, months, days of the week, documents, organizations,* and *holidays*.

1. The *Protestant* church on the corner will offer *Spanish* and *English* courses starting *Thursday, June* 3.

Capitalize the following *only* when they are used as part of a proper noun: *streets, buildings, historical events, titles,* and *family relationships*.

2. We saw *Professor Rodriguez* at *Silver Hall*, where he was delivering a talk on the *Spanish Civil War*.

Do not capitalize these same words when they are used as common nouns:

3. We saw the professor at the lecture hall, where he was delivering a talk on a civil war.

Capitalize geographic locations but not directions:

> 4. The tourists went to the *South* for their winter vacation.
> 5. Go south on this boulevard for three miles.

Capitalize academic subjects only if they refer to a specific named and numbered course:

> 6. Have you ever studied psychology?
> 7. Last semester, I took *Psychology* 101.

PRACTICE 1

Capitalize wherever necessary in the following sentences. Put a C after each correct sentence.

1. Barbara Kingsolver, a well-known novelist, nonfiction writer, and poet, was born on *A*april 8, 1955, in *A*annapolis, *M*maryland.

2. She grew up in rural *K*kentucky and then went to college in *I*indiana; after graduating, she worked in *E*europe and since then has lived in and around *T*tucson, *A*arizona.

3. In college, Kingsolver majored first in music and then in biology; she later withdrew from a graduate program in biology and ecology at the *U*university of *A*arizona to work in its *O*office of *A*arid *L*land *S*studies.

4. Kingsolver's first novel, *The Bean Trees*, has become a classic; it is taught in *E*english classes and has been translated into more than sixty-five languages.

5. The main character, named *T*taylor *G*greer, is considered one of the most memorable women in modern *A*american literature.

6. In a later novel, *The Poisonwood Bible*, Kingsolver follows the family of a *B*baptist minister in its move to the *C*congo.

7. The fanaticism of *R*reverend *P*price brings misery to his family and destruction to the villagers he tries to convert to *C*christianity.

8. Kingsolver's writing always deals with powerful political and social issues, but her novels don't sound preachy because she is a wonderful storyteller. C

9. She has won awards and prizes from the $\overset{A}{\text{american}}$ $\overset{L}{\text{library}}$ $\overset{A}{\text{association}}$ and many other organizations; she also has earned special recognition from the $\overset{U}{\text{united}}$ $\overset{N}{\text{nations}}$ $\overset{N}{\text{national}}$ $\overset{C}{\text{council}}$ of $\overset{W}{\text{women}}$.

10. This gifted writer, who plays drums and piano, performs with a band called $\overset{R}{\text{rock}}$ $\overset{B}{\text{bottom}}$ $\overset{R}{\text{remainders}}$; other band members are also notable writers— $\overset{S}{\text{stephen}}$ $\overset{K}{\text{king}}$, $\overset{A}{\text{amy}}$ $\overset{T}{\text{tan}}$, and $\overset{D}{\text{dave}}$ $\overset{B}{\text{barry}}$.

PART B Titles

Capitalize all the words of a title except short prepositions, short conjunctions, and the articles *the, an,* and *a.* Always capitalize the first and last words of the title, no matter what they are:

> 1. I liked *The Color Purple* but found *The House on the River* slow reading.

Underline the titles of long works: *books,** *newspapers and magazines, television shows, plays, record albums, operas,* and *films.*
Put quotation marks around shorter works or parts of longer ones: *articles, short stories, poems, songs, paintings, scenes from plays,* and *chapters from full-length books.*

> 2. Have you read Hemingway's "The Killers" yet?
> 3. We are assigned "The Money Market" in *Essentials of Economics* for homework in my marketing course.

■ "The Killers" is a short story.
■ "The Money Market" is a chapter in the full-length book *Essentials of Economics.*

Do not underline or use quotation marks around the titles of your own papers.

---

* The titles and parts of sacred books are not underlined and are not set off by quotation marks: Job 5:6, Koran 1:14, and so on.

446 UNIT 6 Reviewing the Basics

PRACTICE 2

Capitalize these titles correctly. Do not underline or use quotation marks in this practice.

1. the first immigrants (T F I)
2. a trip through the Netherlands (A T T)
3. making jams and jellies (M J J)
4. a dangerous game (A D G)
5. why every american should vote (W E A S V)
6. nuclear power: safe or sorry? (N P S S)
7. you can build a sailboat (Y C B S)
8. the quark theory (T Q T)
9. starting over (S O)
10. the millionaire next door (T M N D)
11. parents without partners (P W P)
12. the value of friendship (T V F)
13. what I would do with $50,000 (W W D)
14. three causes of world war II (T C W W)
15. the fate of the earth (T F E)

PRACTICE 3

Wherever necessary, underline or place quotation marks around each title in the sentences below so that the reader will know at a glance what type of work the title refers to. Put a C after any correct sentence.

EXAMPLE Two of the best short stories in that volume are "Rope" and "The New Dress."

1. African-American writer Langston Hughes produced his first novel, <u>Not Without Laughter</u>, when he was a student at Lincoln University in Pennsylvania.

2. By that time, he had already been a farmer, a cook, a waiter, and a doorman at a Paris nightclub; he had also won a prize for his poem "The Weary Blues," which was published in 1925 in the magazine <u>Opportunity</u>.

3. In 1926 Hughes wrote his famous essay "The Negro Artist and the Racial Mountain," which appeared in the *Nation* magazine; he wanted young black writers to write without shame or fear about the subject of race.

4. Because he spoke Spanish, Hughes was asked in 1937 by the newspaper the *Baltimore Afro-American* to cover the activities of blacks in the International Brigades in Spain during the Spanish Civil War.

5. For the rest of his life, he wrote articles in newspapers such as the *San Francisco Chronicle*, the *New York Times*, and the *Chicago Defender*.

6. In fact, for more than twenty years he wrote a weekly column for the *Chicago Defender*, in which he introduced a character named Simple, who became popular because of his witty observations on life.

7. The stories about Simple were eventually collected and published in five books; two of those books are *Simple Speaks His Mind* and *Simple Takes a Wife*.

8. In 1938, Hughes established the Harlem Suitcase Theater in Manhattan, where his play *Don't You Want to Be Free?* was performed.

9. Because Hughes's poetry was based on the rhythms of African-American speech and music, many of his poems have been set to music, including "Love Can Hurt You," "Dorothy's Name Is Mud," and "Five O'Clock Blues."

10. Few modern writers can rival Hughes's enormous output of fine poems, newspaper articles, columns, sketches, and novels. C

PART C Direct Quotations

Use quotation marks to enclose the exact words of the speaker:

> 1. He said, "These are the best seats in the house."

- The direct quotation is preceded by a comma or a colon.
- The first letter of the direct quotation is capitalized.
- Periods always go *inside* the quotation marks.

2. He asked, "Where is my laptop?"
3. Stewart yelled, "I don't like beans!"

■ Question marks and exclamation points go inside the quotation marks if they are part of the direct words of the speaker.

4. "That was meant for the company," he said, "but if you wish, you may have it."
5. "The trees look magnificent!" she exclaimed. "It would be fun to climb them all."

■ In sentence 4, the quotation is one single sentence interrupted by *he said*. Therefore, a comma is used after *he said,* and *but* is not capitalized.

■ In sentence 5, the quotation consists of two different sentences. Thus a period follows *exclaimed,* and the second sentence of the quotation begins with a capital letter.

PRACTICE 4

Insert quotation marks where necessary in each sentence. Capitalize and punctuate correctly.

1. The sign reads don't even think about parking here.
2. Can you direct me to the central bus stop he asked.
3. Alexander Pope wrote to err is human, to forgive divine.
4. Jim wondered why have I been having such good luck lately
5. Well, it takes all kinds she sighed
6. The report stated no one responded to the crisis in time.
7. He exclaimed you look terrific in those jeweled sandals
8. The article said Most American children do poorly in geography.
9. These books on ancient Egypt look interesting he replied but I don't have time to read them now.
10. Although the rain is heavy she said we will continue harvesting the corn.
11. Give up caffeine and get lots of rest the doctor advised.
12. This final is easy he whispered to himself it is a guaranteed A.

13. "We haven't gone fishing for a month," he complained, "and we really miss it."

14. The label warns, "This product should not be taken by those allergic to aspirin."

15. "Red, white, and blue," Hillary said, "are my favorite colors."

PART D — Minor Marks of Punctuation

1. The Colon

Use a colon to show that a direct quotation will follow or to introduce a list:*

> 1. This is the opening line of his essay: "The airplane is humanity's greatest invention."
> 2. There are four things I can't resist in warm weather: fresh mangoes, a sandy beach, cold drinks, and a hammock.

Use a colon to separate the chapter and verse in a reference to the Bible or to separate the hour and minute:

> 3. This quotation comes from Genesis 1:1.
> 4. It is now exactly 4:15 P.M.

2. Parentheses

Use parentheses to enclose a phrase or word that is not essential to the meaning of the sentence:

> 5. Herpetology (the study of snakes) is a fascinating area of zoology.
> 6. She left her hometown (Plunkville) to go to the big city (Fairmount) in search of success.

3. The Dash

Use a dash to emphasize a portion of a sentence or to interrupt the sentence with an added element:

> 7. This is the right method—the only one—so we are stuck with it.

The colon, parentheses, and the dash should be used sparingly.

---

*Avoid using a colon after any form of the verb *to be* or after a preposition.

450 UNIT 6 Reviewing the Basics

PRACTICE 5

Punctuate these sentences with colons, dashes, or parentheses.

1. Calvin asked for the following: two light bulbs, a pack of matches, a lead pencil, and a pound of grapes.
2. They should leave by 11:30 P.M.
3. The designer's newest fashions (magnificent leather creations) were generally too expensive for the small chain of clothing stores.
4. Harvey—the only Missourian in the group—remains unconvinced.
5. She replied, "This rock group (The Woogies) sounds like all the others I've heard this year."
6. If you eat a heavy lunch—as you always do—remember not to go swimming immediately afterward.
7. By 9:30 P.M., the zoo veterinarian (a Dr. Smittens) had operated on the elephant.
8. Note these three tips for hammering in a nail: hold the hammer at the end of the handle, position the nail carefully, and watch your thumb.
9. Whenever Harold Garvey does his birdcalls at parties—as he is sure to do—everyone begins to yawn.
10. Please purchase these things at the hardware store: masking tape, thumbtacks, a small hammer, and some sandpaper.

PRACTICE 6   Review

Proofread the following essay for errors in capitalization, quotation marks, colons, parentheses, and dashes. Correct the errors by writing above the lines.

The Passion of Thomas Gilcrease

(1) Thomas Gilcrease, a descendent of *C*reek *I*ndians, became an instant *M*illionaire when oil was discovered on his homestead in 1907. (2) He spent most of his fortune collecting objects that tell the story of the *A*merican frontier, particularly of the Native American experience. (3) The Thomas Gilcrease *I*nstitute of *A*merican *H*istory and *A*rts in Tulsa, *O*klahoma, is the result of his lifelong passion.

(4) This huge collection, more than 10,000 works of art, 90,000 historical documents, and 250,000 Native American artifacts, spans the centuries from 10,000 B.C. to the 1950s. (5) Awed visitors can view nearly two hundred George Catlin paintings of Native American life. (6) They can walk among paintings and bronze sculptures by Frederic Remington with names like "The Coming and Going of the Pony Express," that call up images of the West. (7) Museumgoers can admire Thomas Moran's watercolors that helped persuade Congress to create Yellowstone, the first national park. (8) In addition, visitors are treated to works by modern Native Americans, such as the display of wood sculptures by the Cherokee Willard Stone.

(9) The museum also houses many priceless documents: an original copy of the Declaration of Independence, the oldest known letter written from the New World, and the papers of Hernando Cortés. (10) A new glass storage area even allows visitors to view the 80 percent of the holdings that are not on display. (11) Thousands of beaded moccasins and buckskin dresses line the shelves, and a collection of magnificent war bonnets hangs from brackets.

(12) When the Gilcrease Institute opened its doors on May 2, 1949, *Life* declared, "It is the best collection of art and literature ever assembled on the American frontier and the Indian." (13) Thousands of visitors agree.

CHAPTER 36

Putting Your Proofreading Skills to Work

After you have written a paragraph or an essay—once you have prewritten, drafted, and revised—you are ready for the next step—**proofreading.**

Proofreading, which takes place at the sentence level, means applying what you have learned in Unit 6. When you proofread, carefully check each sentence for correct grammar, punctuation, and capitalization. Is every sentence complete? Do all verbs agree with their subjects? Are there any comma errors? Do all proper nouns begin with a capital letter?

This chapter gives you the opportunity to put your proofreading skills to work in real-world situations. As you proofread the paragraphs and essays that follow, you must look for any—and every—kind of error, just as you would in the real world of college or work. The paragraph practices tell you what kinds of errors to look for; if you have trouble, go back to those chapters and review. The essay practices, however, contain a random mix of errors and give you no clues at all.

PROOFREADING PRACTICE 1

Proofread this paragraph, correcting any errors above the lines. To review, see these chapters:

Chapter 25   run-ons, comma splices, fragments
Chapter 26   present tense problems, subject-verb agreement
Chapter 27   past tense problems
Chapter 28   past participle problems

 (1) Don't sit in a draft or you'll get a chill, (2) ~~And~~ *and* catch a cold. (3) If you ~~walks~~ *walk* around with wet socks and shoes in winter or don't wear a hat, you'll catch a cold. (4) Sitting in a frosty air-conditioned room is sure to give you a cold. (5) If you haven't ~~gave~~ *given* this advice, you've probably received it at some

452

CHAPTER 36 Putting Your Proofreading Skills to Work   453

time. (6) However, the fact is that the only way to catch a cold is by coming in direct contact with a cold virus when you are susceptible. (7) Cold viruses are called *Rhinoviruses* (*rhin* is Greek for *nose*). (8) ~~Because~~ *because* they ~~have entered~~ *enter* the body through the nose. (9) Colds usually spread when people sneeze or cough, get the virus on their hands or a tissue, and then ~~touches~~ *touch* other people who touch their noses. (10) You can, therefore, sit in a draft or in a too-cold air-conditioned room and not catch a cold. (11) A chill actually ~~be~~ *is* the first symptom of a cold, not the cause. (12) Similarly, you can be outdoors on a freezing day in wet shoes and socks—and without a hat—and not catch a cold if there ~~is~~ *are* no cold germs present. (13) (You would probably be very uncomfortable, though.) (14) What should you do if you have ~~catched~~ *caught* a cold? (15) Unfortunately, there is no magic cure, *The* best advice is to stay indoors, keep warm, and drink lots of fluids.

PROOFREADING PRACTICE 2

Proofread this paragraph, correcting any errors above the lines. To review, see these chapters:

Chapter 25	run-ons, comma splices, fragments
Chapter 26	subject-verb agreement
Chapter 29	noun errors
Chapter 30	pronoun errors
Chapter 35	capitalization

(1) Since ancient times, the Zunis of New Mexico have used *fetishes*, (2) ~~Small~~ *small* objects carved from stone or wood that are believed to have magical powers. (3) The Zuni religion ~~have~~ *has* a complex tradition of fetishes based on the six directions, (4) ~~North~~ *north*, south, east, west, above, and below. (5) Each of the directions ~~are~~ *is* associated with special forces and a guardian animal. (6) The East, for example, where the sun rises, is the source of all life, truth, and new ideas. *It* is represented by a white wolf. (7) Because ~~wolfs~~ *wolves* are highly intelligent, social, and loving as parents, they are good to adopt as a personal fetish if you feel you share these qualities. (8) Likewise, someone facing a big decision or a family problem might seek

the help of ~~their~~ [his or her] wolf fetish. (9) The other five guardian animals are the mountain lion, black bear, badger, eagle, and mole. (10) Additional fetish animals include coyotes, owls, snakes, ~~deers~~ [deer], and rabbits. (11) The Zunis still ~~holds~~ [hold] fetishes sacred in ~~its~~ [their] religion and ~~continues~~ [continue] to carve them. (12) In fact, some Zunis are famous for their distinctive carving. [Their] ~~their~~ fetishes sell all over the world as works of art.

PROOFREADING PRACTICE 3

Proofread this paragraph, correcting any errors above the lines. To review, see these chapters:

Chapter 25   run ons, comma splices, fragments
Chapter 31   preposition errors
Chapter 32   adjective and adverb errors

(1) Florence Griffith Joyner, [was] the fastest woman in track and field history and one of the ~~interestingest~~ [most interesting]. (2) Flo-Jo, as she was known, was a sprinter. [At] ~~at~~ the 1984 Olympics, she won a silver medal running the 200-meter sprint. (3) In the U.S. trials for the 1988 Olympics, she set a world record of 10.49 seconds. (4) ~~For~~ [for] the 100-meter sprint. (5) At the Olympics, she won three gold medals and set a world record of 21.23 seconds for the 200. (6) No other female sprinter has ever run as ~~swift~~ [swiftly]; her records are unbroken. (7) Neither has any track star come close in style. [At] ~~at~~ the starting line, all eyes were on Flo-Jo. (8) Flo-Jo's hair was always the most ~~beautiful~~ [beautifully] styled, her makeup was applied ~~perfect~~ [perfectly], and her nails were long and ~~bright~~ [brightly] polished. (9) Her running gear was the ~~more~~ [most] flamboyant imaginable. (10) At first, spectators were shocked ~~with~~ [by] Flo-Jo's lacey spandex suits and neon-colored unitards. (11) Off the field, Flo-Jo was a business woman who did extremely ~~good~~ [well] marketing her own line of athletic wear. (12) When she died at age 38 ~~on~~ [in] 1998, she was serving on the President's Council on Physical Fitness and Sports. (13) She was a superb athlete and a model for women everywhere.

PROOFREADING PRACTICE 4

Proofread this paragraph, correcting any errors above the lines. To review, see these chapters:

CHAPTER 36 Putting Your Proofreading Skills to Work   455

Chapter 24   commas for subordination
Chapter 25   run-ons, comma splices, fragments
Chapter 33   apostrophe errors
Chapter 34   comma and other punctuation errors
Chapter 35   capitalization, titles, and minor punctuation marks

(1) If you want to eat well and do our planet a favor become a Vegetarian. (2) Most vegetarian's eat eggs, milk, dairy products and fish. (3) All youre giving up are leathery steak's and overcooked chicken. (4) A vegetarian dinner might begin with a greek salad of crisp cucumbers, sweet red onion black olives, and a sprinkling of feta cheese. (5) Youll think you're sitting in a little cafe overlooking the mediterranean sea. (6) For the main course, head to mexico for tamale pie (7) A rich, flavorful dish made of pinto beans's, brown rice, green peppers and tomatoes. (8) On the table of course is a loaf of warm bread. (9) Do you have room for dessert how about some ben and jerrys ice cream, made in vermont? (10) As you linger over a cup of french espresso coffee think how your vegetarian meal was delicious, nutritious, and a help to our planet. (11) If more people ate vegetarian the land given to raising cattle and crops to feed cattle could be used for raising grain many of the worlds hungry people could be fed. (12) To read about vegetarianism, get the best-known guide laurels kitchen: a handbook for vegetarian cookery and nutrition.

PROOFREADING PRACTICE 5

This essay contains many of the errors you learned to avoid in Unit 6. Proofread each sentence carefully, and then correct each error above the line.

Gators and Crocs

(1) With their scaly bodies slit eyes and long tails, alligators and crocodiles look a lot like dinosaurs. (2) In fact alligators and crocodiles descended from the same family as dinosaurs. (3) While its true that alligators and crocodiles look a lot alike, they differ in three ways.

(4) First alligators and crocodiles are found in different parts of the world. (5) Alligators be found in china, central america, and south america. (6) On the other

hand, crocodiles are found in Africa (especially around the Nile River), Australia, southeast Asia, India, Cuba, and the West Indies. (7) Only in the southern United States are both alligators and crocodiles found. (8) In all cases, however, alligators and crocodiles live in hot, tropical regions. (9) Reptiles are cold-blooded, so at temperatures below 65 degrees, alligators and crocodiles get sluggish and cannot hunt.

(10) Alligators and crocodiles also differ in appearance. (11) Alligators have broader, flatter snouts that are rounded at the end. (12) Crocodiles have narrower, almost triangular snouts. (13) The best way to tell the difference is to view both from the side. When they have their mouths closed, you can see only upper teeth on an alligator, but you can also see four lower teeth on a croc. (14) If you get really close, you can see that alligators have a space between their nostrils while the nostrils of crocs are very close together.

(15) Finally, alligators and crocodiles are temperamentally different. (16) Alligators are not aggressive; they are even a bit shy. (17) They will lie in wait along a river bank for prey. When on land, they move slowly and unevenly. (18) Crocodiles, however, are much more aggressive. (19) They are fast, mean, and often stalk their prey. (20) The Australian freshwater crocodile and the Nile crocodile can even run on land, with their front and back legs working together like a dog's. (21) Nile crocodiles kill hundreds of people every year.

(22) Alligators and crocodiles have outlived the dinosaurs, but they might not survive hunters who want to turn them into shoes, wallets, briefcases, and belts. (23) In 1967, the U.S. government declared alligators an endangered species. (24) Fortunately, American alligators have repopulated and are now reclassified as threatened. (25) Importing crocodile and alligator skins is banned worldwide, but some species are still threatened. (26) These frightening and fascinating ancient creatures need help worldwide if they are to survive.

PROOFREADING PRACTICE 6

This essay contains many of the errors you learned to avoid in Unit 6. Proofread each sentence carefully, and then correct each error above the line.

In the Market for a Used Car?

(1) For several year's now, used car sales have exceeded new car sales. (2) Good used cars can be ~~founded~~ *found* at dealers. (3) And through newspaper ads. (4) You might also let your friends know ~~your~~ *you're* in the market for a used car; they might know of someone who wants to sell ~~their~~ *his or her* car. (5) Wherever you look for a used car, keep the following tips in mind.

(6) First, shop before you need the car. (7) This way you can decide exactly what type of car ~~suit~~ *suits* you ~~most~~ best. (8) Do you want a compact, (9) ~~Or~~ *or* a midsize car? (10) What features are important to you? (11) Should you get an ~~american~~-*A* made car or a ~~japanese~~, ~~german~~, or other import? (12) If you shop when you ~~are'nt~~ *aren't* desperate, you are more likely to make a good choice and negotiate ~~good~~ *well*.

(13) Second, narrow your choices to three or four cars, and do some research. (14) Start with the ~~kelley blue book used car price manual~~ *Kelley Blue Book Used Car Price Manual*. (15) The blue book, as its called for short, gives the current value by model, year, and features. (16) Its also a good idea to check ~~consumer reports~~ *Consumer Reports* magazine. (17) Every ~~april~~ *A* issue lists good used car buys and cars to avoid. (18) Based on what you learn, go back and test-drive the cars that interest you the ~~mostest~~ *most*. (19) Drive each for at least an hour; *D* drive in stop-and-go traffic ~~in~~ *on* the highway, ~~in~~ *on* winding roads, and ~~in~~ *on* hills.

(20) When you do decide on a car, ask your mechanic to look at it. (21) Be sure to get a written report that ~~include~~ *includes* an estimate of what repair's will cost. (22) Money spent at this point is money spent ~~wise~~ *wisely*, if the seller wont allow an inspection, take your business elsewhere.

(23) When you buy a used car, you want dependability and value. (24) Follow these tip's, ~~youll~~ *You'll* be able to tell a good buy when you see it.

UNIT 6 WRITERS' WORKSHOP

Adopt a New Point of View

No matter how excellent the content of an essay, report, or business letter, grammatical errors will diminish its impact. Ironically, errors call attention to themselves. Learning to proofread your writing might not seem terribly exciting, but it is an all-important skill.

When this student received the interesting assignment to *write as if you are someone or something else*, he decided to see what it's like to be a roach. His audience: humans. His tone: wacky. In your group or class, read his essay, aloud if possible. Underline details or sentences that are especially effective or humorous, and **proofread** as you go. If you spot any errors, correct them.

It's Not Easy Being a Roach

(1) It's not easy being a roach. My life consist [*consists*] of the constant struggle to survive. We have existed for millions of years, yet we still do not get the respect that we deserve. We have witnessed the dawn of the dinosaur and the coming of Jesus. We have experienced two world wars, enjoyed the benefits of cable television, and feasted our eyes on many women taking showers. Being small has its advantages, and it doesn't hurt to be quick either. Because we have live [*lived*] so long, You [*you*] would think that respect would be ours, but that is not the case.

(2) We are looked upon as pests rather than pets, [*pets. We*] we are quieter than household pets. We don't eat much, and contrary to popular belief, we are very clean. Sure, some of us prefers [*prefer*] the wild life of booze, drugs, and unprotected sex with other insects, but that doesn't mean that most of us are not seeking a happy life that includes love and affection from you humans. I think it's high time that you appreciated our value as insects, pets, and potential lifelong companions.

(3) I might have six legs, but that doesn't mean I can handle all the burdens that come with being a roach. My wife is pregnant again, which means 10,000 more mouths to feed. It's bad enough that I have to find a meal fit for thousands, [*thousands. I*] I also live in fear of becoming a Roach McNugget. For some strange reason, rodents consider us food. Do I look scrumptious to you? Does my body ignite wild fantasies of sinful feasting? I think not. Mice and rats refuse to respect us because they see us as midnight munchies.

(4) I don't ask for much—a home, some food, and maybe an occasional pat on the head. If I can't have these simple things, I would prefer somebody simply step on me. A fast, hard crunch would do—no spraying me with roach spray, no Roach Motel. I may be on the lower end of the species chain, but that doesn't mean I'm not entitled to live out my dreams. I am roach and hear me roar!

> (5) When you humans kill each other off with nuclear bombs, we will still be around. With luck on our side, we will grow into big monsters because of exposure to radiation. Then I don't think those of you who ~~remains~~ *remain* will enjoy being chased around by giant, glowing roaches—all because you humans didn't want to hug a roach when you had the chance.
>
> (6) One more thing: Stop trying to kill us with that pine-scented roach spray. It doesn't kill ~~us it~~ *us. It* just makes us smell bad. If I want to smell like pine trees, I will go and frolic in some wood, naked and free. You people really tick me off.
>
> —Israel Vasquez (Student)

1. How effective is Mr. Vasquez's essay?

   __Y__ Strong thesis statement?   __Y__ Good supporting details?

   __Y__ Logical organization?   __Y__ Effective conclusion?

2. Discuss your underlinings. What details or lines in the essay did you like the most? Explain as exactly as possible why you like something or why it made you laugh.

3. Mr. Vasquez's sense of humor comes through to readers. Does he also achieve his goal of presenting a roach's point of view?

4. Would you suggest any revisions? Is this essay effective or offensive? Why? Does the final paragraph provide a strong and humorous conclusion, or does it seem like an afterthought?

5. This essay contains several serious grammar errors. Can you find and correct them? What two error patterns does this fine writer need to watch out for?
   verb agreement and comma splices; one past participle error

GROUP WORK

In writing as in life, it is often easier to spot other people's errors than our own. In your group or class, discuss *your* particular error patterns and how you have learned to catch them. Do you have problems with comma splices, *-ed* verb endings, or prepositional phrases? Discuss any proofreading tricks and techniques you have learned to spot and correct those errors successfully in your own papers. Have someone jot down the best techniques that your group mates have used, and be prepared to share these with the class.

WRITING AND REVISING IDEAS

1. Adopt a new point of view; discuss your life as a bird, animal, insect, or object.

2. Write as a person of another gender, ethnic group, or period in history.

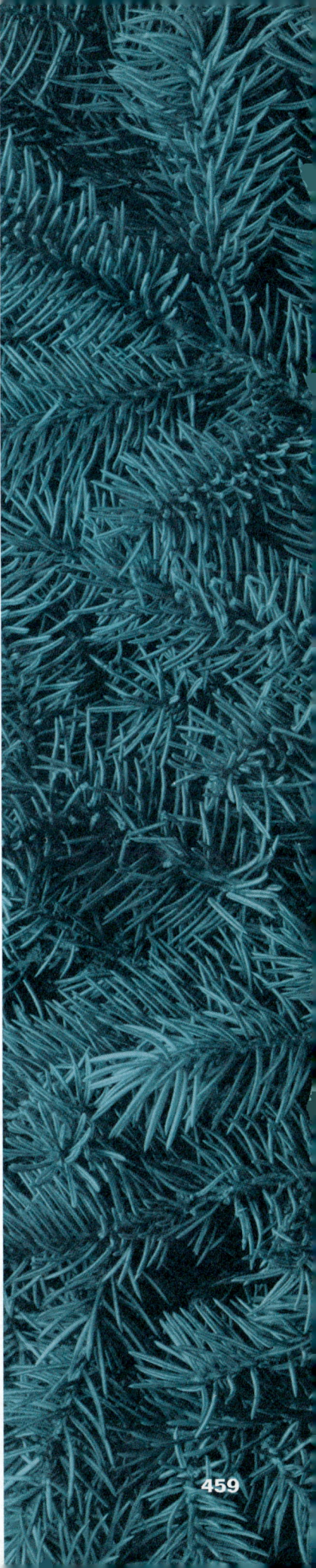

UNIT 7

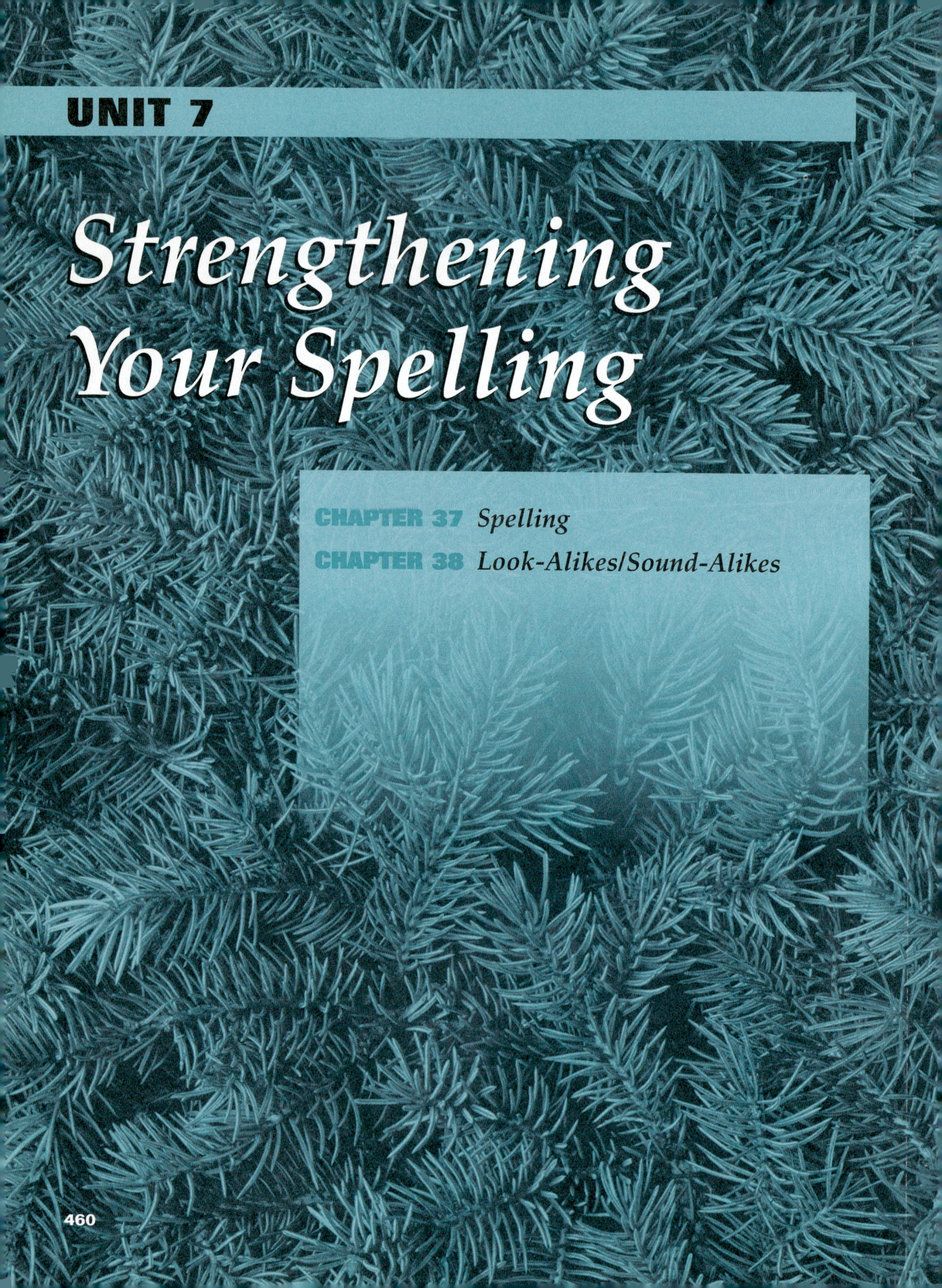

Strengthening Your Spelling

CHAPTER 37 *Spelling*
CHAPTER 38 *Look-Alikes/Sound-Alikes*

CHAPTER 37

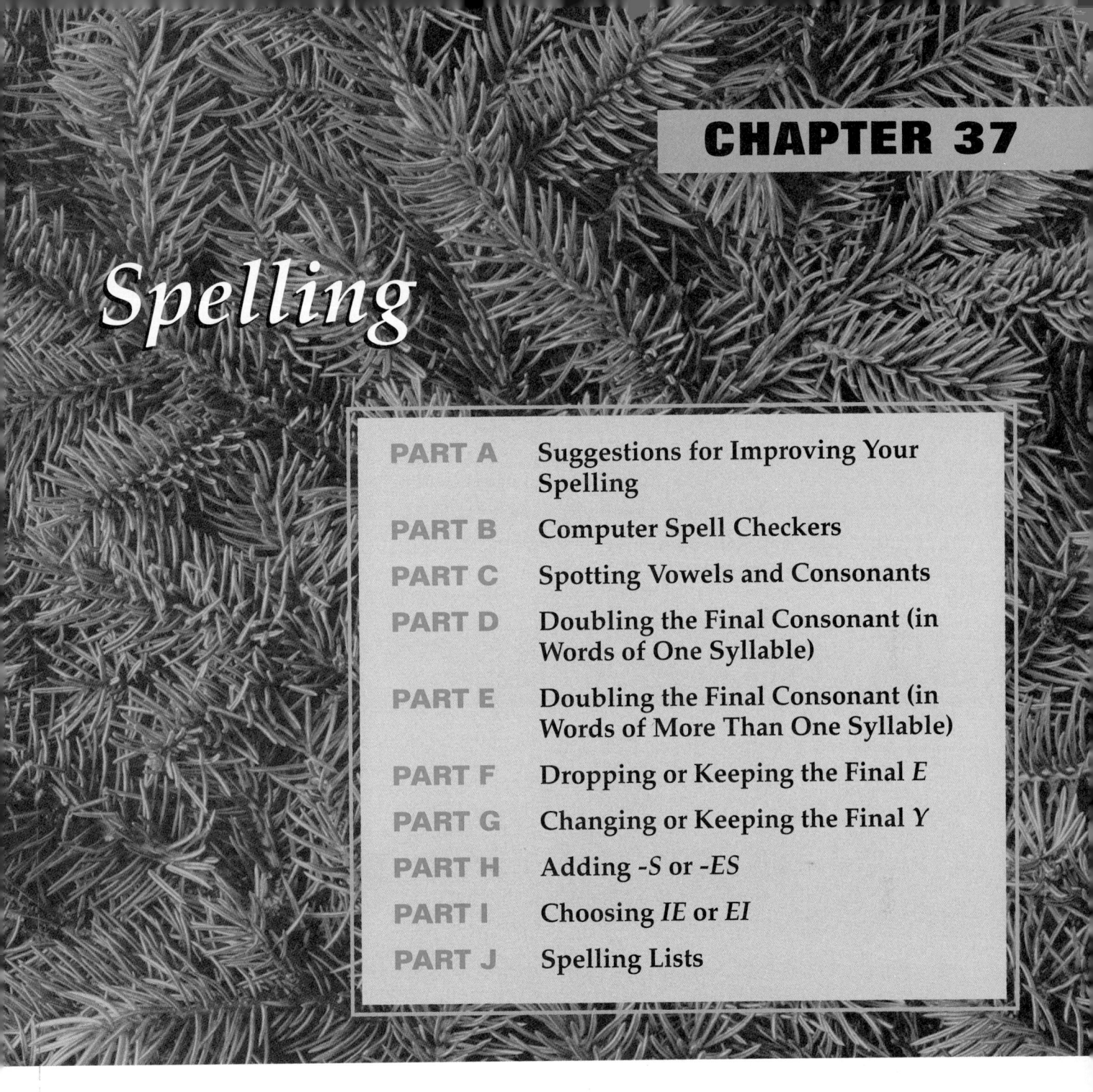

Spelling

PART A	Suggestions for Improving Your Spelling
PART B	Computer Spell Checkers
PART C	Spotting Vowels and Consonants
PART D	Doubling the Final Consonant (in Words of One Syllable)
PART E	Doubling the Final Consonant (in Words of More Than One Syllable)
PART F	Dropping or Keeping the Final *E*
PART G	Changing or Keeping the Final *Y*
PART H	Adding *-S* or *-ES*
PART I	Choosing *IE* or *EI*
PART J	Spelling Lists

PART A Suggestions for Improving Your Spelling

Accurate spelling is an important ingredient of good writing. No matter how interesting your ideas are, if your spelling is poor, your writing will not be effective.

Some Tips for Improving Your Spelling

- **Look closely at the words on the page.** Use any tricks you can to remember the right spelling. For example, "The *a*'s in *separate* are separated by an *r*," or "*Dessert* has two *s*'s because you want two desserts."

- **Use a dictionary.** Even professional writers frequently check spelling in a dictionary. As you write, underline the words you are not sure of and look them up when you write your final draft. If locating words in the dictionary is a real problem for you, consider a "poor speller's dictionary."

- **Use a spell checker.** If you write on a computer, make a habit of using the spell-check software. See Part B for tips and cautions about spell checkers.

- **Keep a list of the words you misspell.** Look over your list whenever you can and keep it handy as you write.

- **Look over corrected papers for misspelled words** (often marked *sp.*). Add these words to your list. Practice writing each word three or four times.

- **Test yourself.** Use flash cards or have a friend dictate words from your list or from this chapter.

- **Review the basic spelling rules explained in this chapter.** Take time to learn the material; don't rush through the entire chapter all at once.

- **Study the spelling list on page 471,** and test yourself on these words.

- **Read through Chapter 38, "Look-Alikes/Sound-Alikes,"** for commonly confused words (*their, there,* and *they're,* for instance). The practices in that chapter will help you eliminate some common spelling errors from your writing.

PART B Computer Spell Checkers

Almost all word-processing programs are equipped with a spell checker. A spell checker picks up spelling errors and gives you alternatives for correcting them. Get in the habit of using this feature as your first and last proofreading task.

Depending on your program and the paper you are writing, determine the best ways to use the spell checker. For example, if your paper repeats an unusual name, use the "ignore all" feature rather than check the name each time it appears. If the name appears when you're using "ignore all," you've spelled the name differently that time.

What a spell checker cannot do is think. If you've mistyped one word for another—*if* for *it,* for example—the spell checker cannot bring it to your attention. If you've written *then* for *than,* the spell checker cannot help. Proofread your paper after using the spell checker. For questions about words that sound the same but are spelled differently, check Chapter 38, "Look-Alikes/Sound-Alikes." Run spell check again after you've made all your corrections. If you've introduced a new error, the spell checker will let you know.

PRACTICE 1

With a group of four or five classmates, read this poem, which "passed" spell check. Can your group find and correct all the errors that the spell check missed?

       I have   *checker*
~~Eye halve~~ a spelling ~~check her~~,
                PC
It came with my ~~pea see~~.
        marks *for*   *review*
It clearly ~~marques four~~ my ~~revue~~,
  Mistakes *I* *cannot* *see*
~~Miss steaks eye can knot sea.~~

            through
I've run this poem ~~threw~~ it.
You're surely pleased to know
~~Your Shirley please too no~~

It's   its   way
Its letter perfect in it's weigh.
         told   so
My checker tolled me sew.

PART C Spotting Vowels and Consonants

To learn some basic spelling rules, you must know the difference between vowels and consonants.

The **vowels** are *a, e, i, o,* and *u.*

The **consonants** are *b, c, d, f, g, h, j, k, l, m, n, p, q, r, s, t, v, w, x,* and *z.*

The letter *y* can be either a vowel or a consonant, depending on its sound:

daisy   **sky**

■ In each of these words, *y* is a vowel because it has a vowel sound: an *ee* sound in *daisy* and an *i* sound in *sky.*

yellow   **your**

■ In both *yellow* and *your*, *y* is a consonant because it has the consonant sound of *y.*

PRACTICE 2

Write *v* for vowel and *c* for consonant in the space on top of each word. Be careful of the *y.*

EXAMPLE $\dfrac{c\ v\ c\ v\ c}{h\ o\ p\ e\ d}$

1. $\dfrac{c\ v\ c\ c}{h\ a\ l\ l}$

2. $\dfrac{c\ v\ c\ v}{r\ e\ l\ y}$

3. $\dfrac{c\ v\ c\ c\ v\ c\ c}{p\ e\ r\ h\ a\ p\ s}$

4. $\dfrac{c\ v\ c\ c}{y\ a\ w\ n}$

5. $\dfrac{v\ c\ c\ c\ v\ c}{i\ n\ s\ t\ e\ a\ d}$

6. $\dfrac{c\ v\ c\ c}{j\ u\ m\ p}$

7. $\dfrac{c\ v\ v\ c\ v\ c\ v}{q\ u\ a\ l\ i\ f\ y}$

8. $\dfrac{c\ v\ c\ c\ v\ c}{h\ i\ d\ d\ e\ n}$

9. $\dfrac{c\ v\ c\ c\ v}{f\ o\ r\ g\ e}$

10. $\dfrac{c\ v\ c\ c\ v\ c\ c\ v\ c}{b\ y\ s\ t\ a\ n\ d\ e\ r}$

PART D Doubling the Final Consonant (in Words of One Syllable)

When you add a suffix or an ending that begins with a vowel (like *-ed, -ing, -er, -est*) to a word of one syllable, double the final consonant *if* the last three letters of the word are *consonant-vowel-consonant* or *c-v-c.*

UNIT 7 Strengthening Your Spelling

plan + ed = planned swim + ing = swimming
thin + est = thinnest light + er = lighter

- *Plan, swim,* and *thin* all end in *cvc;* therefore, the final consonants are doubled.
- *Light* does not end in *cvc;* therefore, the final consonant is not doubled.

PRACTICE 3

Which of the following words should double the final consonant? Check to see whether the word ends in *cvc*. Then add the suffixes *-ed* and *-ing*.

	Word	Last Three Letters	-ed	-ing
EXAMPLE	drop	cvc	dropped	dropping
	boil	vvc	boiled	boiling
1.	tan	cvc	tanned	tanning
2.	brag	cvc	bragged	bragging
3.	rip	cvc	ripped	ripping
4.	mail	vvc	mailed	mailing
5.	stop	cvc	stopped	stopping
6.	peel	vvc	peeled	peeling
7.	shift	vcc	shifted	shifting
8.	wrap	cvc	wrapped	wrapping
9.	ask	vcc	asked	asking
10.	chat	cvc	chatted	chatting

PRACTICE 4

Which of the following words should double the final consonant? Check for *cvc*. Then add the suffixes *-er* or *-est*.

	Word	Last Three Letters	-er	-est
EXAMPLE	wet	cvc	wetter	wettest
	cool	vvc	cooler	coolest
1.	deep	vvc	deeper	deepest
2.	short	vcc	shorter	shortest
3.	fat	cvc	fatter	fattest
4.	slim	cvc	slimmer	slimmest

Word	Last Three Letters	-er	-est
5. red	cvc	redder	reddest
6. green	vvc	greener	greenest
7. moist	vcc	moister	moistest
8. clean	vvc	cleaner	cleanest
9. dim	cvc	dimmer	dimmest
10. bright	ccc	brighter	brightest

PART E — Doubling the Final Consonant (in Words of More Than One Syllable)

When you add a suffix that begins with a vowel to a word of more than one syllable, double the final consonant *if*

(1) the last three letters of the word are *cvc,* and

(2) the accent or stress is on the *last* syllable.

begin + ing = beginning   control + ed = controlled

- *Begin* and *control* both end in *cvc.*
- In both words, the stress is on the last syllable: *be-gin', con-trol'*. (Pronounce the words aloud and listen for the correct stress.)
- Therefore, *beginning* and *controlled* double the final consonant.

listen + ing = listening   visit + ed = visited

- *Listen* and *visit* both end in *cvc.*
- However, the stress is *not* on the last syllable: lis'-ten, vis'-it.
- Therefore, *listening* and *visited* do not double the final consonant.

PRACTICE 5

Which of the following words should double the final consonant? First, check for *cvc;* then check for the final stress. Then add the suffixes *-ed* and *-ing*.

	Word	Last Three Letters	-ed	-ing
EXAMPLE	repel	cvc	repelled	repelling
	enlist	vcc	enlisted	enlisting
1.	expel	cvc	expelled	expelling
2.	happen	cvc	happened	happening
3.	polish	vcc	polished	polishing

466 UNIT 7 Strengthening Your Spelling

Word	Last Three Letters	-ed	-ing
4. admit	cvc	admitted	admitting
5. offer	cvc	offered	offering
6. prefer	cvc	preferred	preferring
7. commit	cvc	committed	committing
8. pardon	cvc	pardoned	pardoning
9. compel	cvc	compelled	compelling
10. answer	cvc	answered	answering

PART F Dropping or Keeping the Final E

When you add a suffix that begins with a vowel (like *-able, -ence, -ing*), drop the final *e*.

When you add a suffix that begins with a consonant (like *-less, -ment, -ly*), keep the final *e*.

move + ing = moving   **pure + ity = purity**

- *Moving* and *purity* both drop the final *e* because the suffixes *-ing* and *-ity* begin with vowels.

home + less = homeless   **advertise + ment = advertisement**

- *Homeless* and *advertisement* keep the final *e* because the suffixes *-less* and *-ment* begin with consonants.

Here are some exceptions to memorize:

argument	judgment	truly
awful	knowledgeable	simply
courageous	manageable	

PRACTICE 6

Add the suffix shown to each word.

EXAMPLE hope + ing = *hoping*
hope + ful = *hopeful*

1. love + able = *lovable*
2. love + ly = *lovely*
3. pure + ly = *purely*
4. pure + er = *purer*
5. complete + ing = *completing*
6. complete + ness = *completeness*
7. enforce + ment = *enforcement*
8. enforce + ed = *enforced*
9. arrange + ing = *arranging*
10. arrange + ment = *arrangement*

PRACTICE 7

Add the suffix shown to each word.

EXAMPLE come + ing = *coming*

rude + ness = *rudeness*

1. guide + ance = *guidance*
2. manage + ment = *management*
3. dense + ity = *density*
4. complete + ly = *completely*
5. motive + ation = *motivation*
6. sincere + ly = *sincerely*
7. like + able = *likable*
8. response + ible = *responsible*
9. judge + ment = *judgment*
10. fame + ous = *famous*

PART G Changing or Keeping the Final Y

When you add a suffix to a word that ends in -y, change the y to i if the letter before the y is a consonant.
  Keep the final y if the letter before the y is a vowel.

happy + ness = happiness   portray + ed = portrayed

- The y in *happiness* is changed to i because the letter before the y is a consonant, p.
- The y in *portrayed* is not changed because the letter before it is a vowel, a.

However, when you add -ing to words ending in y, always keep the y:

copy + ing = copying   delay + ing = delaying

Here are some exceptions to memorize:

day + ly = daily   pay + ed = paid
lay + ed = laid   say + ed = said

PRACTICE 8

Add the suffix shown to each of the following words.

EXAMPLE marry + ed = *married*

buy + er = *buyer*

1. try + ed = *tried*
2. vary + able = *variable*
3. worry + ing = *worrying*
4. pay + ed = *paid*
5. enjoy + able = *enjoyable*
6. wealthy + est = *wealthiest*
7. day + ly = *daily*
8. duty + ful = *dutiful*
9. display + s = *displays*
10. occupy + ed = *occupied*

PRACTICE 9

Add the suffix in parentheses to each word.

1. beauty (fy) _beautify_ 4. angry (er) _angrier_
   (ful) _beautiful_ (est) _angriest_
   (es) _beauties_ (ly) _angrily_
2. lonely (er) _lonelier_ 5. study (es) _studies_
   (est) _loneliest_ (ous) _studious_
   (ness) _loneliness_ (ing) _studying_
3. betray (ed) _betrayed_ 6. busy (ness) _business_
   (ing) _betraying_ (er) _busier_
   (al) _betrayal_ (est) _busiest_

PART H Adding -S or -ES

Nouns usually take an -s or an -es ending to form the plural. Verbs take an -s or -es in the third person singular (*he, she,* or *it*).

Add -es instead of -s if a word ends in *ch, sh, ss, x,* or *z* (the -es adds an extra syllable to the word):

box + es = boxes   **crutch + es = crutches**   **miss + es = misses**

Add -es instead of -s for most words that end in *o*:

do + es = does   **hero + es = heroes**
echo + es = echoes   **tomato + es = tomatoes**
go + es = goes   **potato + es = potatoes**

Here are some exceptions to memorize:

pianos   sopranos
radios   solos

When you change the final *y* to *i* in a word,* add -es instead of -s:

fry + es = fries   **marry + es = marries**   **candy + es = candies**

PRACTICE 10

Add -s or -es to the following nouns and verbs, changing the final *y* to *i* when necessary.

---

* See Part G of this chapter for more on changing or keeping the final *y*.

EXAMPLE sketch _sketches_

echo _echoes_

1. watch _watches_
2. tomato _tomatoes_
3. reply _replies_
4. company _companies_
5. bicycle _bicycles_
6. piano _pianos_
7. donkey _donkeys_
8. dictionary _dictionaries_
9. boss _bosses_
10. hero _heroes_

PART 1 Choosing *IE* or *EI*

Write *i* before *e*, except after *c* or in an *ay* sound like *neighbor* or *weigh*.

achieve, niece   deceive   vein

- *Achieve* and *niece* are spelled *ie*.
- *Deceive* is spelled *ei* because of the preceding *c*.
- *Vein* is spelled *ei* because of its *ay* sound.

However, words with a *shen* sound are spelled with an *ie* after the *c*: *ancient, conscience, efficient, sufficient*.

Here are some exceptions to memorize:

either	seize
neither	society
foreign	their
height	weird

PRACTICE 11

Pronounce each word out loud. Then fill in either *ie* or *ei*.

1. bel _i e_ ve
2. _e i_ ght
3. effic _i e_ nt
4. n _e i_ ther
5. cash _i e_ r
6. th _e i_ r
7. ch _i e_ f
8. soc _i e_ ty
9. rec _e i_ ve
10. fr _i e_ nd
11. consc _i e_ nce
12. h _e i_ ght
13. ach _i e_ ve
14. v _e i_ n
15. for _e i_ gn
16. perc _e i_ ve

UNIT 7 Strengthening Your Spelling

PRACTICE 12 Review

Test your knowledge of the spelling rules in this chapter by adding suffixes to the following words. If you have trouble, the part in which the rule appears is shown in parentheses.

		Part			Part
1. nerve + ous	_nervous_	(F)	11. carry + ing	_carrying_	(G)
2. feed + ing	_feeding_	(D)	12. tomato + s/es	_tomatoes_	(H)
3. beach + s/es	_beaches_	(H)	13. admit + ing	_admitting_	(E)
4. drop + ed	_dropped_	(D)	14. test + er	_tester_	(D)
5. hope + ing	_hoping_	(F)	15. tasty + est	_tastiest_	(G)
6. study + s/es	_studies_	(H)	16. sip + ing	_sipping_	(D)
7. busy + ness	_business_	(G)	17. believe + able	_believable_	(F)
8. manage + ment	_management_	(F)	18. commit + ment	_commitment_	(E)
9. radio + s/es	_radios_	(H)	19. deny + al	_denial_	(G)
10. occur + ed	_occurred_	(E)	20. day + ly	_daily_	(G)

PRACTICE 13 Review

Circle the correctly spelled word in each pair.

1. writting, **(writing)**
2. **(receive)**, recieve
3. begining, **(beginning)**
4. greif, **(grief)**
5. relaid, **(relayed)**
6. **(piece)**, peice
7. **(resourceful)**, resourcful
8. **(argument)**, arguement
9. **(marries)**, marrys
10. thier, **(their)**

PART J Spelling Lists

Commonly Misspelled Words

Following is a list of words that are often misspelled. As you can see, they are words that you might use daily in speaking and writing. The trouble spot, the part of each word that is usually spelled incorrectly, has been put in bold type.

To help yourself learn these words, you might copy each one twice, making sure to underline the trouble spot, or copy the words on flash cards and have someone test you.

1. across
2. a**dd**ress
3. an**sw**er
4. argum**e**nt
5. ath**l**ete
6. begi**nn**ing
7. beha**v**ior
8. calend**a**r
9. ca**r**eer
10. cons**ci**ence
11. crow**ded**
12. defin**ite**
13. de**s**cribe
14. desp**e**rate
15. d**i**fferent
16. disa**pp**oint
17. disa**pp**rove
18. doesn't
19. ei**gh**th
20. embarra**ss**
21. envir**on**ment
22. exa**gg**erate
23. fami**li**ar
24. finally
25. government
26. gram**m**ar
27. hei**gh**t
28. **ill**egal
29. immed**iately**
30. import**ant**
31. int**e**gration
32. int**ell**igent
33. inte**r**est
34. inte**r**fere
35. jew**e**lry
36. jud**gm**ent
37. kno**w**ledge
38. main**tain**
39. mathematics
40. meant
41. ne**cess**ary
42. nerv**ous**
43. occ**a**sion
44. opin**ion**
45. optim**ist**
46. particular
47. per**form**
48. **per**haps
49. personn**el**
50. po**ss**e**ss**
51. possible
52. **pre**fer
53. pre**jud**ice
54. privi**lege**
55. prob**ably**
56. **psych**ology
57. **pur**sue
58. reference
59. rhythm
60. ridiculous
61. separate
62. simil**ar**
63. **since**
64. speech
65. streng**th**
66. suc**c**ess
67. **sur**prise
68. taught
69. temperature
70. thorough
71. thought
72. tired
73. until
74. wei**gh**t
75. written

Personal Spelling List

In your notebook, keep a list of words that *you* misspell. Add words to your list from corrected papers and from the exercises in this chapter. First, copy each word as you misspelled it, underlining the trouble spot; then write the word correctly. Study your list often. Use this form:

As I Wrote It   **Correct Spelling**

1. pro_bly_   probably
2. _____   _____
3. _____   _____

472 UNIT 7 Strengthening Your Spelling

4. _____   _____

5. _____   _____

PRACTICE 14   Review

Proofread the following essay for spelling errors. (Be careful: There are misspelled words from both the exercises in this chapter and the spelling list.) Correct any errors by writing above the lines.

The Cell Phone Explosion

(1) Cellular phones, those ~~lightwieght~~ *lightweight* telephones people carry with them, are becoming more popular all the time. (2) About fifty million people in the United States use them, sometimes at odd times—for example, when they are seated in a crowded restaurant or standing in a ~~crowdded~~ *crowded* elevator. (3) As digital technology keeps ~~improveing~~ *improving*, even more cell phones ~~probly~~ *probably* will appear—in even odder places.

(4) Although analog phones—the older, more ~~familar~~ *familiar* type—transmit voices that usually come ~~accross~~ *across* more clearly, digital phones have several advantages.

(5) For one thing, they protect your privacy. (6) Calls made with analog phones can be picked up by ~~radioes~~ *radios*, other cellular sets, and even old televisions if they are ~~lockked~~ *locked* on the right frequency. (7) Digital technology, however, can prevent people from ~~eavesdroping~~ *eavesdropping* on your conversation.

(8) New digital wireless phone networks also simplify the process of ~~useing~~ *using* cell phones outside your home area. (9) A digital network ~~dosen't~~ *doesn't* charge you for calls made in other ~~citys~~ *cities* or states.

(10) Digital cell phones are growing more high tech every day. (11) Some let you ~~recieve~~ *receive* messages. (12) Others combine a phone, pager, and two-way radio in one unit. (13) Some cell phones even fax, send e-mail, and browse the Web. (14) Furthermore, the phones are ~~definately geting~~ *definitely getting* more fashionable. (15) Some cell phones can be worn like ~~jewlery~~ *jewelry*, ~~prehaps~~ *perhaps* clipped to a belt or ~~straped~~ *strapped* on an arm.

CHAPTER 38
Look-Alikes/Sound-Alikes

A/an/and

1. *A* is used before a word beginning with a consonant or a consonant sound.

   a man   **a** house
   a union (*u* in *union* is pronounced like the consonant *y*)

2. *An* is used before a word beginning with a vowel (*a, e, i, o, u*) or silent *h*.

   an igloo   **an** apple
   an hour (*h* in *hour* is silent)

3. *And* joins words or ideas together.

   Edward **and** Ralph are taking the same biology class.
   He is very honest, **and** most people respect him.

PRACTICE 1

Fill in *a*, *an*, or *and*.

1. The administration building is __an__ old brick house on top of __a__ hill.

2. __An__ artist __and__ two students share that studio.

3. The computer in my office has __an__ amber screen __and__ __a__ hard-disk drive.

4. Joyce __and__ Luis bought __a__ lovely old rocker at the garage sale.

5. For lunch, Ben ate __a__ ham sandwich, __an__ apple, __and__ two bananas.

473

Accept/except

1. *Accept* means to receive.

   That college *accepts* only women.   **I *accepted* his offer of help.**

2. *Except* means other than or excluding.

   Everyone *except* Ron thinks it's a good idea.

PRACTICE 2

Fill in *accept* or *except*.

1. Jan has read all of Shakespeare's comedies __except__ one.
2. Please __accept__ my apologies.
3. Unable to __accept__ defeat, the boxer protested the decision.
4. Sam loves all his courses __except__ chemistry.
5. __Except__ for Elizabeth, all of my friends went home after the intermission.

Affect/effect

1. *Affect* (verb) means to have an influence on or to change.

   Her father's career as a lawyer *affected* her decision to go to law school.

2. *Effect* (noun) means the result of a cause or an influence.

   Careful proofreading had a positive *effect* on the grades Carl received for his compositions.

3. *Effect* is also a verb that means to cause.

   The U.S. Senate is attempting to *effect* changes in foreign policy.

PRACTICE 3

Fill in *affect* or *effect*.

1. You are mistaken if you think alcohol will not __affect__ your judgment.
2. Attractive, neat clothing will have a positive __effect__ on an employment interviewer.
3. Your cigarette smoke __affects__ my ability to think straight.
4. Hot, humid summers always have the __effect__ of making me lazy.
5. We will not be able to __effect__ these changes without the cooperation of the employees and the union.

Been/being

1. *Been* is the past participle form of *to be*. *Been* is usually used after the helping verb *have, has,* or *had*.

   I *have been* to that restaurant before.

   She *has been* a poet for ten years.

2. *Being* is the *-ing* form of *to be*. *Being* is usually used after the helping verb *is, are, am, was,* or *were*.

   They *are being* helped by the salesperson.

   Rhonda *is being* foolish and stubborn.

PRACTICE 4

Fill in *been* or *being*.

1. Have you __been__ to Rib Heaven yet?
2. Pete thinks his phone calls are __being__ taped.
3. Are you __being__ secretive, or have I __been__ imagining it?
4. Yoko has never __been__ to Omaha!
5. __Being__ a dynamic teacher is Jenny's goal.

Buy/by

1. *Buy* means to purchase.

   She *buys* new furniture every five years.

2. *By* means near, by means of, or before.

   He walked right *by* and didn't say hello.

   ***By* sunset, we had finished the harvest.**

PRACTICE 5

Fill in *buy* or *by*.

1. You can't __buy__ happiness, but many people try.
2. Lee __buys__ sand __by__ the ton for his masonry business.
3. Please drop __by__ the video store and __buy__ some blank tapes; I want to tape the football game.
4. __By__ __buying__ out his partners, Joe became sole owner of the firm.
5. __By__ the time he is thirty, Emil will have earned his M.A.

It's/its

1. *It's* is a contraction of *it is* or *it has*. If you cannot substitute *it is* or *it has* in the sentence, you cannot use *it's*.

   It's a ten-minute walk to my house.   **It's been a nice party.**

2. *Its* is a possessive and shows ownership.

   The kitten rolled playfully on *its* side.

   Industry must do *its* share to curb inflation.

Practice 6

Fill in *it's* or *its*.

1. Put the contact lens in __its__ case, please.

2. __It's__ about time H.T. straightened up the rubble in his room.

3. Dan's truck has a dent in __its__ fender.

4. The company offered some of __its__ employees an early retirement option.

5. You know __it's__ cold when the pond has ice on __its__ surface.

Know/knew/no/new

1. *Know* means to have knowledge or understanding.

2. *Knew* is the past tense of the verb *know*.

   Carl *knows* he has to finish by 6 P.M.

   The police officer *knew* the quickest route to the pier.

3. *No* is a negative.

   He is *no* longer dean of academic affairs.

4. *New* means recent, fresh, unused.

   I like your *new* hat.

Practice 7

Fill in *know, knew, no,* or *new*.

1. I __know__ he's __new__ in town, but this is ridiculous.

2. If I __knew__ then what I __know__ now, I wouldn't have made so many mistakes when I was young.

3. Abe and Gabe __know__ that they have __no__ chance of winning the marathon.

4. Fran _knew_ when she bought this _new_ chair that it was too big for the room.

5. _No_, I don't _know_ the way to Grandma's house, you hairy weirdo.

Lose/loose

1. *Lose* means to misplace or not to win.

   Be careful not to *lose* your way on those back roads.

   George hates to *lose* at cards.

2. *Loose* means too large, not tightly fitting.

   That shirt is not my size; it's *loose*.

PRACTICE 8

Fill in *lose* or *loose*.

1. When Ari studies in bed, he _loses_ the _loose_ change from his pockets.

2. Several layers of _loose_ clothing can warm you in winter.

3. Whenever my dog Rover gets _loose_ in the streets, all the neighborhood cats stay in hiding.

4. Don't _lose_ any sleep over tomorrow's exam.

5. If you _lose_ that _loose_ screw, the handle will fall off.

Past/passed

1. *Past* is that which has already occurred; it is over with.

   His *past* work has been satisfactory.

   Never let the *past* interfere with your hopes for the future.

2. *Passed* is the past tense of the verb *to pass*.

   She *passed* by and nodded hello.   **The wild geese *passed* overhead.**

PRACTICE 9

Fill in *past* or *passed*.

1. As Jake _passed_ the barn, he noticed a man talking to the reindeer.

2. To children, even the recent _past_ seems like ancient history.

3. Mia _passed_ up the opportunity to see a friend from her _past_.

4. The quarterback _passed_ the ball fifty yards for a touchdown.

5. This Bible was _passed_ down to me by my mother; it contains records of our family's _past_.

Quiet/quit/quite

1. *Quiet* means silent, still.

   The woods are *quiet* tonight.

2. *Quit* means to give up or to stop doing something.

   Last year I *quit* drinking.

3. *Quite* means very or exactly.

   He was *quite* tired after playing handball for two hours.
   That's not *quite* right.

PRACTICE 10

Fill in *quiet*, *quit*, or *quite*.

1. The cottage is a _quiet_ and beautiful place to study.

2. Nora is _quite_ dedicated to her veterinary career.

3. Don't _quit_ your job, even though you aren't _quite_ happy with the working conditions.

4. Each day when he _quits_ work, Dan visits a _quiet_ spot in the park.

5. She made _quite_ an impression in red fake fur and a blond wig.

Rise/raise

1. *Rise* means to get up by one's own power.
   The past tense of *rise* is *rose*.
   The past participle of *rise* is *risen*.

   The sun *rises* at 6 A.M.

   Daniel *rose* early yesterday.

   He has *risen* from the table.

2. *Raise* means to lift an object or to grow or increase.
   The past tense of *raise* is *raised*.
   The past participle of *raise* is *raised*.

Raise your right hand.

She *raised* the banner over her head.

We have *raised* one thousand dollars.

PRACTICE 11

Fill in the correct form of *rise* or *raise*.

1. The loaves of bread have __risen__ perfectly.
2. The new mayor __raised__ his arms in a victory salute.
3. Once the sun has __risen__, Pete __raises__ the shades and opens the window.
4. We all __rose__ as the bride walked down the aisle.
5. The money we have __raised__ will help build a shelter.

Sit/set

1. *Sit* means to seat oneself.
   The past tense of *sit* is *sat*.
   The past participle of *sit* is *sat*.

   Sit up straight!

   He *sat* down on the porch and fell asleep.

   She has *sat* reading that book all day.

2. *Set* means to place or put something down.
   The past tense of *set* is *set*.
   The past participle of *set* is *set*.

   Don't *set* your books on the dining room table.

   She *set* the package down and walked off without it.

   She had *set* the timer on the stove.

PRACTICE 12

Fill in *sit* or *set*.

1. Please __set__ your briefcase here. Would you like to __sit__ down?
2. Have they __sat__ in on a rehearsal before?
3. Tom __set__ the chair by the window and __sat__ down.
4. Maria __set__ her alarm clock for 6:30 A.M.
5. Sorry, I wouldn't have __sat__ here if I had known you were returning.

Suppose/supposed

1. *Suppose* means to assume or guess.
   The past tense of *suppose* is *supposed*.
   The past participle of *suppose* is *supposed*.

   Brad *supposes* that the teacher will give him an A.

   We all *supposed* she would win first prize.

   I had *supposed* Dan would bring his trumpet.

2. *Supposed* means ought to or should; it is followed by *to*.

   He is *supposed* to meet us after class.

   You were *supposed* to wash and wax the car.

Remember: When you mean *ought to* or *should*, always use the *-ed* ending—*supposed*.

Practice 13

Fill in *suppose* or *supposed*.

1. Why do you __suppose__ wolves howl at the moon?

2. I __suppose__ you enjoy reggae.

3. Detective Baker is __supposed__ to address the Citizens' Patrol tonight.

4. Wasn't Erik __supposed__ to meet us at five?

5. Ms. Ita says we're not __supposed__ to guess in computer science class; we're __supposed__ to know.

Their/there/they're

1. *Their* is a possessive and shows ownership.

   They couldn't find *their* wigs.   ***Their* children are charming.**

2. *There* indicates a direction.

   I wouldn't go *there* again.   **Put the lumber down *there*.**

   There is also a way of introducing a thought.

   There is a fly in my soup.

   There are two ways to approach this problem.

3. *They're* is a contraction: *they + are = they're*. If you cannot substitute *they are* in the sentence, you cannot use *they're*.

   They're the best tires money can buy.   **If *they're* coming, count me in.**

PRACTICE 14

Fill in *their*, *there*, or *they're*.

1. If __they're__ not __there__ on time, we will have to leave without them.
2. __They're__ two of the most amusing people I know.
3. __There__ are two choices you can make, and __they're__ both risky.
4. Two mail carriers left __their__ mail bags __there__ on the post office steps.
5. Is __there__ a doctor in the house?
6. The motorcycles roared __their__ way into town.
7. __Their__ phone usually rings seven or eight times before they answer.
8. Don't worry about __their__ performance in the race because __they're__ both tough.

Then/than

1. *Then* means afterward or at that time.

   First we went to the theater, and *then* we went out for a pizza and champagne.

   I was a heavyweight boxer *then*.

2. *Than* is used in a comparison.

   She is a better student *than* I.

PRACTICE 15

Fill in *then* or *than*.

1. First, Cassandra kicked off her shoes; __then__ she began to dance.
2. Jupiter's diameter is eleven times larger __than__ Earth's.
3. If you're more familiar with this trail __than__ I, __then__ you should lead the way.
4. Fran lived in Chicago __then__; now she lives in Miami.
5. If he is better prepared __than__ you, what will you do __then__?

Through/though

1. *Through* means in one side and out the other, finished, or by means of.

   The rain came *through* the open window.

   We should be *through* soon.

   ***Through* practice, I can do anything.**

2. *Though* means although. Used with *as*, *though* means as if.

   ***Though* he rarely speaks, he writes terrific letters.**

   It was as *though* I had never ridden a bicycle before.

PRACTICE 16

Fill in *through* or *though*.

1. __Through__ study and perseverance, Charelle earned her degree in three years.

2. Dee usually walks to work __though__ she sometimes rides the bus.

3. Julio strode __through__ the bank as __though__ he owned it.

4. Clayton is a Texan __through__ and __through__.

5. I'm not really hungry; I will have an apple, __though__.

To/too/two

1. *To* means toward.

   We are going *to* the stadium.

   To can also be combined with a verb to form an infinitive.

   Where do you want *to go* for lunch?

2. *Too* means also or very.

   Roberto is going to the theater *too*.

   They were *too* bored to stay awake.

3. *Two* is the number 2.

   There are *two* new accounting courses this term.

PRACTICE 17

Fill in *to*, *too*, or *two*.

1. Please take my daughter __to__ the movies __too__.

2. We'd like a table for __two__ with a view of the sea.

3. Dan, __too__, took __two__ hours __to__ complete the exam.

CHAPTER 38 Look-Alikes/Sound-Alikes   483

4. Luis went __to__ Iowa State for __two__ semesters.

5. This curry is __too__ hot __to__ eat and __too__ good __to__ resist.

Use/used

1. *Use* means to make use of.
   The past tense of *use* is *used*.
   The past participle of *use* is *used*.

   Why do you *use* green ink?

   He *used* the wrong paint in the bathroom.

   I have *used* that brand of toothpaste myself.

2. *Used* means in the habit of or accustomed to; it is followed by *to*.

   I am not *used* to getting up at 4 A.M.   They got *used* to the good life.

Remember: When you mean *in the habit of* or *accustomed to*, always use the *-ed* ending—*used*.

PRACTICE 18

Fill in *use* or *used*.

1. Marie __used__ to drive a jalopy that she bought at a __used__ car lot.

2. We will __use__ about three gallons of paint on this shed.

3. Can you __use__ a __used__ computer?

4. Pam __used__ to __use__ a pick to strum her guitar.

5. Shall I __use__ contrast or illustration to develop this essay?

Weather/whether

1. *Weather* refers to atmospheric conditions.

   In June, the *weather* in Spain is lovely.

2. *Whether* implies a question.

   Whether or not you pass depends on you.

PRACTICE 19

Fill in *weather* or *whether*.

1. In fine __weather__, we take long walks in the woods.

2. __Whether__ or not you like Chinese food, you'll love this dish.

484 UNIT 7 Strengthening Your Spelling

3. The __weather__ person never said __whether__ or not it would snow.

4. I can't recall __whether__ you prefer tea or coffee.

5. In 1870 a national __weather__ service was established.

Where/were/we're

1. *Where* implies place or location.

   Where have you been all day?   **Home is *where* you hang your hat.**

2. *Were* is the past tense of *are*.

   We *were* on our way when the hurricane hit.

3. *We're* is a contraction: *we* + *are* = *we're*. If you cannot substitute *we are* in the sentence, you cannot use *we're*.

   We're going to leave now.   **Since *we're* in the city, let's go to the zoo.**

Practice 20

Fill in *where*, *were*, or *we're*.

1. __We're__ going to Hawaii __where__ the sun always shines.

2. __Were__ you standing __where__ we agreed to meet?

3. __We're__ working out three times a week.

4. There __were__ two high-rise apartment houses __where__ the ballpark used to be.

5. __We're__ determined to attend college though we don't yet know __where__.

Whose/who's

1. *Whose* implies ownership and possession.

   Whose term paper is that?

2. *Who's* is a contraction of *who is* or *who has*. If you cannot substitute *who is* or *who has*, you cannot use *who's*.

   Who's knocking at the window?

   Who's seen my new felt hat with the red feathers?

Practice 21

Fill in *whose* or *who's*.

1. __Whose__ Probe convertible is this?

2. Tanya, __who's__ in my history class, will join us for dinner.

3. We need someone in that position __who's__ dependable, someone __whose__ abilities have already been proven.

4. __Whose__ biology textbook is this?

5. __Who's__ going to clean the oven?

Your/you're

1. *Your* is a possessive and shows ownership.

   Your knowledge astonishes me!

2. *You're* is a contraction: *you + are = you're*. If you cannot substitute *you are* in the sentence, you cannot use *you're*.

   You're the nicest person I know.

PRACTICE 22

Fill in *your* or *you're*.

1. __You're__ sitting on __your__ hat.

2. When __you're__ ready to begin __your__ piano lesson, we'll leave.

3. Let __your__ adviser help you plan __your__ course schedule.

4. When __you're__ with __your__ friends, __you're__ a different person.

5. If you think __you're__ lost, why not use __your__ map?

Personal Look-Alikes/Sound-Alikes List

In your notebook, keep a list of look-alikes and sound-alikes that *you* have trouble with. Add words to your list from corrected papers and from the exercises in this chapter; consider such pairs as *adapt/adopt, addition/edition, device/devise, stationery/stationary*, and so forth.

First, write the word you used incorrectly; then write its meaning or use it correctly in a sentence, whichever best helps you remember. Now do the same with the word you meant to use.

Word	Meaning
1. though	means although
through	I drove through the woods.
2.	

PRACTICE 23

Write ten sentences using as many of the look-alikes and sound-alikes as possible. Exchange sentences with a classmate and check each other's work.

PRACTICE 24 — Review

The following essay contains a number of look-alike/sound-alike errors. Proofread for these errors, writing the correct word above the line.

Isabel Allende

(1) Possibly the best-known female writer of Latin-American literature, Isabel Allende has survived many political and personal tragedies. (2) Most of those events have found ~~there~~ [their] way into her books. (3) Allende was born in Chile in 1942, but she fled after her uncle, President Salvador Allende, was killed during a military coup in 1973. (4) For the next seventeen years, she lived in Venezuela, ~~were~~ [where] she couldn't find work and felt trapped in ~~a~~ [an] unhappy marriage.

(5) Eventually, Allende started writing a letter to her grandfather, who was still in Chile; when he died, that letter grew until it became her first novel. (6) Still her most famous book, *The House of the Spirits* established Allende's style of writing, which combines political realism and autobiography with dreams, spirits, ~~an~~ [and] magic. (7) The novel, which was banned in Chile, was translated into more ~~then~~ [than] twenty-five languages and in 1994 was made into a movie.

(8) ~~Buy~~ [By] 1988, Allende had moved to northern California, divorced, remarried, and written her fifth novel, *The Infinite Plan*, which is her second husband's story. (9) Her next book traced the profound ~~affect~~ [effect] on Allende of the death of her daughter, Paula. (10) The book *Paula*, like *The House of the Spirits*, was ~~suppose~~ [supposed] ~~two~~ [to] be a letter, this time ~~two~~ [to] her daughter, who lay in a coma in a Madrid hospital.

(11) After *Paula* was published, Allende stopped writing for several years. (12) She started again in 1996, on January 8, the same day of the year that she had begun every one of her books. (13) The result was *Aphrodite*. (14) A nonfiction book about food and sensuality, *Aphrodite* was ~~quiet~~ [quite] different from anything Allende had written in the ~~passed~~ [past].

(15) Isabel Allende is famous for ~~been~~ *being* a passionate storyteller ~~who's~~ *whose* writing captures both the Latin-American and the universal human experience. (16) As the first Latina to write a major novel in the mystical tradition, she not only created a sensation, but she paved the way for other female Hispanic writers, including Julia Alvarez and Sandra Cisneros.

UNIT 7   WRITERS' WORKSHOP

Discuss a Time When Diverse People Were United

Some writers are naturally good spellers, and others are not. If you belong to the latter group, this unit has given you some techniques and tools for overcoming your spelling problems.

In your group or class, read this student's essay, aloud if possible. Underline the ideas and sentences you find especially effective. If you spot any spelling errors, correct them.

A Community of Fishermen

(1) Although City Island is probably best known for it's [*its*] seafood restaurants, it's just before dinnertime that I most enjoy the island. That's when the fishing boats leave. The *Riptide, Apache,* and *Daybreak* all cruise out of their slips and head for the hot spot of the day. These large vessels can pack up to a hundred passengers on board, and the crowd is usualy [*usually*] more diversifyd [*diversified*] than all the fish being hoisted over the railing.

(2) Anglers from all walks of life compete for the prize money that is awarded for catching the bigest [*biggest*] fish. The anglers are black, white, brown, and yellow, but they leave any thoughts about their skin pigment back at the dock alongside there [*their*] problems. What these fishermen do for a living, where they come from, and what kind of car they'll drive home that night are concepts of little importance. The things that count now are catching big fish, learning new tricks to catch them, and above all, having a good time. Men of all diffrent [*different*] races and religions now have something in common; they are all fishermen.

(3) The passengers might be culturally diverse, but with the exception of an ocasional [*occasional*] girlfriend or wife, they're all men. Grandfathers show sons and grandsons the ropes. Veterans give tips to the newer guys next to them, and as they hold their fishing poles over the side of the boat, elbow to elbow, they link together in a chain of masculinity.

(4) It's an eight-hour trip, and with a couple of hours down, you'll actually observe the passengers coming together. Almost everyone is drinking beer, and everyone likes to team up and tease land-lovers who get seasick. Salty old men swap fish tales and complain that the fishing is not what it used to be. Fathers talk shop and exchange jokes and busness [*business*] cards. Younger men play pranks, like sliping [*slipping*] bait into an old-timer's pocket when he's not looking. Naturally, they'll take things too far and get found out, but old-timers were not always old and will usually find humor in the gag. Toward the end of the trip, everyone congratulates the winner of the pool and slips in the last few jokes. Clearly, the conflicts that are so common in life are almost nonexistant [*nonexistent*] when your [*you're*] out on a boat in the middle of Long Island Sound.

(5) Something about sharing close quarters and a passion for the same sport makes men feel like equals. The unity seen on a fishing boat is proof that people can blend without having problems as long as they have something in common. As Anna Quindlen writes in her essay "Melting Pot," "We melt together, then draw apart."

—Paul La Valle (Student)

1. How effective is Mr. La Valle's essay?

   __Y__ Strong thesis statement?   __Y__ Good supporting details?

   __Y__ Logical organization?   __Y__ Effective conclusion?

2. Discuss your underlinings. What details or lines in the essay did you like the most? Explain as exactly as possible why something struck you as interesting or moving.

3. What is the main idea of paragraph 2? Which sentence, if any, is the topic sentence? What is the main idea of paragraph 3? What is the main idea of paragraph 4? *

4. This student ends his essay with a correctly punctuated quotation. Who is the source of the quotation? Does it provide a strong conclusion for the essay? Why or why not? *Anna Quindlen, "Melting Pot"*

5. Give examples of times when or places where diverse people have united to become a true community.

6. This student's spelling errors are distracting in an otherwise thoughtful and very well written essay. What suggestions would you make to him for improving his spelling?

Group Work

In your group, find and correct the spelling errors in this essay. See if your group can find every error. Hint: There are eleven misspelled or confused words.

Writing and Revising Ideas

1. Discuss a time when diverse people were united.

2. Write an essay that concludes with a quotation. Use Anna Quindlen's words, "We melt together, then draw apart," or choose another quotation from the Quotation Bank at the end of this book or elsewhere.

---

* *Paragraph 2 discusses the way fishing is more important than any differences among passengers. Last sentence is topic sentence. Paragraph 3 discusses the male unity on this boat. Paragraph 4 is about the way the group comes together as the hours pass.*

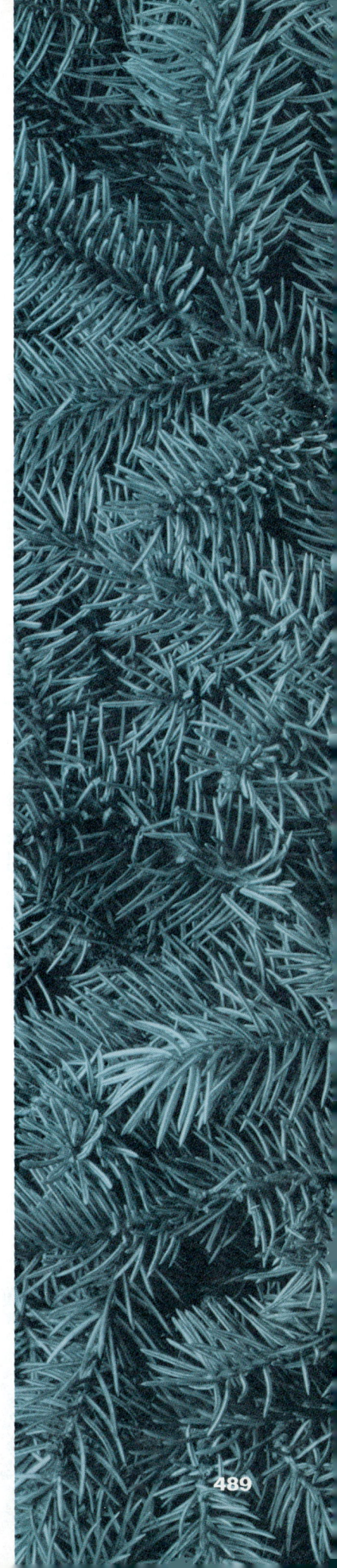

489

UNIT 8

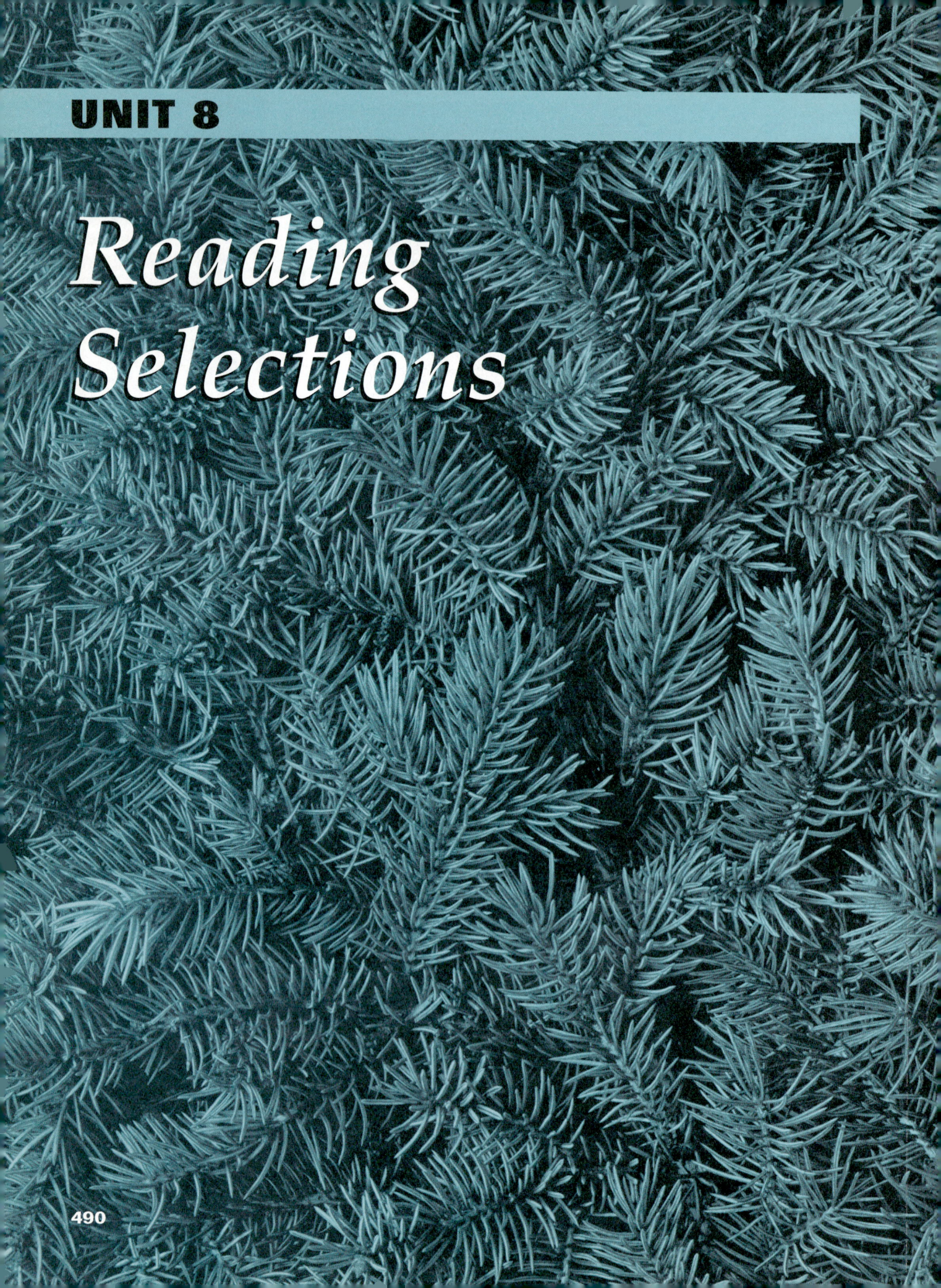

Reading Selections

Reading Strategies for Writers

We hope you will enjoy the reading selections that follow. These essays deal with many of the concerns you have as a student, as a worker, and as a member of a family. Your instructor may ask you to read and think about a selection for class discussion or for a composition either at home or in class.

The more carefully you read these selections, the better you will be able to discuss and write about them. Below are ten strategies that can help you become a more effective reader and writer:

1. **Note the title.** A title, of course, is your first clue as to what the selection is about. For example, the title "Strike Out Little League" lets you know that the selection will discuss negative aspects of organized sports for children.

   A title may also tell you which method of development the author is using. For instance, a selection entitled "Husbands and Wives: Different as Night and Day" might be a comparison/contrast essay; one entitled "Using the Library—Electronically" might be a process piece explaining how to use a computerized library catalogue.

2. **Underline main ideas.** If you read a long or difficult selection, you may forget some of the important ideas soon after you have finished the essay. However, underlining or highlighting these key ideas as you read will later help you review more easily. You may wish to number main ideas to help you follow the development of the author's thesis.

3. **Write your reactions in the margins.** Feel free to express your agreement or disagreement with the ideas in a selection by commenting "yes," "no," "Important—compare with Alice Walker's essay," or "Is he kidding?" in the margins.

   You will often be asked to write a "reaction paper," a composition explaining your thoughts about or reaction to the author's ideas. The comments that you have recorded in the margins will help you formulate a response.

4. **Prepare questions.** As you tackle more difficult reading selections, you may come across material that is hard to follow. Of course, reread the passage to see if a second reading helps. If it does not, put a question mark in the margin.

   Ask a friend or the instructor to help answer your questions. Do not be embarrassed to ask for explanations in class. Instructors appreciate careful readers who want to be sure that they completely understand what they have read.

5. **Note possible composition topics.** As you read, you may think of topics for compositions related to the ideas in the selection. Jot these topics in the margins or write about them in your journal. They may become useful if your instructor asks you for an essay based on the selection.

6. **Note effective writing.** If you are particularly moved by a portion of the selection—a phrase, a sentence, or an entire paragraph—underline or highlight it. You may wish to quote it later in class or use it in your composition.

7. **Circle unfamiliar words.** As you read, you will occasionally come across unfamiliar words. If you can guess what the word means from its context—from how it is used in the sentence or in the passage—do not interrupt your reading to look it up. Interruptions can cause you to lose the flow of ideas in the selection. Instead, circle the word and check it in a dictionary later.

8. **Vary your pace.** Some essays can be read quickly and easily. Others may require more time if the material is difficult or if much of the subject matter is unfamiliar to you. Be careful not to become discouraged, skimming a particularly difficult section just to get through with it. Extra effort will pay off.

9. **Reread.** If possible, budget your time so you can read the selection a second or even a third time. One advantage of rereading is that you will be able to discuss or write about the essay with more understanding. Ideas that were unclear may become obvious; you may even see new ideas that you failed to note the first time around.

    Another advantage is that by the second or third reading, your responses may have changed. You may agree with ideas you rejected the first time; you may disagree with ones you originally agreed with. Rereading gives you a whole new perspective!

10. **Do not overdo it.** Marking the selection as you read can help you become a better reader and writer. However, too many comments may defeat your purpose. You may not be able to decipher the mass—or mess—of underlinings, circles, and notes that you have made. Be selective.

The following essay has been marked, or annotated, by a student. Your responses might be different. Use this essay as a model to help you annotate other selections in this book—and reading material for your other courses as well.

How Sunglasses Spanned the World

Could be a process essay

Like many of the world's inhabitants, you probably own at least one pair of sunglasses, chosen as much for the image they project as for their ability to protect your eyes from the sun. In fact, sunglasses have become a staple in almost every country; it is no longer surprising to spot sunglasses on robed Arabian sheiks, Bolivian grandmothers, or Inuit fishermen tramping Arctic snows. The process by which sunglasses have gained worldwide popularity is a fascinating one that began, surprisingly, in the justice system of medieval China. 1

staple—standard item

Inuit—Eskimo

Step 1—really Stage 1

Dark glasses with smoke-tinted quartz lenses existed for centuries in China prior to 1430, but they were not used for sun protection. Chinese judges wore the darkened lenses in court to conceal their eye expressions and keep secret their reactions to evidence until the end of a trial. In 1430, when vision-correcting glasses were introduced into China from Italy, these lenses, too, were smoke-tinted, but almost entirely for judicial use. Some people wore the darkened lenses for sun protection, but the idea never really caught on. 2

This is a great idea. judicial— relating to court

Stage 2—aviator glasses invented

Five hundred years passed before the popularity of sunglasses began to grow. In the 1930s, the U.S. Army Air Corps asked the optical firm of Bausch & Lomb to produce a highly effective spectacle that would protect pilots from the dangers of high-altitude glare. Company scientists perfected a special dark-green tint that absorbed yellow light from the spectrum. They also designed a slightly drooping metal frame to protect the aviator's eyes, which repeatedly glanced down at the plane's instrument panel. 3

I wonder why . . .

spectrum— range or band (light breaks into a series of colors)

I own a pair just like this!

Stage 3

4   Soon this type of sunglasses was offered to the public as Ray Ban aviators, scientifically designed to ban the sun's rays. For the first time in history, large numbers of people began to purchase sunglasses.

Stage 4—sunglasses are chic

5   The next step in the process—making sunglasses chic—was the result of a clever 1960s advertising campaign by the firm of Foster Grant. Determined to increase its share of the sunglass market, the company began to feature the faces of Hollywood celebrities wearing sunglasses above a slogan that read, "Isn't that . . . behind those Foster Grants?" Big stars of the day like Peter Sellers, Anita Ekberg, and Elke Sommer posed for the ads, and the public love affair with sunglasses took off. Behind those Foster Grants, everyone now could feel like a movie star.

Ah, yes. What makes anything span the world? Advertising.

Stage 5—designer shades

6   In the 1970s, the trend escalated further when well-known fashion designers and Hollywood stars introduced their own brand-name lines, charging high prices for status sunglasses in the latest styles. A giant industry developed where only a few decades earlier none had existed, and shades became big business.

True. I know people who spend $200 for wrap-arounds to wear dancing—at night!

Stage 6

parasol—umbrella for the sun

7   Today sunglasses—like blue jeans and Coca Cola—circle the globe. Protection against solar radiation is just part of their appeal. As women in ancient times had hidden seductively behind an expanded fan or a tipped parasol, modern women and men all over the world have discovered the mystery, sex appeal, and cosmopolitan cool of wearing sunglasses.

Writing ideas—
- *Research the development of origin of another popular item.*
- *Think more about the power of advertising to influence us.*
- *Observe sunglass wearers and write about them.*

Only Daughter
Sandra Cisneros

Sandra Cisneros is one of a growing number of Hispanic writers in English. The author of The House on Mango Street *and other books, she often writes in prose and poetry about the experience of being bicultural, bilingual, and female. In this essay, she explores the ways in which her birth family helped define who she is—and is not. Today Cisneros lives in San Antonio, Texas, in a large Victorian house that she has painted purple.*

Once, several years ago, when I was just starting out my writing career, I was asked to write my own contributor's note for an anthology I was part of. I wrote: "I am the only daughter in a family of six sons. *That* explains everything."

Well, I've thought about that ever since, and yes, it explains a lot to me, but for the reader's sake I should have written: "I am the only daughter in a *Mexican* family of six sons." Or even: "I am the only daughter of a Mexican father and a Mexican-American mother." Or: "I am the only daughter of a working-class family of nine." All of these had everything to do with who I am today.

I was/am the only daughter and *only* a daughter. Being an only daughter in a family of six sons forced me by circumstance to spend a lot of time by myself because my brothers felt it beneath them to play with a *girl* in public. But that aloneness, that loneliness, was good for a would-be writer—it allowed me time to think and think, to imagine, to read and prepare myself.

Being only a daughter for my father meant my destiny would lead me to become someone's wife. That's what he believed. But when I was in the fifth grade and shared my plans for college with him, I was sure he understood. I remember my father saying, "*Que bueno, mi'ja,* that's good." That meant a lot to me, especially since my brothers thought the idea hilarious. What I didn't realize was that my father thought college was good for girls—good for finding a husband. After four years in college and two more in graduate school, and still no husband, my father shakes his head even now and says I wasted all that education.

In retrospect, I'm lucky my father believed daughters were meant for husbands. It meant it didn't matter if I majored in something silly like English. After all, I'd find a nice professional eventually, right? This allowed me the liberty to putter about embroidering my little poems and stories without my father interrupting with so much as a "What's that you're writing?"

But the truth is, I wanted him to interrupt. I wanted my father to understand what it was I was scribbling, to introduce me as "My only daughter, the writer." Not as "This is only my daughter. She teaches." *Es maestra*—teacher. Not even *profesora*.

In a sense, everything I have ever written has been for him, to win his approval even though I know my father can't read English words, even though my father's only reading includes the brown-ink *Esto* sports magazines from Mexico City and the bloody ¡*Alarma!* magazines that feature yet another sighting of *La Virgen de Guadalupe* on a tortilla or a wife's revenge on her philandering[1] husband by bashing his skull in with a *molcajete* (a kitchen mortar made of volcanic rock). Or the *fotonovelas,* the little picture paperbacks with tragedy and trauma erupting from the characters' mouths in bubbles.

My father represents, then, the public majority. A public who is uninterested in reading, and yet one whom I am writing about and for, and privately trying to woo.

---
1. philandering: unfaithful

9 When we were growing up in Chicago, we moved a lot because of my father. He suffered bouts of nostalgia. Then we'd have to let go our flat, store the furniture with mother's relatives, load the station wagon with baggage and bologna sandwiches and head south. To Mexico City.

10 We came back, of course. To yet another Chicago flat, another Chicago neighborhood, another Catholic school. Each time, my father would seek out the parish priest in order to get a tuition break, and complain or boast: "I have seven sons."

11 He meant *siete hijos*, seven children, but he translated it as "sons." "I have seven sons." To anyone who would listen. The Sears Roebuck employee who sold us the washing machine. The short-order cook where my father ate his ham-and-eggs breakfasts. "I have seven sons." As if he deserved a medal from the state.

12 My papa. He didn't mean anything by that mistranslation, I'm sure. But somehow I could feel myself being erased. I'd tug my father's sleeve and whisper: "Not seven sons. Six! and *one daughter.*"

13 When my oldest brother graduated from medical school, he fulfilled my father's dream that we study hard and use this—our heads, instead of this—our hands. Even now my father's hands are thick and yellow, stubbed by a history of hammer and nails and twine and coils and springs. "Use this," my father said, tapping his head, "and not this," showing us those hands. He always looked tired when he said it.

14 Wasn't college an investment? And hadn't I spent all those years in college? And if I didn't marry, what was it all for? Why would anyone go to college and then choose to be poor? Especially someone who had always been poor.

15 Last year, after ten years of writing professionally, the financial rewards started to trickle in. My second National Endowment for the Arts Fellowship. A guest professorship at the University of California, Berkeley. My book, which sold to a major New York publishing house.

16 At Christmas, I flew home to Chicago. The house was throbbing, same as always; hot *tamales* and sweet *tamales* hissing in my mother's pressure cooker, and everybody—my mother, six brothers, wives, babies, aunts, cousins—talking too loud and at the same time, like in a Fellini[2] film, because that's just how we are.

17 I went upstairs to my father's room. One of my stories had just been translated into Spanish and published in an anthology of Chicano writing, and I wanted to show it to him. Ever since he recovered from a stroke two years ago, my father likes to spend his leisure hours horizontally. And that's how I found him, watching a Pedro Infante movie on Galavisión and eating rice pudding.

18 There was a glass filmed with milk on the bedside table. There were several vials of pills and balled Kleenex. And on the floor, one black sock and a plastic urinal that I didn't want to look at but looked at anyway. Pedro Infante was about to burst into song, and my father was laughing.

19 I'm not sure if it was because my story was translated into Spanish, or because it was published in Mexico, or perhaps because the story dealt with Tepeyac, the *colonia* my father was raised in and the house he grew up in, but at any rate, my father punched the mute button on his remote control and read my story.

20 I sat on the bed next to my father and waited. He read it very slowly. As if he were reading each line over and over. He laughed at all the right places and read lines he liked out loud. He pointed and asked questions: "Is this So-and-so?" "Yes," I said. He kept reading.

---

2. Fellini: an Italian movie director whose films were full of strange, unforgettable characters

When he was finally finished, after what seemed like hours, my father 21
looked up and asked: "Where can we get more copies of this for the relatives?"

Of all the wonderful things that happened to me last year, that was the 22
most wonderful.

Discussion and Writing Questions

1. In what two ways can the title of this essay, "Only Daughter," be interpreted?

2. What expectations did the author's father have for his daughter? Did his limited expectations create any advantages for her? Why did the father's comment "I have seven sons" bother her so much?

3. In paragraphs 16 through 18, Cisneros describes one of her trips home. She includes vivid details that help the reader "see" and "feel" life inside her parents' house. Which details do you find especially effective? Although the home is in Chicago, which details capture the family's Mexican heritage?

4. For years, the author wanted her father's attention and approval. Why do you think he finally appreciated her achievement as a writer?

Writing Assignments

1. In a group with three or four classmates, share statements about your personal history like those in Cisneros's opening paragraphs. First, take five minutes working on your own, and then define yourself, using a

   two- or three-sentence pattern: "I am _____

   _____.

   That explains everything."
   Revise your sentences until you feel they capture a truth about you. Now share and discuss these statements with your group. What is most and least effective or intriguing about each? Use your definition as the main idea for a paper to be written at home.

2. Have you (or has someone you know) wanted another person's approval so badly that it influenced how you conducted your life? Who was the person whose approval you sought, and why was that approval so important? What did you do to please him or her and what happened? Was it worth it?

3. What were your family's expectations for you as you grew up, and how did those expectations affect your life choices? Were the expectations high or low? Did your gender or place in the family (oldest, middle, youngest) affect them? Did you accept or reject the family's vision for you?

My Outing[1]

Arthur Ashe

Arthur Ashe was the first African American male to become a great tennis champion. After a heart attack ended his career, he contracted AIDS through a tainted blood transfusion. He kept his illness private for years while he pursued many business interests and human-rights projects. Then the possibility of a newspaper report forced him to reveal his condition to the public. The press conference he refers to in the essay was held in April 1992. Ashe died on February 6, 1993.

1 The day after my press conference, I made sure to keep the two appointments on my calendar because I was anxious to see how people would respond to me after the announcement. I was thinking not only about the people I knew personally, even intimately, but also about waiters and bartenders, doormen and taxi drivers. I knew all the myths and fears about AIDS. I also understood that if I hadn't been educated in the harshest possible way—by contracting the disease and living with it—I would probably share some of those myths and fears. I knew that I couldn't spread the disease by coughing or breathing or using plates and cups in a restaurant, but I knew that in some places my plates and cups would receive special attention, perhaps some extra soap and hot water. Perhaps they would be smashed and thrown away.

2 That morning, I accompanied Donald M. Stewart, head of the College Board Testing Service, on a visit to the offices of the New York Community Trust. We were seeking a grant of $5,000 to support the publication of a handbook aimed at student-athletes. The appointment went well; we got the money. And in the evening, I went in black tie to a gala dinner to celebrate the eightieth birthday of a man I had known for thirty years and regarded as one of my key mentors in New York City, Joseph Cullman III, a former chairman of Philip Morris. At the event, which took place at the Museum of Natural History in Manhattan, I felt anxiety rising as our taxi drew up to the curb. How would the other guests respond to me? The first person I saw was an old friend, John Reese. An investment banker now, in his youth John had been an up-and-coming star with me in junior tennis. He saw me, and hurried over. There was no mistaking the warmth of his greeting, his genuine concern but also his understanding of my predicament. We walked inside together and I had a fine time at the celebration....

3 I was glad, in this context, that I had not concealed my condition from certain people. I had reminded myself from the outset[2] that I had an obligation to tell anyone who might be materially hurt by the news when it came out. I have been both proud of my commercial connections and grateful to the people who had asked me to represent them or work for them in some other way. Several of them had taken a chance on me when they knew full well, from the most basic market research in the early 1970s, that having an African American as a spokesman or an officer might cost them business.

4 Among these organizations, the most important were the Aetna Life and Casualty Company, where I was a member of the board of directors; Head USA, the sports-equipment manufacturer that had given me my first important commercial endorsement, a tennis racquet with my very own autograph on it; the Doral Resort and Country Club in Florida, where I had directed the tennis program; Le Coq Sportif, the sports-clothing manufacturer; Home Box Office (HBO), the cable-television network for which I worked as an analyst

---

1. "Outing" someone usually means revealing publicly, without permission, that he or she is homosexual. Although Ashe was not gay, he was "outed" as a person with AIDS.
2. outset: beginning

at Wimbledon;[3] and ABC Sports, for which I also served as a commentator.

Not one of these companies had dropped me after I quietly revealed to their most important executives that I had AIDS. Now those executives had to deal with the response of the public. I would have to give them a chance to put some distance between their companies and me because I now carried the most abominable and intimidating medical virus of our age. In business, image is everything. And one would have to go back to leprosy, or the plague, to find a disease so full of terrifying implications as AIDS carries. AIDS was a scientific mystery that defied our vaunted[4] claims for science, and also a religious or spiritual riddle—at least to those who insisted on thinking of it as possibly a punishment from God for our evil on earth, as more than one person had publicly suggested. . . .

I waited for the phone calls and the signs that my services were no longer needed. None came.

I read somewhere that in the two weeks following his announcement that he was HIV-positive, Earvin "Magic" Johnson received thousands of pieces of mail, and that months later he was still receiving hundreds of letters a week. Well, I received nothing approaching that volume of correspondence following my press conference, but I certainly had a mountain of reading and writing to do in its aftermath. And every time I appeared on one of the few television interview shows I agreed to do, such as with Barbara Walters or Larry King, there was another surge of correspondence. I heard from the famous and the completely unknown, people I knew and people I had never met.

The most moving letters, without a doubt, came from people who had lived through an AIDS illness, either their own or that of a loved one. Often the loved one was now dead. These writers, above all, understood why I had made such a fuss about the issue of privacy. Many probably understood better than I did, because they were more vulnerable than I am, and had suffered more. One Manhattan woman wrote to tell me about her father, who had received HIV-tainted blood, as I had, through a blood transfusion following heart surgery. Without knowing it, he had passed the infection on to her mother. For some years, they had kept their illness a secret from their daughter. After they could keep the secret from her no longer, she in turn had worked to keep their secret from other family members and friends, and from the world. Although both parents were now dead, she wrote, "I share your anger at that anonymous person who violated either your trust or their professional ethics." . . .

A grandmother in New England, HIV-positive after a transfusion, shared with me her terror that the company she worked for would dismiss her if they found out; she was awaiting the passage of a law that might protect her. From Idaho, a mother told me about her middle-aged son, who had tried to keep his AIDS condition a secret even from her. "My son kept it to himself for six months before he told me and I'll never forget that day as we cried together." His ordeal included dementia,[5] forced incarceration in a state asylum, and ostracism[6] by relatives and friends. But mother and son had spent his last "four difficult months" together. "I'm so thankful to have had those days with him."

I heard from people whom I had not thought of in years, and some of them had been touched by their own tragedy. A woman I remembered as a stunningly beautiful UCLA coed, as we called them in those days, told me about her younger brother, who had been diagnosed with full-blown AIDS about five

---

3. Wimbledon: London, England, district where a major tennis tournament is held each year
4. vaunted: boastful
5. dementia: insanity
6. ostracism: exclusion, banishment

years before. "He is gay," she reported, "and I saw how he lost so much self-esteem and hope" because of intolerance. "No one can speak as eloquently[7] as you and Magic to allow the stigma[8] to disperse[9] regarding this situation." Another letter illustrated the power of the stigma. Signed simply, "Sorry I can't identify myself, but you understand," it came from a man who had been diagnosed with HIV three years ago. "I'm the father of six children and many grandchildren. I'm not into needles or the gay life. Don't know where it came from (really)."

As for my daughter, Camera, more than one writer underscored my fears about what she might have to undergo from insensitive people in the future. A woman whose son had died of AIDS about a year before, following the death of his wife, was now bringing up their young son: "I struggle with how this little child is going to deal with the insults and rejections that people will inflict on him when they find out that his father died from AIDS." ...

Needless to say, I am grateful to all those who have taken the trouble to write. Most of the letters left me humbled.

Discussion and Writing Questions

1. In paragraph 3, Ashe says that he had told some business associates about his illness early on. Why had he done that? How had they reacted? Why, then, was Ashe concerned about the business community's reaction to his *public* announcement?

2. How did the general public react to Ashe's announcement? Which letters did Ashe find most moving? Why?

3. The privacy issue was extremely important to Ashe, who felt that he had been forced by the press to make an announcement he had not wanted to make. One letter he received said, "I share your anger at that anonymous person who violated either your trust or their professional ethics" (paragraph 8). What did the letter writer mean by this statement?

4. Arthur Ashe called his life story *Days of Grace.* On the basis of this essay, why do you think he chose that title? What example or examples of "grace" did he tell about?

Writing Assignments

1. Have you ever prepared yourself for the worst—the ending of a relationship, a frightening medical test result, or other bad news—only to find that the worst did not happen? Discuss such a time: why you expected the worst, what you did to prepare, and what really happened.

2. Serious illness can force people to reevaluate their lives—their aspirations and their goals. Have you, or has someone you know, looked at life differently because of an illness or accident? Write a short account of your own or the other person's experience.

3. In a group with three or four classmates, discuss Ashe's belief that no newspaper had the right to tell the world that he had AIDS. Do you think the press was justified in revealing Ashe's condition? Why or why not? Ashe believed that his right to privacy was greater than the public's need to know. The press argued that Ashe was a public figure and that

---

7. eloquently: skillfully, persuasively
8. stigma: mark of disgrace
9. disperse: disappear

whenever a public figure is ill, his or her condition is legitimate news. Write your own essay about this issue, based on the conclusions you come to after your group's discussion.

The Lady of the Ring

Rene Denfeld

What happens when a woman enters a traditionally male arena—specifically, a boxing ring? Rene Denfeld did just that, but the experience was far different from what she had expected. This article was first published in the *New York Times Magazine*.

I started boxing as a lark, a fantasy. I saw myself becoming glistening, fit and tough—a woman fighter. I saw myself rising from the canvas and fighting back, delivering amazing combinations until my opponent fell among the ropes, vanquished.

My first week in the gym in a run-down neighborhood in Portland, Ore., squashed my fantasy as I began to understand the long, difficult training regimen ahead of me. But I fell in love with the sport: the sound of the timer and the guys talking; the flying, hissing jump ropes; the punishment of the heavy bags, and, above all, the relationships between the fighters and our trainer, Jess Sandoval.

When I first went into the gym, Jess was in his 70s and increasingly infirm. He had lost his own professional career when he shipped out during World War II, but taught the sport afterward. He was shy around me, his only female fighter. We were all drawn close to Jess, though, an uneasy group, grieving in advance for the frail, titular[1] head of our family.

Most of the other fighters were Mexican immigrants like Jess. Sometimes, when they were away for a while, Jess would make sad remarks about prison. Still, their lives were not the easy, cheap simplifications about laziness and crime that many Americans believe about immigrants and illegal aliens. The younger ones seemed touchingly self-conscious despite their macho baggy pants and careful gang attire. Alberto worked at McDonald's and attended school. Bob supported his family by working as a janitor, while his wife sewed satin trunks for the fighters—$25 a pair.

Immigration got Ernesto, Jess told us grimly. But one day Ernesto was back. He snuck in, Jess said, triumphant. I still think about how hard it must be for these young men, who are torn between a love for their native country (he changed flags, they said contemptuously of one Mexican fighter who trains under a gringo[2] coach) and a longing to be wanted and appreciated right here.

I understand. As a woman in a boxing gym, I had changed flags, too. I'm sure Jess never imagined training a woman, and I'm sure the other fighters never imagined having to spar with one. Ernesto would hit me as hard as he would a man—hard enough to bruise my ribs, water my eyes, cut my lips and make my nose bleed. He had to, you see: if he didn't hit back, I would beat him. This is the dilemma I forced on these men. Hitting a woman? They think that only a bully, a wife beater, does that. But the prospect of being beaten by a woman? Only a sissy, a punk. And yet we found a way to manage. There in that safe place, we had an unspoken truce.

Sparring with men, I felt liberated from generations of fear, self-doubt,

---

1. titular: existing in name, or title, only
2. gringo: in Latin America, slang for a person from the United States or England (offensive)

finger-waving and genteel[3] restrictions: men aren't so tough, I found, once you get close enough. Perhaps women's fear has been misplaced, conferring a malignant power on those who neither deserve nor desire it.

In entering this world, I lost more than superficial fantasy and gained more than physical self-confidence. My perceptions of the sexes have been altered, and this has affected nearly every aspect of my life. I feel differently when I walk down the street alone—stronger, less fearful. No longer do I assume that I am less capable of handling anger and conflict.

But the greatest challenge was to the male fighters. I imagined their worries: What will she think of us when she realizes we are not as tough, as cold or as mean as women everywhere have been led to believe? Will she breathe a sigh of relief, or laugh in contempt?

A boxing gym is only one of many places where the myth of male superiority in strength and aggressiveness remains unquestioned. But it is also a place where the myth can begin to unravel. Just as I have always been strong, and never realized it, men have always been vulnerable and complicated.

Now the fighter of my dreams is replaced by myself, in honest memory, leaning over the ropes at the Golden Gloves after having won the title. My opponent was already receding, like a vapor[4] behind me, while the men from the gym cheered in the audience. But there was only me, and Jess, and I was kissing his face, in thanks.

Not long ago, Jess passed away. When I heard the news, I put down the phone and cried, thinking, with surprise, I've lost my father. I had gone into a boxing gym to learn how to be tough. But I also found affection, sincerity and caring—and the deep bond between athlete and coach. Boxing has, in the end, left me softer.

Discussion and Writing Questions

1. What was Denfeld's first fantasy about becoming a boxer (paragraph 1)? What replaced that fantasy?

2. What did boxing teach Denfeld about men? What did boxing teach her about herself?

3. What do the Mexican fighters mean when they say someone has "changed flags" (paragraph 5)? Why, according to the author, would someone do that? What does she mean when she says, "As a woman in a boxing gym, I had changed flags, too" (paragraph 6)?

4. Denfeld ends her narrative with Jess's death (paragraph 12). This event is *foreshadowed*, or hinted at, beforehand. Where in the article does Denfeld foreshadow Jess's death?

Writing Assignments

1. Did you ever participate in a sport, take a class, or work on a project that liberated you from "fear" and "self-doubt," as boxing liberated Denfeld? What kind of person were you before? What specifically gave you confidence? In what specific ways did this sport, class, or project change your life?

2. Jess was a hero, a role model, and possibly a father figure for Denfeld. Did you ever know someone who functioned in one or more of these ways for you or someone else? Write about that person and discuss the role he or she played in another's life.

---

3. genteel: polite, refined
4. vapor: mist, smoke

3. In a group with three or four classmates, discuss possible reasons why a boxing gym might be a place where sexual stereotypes can be faced and dropped. Did new understanding happen because of the place, the activity of boxing, the particular people?

Have you ever been in a situation or place where you were able to see through some stereotype—about gender, race, money, or academic achievement—to the truth? List the places and situations that your group members discuss. On your own, write a paper in which you describe a situation or place where stereotypes were set aside. Where and how did this happen?

Neat People Versus Sloppy People

Suzanne Britt

Suzanne Britt is a humorist and writer who likes to analyze people's behavior. In this essay from her book Show and Tell, *she turns the commonly accepted judgments about neatness and sloppiness upside down.*

1. I've finally figured out the difference between neat people and sloppy people. The distinction is, as always, moral. Neat people are lazier and meaner than sloppy people.

2. Sloppy people, you see, are not really sloppy. Their sloppiness is merely the unfortunate consequence of their extreme moral rectitude.[1] Sloppy people carry in their mind's eye a heavenly vision, a precise plan, that is so stupendous, so perfect, it can't be achieved in this world or the next.

3. Sloppy people live in Never-Never Land. Someday is their métier.[2] Someday they are planning to alphabetize all their books and set up home catalogs. Someday they will go through their wardrobes and mark certain items for tentative mending and certain items for passing on to relatives of similar shape and size. Someday sloppy people will make family scrapbooks into which they will put newspaper clippings, postcards, locks of hair, and the dried corsage from their senior prom. Someday they will file everything on the surface of their desks, including the cash register receipts from coffee purchases at the snack shop. Someday they will sit down and read all the back issues of *The New Yorker*.

4. For all these noble reasons and more, sloppy people never get neat. They aim too high and wide. They save everything, planning someday to file, order, and straighten out the world. But while these ambitious plans take clearer and clearer shape in their heads, the books spill from the shelves onto the floor, the clothes pile up in the hamper and closet, the family mementos accumulate in every drawer, the surface of the desk is buried under mounds of paper and the unread magazines threaten to reach the ceiling.

5. Sloppy people can't bear to part with anything. They give loving attention to every detail. When sloppy people say they're going to tackle the surface of the desk, they really mean it. Not a paper will go unturned; not a rubber band will go unboxed. Four hours or two weeks into the excavation, the desk looks exactly the same, primarily because the sloppy person is meticulously[3] creating new piles of papers with new headings and scrupulously[4] stopping to read all the old book catalogs before he throws them away. A neat person would just bulldoze the desk.

---

1. rectitude: righteousness, correctness
2. métier: specialty; work for which someone is especially suited
3. meticulously: very carefully
4. scrupulously: conscientiously

Neat people are bums and clods at heart. They have cavalier[5] attitudes toward possessions, including family heirlooms. Everything is just another dust-catcher to them. If anything collects dust, it's got to go and that's that. Neat people will toy with the idea of throwing the children out of the house just to cut down on the clutter.

Neat people don't care about process. They like results. What they want to do is get the whole thing over with so they can sit down and watch the rasslin' on TV. Neat people operate on two unvarying principles: Never handle any item twice, and throw everything away.

The only thing messy in a neat person's house is the trash can. The minute something comes to a neat person's hand, he will look at it, try to decide if it has immediate use and, finding none, throw it in the trash.

Neat people are especially vicious with mail. They never go through their mail unless they are standing directly over a trash can. If the trash can is beside the mailbox, even better. All ads, catalogs, pleas for charitable contributions, church bulletins and money-saving coupons go straight into the trash can without being opened. All letters from home, postcards from Europe, bills and paychecks are opened, immediately responded to, then dropped in the trash can. Neat people keep their receipts only for tax purposes. That's it. No sentimental salvaging[6] of birthday cards or the last letter a dying relative ever wrote. Into the trash it goes.

Neat people place neatness above everything, even economics. They are incredibly wasteful. Neat people throw away several toys every time they walk through the den. I knew a neat person once who threw away a perfectly good dish drainer because it had mold on it. The drainer was too much trouble to wash. And neat people sell their furniture when they move. They will sell a La-Z-Boy recliner while you are reclining in it.

Neat people are no good to borrow from. Neat people buy everything in expensive little single portions. They get their flour and sugar in two-pound bags. They wouldn't consider clipping a coupon, saving a leftover, reusing plastic non-dairy whipped cream containers or rinsing off tin foil and draping it over the unmoldy dish drainer. You can never borrow a neat person's newspaper to see what's playing at the movies. Neat people have the paper all wadded up and in the trash by 7:05 A.M.

Neat people cut a clean swath[7] through the organic[8] as well as the inorganic[9] world. People, animals, and things are all one to them. They are so insensitive. After they've finished with the pantry, the medicine cabinet, and the attic, they will throw out the red geranium (too many leaves), sell the dog (too many fleas), and send the children off to boarding school (too many scuffmarks on the hardwood floors).

Discussion and Writing Questions

1. Britt says that the difference between neat and sloppy people is "moral" (paragraph 1). Which type of person does she claim to believe is superior? Is she serious about this? How do you know?

2. What does Britt mean when she says that "someday" is the "métier" for sloppy people (paragraph 3)?

---

5. cavalier: showing disregard; not having respect
6. salvaging: rescuing, saving
7. swath: path, strip
8. organic: living
9. inorganic: nonliving

3. The author characterizes neat people as "bums and clods" (paragraph 6). In what ways does she see neat people as heartless?

4. From her contrast essay, do you think Suzanne Britt is a neat or a sloppy person? Why do you think so?

Writing Assignments

1. Are you neat or sloppy? If Britt does not accurately describe the reasons behind your behavior, write about those reasons. Alternatively, you might want to write a defense of neatness. Explain from a neat person's point of view why neat people do what they do and how they are more "moral" than sloppy people.

2. Contrast the different personalities of two people you know. For instance, you might discuss two members of your study group, one a careless worker and one a perfectionist. You might contrast twins, one of whom is almost a hermit while the other is very sociable. You might want to describe the differences between your mountain-climbing aunt and her stay-at-home husband. Use humor if you wish.

3. Write a one- or two-paragraph summary of "Neat People Versus Sloppy People." Refer to Chapter 18 on summary writing. Be sure to include Britt's main idea and her most important supporting points, all in your own words. Remember, you are summarizing Britt's ideas, not adding your own.

How to Get the Most Out of Yourself

Alan Loy McGinnis

Why are some persons successful and productive while others struggle along unhappily? Alan Loy McGinnis, a psychotherapist, believes that the answer lies in self-image. In this essay, he presents numerous ways people can strengthen their self-image.

Our success at business, sports, friendship, love—nearly every enterprise we attempt—is largely determined by our own self-image. People who have confidence in their personal worth seem to be magnets for success and happiness. Good things drop into their laps regularly, their relationships are long-lasting, their projects are usually carried to completion. To use the imagery of English poet William Blake, they "catch joy on the wing."

Conversely, some people seem to be magnets for failure and unhappiness. Their plans go awry,[1] they have a way of torpedoing their own potential successes, and nothing seems to work out for them. As a counselor, I see many such persons. Their problems usually stem from a difficulty with self-acceptance. When I am able to help them gain more confidence, often their troubles take care of themselves.

I believe that anyone can change his self-perception. A person with low self-image is not doomed to a life of unhappiness and failure. It *is* possible to

---

1. go awry: go off course

get rid of negative attitudes and gain the healthy confidence needed to realize one's dreams. Here's how:

Focus on your potential—not your limitations. When Helen Hayes was a young actress, producer George Tyler told her that, were she four inches taller, she could become one of the great actresses of her time. "I decided," she says, "to lick my size. A string of teachers pulled and stretched till I felt I was in a medieval torture chamber. I gained nary[2] an inch—but my posture was military-straight. I became the tallest five-foot woman in the world. And my refusal to be limited by my limitations enabled me to play Mary of Scotland, one of the tallest queens in history."

Helen Hayes succeeded because she chose to focus on her strong points, not her weak ones.

Many clients tell me that because they are not as smart or good-looking or witty as others, they feel inferior. Probably no habit chips away at our self-confidence quite so effectively as that of scanning the people around us to see how we compare. And when we find that someone is indeed smarter, better-looking or wittier, it diminishes our sense of self-worth.

The Hasidic rabbi Zusya was asked on his deathbed what he thought the kingdom of God would be like. "I don't know," he replied. "But one thing I *do* know. When I get there I am not going to be asked, 'Why weren't you Moses? Why weren't you David?' I am only going to be asked, 'Why weren't you Zusya? Why weren't you fully you?'"

Devote yourself to something you do well. There is nothing so common as unsuccessful people with talent. Usually the problem lies not in discovering our natural aptitude but in developing that skill.

Young surgeons practice skills for months on end, such as tying knots in a confined space or suturing. The refining of these skills is the surgeon's main method of improving total performance.

Many of us get interested in a field, but then the going gets tough, we see that other people are more successful, and we become discouraged and quit. But it is often the boring, repetitive sharpening of our skills that will ultimately enable us to reach our goals.

Horace Bushnell, the great New England preacher, used to say, "Somewhere under the stars God has a job for you to do, and nobody else can do it." Some of us must find our place by trial and error. It can take time, with dead ends along the way. But we should not get discouraged because others seem more skilled. Usually it is not raw talent but drive that makes the difference.

See yourself as successful. If I could plug into the minds of my patients and listen to the statements they make to themselves, I am convinced that the majority of them would be negative: "I'm running late again—as usual." "My hair looks terrible this morning." "That was a stupid remark I made—she probably thinks I'm a dummy." Since thousands of these messages flash across our brains every day, it is small wonder that the result is a diminished self-image.

One daily exercise for building self-confidence is called "imaging" or "visualization." In order to succeed, you must *see* yourself succeeding. Picture yourself approaching a difficult challenge with poise[3] and confidence. Athletes often visualize a move over and over in their minds; they see themselves hitting the perfect golf or tennis shot. When we burn such positive images into our minds deeply enough, they become a part of the unconscious, and we begin to expect to succeed.

Author and editor Norman Cousins wrote: "People are never more insecure than when they become obsessed with their fears at the expense of their

---

2. nary: not even one

3. poise: a look and feeling of self-assurance, calmness

dreams." There is no doubt that if we can envision beneficial things happening, they have a way of actually occurring.

Break away from other people's expectations. It is a liberating step when we decide to stop being what other people want us to be. Although opera singer Risë Stevens performed onstage with great poise, the self-confidence she felt before audiences evaporated in social situations. "My discomfort," she says, "came from trying to be something I was not—a star in the drawing room as well as onstage. If a clever person made a joke, I tried to top it—and failed. I pretended to be familiar with subjects I knew nothing of."

Stevens finally had a heart-to-heart talk with herself: "I realized that I simply wasn't a wit or an intellectual and that I could succeed only as myself. I began listening and asking questions at parties instead of trying to impress the guests. When I spoke, I tried to contribute, not to shine. Almost at once I started to feel a new warmth in my social contacts. They liked the real me better."

If we are true to our instincts, most of us will find that we naturally develop certain trademarks. The discovery and expression of that uniqueness is one reason we are on this planet. Resisting conformity and developing some small eccentricities[4] are among the steps to independence and self-confidence.

Build a network of supportive relationships. Many of my clients scramble to shore up[5] their self images with various techniques, overlooking the source from which they will get help most readily—good friendships.

One of the surest ways to improve confidence is to make certain you have lots of love in your life, to go to whatever lengths are necessary to construct a network of sustaining and nurturing relationships. In building such supportive relationships, most of my patients think their problem is in meeting new people. But the answer, really, is in deepening the friendships you presently have.

The extended family can be a major source of support and nurture. A friend who is 45 tells me that visiting her parents in Indiana is always "a mixed bag." She makes connections with some relatives she'd just as soon not see anymore, and she usually has at least one blow-up with her parents. "But it's important to be around my family," she says. "I always come back feeling that I have a clearer idea of who I am, where I came from, and where I want to go."

She is a wise woman. Such connections with our heritage make our identities more secure. As author John Dos Passos said, "A sense of continuity with the generations gone before can stretch like a lifeline across the scary present."

The distribution of talents in this world should not be our concern. Our responsibility is to take the talents we have and ardently parlay them[6] to the highest possible achievement.

When Yoshihiko Yamamoto of Nagoya City, Japan, was six months old, physicians told his parents that he was mentally retarded. With a hearing loss that strangled his speech and an I.Q. that tested very low, Yamamoto faced a bleak future.

But a new special-education teacher, Takashi Kawasaki, took a special interest in the boy. Gradually Yamamoto began to smile in class. He learned to copy the characters from the blackboard and cartoons from magazines. One day, Yamamoto drew an accurate sketch of Nagoya Castle. Kawasaki had the boy transfer his design to a wood block and encouraged him to concentrate

---

4. eccentricities: unusual or quirky personality traits or behavior
5. shore up: support, strengthen
6. parlay them: turn them into

on printmaking. Eventually Yamamoto won first prize in an art contest. Today, his work is much sought after.

It is not important that Yoshihiko Yamamoto has limitations. The important thing is that he has capitalized on his potential. 25

Self-confidence, like happiness, is slippery when we set out to grab it for its own sake. Usually it comes as a by-product. We lose ourselves in service or work, friendship or love, and suddenly one day we realize that we are confident and happy. 26

Discussion and Writing Questions

1. McGinnis discusses several ways of overcoming poor self-esteem. What are these ways? Can you think of any he doesn't mention?

2. Which of these ways do you think is the most effective? The least effective? Why?

3. Identify the paragraphs in which McGinnis uses an anecdote, or brief story, to illustrate the topic sentence(s) of the paragraph. Choose one or two of these paragraphs and illustrate the topic sentence with anecdotes from your own experience.

4. What is the most important point McGinnis illustrates with Yamamoto's story (paragraphs 23–26)?

Writing Assignments

1. Write about someone you consider successful. What qualities or characteristics distinguish this person from others? The person need not be someone you know directly; he or she could be a politician, a rock star, a local personality, or a teacher. Be sure to choose someone about whom you know interesting details, so that your writing will engage your reader.

2. Choose one of the methods the author presents for improving self-esteem and restate the method as a topic sentence. Then write a paragraph that fully develops that topic sentence. For example, you could restate "Break away from other people's expectations" (paragraph 15) this way: "In order for me to break away from other people's expectations, I have to concentrate on what I want in life." The supporting details would then show how you concentrate on what you want. Remember to use details that clearly support the topic sentence.

3. Write a one- or two-paragraph summary of "How to Get the Most Out of Yourself." Refer to Chapter 18 on summary writing. Be sure to include McGinnis's main idea and his most important points so that someone who has not read the essay will know what it is about. Remember, you are summarizing McGinnis's ideas, not adding your own ideas or opinions.

Beauty:
When the Other Dancer Is the Self

Alice Walker

> Being physically injured can be terrifying; coming to terms with a permanent disability can be a painful, difficult process. Alice Walker, a noted fiction writer, poet, and author of *The Color Purple*, tells of her feelings and experiences before, during, and after an injury that changed her life.

It is a bright summer day in 1947. My father, a fat, funny man with beautiful eyes and a subversive wit,[1] is trying to decide which of his eight children he will take with him to the county fair. My mother, of course, will not go. She is knocked out from getting most of us ready: I hold my neck stiff against the pressure of her knuckles as she hastily completes the braiding and then beribboning of my hair.

My father is the driver for the rich old white lady up the road. Her name is Miss Mey. She owns all the land for miles around, as well as the house in which we live. All I remember about her is that she once offered to pay my mother thirty-five cents for cleaning her house, raking up piles of her magnolia leaves, and washing her family's clothes, and that my mother—she of no money, eight children, and a chronic earache—refused it. But I do not think of this in 1947. I am two and a half years old. I want to go everywhere my daddy goes. I am excited at the prospect of riding in a car. Someone has told me fairs are fun. That there is room in the car for only three of us doesn't faze[2] me at all. Whirling happily in my starchy frock, showing off my biscuit-polished patent-leather shoes and lavender socks, tossing my head in a way that makes my ribbons bounce, I stand, hands on hips, before my father. "Take me, Daddy," I say with assurance; "I'm the prettiest!"

Later, it does not surprise me to find myself in Miss Mey's shiny black car, sharing the back seat with the other lucky ones. Does not surprise me that I thoroughly enjoy the fair. At home that night I tell the unlucky ones all I can remember about the merry-go-round, the man who eats live chickens, and the teddy bears, until they say: that's enough, baby Alice. Shut up now, and go to sleep.

It is Easter Sunday, 1950. I am dressed in a green, flocked, scalloped-hem dress (handmade by my adoring sister, Ruth) that has its own smooth satin petticoat and tiny hot-pink roses tucked into each scallop. My shoes, new T-strap patent leather, again highly biscuit-polished. I am six years old and have learned one of the longest Easter speeches to be heard that day, totally unlike the speech I said when I was two: "Easter lilies / pure and white / blossom in / the morning light." When I rise to give my speech I do so on a great wave of love and pride and expectation. People in the church stop rustling their new crinolines. They seem to hold their breath. I can tell they admire my dress, but it is my spirit, bordering on sassiness (womanishness), they secretly applaud.

"That girl's a little *mess*," they whisper to each other, pleased.

Naturally I say my speech without stammer or pause, unlike those who stutter, stammer, or, worst of all, forget. This is before the word "beautiful" exists in people's vocabulary, but "Oh, isn't she the *cutest* thing!" frequently floats my way. "And got so much sense!" they gratefully add . . . for which thoughtful addition I thank them to this day.

---

1. subversive wit: sarcastic, sharp sense of humor
2. faze: discourage

It was great fun being cute. But then, one day, it ended.

I am eight years old and a tomboy. I have a cowboy hat, cowboy boots, checkered shirt and pants, all red. My playmates are my brothers, two and four years older than I. Their colors are black and green, the only difference in the way we are dressed. On Saturday nights we all go to the picture show, even my mother; Westerns are her favorite kind of movie. Back home, "on the ranch," we pretend we are Tom Mix, Hopalong Cassidy, Lash LaRue (we've even named one of our dogs Lash LaRue); we chase each other for hours rustling cattle, being outlaws, delivering damsels from distress. Then my parents decide to buy my brothers guns. These are not "real" guns. They shoot "BBs," copper pellets my brothers say will kill birds. Because I am a girl, I do not get a gun. Instantly I am relegated to[3] the position of Indian. Now there appears a great distance between us. They shoot and shoot at everything with their new guns. I try to keep up with my bow and arrows.

One day while I am standing on top of our makeshift "garage"—pieces of tin nailed across some poles—holding my bow and arrow and looking out toward the fields, I feel an incredible blow in my right eye. I look down just in time to see my brother lower his gun.

Both brothers rush to my side. My eye stings, and I cover it with my hand. "If you tell," they say, "we will get a whipping. You don't want that to happen, do you?" I do not. "Here is a piece of wire," says the older brother, picking it up from the roof; "say you stepped on one end of it and the other flew up and hit you." The pain is beginning to start. "Yes," I say. "Yes, I will say that is what happened." If I do not say this is what happened, I know my brothers will find ways to make me wish I had. But now I will say anything that gets me to my mother.

Confronted by our parents we stick to the lie agreed upon. They place me on a bench on the porch and I close my left eye while they examine the right. There is a tree growing from underneath the porch that climbs past the railing to the roof. It is the last thing my right eye sees. I watch as its trunk, its branches, and then its leaves are blotted out by the rising blood.

I am in shock. First there is intense fever, which my father tries to break using lily leaves bound around my head. Then there are chills: my mother tries to get me to eat soup. Eventually, I do not know how, my parents learn what has happened. A week after the "accident" they take me to see a doctor. "Why did you wait so long to come?" he asks, looking into my eye and shaking his head. "Eyes are sympathetic,[4]" he says. "If one is blind, the other will likely become blind too."

This comment of the doctor's terrifies me. But it is really how I look that bothers me most. Where the BB pellet struck there is a glob of whitish scar tissue, a hideous cataract, on my eye. Now when I stare at people—a favorite pastime, up to now—they will stare back. Not at the "cute" little girl, but at her scar. For six years I do not stare at anyone, because I do not raise my head.

Years later, in the throes[5] of a mid-life crisis, I ask my mother and sister whether I changed after the "accident." "No," they say, puzzled. "What do you mean?"

What do I mean?

I am eight, and, for the first time, doing poorly in school, where I have been something of a whiz since I was four. We have just moved to the place where the "accident" occurred. We do not know any of the people around us

---

3. relegated to: assigned
4. sympathetic: closely connected
5. throes: a condition of struggle

because this is a different county. The only time I see the friends I knew is when we go back to our old church. The new school is the former state penitentiary. It is a large stone building, cold and drafty, crammed to overflowing with boisterous,[6] ill-disciplined children. On the third floor there is a huge circular imprint of some partition that has been torn out.

"What used to be there?" I ask a sullen girl next to me on our way past it to lunch.

"The electric chair," says she.

At night I have nightmares about the electric chair, and about all the people reputedly[7] "fried" in it. I am afraid of the school, where all the students seem to be budding criminals.

"What's the matter with your eye?" they ask, critically.

When I don't answer (I cannot decide whether it was an "accident" or not), they shove me, insist on a fight.

My brother, the one who created the story about the wire, comes to my rescue. But then brags so much about "protecting" me, I become sick.

After months of torture at the school, my parents decide to send me back to our old community, to my old school. I live with my grandparents and the teacher they board. But there is no room for Phoebe, my cat. By the time my grandparents decide there *is* room, and I ask for my cat, she cannot be found. Miss Yarborough, the boarding teacher, takes me under her wing, and begins to teach me to play the piano. But soon she marries an African—a "prince," she says—and is whisked away to his continent.

At my old school there is at least one teacher who loves me. She is the teacher who "knew me before I was born" and bought my first baby clothes. It is she who makes life bearable. It is her presence that finally helps me turn on the one child at the school who continually calls me "one-eyed bitch." One day I simply grab him by his coat and beat him until I am satisfied. It is my teacher who tells me my mother is ill.

My mother is lying in bed in the middle of the day, something I have never seen. She is in too much pain to speak. She has an abscess in her ear. I stand looking down on her, knowing that if she dies, I cannot live. She is being treated with warm oils and hot bricks held against her cheek. Finally a doctor comes. But I must go back to my grandparents' house. The weeks pass but I am hardly aware of it. All I know is that my mother might die, my father is not so jolly, my brothers still have their guns, and I am the one sent away from home.

"You did not change," they say.

Did I imagine the anguish of never looking up?

I am twelve. When relatives come to visit I hide in my room. My cousin Brenda, just my age, whose father works in the post office and whose mother is a nurse, comes to find me. "Hello," she says. And then she asks, looking at my recent school picture, which I did not want taken, and on which the "glob," as I think of it, is clearly visible, "You still can't see out of that eye?"

"No," I say, and flop back on the bed over my book.

That night, as I do almost every night, I abuse my eye. I rant and rave at it, in front of the mirror. I plead with it to clear up before morning. I tell it I hate and despise it. I do not pray for sight. I pray for beauty.

"You did not change," they say.

I am fourteen and baby-sitting for my brother Bill, who lives in Boston. He is

---

6. boisterous: rowdy and noisy
7. reputedly: supposedly

my favorite brother and there is a strong bond between us. Understanding my feelings of shame and ugliness he and his wife take me to a local hospital, where the "glob" is removed by a doctor named O. Henry. There is still a small bluish crater where the scar tissue was, but the ugly white stuff is gone. Almost immediately I become a different person from the girl who does not raise her head. Or so I think. Now that I've raised my head I win the boyfriend of my dreams. Now that I've raised my head I have plenty of friends. Now that I've raised my head classwork comes from my lips as faultlessly as Easter speeches did, and I leave high school as valedictorian, most popular student, and *queen,* hardly believing my luck. Ironically, the girl who was voted most beautiful in our class (and was) was later shot twice through the chest by a male companion, using a "real" gun, while she was pregnant. But that's another story in itself. Or is it?

"You did not change," they say. 33

It is now thirty years since the "accident." A beautiful journalist comes to visit and to interview me. She is going to write a cover story for her magazine that focuses on my latest book. "Decide how you want to look on the cover," she says. "Glamorous, or whatever." 34

Never mind "glamorous," it is the "whatever" that I hear. Suddenly all I can think of is whether I will get enough sleep the night before the photography session: if I don't, my eye will be tired and wander, as blind eyes will. 35

At night in bed with my lover I think up reasons why I should not appear on the cover of a magazine. "My meanest critics will say I've sold out," I say. "My family will now realize I write scandalous books." 36

"But what's the real reason you don't want to do this?" he asks. 37

"Because in all probability," I say in a rush, "my eye won't be straight." 38

"It will be straight enough," he says. Then, "Besides, I thought you'd made your peace with that." 39

And I suddenly remember that I have. 40

I remember: 41

I am talking to my brother Jimmy, asking if he remembers anything unusual about the day I was shot. He does not know I consider that day the last time my father, with his sweet home remedy of cool lily leaves, chose me, and that I suffered and raged inside because of this. "Well," he says, "all I remember is standing by the side of the highway with Daddy, trying to flag down a car. A white man stopped, but when Daddy said he needed somebody to take his little girl to the doctor, he drove off." 42

I remember: 43

I am in the desert for the first time. I fall totally in love with it. I am so overwhelmed by its beauty, I confront for the first time, consciously, the meaning of the doctor's words years ago: "Eyes are sympathetic. If one is blind, the other will likely become blind too." I realize I have dashed about the world madly, looking at this, looking at that, storing up images against the fading of the light. *But I might have missed seeing the desert!* The shock of that possibility—and gratitude for over twenty-five years of sight—sends me literally to my knees. Poem after poem comes—which is perhaps how poets pray. 44

On Sight

I am so thankful I have seen
The Desert
And the creatures in the desert
And the desert Itself.

The desert has its own moon
Which I have seen

With my own eye.
There is no flag on it.

Trees of the desert have arms
All of which are always up
That is because the moon is up
The sun is up
Also the sky
The stars
Clouds
None with flags.
If there *were* flags, I doubt
the trees would point.
Would you?

But mostly, I remember this:

45

I am twenty-seven, and my baby daughter is almost three. Since her birth I have worried about her discovery that her mother's eyes are different from other people's. Will she be embarrassed? I think. What will she say? Every day she watches a television program called "Big Blue Marble." It begins with a picture of the earth as it appears from the moon. It is bluish, a little battered-looking, but full of light, with whitish clouds swirling around it. Every time I see it I weep with love, as if it is a picture of Grandma's house. One day when I am putting Rebecca down for her nap, she suddenly focuses on my eye. Something inside me cringes, gets ready to try to protect myself. All children are cruel about physical differences, I know from experience, and that they don't always mean to be is another matter. I assume Rebecca will be the same.

46

But no-o-o-o. She studies my face intently as we stand, her inside and me outside her crib. She even holds my face maternally between her dimpled little hands. Then, looking every bit as serious and lawyerlike as her father, she says, as if it may just possibly have slipped my attention: "Mommy, there's a *world* in your eye." (As in, "Don't be alarmed, or do anything crazy.") And then, gently, but with great interest: "Mommy, where did you *get* that world in your eye?"

47

For the most part, the pain left then. (So what, if my brothers grew up to buy even more powerful pellet guns for their sons and to carry real guns themselves. So what, if a young "Morehouse man" once nearly fell off the steps of Trevor Arnett Library because he thought my eyes were blue.) Crying and laughing I ran to the bathroom, while Rebecca mumbled and sang herself to sleep. Yes indeed, I realized, looking into the mirror. There *was* a world in my eye. And I saw that it was possible to love it: that in fact, for all it had taught me of shame and anger and inner vision, I *did* love it. Even to see it drifting out of orbit in boredom, or rolling up out of fatigue, not to mention floating back at attention in excitement (bearing witness, a friend has called it), deeply suitable to my personality, and even characteristic of me.

48

That night I dream I am dancing to Stevie Wonder's song "Always" (The name of the song is really "As," but I hear it as "Always"). As I dance, whirling and joyous, happier than I've ever been in my life, another bright-faced dancer joins me. We dance and kiss each other and hold each other through the night. The other dancer has obviously come through all right, as I have done. She is beautiful, whole and free. And she is also me.

49

Discussion and Writing Questions

1. When did the author stop being "cute"? Is she happy about this change?

2. Why do you think her family insists that she did not change after the shooting?

3. Until her operation at age fourteen, Walker speaks of hating her injured eye. By the end of the essay, she dances with another "dancer," who is "beautiful, whole and free. And she is also me." What makes the author change her mind about her "deformity"?

4. The author uses particular words and phrases to indicate time or chronological order in her narrative. Find the words that indicate time order. At one point in her narrative, she breaks this time order to skip back into the past. In which paragraph does this flashback occur?

Writing Assignments

1. Write about an unpleasant event or experience that resulted in personal growth for you. Your writing need not focus on something as painful as Alice Walker's injury. What is important is how you came to terms with the experience and what you ultimately learned from it.

2. Tell a story about being thrust into a completely unfamiliar situation. You might describe your reaction to attending a new school, starting a new job, or moving to a new city. Present concrete details of your experience. Organize the story around your most vivid memories, like meeting new classmates for the first time, or your first few days on the new job.

3. In a group with three or four classmates, discuss the accident that injured Walker's eye and the children's cover-up (paragraphs 8–11). Her brothers, ten and twelve, were given BB guns. How did these guns change the relationships among siblings even before the accident? Why did this happen? Are BB guns "real guns"? Have you known someone injured by "gun play"? How can such accidents be prevented? Write a paper on your own in which you present one to three ways in which Walker's injury—or one that you know about—could have been prevented.

Hunger of Memory

Richard Rodriguez

Growing up in California as a second-generation Mexican American, Richard Rodriguez wanted to understand the lives of *los pobres*, the poor Mexican laborers he saw around him. In this selection from *Hunger of Memory*, he tells of taking a summer job as a laborer and of learning about himself in the process.

It was at Stanford, one day near the end of my senior year, that a friend told me about a summer construction job he knew was available. I was quickly alert. Desire uncoiled[1] within me. My friend said that he knew I had been looking for summer employment. He knew I needed some money. Almost apologetically he explained: It was something I probably wouldn't be interested in, but a friend of his, a contractor, needed someone for the summer to do

---

1. uncoiled: loosened, unwound

menial[2] jobs. There would be lots of shoveling and raking and sweeping. Nothing too hard. But nothing more interesting either. Still, the pay would be good. Did I want it? Or did I know someone who did?

I did. Yes, I said, surprised to hear myself say it.

In the weeks following, friends cautioned that I had no idea how hard physical labor really is. ("You only *think* you know what it is like to shovel for eight hours straight.") Their objections seemed to me challenges. They resolved the issue. I became happy with my plan. I decided, however, not to tell my parents. I wouldn't tell my mother because I could guess her worried reaction. I would tell my father only after the summer was over, when I could announce that, after all, I did know what "real work" is like.

The day I met the contractor (a Princeton graduate, it turned out), he asked me whether I had done any physical labor before. "In high school, during the summer," I lied. And although he seemed to regard me with skepticism,[3] he decided to give me a try. Several days later, expectant, I arrived at my first construction site. I would take off my shirt to the sun. And at last grasp desired sensation. No longer afraid. At last become like a *bracero*.[4] "We need those tree stumps out of here by tomorrow," the contractor said. I started to work.

I labored with excitement that first morning—and all the days after. The work was harder than I could have expected. But it was never as tedious as my friends had warned me it would be. There was too much physical pleasure in the labor. Especially early in the day, I would be most alert to the sensations of movement and straining. Beginning around seven each morning (when the air was still damp but the scent of weeds and dry earth anticipated the heat of the sun), I would feel my body resist the first thrusts of the shovel. My arms, tightened by sleep, would gradually loosen; after only several minutes, sweat would gather in beads on my forehead and then—a short while later—I would feel my chest silky with sweat in the breeze. I would return to my work. A nervous spark of pain would fly up my arm and settle to burn like an ember in the thick of my shoulder. An hour, two passed. Three. My whole body would assume regular movements; my shoveling would be described by identical, even movements. Even later in the day, my enthusiasm for primitive sensation would survive the heat and the dust and the insects pricking my back. I would strain wildly for sensation as the day came to a close. At three-thirty, quitting time, I would stand upright and slowly let my head fall back, luxuriating[5] in the feeling of tightness relieved.

Some of the men working nearby would watch me and laugh. Two or three of the older men took the trouble to teach me the right way to use a pick, the correct way to shovel. "You're doing it wrong, too hard," one man scolded. Then proceeded to show me—what persons who work with their bodies all their lives quickly learn—the most economical way to use one's body in labor.

"Don't make your back do so much work," he instructed. I stood impatiently listening, half listening, vaguely watching, then noticed his work-thickened fingers clutching the shovel. I was annoyed. I wanted to tell him that I enjoyed shoveling the wrong way. And I didn't want to learn the right way. I wasn't afraid of back pain. I liked the way my body felt sore at the end of the day.

I was about to, but, as it turned out, I didn't say a thing. Rather it was at

---

2. menial: lowly, lacking status
3. skepticism: doubt
4. *bracero:* a Mexican living and working in the United States for a period of time
5. luxuriating: enjoying with deep pleasure

that moment I realized that I was fooling myself if I expected a few weeks of labor to gain me admission to the world of the laborer. I would not learn in three months what my father had meant by "real work." I was not bound to this job; I could imagine its rapid conclusion. For me the sensations of exertion and fatigue could be savored. For my father or uncle, working at comparable jobs when they were my age, such sensations were to be feared. Fatigue took a different toll on their bodies—and minds.

9   It was, I know, a simple insight. But it was with this realization that I took my first step that summer toward realizing something even more important about the "worker." In the company of carpenters, electricians, plumbers, and painters at lunch, I would often sit quietly, observant. I was not shy in such company. I felt easy, pleased by the knowledge that I was casually accepted, my presence taken for granted by men (exotics[6]) who worked with their hands. Some days the younger men would talk and talk about sex, and they would howl at women who drove by in cars. Other days the talk at lunchtime was subdued;[7] men gathered in separate groups. It depended on who was around. There were rough, good-natured workers. Others were quiet. The more I remember that summer, the more I realize that there was no single *type* of worker. I am embarrassed to say I had not expected such diversity. I certainly had not expected to meet, for example, a plumber who was an abstract painter in his off hours and admired the work of Mark Rothko. Nor did I expect to meet so many workers with college diplomas. (They were the ones who were not surprised that I intended to enter graduate school in the fall.) I suppose what I really want to say here is painfully obvious, but I must say it nevertheless: The men of that summer were middle-class Americans. They certainly didn't constitute[8] an oppressed society. Carefully completing their work sheets; talking about the fortunes of local football teams; planning Las Vegas vacations; comparing the gas mileage of various makes of campers—they were not *los pobres*[9] my mother had spoken about.

10   On two occasions, the contractor hired a group of Mexican aliens. They were employed to cut down some trees and haul off debris. In all, there were six men of varying age. The youngest in his late twenties; the oldest (his father?) perhaps sixty years old. They came and they left in a single old truck. Anonymous men. They were never introduced to the other men at the site. Immediately upon their arrival, they would follow the contractor's directions, start working—rarely resting—seemingly driven by a fatalistic[10] sense that work which had to be done was best done as quickly as possible.

11   I watched them sometimes. Perhaps they watched me. The only time I saw them pay me much notice was one day at lunchtime when I was laughing with the other men. The Mexicans sat apart when they ate, just as they worked by themselves. Quiet. I rarely heard them say much to each other. All I could hear were their voices calling out sharply to one another, giving directions. Otherwise, when they stood briefly resting, they talked among themselves in voices too hard to overhear.

12   The contractor knew enough Spanish, and the Mexicans—or at least the oldest of them, their spokesman—seemed to know enough English to communicate. But because I was around, the contractor decided one day to make me his translator. (He assumed I could speak Spanish.) I did what I was told. Shyly I went over to tell the Mexicans that the *patrón*[11] wanted them

---

6. exotics: people who are quite unfamiliar
7. subdued: quiet, constrained
8. constitute: make up
9. *los pobres*: the poor people
10. fatalistic: believing events to be predetermined; yielding to one's fate
11. *patrón*: boss

to do something else before they left for the day. As I started to speak, I was afraid with my old fear that I would be unable to pronounce the Spanish words. But it was a simple instruction I had to convey. I could say it in phrases.

The dark sweating faces turned toward me as I spoke. They stopped their work to hear me. Each nodded in response. I stood there. I wanted to say something more. But what could I say in Spanish, even if I could have pronounced the words right? Perhaps I just wanted to engage them in small talk, to be assured of their confidence, our familiarity. I thought for a moment to ask them where in Mexico they were from. Something like that. And maybe I wanted to tell them (a lie, if need be) that my parents were from the same part of Mexico.

I stood there.

Their faces watched me. The eyes of the man directly in front of me moved slowly over my shoulder, and I turned to follow his glance toward *el patrón* some distance away. For a moment I felt swept up by that glance into the Mexicans' company. But then I heard one of them returning to work. And then the others went back to work. I left them without saying anything more.

When they had finished, the contractor went over to pay them in cash. (He later told me that he paid them collectively—"for the job," though he wouldn't tell me their wages. He said something quickly about the good rate of exchange "in their own country.") I can still hear the loudly confident voice he used with the Mexicans. It was the sound of the *gringo*[12] I had heard as a very young boy. And I can still hear the quiet, indistinct sounds of the Mexican, the oldest, who replied. At hearing that voice I was sad for the Mexicans. Depressed by their vulnerability. Angry at myself. The adventure of the summer seemed suddenly ludicrous. I would not shorten the distance I felt from *los pobres* with a few weeks of physical labor. I would not become like them. They were different from me.

Discussion and Writing Questions

1. Why does the author decide to take the summer construction job?

2. Why does Rodriguez say he didn't mind shoveling the wrong way? As he says this, what does he realize about the men he works with?

3. Why does the experience with the Mexican laborers have such an impact on Rodriguez?

4. Rodriguez might have written his essay using comparison or contrast, discussing his feelings before and after his work on the summer construction crew. Why do you think he chose to write it as a narrative?

Writing Assignments

1. Retell Rodriguez's narrative from the point of view of one of the Mexican laborers. You could retell the story Rodriguez tells about speaking with the men, but this time from *your* point of view as a laborer, or you could describe a typical day working for the *patrón*, doing various jobs at the construction site.

2. Tell what it is like to do a particular kind of work. You may choose, like

---

12. gringo: in Latin America, slang for a person from the United States or England (offensive)

Rodriguez, to describe hard, manual labor, or you may have a less strenuous form of work in mind. Whatever work you tell about, be sure to describe it in detail, so that your audience can picture exactly what the job involves.

3. In a group with three or four classmates, discuss the work of someone who was born a generation before you. What kind of work did he or she do? Consider that person's job opportunities or lack of them. Then write your own essay about that person and his or her work.

Some Thoughts About Abortion

Anna Quindlen

Since the *Roe vs. Wade* Supreme Court decision of 1973, the issue of abortion has gripped the United States as perhaps never before. In this essay, noted *New York Times* columnist Anna Quindlen describes her own mixed feelings about the subject and at the same time gives persuasive reasons for keeping abortion legal.

1 It was always the look on their faces that told me first. I was the freshman dormitory counselor and they were the freshmen at a women's college where everyone was smart. One of them would come into my room, a golden girl, a valedictorian, an 800 verbal score on the S.A.T.'s, and her eyes would be empty, seeing only a busted future, the devastation of her life as she knew it. She had failed biology, messed up the math; she was pregnant.

2 That was when I became pro-choice.

3 It was the look in his eyes that I will always remember, too. They were as black as the bottom of a well, and in them for a few minutes I thought I saw myself the way I had always wished to be—clear, simple, elemental, at peace. My child looked at me and I looked back at him in the delivery room, and I realized that out of a sea of infinite possibilities it had come down to this: a specific person, born on the hottest day of the year, conceived on a Christmas Eve, made by his father and me miraculously from scratch.

4 Once I believed that there was a little blob of formless protoplasm[1] in there and a gynecologist went after it with a surgical instrument, and that was that. Then I got pregnant myself—eagerly, intentionally, by the right man, at the right time—and I began to doubt. My abdomen still flat, my stomach roiling with morning sickness, I felt not that I had protoplasm inside, but, instead, a complete human being in miniature to whom I could talk, sing, make promises. Neither of these views was accurate; instead, I think, the reality is something in the middle. And that is where I find myself now, in the middle—hating the idea of abortions, hating the idea of having them outlawed.

5 For I know it is the right thing in some times and places. I remember sitting in a shabby clinic far uptown with one of those freshmen, only three months after the Supreme Court had made what we were doing possible, and watching with wonder as the lovely first love she had had with a nice boy unraveled[2] over the space of an hour as they waited for her to be called,

---
1. protoplasm: living matter
2. unraveled: came apart

degenerated[3] into sniping[4] and silences. I remember a year or two later seeing them pass on campus and not even acknowledge each other because their conjoining had caused them so much pain, and I shuddered to think of them married, with a small psyche in their unready and unwilling hands.

I've met fourteen-year-olds who were pregnant and said they could not have abortions because of their religion, and I see in their eyes the shadows of twenty-two-year-olds I've talked to who lost their kids to foster care because they hit them or used drugs or simply had no money for food and shelter. I read not long ago about a teenager who said she meant to have an abortion but she spent the money on clothes instead: now she has a baby who turns out to be a lot more trouble than a toy. The people who hand out those execrable[5] little pictures of dismembered fetuses at abortion clinics seem to forget the extraordinary pain children may endure after they are born when they are unwanted, even hated, or simply tolerated.

I believe that in a contest between the living and the almost living, the latter must, if necessary, give way to the will of the former. That is what the fetus is to me, the almost living. These questions began to plague me—and, I've discovered, a good many other women—after I became pregnant. But they became even more acute after I had my second child, mainly because he is so different from his brother. On two random nights eighteen months apart the same two people managed to conceive, and on one occasion the tumult[6] within turned itself into a curly-haired brunet with merry black eyes who walked and talked late and loved the whole world, and on another it became a blond with hazel Asian eyes and a pug nose who tried to conquer the world almost as soon as he entered it.

If we were to have an abortion next time for some reason or another, which infinite possibility becomes, not a reality, but a nullity?[7] The girl with the blue eyes? The improbable redhead? The natural athlete? The thinker? My husband, ever at the heart of the matter, put it another way. Knowing he is finding two children somewhat more overwhelming than he expected, I asked if he would want me to have an abortion if I accidentally became pregnant again right away. "And waste a perfectly good human being?" he said.

Coming to this quandary[8] has been difficult for me. In fact, I believe the issue of abortion is difficult for all thoughtful people. I don't know anyone who has had an abortion who has been casual about it. If there is one thing I find intolerable about most of the so-called right-to-lifers, it is that they try to portray abortion rights as something that feminists thought up on a slow Saturday over a light lunch. That is nonsense. I also know that some people who support abortion rights are most comfortable with a monolithic[9] position because it seems the strongest front against the smug and sometimes violent opposition.

But I don't feel all one way about abortion anymore, and I don't think it serves a just cause to pretend that many of us do. For years I believed that a woman's right to choose was absolute, but now I wonder. Do I, with a stable home and marriage and sufficient stamina and money, have the freedom to choose abortion because a pregnancy is inconvenient just now? Legally I do have the right; legally I want always to have that right. It is the morality of exercising it under those circumstances that makes me wonder.

---

3. degenerated: became worse
4. sniping: bickering, arguing
5. execrable: disgusting
6. tumult: energetic movement
7. nullity: nonexistence
8. quandary: tough spot, predicament
9. monolithic: unified and solid

Technology has foiled[10] us. The second trimester has become a time of resurrection; a fetus at six months can be one woman's late abortion, another's premature, viable[11] child. Photographers now have film of embryos the size of a grape, oddly human, flexing their fingers, sucking their thumbs. Women have amniocentesis[12] to find out whether they are carrying a child with birth defects that they may choose to abort. Before the procedure, they must have a sonogram, one of those fuzzy black-and-white photos like a love song heard through static on the radio, which shows someone is in there.

I have taped on my VCR a public television program in which somehow, inexplicably,[13] a film is shown of a fetus *in utero*[14] scratching its face, seemingly putting up a tiny hand to shield itself from the camera's eye. It would make a potent weapon in the arsenal of the antiabortionists. I grow sentimental about it as it floats in the salt water, part fish, part human being. It is almost living, but not quite. It has almost turned my heart around, but not quite turned my head.

Discussion and Writing Questions

1. Quindlen describes two positions she has taken about abortion. What are they?
2. In which paragraph does the author begin to express doubts about abortion? Why does she have these doubts?
3. By the end of her essay, how does Quindlen feel about abortion?
4. What types of proof does the author use in her argument?

Writing Assignments

1. Write on an issue about which you are, like Quindlen, undecided. Choose a topic you know fairly well so that you can present solid arguments for both sides. Be objective, but let your reader know which side you finally find more persuasive.
2. Do you believe that teenagers should be required to inform their parents before obtaining an abortion? Argue in favor of or against this position.
3. Quindlen first gained experience with the abortion issue as a freshman dorm counselor. Write about a time that you once counseled, or gave advice, to a friend in need. Your friend might have been contemplating an abortion, like some of the young women Quindlen describes. She or he may have been fighting with a mate or having a problem with money, career decisions, or school.

---

10. foiled: blocked, confused
11. viable: able to live
12. amniocentesis: a medical procedure for checking the amniotic fluid in the uterus
13. inexplicably: unexplainably
14. *in utero*: in the mother's uterus

Food for Thought

Dave Barry

Humorist Dave Barry writes that he was "born in Armonk, NY, in 1947 and has been steadily growing older ever since without ever actually reaching maturity." He is a Pulitzer Prize–winning columnist for the Miami Herald. *Although Barry's columns and books often make us laugh out loud, his humor always has a point. Here he takes on science fair projects.*

It's getting late on a school night, but I'm not letting my son go to bed yet, because there's serious work to be done.

"Robert!" I'm saying, in a firm voice. "Come to the kitchen right now and blow-dry the ant!"

We have a large ant, about the size of a mature raccoon, standing on our kitchen counter. In fact, it *looks* kind of like a raccoon, or possibly even a mutant[1] lobster. We made the ant out of papier-mâché, a substance you create by mixing flour and water and newspapers together into a slimy goop that drips down and gets licked up by your dogs, who operate on the wise survival principle that you should immediately eat everything that falls onto the kitchen floor, because if it turns out not to be food, you can always throw it up later.

The ant, needless to say, is part of a Science Fair project. We need a big ant to illustrate an important scientific concept, the same concept that is illustrated by *all* Science Fair projects, namely: "Look! I did a Science Fair project!"

(I know how we can solve our national crisis in educational funding: Whenever the schools needed money, they could send a letter to all the parents saying: "Give us a contribution right now, or we're going to hold a Science Fair." They'd raise billions.)

Our Science Fair project is due tomorrow, but the ant is still wet, so we're using a hair dryer on it. Science Fair judges *hate* a wet ant. Another problem is that our ant is starting to sag, both in the front (or, in entomological[2] terms, the "prognosis") and in the rear (or "butt"). It doesn't look like one of those alert, businesslike, "can-do" ants that you see striding briskly around. It looks depressed, like an ant that has just been informed that all 86,932 members of its immediate family were crushed while attempting to lift a Tootsie Roll.

While Robert is drying the ant, I get a flashlight and go outside to examine the experiment portion of our project, which is entitled "Ants and Junk Food." On our back fence we put up a banner that says, in eight-inch-high letters, WELCOME ANTS. Under this is a piece of cardboard with the following snack substances scientifically arranged on it: potato chips, a spicy beef stick, a doughnut, a Snickers candy bar, chocolate-filled cookies, Cheez Doodles, Cocoa Krispies, and Screaming Yellow Zonkers. If you were to eat this entire experiment, you would turn into a giant pimple and explode.

We figured this experiment would attract ants from as far away as Indonesia, and we'd note which junk foods they preferred, and this would prove our basic scientific point ("Look! I did a Science Fair project!"). Of course you veteran parents know what actually happened: The ants didn't show up. Nature has a strict rule against cooperating with Science Fair projects. This is why, when you go to a Science Fair, you see 200 projects designed to show you how an electrical circuit works, and not one of them can actually make the little bulb light up. If you had a project that was supposed to demonstrate the law of gravity using heavy lead weights, they would fall *up*.

---

1. mutant: biologically changed or altered
2. entomological: having to do with the scientific study of insects

So when the ants saw our banner, they said: "Ah-hah! A Science Fair project! Time for us to act in a totally unnatural manner and stay away from the food!"

The irony is, I knew where some ants were: in my office. They live in one of the electrical outlets. I see them going in there all day long. I think maybe they're eating electrons, which makes me nervous. I seriously considered capturing one of the office ants and carrying it out to the science experiment, and if necessary giving it broad hints about what to do ("Yum! Snickers!"). But I was concerned that if I did this, the ants might become dependent on me, and every time they got hungry they'd crawl onto my desk and threaten to give me electrical stings if I didn't carry them to a snack.

Fortunately, some real outdoor ants finally discovered our experiment, and we were able to observe their behavior at close range. I had been led to believe, by countless public-television nature shows, that ants are very organized, with the colony divided into specialized jobs such as drones, workers, fighters, bakers, consultants, etc., all working together with high-efficiency precision. But the ants that showed up at our experiment were total morons. You'd watch one, and it would sprint up to a Cocoa Krispie, then stop suddenly, as if saying: "Yikes! Compared with me, this Cocoa Krispie is the size of a Buick!" Then it would sprint off in a random direction. Sometimes it would sprint back; sometimes it would sprint to another Cocoa Krispie and act surprised again. But it never seemed to *do* anything. There were thousands of ants behaving this way, and every single time two of them met, they'd both stop and exchange "high-fives" with their antennas, along with, I assume, some kind of ant pleasantries ("Hi Bob!" "No, I'm Bill!" "Sorry! You look just like Bob!"). This was repeated *millions of times.* I watched these ants for two days, and they accomplished nothing. It was exactly like highway construction. It wouldn't have surprised me if some ants started waving orange flags to direct other insects around the area.

But at least there were ants, which meant we could do our project and get our results. I'd tell you what they were, but I really think you should do your own work. That's the whole point of a Science Fair, as I keep telling my son, who has gone to bed, leaving me to finish blow-drying the ant.

Discussion and Writing Questions

1. Although Dave Barry writes humorously, his essay makes a serious point. What is he really saying about science fair projects?

2. Which do you think are the funniest lines in this essay? Explain as specifically as possible why you think those sentences are so funny. What words does Barry use to add to the humor? For example, in paragraph 3, he describes the large ant as "about the size of a mature raccoon."

3. Barry's piece is filled with *irony:* his words express something other than their literal meaning. One such example appears in paragraph 4, where he writes that a *big* ant is needed to illustrate the importance of the scientific concept—as if *big* had anything to do with importance. What other examples of irony do you find?

4. Have you ever been assigned a project at school or work that seemed meaningless at first, yet later you found a way to make it interesting or meaningful? What was the project, and what did you do to make it work?

Writing Assignments

1. Have you ever taken on a serious project—sewing or building something, starting a fitness program, throwing a party—only to have it turn out

very differently from what you imagined? Using humor if you wish, describe your initial goal, the steps you took to achieve it, and the ways in which it all went wrong.

2. When parents help their children complete a school project or homework assignment, is this cheating? Write an essay advising parents how to help their child learn without doing the work for the child. You might wish to present your advice in three or four steps or guidelines. Or you might take a particular homework assignment and explain the difference between helping and cheating.

3. In a group with three or four classmates, discuss Barry's attitude toward science fair projects. Do you agree with Barry about the futility of such projects—or do you see value in them? Write your own essay, incorporating ideas from your group discussion if you wish, that either agrees with or contradicts Barry's argument.

One More Lesson

Judith Ortiz Cofer

Judith Ortiz Cofer attended Augusta College, Florida Atlantic University, and Oxford University in England. Here she contrasts her memories of holidays in her native Puerto Rico and of later school experiences in Paterson, New Jersey, telling what she learned about love, prejudice, and the power of words. Her essay sheds light, too, on her decision to become a writer.

I remember Christmas on the Island by the way it felt on my skin. The temperature dropped into the ideal seventies and even lower after midnight when some of the more devout Catholics, mostly older women, got up to go to church—*misa del gallo,* they called it; mass at the hour when the rooster crowed for Christ. They would drape shawls over their heads and shoulders and move slowly toward town. The birth of Our Savior was a serious affair in our town.

At Mamá's house, food was the focal point of *Navidad.* There were banana leaves brought in bunches by the boys, spread on the table, where the women would pour coconut candy steaming hot, and the leaves would wilt around the sticky lumps, adding an extra tang of flavor to the already irresistible treat. Someone had to watch the candy while it cooled, or it would begin to disappear as the children risked life and limb for a stolen piece of heaven. The banana leaves were also used to wrap the traditional food of holidays in Puerto Rico: *pasteles,* the meat pies made from grated yucca[1] and plantain[2] and stuffed with spiced meats.

Every afternoon during the week before Christmas Day, we would come home from school to find the women sitting around in the parlor with bowls on their laps, grating pieces of coconut, yuccas, plantains, cheeses—all the ingredients that would make up our Christmas Eve feast. The smells that filled Mamá's house at that time have come to mean anticipation and a sensual joy during a time in my life, the last days of my early childhood, when I could absorb joy through my pores—when I had not yet learned that light is followed by darkness, that all of creation is based on that simple concept, and maturity is a discovery of that natural law.

---

1. yucca: a thick-stemmed tropical plant
2. plantain: a banana-like fruit

It was in those days that the Americans sent baskets of fruit to our barrio[3]—apples, oranges, grapes flown in from the States. And at night, if you dared to walk up to the hill where the mango tree stood in the dark, you could see a wonderful sight: a Christmas tree, a real pine, decorated with lights of many colors. It was the blurry outline of this tree you saw, for it was inside a screened-in porch, but we had heard a thorough description of it from the boy who delivered the fruit, a nephew of Mamá's, as it had turned out. Only, I was not impressed, since just the previous year we had put up a tree ourselves in our apartment in Paterson.

Packages arrived for us in the mail from our father. I got dolls dressed in the national costumes of Spain, Italy, and Greece (at first we could not decide which of the Greek dolls was the male, since they both wore skirts); my brother got picture books; and my mother, jewelry that she would not wear, because it was too much like showing off and might attract the Evil Eye.

Evil Eye or not, the three of us were the envy of the pueblo.[4] Everything about us set us apart, and I put away my dolls quickly when I discovered that my playmates would not be getting any gifts until *Los Reyes*—the Day of the Three Kings, when Christ received His gifts—and that even then it was more likely that the gifts they found under their beds would be practical things like clothes. Still, it was fun to find fresh grass for the camels the night the Kings were expected, tie it in bundles with string, and put it under our beds along with a bowl of fresh water.

The year went by fast after Christmas, and in the spring we received a telegram from Father. His ship had arrived in Brooklyn Navy Yard. He gave us a date for our trip back to the States. I remember Mother's frantic packing, and the trips to Mayagüez for new clothes; the inspections of my brother's and my bodies for cuts, scrapes, mosquito bites, and other "damage" she would have to explain to Father. And I remember begging Mamá to tell me stories in the afternoons, although it was not summer yet and the trips to the mango tree had not begun. In looking back I realize that Mamá's stories were what I packed—my winter store.

Father had succeeded in finding an apartment outside Paterson's "vertical barrio," the tenement Puerto Ricans called *El Building*. He had talked a candy store owner into renting us the apartment above his establishment, which he and his wife had just vacated after buying a house in West Paterson, an affluent suburb. Mr. Schultz was a nice man whose melancholy[5] face I was familiar with from trips I had made often with my father to his store for cigarettes. Apparently, my father had convinced him and his brother, a look-alike of Mr. Schultz who helped in the store, that we were not the usual Puerto Rican family. My father's fair skin, his ultra-correct English, and his Navy uniform were a good argument. Later it occurred to me that my father had been displaying me as a model child when he took me to that store with him. I was always dressed as if for church and held firmly by the hand. I imagine he did the same with my brother. As for my mother, her Latin beauty, her thick black hair that hung to her waist, her voluptuous[6] body which even the winter clothes could not disguise, would have been nothing but a hindrance to my father's plans. But everyone knew that a Puerto Rican woman is her husband's satellite; she reflects both his light and his dark sides. If my father was respectable, then his family would be respectable. We got the apartment on Park Avenue.

---

3. barrio: district or neighborhood
4. pueblo: town or community
5. melancholy: sad
6. voluptuous: having a rounded, full shape

Unlike El Building, where we had lived on our first trip to Paterson, our new home was truly in exile. There were Puerto Ricans by the hundreds only one block away, but we heard no Spanish, no loud music, no mothers yelling at children, nor the familiar ¡Ay Bendito!, that catch-all phrase of our people. Mother lapsed into silence herself, suffering from La Tristeza, the sadness that only place induces and only place cures. But Father relished[7] silence, and we were taught that silence was something to be cultivated and practiced.

Since our apartment was situated directly above where the Schultzes worked all day, our father instructed us to remove our shoes at the door and walk in our socks. We were going to prove how respectable we were by being the opposite of what our ethnic group was known to be—we would be quiet and inconspicuous.[8]

I was escorted each day to school by my nervous mother. It was a long walk in the cooling air of fall in Paterson and we had to pass by El Building where the children poured out of the front door of the dilapidated[9] tenement still answering their mothers in a mixture of Spanish and English: "Sí, Mami, I'll come straight home from school." At the corner we were halted by the crossing guard, a strict woman who only gestured her instructions, never spoke directly to the children, and only ordered us to "halt" or "cross" while holding her white-gloved hand up at face level or swinging her arm sharply across her chest if the light was green.

The school building was not a welcoming sight for someone used to the bright colors and airiness of tropical architecture. The building looked functional. It could have been a prison, an asylum, or just what it was: an urban school for the children of immigrants, built to withstand waves of change, generation by generation. Its red brick sides rose to four solid stories. The black steel fire escapes snaked up its back like an exposed vertebra. A chain-link fence surrounded its concrete playground. Members of the elite safety patrol, older kids, sixth graders mainly, stood at each of its entrances, wearing their fluorescent white belts that criss-crossed their chests and their metal badges. No one was allowed in the building until the bell rang, not even on rainy or bitter-cold days. Only the safety-patrol stayed warm.

My mother stood in front of the main entrance with me and a growing crowd of noisy children. She looked like one of us, being no taller than the sixth-grade girls. She held my hand so tightly that my fingers cramped. When the bell rang, she walked me into the building and kissed my cheek. Apparently my father had done all the paperwork for my enrollment, because the next thing I remember was being led to my third-grade classroom by a black girl who had emerged from the principal's office.

Though I had learned some English at home during my first years in Paterson, I had let it recede deep into my memory while learning Spanish in Puerto Rico. Once again I was the child in the cloud of silence, the one who had to be spoken to in sign language as if she were a deaf-mute. Some of the children even raised their voices when they spoke to me, as if I had trouble hearing. Since it was a large troublesome class composed mainly of black and Puerto Rican children, with a few working-class Italian children interspersed,[10] the teacher paid little attention to me. I re-learned the language quickly by the immersion method.[11] I remember one day, soon after I joined

---

7. relished: enjoyed
8. inconspicuous: hard to notice
9. dilapidated: run-down
10. interspersed: mixed in
11. immersion method: method of learning a new language in which the student is surrounded only by speakers of that language

the rowdy class, when our regular teacher was absent and Mrs. D., the sixth-grade teacher from across the hall, attempted to monitor both classes. She scribbled something on the chalkboard and went to her own room. I felt a pressing need to use the bathroom and asked Julio, the Puerto Rican boy who sat behind me, what I had to do to be excused. He said that Mrs. D. had written on the board that we could be excused by simply writing our names under the sign. I got up from my desk and started for the front of the room when I was struck on the head hard with a book. Startled and hurt, I turned around expecting to find one of the bad boys in my class, but it was Mrs. D. I faced. I remember her angry face, her fingers on my arms pulling me back to my desk, and her voice saying incomprehensible things to me in a hissing tone. Someone finally explained to her that I was new, that I did not speak English. I also remember how suddenly her face changed from anger to anxiety. But I did not forgive her for hitting me with that hard-cover spelling book. Yes, I would recognize that book even now. It was not until years later that I stopped hating that teacher for not understanding that I had been betrayed by a classmate, and by my inability to read her warning on the board. I instinctively understood then that language is the only weapon a child has against the absolute power of adults.

I quickly built up my arsenal[12] of words by becoming an insatiable[13] reader of books. 15

Discussion and Writing Questions

1. Cofer writes that at some point after her early childhood she "learned that light is followed by darkness" (paragraph 3). What do you suppose she means by this?

2. How does the author seem to feel about her memories of Christmas in Puerto Rico? Is this feeling different from the one that she seems to have about her memories of Paterson?

3. Why does Cofer title her essay "One More Lesson"? What lesson does she learn? Why do you think she responded to her school experience by becoming a reader (and later, a writer) when another child might have learned to hate school?

4. Cofer uses rich description in this essay. Choose one paragraph that you think contains excellent description. What words and details help you "see" Cofer's young world?

Writing Assignments

1. Compare two places that have been important to you. You may want to concentrate on the people in those two places, or you might discuss the smells and sounds or other physical details of each location. Focus on the most important details.

2. Write about a lesson you learned, especially an experience of prejudice, misunderstanding, or achievement that strongly affected your attitude toward English class, reading, or school.

---

12. arsenal: stockpile of weapons
13. insatiable: unable to be satisfied

3. In a group of three or four classmates, discuss how English should be taught to speakers of other languages. Some educators believe in bilingual education, in which students are taught in their native language as well as in English. Others believe in the "immersion method" that Cofer writes about. Then write your own essay. Take a stand for bilingual education or for the immersion method. Which do you think is better for students in the long run?

A Brother's Murder

Brent Staples

Brent Staples grew up in a rough, industrial city. He left to become a successful journalist, but his younger brother remained. Staples's story of his brother is a reminder of the grim circumstances in which so many young black men of the inner city find themselves today.

It has been more than two years since my telephone rang with the news that my younger brother Blake—just twenty-two years old—had been murdered. The young man who killed him was only twenty-four. Wearing a ski mask, he emerged from a car, fired six times at close range with a massive .44 Magnum, then fled. The two had once been inseparable friends. A senseless rivalry—beginning, I think, with an argument over a girlfriend—escalated[1] from posturing,[2] to threats, to violence, to murder. The way the two were living, death could have come to either of them from anywhere. In fact, the assailant had already survived multiple gunshot wounds from an accident much like the one in which my brother lost his life.

As I wept for Blake I felt wrenched backward into events and circumstances that had seemed light-years gone. Though a decade apart, we both were raised in Chester, Pennsylvania, an angry, heavily black, heavily poor, industrial city southwest of Philadelphia. There, in the 1960s, I was introduced to mortality, not by the old and failing, but by beautiful young men who lay wrecked after sudden explosions of violence. The first, I remembered from my fourteenth year—Johnny, brash lover of fast cars, stabbed to death two doors from my house in a fight over a pool game. The next year, my teenage cousin, Wesley, whom I loved very much, was shot dead. The summers blur. Milton, an angry young neighbor, shot a crosstown rival, wounding him badly. William, another teenage neighbor, took a shotgun blast to the shoulder in some urban drama and displayed his bandages proudly. His brother, Leonard, severely beaten, lost an eye and donned a black patch. It went on.

I recall not long before I left for college, two local Vietnam veterans—one from the Marines, one from the Army—arguing fiercely, nearly at blows about which outfit had done the most in the war. The most killing, they meant. Not much later, I read a magazine article that set that dispute in a context. In the story, a noncommissioned officer—a sergeant, I believe—said he would pass up any number of affluent, suburban-born recruits to get hard-core soldiers from the inner city. They jumped into the rice paddies with "their manhood

---

1. escalated: increased
2. posturing: trying to appear tough

on their sleeves," I believe he said. These two items—the veterans arguing and the sergeant's words—still characterize for me the circumstances under which black men in their teens and twenties kill one another with such frequency. With a touchy paranoia born of living battered lives, they are desperate to be *real* men. Killing is only machismo taken to the extreme. Incursions[3] to be punished by death were many and minor, and they remain so: they include stepping on the wrong toe, literally; cheating in a drug deal; simply saying "I dare you" to someone holding a gun; crossing territorial lines in a gang dispute. My brother grew up to wear his manhood on his sleeve. And when he died, he was in that group—black, male and in its teens and early twenties—that is far and away the most likely to murder or be murdered.

I left the East Coast after college, spent the mid- and late 1970s in Chicago as a graduate student, taught for a time, then became a journalist. Within ten years of leaving my hometown, I was overeducated and "upwardly mobile," ensconced[4] on a quiet, tree-lined street where voices raised in anger were scarcely ever heard. The telephone, like some grim umbilical, kept me connected to the old world with news of deaths, imprisonings and misfortune. I felt emotionally beaten up. Perhaps to protect myself, I added a psychological dimension to the physical distance I had already achieved. I rarely visited my hometown. I shut it out.

As I fled the past, so Blake embraced it. On Christmas of 1983, I traveled from Chicago to a black section of Roanoke, Virginia, where he then lived. The desolate public housing projects, the hopeless, idle young men crashing against one another—these reminded me of the embittered town we'd grown up in. It was a place where once I would have been comfortable, or at least sure of myself. Now, hearing of my brother's forays[5] into crime, his scrapes with police and street thugs, I was scared, unsteady on foreign terrain.[6]

I saw that Blake's romance with the street life and the hustler image had flowered dangerously. One evening that late December, standing in some Roanoke dive among drug dealers and grim, hair-trigger losers, I told him I feared for his life. He had affected the image of the tough he wanted to be. But behind the dark glasses and the swagger, I glimpsed the baby-faced toddler I'd once watched over. I nearly wept. I wanted desperately for him to live. The young think themselves immortal, and a dangerous light shone in his eyes as he spoke laughingly of making fools of the policemen who had raided his apartment looking for drugs. He cried out as I took his right hand. A line of stitches lay between the thumb and index finger. Kickback from a shotgun, he explained, nothing serious. Gunplay had become part of his life.

I lacked the language simply to say: Thousands have lived this for you and died. I fought the urge to lift him bodily and shake him. This place and the way you are living smells of death to me, I said. Take some time away, I said. Let's go downtown tomorrow and buy a plane ticket anywhere, take a bus trip, anything to get away and cool things off. He took my alarm casually. We arranged to meet the following night—an appointment he would not keep. We embraced as though through glass. I drove away.

As I stood in my apartment in Chicago holding the receiver that evening in February 1984, I felt as though part of my soul had been cut away. I questioned myself then, and I still do. Did I not reach back soon enough or earnestly enough for him? For weeks I awoke crying from a recurrent dream in which I chased him, urgently trying to get him to read a document I had, as though reading it would protect him from what had happened in waking life.

---

3. incursions: attacks, violations
4. ensconced: settled comfortably
5. forays: undertakings, trips
6. terrain: ground

His eyes shining like black diamonds, he smiled and danced just beyond my grasp. When I reached for him, I caught only the space where he had been.

Discussion and Writing Questions

1. Staples says that he was "introduced to mortality" in Chester, Pennsylvania, in the 1960s (paragraph 2). What does he mean?

2. What does the author mean when he says his brother grew up to "wear his manhood on his sleeve" (paragraph 3)? Does he imply that there are other ways of expressing masculinity?

3. Staples speaks of a dream in which he holds a document for his brother to read (paragraph 8). What do you suppose that document might say? What does this dream seem to say about communication between the two brothers?

4. Staples begins his narrative by describing the moment at which he hears of Blake's death. Why does he *start* with this event, instead of moving toward it?

Writing Assignments

1. Write a narrative about a shocking incident that took place in your neighborhood. Like Staples, you may want to start with the incident, and then narrate the smaller events in the story that led up to it. Or you can follow time order and end with the incident.

2. Do you think Brent Staples could have done more to change his brother? Can we really influence others to change their lives?

3. In a group with three or four classmates, discuss the most significant problem facing young people in the inner city today. Is it crime? Drugs? Lack of educational or employment opportunities? Choose one problem and decide how it can be solved. Your instructor may ask you to share your solution with the class. Then write your own paper, discussing the problem you think is most significant and proposing a solution.

In Search of Bruce Lee's Grave

Shanlon Wu

Most young people need heroes to respect or imitate. In this essay, Shanlon Wu discusses the lack of Asian heroes as he grew up in suburban New York in the 1950s. Then he saw his first Bruce Lee movie.

It's Saturday morning in Seattle, and I am driving to visit Bruce Lee's grave. I have been in the city for only a couple of weeks and so drive two blocks past the cemetery before realizing that I've passed it. I double back and turn through the large wrought-iron gate, past a sign that reads: "Open to 9 P.M. or dusk, whichever comes first."

It's a sprawling cemetery, with winding roads leading in all directions. I feel silly trying to find his grave with no guidance. I think that my search for his grave is similar to my search for Asian heroes in America.

I was born in 1959, an Asian-American in Westchester County, N.Y. During my childhood there were no Asian sports stars. On television, I can recall only that most pathetic of Asian characters, Hop Sing, the Cartwright family houseboy on "Bonanza." But in my adolescence there was Bruce.

I was 14 years old when I first saw "Enter the Dragon," the granddaddy of martial-arts movies. Bruce had died suddenly at the age of 32 of cerebral edema, an excess of fluid in the brain, just weeks before the release of the film. Between the ages of 14 and 17, I saw "Enter the Dragon" 22 times before I stopped counting. During those years I collected Bruce Lee posters, putting them up at all angles in my bedroom. I took up Chinese martial arts and spent hours comparing my physique with his.

I learned all I could about Bruce: that he had married a Caucasian, Linda; that he had sparred with Kareem Abdul-Jabbar; that he was a buddy of Steve McQueen and James Coburn, both of whom were his pallbearers.

My parents, who immigrated to America and had become professors at Hunter College, tolerated my behavior, but seemed puzzled at my admiration of an "entertainer." My father jokingly tried to compare my obsession with Bruce to his boyhood worship of Chinese folk-tale heroes.

"I read them just like you read American comic books," he said.

But my father's heroes could not be mine; they came from an ancient literary tradition, not comic books. He and my mother had grown up in a land where they belonged to the majority. I could not adopt their childhood and they were wise enough not to impose it upon me.

Although I never again experienced the kind of blind hero worship I felt for Bruce, my need to find heroes remained strong.

In college, I discovered the men of the 442d Regimental Combat Team, a United States Army all-Japanese unit in World War II. Allowed to fight only against Europeans, they suffered heavy casualties while their families were put in internment camps. Their motto was "Go for Broke."

I saw them as Asians in a Homeric epic, the protagonists[1] of a Shakespearean tragedy; I knew no Eastern myths to infuse them with.[2] They embodied my own need to prove myself in the Caucasian world. I imagined how their American-born flesh and muscle must have resembled mine: epicanthic folds[3] set in strong faces nourished on milk and beef. I thought how much they had proved where there was so little to prove.

After college, I competed as an amateur boxer in an attempt to find my self-image in the ring. It didn't work. My fighting was only an attempt to copy Bruce's movies. What I needed was instruction on how to live. I quit boxing after a year and went to law school.

I was an anomaly[4] there: a would-be Asian litigator.[5] I had always liked to argue and found I liked doing it in front of people even more. When I won the first-year moot court competition in law school, I asked an Asian classmate if he thought I was the first Asian to win. He laughed and told me I was probably the only Asian to even compete.

The law-firm interviewers always seemed surprised that I wanted to litigate.

"Aren't you interested in Pacific Rim trade?" they asked.

"My Chinese isn't good enough," I quipped.

My pat response seemed to please them. It certainly pleased me. I thought I'd found a place of my own—a place where the law would insulate[6] me from

---

1. protagonists: main characters
2. infuse them with: put into them
3. epicanthic folds: folds of the upper eyelid skin found in many Asian people
4. anomaly: oddity, unusual person
5. litigator: one who argues legal matters
6. insulate: isolate and protect

the pressure of defining my Asian maleness. I sensed the possibility of merely being myself.

But the pressure reasserted itself. One morning, the year after graduating from law school, I read the obituary of Gen. Minoru Genda—the man who planned the Pearl Harbor attack. I'd never heard of him and had assumed that whoever did that planning was long since dead. But the general had been alive all those years—rising at 4 every morning to do his exercises and retiring every night by 8. An advocate of animal rights, the obituary said.

I found myself drawn to the general's life despite his association with the Axis powers. He seemed a forthright, graceful man who died unhumbled. The same paper carried a front-page story about Congress's failure to pay the Japanese-American internees their promised reparation[7] money. The general, at least, had not died waiting for reparations.

I was surprised and frightened by my admiration for General Genda, by my still-strong hunger for images of powerful Asian men. That hunger was my vulnerability manifested,[8] a reminder of my lack of place.

The hunger is eased this gray morning in Seattle. After asking directions from a policeman—Japanese—I easily locate Bruce's grave. The headstone is red granite with a small picture etched into it. The picture is very Hollywood—Bruce wears dark sunglasses—and I think the calligraphy[9] looks a bit sloppy. Two tourists stop but leave quickly after glancing at me.

I realize I am crying. Bruce's grave seems very small in comparison to his place in my boyhood. So small in comparison to my need for heroes. Seeing his grave, I understand how large the hole in my life has been, and how desperately I'd sought to fill it.

I had sought an Asian hero to emulate.[10] But none of my choices quite fit me. Their lives were defined through heroic tasks—they had villains to defeat and wars to fight—while my life seemed merely a struggle to define myself.

But now I see how that very struggle has defined me. I must be my own hero even as I learn to treasure those who have gone before.

I have had my powerful Asian male images: Bruce, the men of the 442d and General Genda; I may yet discover others. Their lives beckon like fireflies on a moonless night, and I know that they—like me—may have been flawed by foolhardiness and even cruelty. Still, their lives were real. They were not houseboys on "Bonanza."

Discussion and Writing Questions

1. Why did Wu see *Enter the Dragon* so many times?

2. Why did the author need so badly to find heroes? How did his situation differ from that of his parents?

3. Does Wu conclude his search for heroes?

4. This narrative begins in the present, then switches to the past, and then ends in the present. Why does the author switch tenses this way?

---

7. reparation: compensation
8. manifested: revealed, made apparent
9. calligraphy: art of fine handwriting
10. emulate: imitate

Writing Assignments

1. Write about a longing you felt as a child that was important in your development as a person—perhaps to have friends, to play music, or to make your parents happy. Was this longing ever filled? Do you think this longing has helped shape the person you are today?

2. Discuss how it feels to be a stranger or an outsider. Perhaps you have felt like an outsider because your interests or ways of dressing are different from those of your classmates or neighbors; perhaps you have felt left out by your coworkers; or perhaps you have been treated as "different" because of your ethnic group or even your gender.

3. Write a one- or two-paragraph summary of "In Search of Bruce Lee's Grave." Refer to Chapter 18 on summary writing. Be sure to include Wu's main idea and his most important supporting points, all in your own words.

The Plot Against People

Russell Baker

Have you ever suspected that your appliances *plan* their breakdowns for the sole purpose of driving you crazy? Here, the Pulitzer Prize–winning author and humorist Russell Baker argues an absurd thesis: objects are out to defeat us.

1 Inanimate[1] objects are classified scientifically into three major categories—those that break down, those that get lost, and those that don't work.

2 The goal of all inanimate objects is to resist man and ultimately to defeat him, and the three major classifications are based on the method each object uses to achieve its purpose. As a general rule, any object capable of breaking down at the moment when it is most needed will do so. The automobile is typical of the category.

3 With the cunning peculiar to its breed, the automobile never breaks down while entering a filling station which has a large staff of idle mechanics. It waits until it reaches a downtown intersection in the middle of the rush hour, or until it is fully loaded with family and luggage on the Ohio Turnpike. Thus it creates maximum inconvenience, frustration, and irritability, thereby reducing its owner's lifespan.

4 Washing machines, garbage disposals, lawn mowers, furnaces, TV sets, tape recorders, slide projectors—all are in league with the automobile to take their turn at breaking down whenever life threatens to flow smoothly for their enemies.

5 Many inanimate objects, of course, find it extremely difficult to break down. Pliers, for example, and gloves and keys are almost totally incapable of breaking down. Therefore, they have had to evolve[2] a different technique for resisting man.

6 They get lost. Science has still not solved the mystery of how they do it,

---
1. inanimate: nonliving
2. evolve: develop

and no man has ever caught one of them in the act. The most plausible[3] theory is that they have developed a secret method of locomotion which they are able to conceal from human eyes.

It is not uncommon for a pair of pliers to climb all the way from the cellar to the attic in its single-minded determination to raise its owner's blood pressure. Keys have been known to burrow three feet under mattresses. Women's purses, despite their great weight, frequently travel through six or seven rooms to find hiding space under a couch.

Scientists have been struck by the fact that things that break down virtually never get lost, while things that get lost hardly ever break down. A furnace, for example, will invariably break down at the depth of the first winter cold wave, but it will never get lost. A woman's purse hardly ever breaks down; it almost invariably chooses to get lost.

Some persons believe this constitutes evidence that inanimate objects are not entirely hostile to man. After all, they point out, a furnace could infuriate a man even more thoroughly by getting lost than by breaking down, just as a glove could upset him far more by breaking down than by getting lost.

Not everyone agrees, however, that this indicates a conciliatory[4] attitude. Many say it merely proves that furnaces, gloves and pliers are incredibly stupid.

The third class of objects—those that don't work—is the most curious of all. These include such objects as barometers, car clocks, cigarette lighters, flashlights and toy-train locomotives. It is inaccurate, of course, to say that they *never* work. They work once, usually for the first few hours after being brought home, and then quit. Thereafter, they never work again.

In fact, it is widely assumed that they are built for the purpose of not working. Some people have reached advanced ages without ever seeing some of these objects—barometers, for example—in working order.

Science is utterly baffled by the entire category. There are many theories about it. The most interesting holds that the things that don't work have attained the highest state possible for an inanimate object, the state to which things that break down and things that get lost can still only aspire.[5]

Discussion and Writing Questions

1. Part of the humor in this essay comes from Baker's imitation of scientific writing. Which sentence introduces the "scientific tone"? Which words establish that tone? Why is the end of that sentence funny?

2. How does Baker classify objects? That is, according to Baker, what are the three major categories into which objects can be divided?

3. Which category does Baker suggest is the "highest" of the three? Why?

4. "Objects" are nonliving things, but Baker constantly refers to them as "*inanimate* objects"—as if he needs to remind us that the objects are not alive. Why would he want to do that? How does he also suggest that the objects really are alive? What is his purpose in doing so?

---

3. plausible: likely, apparently true
4. conciliatory: trying to be friendly
5. aspire: hope to achieve

Writing Assignments

1. Have you had any frustrating experiences with objects such as Baker describes? Write about one object that always seems to get the better of you. What problems do you have with it? Do you ever feel that it has a mind of its own?

2. Have you developed a creative technique for finding lost or misplaced objects? For example, some people ask themselves where they might go if they were their own missing car keys. Describe a situation in which you lost something and then were able to find it by using an unusual or imaginative process.

3. Write a one- or two-paragraph summary of "The Plot Against People." Refer to Chapter 18 on summary and quotation. Be sure to include Baker's main idea and his most important supporting points and categories, all in your own words.

Road Rage

Andrew Ferguson

Although the term *road rage* only recently entered our language, many of us already have experienced it firsthand—either in ourselves or in another driver who has targeted us as the enemy. In this *Time* magazine story, Andrew Ferguson examines the causes of this new tragedy—and insanity—on our highways.

1   It's a jungle out there. Well, not really: it's worse than a jungle. It's a stretch of roadway anywhere in America, and in place of the ravenous tigers and stampeding rhinos and slithery anacondas are your friends and neighbors and co-workers, that nice lady from the church choir and the cheerful kid who bags your food at the local Winn Dixie—even Mom and Dad and Buddy and Sis. They're in a hurry. And you're in their way. So step on it! That light is not going to get any greener! Move it or park it! Tarzan had it easy. Tarzan didn't have to drive to work.

2   It may be morning in America—crime down, incomes up, inflation nonexistent—but it's high noon on the country's streets and highways. This is road recklessness, auto anarchy,[1] an epidemic of wanton[2] carmanship. Almost everyone from anywhere has a story about it, as fresh as the memory of this morning's commute. And no wonder. Incidents of "road rage" were up 51% in the first half of the decade, according to a report from the AAA Foundation for Traffic Safety. Some occurrences are grisly enough to make the headlines. Last year a high-speed racing duel on the George Washington Memorial Parkway outside Washington killed two innocent commuters, including a mother of two, traveling in the opposite direction.

3   More often the new road anarchy manifests itself in the mundane:[3] the unsignaled lane change by the driver next to you, the guy who tailgates you if you go too slow, and the person ahead who brakes abruptly if you go too fast—each transgression[4] accented by a flip of the bird or a blast of the horn. Sixty-four percent of respondents to a recent Coalition for Consumer Health

---

1. anarchy: chaos, disorder
2. wanton: reckless
3. mundane: common, everyday
4. transgression: a violation of law

and Safety poll say people are driving less courteously and more dangerously than they were five years ago.

And the enemy is us. Take a ride with "Anne," a 40-year-old mother of three who would rather we not use her real name, as she steers her 2½-ton black Chevy Suburban out of her driveway on a leafy street in residential Washington. The clock on the dashboard reads 2:16. She has 14 minutes to make it to her daughter's game. Within a block of her house she has hit 37 m.p.h., taking stop signs as suggestions rather than law. She has a lot on her mind. "I'm not even thinking of other cars," Anne admits cheerfully as she lays on the horn. An oldster in an econo-box ahead of her has made the near fatal mistake of slowing at an intersection with no stop sign or traffic light. Anne swears and peels off around him.

Anne has a clean driving record with scarcely even a fender bender to her name. But when she takes to the highway, even her kids join the fun. "Make him move over!" they shout as she bears down on a 55-m.p.h. sluggard in the fast lane. She flashes her headlights. The kids cheer when the unlucky target gives in and moves aside. Back in town, Anne specializes in near misses. "Jeez, I almost hit that woman," she chirps, swinging the Suburban into the right lane to pass a car turning left at an intersection. She makes the game two minutes late. "I don't think I'm an aggressive driver," Anne says. "But there are a lot of bad drivers out there."

Residents of late 20th century America are arguably the luckiest human beings in history: the most technologically pampered, the richest, the freest things on two legs the world has ever seen. Then why do we drive like such jerks? The most common answer: What do you mean we, Kemo Sabe? Of course, you don't drive like a jerk. Very few drivers admit to being an obnoxious road warrior. There seem to be only three types of people on the road these days: the insane (those who drive faster than you), the moronic (those who drive slower than you) and . . . you. But this merely confuses the issue. Surely someone is doing all that speeding, tailgating, headlight flashing and abrupt lane changing, not to mention the bird flipping and horn blasting.

Aggressive driving, of course, has been around since the early decades of this century, from the moment when the average number of automobiles on any given roadway rose from 1 to 2. It is partly a matter of numbers. There are 17% more cars in America than there were 10 years ago, while the number of drivers is up 10%. More to the point: the number of miles driven has increased 35% since 1987, while only 1% more roads have been built.

But as the quantity of cars has risen, the nature of the problem has changed qualitatively as well. Maybe the congestion is making everyone cranky. Americans are famously attached to their cars; it's just the driving they can't stand. "Driving and habitual road rage have become virtually inseparable," says Leon James, a professor of psychology at the University of Hawaii who specializes in the phenomenon.

In the most comprehensive national survey on driving behavior so far, a Michigan firm, EPIC-MRA, found that an astounding 80% of drivers are angry most or all of the time while driving. Simple traffic congestion is one cause of irritation, but these days just about anything can get the average driver to tap his horn. More than one-third of respondents to the Michigan survey said they get impatient at stoplights or when waiting for a parking space; an additional 25% can't stand waiting for passengers to get in the car. And 22% said they get mad when a multi-lane highway narrows.

So not only are roads more crowded than ever, but they are crowded with drivers whom science has now discovered to be extremely touchy. Modern life offers plenty of ready-made excuses for bad driving, and here as elsewhere time seems to be of the essence: there's just not enough of it.

So many miles, so little time. For Ron Remer, 47, a soft-spoken salesman, offensive driving was simply part of the job. From his home in New Haven,

Conn., he logged 30,000 miles a year selling promotional products. "People on the road were an impediment[5] to my progress," he says. "If I was late, it would reflect badly on me. Maybe the customer wouldn't want the products, and I'd be out of a sale. Getting there was the only thing that was important. If I met you in person, I might invite you for coffee or something. But on the road, you were in my way."

Remer says he's reformed now. He was stopped one night on the narrow and unlighted Merritt Parkway in Connecticut after a high-speed race with another car, and soon thereafter he enrolled in a seminar for aggressive drivers. "I was lucky to recognize my problem and try to fix it," he says.

Other road warriors are unrepentant. Alan Carter, 43, a computer specialist from North Carolina and a self-described "aggressive driver," has his own vision of a perfect commute: one with no other cars in sight. "I don't want anyone in front of me. Any time. I think maybe this type of thinking has its roots in the minutiae[6] of territorial rights and typical American individualism. But I don't really think about the deeper meanings. I just know that someone else is in my space or in the space I want."

Carter doesn't have to search for deeper meanings; that is a job for paid professionals, of whom, in America, there are many. Their theories range from the sociological to the psychological to the quasi political. "There is a greater diversity of road users now than at any other time in history," says Hawaii's James. "Therefore streets are not reserved for the optimum, skilled driver but accommodate a variety of driver groups with varying skill, acuity[7] and emotional control"—jerks, in nontechnical lingo. And unlike in previous generations, the willingness to be a jerk on the road is no longer confined to a single sex.

Ed Sarpolus, the head researcher for the Michigan study of driving behavior, was struck by the gender breakdown of aggressive drivers: 53% of them are women. "There is a tremendous cultural shift taking place," he says. "Men still outnumber women in pure numbers, but women are not only increasing, they are not falling off as they get older. Women have fought to be equal in the workplace and in society, and now they're fighting to be equal behind the wheel. [Our] data are full of soccer moms."

This democratization of the highway has occurred simultaneously [with] a decline in traditional driver's education, once a near universal part of the curriculum in America's secondary schools—and a course beloved by generations of high schoolers, since the only way you could fail was by running over the instructor's cat. Some states have backed off mandatory driver training altogether, and elsewhere most courses demand no more than six hours behind the wheel.

Driving is a curious combination of public and private acts. A car isolates a driver from the world even as it carries him through it. The sensation of personal power is intoxicating. Sealed in your little pod, you control the climate with the touch of a button, from Arctic tundra to equatorial tropic. The cabin is virtually soundproof. Your "pilot's chair" has more positions than a Barcalounger. You can't listen to that old Sammy Davis Jr. tape at home because your kids will think you're a dweeb, but in the car, the audience roars as you belt out I've Gotta Be Me. Coffee steams from the cup holder, a bag of Beer Nuts sits open at your side, and God knows you're safe. The safety belt is strapped snugly across your body, and if that fails, the air bag will save your life—if it doesn't decapitate you. Little bells and lights go off if you make a mistake: don't forget to buckle up! Change your oil, you sleepyhead!

---

5. impediment: blockage, obstruction
6. minutiae: small details
7. acuity: sharpness of vision

The illusions—of power, of anonymity,[8] of self-containment—pile up. You are the master of your domain. Actually driving the car is the last thing you need to worry about. So you can pick your nose, break wind, fantasize to your heart's content. Who's to know?

The fantasies are shaped not only by the comforts of the cars but by their sheer tonnage as well. Affluent Americans of the 1990s—so responsible at home, so productive in the workplace—want a car designed for war. With its four-wheel drive and tons of torque and booster-rocket horsepower, today's sports-utility vehicle would have come in handy at the Battle of the Bulge. "There is a real illusion of anonymity combined with potency because you have a machine you can command," says Jack Levin, a sociologist at Northeastern University's Program for the Study of Violence. "Top it off with the stress of work and people perhaps feeling insecure there, or with troubles at home, and it can make for a dangerous combination."

Road-rage experts have come up with various solutions to the anarchy of our streets and highways. We could legislate it (lower speed limits, build more roads to relieve congestion), adjudicate it (more highway cops, stiffer penalties), regulate it (more elaborate licensing procedures) or educate it away (mandatory driver's ed). Others suggest an option perhaps more typical of America circa 1998: therapize it.

"The road rage habit can be unlearned," says James of the University of Hawaii, "but it takes more than conventional driver's ed." He calls for a new driver's ed program from kindergarten on—to teach "a spirit of cooperation rather than competition"—and grass-roots organizations called Quality Driving Circles. These, he told a radio station, would be "small groups of people meeting regularly together to discuss their driving problems and help one another do driving-personality makeovers."

Will it work? A better question might be, Do we want it to? Road-rage therapists come perilously close to calling for a transformation of the national character—remaking our rough-and-tumble, highly individualistic country into a large-scale version of a college town where everyone recycles kitty litter, drinks latte, listens to Enya[9] and eats whole grains. Is that really what we want? For all its dangers, road rage may simply be a corruption of those qualities that Americans have traditionally, and rightly, admired: tenacity,[10] energy, competitiveness, hustle—something, in other words, to be contained and harnessed by etiquette and social censure rather than eradicated[11] outright. Until then, alas, anyone braving the streets and highways of America would be well advised to employ a technique older than therapy: prayer.

Discussion and Writing Questions

1. According to Andrew Ferguson, what kinds of people are affected by road rage? Do they consider themselves dangerous drivers?

2. What are the main causes of road rage?

3. Ferguson uses illustration well to strengthen and humanize his argument; examples of drivers include "Anne," Ron Remer, Alan Carter, and others. Which examples did you find most effective? Explain why, as specifically as possible.

---

8. anonymity: the state of being unknown, unnamed
9. Enya: New Age singer
10. tenacity: persistence, refusal to give up
11. eradicated: eliminated

4. Paragraphs 17 and 18 skillfully describe driving as a "curious combination of public and private acts." What details does Ferguson include that especially capture the isolation, enjoyment, and power of driving alone in one's car? Do you agree with Ferguson that Americans "want a car designed for war"?

5. What kinds of solutions have been proposed for road rage? Will they work?

Writing Assignments

1. Have you or has someone you know experienced road rage? Describe what happened. Were you able to control your anger? How did you do so?

2. Ferguson says that cars give drivers a dangerous and false sense of control and power. Guns too can give a false sense of control and power, with similarly deadly results. Does wielding a deadly weapon give us real power? Many religions tell us that real power lies in kindness, forgiveness, and serenity. Who is right?

3. In a group with three or four classmates, discuss how you and others you know have handled road rage. Discuss any programs you know of and their procedures and results. Then write your own paper on solutions for road rage. You can use information you learned from your group, as well as anecdotes, examples, or research (studies, experts' opinions, statistics, and so on).

Quotation Bank

This collection of wise and humorous statements has been assembled for you to read, enjoy, and use in a variety of ways as you write. You might choose quotations that you particularly agree or disagree with and use them as the basis of journal entries and writing assignments. Sometimes when writing a paragraph or an essay, you may find it useful to include a quotation to support a point you are making. Alternatively, you may simply want to read through these quotations for ideas and for fun. As you come across other intriguing statements by writers, add them to the list—or write some of your own.

Education

1. Knowledge is power.
   —*Francis Bacon*

2. Everyone is ignorant, only on different subjects.
   —*Will Rogers*

3. The children need the bread of the mind.
   —*Rafael Cordero y Molina*

4. Never be afraid to sit awhile and think.
   —*Lorraine Hansberry*

5. A mind stretched by a new idea can never go back to its original dimensions.
   —*Oliver Wendell Holmes, Jr.*

6. The contest between education and TV . . . has been won by television.
   —*Robert Hughes*

7. Our minds are lazier than our bodies.
   —*François, Duc de la Rochefoucauld*

8. This thing called "failure" is not the falling down, but the staying down.
   —*Mary Pickford*

9. Tell me what you pay attention to, and I will tell you who you are.
   —*José Ortega y Gasset*

10. Wisdom consists of anticipating the consequences.
    —*Norman Cousins*

11. We learn something by doing it. There is no other way.
    —*John Holt*

Work and Success

12. He who does not hope to win has already lost.
    —*José Joaquin de Olmedo*

13. The harder you work, the luckier you get.
    —*Gary Player*

Float like a butterfly, sting like a bee.   14
—*Muhammad Ali*

All glory comes from daring to begin.   15
—*Anonymous*

Have a vision not clouded by fear.   16
—*Old Cherokee saying*

Show me a person who has never made a mistake, and I'll show you a person who has never achieved much.   17
—*Joan Collins*

To me, success means effectiveness in the world, that I am able to carry out my ideas and values into the world—that I am able to change it in positive ways.   18
—*Maxine Hong Kingston*

Nice guys finish last.   19
—*Leo Durocher*

Do as the bull in the face of adversity: charge.   20
—*José de Diego*

Life is a succession of moments. To live each one is to succeed.   21
—*Corita Kent*

Should you not find the pearl after one or two divings, don't blame the ocean! Blame your diving! You are not going deep enough.   22
—*P. Yogananda*

It is good to have an end to journey towards, but it is the journey that matters in the end.   23
—*Ursula K. LeGuin*

Nothing is really work unless you would rather be doing something else.   24
—*J. M. Barrie*

I merely took the energy it takes to pout and wrote some blues.   25
—*Duke Ellington*

I write when I'm inspired, and I see to it that I'm inspired at nine o'clock every morning.   26
—*Peter De Vries*

Love

If you want to be loved, be lovable.   27
—*Ovid*

After ecstasy, the laundry.   28
—*Zen saying*

The first duty of love is to listen.   29
—*Paul Tillich*

The way is not in the sky. The way is in the heart.
—*Dhammapada*

A successful marriage requires falling in love many times, always with the same person.
—*Mignon McLaughlin*

Love is a fire, but whether it's going to warm your hearth or burn down your house, you can never tell.
—*Dorothy Parker*

The old Lakota was wise. He knew that man's heart away from nature becomes hard.
—*Standing Bear*

The way to love anything is to realize that it might be lost.
—*G. K. Chesterton*

It's like magic. When you live by yourself, all your annoying habits are gone!
—*Merrill Marko*

Love does not consist in gazing at each other but in looking together in the same direction.
—*Antoine de Saint-Exupéry*

The story of a love is not important—what is important is that one is capable of love. It is perhaps the only glimpse we are permitted of eternity.
—*Helen Hayes*

To deserve a people's love, you must know them. You must learn to appreciate their history, their culture, their values, their aspirations for human advancement and freedom.
—*Jesus Colon*

Friends and Family

Love is blind; friendship closes its eyes.
—*Anonymous*

Friendship with oneself is all important because without it one cannot be friends with anyone else in the world.
—*Eleanor Roosevelt*

What is a friend? A single soul dwelling in two bodies.
—*Aristotle*

You do not know who is your friend and who is your enemy until the ice breaks.
—*Eskimo proverb*

What's more important? Building a bridge or taking care of a baby?
—*June Jordan*

Your children need your presence more than your presents.
—*Jesse Jackson*

The peace and stability of a nation depend upon the proper relationships established in the home.
—*Jade Snow Wong*
45

How times change: it used to be kids would ask where they came from. Now they tell you where to go.
—*Ann Landers*
46

Children need love, especially when they do not deserve it.
—*Harold S. Hulbert*
47

Ourselves in Society

America is not a melting pot. It is a sizzling cauldron.
—*Barbara Ann Mikulski*
48

When spider webs unite, they can tie up a lion.
—*Ethiopian proverb*
49

We can do no great things, only small things with great love.
—*Mother Teresa*
50

A smile is the shortest distance between two people.
—*Victor Borge*
51

Whether we're laughing or crying, the reality of the streets persists.
—*Roberto Santiago*
52

Freedom does not always win. This is one of the bitterest lessons of history.
—*A. J. P. Taylor*
53

If you think you're too small to have an impact, try going to bed with a mosquito.
—*Anita Koddick*
54

Courage isn't the absence of fear; it is action in the face of fear.
—*S. Kennedy*
55

Racism is still a major issue because it is a habit.
—*Maya Angelou*
56

What women want is what men want: they want respect.
—*Marilyn Vos Savant*
57

The same heart beats in every human breast.
—*Matthew Arnold*
58

Basically people are people . . . but it is our differences which charm, delight, and frighten us.
—*Agnes Newton Keith*
59

I can think of no greater honor than to help others fight to survive.
—*Helen Cahlakee Burgess*
60

Wisdom for Living

61. Look within! The secret is inside you!
—Hui Neng

62. One who wants a rose must respect the thorn.
—Persian proverb

63. To live a creative life, we must lose our fear of being wrong.
—Joseph Chilton Pearce

64. Laughter can be more satisfying than honor, more precious than money, more heart cleansing than prayer.
—Harriet Rochlin

65. People who keep stiff upper lips find that it's damn hard to smile.
—Judith Guest

66. The way to get things done is not to mind who gets the credit of doing them.
—Benjamin Jowett

67. Self-pity in its early stages is as snug as a feather mattress. Only when it hardens does it become uncomfortable.
—Maya Angelou

68. When three people call you a donkey, put on a saddle.
—Spanish proverb

69. Never criticize a man until you have walked a mile in his moccasins.
—Native American proverb

70. Everyone is a moon and has a dark side which he never shows to anybody.
—Mark Twain

71. Self-examination—if it is thorough enough—is always the first step towards change.
—Thomas Mann

72. If you can't change your fate, change your attitude.
—Amy Tan

73. Time is a dressmaker specializing in alterations.
—Faith Baldwin

74. Money can't buy friends, but you can get a better class of enemy.
—Spike Milligan

75. Living in the lap of luxury isn't bad, except you never know when luxury is going to stand up.
—Orson Welles

76. Egoist. A person of low taste, more interested in himself than me.
—Ambrose Bierce

77. Envy is a kind of praise.
—John Gay

What doesn't destroy me strengthens me. 78
—*Friedrich Nietzsche*

Life shrinks and expands in proportion to one's courage. 79
—*Anaïs Nin*

I'm not afraid to die. I just don't want to be there when it happens. 80
—*Woody Allen*

Acknowledgments

(continued from copyright page)

Pages 494–496: "Only Daughter" © 1990 by Sandra Cisneros. First published in *Glamour*, November 1990. Reprinted by permission of Susan Bergholz Literary Services, New York. All rights reserved.

Pages 497–499: "My Outing" from *Days of Grace* by Arthur Ashe and Arnold Rampersad. Copyright © 1993 by Jeanne Moutoussamy-Ashe and Arnold Rampersad. Reprinted by permission of Alfred A. Knopf, Inc.

Pages 500–501: "The Lady of the Ring" by Rene Denfeld. Rene Denfeld is the author of "The New Victorians" and "Kill the Body, The Head Will Fall."

Pages 502–503: "Neat People Versus Sloppy People" by Suzanne Britt. Copyright © 1993 by Suzanne Britt. Reprinted by permission of the author.

Pages 504–507: "How to Get the Most out of Yourself" from *Confidence: How to Succeed at Being Yourself* by Alan Loy McGinnis. Copyright © 1987 Augsburg Publishing House. Used by permission of Augsburg Fortress and from the March 1988 Reader's Digest.

Pages 508–512: "Beauty: When the Other Dancer Is the Self" from *In Search of Our Mothers' Gardens: Womanist Prose*, copyright © 1983 by Alice Walker, reprinted by permission of Harcourt Brace & Company and David Hingham Associates.

Pages 513–516: From *Hunger of Memory* by Richard Rodriguez. Copyright © 1982 by Richard Rodriguez. Reprinted by permission of David R. Godine, Publisher.

Pages 517–519: "Some Thoughts About Abortion" from *Living Out Loud* by Anna Quindlen. Copyright © 1987 by Anna Quindlen. Reprinted by permission of Random House, Inc. and International Creative Management.

Pages 520–521: "Food for Thought" from *Dave Barry Is Not Making this Up* by Dave Barry. Copyright © 1994 by Dave Barry. Reprinted by permission of Crown Publishers, Inc.

Pages 522–525: "One More Lesson" by Judith Ortiz Cofer is reproduced with permission from the publisher of *Silent Dancing: A Partial Remembrance of a Puerto Rican Childhood* (Houston: Arte Publico Press-University of Houston, 1990).

Pages 526–528: "A Brother's Murder" by Brent Staples. Copyright © 1986 by The New York Times. Reprinted by permission.

Pages 528–530: "In Search of Bruce Lee's Grave" by Shanlon Wu. Copyright © 1990 by The New York Times. Reprinted by permission.

Pages 531–532: "The Plot Against People" by Russell Baker. Copyright © 1968 by The New York Times. Reprinted by permission.

Pages 533–536: "Road Rage" by Andrew Ferguson. Copyright © 1998 Time, Inc. Reprinted by permission.

ESL Reference Guide

A/an/and, 473
Active voice, 385
Adjectives, 387, 418–421, 423
Adverbs, 270–271, 335, 418–421, 423
Agreement, subject-verb, 356–357
Apostrophes, 427–431

Capitalization, 443–445, 447, 448
Clauses, 287–288, 327, 330, 349, 437
Collective nouns, 400
Commands, 270
Commas, 271, 273, 278, 284, 328, 330, 433–440, 447
Concise language, 301
Conjunctions, 327–328, 330, 343
Conjunctive adverbs, 335, 343
Consistency in number, 256–259
Coordinating conjunctions, 327–328, 343
Coordination, 327–328

Dependent clauses, 327, 330, 349
Direct quotations, 223, 243–244, 447–449. *See also* Quotations
-ed/-d endings, 367, 376
-er/-est endings, 421

Exact language, 174

Fragments. *See* Sentence fragments

Helping verbs, 324–325, 376
Here, 363

Independent clauses, 327
Indirect quotations, 244. *See also* Quotations
Infinitives, 349, 404
-ing modifiers, 277–278, 349
Irregular verbs, 368–369, 378–380. *See also* specific verbs

Linking verbs, 324
Look-alikes/sound-alikes
a/an/and, 473
accept/except, 474
affect/effect, 474
been/being, 475
buy/by, 475
it's/its, 476
know/knew/no/new, 476
lose/loose, 477
past/passed, 477
quiet/quit/quite, 478
rise/raise, 478–479
sit/set, 479
suppose/supposed, 480
their/there/they're, 480
then/than, 481
through/though, 482
to/too/two, 482
use/used, 483
weather/whether, 483
where/were/we're, 484
whose/who's, 484
your/you're, 485

Metaphors, 306
Myself, 405

Nouns, 390–394, 400

Order
of importance, 51–52, 146, 184
of paragraphs, 184–185
space, 47–48, 87, 184
time, 43–44, 79, 184

Parallelism, 261–262
Passive voice, 385
Past participial modifiers, 280–281
Past participles, 376, 378–380, 387
Past perfect tense, 384
Past tense, 367–369, 371–373
Perfect tenses, 382–384
Person, consistency in, 256–259
Prepositional phrases, 272–273, 322–323, 411
Prepositions, 272, 322, 323, 411–415
Present perfect tense, 382–383
Present tense, 356–357, 359, 361–365
Pronouns, 396–398, 401, 404–405, 407–408

Questions, 11–12, 224, 227, 230, 233–237, 269, 364, 440
Quotations, 223, 243–244, 447–449

Regular verbs
in past tense, 367
Relative clauses, 287–288, 349, 365, 437
Religions, capitalization of, 443
Repetition
avoiding unnecessary, 301
of important words and ideas, 55–56
Restrictive clauses, 437
Restrictive relative clauses, 327
Run-on sentences, 342–343

Semicolons, 333–334, 343
Sentence fragments, 346–349
Signal words, 392–394
Similes, 306
Sound-alikes. *See* Look-alikes/sound-alikes
Spelling, 461–471
Subordinate clauses. *See* Dependent clauses
Subordinating conjunctions, 330, 343

Transitional expressions, 60–61, 72, 79, 87–88, 100, 113, 122–123, 136–137, 146, 154–155, 187, 434

Verbs, 324–325, 361, 362
Voice, active and passive, 385

Wordiness, 301

Index

A/an/and, 473
Accept/except, 474
Action, calls to, 224
Action verbs, 324
Active voice, 385
Addresses, commas with, 438, 439
Adjectives
   changed into adverbs, 419
   comparative of, 420, 421
   explanation of, 418
   good/well, 423
   past participles as, 387
   superlative of, 420, 421
Adverbs
   beginning sentences with, 270–271
   comparative of, 420, 421
   conjunctive, 335
   explanation of, 418–419
   good/well, 423
   superlative of, 420, 421
Affect/effect, 474
Agreement
   between pronouns and antecedents, 397–398, 401
   in questions, 364
   in relative clauses, 365
   subject-verb, 356–357
Antecedents
   agreement between pronouns and, 397–398, 401
   explanation of, 396
   referring to, 401
   singular, 399
Anyone, 398
Apostrophe
   for contractions, 427
   for ownership, 428–430
   special uses for, 431
Appositives
   commas for, 436
   explanation of, 283
   joining ideas with, 284
Audience
   determining one's, 4
   for persuasive paragraphs, 156
Authorities, references to, 153, 155
Authors
   giving credit to, 243, 244

Been/being, 475
Body of essays
   elements of, 170
   generating ideas for, 177–183
Body of paragraphs
   elements of, 20, 21
   generating ideas for, 29–30
Brainstorming
   explanation of, 9–10
   function of, 29–30
   ideas for body of essays, 177–178
Buy/by, 475

Calls to action, 224
Can/could, 372
Capitalization
   of direct quotations, 447, 448
   explanation of, 443–444
   of titles, 445
Case
   in comparisons, 405–406
   in compound constructions, 405
   of pronouns, 404–405
Cause and effect essays, 213–215
Cause and effect paragraphs
   checklist for writing, 150
   plan for, 144–146
   problems to avoid in, 146
   suggested topics for, 151
   topic sentences for, 143–144
   transitional expressions in, 146
Causes
   confusion between effects and, 146
   explanation of, 143
Chronological order. *See* Time order
Cities, capitalization of, 443
Class, definitions by, 107–109
Classification, 134
Classification essays, 211–213
Classification paragraphs
   checklist for writing, 141–142
   plan for, 135–136
   suggested topics for, 142
   topic sentences for, 134–136
   transitional expressions for, 136–137
Clauses
   dependent, 327, 330, 349
   explanation of, 327
   independent, 327
   relative, 287–288, 365, 437
Clichés, 304–305
Clustering, 10, 11
Coherence
   of essays, 183
   order of importance arrangement to achieve, 51–52
   repetition of words and ideas to achieve, 55–56
   space order to achieve, 47–48
   synonyms and substitutions to achieve, 57–58
   time order to achieve, 43–44
   transitional expressions to achieve, 61–62
Collaborative work. *See* Group work
Collective nouns, 400
Colons, 449
Commands, 270
Commas
   with adverbs that introduce sentences, 271
   with appositives, 284, 436
   with coordinating conjunctions, 328
   with dates and addresses, 438–439
   with dependent clauses, 330
   with direct quotations, 447
   with *-ing* modifiers, 278
   with introductory phrases, 434
   with items in series, 433
   minor uses of, 440
   with nonrestrictive and restrictive clauses, 437
   with parenthetical expressions, 435
   with prepositional phrases that introduce sentences, 273
   with transitional expressions, 435
Comma splices, 342–343
Comparative
   of adjectives, 420, 421
   of adverbs, 420, 421
Comparison
   in definition paragraphs, 113
   explanation of, 118
   pronoun case in, 405
Comparison-contrast paragraphs
   plan for, 129–130
   steps for, 132
   suggested topics for, 133
   topic sentences for, 130
Comparison essays, 208–211
Comparison paragraphs
   plan for, 121–122
   process of writing, 128
   suggested topics for, 128–129
   transitional expressions for, 122–123
Complete sentences, 26–27
Compound constructions, 405
Compound predicates, 275
Compound subjects, 321
Computer spell checkers, 462
Concise language, 301
Conclusion, of essays, 170, 223–224
Conjunctions
   coordinating, 327–328, 343
   subordinating, 330, 343
Conjunctive adverbs, 335, 343
Consequences, prediction of, 153, 155–156
Consistency in number, 256–259
Consonants
   doubling final, 463–465
   explanation of, 463
Contractions, 427
Contradictions, 222
Contrast
   in definition paragraphs, 113
   explanation of, 118
   use of commas to, 440
Contrast essays, 208–211
Contrast paragraphs. *See also* Comparison-contrast paragraphs; Comparison paragraphs
   plan for, 119–121
   process of writing, 128
   suggested topics for, 128–129
   topic sentences for, 118–119
   transitional expressions for, 122, 123
Controlling ideas
   in essays, 174
   in paragraphs, 25
Coordinating conjunctions, 327–328, 343
Coordination, 327–328
Countries, capitalization of, 443

Dashes, 449
Dates, commas with, 439
Days of week, capitalization of, 443
Definition

547

by class, 107–109
explanation of, 106
by negation, 109
by synonym, 106–107
Definition essays, 206–208
Definition paragraphs
  checklist for writing, 116
  plan for, 112–113
  suggested topics for, 117
  topic sentences for, 112
Dependent clauses, 327, 330, 349
Description, 85
Descriptive essays, 202–204
Descriptive paragraphs
  checklist for writing, 94–95
  plan for, 86–87
  suggested topics for, 95
  topic sentences for, 85–86
  transitional expressions for, 87–88
Dictionary use, 392, 462
Direct quotations
  in introduction to essays, 223
  punctuation of, 447–449. *See also* Quotations
  use of, 243–244
Documents, capitalization in, 443
Drafts of essays
  final, 190
  first, 189
  proofreading, 190
  revising, 190, 192–193
Drafts of paragraphs
  elements of revising, 35–36
  first, 33
  peer feedback for, 37–38
  proofreading final, 39
  writing final, 38–39

Each, 361
-ed/-d endings, 367, 376
Effects
  confusion between causes and, 146
  explanation of, 143
Either, 361
-er/-est endings, 421
Essay examinations, 227, 228
Essay questions
  checklist for writing, 236–237
  common instructions in, 233–234
  explanation of, 227
  reading and understanding, 230
  writing topic sentences or thesis statements in response to, 235
Essays
  checklist for writing, 195–196
  conclusion to, 223–225
  explanation of, 169
  generating ideas for body of, 177–181
  introduction to, 220–223
  looking at, 169–172
  narrowing topic for, 173–174
  ordering and linking paragraphs of, 183–188
  proofreading and writing final draft of, 190
  revising, 190
  sample, 191–194
  suggested topics for, 196

title of, 225–226
writing first draft of, 189
writing thesis statement for, 174–175
Essay types
  cause and effect, 213–215
  classification, 211–213
  comparison or contrast, 208–211
  definition, 206–208
  descriptive, 202–204
  illustration, 197–199
  narrative, 200–202
  persuasive, 216–219
  process, 204–206
Everybody, 398
Every one, 361
Everyone, 398
Every one, 399
Exact language, 174
Examples
  of definition paragraphs, 112
  developing paragraphs by using, 180
  of persuasive paragraphs, 154, 155
Exclamation points, 448
Explanation paragraphs
  explanation of, 96
  plan for, 98–99

Facts
  in persuasive paragraphs, 153, 155
  use of surprising, 222
Final points, 224
Focused freewriting, 8
Fragments. *See* Sentence fragments
Freewriting
  explanation of, 6–7
  focused, 8
  function of, 30

Good/well, 423
Group work, 17, 67, 167, 249, 319, 459, 489

Helping verbs
  explanation of, 324–325
  with past participles, 376
Here, 363
Holidays, capitalization of, 443
How-to paragraphs
  explanation of, 96
  plan for, 97–98
  topic sentences for, 96–97

Ideas
  asking questions to generate, 11–12
  brainstorming to generate, 29–30
  controlling, 25
  freewriting to generate, 30
  keeping journal to generate, 13–14
  selecting and dropping, 30–31
  use of surprising, 222
  using outlines to arrange, 31–32
ie/ei, 469
Illustration
  explanation of, 69
  in introductions to essays, 221
Illustration essays, 197–199
Illustration paragraphs
  checklist for writing, 76
  plan for, 70–71

suggested topics for, 76
topic sentences for, 69
transitional expressions to introduce, 72
Importance, order of
  in cause and effect paragraphs, 146
  coherence through, 51–52
  paragraphs arranged by, 184
Indefinite pronouns, 398
Indents, paragraph, 20
Independent clauses, 327
Indirect quotations, 244. *See also* Quotations
Infinitives, 349, 404
-ing modifiers, 277–278, 349
In/on (place), 412–413
In/on (time), 412
Instruction words, 233–234
Intensive pronouns, 407–408
Interjections, commas after, 440
Introductions, to essays, 220–223
Introductory paragraphs, 170
Introductory phrases, 434
Irregular verbs. *See also specific verbs*
  lists of, 369, 378–380
  past participles of, 378–380
  in past tense, 368, 369
It's/its, 476

Journals
  generating ideas by keeping, 13–14
  uses for, 14–15

Key words
  repetition of, 55
  from thesis statements, 186
  of topic sentence, 31
Know/knew/no/new, 476

Language
  figurative, 306–307
  triteness in, 304–305
  vagueness in, 295–297
  wordiness in, 301
Letters, apostrophe to pluralize, 431
Linking verbs, 324
Lists, 449
Look-alikes/sound-alikes
  a/an/and, 473
  accept/except, 474
  affect/effect, 474
  been/being, 475
  buy/by, 475
  it's/its, 476
  know/knew/no/new, 476
  lose/loose, 477
  past/passed, 477
  quiet/quit/quite, 478
  rise/raise, 478–479
  sit/set, 479
  suppose/supposed, 480
  their/there/they're, 480
  then/than, 481
  through/though, 482
  to/too/two, 482
  use/used, 483
  weather/whether, 483
  where/were/we're, 484
  whose/who's, 484
  your/you're, 485

Lose/loose, 477
-ly, 419

Main ideas
   in essays, 170
   in paragraphs, 20–22
Mapping. *See* Clustering
Metaphors, 306
Months, capitalization of, 443
Myself, 405

Names, capitalization of, 443
Narration, 77
Narrative essays, 200–202
Narrative paragraphs
   checklist for writing, 83–84
   plan for, 78–79
   suggested topics for, 84
   topic sentences for, 77
   transitional expressions for, 79
Nationalities, capitalization of, 443
Negation, definitions by, 109
Neither, 361, 399
Nonrestrictive relative clauses, 437
Nouns
   collective, 400
   explanation of, 390
   hyphenated, 391
   signal words preceding, 392–394
   singular and plural, 390–392, 394
Number
   consistency in, 256–259
   subject-verb agreement, 356–357
Numbers, apostrophe with, 431

Objective case, 404, 405
Objects
   explanation of, 322
   of preposition, 323, 411
   pronouns as, 404
of/of the, 394
One, 361
Opposition, answering to, 153, 156
Order
   of importance, 51–52, 146, 184
   of paragraphs, 184–185
   space, 47–48, 87, 184
   time, 43–44, 79, 184
Organizations, capitalization of, 443
Outlines, 31–32
Outside sources, quoting, 243–244. *See also* Quotations
Oversimplification, 146
Ownership
   apostrophe for, 428–429
   pronouns showing, 404–405

Paragraphs
   arranging ideas in plan of outline for, 31–32
   body of, 20, 21, 29–30
   explanation of, 19–20
   final draft of, 38–39
   introductory, 170
   methods of linking, 186–188
   narrowing topic for, 24–25
   order of, 184–185
   proofreading, 39
   revising, 33
   revising for support, 33–34
   revising for unity, 35–36
   revising with peer feedback, 37–38
   sample, 38–39
   selecting and dropping ideas for, 30–31
   steps prior to writing, 24
   topic sentence of, 20, 21, 25–27
   writing first draft of, 33
Paragraph types
   cause and effect, 143–150
   classification, 134–142
   comparison, 121–123, 128–129
   comparison-contrast, 129–130, 132, 133
   contrast, 118–123, 128–129
   definition, 112–117
   descriptive, 85–95
   explanation of, 96, 98–99
   illustration, 69–76
   narrative, 77–84
   persuasive, 152–165
   process, 96–105
Parallelism, 261–262
Parentheses, 449
Parenthetical expressions, 435
Passive voice, 385
Past participial modifiers, 280–281
Past participles
   as adjectives, 387
   of irregular verbs, 378–380
   of regular verbs, 376
Past/passed, 477
Past perfect tense, 384
Past tense
   to be in, 371
   can/could in, 372
   irregular verbs in, 368–369
   regular verbs in, 367
   will/would in, 373
Peer feedback sheet, 37
Peer review
   of essays, 190
   of paragraphs, 37–38
Perfect tenses, 382–384
Periods, 447
Person, consistency in, 256–259
Persuasion
   definition combined with, 112
   explanation of, 152
   methods of, 155–156
Persuasive essays, 216–219
Persuasive paragraphs
   checklist for writing, 164–165
   considering audience when writing, 156
   plan for, 153–154
   suggested topics for, 165
   topic sentences for, 152, 154
   transitional expressions for, 154–155
Phrases, 349. *See also* Preopsitional phrases
Plagiarism
   explanation of, 238–239
   guidelines for avoiding, 239, 240, 243
Plural nouns
   explanation of, 390
   one of the and *each of the* with, 394
Possessive case, 404–405
Prepositional phrases
   beginning sentences with, 272–273
   explanation of, 272, 322–323, 411
Prepositions
   in common expressions, 413–415
   explanation of, 322, 411
   in/on (place), 412–413
   in/on (time), 412
   list of common, 272, 323
   objects of, 322
Present perfect tense, 382–383
Present tense
   agreement in questions in, 364
   agreement in relative clauses in, 365
   to be, to have, and *to do in,* 359
   sentences beginning with *there* and *here* in, 363
   separation of subject and verb in, 362
   singular constructions in, 361
   subject-verb agreement in, 356–357
Prewriting
   asking questions as, 11–13
   brainstorming as, 9–10
   clustering as, 10–11
   freewriting as, 6–9
   keeping a journal as, 13–15
   steps of, 3, 4
Process essays, 204–206
Process paragraphs
   checklist for writing, 104–105
   in essays, 180
   explanation of, 96
   plans for, 97–99
   suggested topics for, 105
   topic sentences for, 96–97
   transitional expressions for, 100
Pronouns
   agreement between antecedents and, 397–398, 401
   cases of, 404–405
   explanation of, 396
   indefinite, 398
   intensive, 407–408
   reflexive, 407, 408
   with *-self/-selves,* 407–408
Proofreading
   elements of, 39
   explanation of, 4, 452
   function of, 190
Punctuation. *See specific punctuation*
Purpose, of writing, 4–5

Question marks, 448
Questions
   agreement in, 364
   commas when answering, 440
   ending with, 224
   essay, 227, 230, 233–237. *See also* Essay questions
   generating ideas by asking, 11–12
   rhetorical, 269
   sentence variety by using, 269
Quiet/quit/quite, 478
Quotation Bank, 543–548
Quotation marks, 445, 447
Quotations
   avoiding plagiarism in, 243
   direct, 223, 243–244, 447–449
   indirect, 244
   in introduction to essays, 223

punctuation of, 244, 447–448
use of, 243–244

Races, capitalization of, 443
Reflexive pronouns, 407, 408
Regular verbs
  past participles of, 376
  in past tense, 367
Relative clauses
  agreement in, 365
  explanation of, 287
  joining ideas with, 287–288, 349
  restrictive and nonrestrictive, 437
Religions, capitalization of, 443
Repetition
  avoiding unnecessary, 301
  of important words and ideas, 55–56
Restrictive relative clauses, 327
Revision
  for consistent number and person, 256–259
  for consistent tense, 251–252
  explanation of, 33
  for parallelism, 261–262
  peer feedback for, 37–38
  samples of, 312–314
  for sentence variety. *See* Sentence variety
  steps of, 3, 4
  for support, 33–34
  for unity, 35–36
Rhetorical questions, 269
Rise/raise, 478–479
Run-on sentences, 342–343
-self/-selves, 407–408

Semicolons, 333–334, 343
's ending, 428
Sentence fragments
  correction of, 347–349
  explanation of, 346–347
  quick review chart for, 349
Sentences. *See also* Topic sentences
  complete, 26–27
  length of, 267–268
  prepositional phrases in, 322–323
  run-on, 342–343
  subjects of, 321–322
  transitional, 187–188
  verbs in, 324–325
Sentence variety
  beginning with adverbs for, 270–271
  beginning with prepositional phrases for, 272–273
  importance of, 267
  joining ideas with appositives for, 283–284
  joining ideas with compound predicates for, 275
  joining ideas with *-ing* modifiers for, 277–278
  joining ideas with past participial modifiers for, 280–281
  joining ideas with relative clauses for, 287–288
  mixing long and short sentences for, 267–268
  summary of techniques for, 290

using commands and exclamations for, 269–270
using questions for, 269
Series, 433
-s/-es endings, 390–392, 468
Signal words
  with *of*, 394
  singular and plural indicated by, 392–393
Similes, 306
Simple sentences
  prepositional phrases in, 322–323
  subjects of, 321–322
  verbs in, 324–325
Singular antecedents, 399
Singular nouns, 390
Sit/set, 479
Somebody, 398
Sound-alikes. *See* Look-alikes/sound-alikes
Space order
  coherence through, 47–48
  of descriptive paragraphs, 87
  paragraphs arranged by, 184
Spell checkers, computer, 462
Spelling
  adding *-s* or *es* and, 468
  changing or keeping final *y* and, 467
  choosing *i* or *ie* and, 469
  computer programs to check, 462
  doubling final consonants and, 463–465
  dropping or keeping final *e* and, 466
  list of commonly misspelled words and, 470–471
  tips for improving, 461–462
  vowels and consonants and, 463
Subjective case
  pronouns in, 404, 405
  who and *whoever* in, 406, 407
Subjects
  compound, 321
  explanation of, 321–322
  pronouns as, 404
  separation of verbs from, 362
Subjects (of writing). *See* Topics
Subject-verb agreement, 356–357
Subordinate clauses. *See* Dependent clauses
Subordinating conjunctions, 330, 343
Subordination, 330
Substitutions, 57–58
Summaries
  avoiding plagiarism in, 240
  checklist for writing, 242–243
  elements of, 239–240
  examples of, 240–241
  explanation of, 239
  preparation for writing, 240
Superlative
  of adjectives, 420, 421
  of adverbs, 420, 421
Support, for paragraph, 33–34
Suppose/supposed, 480
Synonyms
  coherence through use of, 57–58
  definitions by, 106–107
  explanation of, 57

Tense
  past, 367–373
  past perfect, 384

present, 356–365
present perfect, 382–383
revision for consistent, 251–252
That, 365
Their/there/they're, 480
Then/than, 481
There, 363
Thesis statements
  in cause and effect essays, 214
  in classification essays, 212
  in comparison essays, 209, 210
  composing topic sentences from, 179–180
  in contrast essays, 209, 210
  in definition essays, 207–208
  in descriptive essays, 203, 204
  elements of writing, 174–175
  in essay exams, 235
  explanation of, 170, 174
  general ideas leading to, 221
  in illustration essays, 199
  illustrations leading to, 221
  in narrative essays, 201
  order of paragraphs and, 184
  in persuasive essays, 217
  in process essays, 205, 206
  repeating key words from, 186
  single-sentence, 220–221
Through/though, 482
Timed papers, 227. *See also* Essay questions
Time expressions, 431
Time order
  causation confused with, 146
  in cause and effect paragraphs, 146
  coherence through, 43–44
  in narrative paragraphs, 79
  paragraphs arranged of, 184
  in process paragraphs, 100
Titles
  capitalization of, 445
  guidelines for, 225
  types of, 225–226
To be
  passive voice and, 385
  past tense of, 371
  present tense of, 359
To do, 359
To have
  in past perfect tense, 384
  in present perfect tense, 382–383
  present tense of, 359
Topics
  choosing one's, 4
  narrowing essay, 173–174
  narrowing paragraph, 24–25
Topic sentences
  in classification paragraphs, 134–136
  in comparison-contrast paragraphs, 130
  in definition paragraphs, 112
  in descriptive paragraphs, 85–86
  in essay exams, 235
  in essays, 179 (*See also* Essays)
  explanation of, 20, 21, 25
  in illustration paragraphs, 69
  key words of, 31
  in narrative paragraphs, 77
  in persuasive paragraphs, 152, 154
  in process paragraphs, 96–97
To/too/two, 482

Transitional expressions
- in cause and effect paragraphs, 146
- in classification paragraphs, 136–137
- coherence through, 61–62
- commas to set off, 434
- in comparison paragraphs, 122–123
- in contrast paragraphs, 122, 123
- in definition paragraphs, 113
- in descriptive paragraphs, 87–88
- in illustration paragraphs, 72
- linking paragraphs with, 187
- list of, 61
- in narrative paragraphs, 79
- in persuasive paragraphs, 154–155
- in process paragraphs, 100

Transitional sentences, 187–188
Trite expressions, 304–305

Underlining, 445
Unity, 35–36
Use/used, 483

Vagueness
- methods to avoid, 295–297
- in thesis statements, 174

Verbs
- action, 324
- explanation of, 324
- helping, 324–325
- linking, 324
- separation of subjects from, 362
- singular constructions for, 361

Voice, active and passive, 385
Vowels, 463

Weather/whether, 483
Well/good, 423
Where/were/we're, 484
Which, 365
Which one, 361
Who
- relative clauses beginning with, 365
- subjective case and, 406, 407

Whoever, 406, 407
Whom, 406, 407
Whomever, 406, 407
Whose/who's, 484
Will/would, 373
Wordiness, 301
Writing process, 3–4
Your/you're, 485

Rhetorical Index

The following index first classifies the paragraphs and essays in this text according to rhetorical mode and then according to rhetorical mode by chapter. (Those paragraphs with built-in errors for students to correct are not included.)

Rhetorical Modes

Illustration

At local noontime, 22
John Bryant is, 35
Louis Pasteur is revered, 51
El Niño, an unusual, 52
I have always considered my father, 56
According to sports writer, 58
More important perhaps, 65
Making Mittens Out of Sweaters, 66
Great athletes, 69, 70
Many schools in the twenty-first century, 71
Aggressive drivers, 71
Random acts of kindness, 72
There are many quirky variations, 72
Sunlight, 170–171
Libraries of the Future—Now, 198
Lisette Flores-Nieves, 221
In most cultures, 244
Immortality in Wax, 260
Dr. Alice Hamilton, Medical Pioneer, 303
My Outing (Arthur Ashe), 497–499
How to Get the Most Out of Yourself (Alan Loy McGinnis), 504–507
Some Thoughts About Abortion (Anna Quindlen), 517–519
Road Rage (Andrew Ferguson), 533–536

Narration

In 1905, a poor washerwoman, 44
James Escalante, 63
A birthday gift, 77, 78
Horace Bristol might be the only, 79
Maya Lin's Vietnam War Memorial, 200
It was 1850, 253
On the night of December 2, 1777, 254
Nelly Bly, 265
Little Richard, the King of Rock'n'Roll, 291
Visiting my grandparents, 313, 314
Only Daughter (Sandra Cisneros), 494–496
My Outing (Arthur Ashe), 497–499
Hunger of Memory (Richard Rodriguez), 513–516
Food for Thought (Dave Barry), 520–521
One More Lesson (Judith Ortiz Cofer), 522–525
A Brother's Murder (Brent Staples), 526–528
In Search of Bruce Lee's Grave (Shanlon Wu), 528–530
Beauty: When the Other Dancer Is the Self (Alice Walker), 508–512

Description

Mr. Martin, the reason, 8
Noises in My Village, 16
We lived on the top floor, 47
On my right a woods, 48
On September 10, 1990, 57
Rocky Mountain bighorn sheep, 58
Mrs. Zajac seemed to have, 64
On November 27, when archaeologist, 85, 86
The woman who met us, 88
The Day of the Dead, 202
Two Childhoods, 209
The tension built, 254
I recall being told, 268
Little Richard, the King of Rock'n'Roll, 291
It is called the suburbs now, 296, 297
He was a large, juicy man, 307
You have to know the feel of a baseball, 309
Visiting my grandparents, 313, 314
One More Lesson (Judith Ortiz Cofer), 522–525

Process

Most Westerners are fascinated, 44
More important perhaps, 65
Luck is preparation, 97
Many experts believe, 98
If your dog barks too much, 100
Bottle Watching, 172
Skin Deep, 188
How to Prepare for a Final Exam, 204
It was 1850, 253
A Quick History of Chocolate, 255
In order to give my best performance, 313
How Sunglasses Spanned the World, 492–493
Lady of the Ring (Rene Denfeld), 500–501
Food for Thought (Dave Barry), 520–521

Definition

A grand jury is an investigative body, 55
Ambivalence can be defined, 112
A feminist is not a man-hater, 114
Induction is reasoning, 115
Would you rather, 187
Winning, 207
Besides the nine known planets, 246
Only Daughter (Sandra Cisneros), 494–496
How to Get the Most Out of Yourself (Alan Loy McGinnis), 504–507
Road Rage (Andrew Ferguson), 533–536

Comparison and Contrast

Zoos in the past, 60
Christopher Reeve's story, 59
Although soul and hip-hop, 118, 119, 120
Two birds of a feather, 121
Certain personality traits, 123
The city of Bangalore, 124
Although contemporary fans, 129
No meal eaten in the Middle East, 130–131
The house where I grew up, 187
Two Childhoods, 209
Almost all of us, 222
Speech is silver, 223
He was a large, juicy man, 307
Neat People Versus Sloppy People (Suzanne Britt), 502–503
One More Lesson (Judith Ortiz Cofer), 522–525

Classification

Gym-goers can be classified, 134, 135
Judges can be divided, 137
The Potato Scale, 211
The Plot Against People (Russell Baker), 531–532

Cause and Effect

El Nino, an unusual, 52
What killed off the dinosaurs, 143, 144
For Christy Haubegger, 145
Sadly, this college, 147
Bottle Watching, 172
Dee Kantner and Violet Palmer, 187
Why I Stayed and Stayed, 213
Identical twins, 245
One cause of the falling crime rate, 268
Only Daughter (Sandra Cisneros), 494–496
Lady of the Ring (Rene Denfeld), 500–501
Road Rage (Andrew Ferguson), 533–536

Persuasion

Something strange and wonderful, 21

Eating sugar can be worse, 21
Passengers should refuse to ride, 152, 153
American women should stop buying, 156
This state should offer, 157
English Students, Listen Up! 166
Sunlight, 170–171
Stopping Youth Violence: An Inside Job, 216
Few Americans stay put, 221
Millions of law-abiding Americans, 222
Speech is silver, 223
Thus, bird watchers, 224
Students who follow their hearts, 224
Illness related to, 224
It's Great to Get Old, 248

The salesperson is crucial, 260
Try to imagine using failure, 269
It's Not Easy Being a Roach, 458
How to Get the Most Out of Yourself (Alan Loy McGinnis), 504–507
Some Thoughts About Abortion (Anna Quindlen), 517–519
Road Rage (Andrew Ferguson), 533–536

Mixed Modes

Two weeks ago, 14
I allow the spiders, 20

The summer picnic gave ladies, 21
Pete's sloppiness, 38
When Lewis and Clark, 58
The blues is the one truly American, 64
Bottle Watching, 172
The house where I grew up, 187
Skin Deep, 188
Portrait of a Bike Fanatic, 191, 193
Family Secrets: Don't You Go Talking, 318–319
A Community of Fishermen, 488–489

Rhetorical Modes by Chapter

2 Prewriting to Generate Ideas

Description

Mr. Martin, the reason, 8
Noises in My Village, 16

Mixed Modes

Two weeks ago, 14

3 The Process of Writing Paragraphs

Illustration

At local noontime, 22
John Bryant is, 35

Persuasion

Something strange and wonderful, 21
Eating sugar can be worse, 21

Mixed Modes

I allow the spiders, 20
The summer picnic gave ladies, 21
Pete's sloppiness, 38

4 Achieving Coherence

Illustration

Louis Pasteur is revered, 51
El Niño, an unusual, 52
I have always considered my father, 56
According to sports writer, 58
More important perhaps, 65
Making Mittens Out of Sweaters, 66

Narration

In 1905, a poor washerwoman, 44
James Escalante, 63

Description

We lived on the top floor, 47
On my right a woods, 48
On September 10, 1990, 57
Rocky Mountain bighorn sheep, 58
Mrs. Zajac seemed to have, 64

Process

Most Westerners are fascinated, 44
More important perhaps, 65

Definition

A grand jury is an investigative body, 55

Comparison and Contrast

Zoos in the past, 60
Christopher Reeve's story, 59

Cause and Effect

El Niño, an unusual, 52

Mixed Modes

When Lewis and Clark, 58
The blues is the one truly American, 64

5 Illustration

Illustration

Great athletes, 69, 70

Many schools in the twenty-first century, 71
Aggressive drivers, 71
Random acts of kindness, 72
There are many quirky variations, 72

6 Narration

Narration

A birthday gift, 77, 78
Horace Bristol might be the only, 79

7 Description

Description

On November 27, 1922, when archaeologist, 85, 86
The woman who met us, 88

8 Process

Process

Luck is preparation, 97
Many experts believe, 98
If your dog barks too much, 100

9 Definition

Definition

Ambivalence can be defined, 112
A feminist is not a man-hater, 114
Induction is reasoning, 115

10 Comparison and Contrast

Comparison and Contrast

Although soul and hip-hop, 118, 119, 120
Two birds of a feather, 121
Certain personality traits, 123
The city of Bangalore, 124
Although contemporary fans, 129
No meal eaten in the Middle East, 130–131

11 Classification

Classification

Gym-goers, 134, 135
Judges can be divided, 137

12 Cause and Effect

What killed off the dinosaurs, 143, 144
For Christy Haubegger, 145
Sadly, this college, 147

13 Persuasion

Persuasion

Passengers should refuse to ride, 152, 153
American women should stop buying, 156
This state should offer, 157
English Students, Listen Up! 166

14 The Process of Writing an Essay

Illustration

Sunlight, 170–171

Process

Bottle Watching, 172
Skin Deep, 188

Definition

Would you rather, 187

Comparison and Contrast

The house where I grew up, 187

Cause and Effect

Bottle Watching, 172
Dee Kantner and Violet Palmer, 187

Persuasion

Sunlight, 170–171

Mixed Modes

Bottle Watching, 172
The house where I grew up, 187
Skin Deep, 188
Portrait of a Bike Fanatic, 191, 193

15 Types of Essays

Illustration

Libraries of the Future—Now, 198

Narration

Maya Lin's Vietnam War Memorial, 200

Description

The Day of the Dead, 202
Two Childhoods, 209

Process

How to Prepare for a Final Exam, 204

Definition

Winning, 207

Comparison and Contrast

Two Childhoods, 209

Cause and Effect

Why I Stayed and Stayed, 213

Classification

The Potato Scale, 211

Persuasion

Stopping Youth Violence: An Inside Job, 216

16 The Introduction, the Conclusion, and the Title

Illustration

Lisette Flores-Nieves, 221

Comparison and Contrast

Almost all of us, 222
Speech is silver, 223

Persuasion

Few Americans stay put, 221
Millions of law-abiding Americans, 222
Speech is silver, 223
Thus, bird watchers, 224
Students who follow their hearts, 224
Illness related to, 224

18 Special College Skills: Summary and Quotation

Illustration

In most cultures, 244

Definition

Besides the nine known planets, 246

Cause and Effect

Identical twins, 245

Persuasion

It's Great to Get Old, 248

19 Revising for Consistency and Parallelism

Illustration

Immortality in Wax, 260

Narration

It was 1850, 253
On the night of December 2, 1777, 254
Nelly Bly, 265

Description

The tension built, 254

Process

It was 1850, 253
A Quick History of Chocolate, 255

Persuasion

The salesperson is crucial, 260

20 Revising for Sentence Variety

Narration

Little Richard, the King of Rock'n'Roll, 291

Description

I recall being told, 268
Little Richard, the King of Rock'n'Roll, 291

Cause and Effect

One cause of the falling crime rate, 268

Persuasion

Try to imagine using failure, 269

21 Revising for Language Awareness

Illustration

Dr. Alice Hamilton, Medical Pioneer, 303

Description

It is called the suburbs now, 296, 297
He was a large, juicy man, 307
You have to know the feel of a baseball, 309

Comparison and Contrast

He was a large, juicy man, 307

22 Putting Your Revision Skills to Work

Description and Narration

Visiting my grandparents, 314

Process

In order to give my best performance, 313

Mixed Modes

Family Secrets: Don't You Go Talking, 318–319

36 Putting Your Proofreading Skills to Work

Persuasion

It's Not Easy Being a Roach, 458

38 Look-Alikes/Sound-Alikes

Mixed Modes

A Community of Fishermen, 488–489

Rhetorical Modes in the Reading Selections

Illustration

My Outing (Arthur Ashe), 497
How To Get the Most Out of Yourself (Alan Loy McGinnis), 504
Some Thoughts About Abortion (Anna Quindlen), 517
Road Rage (Andrew Ferguson), 533

Narration

Only Daughter (Sandra Cisneros), 494
My Outing (Arthur Ashe), 497
Hunger of Memory (Richard Rodriguez), 513
Food for Thought (Dave Barry), 520
One More Lesson (Judith Ortiz Cofer), 522
A Brother's Murder (Brent Staples), 526
In Search of Bruce Lee's Grave (Shanlon Wu), 528
Beauty: When the Other Dancer Is the Self (Alice Walker), 508

Description

One More Lesson (Judith Ortiz Cofer), 522

Process

How Sunglasses Spanned the World, 492
Lady of the Ring (Rene Denfeld), 500
Food for Thought (Dave Barry), 520

Definition

Only Daughter (Sandra Cisneros), 494
How To Get the Most Out of Yourself (Alan Loy McGinnis), 504
Road Rage (Andrew Ferguson), 533

Comparison and Contrast

Neat People Versus Sloppy People (Suzanne Britt), 502
One More Lesson (Judith Ortiz Cofer), 522

Classification

The Plot Against People (Russell Baker), 531

Cause and Effect

Only Daughter (Sandra Cisneros), 494
Lady of the Ring (Rene Denfeld), 500
Road Rage (Andrew Ferguson), 533

Persuasion

How to Get the Most Out of Yourself (Alan Loy McGinnis), 504
Some Thoughts About Abortion (Anna Quindlen), 517
Road Rage (Andrew Ferguson), 533

Evergreen with Readings, Sixth Edition

To the instructor:

One of the best ways to improve the next edition of our textbook is to get reactions and suggestions from you, the instructor. You have worked with *Evergreen with Readings*, Sixth Edition, and we want to know what you like about the book and what can be improved. Please answer the questions below. Tear out this page and mail it to

Susan Fawcett and Alvin Sandberg
c/o Marketing Services
College Division
Houghton Mifflin Company
222 Berkeley Street
Boston, MA 02116

Be honest and specific in your comments. Tell us both what is good about *Evergreen with Readings* and what could be better. Thank you.

1. Overall, how would you rate *Evergreen with Readings*? (Check one.)
   ☐ excellent   ☐ average
   ☐ good   ☐ poor

2. Which chapters did you find especially helpful? Why? _____
   _____
   _____
   _____

3. Which chapters did you find least helpful? Why? _____
   _____
   _____
   _____

4. Were any chapters too difficult or confusing for your students? Which ones?
   _____
   _____
   _____

5. Do any chapters need more explanation or practices? Which ones and why?
   _____
   _____
   _____

6. What material would you like to see added to or deleted from future editions of *Evergreen with Readings*? _____

   _____

   _____

   _____

7. Do you have any additional reactions to *Evergreen with Readings*? _____

   _____

   _____

   _____

8. How can we improve the Instructor's Annotated Edition? _____

   _____

   _____

   _____

9. Please rate the Reading Selections.

	Excellent	Good	Fair	Poor	Didn't read
How Sunglasses Spanned the World	☐	☐	☐	☐	☐
Only Daughter	☐	☐	☐	☐	☐
My Outing	☐	☐	☐	☐	☐
The Lady of the Ring	☐	☐	☐	☐	☐
Neat People Versus Sloppy People	☐	☐	☐	☐	☐
How to Get the Most out of Yourself	☐	☐	☐	☐	☐
Beauty: When the Other Dancer Is the Self	☐	☐	☐	☐	☐
Hunger of Memory	☐	☐	☐	☐	☐
Some Thoughts About Abortion	☐	☐	☐	☐	☐
Food for Thought	☐	☐	☐	☐	☐
One More Lesson	☐	☐	☐	☐	☐
A Brother's Murder	☐	☐	☐	☐	☐
In Search of Bruce Lee's Grave	☐	☐	☐	☐	☐
The Plot Against People	☐	☐	☐	☐	☐
Road Rage	☐	☐	☐	☐	☐

Revising and Proofreading Symbols

The following chart lists common writing errors and the symbols that instructors often use to mark them. For some errors, your instructor may wish to use symbols other than the ones shown. You may wish to write these alternate symbols in the blank column.

Standard Symbol	Instructor's Alternate Symbol	Error	For help, see Chapter
adj		Incorrect adjective form	32
adv		Incorrect adverb form	32
agr		Incorrect subject-verb agreement	26; 23
		Incorrect pronoun-antecedent agreement	30, Parts A and B
apos		Missing or incorrect apostrophe	33
awk		Awkward expression	3, Part F; 21
cap		Missing or incorrect capital letter	35, Parts A and B
case		Incorrect pronoun case	30, Part D
⊙ (,)		Missing or incorrect comma	34; 24, Parts A and B
coh		Lack of coherence	4
⊙ (:)		Missing or incorrect colon	35, Part D
con d		Inconsistent discourse	18, Part C
con p		Inconsistent person	19, Part B
con t		Inconsistent verb tense	19, Part A
coord		Incorrect coordination	24, Part A
cs		Comma splice	25, Part A
⊖		Missing or incorrect dash	35, Part D
dev		Incomplete paragraph or essay development	3, Parts C, D, and E; 14, Parts C, D, and E
dm		Dangling or confusing modifier	20, Part D
ed		Missing -ed, past tense or past participle	27, Part A; 28, Part A
frag		Sentence fragment	25, Part B; 20, Part D; 24, Part B
¶		Missing indentation for new paragraph	3, Part A
( )		Missing or incorrect parenthesis	35, Part D
‖		Faulty parallelism	19, Part C
pl		Missing or incorrect plural form	29
pp		Incorrect past participle form	28
⊙ ! ?		Missing or incorrect end punctuation	20, Part B
quot		Missing or incorrect quotation marks	35, Part C
rep		Unnecessary repetition	3, Parts D and F
ro		Run-on sentence	25, Part A
⊙ (;)		Missing or incorrect semicolon	24, Parts C and D
sub		Incorrect subordination	24, Part B
sp		Spelling error	37
		Look-alike, sound-alike error	38
sup		Inadequate support	3, Part F
title		Title needed	16, Part C
trans		Transition needed	3, Part E; 14, Part D
trite		Trite expression	21, Part C
ts		Poor or missing topic sentence or thesis statement	3, Parts A and B; 14, Part B
u		Lack of paragraph or essay unity	3, Part F; 14, Parts C, D, and E
w		Unnecessary words	21, Part B
⌒		Too much space	
℘		Words or letters to be deleted	
?		Unclear meaning	21, Part A
		Omitted words	
		Words or letters in reverse order	